*Letters on Ethics*

THE COMPLETE WORKS OF LUCIUS ANNAEUS SENECA

*Edited by Elizabeth Asmis, Shadi Bartsch, and Martha C. Nussbaum*

# *Seneca*
## Letters on Ethics
## To Lucilius

TRANSLATED WITH AN INTRODUCTION
AND COMMENTARY BY MARGARET
GRAVER AND A. A. LONG

*The University of Chicago Press* CHICAGO AND LONDON

*Publication of this book has been aided by a gift from Ruth O'Brien.*

The University of Chicago Press, Chicago 60637
The University of Chicago Press, Ltd., London
© 2015 by The University of Chicago
All rights reserved. Published 2015.
Paperback edition 2017
Printed in the United States of America

23 22 21 20 19     2 3 4 5 6

ISBN-13: 978-0-226-26517-9 (cloth)
ISBN-13: 978-0-226-52843-4 (paper)
ISBN-13: 978-0-226-26520-9 (e-book)
DOI: 10.7208/chicago/9780226265209.001.0001

Library of Congress Cataloging-in-Publication Data

Seneca, Lucius Annaeus, approximately 4 B.C.–65 A.D.,
author.
    [Epistulae morales ad Lucilium. English]
    Letters on ethics : to Lucilius / Seneca ; translated with
an introduction and commentary by Margaret Graver and
A. A. Long.
        pages cm — (The complete works of Lucius Annaeus
Seneca)
        ISBN 978-0-226-26517-9 (hardcover : alk. paper) —
    ISBN 978-0-226-26520-9 (e-book)  1. Ethics—Early works
to 1800.  I. Graver, Margaret, translator.  II. Long, A. A.,
translator.  III. Title.  IV. Series: Seneca, Lucius Annaeus,
approximately 4 B.C. –65 A.D. Works. English. 2010.
    PA6665.A1G739 2015
    188—dc23

                                        2014044259

♾ This paper meets the requirements of ANSI/NISO Z39.48-
1992 (Permanence of Paper).

# Contents

# Seneca and His World

ELIZABETH ASMIS, SHADI BARTSCH, AND MARTHA C. NUSSBAUM

Seneca once remarked of Socrates that it was his death by hemlock that made him great (*Letter* 13.14). With reason: Socrates' death demonstrated the steadfastness of his philosophical principles and his belief that death offered nothing to fear. When Seneca himself, then, was ordered to commit suicide by Nero in 65 CE, we might well believe Tacitus's account in his *Annals* (15.63) that the Roman Stoic modeled his death on that of Socrates, discoursing calmly about philosophy with his friends as the blood drained out of his veins. In Tacitus's depiction we see, for once, a much-criticized figure living up to the principles he preached.

Seneca's life was mired in political advancement and disappointment, shaped by the effects of exile and return, and compromised by his relationship with the emperor Nero—first his pupil, then his advisee, and finally his murderer. But his many writings say little about his political career and almost nothing about his relationship with Nero except for what can be gleaned from his essay *On Clemency*, leaving us to turn to later sources for information—Tacitus, Suetonius, and Dio Cassius in particular. We know that Seneca was born to a prominent equestrian family in Corduba, Spain, some time between 4 and 1 BCE. He was the second of three sons of Helvia and Lucius Annaeus Seneca (the youngest son, Annaeus Mela, was the father of the poet Lucan). The elder Seneca had spent much of his life in Rome, and Seneca himself was brought to Rome as a young boy. There he was educated in rhetoric and later became a student of the philosopher Sextius. But his entry into political life was delayed, and when he did enter upon the *cursus honorum* late in Tiberius's reign, his ill health (he had asthma and possibly tuberculosis) was a source of difficulty. In any case his career was cut short. He survived Caligula's hostility, which the sources tell us was thanks to his talents in oratory, but was sent into exile on Corsica by Claudius shortly after Caligula's death in 41 CE. The charge, almost certainly false, was adultery with Caligula's younger sister, Julia Livilla. Seneca spent his time in exile in philosophical and natural study and wrote the *Consolations* to Helvia (his mother) and to Polybius (Claudius's freedman secretary), revealing in the latter how desperately he hoped to be recalled to Rome.

When Seneca did return in 49 CE, it was under different auspices. Claudius had recently remarried, to Germanicus's daughter Agrippina, and she urged him to recall Seneca as tutor to her son, the twelve-year-old Nero. Claudius already had a younger son, Britannicus, but it was clear that the wily Agrippina wished to see her own flesh and blood on the throne. When Claudius died five years later, Agrippina was able to maneuver Nero into position as emperor—and Britannicus was dispatched by poison shortly after, in 55 CE.

From 54 until his influence waned at the end of the decade, Seneca acted as Nero's adviser, together with the praetorian prefect Sextus Afranius Burrus. We know he wrote a speech on clemency for Nero to deliver to the Roman senate soon after his accession, and Seneca's own essay *On Clemency* may contain some inkling of his strategy to keep the young emperor from running amok. Seneca's use of the term *rex*, or king, applied to Nero by analogy in this piece, is surprising from a Roman senator, but he seems to have hoped that flattering Nero by pointing to his limitless power and the value of clemency would be one way to keep him from abusing that power. Both Seneca and Burrus also helped with the civil and judicial administration of the empire.

Many historians, ancient and modern, feel that this early part of Nero's reign, moderated by Seneca and Burrus, represented a period of comparative good rule and harmony (the "*quinquennium Neronis*"). The decline started in 59 CE with Nero's murder of Agrippina, after which Seneca wrote the emperor's speech of self-exculpation—perhaps the most famous example of how the philosopher found himself increasingly compromised in his position as Nero's chief counsel. Certainly as a Stoic, Seneca cuts an ambiguous figure next to the others who made their opposition to Nero clear, such as Thrasea Paetus and Helvidius Priscus. His participation in court politics probably led him to believe that he could do more good from where he stood than by abandoning Nero to his own devices—if he even had this choice.

In any case, Seneca's influence over Nero seems to have been considerably etiolated after the death of Burrus in 62. According to Tacitus, Seneca tried to retire from his position twice, in 62 and

64. Although Nero refused him on both occasions, Seneca seems to have largely absented himself from the court after 64. In 65 CE came the Pisonian conspiracy, a plot to kill Nero and replace him with the ringleader, C. Calpurnius Piso. Although Seneca's nephew Lucan was implicated in this assassination attempt, Seneca himself was probably innocent. Nonetheless, Nero seized the opportunity to order his old adviser to kill himself. Seneca cut his own veins, but (so Tacitus tells us) his thinness and advanced age hindered the flow of blood. When a dose of poison also failed to kill him, he finally sat in a hot bath to make the blood flow faster. His wife, Pompeia Paulina, also tried to commit suicide but was saved on orders from Nero.

Because of his ethical writings, Seneca fared well with the early Christians—hence the later forging of a fake correspondence with St. Paul—but already in antiquity he had his fair share of critics, the main charge arising from the apparent contradiction between his Stoic teachings on the unimportance of "externals" and his own amassing of huge wealth. Perhaps for this reason he never gained the respect accorded the "Roman Socrates," the Stoic C. Musonius Rufus, banished by Nero in 65, even though Seneca's writings have had far more influence over the centuries. In Seneca's own lifetime one P. Suillius attacked him on the grounds that, since Nero's rise to power, he had piled up some 300 million sesterces by charging high interest on loans in Italy and the provinces—though Suillius himself was no angel and was banished to the Balearic Islands for being an embezzler and informant. In Seneca's defense, he seems to have engaged in ascetic habits throughout his life and despite his wealth. In fact, his essay *On the Happy Life* (*De vita beata*) takes the position that a philosopher may be rich as long as his wealth is properly gained and spent and his attitude to it is appropriately detached. Where Seneca finally ranks in our estimation may rest on our ability to tolerate the various contradictions posed by the life of this philosopher in politics.

## A Short Introduction to Stoicism

Stoicism is one of the world's most influential philosophical movements. Starting from the works and teaching of the three original heads of the Greek Stoic school—Zeno of Citium (335–263 BCE), Cleanthes (331–232 BCE), and Chrysippus (ca. 280–207 BCE)—it became the leading philosophical movement of the ancient Greco-Roman world, shaping the development of thought well into the Christian era. Later Greek Stoics Panaetius (ca. 185–109 BCE) and Posidonius (ca. 135–51 BCE) modified some features of Stoic doctrine. Roman thinkers then took up the cause, and Stoicism became the semiofficial creed of the Roman political and literary world. Cicero (106–43 BCE) does not agree with the Stoics on metaphysical and epistemological matters, but his ethical and political positions lie close to theirs, and even when he does not agree, he makes a concerted effort to report their positions sympathetically. Roman Stoics Seneca, Epictetus (mid-first to early second century CE), Musonius Rufus (ca. 30–ca. 102 BCE), and the emperor Marcus Aurelius (121–80 CE, emperor 161–80) produced Stoic works of their own (the last three writing in Greek).

The philosophical achievement of the Greek Stoics, and especially that of Chrysippus, was enormous: the invention of propositional logic, the invention of the philosophy of language, unprecedented achievements in moral psychology, distinction in areas ranging from metaphysics and epistemology to moral and political philosophy. Through an accident of history, however, all the works of all the major Greek Stoics have been lost, and we must recover their thoughts through fragments, reports (particularly the lengthy accounts in Diogenes Laertius's *Lives of the Philosophers*, in Cicero, and in Sextus Empiricus's skeptical writings, since the Stoics are his primary target), and the works of the Roman thinkers—who often are adjusting Stoic doctrines to fit Roman reality and probably contributing creative insights of their own. This also means that we know somewhat less about Stoic logic or physics than about Stoic ethics, since the Romans took a particular interest in the practical domain.

The goal of Stoic philosophy, like that of other philosophical schools of the Hellenistic era, was to give the pupil a flourishing life free from the forms of distress and moral failure that the Stoics thought ubiquitous in their societies. Unlike some of their competitor schools, however, they emphasized the need to study all parts of their threefold system—logic, physics, and ethics—in order to understand the universe and its interconnections. To the extent that a Roman such as Cicero believed he could uphold the moral truths of Stoicism without a confident belief in a rationally ordered universe, he held a heretical position (one shared many centuries later by Immanuel Kant).

Stoic physics held that the universe is a rationally ordered whole, and that everything that happens in it happens for the best of reasons. (It is this position, in its Leibnizian incarnation, that is pilloried in Voltaire's *Candide*.) Rejecting traditional anthropomorphic religion, the Stoics gave the name Zeus to the rational and providential principle animating the universe as a whole, and they could find even in the most trivial or distressing events (such as earthquakes and thunderbolts) signs of the universe's overall good order. This order was also a moral order based on the inherent dignity and worth of the moral capacities of each and every rational being. The Stoics believed that this order was deterministic: everything happens of necessity. But they were also "compatibilists," believing that human free will is compatible with the truth of determinism. They engaged in spirited debates with "incompatibilist" Aristotelians, making lasting contributions to the free will controversy.

Stoic ethics begins from the idea of the boundless worth of the rational capacity in each and every human being. The Roman Stoics understood this capacity to be centrally practical and moral. (Thus, unlike Plato, they did not think that people who had a natural talent for mathematics were better than people who didn't, and they became more and more skeptical that even the study of logic had much practical value.) They held that all human beings are equal in worth by virtue of their possession of the precious capacity to choose and direct their lives, ranking some ends ahead of others. This, they said, was what distinguished human beings from animals: this power of selection and rejection. (Unlike most other ancient schools, they had little concern for the morality of animal treatment, since they thought that only moral capacity entitled a being to respect and good treatment.) Children, they said, come into the world like little animals, with a natural orientation toward self-preservation but no understanding of true worth. Later, however, a remarkable shift will take place, already set up by their possession of innate human nature: they will be able to appreciate the beauty of the capacity for choice and the way in which moral reason has shaped the entire universe. This recognition, they said, should lead people to respect both self and others in an entirely new way. Stoics were serious about (human) equality: they urged the equal education of both slaves and women. Epictetus himself was a former slave.

Stoicism looks thus far like an ethical view with radical political consequences, and so it became during the Enlightenment, when its distinctive emphases were used to argue in favor of equal political rights and more nearly equal economic opportunities. However, the original Stoics maintain a claim of great significance for politics: moral capacity is the only thing that has intrinsic worth. Money, honor, power, bodily health, and even the love of friends, children, and spouse—all these are held to be things that one may reasonably pursue if nothing impedes (they are called "preferred indifferents"), but they have no true intrinsic worth. They should not even be seen as commensurate with moral worth. So when they do not arrive as one wishes, it is wrong to be distressed.

This was the context in which the Stoics introduced their famous doctrine of *apatheia*, freedom from the passions. Defining the major emotions or passions as all involving a high valuation of "external goods," they argue that the good Stoic will not have any of these disturbances of the personality. Realizing that chance events lie beyond our control, the Stoic will find it unnecessary to experience grief, anger, fear, or even hope: all these are characteristic of a mind that waits in suspense, awestruck by things indifferent. We can have a life that truly involves joy (of the right sort) if we appreciate that the most precious thing of all, and the only truly precious thing, lies within our control at all times.

Stoics do not think that it is at all easy to get rid of the cultural errors that are the basis of the rejected passions: thus a Stoic life is a constant therapeutic process in which mental exercises are devised to wean the mind from its unwise attachments. Their works depict processes of therapy through which the reader may make progress in the direction of Stoic virtue, and they often engage their reader in just such a process. Epictetus and Marcus Aurelius describe processes of repeated meditation; Seneca (in *On Anger*) describes his own nightly self-examination. Seneca's *Letters* show the role that a wiser teacher can play in such a therapeutic process, but Seneca evidently does not think that even he himself is free from erroneous attachments. The "wise man" is in that sense a distant ideal, not a worldly reality, particularly for the Roman Stoics. A large aid in the therapeutic process is the study of the horrible deformities that societies (including one's own) suffer by caring too much about external goods. If one sees the ugly face of power, honor, and even love clearly enough, this may assist one in making the progress toward true virtue. Thus Seneca's *On Anger* is an example of a genre that we know to have been common in Stoicism.

Because of their doctrine of value, the Stoics actually do not propose radical changes in the distribution of worldly goods, as one might suppose equal regard for the dignity of all human beings would require. They think that equal respect does require dignified treatment of each person; thus Seneca urges masters not to beat their slaves or use them as sexual tools. About the institution of slavery, however, there is silence, and worse than silence: Seneca argues that true freedom is internal freedom, so the external sort does not really matter. Musonius, similarly, advocates respectful treatment for women, including access to a Stoic education. But as for changes in the legal arrangements that confined women to a domestic role and gave males power of life and death over them, he too is silent, arguing that women will manifest their Stoic virtue in the domestic context. Some Roman Stoics do appear to have thought that political liberty is a part of dignity, and thus died supporting republican institutions, but whether this attention to external conditions was consistent with Stoicism remains unclear. (Certainly Cicero's profound grief over the loss of political freedom was not the attitude of a Stoic, any more than was his agonizing grief over his daughter's death.)

There was also much debate about whether the Stoic norm of *apatheia* encouraged people to detach themselves from bad political events in a way that gave aid and comfort to bad politics. Certainly Stoics were known to counsel retirement from politics (a theme in Seneca's own life as he sought Nero's permission for retirement, unsuccessfully), and they were thought to believe that upheaval is worse than lawless tyranny. Plutarch reports that Brutus (a Platonist) questioned potential coconspirators in the assassination of Julius Caesar by trying to determine whether they accepted that Stoic norm or believed, with him, that lawless tyranny is worse than civil strife; only non-Stoics were selected for the group of assassins. During Nero's reign, however, several prominent Stoics—including Seneca and his nephew Lucan—joined republican political movements aimed at overthrowing Nero and lost their lives for their efforts, by politically ordered suicide.

Stoics believed that from the moral point of view, national boundaries are as irrelevant as honor, wealth, gender, and birth. They held that we are, first and foremost, citizens of the universe as a whole. (The term *kosmou polites*, citizen of the universe, was apparently first used by Diogenes the Cynic, but the Stoics took it up and were the real forefathers of modern cosmopolitanism.) What cosmopolitanism meant in practical terms was unclear, for the reasons already given—but Cicero thinks, at any rate (in *On Duties*, a highly Stoic work), that our common human dignity entails some very strict limits on the reasons for going to war and the sort of conduct that is permissible in it. He thus adumbrated the basis of the modern law of war. Cicero denied, however, that our common humanity entails any duty to distribute material goods beyond our own borders, thus displaying the unfortunate capacity of Stoic doctrine to support the status quo. Cicero's *On Duties* has had such an enormous influence on posterity in this that it is scarcely an exaggeration to blame the Stoics for the fact that we have well-worked-out doctrines of international law in the area of war and peace, but no well-established understanding of our material duties to one another.

Stoicism's influence on the development of the entire Western intellectual tradition cannot be underestimated. Christian thought owes it a large debt. Clement of Alexandria is just one example of a Christian thinker steeped in Stoicism; even a thinker such as Augustine, who contests many Stoic theses, finds it natural to begin from Stoic positions. Even more strikingly, many philosophers of the early modern era turn to Stoicism for guidance—far more often than they turn to Aristotle or Plato. Descartes' ethical ideas are built largely on Stoic models; Spinoza is steeped in Stoicism at every point; Leibniz's teleology is essentially Stoic; Hugo Grotius bases his ideas of international morality and law on Stoic models; Adam Smith draws more from the Stoics than from other ancient schools of thought; Rousseau's ideas of education are in essence based on Stoic models; Kant finds inspiration in the Stoic ideas of human dignity and the peaceful world community; and the American founders are steeped in Stoic ideas, including the ideas of equal dignity and cosmopolitanism, which also deeply influence the American transcendentalists

Emerson and Thoreau. Because the leading works of Greek Stoicism had long been lost, all these thinkers were reading the Roman Stoics. Because many of them read little Greek, they were primarily reading Cicero and Seneca.

The Stoic influence on the history of literature has also been immense. In the Roman world, all the major poets, like other educated Romans, were acquainted with Stoic ideas and alluded to them often in their work. Virgil and Lucan are perhaps particularly significant in this regard. Later European literary traditions also show marked traces of Stoic influence—in part via the influence of Roman literature, and in part through the influence of philosophers in their own time who were themselves influenced by Stoic thought, but often also through their own reading of the influential works of Cicero, Seneca, and Marcus Aurelius.

### Seneca's Stoicism

Seneca identifies himself as a Stoic. He declares his allegiance by repeatedly referring to "our people" (*nostri*)—the Stoics—in his writings. Yet he exercises considerable independence in relation to other Stoics. While he is committed to upholding basic Stoic doctrines, he recasts them on the basis of his own experience as a Roman and a wide reading of other philosophers. In this respect he follows a tradition of Stoic philosophical innovation exemplified most clearly by Panaetius and Posidonius, who introduced some Platonic and Aristotelian elements while adapting Stoicism to Roman circumstances. Seneca differs from previous Stoics by welcoming some aspects of Epicurean philosophy along with other influences.

Seneca is concerned above all with applying Stoic ethical principles to his life and to the lives of others like him. The question that dominates his philosophical writings is how an individual can achieve a good life. In his eyes, the quest for virtue and happiness is a heroic endeavor that places the successful person above the assaults of fortune and on a level with god. To this end, Seneca transforms the sage into an inspirational figure who can motivate others to become like him by his gentle humanity and joyful tranquility. Key topics are how to reconcile adversity with providence, how to free oneself from passions (particularly anger and grief), how to face death, how to disengage oneself from political involvement, how to practice poverty and use wealth, and how to benefit others. All these endeavors are viewed within the context of a supreme, perfectly rational and virtuous deity who looks with favor on the efforts of humans to attain the same condition of virtue. In the field of politics, Seneca argues for clemency on the part of the supreme ruler, Nero. In human relations, he pays special attention to friendship and the position of slaves. Overall, he aims to replace social hierarchies, with their dependence on fortune, with a moral hierarchy arranged according to proximity to the goal of being a sage.

Seneca's own concerns and personality permeate his writings. The modern reader learns much about the life of an aristocrat in the time of Claudius and Nero, and much about Seneca's personal strengths and weaknesses. At the same time, there is also much in the work that transcends the immediate concerns of Seneca and his period. Some topics that resonate especially with a modern audience are his vision of humans as members of a universal community of mankind, the respect he demands for slaves, his concern with human emotions, and, in general, his insistence on looking within oneself to find happiness. What is perhaps less appealing to the modern reader is the rhetorical elaboration of his message, which features an undeniable tendency toward hyperbole. Most of all, Seneca's own character strikes many readers as problematic. From his own time onward, he was perceived by some as a hypocrite who was far from practicing what he preached. Some of Seneca's writings (in particular, his *Consolations* to Polybius and his mother Helvia, and his essay *On the Happy Life*) are obviously self-serving. As Seneca himself suggests (*Letters* 84), he has transformed the teachings he has culled, in the manner of bees, into a whole that reflects his own complex character.

The Stoics divided logic into dialectic (short argument) and rhetoric (continuous exposition). There is not much to be said on dialectic in Seneca's writings except that he shuns it, along with formal logic in general. Every so often, however, he engages in a satirical display of fine-grained Stoic-type reasoning. The point is that carrying logical precision to excess is futile: it does not make a person any better. Quibbles of all kinds should be avoided, whether they involve carrying through a minute line of argument, making overly subtle verbal distinctions, or indulging in abstruse philological interpretation. While making the point, Seneca makes sure the reader knows he could beat the quibbler at his own game if he wanted to.

We have only sparse details about how the Stoics viewed rhetoric. What is clear about Seneca, however, is that he used the full panoply of Roman rhetorical methods to persuade readers of his philosophical message. His writings are full of vivid examples, stunning metaphors, pointed sayings, ringing sound effects. He knows how to vary his tone, from casual conversation to soaring exhortation and bitter denunciation. He peoples his text with a varied cast of characters: the addressee, the implied audience, hypothetical objectors, friends, opponents, historical figures. He himself hovers over the proceedings as watchful friend and sometime foe. Following Cleanthes, he intersperses poetry into his prose to impel the reader even more forcefully toward the task of self-improvement.

Given Seneca's ethical aims, it is perhaps surprising that he devotes a large work, *Natural Questions*, to physics. Yet the entire work has an overarching ethical aim. As Seneca insists repeatedly, the mind is uplifted by venturing beyond narrowly human concerns to survey the world as a whole. The contemplation of the physical world complements moral action by showing the full context of human action: we see god in his full glory, caring for human lives as he administers the world as a whole. In the spirit of Lucretius (who championed a rival philosophy), Seneca also intersperses ethical messages throughout his physical inquiries. Thus he emphasizes that humans must confront natural events, such as death and natural disasters, with courage and gratitude to god; and he warns against human misuse of natural resources and the decadence that accompanies progress. Of all areas of inquiry, physics affords Seneca the greatest scope for making additions and corrections to Stoic doctrine. He ranges over the whole history of physical inquiries, from the Pre-Socratics to his own time, to improve on the Stoics.

Seneca writes (*Letters* 45.4) that while he believes "in the judgment of great men," he also claims something for his own judgment: previous philosophers left some things to be investigated by us, which they might indeed have discovered for themselves if they hadn't engaged in useless quibbles. Granted that Seneca shows special investigative fervor in his cosmological inquiries, his moral teachings too are a product of his own judgment and innovation.

What he contributes is a new vision rather than new theories. Using certain strict Stoic distinctions as a basis, he paints a new picture of the challenges that humans face and the happiness that awaits those who practice the correct philosophy. In agreement with Stoic orthodoxy, Seneca is uncompromising about differentiating between external advantages and the good, about the need to eradicate the passions, about the perfect rationality of the wise person, about the identity of god with fate. What he adds is a moral fervor, joined by a highly poetic sensibility, that turns these distinctions into springboards for action.

The Stoic sage was generally viewed by critics as a forbidding figure, outside the reach of human capabilities and immune to human feeling. Seneca concedes, or rather emphasizes, that the sage is indeed rare; he remarks that the sage is like a phoenix, appearing perhaps every five hundred years (*Letters* 42.1). As he sees it, the sage's exceptional status is not a barrier to improvement; it inspires. Seneca gives real-life immediacy to the sage by citing the younger Cato, opponent of Julius Caesar, as an example. Cato, indeed, is not just any sage; Seneca says he is not sure whether Cato might even surpass *him* (*On Constancy* 7.1). In this he is not blurring Stoic distinctions but highlighting the indomitable moral strength of a sage. Through Cato and numerous other examples from the Roman past, Seneca fuses the Stoic sage with the traditional image of a Roman hero, thus spurring his Roman readers to fulfill their duties by emulating both at once.

Below the level of sage, Seneca outlines three stages of moral progress, demarcated according to our vulnerability to irrational emotions (*Letters* 75). There is the condition very near to that of being a sage, in which a person is not yet confident of being able to withstand irrational emotions (the so-called passions, *pathê*). Just below it is the stage in which a person is still capable of lapsing, and at the lowest level of progress a person can avoid most irrational emotions, but not all. Below these are the innumerable people who have yet to make progress. Seneca has nothing to say to them; he wants to avoid them, lest he be contaminated. What he does allow is that persons who are still struggling to become good may give way to grief initially; but he insists that this period must be brief. The Stoics talk "big words," he says, when they forbid moans and groans; he'll adopt a more gentle tone (*Letters* 23.4). Still, he insists, these words are "true"; and his aim is to lead, as much as he can, to the goal of a dispassionate attitude toward externals. Like everyone, the wise person is prone to initial shocks—reactions that look momentarily like irrational emotions—but these are involuntary responses to be succeeded immediately by the calmness of judgment. Seneca's sage is kind to others and is filled with a serene joy that has nothing to do with the ephemeral pleasure that other people take in externals.

Looking toward Roman heroism, Seneca portrays moral progress as an arduous struggle, like a military campaign or the uphill storming of an enemy's position. The enemy is fortune, viciously attacking its victim in the form of the most cruel disasters. Its opponent may succumb, but he will have conquered fortune if he resists to the end. In reality, the disasters come from other people or simply from circumstances. Seneca commonly cites death (whether one's own or that of a loved one), exile, torture, and illness. His own life is rich with examples. He goes so far as to advocate adversity as a means of making moral progress, but he also allows (with a view to his own wealth) that favorable circumstances are a help to the person who is still struggling to make progress.

To make progress, a person must not only confront externals but also, above all, look within oneself. Drawing inspiration from Plato, Seneca tells us there is a god inside; there is a soul that seeks to free itself from the dross of the body. Seneca invites the reader to withdraw into this inner self, so as to both meditate on one's particular condition and take flight in the contemplation of god. This withdrawal can occur in the press of a very active life. But it's easier when one is no longer fully caught up in politics, and so Seneca associates moral withdrawal with his own attempt to withdraw from politics toward the end of his life. He insists that he will continue to help others through his philosophical teachings, like other Stoics.

## Senecan Tragedy

From Seneca's hand there survive eight tragedies (*Agamemnon, Thyestes, Oedipus, Medea, Phaedra, Phoenissae, Troades, Hercules Furens*), not including the spurious *Octavia* and the probably spurious *Hercules Oetaeus*; of the *Phoenissae* there remain only fragments. These dramas have undergone many vicissitudes in fortune throughout the centuries; however, they are no longer criticized as being mere flawed versions of the older Greek dramas in which much of Seneca's subject matter had already been treated. While Seneca's plays were once mined only for the light they shed on Roman Stoic philosophy, for examples of rhetorical extravagance, or for the reconstruction of missing plays by Sophocles and his fellows, the traits that once marked the dramas as unworthy of critical attention now engage us in their own right. Indeed, they are the only extant versions of any Roman tragedy, the writings of other dramatists such as Marcus Pacuvius (ca. 220–130 BCE) and Lucius Accius (ca. 170–86 BCE) having been lost to posterity. It is thus only Seneca's version of Roman drama, translated into English as the *Tenne Tragedies* in 1581, that so influenced the tragedians of the Elizabethan era.

Seneca may have turned his hand to writing drama as early as the reign of Caligula (37–41 CE), although there is no way of determining exactly when he began. Our first reference to the plays comes from a famous graffito from the *Agamemnon* preserved on a wall in Pompeii, but we can only deduce that this was written before the eruption of Vesuvius in 79 CE; it is of little actual use in trying to date the dramas. Stylistic analysis has not provided us with a sure order of composition, though scholars seem to agree that the *Thyestes* and the *Phoenissae* are late efforts. Certainly we are unable to make claims about their dating with respect to the *Essays* and *Letters*, despite the very different tones of Seneca's prose and his poetry—a difference that led some readers, including the fifth-century churchman and orator Sidonius Apollinaris and after him Erasmus and Diderot, to speculate (erroneously) that there might have been two Lucius Annaeus Senecas at work on them rather than one.

This confusion about the authorship of Seneca's writing may seem natural, given the argument that Stoicism fails as a way of life in the dramas. Whether it fails because its adherents are too weak to resist the pull of desire or emotion, because Stoicism itself is too difficult to practice successfully, because the universe is not the locus of a divine providence, or because the protagonists are so evil that they fail to see providence in action is open to argument; a metaliterary view might even suggest that plotlines inherited from mythology provide the force that condemns a Cassandra or a Polyxena to death at the hands of a Clytemnestra or a Ulysses, with Seneca taking advantage of this dramatic fact to suggest the inexorable workings of Fate and the futility of struggle against it. Consider the *Thyestes* (a topic often dramatized in the Late Republic, though Seneca's version is the only one we have). We meet the eponymous exile as he praises the pauper's life to his children—only the man who drinks out of earthenware cups can be truly happy and without fear, he reminds them—but when invited to return to the palace at Argos by his conniving brother Atreus, the source of his exile, he allows himself to be lured back after only a token hesitation about giving up his newfound equanimity. "Sequor," he says to his son, "I follow you"; but in following his appetite for the luxurious life he does the opposite of the good Stoic.

The rest is, well, the stuff of myth. Dressed in royal regalia, Thyestes sits down to enjoy a hearty stew and some fine red wine, but his satiated belches soon turn into howls of horror as the delighted Atreus informs him of his dinner's provenance: the meal is made up of the dismembered bodies of Thyestes' own sons. Is there an explicit ethical or philosophical message here? If we followed the view of another Stoic, Epictetus (ca. 55–ca. 135 CE), who defined tragedy as what happens "when chance events befall fools" (*Discourses* 2.26.31 ), we might conclude that the story of Thyestes precisely illustrates the folly of giving in to a desire for power (or haute cuisine). In Seneca's treatment, however, such a clear object lesson seems undermined by a number of factors: the fact that Atreus reigns triumphant as the drama ends; the undeniable echoes of Stoic exhortation in the impotent counsels of Atreus's adviser; and the fragility of civic and religious values—the hellish scene in which Atreus sacrifices the children represents precisely a travesty of sacrifice itself, while *xenia* (the ancient tradition of hospitality) fares still worse. The adviser or a nurse mouthing Stoic platitudes without effect is featured in many of the plays: Phaedra, Clytemnestra, and Medea all have nurses to counsel them against their paths of action, even though their advice is invariably distorted and thrown back in their faces. Creon plays a similar role in the *Agamemnon*.

Other Senecan protagonists have more lasting doubts than Thyestes about the value of earthly success. Oedipus asks: "Joys any man in power?" And unlike his more confident Sophoclean manifestation, he feels the answer is clearly no. From the beginning of the play, the

*Oedipus* provides striking contrasts to its Greek precedent, whose emphasis on the discovery of identity yields here to the overwhelming sense of pollution affecting Oedipus. The king, anxious even as the drama opens, worries that he will not escape the prophecy of his parricide, and suspects he is responsible for the plague ravaging Thebes. Despondent, he hopes for immediate death; his emotional state is far different from that of the character at the center of Sophocles' play. Seneca's version also features Creon's report of the long necromantic invocation of Laius's ghost in a dark grove, something absent in Sophocles. Even the sense that the characters' interaction onstage fails to drive the drama makes sense in the context of Seneca's forbidding and inexorable dramatic world. Causality and *anagnorisis* (dramatic recognition) are put aside in favor of the individual's helplessness before what awaits him, and the characters' speeches react to the violence rather than motivate it.

The pollution of the heavens by humans goes against Stoic physics but finds its place in the plays. The Stoics posited a tensional relationship between the cosmos and its parts; according to this view, the *pneuma*, or vital spirit, that subtends all matter results in a cosmic sympathy of the parts with the whole. "All things are united together . . . and earthly things feel the influence of heavenly ones," as Epictetus (*Discourses* 1.4.1) puts it. But what we see in the dramas is a disquieting manifestation of this *sympatheia*: the idea that the wickedness of one or a few could disrupt the rational and harmonic logos of the entire cosmos represents a reversal of the more orthodox Stoic viewpoint that the world is accessible to understanding and to reason. Thus we see the universe trembling at Medea's words, and the law of heaven in disorder. In the *Thyestes*, the sun hides its face in response to Atreus's crime; in the *Phaedra*, the chorus notes an eclipse after Phaedra's secret passion is unveiled. Horrific portents presage what is to come in the *Troades*. In Seneca's dramas, unlike in Greek tragedy, there is no role for civic institutions or the city to intervene in this relationship. The treatment of the gods is similarly unorthodox. Although Jason calls on Medea to witness that there are no gods in the heavens, the very chariot in which she flies away is evidence of the assistance given her by her divine father. The gods are there; the problem is that they are unrecognizable.

Seneca's great antiheroes like Medea and Thyestes are troubling not only because they often triumph, but because the manner of their triumph can resemble the goal point of the aspiring Stoic: in exhorting themselves to take up a certain stance toward the world, in abandoning familial and social ties, in rejecting the moral order of the world around them, and in trying to live up to a form of selfhood they have judged to be "better," Seneca's tyrants, just like his sages, construct a private and autonomous world around themselves which nothing can penetrate. Not only do they borrow the self-exhortations and self-reproving of the Stoic's arsenal, in which the dialogue conducted with the self suggests a split between a first-order desiring self and a second-order judging self, but they also adopt the consideration of what befits or is worthy of them as a guiding principle always with a negative outcome.

This leads in turn to a metatheatrical tinge in several of the plays. In the *Medea*, for example, Medea seems to look to prior versions of her own story to discover what exactly is appropriate for her persona, in the same way that Oedipus, after putting out his eyes, remarks, "*This* face befits (an) Oedipus" (*Oedipus* 1000) or that Atreus says of his recipe, "This is a crime that befits Thyestes—and befits Atreus" (*Thyestes* 271). Such metatheatricality seems to draw on the concern of the traditional Roman elite to perform exemplary actions for an approving audience, to generate one's ethical exemplarity by making sure that spectators for it exist.

And spectators do exist—we, the theater audience or the recitation audience. Scholars have long debated the question of whether Seneca's dramas were staged in antiquity. It is possible, as argued by the nineteenth-century German scholar Friedrich Leo, the tragedies were written for recitation only; inter alia, it would be unusual (but not impossible) to represent animal sacrifice and murder onstage. The question is unresolvable, but whether the original audiences were in the theater or in the recitation room, they shared with us the full knowledge of how the story would turn out, and in this they uncomfortably resembled some of the plotting antiheroes themselves. Indeed, our pleasure in watching Senecan tragedy unfold might seem to assimilate us to the pleasure these characters take in inflicting suffering on one another. In a famous line from the *Troades*, the messenger who brings news of Astyanax's murder reports of the scene of his death—which he has already compared to a theater—that "the greater part of the fickle crowd abhors the crime—and watches it" (1128–29). Here, in the tension between sadistic voyeurism and horror at what the drama unfolds, we can recognize the uncomfortable position of the spectator of Seneca's despairing plays.

## Senecan Drama after the Classical Period

The fortunes of Senecan drama have crested twice: once during the Elizabethan period, and again in our own day. Although Seneca himself never refers to his tragedies, they were known in antiquity at least until Boethius (ca. 480–524 CE), whose *Consolation of Philosophy* draws on the themes of Seneca's choral odes. The dramas then largely dropped from sight, to reemerge in 1300 in a popular edition and commentary by Nicholas Trevet, a Dominican scholar at Oxford. Trevet's work was followed by vernacular translations in Spain, Italy, and France over the next two centuries. In Italy, an early imitator was Albertino Mussato (1261–1329), who wrote his tragic drama *Ecerinis* to alert his fellow Paduans to the danger presented by the tyrant of Verona. In England, the Jesuit priest and poet Jasper Heywood (1535–1598) produced translations of three of the plays; these were followed by Thomas Newton's *Seneca His Tenne Tragedies Translated into English* in 1581—of which one tragedy was Newton's own *Thebais*. The dramas were considered to be no mere pale shadow of their Greek predecessors: Petrarch, Salutati, and Scaliger all held Seneca inferior to none on the classical stage. In Scaliger's influential treatise on poetry, the *Poetices libri septem* (1561), he ranks Seneca as the equal of the Greek dramatists in solemnity and superior to Euripides in elegance and polish (6.6).

The Elizabethan playwrights in particular took up Seneca as a model for translation or imitation. T. S. Eliot claimed, "No author exercised a wider or deeper influence on the Elizabethan mind or on the Elizabethan form of tragedy than did Seneca," and the consensus is that he was right. It is perhaps little wonder that Seneca appealed to an age in which tragedy was seen as the correct vehicle for the representation of "haughtinesse, arrogancy, ambition, pride, iniury, anger, wrath, envy, hatred, contention, warre, murther, cruelty, rapine, incest, rovings, depredations, piracyes, spoyles, robberies, rebellions, treasons, killings, hewing, stabbing, dagger-drawing, fighting, butchery, treachery, villainy, etc., and all kind of heroyicke evils whatsoever" (John Greene, *A Refutation of the Apology for Actors*, 1615, p. 56). Kyd, Marlowe, Marston, and Shakespeare all read Seneca in Latin at school, and much of their drama shows his influence in one form or another. The itinerant players at Elsinore in Shakespeare's *Hamlet* famously opine that "Seneca cannot be too heavy nor Plautus too light" (2.2.400–401), but it is Shakespeare's *Titus Andronicus* that shows the greatest Senecan influence with its taste for revenge, rape, decapitation, human cookery, and insanity. Richard III and Macbeth, on the other hand, exemplify the presence of unrestrained, brooding ambition in the power-hungry protagonist. Similarly, in such plays as Thomas Kyd's *The Spanish Tragedy* and John Marston's *Antonio's Revenge* we see the influence of such Senecan fixtures as ghosts speaking from beyond the grave, graphic violence, obsession with revenge, and even structural features such as choruses, use of stichomythia, and division into five acts.

The bleak content of the dramas was often tied to the notion of a moral lesson. Already Trevet's preface to the *Thyestes* argued that the play taught the correction of morals by example, as well as simply offered the audience enjoyment. The Jesuit Martín Antonio Delrio (1551–1608) defended the use of Roman drama in a Christian education by suggesting that it provided a masked instruction in wisdom, as did Mussato before him. Nonetheless, after the middle of the seventeenth century Seneca's drama fell largely into disrepute. The Restoration poet John Dryden (1631–1700) took the opportunity in the preface to his own *Oedipus* to criticize both Seneca's and Corneille's versions; of the former, he wrote that "Seneca . . . is always running after pompous expression, pointed sentences, and Philosophical notions, more proper for the Study than the Stage." The French dramatist Jean Racine (1639–1699) used Seneca as a model for his *Phèdre*, but at the same time claimed that his main debt was to Euripides. Not surprisingly, the Romantics did not find much to like in Seneca. Recently, however, an efflorescence of interest in both the literary and the performance aspects of Senecan drama has produced new editions, scholarly monographs, and the staging of some of the plays. Noteworthy here are Sarah Kane's adaptation *Phaedra's Love*, performed in New York in May 1996; Michael Elliot

Rutenberg's May 2005 dramatization of a post-Holocaust *Oedipus* at Haifa University in Israel; and a 2007 Joanne Akalaitis production of the *Thyestes* at the Court Theatre in Chicago.

A note on the translations: they are designed to be faithful to the Latin while reading idiomatically in English. The focus is on high standards of accuracy, clarity, and style in both the prose and the poetry. As such, the translations are intended to provide a basis for interpretive work rather than to convey personal interpretations. They eschew terminology that would imply a Judeo-Christian moral framework (e.g., "sin"). Where needed, notes have been supplied to explain proper names in mythology and geography.

### For Further Information

On Seneca's life: Miriam T. Griffin, *Seneca: A Philosopher in Politics* (Oxford: 1976), and Paul Veyne, *Seneca: The Life of a Stoic*, translated from the French by David Sullivan (New York: 2003). On his philosophical thought: Brad Inwood, *Seneca: Stoic Philosophy at Rome* (Oxford: 2005), and Shadi Bartsch and David Wray, *Seneca and the Self* (Cambridge: 2009). On the dramas: A. J. Boyle, *Tragic Seneca: An Essay in the Theatrical Tradition* (New York and London: 1997); C. A. J. Littlewood, *Self-Representation and Illusion in Senecan Tragedy* (Oxford: 2004); and Thomas G. Rosenmeyer, *Senecan Drama and Stoic Cosmology* (Berkeley: 1989). On Seneca and Shakespeare: Robert S. Miola, *Shakespeare and Classical Tragedy: The Influence of Seneca* (Oxford: 1992), and Henry B. Charlton, *The Senecan Tradition in Renaissance Tragedy* (Manchester: 1946).

# Introduction to the Letters on Ethics

MARGARET GRAVER AND A. A. LONG

Late in life, Seneca developed a new format for philosophical writing that he found especially congenial to his talents. Like the philosopher Epicurus, he would compose a series of letters on philosophical topics, using the intimacy of the personal letter as a vehicle for a searching examination of values and life choices. Unlike Epicurus, though, he would address his letters not to several different people but all to one individual, his younger friend Gaius Lucilius Iunior. In this way, he could replicate the sense of ongoing relationship that is strongly present in the letters written by Cicero to his close friend Atticus. Seneca's correspondence would not include any letters written by the addressee; but anyone reading it would nonetheless be constantly aware of Lucilius through frequent mentions of his name and references to his questions and concerns. Composed over the two to three years[1] before Seneca's death in the spring of 65 CE, the *Letters on Ethics to Lucilius* are their author's most significant philosophical contribution and, at the same time, his most innovative venture in literary composition.

The premise of the entire collection is stated in 8.2, where Seneca writes,

> The work that I am doing is for posterity: it is they who can benefit from what I write. I am committing to the page some healthful admonitions, like the recipes for useful salves. I have found these effective on my own sores, which, even if not completely healed, have ceased to spread. The right path, that I myself discovered late in life when weary from wandering, I now point out to others.

1. The period of composition must be after Seneca's retirement in 62 CE; it is concurrent with that of the *Natural Questions*, likewise referring to Lucilius's governorship. Of events mentioned in the correspondence, only the fire at Lyon (91.1) is datable, to late summer of 64 CE, but some letters mention the passage of the seasons, suggesting a rough chronology that spans either 63–65 (if the springtime of 23.1 is the same as that of 67.1) or 62–65 (if they are in successive years).

In his claim to benefit large numbers of people through his writing, Seneca offers an answer to a problem that had long been debated among philosophers. If it is incumbent on every human being to serve the community—a point emphasized in Stoic ethics—then what justification can there be for spending large amounts of time in philosophical study and reflection? This is the question investigated in Seneca's brief essay *On Leisure*. There he explains that a life spent in scholarly retreat may sometimes do more for others than another person's life of activity. The founders of Stoicism, he argues, did not serve in the military or hold public office, yet their work was beneficial to the entire human race; for one who writes on important philosophical topics addresses readers of every time and place. The *Letters on Ethics* claim to justify Seneca's retirement in the same way, by teaching Roman readers how to live happy and productive lives.

This stated purpose implies a rather limited range of objectives for philosophical writing. If the philosopher is to aid others in managing their emotions and making important life decisions, his concern should be with the most basic themes of ethics: the importance of personal integrity, the foundations of friendship, the reasons not to fear pain and death, and so on. Some such immediately applicable material is included in every one of the letters. It is in this sense that they are what the title promises: letters *on ethics*.[2] The premise of the collection allows, however, that the matters of practical ethics will be surrounded and enlivened by much material drawn from the author's personal experience and that of the recipient. Seneca describes his daily routine (80, 82), his trips through the countryside (52, 53, 87), his interactions with his wife (104). He evokes vivid scenes he has encountered: night singing over the lagoon at Baiae (51), the cacophony inside a bathhouse (56), the arrival of mail boats into harbor (77), the transplanting of a tree (86). Such highly engaging material ensures that the collection will remain attractive even to those with no prior

2. The title *Letters on Ethics to Lucilius* (*Epistulae Morales ad Lucilium*) is attested already in the second century (Aulus Gellius 12.2) and is given in the oldest surviving manuscript copies, dating to the ninth century; see Reynolds 1965a. Whether or not Seneca himself referred to his work by that title, he makes clear that the project is defined by its epistolary format (21, 38, 40, 75, 118) and by its prevailing interest in ethics (102.3, 121.1).

interest in philosophy, and assists as well in demonstrating the relevance of abstract principles to the business of daily living.

## Philosophy in Letters

The notion that material of high quality and lasting importance might be presented in the form of letters was one that could arise quite naturally in a Roman context. It was not only that Epicurus and other Greeks had sometimes written philosophical letters. Roman literary conventions allowed for works aimed at a wide readership to carry a formal dedication to some prominent individual whose name would appear, in the form used for direct address, in the first line or paragraph. Cicero's philosophical treatises had all begun in this way, as had Seneca's earlier essays on philosophical topics. Such dedications did not convey that the person named was actually in need of the information the work contained; rather, they offered a compliment to that person's literary taste and a promise to preserve his name for posterity. To some extent, this must also be the message conveyed to Lucilius in these letters. In letter 21, Seneca tells Lucilius,

> What Epicurus was able to promise his friend, I promise to you, Lucilius: I shall find favor with posterity, and I can bring others' names along with me, so that they will endure as well. (21.5)

Like the letters of Epicurus and even like Virgil's *Aeneid*, Seneca's letters will achieve a kind of immortality; in them, Seneca will live on after death, and Lucilius will live alongside him.

One may still ask whether the letters to Lucilius are real letters, in the sense that a real letter is one that is not only sent to the addressee but composed with an exclusive eye to that person's specific needs, interests, and knowledge. To this question the answer is surely no. Aspects of Lucilius's life are indeed featured: Seneca makes a point of mentioning his career in government (19, 31.9), his travels (14, 51, 79), his hometown of Pompeii (49, 53, 70), and his writings (8, 24, 46, 79). But such observations do not restrict the work to Lucilius's sole perspective; on the contrary, they honor him by sharing information about him with a wide audience. Nor do we find material in the work that is of merely topical significance. In contrast to the highly particularized letters of Cicero, which constantly refer to circumstances, persons, and events that will be understood only by the named addressee (118), those of Seneca make a conspicuous effort to be intelligible to a broad readership. Particulars that might not be understood outside the author's immediate circle are either reduced to the generic ("a friend of yours" in 3.1) or explained: Cornelius Senecio, for instance, is identified as "a prominent and conscientious Roman equestrian" (101.1). Material directed ostensibly to Lucilius alone is thus overheard, as it were, by other readers, who will find in it their own forms of benefit or amusement. Concern for the perspective of the general reader can be made explicit: in letter 17, for instance, Seneca explains that modest means are no obstacle to practicing philosophy, but then remarks to Lucilius that this point "applies to others, for *you* are more nearly among the wealthy" (17.10). As the more general perspective is compatible with Seneca's retaining a genuine interest in the problems and motivations of the real Lucilius, it is often impossible to say whether Lucilius actually experienced the events described—the hostile lawsuit of letter 24, for instance—or whether these are only typical situations that any reader might be likely to confront.

A new literary endeavor demands some kind of introduction, but the notion of a correspondence with an intimate friend precludes the usual formal opening: such close friends as Seneca and Lucilius ought already to have been corresponding for some time. Seneca gets around this difficulty by means of a stylized device like the *in medias res* openings of epic poems. The opening words of letter 1, "Do that," seem to refer to something Lucilius has said in a previous letter to Seneca, and yet the thing Lucilius is supposed to do is precisely to *begin* thinking about the matters Seneca is able to teach. In a powerful metaphor, this beginning is represented as an act of self-liberation. In Roman law, a slave was set free by the act of a vindicator (*vindex*), who formally claimed him or her into freedom; Lucilius, however, is told to "assert your own freedom" (*vindica te tibi*). He has been enslaved by various demands on his time; now he must lay claim to himself, by drawing back from his previous occupations and devoting himself to a course of reading and study.

Nor will he be reading just any sort of book. In the letter that immediately follows, Seneca instructs him not to go abroad, as it were, with his reading, but to settle down to one or two authors with whom he can become intimate, finding in their books a home and a source of sustenance. Further, he should extract from each day's reading some short maxim for subsequent reflection. To illustrate, Seneca provides a suitable example from his own reading, together with a brief reflection on it. Thus the letter itself enacts the recommended process of reading. As if to inculcate the practice, a similar maxim is provided at the close of every letter down to 29 at the end of book 3. It becomes a joke—Lucilius's "little gift" or "payment" or his "daily dole"—but it also serves to establish an important link between the reading of books and the business of living.[3]

One distinct advantage of the epistolary format is that it is open-ended. Virtually anything in Roman life might be made relevant to ethics, and even themes that have already been introduced can be developed further or taken in a different direction. There is no obvious reason why the sequence needs ever to end. To some extent, the format itself can also be altered without fundamentally changing the character of the correspondence. The initial practice of providing maxims for daily meditation is abandoned at the beginning of book 4, allowing for greater variety in the endings of letters. Longer and more demanding letters begin to appear; and some discussions develop more in the manner of a philosophical treatise, with problems clearly stated and arguments and counterarguments defending various positions. Seneca is careful, however, to maintain his practice of including some letters that are very short and some that treat the more colorful and amusing aspects of Roman life. He is intensely serious about philosophical matters, but the letters are never to become just another philosophical treatise.

A skilled rhetorician can find ways to include what he wishes to include even where the very premise of his work seems to exercise constraint. Despite the restrictive nature of the justification offered in letter 8, Seneca finds excuses to incorporate a wide variety of philosophical material, from tricks of logic (48 and 49) to the philosophical analysis of causation (65) and even the incorporeality of predicates (117). One of his favorite devices is to make a show of pulling him-

---

3. In the context of this running joke about reading material as a commodity for exchange, the phrase "your dear Epicurus" (23.9) can hardly be taken as evidence of a commitment to Epicurean philosophy on the part of Lucilius. It is, rather, Seneca himself who is interested in exploring Epicurean philosophy from the perspective of a Stoic.

self back from some fascinating topic that has no immediate ethical payoff. At 58.25, for instance, he interrupts himself in the midst of explaining some points in metaphysics with an elaborate apology ("'What have I to gain,' you say, 'from these fine distinctions of yours?' Nothing"), as if he thinks such topics do not properly belong in his letters.[4] Another verbal dodge is the ventriloquized question, in which the topic to be treated is presented as a response to some inquiry by Lucilius. Letter 113, for instance, begins by complaining that Lucilius is overly curious: the topic Seneca is about to treat is one of those that "are only right for people who go in for Greek shoes and cloaks"—yet he will treat it nonetheless. These and similar devices allow Seneca to take credit for the specialized knowledge of philosophy he really possesses while still preserving the epistolary decorum he has established.

Although the *Letters on Ethics* are the longest of Seneca's surviving works, the extant collection comes short of what Seneca actually wrote. A later Roman author, Aulus Gellius, quotes an excerpt from what he says is "the 22nd book of the letters on ethics that he wrote for Lucilius"; the work we have ends with book 20.[5] There cannot have been a great many additional letters, however, because Seneca did not have much time left to live: the fire at Lyon, mentioned in letter 91, took place only a few months before his death in 65 CE.

## Politics and Society

The Seneca of the *Letters on Ethics* was not only a scholarly retiree from public life but also a man who, as Nero's tutor and subsequent advisor, had lived and worked at the hub of political power. On a cursory sampling, the letters may give the impression that their author has quite detached himself from this extraordinary career, choosing the quiet life of a scholar over the political life. Many of the ethical concerns he airs to Lucilius transcend the particularities of time and place, making these items of the correspondence a universalist guide to life on such topics as happiness, friendship, fear, and death. At the same time, however, a discerning reader will find in the collection a range of historical and political themes that are highly revealing of

4. Additional examples include 65.15, 106.11–12, 113.21–22.
5. The quoted material is given here as fragments 1 and 2.

Seneca's personal values and outlook. This material is an essential component of Seneca's biography.

The political element of the work resonates in the constant presence of Lucilius, like Seneca a member of the equestrian order (44) who has been a government official: at the time the correspondence opens, Lucilius holds a high position as procurator (civil governor) of the province of Sicily. Seneca honors the personal characteristics that have enabled Lucilius to rise politically, and mentions his "distinguished connections" (19.3). At the same time, he consistently represents political influence as a dangerous acquisition that is best avoided. A parallel can be drawn to the *Natural Questions*, composed at around the same time as the *Letters on Ethics* and likewise dedicated to Lucilius. There Seneca praises Lucilius for his selfless loyalty to friends threatened with execution during the rule of Caligula; simultaneously, he reminds him of the tortures and fires he witnessed at the imperial court (*Natural Questions* 4a pref.). One should withdraw from public life not only for the sake of philosophical study but also to avoid the dangers and sheer sordidness of public life (68). Alluding perhaps to his own experience, he warns Lucilius of the recrudescence of ambition during retirement (56.9).

While Seneca is reticent concerning the activities of the Julio-Claudian imperial dynasty, his nostalgia for the Roman Republic is evident in his negative remarks about Pompey and Julius Caesar (94.65, 95.70) and his admiration for such figures as Scipio Africanus (86), Quintus Aelius Tubero (95.72), and Publius Rutilius Rufus (24.4). Above all, he is fascinated by the career of Cato the Younger, whom he admires not only for his courageous suicide but also for his patient endurance of political setbacks (14, 24, 71, 104). Seneca extols the values of public peace and freedom, remarking that philosophers, who make good use of those benefits, should be especially grateful for them (73). He weighs the importance of good political administration and its benefits to private citizens against mere ambition for power and electioneering (118). Political threats to life and limb, which were soon to bring about his own death, are vividly set before the reader along with stark mentions of torture and its implements, execution, and pain (e.g., 14, 66, 67, 70, 78). The violence and cruelty of Roman reality are constantly brought to the fore, notably as concerns the gladiatorial contests (7), the harsh treatment of slaves and prisoners (47, 70.19–23), and the sexual exploitation of women and teenage boys (97, 122.7).

Seneca uses his rhetorical skills and satirical wit to attack the decadence of the elite society of his times. Imagining the impossible, he invents an emblematic meeting on the highway: on one side a troop of modern youths, fashionably mounted and surrounded with attendants and clouds of dust, and on the other Cato the Censor on a single packhorse hung about with various useful articles (87). He is especially tart in pillorying gluttony, displays of wealth, and luxurious excess of every kind. Instances of his satirical technique include letter 51, on the depravity of a fashionable resort; 95.15–28, on the excesses of the table; and the lampoon in letter 122 of aristocrats who keep late hours. Yet it is not the times alone that are at fault, for the letters of Cicero report shocking moral degeneracy even in the time of Cato the Younger (97). The values and practices of contemporary Roman society are completely out of joint, but the corruption that pervades Rome affects human societies in all time periods.

Seneca makes this point pithily and repetitively by dwelling on both the pathos and the absurdity of grounding the goodness of a life in external contingencies and nonmoral values. Overnight, a disaster may afflict an entire populace, as it did in the fire that destroyed the city of Lyon (91). Fortune cannot be trusted, but it can be vanquished if individual persons come to terms with reality by cultivating virtue and reason. Existing human societies do not provide us with appropriate standards of conduct, but our innate sociability is nonetheless a guide to action: public and private utility are linked, for we are born for mutual aid (66.10, 73.7, 95.53). These are the Stoic values that Seneca finds quite absent from the dominant ideology of his own time. If we take politics to be entirely a matter of constitutional rules, administration, and popular participation, the *Letters on Ethics* have little or no political content. If, on the other hand, we think that politics must start from principles such as universal human rights, Seneca's work does have a significant political dimension.

### The Literary Scene

Throughout the letters, Seneca's knowledge of Roman literature and the current literary scene is much in evidence. He is constantly quoting poetry, especially favoring Virgil's *Aeneid* but also including the

*Eclogues* and *Georgics*, the *Metamorphoses* of Ovid, the *Satires* of Horace, and the Epicurean poem *On the Nature of Things* by Lucretius. Comparison with surviving texts of those authors suggests that he quotes from memory, for there are several instances in which he substitutes a word or splices together two similar passages.[6] On occasion his letters have provided modern scholars with valuable information also about poems in Latin that do not otherwise survive: bits of Ennius in 108, Julius Montanus in 122, and Maecenas in three letters, 19, 92, and 101. Among the Greek authors, he often refers to Homer but does not quote him at length; he does, however, quote Euripides in Latin translation (115), and in letter 107 supplies his own metrical translation from the Stoic poetry of Cleanthes.

But his knowledge extends well beyond the works of the poets. He knows a great deal about oratory both from his own experience as a speaker and hearer and from his reading; for he refers not only to the speeches of Cicero and Asinius Pollio but also to a number of older figures, and gives a crisp assessment of technical features of Latin prose style (114, 100). His appreciation for the "facility and elegance" of Papirius Fabianus does not blind him to the stylistic errors of that philosopher (40, 58.6, 100). For the prose writings of Maecenas, he has much contempt, but he finds them interesting nonetheless, and provides the reader with half a dozen specimens of their flamboyant style (114). Further, he knows something of the writings of contemporary critics and antiquarians, since he is able to comment on methods of interpreting literature (88, 108) and to cite specific anomalies of usage in the manner of the literary scholar (17.2, 58.2–5, frag. 1).

It was a convention of Roman literary culture to offer a compliment to the literary achievements of one's addressee. Seneca does as much for Lucilius, whose prose writing he praises in a charming note of thanks (46), and whose poetic efforts he admires (8.10, 24.21) and encourages (79). There is an implied compliment too in the advice he gives in letter 84 about nurturing one's own literary talent through a varied course of reading. Like the honeybee, Lucilius will find nourishment in many different places but will combine what he has taken into "one savor," which is his own distinctive style. By

6. See the notes on 82.16, 90.20, 92.30, 92.34.

writing, he will give proof of his inner harmony and of his ability to impose order on the world, becoming the "greatly talented man" who "stamps his own form upon all the elements that he draws from his chosen model" (84.8).

This last point applies also to Seneca himself, for it is obvious that he means the *Letters on Ethics* to be a highly literary work. Touches of artistry are noticeable throughout, especially in his detailed descriptions of places, in lively passages of narrative, and in extended metaphors that recall the similes of the epic poets. Passages of satire are frequent, including some that are similar in tone and content to the poetic satires of Horace. In keeping with Roman literary principles, Seneca is careful to vary the subject matter from one letter to the next while still arranging his material in such a way as to suggest connections between letters. His ambitions for his work are also evident in passages where the writing takes on a more elevated style. Paragraphs like 41.2–4, on the majesty of forests and the grandeur of the human mind, leave us in no doubt that Seneca meant his letters to be admired as fine writing. But the intervening passages of plain and sometimes breezy and colloquial style are no less deliberately and artfully composed. His aim, he says, is that the letters should be easy and unstudied, like the conversation of two people walking together: at the same time, however, they should not be "jejune and arid." "There is a place for literary talent even in philosophy" (75.3).

### Teachers and Learners

In keeping with the stated purpose of the *Letters*, but also because of his own literary bent, Seneca shows a strong interest in the activities of teaching through various oral and written forms of discourse. Lucilius, of course, is a learner; but he has pupils of his own as well (36), and Seneca admits that he is still learning himself. Although the youthful enthusiasm he remembers in letter 108 has quieted with age, he is still deeply moved by a reading from Quintus Sextius, who was his initial inspiration toward philosophical study (64), and he does not consider himself too old to sit in a classroom alongside the younger generation (76). "Why should I not have many characteristics to sort through and either reduce or heighten?" he writes in the opening of letter 6. But an equally important aim is to teach others. "If wisdom were given to me with this proviso, that I should keep it shut up in myself and never express it to anyone else, I should refuse it: no good is enjoyable to possess without a companion" (6.4).

If Seneca in the early letters often expresses appreciation for Epicurean writings—"the other camp," as he calls them—it can only be for their effectiveness in drawing the pupil toward a philosophical way of life. The works of Epicurus and others of his school are valuable because they are full of well-phrased remarks like "cheerful poverty is an honorable thing" or "anger beyond bounds begets insanity," points that are easy to memorize and incorporate into one's daily reflections. Epicurus himself had encouraged memorization of epitomes of his teachings (*Letter to Herodotus* 35, *Letter to Menoeceus* 135); and Seneca considers the method helpful, but only for beginners. In letter 33, having now ceased to end every letter with a maxim for reflection, he addresses directly the question of whether memorization can ever be an effective means of learning. New recruits may find that isolated sayings take hold easily; one who is beginning to make progress must become a more independent learner. "Let there be some distance between you and the book!" In other words, students must learn to think for themselves and to reason out an appropriate course of action amid the manifold complexities of real situations. Mere familiarity with texts will not do: there must be an increased capacity to make well-reasoned judgments.

For these purposes, an exchange of letters can be a highly effective kind of philosophical writing. Brief and relatively simple, a letter may yet unfold within the mind of the reader, and the back-and-forth of correspondence allows opportunity for the learner's own ideas to develop. So Seneca indicates in letter 38, itself the shortest in the collection. But he recognizes also a need for systematic progress through a more sustained course of reading, the kind of course outlined in letters 39 and 45. One sort of philosophical teaching that is not helpful is the devising of clever syllogisms to prove an absurd conclusion (48, 49). Such "sophistical arguments" do nothing to develop one's good qualities or to help one deal with difficult situations. As far as Seneca is concerned, they are a waste of time.

The two longest letters in the collection, the paired 94 and 95, represent two sides of an intense debate over the form philosophical instruction is to take. Does the philosopher need to supply precepts—that is, instructions on how to behave in specific situations—or will a thorough understanding of the principles of philosophy enable students to decide for themselves what their responsibilities are? Seneca strongly favors the inclusion of precepts, which he feels can be highly effective in daily life, especially if expressed as memorable sayings or lines of verse. But it does not follow that precepts are sufficient by themselves to enable a person to behave honorably, especially in the complex and decadent world of imperial Rome. A theoretical grounding in the principles of philosophy remains indispensable: without it, one is "weak and rootless" (95.12). He draws an analogy to the practice of medicine, where simple techniques for first aid are highly useful but are no replacement for a deep knowledge of human physiology. It is perhaps for this reason that Seneca plans eventually to compose a systematic work on ethics (106, 108, 109), a work that will be of a character very different from the *Letters on Ethics*.

### Seneca's Philosophical Stance

At first the philosophical material contained in the *Letters* is of the most general kind, exhorting readers to begin a course of study rather than providing them with technical details, and steering clear of any single doctrinal perspective. Indeed, it is not until the ninth letter that Seneca gives clear indication of his own commitment to Stoicism. When he does so, however, he speaks firmly and with some philosophical elaboration. The topic he addresses is one that will frequently occupy his attention: the kind of concern one should ideally feel for one's friends or for any of one's nearest personal connections. The Stoic view is differentiated first from that of the old Cynic philosophers, who when they speak of "impassivity" (*apatheia*) mean that one should be insensitive to all adversities, including the death of one's friends. This is not what Stoics have in mind: for them, the ideal person does feel such a loss but can still lead a fulfilled life. From here the letter goes on to explain the difference between an Epicurean conception of friendship, which as Seneca understands it is grounded in each person's self-interest, and the Stoic conception, which is grounded in the good qualities of each and expresses the natural kinship of all human beings. The implied notions of service and mutual aid will eventually be developed in detail, especially in letters 81 and 109.

A related issue explored at intervals throughout the collection concerns the inner life of the "wise" person, that is, the one whose moral and intellectual development is complete. That such a person will not experience desire or fear in relation to typical objects of pursuit and avoidance—wealth, reputation, pain—is a familiar contention of Stoic ethics. Seneca emphasizes, however, that one can be truly wise and still subject to emotion-like reactions such as blushing, shuddering, and shedding tears (11, 57, 71, 99). These sensations are not, properly speaking, emotions, since they do not necessarily express a belief in the value of some external object. Seneca sometimes refers to them as merely corporeal reactions. Nonetheless, they are important, for they give evidence that one who is wise can still be sensitive to the inevitable vagaries of human life. The wise person's most characteristic affective response, however, is different from these: it is a deep and heartfelt sensation of joy. In keeping with earlier Stoic doctrine, but with much greater emphasis, Seneca develops the notion of a joy that does not come and go, as ordinary pleasures do, but remains with a good person always, because it arises from the real and stable goods that belong to the perfected mind itself (23, 59). In a word, Senecan joy comes from within, from a good person's own character and conduct: it arises from goodness itself and from right actions that one performs. This means that joy will not always be a matter of smiles and laughter, for good actions may be difficult and unpleasant: one may have to accept poverty, endure pain, even die for one's country (76.27). A good person does these things only when they are right, and only for that reason, but the doing is itself a good and a reason to rejoice.

Long, searching letters probe deeply into the nature of this Stoic good. How exactly does the claim that virtue is the sole good differ from the rival claim associated with the Peripatetic school, that virtue is the most important of many goods? On what basis can the Stoic account be defended? If some goods are dangerous or painful, how can it be the case that all goods are choiceworthy and of equal value? Seneca argues at length in letters 71, 74, and 76 that the radical Stoic position is the only one that is philosophically defensible. Only this view, he feels, gives full weight to the distinctive nature of the human as a *rational* being, a creature that decides and judges what actions to perform. Further, this is the only position that satisfies the conceptual requirement that the endpoint of human development should be perfect and complete. Like earlier Stoics, Seneca does not doubt that such advantages as health, financial security, and physical comfort are in accordance with our nature and worth pursuing, but he does insist that such things are not intrinsically desirable. Knowledge is an absolute: it is a limit, like the straightness of a straight line, and the virtues are in essence forms of ethical knowledge (66, 71). From this it would seem to follow that the human good is virtually unattainable, and Seneca concedes that actually to attain the ideal is at least extremely rare (42). But even ordinary, very imperfect people can make progress toward that goal (52, 75).

Since our knowledge of the world is necessarily derived from experience, it remains to be explained how human beings can develop a conception of a good that is so rarely exhibited in fact. Seneca investigates this epistemological issue in several of the latest letters. Such mental operations as analogy and extrapolation must play a role here (120), for it is not the sensory faculty that grasps what goodness is but rather the intellectual (124). But our awareness of our own nature as rational beings must also be involved, and this presents a puzzle. Human beings come under the general rule that every animal directs its activities through an instinctive sense of "attachment" to its own constitution. But an infant is not yet able to reason, so how can it be attached to the rational nature of a human being? In accordance with earlier Stoic thought, Seneca argues that our constitution changes in the course of our development. We are at first attached only to our animal nature, but as we mature we transfer our allegiance to the rational capacities that then appear in us (121).

While Seneca sometimes makes a point of declaring his intellectual independence from earlier representatives of his school (33, 45, 64), there are only a few instances in which he moves outside the realm of Stoic thought as we know it from other sources. Such interest as he shows in Platonic and Aristotelian metaphysics does not constitute a departure from Stoicism, since he does not endorse the views of Plato and Aristotle that he summarizes in letters 58 and 65. Nor should his remark about the different "parts" of the mind (92) be taken as evidence of Platonic leanings, for unlike Plato he does not speak of a power struggle among the parts; instead, he assumes that the mind's thinking and reasoning part is alone responsible for directing the activities of the person. Platonic influence is more notable in Seneca's inclination to speak of the human mind as a divine power which has descended from above to take residence within the body, and of abstract studies as the means by which this divine spirit can gain escape and immortality (41, 58, 102). With some justification, he considers this view of the mind to be compatible with a Stoic understanding of divinity and of human wisdom—as long as one does not insist on personal immortality, which he does not (24, 57). His independence from Stoic tradition consists primarily in taking his own positions on such technical points as whether the virtues are animate creatures (113) or whether an incorporeal predicate can count as a good (117).

Even though he objects very strongly to the hedonism of Epicurus as a system of ethics,[7] Seneca is willing to endorse some elements of Epicurean philosophy where he feels he can do so without inconsistency. Concerning the anxiety of malefactors, for instance, he objects to Epicurus's view that nothing is just by nature, but agrees with him that wrongdoers are invariably tormented by their misdeeds (97, 105). More than once we see him take over a point that he knows is Epicurean and adapt it to his own Stoic framework. This happens, for instance, with Epicurus's arguments against the fear of death and pain (30, 36), with his encouragement to his followers to stay out of the public eye (105; cf. 68.10), and with his remarks on natural wealth (4, 25, 119).

## A Roman Philosopher at Work

Because they mingle philosophical concerns with a representation of the author's own life, the *Letters on Ethics* offer an unparalleled opportunity to study the working methods of a philosopher in a Roman setting. We must remember, of course, that what Seneca says about his habits is just the narrative frame that he uses to give a compelling presentation to his material. But we can assume a fair measure of verisimilitude; for the picture had to be recognizable to readers of his own time, who knew his habits and those of other philosophers. In addition, we can sometimes draw inferences that tell us more than our author means to reveal.

At the time Seneca wrote the *Letters on Ethics*, he already possessed a thorough knowledge of many arguments in philosophy, not

7. See for instance 90.35, and compare *On Benefits* 4.2.

only the Stoic positions but those of their chief opponents as well. Memory alone would have enabled him to cite standard explanations of doctrine and such definitions as that of joy (59) or of mental infirmity (75). Even verbatim quotations, like Epicurus's fourth *Principal Doctrine* in 30.14 or the specific remarks credited to Chrysippus in 9.14 and 113.23, might have been supplied from his capacious memory. There are, however, a number of letters in which Seneca supplies an extended discussion of a topic that is not in his usual manner or that he never addresses elsewhere. At these points we should consider the possibility that his information has been drawn in a more immediate way from a specific source, whether oral or written.

Sometimes he tells us directly what book has supplied the material in question. He mentions several specific letters written by Epicurus, naming their recipients and in 18.9 even referring to a date of composition.[8] The letter by Metrodorus quoted in letters 98 and 99 is probably known to him from the same collection. These passages are interesting because in them we can observe Seneca's manner of working with a text, even though the texts themselves are no longer available for comparison. We can see how he names the author, quotes passages—sometimes translating directly from the Greek originals—and then goes on to discuss the point, offering specific objections of his own devising.[9] Nor is it only Epicurean material he handles in this way. A long account in letter 90 of the influence of wise individuals in human history repeatedly mentions an unnamed work by the Stoic Posidonius; and here too the treatment is critical, with many of Posidonius's views rejected out of hand. In letter 88, by contrast, he approves the view of Posidonius mentioned in sections 21–23, but presents it as just one supporting element in a longer discussion for which he himself is responsible.

In some instances, though, his discussion mentions more than one earlier work, and it is up to us to infer whether he has read both authors directly or only knows about the earlier author from references in the later one's work. In letter 83, for example, he quotes a syllogism on drunkenness by Zeno of Citium and then without citation an-

---

8. The clearest examples are in letters 9, 18 (which gives a date), 21, 22, 52, and 79.

9. Clear instances of translation from Greek include 9.20, 97.13, 99.25–26.

other refuting it; immediately afterward, he reports how Posidonius attempted to defend Zeno's argument. Here it is reasonable to conclude that he has before him just one book, that of Posidonius, and knows about the two syllogisms from that source. Similarly in letter 87, he explains how Posidonius critiques a set of syllogisms on the value of wealth, then goes on to repeat a paragraph that Posidonius had quoted from another Stoic, Antipater. Again he must be translating directly, for he comments on the difficulty of rendering certain of Antipater's Greek terms into Latin. A third case of close engagement with multiple authors is the long discussion in letters 94 and 95 of the role of precepts in education. Seneca now quotes a long paragraph of his principal source, Aristo of Chios, right at the outset, and mentions also the position of Aristo's contemporary Cleanthes. It would perhaps be possible to conclude that Aristo's views are known to Seneca because of extensive quotations in a rival work by Cleanthes, whose views seem to coincide with his own. Alternatively, he may be working from an extensive account of both authors by Posidonius, whose opinion on the issue he mentions lower down (94.38, 95.65). On any scenario, it is clear that Seneca is much more than a reporter of older views: whatever the source, he himself understands well the discussion he has read and has ideas of his own to contribute to it.

Another very real possibility is that the letters may incorporate knowledge recently gained from oral teaching and live discussion. Seneca mentions attending lectures (40, 76), and speaks often of philosophical conversations with friends, including conversations about books: deep reflections on the fear of death with the elderly Epicurean Aufidius Bassus (30), a dinner party at his home with a reading from Quintus Sextius (64), a leisurely afternoon visit with much talk about theories of causation (65). We need not doubt that Seneca had such conversations, and learned from them. Just as he must have shared what he knew of Stoic doctrine orally with such friends as Annaeus Serenus (the addressee of *On Tranquility of Mind* whose death is mentioned in letter 63) and Lucilius himself, so others might have shared with him their knowledge of other philosophical systems, including perhaps the Platonic and Aristotelian material summarized in letters 58 and 65. On the other hand, the supposed conversations might be semifictional devices meant to provide an attractive frame for material Seneca knows from some unnamed written source. Thus while letter 66 purports to describe a visit with Seneca's friend Claranus, its exceptionally long and elaborate argument looks more like a résumé of some Stoic treatise than a record of a conversation, especially as letter 67 continues the same topic without further mention of Claranus.

A point of particular interest concerns Seneca's knowledge of the philosophical writings of Cicero. One work he does certainly know is Cicero's *On the Republic*, since he cites it by title in letter 108 and gives some details of it in fragment 1. Unfortunately this treatise, the keystone of Cicero's philosophical reputation in antiquity, now survives only in part, so that Seneca's use of it is hard to assess. Beyond *On the Republic*, we can infer from fragment 1 that Seneca probably knew Cicero's *Brutus*, on the history of oratory at Rome. Concerning the philosophical treatises of 45 BCE, however, the ones in which Cicero gave his most extensive treatment of the systems of thought that are of central concern to the *Letters on Ethics*, Seneca is strangely silent. It is indeed possible that he has not read these works, or does not consider them important; for he has available to him a number of Greek treatises, no doubt including some of those Cicero himself consulted. It is surely significant that on some points treated by both authors, Seneca includes details he could not have found in Cicero, and that on others he omits elements one would have expected him to find interesting.[10] Among the Latin authors, Seneca shows more definite connection with the philosophical writings of Brutus and even with the philosophical dialogues of Livy than he does with these important works of Cicero.[11]

---

10. For instance, in 85.2, where he discusses the same syllogism as is reported by Cicero in *Tusculan Disputations* 3.18, Seneca also gives the Peripatetic refutation of it. Conversely, Seneca in letter 9 fails to mention the alternative Epicurean accounts of friendship, an egregious omission if he has read books 1 and 2 of Cicero's treatise *On Ends*. It is noteworthy too that Seneca never mentions Antiochus of Ascalon, who plays an important role both in *On Ends* and in the *Academics*. A familiarity with the *Academics* might have been inferred from his discussion of the word *cavillationes* in 111.1, were it not for the fact that Cicero does not use that word in surviving portions of the work. See also the notes on 17.2 and 58.6, for the allegedly Ciceronian terms *opitulari* and *essentia*.

11. Livy's philosophical writings are mentioned in 100.9 (and compare 46.1), Brutus's *On Appropriate Action* in 95.45 (but see the note on the passage).

## Seneca's Letters after the Classical Period

The *Letters on Ethics* were widely studied by Roman readers as much for their sparkling prose as for their content. This is evident even in later authors who were eager to contest his influence. As a teacher of public speaking, Quintilian warns against imitating Seneca's mannerisms—and thus reveals their popularity among his contemporaries a generation after Seneca's death (10.1.128–30). The same can be said of Fronto, the instructor of Marcus Aurelius during the second century, when he warns the emperor against reading Seneca's works in his *Epistle on Orations*. For both Quintilian and Fronto, Seneca represents a flashy and modern style of writing in contrast to the rugged vigor of Cicero and other authors of the Roman Republic. A preference for the archaic also informs the judgment of Fronto's contemporary Aulus Gellius, who complains bitterly about certain remarks of Seneca concerning Cicero's writings and those of Quintus Ennius, Rome's national poet in the age before Virgil (fragment 1). In a period that finds nothing that is not admirable in the old Republican authors, Seneca's more nuanced judgment was bound to offend some readers, yet clearly he was still regarded as an important figure whom educated people were expected to know about.

Seneca was highly esteemed among early Christian authors. Lactantius, writing in the third century, judges him "the sharpest of all Stoics"; Tertullian calls him "frequently one of us"; and Jerome actually lists him among "the sacred," that is, among those who write on Christian topics.[12] For Jerome, and probably for others as well, Seneca appeared acceptable in part because he was thought to have corresponded with the apostle Paul, who was his contemporary. Equally important, however, was the general tenor of his Stoic ethics, which was compatible with many of the ethical teachings of Christianity. The notable exception to this Christian regard for Seneca was his approval of suicide *in extremis*; there the patristic authors were careful to distance themselves from him.

Knowledge of the *Letters* is less in evidence for the latest period of antiquity and the early Middle Ages; yet there are indications that

---

12. Lactantius, *Divine Institutes* 2.8.23; Tertullian, *On the Soul* 20.1; Jerome, *On Illustrious Men* 12.

some well-educated readers still knew and admired the work. Macrobius, writing in the early fifth century, provides a striking instance of appreciation for Seneca's literary talents in his dialogue *Saturnalia*, where he quotes without attribution from letters 84 and 47. Seneca's comparison to the honeybee in 84.5–7 indeed has programmatic significance for Macrobius's work, which is a kind of compendium of material drawn from the author's varied reading (Trillitzsch 1971, 194). Perhaps a century later, a poet-scholar named Honorius Scholasticus compares his earlier reading in the *Letters on Ethics* to the instruction he expects to receive in Christian doctrine. He will be a second Lucilius; his correspondent, the bishop Jordanes, will teach him "to surpass even Seneca through the talents of faith."[13] Evidence of familiarity with the collection can also be found in anthologies of excerpts and maxims that circulated under Seneca's name throughout the Middle Ages. In this form, Seneca's reputation as a moralist was long perpetuated among readers who had no access to his complete writings.

The oldest surviving manuscripts of the *Letters on Ethics* date from the ninth century. However, none of the oldest copies include all the surviving letters: some contain only 1–88, others only 89–124. This suggests that the early tradition must have preserved the *Letters* in two separate volumes, or more likely three, since there are also copies that contain only 1–52 or 53–88 (Reynolds 1965b, 17). A point of some significance for the prior history of the transmission is that the headings dividing the letters into books are imperfectly preserved in our existing manuscripts. Such headings do appear at intervals up through book 20; however, no indication is to be found for books 12, 13, and 18, and the irregular spacing of those that remain suggests that some letters may be missing internally as well as at the end.[14] The full corpus of extant material did not circulate as a unit

13. The poem appears as number 666 in Buecheler and Riese 1894–1926; see Mastandrea 1988, 70–73.

14. The length of books in the first main division is between 21 and 32 pages in Reynolds's edition, with book 11 (ending with 88) significantly longer at 39 pages. In the second division, the length of most of the books is between 36 and 46 pages, with the exception of book 16 at only 20 pages. Not coincidentally, the one point where there is an unmistakable gap in the received text is found in book 16, at 98.15.

until the twelfth century, when the *Letters*, together with *On Clemency* and *On Benefits*, began to be widely copied and disseminated throughout Europe.

It was in that period that the *Letters on Ethics* began to have significant influence on European thought. Seneca was especially appealing to the monastic reformers of the Cistercian order, who appreciated his emphasis on living in accordance with nature, on friendship, and on moderation in food and drink. And there were some who engaged quite deeply with Seneca's ideas. John of Salisbury, for instance, quotes with approval Seneca's claim that "reason is nothing other than a portion of the divine breath submerged in the human body" (66.12), but adds further explanation to make the statement accord with Christian doctrine (Lapidge 1992). Among those who studied the *Letters* extensively in this period were Peter Abelard, the Cistercian William of Saint-Thierry, and William of Malmesbury (Reynolds 1965b, 115).

Seneca's influence was at its strongest from about 1450 to 1650. The first printed text of the *Letters* appeared in 1475, to be followed in 1529 by the much superior edition of Erasmus. The *Essays* of Montaigne, written in the last decades of the sixteenth century, are modeled on Seneca's *Letters* to a considerable extent, as the author himself acknowledged, coupling him with Plutarch:

> I have not devoted myself to any serious work except Plutarch and Seneca; but upon them, I draw as do the Danaids, endlessly refilling my sieve and emptying it again. (*Essays* 1.25)

But it was the humanist scholar Justus Lipsius (1547–1606), a correspondent of Montaigne, who was Seneca's most accomplished and effective publicist. In addition to his celebrated *On Constancy*, modeled on Seneca's *On the Constancy of the Wise Person*, Lipsius authored two influential studies of Stoicism, and in the last year of his life produced a complete edition of all Seneca's prose works including the *Letters*, meant "to publicize Seneca and put him into the hands of the general public." The Dutch artist Rubens, a great admirer of Lipsius, was likewise much influenced by Seneca's ethics. In his painting *The Four Philosophers*, Rubens included a clearly identifiable bust of Seneca in an alcove, as if presiding over the meeting of Lipsius's circle. This was the high point of Seneca's influence on early modern thought and literature. Some eighteenth-century authors, notably Diderot, Rousseau, and Gibbon, mention Seneca approvingly, but thereafter his influence declines. For the next two centuries, he largely drops out of general circulation and citation.

Since the second half of the twentieth century, the *Letters on Ethics* have begun again to attract an appreciative readership. Seneca's renewed popularity is due in part to the resurgence of work on ancient Stoicism, but to a great extent it is also due to a fresh appreciation of his literary genius. Seminal figures in this renewal of interest were the classicists Ilsetraut and Pierre Hadot, whose work on Seneca's letters and on ascetic practices in ancient philosophy captured the attention of Michel Foucault at the beginning of the 1980s. Foucault saw connections with his own developing idea of a "hermeneutics of the subject," and in the last years of his life he frequently referred to Seneca in lectures and writings.[15] The burgeoning of interest in Stoicism in the most recent generation of readers has led many to turn to the *Letters* specifically for their philosophical content. It is our hope that the present volume, the first complete English translation since the 1930s, will enable a much wider community of readers to study and appreciate the best work of one of Roman antiquity's most brilliant writers.

## Modern Scholarship on the Letters

The works of Seneca are today a very active area in classical scholarship. The References section in this volume gives some indication of the resources available for further study. An especially important work on Seneca's political career, with much information also on his education and writings, is Griffin 1992 (first published in 1976); and see also Inwood 1995 on his relations to other intellectuals of the period. Seneca's objectives as a writer of letters have been treated recently in Graver 2012 and 2014; see also Wilcox 2012 on the dynamics of correspondence. On the importance of Epicurus as a literary model, see Inwood 2007b and Setaioli 2014; the last also provides a balanced overview of historical and literary issues. Seneca's prose

15. See Foucault 2001, and note the influence of Foucault on Paul Veyne, who in 1993 produced a richly annotated edition of the *Dialogues* and *Letters*, revising older French translations. Veyne remarks on Foucault's role in his introduction (v).

style has been the object of intensive study, especially in Italy: Traina 1995 and Setaioli 2000 are the basic works, and in English see von Albrecht 2014.

Among recent studies of Seneca's educational method are Schafer 2009 (which treats especially 94–95), Hachmann 1995, Schafer 2011, and Griffin 2013, 125–48. Considerable attention has been given to Seneca's role in the development of conceptions of the self: see Edwards 1997; Long 2006, 312–26; Gill 2009. Many specifics concerning Seneca's handling of Stoic philosophy can be found in Inwood 2005, Wildberger 2006, and in the relevant portions of Damschen and Heil 2014. More generally on Stoic philosophy, see Long 1996, Inwood 2003, Brennan 2005, Graver 2007, and Cooper 2012; on Platonic influences, Reydams-Schils 2010; on Epicurean, Graver 2015. Most of the ancient evidence for the Hellenistic philosophical schools may be found in English translation either in Long and Sedley 1987 or in Inwood and Gerson 1997. Inwood 2007a provides a detailed philosophical commentary on some of the more difficult letters; included are 58, 65, 66, 71, 76, 85, 87, 106, 113, and 117–24.

A thorough study by Reynolds (1965b) gives much essential information concerning the manuscript tradition of the *Letters* and also their influence from late antiquity to the twelfth century. Trillitzsch 1971 treats the influence of the *Letters* as well as of Seneca's other works, and includes an extensive list of passages; in English on the same topic, see also Ross 1974 and Laarman 2014.

## About This Edition

The translation follows the Latin text as given in Reynolds 1965a, omitting without comment words and phrases marked by Reynolds as spurious. In those few places where we differ from Reynolds as to what Latin text best represents Seneca's intentions, the word or phrase that renders the different Latin wording is marked with a superscript circle, and our reading given in the Textual Notes section. Where there is uncertainty, we have generally preferred to accept one of the reasonable suggestions of textual critics rather than mark a passage as corrupt. At 98.15, however, a paragraph or more of the original must have dropped out in transmission, and the passage is so marked. Further information about the transmission of the text and about the origins of the readings we adopt will be found in the critical apparatus to Reynolds 1965a or in the editions by Préchac, Beltrami, and Hense that are listed in the References section.

Our aim as translators is to convey Seneca's ideas exactly while also giving some sense of his ever-changing style and mood. Seneca himself found, when translating Greek texts, that he sometimes needed to rearrange an expression to render its meaning exactly in Latin. "Our service should be given to thoughts, not words," he writes in 9.20. We have taken the same approach to his Latin, first pondering the thought expressed and then seeking natural English to match the stylistic register. In most instances we strive for consistency, keeping lists of key words and taking pains especially with philosophical terms. But there are cases in which we choose to vary the rendering to bring out the nuances of a word. For example, the subtle adjective *delicatus* is rendered in numerous ways, including "decadent," "fashionable," "finicky," and "lascivious." A more difficult decision was the translation to be used for *sapiens*, which Seneca occasionally varies with the gendered expression *sapiens vir*. Here we usually write "wise person" or "sage," since Seneca's principal concern is with the ideal human being of Hellenistic moral philosophy, but sometimes "wise man," since it is part of his cultural bias to represent this figure as male.

The actual work of translation has been collaborative through and through. While each of us has taken primary responsibility for certain of the letters, we have both worked on the volume in its entirety, and we have constantly conferred with each other on difficult passages. For many particular translation problems, our solution has been the result of intense discussion and negotiation. Portions of the translation, notes, and index have been improved as well by the acumen of undergraduate research assistants funded through the James O. Friedman Presidential Scholars Program at Dartmouth College: Brian Howe, John Kee, Michael Konieczny, Karen Laakko, Aaron Pellowski, Lea Schröder, and Leslie Shribman.

In preparing the explanatory notes, we have relied mainly on our own judgment, but we are often indebted to earlier commentators for assistance in locating the relevant ancient evidence. For historical and biographical matters, we have frequently consulted the comprehensive *Brill's New Pauly* (Cancik and Schneider 2002–10).

The labels given to individual letters in the Table of Contents are supplied by us for ease of reference; they are not authorial.

# BOOK ONE

# *Letter 1*

*From Seneca to Lucilius*
*Greetings*

1 Do that, dear Lucilius: assert your own freedom.* Gather and guard the time that until now was being taken from you, or was stolen from you, or that slipped away. Convince yourself that what I write is true: some moments are snatched from us, some are filched, and some just vanish. But no loss is as shameful as the one that comes about through carelessness. Take a close look, and you will see that when we are not doing well, most° of life slips away from us; when we are inactive, much of it—but when we are inattentive, we miss it all. 2 Can you show me even one person who sets a price on his time, who knows the worth of a day, who realizes that every day is a day when he is dying? In fact, we are wrong to think that death lies ahead: much of it has passed us by already, for all our past life is in the grip of death.*

And so, dear Lucilius, do what your letter says you are doing: embrace every hour. If you lay hands on today, you will find you are less dependent on tomorrow. While you delay, life speeds on by. 3 Everything we have belongs to others, Lucilius; time alone is ours. Nature has put us in possession of this one thing, this fleeting, slippery thing—and anyone who wants to can dispossess us. Such is the foolishness of mortal beings: when they borrow the smallest, cheapest items, such as can easily be replaced, they acknowledge the debt, but no one considers himself indebted for taking up our time. Yet this is the one loan that even those who are grateful cannot repay.

4 You ask, perhaps, what I am doing—I, who give you these instructions. I am a big spender, I freely admit, but a careful one: I have kept my accounts. I cannot say that nothing has been wasted, but at least I can say what, and why, and how; I can state the causes of my impoverishment. But it is with me as with many others who have been reduced to penury through no fault of their own: everyone forgives them, but no one comes to their assistance.

**5** What of it? A person is not poor, I think, as long as what little he has left is enough for him. Still, I prefer that you, for your part, conserve what you have. And make an early start. For in the words of our ancestors, "Thrift comes late when stocks are low."* Not only is there very little left at the bottom of the jar, but its quality is the worst.

Farewell.

## Letter 2

*From Seneca to Lucilius*
*Greetings*

**1** From your letter and from what I hear, I am becoming quite hopeful about you: you are not disquieting yourself by running about from place to place. Thrashing around in that way indicates a mind in poor health. In my view, the first sign of a settled mind is that it can stay in one place and spend time with itself.

**2** Be careful, though, about your reading in many authors and every type of book. It may be that there is something wayward and unstable in it. You must stay with a limited number of writers and be fed by them if you mean to derive anything that will dwell reliably with you. One who is everywhere is nowhere. Those who travel all the time find that they have many places to stay, but no friendships. The same thing necessarily happens to those who do not become intimate with any one author, but let everything rush right through them. **3** Food does not benefit or become part of the body when it is eaten and immediately expelled. Nothing impedes healing as much as frequent change of medications. A wound does not close up when one is always trying out different dressings on it; a seedling that is transplanted repeatedly will never grow strong. Nothing, in fact, is of such utility that it benefits us merely in passing. A large number of books puts a strain on a person. So, since you cannot read everything you have, it is sufficient to have only the amount you can read.

**4** "But I want to read different books at different times," you say. The person of delicate digestion nibbles at this and that; when the diet is too varied, though, food does not nourish but only upsets the stomach. So read always from authors of proven worth; and if ever you are inclined to turn aside to others, return afterward to the previous ones. Obtain each day some aid against poverty, something against death, and likewise against other calamities. And when you have moved rapidly through many topics, select one to ponder that day and digest.

5 This is what I do as well, seizing on some item from among several things I have read. Today it is this, which I found in Epicurus—for it is my custom to cross even into the other camp,* not as a deserter but as a spy:

Cheerful poverty is an honorable thing.

6 Indeed, it is not poverty if it is cheerful: the pauper is not the person who has too little but the one who desires more. What does it matter how much is stashed away in his strongbox or his warehouses, how much he has in livestock or in interest income, if he hangs on another's possessions, computing not what has been gained but what there is yet to gain? Do you ask what is the limit of wealth? Having what one needs, first of all; then, having enough.

Farewell.


## Letter 3

*From Seneca to Lucilius*
*Greetings*

1 You gave letters to a friend of yours—so you write—to bring to me, and then you advise me not to tell him all your affairs, since you yourself are not in the habit of doing so. Thus in one and the same letter you have said both that he is your friend and that he is not. Well, if you used that word not with its proper meaning but as if it were public property, calling him a friend in the same way as we call all candidates "good men" or address people as "sir" when we don't remember their names, then let it go. 2 But if you think that a person is a friend when you do not trust him as much as you trust

yourself, you are seriously mistaken; you do not know the meaning of real friendship.

Consider every question with a friend; but first, consider the friend. After you make a friend, you should trust him—but before you make a friend, you should make a judgment. People who love someone and then judge that person are mixing up their responsibilities: they should judge first, then love, as Theophrastus advised.* Take time to consider whether or not to receive a person into your friendship; but once you have decided to do so, receive him with all your heart, and speak with him as candidly as with yourself.

3 Live in such a way that anything you would admit to yourself could be admitted even to an enemy. Even so, there are things that are customarily kept private; with a friend, though, you should share all your concerns, all your thoughts. If you believe him loyal, you will make him so. Some people teach their friends to betray them by their very fear of betrayal: by being suspicious, they give the other person the right to transgress. He is my friend: why should I hold back my words in his presence? When I am with him, why is it not as if I am alone?

4 There are those who unload their worries into every available ear, telling anyone they meet what should be entrusted only to friends. Others are reluctant to confide even in those who are closest to them; they press every secret to their chest, and would keep it even from themselves if they could. Neither alternative is appropriate—to trust everyone or to trust no one; both are faults, but the former is what I might call a more honorable fault, the latter a safer one.

5 Similarly, there is reason to criticize both those who are always on the move and those who are always at rest. Liking to be in the fray does not mean that one is hardworking; it is only the hustle and bustle of an agitated mind. Finding every movement a bother does not mean that one is tranquil; it is just laxity and idleness. 6 So let's keep in mind this saying I have read in Pomponius:

> Some flee so far into their dens that they think everything outside is turmoil.*

There should be a mix: the lazy one should do something, the busy one should rest. Consult with nature: it will tell you that it made both day and night.

Farewell.

# Letter 4

*From Seneca to Lucilius*
*Greetings*

1 Persevere in what you have begun; hurry as much as you can, so that you will have more time to enjoy a mind that is settled and made flawless. To be sure, you will have enjoyment even as you make it so; but there is quite another pleasure to be gained from the contemplation of an intellect that is spotlessly pure and bright.*

2 Surely you remember what joy you felt when you set aside your boy's clothes and put on a man's toga for your first trip down to the Forum. A greater joy awaits you once you set aside your childish mind, once philosophy registers you as a grown man. For childhood—or rather, childishness, which is worse—has not yet left us. Worse yet, we have the authority of grown men but the faults of children, of infants even. Children are terrified of trivial things, infants of imagined things, and we of both. 3 Just make some progress, and you will understand that if some things seem very frightening, that is all the more reason why we should not fear them.

No evil is great if it is an ending. Death is on its way to you. You would have reason to fear it if it could ever be present with you; necessarily, though, it either does not arrive or is over and gone.*

4 "It is hard," you say, "to get one's mind to despise life." But don't you see, people do sometimes despise it, and for trivial reasons. One person hangs himself outside his girlfriend's door; another hurls himself from a rooftop so as not to have to listen any longer to his master's complaints; a runaway slave stabs himself in the belly to avoid being recaptured. Don't you agree that courage will achieve what overwhelming terror manages to do? One cannot attain a life free of anxiety if one is too concerned about prolonging it—if one counts living through many consulships as an important good.

5 Rehearse this every day, so that you will be able to let go of life with equanimity. Many people grasp and hold on to life, like those caught by a flash flood who grasp at weeds and brambles. Most are tossed about between the fear of death and the torments of life: they do not want to live but do not know how to die. 6 Cast off your so-

licitude for life, then, and in doing so make life enjoyable for yourself. No good thing benefits us while we have it unless we are mentally prepared for the loss of it. And of all losses this is the easiest to bear, since once life is gone, you cannot miss it.

Exhort yourself, toughen yourself, against such events as befall even the most powerful. 7 Pompey lost his life to the decree of a young boy and a eunuch; Crassus lost his to the cruel and uncouth Parthians.* Gaius Caesar commanded Lepidus to yield his neck to the tribune Dexter—then gave his own to Chaerea.* No one has ever reached a point where the power fortune granted was greater than the risk. The sea is calm now, but do not trust it: the storm comes in an instant. Pleasure boats that were out all morning are sunk before the day is over.

8 Think: a robber, as well as a foe, can put a knife to your throat. In the absence of any greater authority, any slave holds the power of life or death over you. That's right: anyone who despises his own life is master of yours. Call to mind the stories of people whose house servants plotted to kill them, some by stealth and some in broad daylight, and you will realize that just as many people have died from the anger of slaves as from the anger of kings. So why should you bother to fear those who are especially powerful, when the thing you are afraid of is something anyone can do?

9 And suppose you should fall into the hands of the enemy, and the victor should order you to be put to death. Death is where you are headed anyway! Why do you deceive yourself? Do you realize now for the first time what has in fact been happening to you all along? So it is: since the moment of birth, you have been moving toward your execution. These thoughts, and others like them, are what we must ponder if we want to be at peace as we await the final hour. For fear of that one makes all our other hours uneasy.

10 To bring this letter to an end, here is what I liked from today's reading. This too is lifted from another's Garden:*

Poverty is great wealth when it adjusts to nature's law.

Do you know what boundaries nature's law imposes? Not to be hungry, not to be thirsty, not to be cold.* To keep back hunger and thirst, you need not hang about the thresholds of the proud, nor endure the scorn of those whose very kindness is insulting; you need not brave the seas nor follow the camps of the army. What nature requires is close by and easy to obtain. 11 All that sweat is for superfluities. We wear out our fine clothes, grow old in army tents, hurl ourselves against foreign shores, and for what? Everything we need is already at hand. Anyone who is on good terms with poverty is rich.

Farewell.

## Letter 5

*From Seneca to Lucilius*
*Greetings*

1 You are hard at work, forgetting everything else and sticking to the single task of making yourself a better person every day. This I approve, and rejoice in it too. I urge you, indeed plead with you, to persevere. All the same, I have a warning for you. There are those whose wish is to be noticed rather than to make moral progress. Don't be like them, altering your dress or way of life so as to attract attention. 2 The rough clothes, the rank growth of hair and beard, the sworn hatred of silverware, the pallet laid on the ground: all these and any other perverse form of self-aggrandizement are things you should avoid.

The word "philosophy" makes people uncomfortable enough all by itself, even when used modestly. How would it be if we were to begin exempting ourselves from the conventions people usually observe? Within, let us be completely different, but let the face we show to the world be like other people's. 3 Our clothes should not be fine, but neither should they be filthy; we should not own vessels of silver engraved with gold, but neither should we think that the mere fact that one lacks gold and silver is any indication of a frugal nature. The life we endeavor to live should be better than the general practice, not contrary to it. Otherwise we frighten off the very people we want to correct: by making them afraid that they will have to imitate everything about us, we make them unwilling to imitate us in any way at all. 4 The very first thing philosophy promises is fellow feeling, a sense of togetherness among human beings. By becoming different, we will be cut off from this. If we are not careful, the very measures that are meant to win us admiration will instead make us objects of hatred and ridicule.

Our aim is to live in accordance with nature, is it not? This is contrary to nature: tormenting one's body, swearing off simple matters of grooming, affecting a squalid appearance, partaking of foods that are not merely inexpensive but rancid and coarse. 5 A hankering after delicacies is a sign of self-indulgence; by the same token, avoidance of those comforts that are quite ordinary and easy to obtain is an indication of insanity. Philosophy demands self-restraint, not self-abnegation—and even self-restraint can comb its hair. The limit I suggest is this: our habits should mingle the ideal with the ordinary in due proportion, our way of life should be one that everyone can admire without finding it unrecognizable.

6 "What do you mean? Are we to act just like other people? Is there to be no difference between us and them?" A very great difference, but a difference that will be evident only on close inspection. A person entering our house should marvel at the inhabitant, not at the dinnerware. One who uses earthenware as if it were silver is indeed a great person; equally great, though, is the one who uses silver as if it were earthenware. Not being able to cope with wealth is an indication of weakness.

7 But let me share with you the little profit I made today as well. In the writings of our own Hecaton I find it said that limiting one's desires is beneficial also as a remedy for fear.* "You will cease to fear," he says, "if you cease to hope."

"The two feelings are very different," you say. "How is it that they occur together?" But so it is, dear Lucilius: although they seem opposed, they are connected. Just as the prisoner and the guard are bound to each other by the same chain, so these two that are so different nonetheless go along together: where hope goes, fear follows. 8 Nor do I find it surprising that it should be so. Both belong to the mind that is in suspense, that is worried by its expectation of what is to come. The principal cause of both is that we do not adapt ourselves to the present but direct our thoughts toward things far in the future. Thus foresight, which is the greatest good belonging to the human condition, has become an evil.* 9 Animals in the wild flee the dangers they see and are tranquil once they have escaped; we, though, are tormented both by what is to come and by what has been. Often, our goods do us harm: memory recalls the stab of fear; foresight anticipates it. No one is made wretched merely by the present.

Farewell.

## Letter 6

*From Seneca to Lucilius*
*Greetings*

1 My understanding is, Lucilius, that what is happening in me is not merely a removal of flaws, but a transformation. Not that there is nothing left in me to be amended! At this point I don't promise that, nor do I expect it. Why should I not have many characteristics to sort through and either reduce or heighten? This is itself an indication that the mind has reached a better place, when it perceives faults in itself that previously went unrecognized. With some patients, it is cause for congratulation when they realize that they are ill.

2 If only I *could* share such a sudden transformation with you—that's what I would like. In that case, I would begin to have more confidence in our friendship. For it would then be true friendship, such as no hope, no fear, no self-interest can sever. That is a friendship that stays with people until they die—and that people die for. 3 I can name you many people who have friends and yet are without friendship; this is not the case, though, where equal willingness draws minds into a companionship of honorable intentions.* How could it be? For they know that everything they have is held in common, and especially their trials.

You cannot imagine how much progress I see myself making every day. 4 "What remedies are these that have done so much for you?" you say. "Send them to me too!" Indeed, I am longing to shower you with all of them. What gives me pleasure in learning something is that I can teach it. Nothing will ever please me, not even what is remarkably beneficial, if I have learned it for myself only. If wisdom were given to me with this proviso, that I should keep it shut up in myself and never express it to anyone else, I should refuse it: no good is enjoyable to possess without a companion. 5 So I will send you the books themselves; and I will annotate them too, so that you need not expend much effort hunting through them for the profitable bits, but can get right away to the things that I endorse and am impressed with.

But formal discourse will not do as much for you as direct contact, speaking in person and sharing a meal. You must come and see me face to face—first of all, because humans believe their eyes much more than their ears, and second, because learning by precepts is the long way around. The quick and effective way is to learn by example. 6 If Cleanthes had merely listened to Zeno, he would not have been molded by him; instead, he made himself a part of Zeno's life, looking into his inmost thoughts and seeing whether he lived in accordance with his own rule.* Plato and Aristotle and the whole crowd of philosophers who would later go their separate ways all derived more from Socrates' conduct than from his words. Metrodorus, Hermarchus, and Polyaenus were made great men not by Epicurus's formal instruction but by living together with him.* Nor do I summon you to me only for your own benefit. It is for my benefit as well: each of us has much to bestow on the other.

7 Meanwhile, as I owe you the daily dole, I will tell you what pleased me today in the writings of Hecaton:

Do you ask what progress I have made? I have begun to be a friend to myself.*

Valuable progress indeed: he will never be alone. Believe me, such a person will be a friend to everyone.

Farewell.

## Letter 7

*From Seneca to Lucilius*
*Greetings*

1 Do you ask what you should avoid more than anything else? A crowd. It is not yet safe for you to trust yourself to one.

I'll freely admit my own weakness in this regard. Never do I return home with the character I had when I left; always there is something I had settled before that is now stirred up again, something I had gotten rid of that has returned. As with invalids, who are so affected by a lengthy convalescence that they cannot be moved outdoors without taking some harm, so it is with us: our minds are recovering from a long illness; **2** contact with the many is harmful to us. Every single person urges some fault upon us, or imparts one to us, or contaminates us without our even realizing it.

Without doubt, the larger the group we associate with, the greater the danger. Nothing, though, is as destructive to good character as occupying a seat in some public spectacle, for then the pleasure of the sight lets the faults slip in more easily. **3** What do you suppose I mean? Do I come home greedier, more power-hungry, more self-indulgent? Worse than that! I become more cruel and inhumane, just because I have been among humans.

Purely by chance, I found myself at the midday show, expecting some amusement or wit, something relaxing to give people's eyes a rest from the sight of human blood. On the contrary! The fights that preceded turned out to have been downright merciful. The trifling was over: now it was unmitigated slaughter. They are not provided with any protective armor: their bodies are completely exposed, so that the hand never strikes in vain. **4** This is generally liked better than the usual matches between even the most popular gladiators. And why not? There is no helmet, no shield to stop the blade. Why bother with defenses? Why bother with technique? All that stuff just delays the kill. In the morning, humans are thrown to the lions or to the bears; at noon, they are thrown to their own spectators! Those who do the killing are made to submit to others who will kill them; the victor is detained for further slaughter. The only way out of the ring is to die. Steel and flames are the business of the hour. And this is what goes on when the arena is empty!

**5** "But one of them committed a robbery! He killed somebody!" So what? He is a murderer, and therefore deserves to have this done to him, but what about you? What did you do, poor fellow, to make you deserve to watch?

"Kill him! Whip him! Burn him! Why is he so timid about running onto the sword? Why does he not succumb more bravely? Why is he not more willing to die? Let him be driven with lashes into the fray! Let them receive each other's blows with their chests naked and exposed!" A break in the action: "Cut some throats in the meantime, just so there will be something going on!" Come, now, don't you understand this, even, that bad examples redound upon those who set them? Thank the gods that the person you are teaching to be cruel is not capable of learning!*

6 The mind that is young and not yet able to hold on to what is right must be kept apart from the people. It is all too easy to follow the many. Even Socrates, Cato, or Laelius could have had their character shaken out of them by the multitude that was so different.* All the more, then, we who are just now beginning to establish inner harmony cannot possibly withstand the attack of faults that bring so much company along. 7 A single example of self-indulgence or greed does a great deal of harm. A dissipated housemate makes one become less strong and manly over time; a wealthy neighbor inflames one's desires; a spiteful companion infects the most open and candid nature with his own canker. What do you suppose happens to the character that is under attack by the public at large? You must either imitate them or detest them.

8 Both are to be avoided: you should not imitate those who are bad because they are many, and neither should you become hateful to the many because they are unlike you. Retreat into yourself, then, as much as you can. Spend your time with those who will improve you; extend a welcome to those you can improve. The effect is reciprocal, for people learn while teaching.

9 There is no reason for you to be enticed into the midst of the people by a prideful wish to display your talent for public recitation or debate. I would want you to do that if you had any merchandise suitable for this populace; as it is, there is nobody capable of understanding you. Perhaps somebody or other will show up, and even that one will need to be instructed, to teach him how to understand you.

"For whom, then, did I learn these things?" You need not fear that your time has been wasted so long as you have learned them for yourself.

10 And so that my own learning today will not be for myself alone, I will share with you three exceptionally fine sayings that come

to mind as having some bearing on the point at hand. One shall pay what is due with this letter, and the other two you may credit to my account. Democritus says,

> One person counts as a nation with me, a nation as one person.*

11 Also well spoken is the remark of whoever it was (for there is some dispute as to the author) who said, when asked why he expended such efforts over a work of art that very few would ever see,

> A few are enough; one is enough; not even one is also enough.

The third is especially good. Epicurus, writing to one of his companions in philosophy, said,

> I write this not for the many but for you: you and I are audience enough for one another.*

12 Take these words to heart, dear Lucilius, so that you may think little of the pleasure that comes from the acclaim of the many. Many people do praise you: does it give you reason to be satisfied with yourself if you are one whom many people can understand? Direct your goods inward.

Farewell.


## Letter 8

*From Seneca to Lucilius*
*Greetings*

1 "Are you, then, telling me to avoid the crowd, retire, and content myself with my private thoughts? What about those instructions of your school that bid us die in action?"*

Well, do you think this is inaction that I am urging upon you? Here is the reason I have hidden myself away and closed the doors: to benefit the greater number. Not one of my days is spent in leisure, and I claim a part of the nights for study. I have no time for sleep, until it overcomes me; my eyes are exhausted and drooping with late hours, but I keep them to the task. **2** I have withdrawn not only from society but from business, and especially from my own business. The work that I am doing is for posterity: it is they who can benefit from what I write. I am committing to the page some healthful admonitions, like the recipes for useful salves. I have found these effective on my own sores, which, even if not completely healed, have ceased to spread. **3** The right path, which I myself discovered late in life when weary from wandering, I now point out to others.

My cry is this:*

"Avoid those things that please the many, the gifts that fortune brings. Be suspicious; be timid; resist every good that comes by chance. It is by the allurements of hope that the fish is caught, the game snared. Do you think these are the blessings of fortune? They are traps. Any one of you who wants to live in safety must make every effort to shun those baited favors amidst which we, poor creatures, are deceived. We think we have hold of them, when in fact they have hold of us.

**4** "That career of yours leads over a cliff. To leave such an exalted life, you have to fall. And once prosperity begins to push us over, we cannot even resist. We could wish to fall only once, or at least to fall from an upright position, but we are not allowed. Fortune does not only overturn us: it upends us, and then smashes us.

**5** "Hold therefore to this sound and saving rule of life: indulge the body only to the extent that suffices for health. Deal sternly with it, lest it fail to obey the mind. Let food be for appeasing hunger, drink for satisfying thirst, clothing a protection against cold, a house a shelter against inclement weather. Whether that house is built of sod or of variegated marble from foreign lands is of no significance: believe me, a person can be sheltered just as well with thatch as with gold. Scorn all those things that superfluous labor sets up for decoration and for show: keep in mind that nothing but the mind is marvelous, that to the great mind, nothing else is great."

**6** If I am saying all this to myself and to posterity, do you not think that I am doing more to benefit them than I used to when I was an advocate, going down to post bail or affixing a seal to someone's will or lending my voice and aid to some senatorial candidate? Believe me: those who appear to be doing nothing are doing greater things— they are dealing with matters both human and divine.

7 But now I must make an end; and as has become my custom, I must pay for my letter. This will be done, but not on my own charge. I am still plundering Epicurus, in whose work I today found this saying:

> You should become a slave to philosophy, that you may attain true liberty.*

Those who give themselves in obedient service to philosophy are not put off from day to day: they have their liberty-turn* at once, for this slavery to philosophy is true freedom.

8 Perhaps you will ask me why I mention so many fine sayings from Epicurus rather than from our own school. But is there any reason why you should consider them to belong to Epicurus rather than to the public? So many poets say things that philosophers have said, or that they ought to have said! I need not refer to the tragedians or to the authors of our *fabulae togatae* (for those plays too have a serious element; they are in between tragedy and comedy).* Plenty of highly eloquent verses are to be found even in the mime. Many lines of Publilius are such as would befit not only the writer of comedy but even the tragedian. 9 I will report one verse of his that is relevant to philosophy and indeed to the topic I was just discussing. In it he asserts that things that come by chance ought not to be regarded as belonging to us:

> Whatever comes by wishing is not your possession.*

10 I remember that you yourself expressed the same idea in a much better and more concise way:

> What fortune makes your own is not your own.

Nor will I omit another, even better saying of yours:

> The good that can be given can be taken.*

I am not charging these against your account: they come to you from yourself.

Farewell.

# Letter 9

*From Seneca to Lucilius*
*Greetings*

1 You are eager to know whether Epicurus was justified in the criticism expressed in one of his letters* against those who say that the wise person is self-sufficient and for this reason has no need of a friend.* It is a charge made by him against Stilpo* and others who say that the highest good is an impassive mind. 2 (If we choose to express the Greek word *apatheia* by a single term and say *impatientia*, we cannot help but create ambiguity, for *impatientia* can also be understood in the opposite sense to what we intend: we mean by it a person who refuses to feel any misfortune, but it will be taken to refer to one who cannot bear any misfortune.* Consider, then, whether it might not be better to speak of the invulnerable mind or the mind set beyond all suffering.) 3 Our position is different from theirs in that our wise person conquers all adversities, but still feels them; theirs does not even feel them.* That the sage is self-sufficient is a point held in common between us; yet even though he is content with himself, he still wishes to have a friend, a neighbor, a companion.*

4 To see how self-sufficient he is, consider this: there are times when he is satisfied with just part of himself. If his hand were cut off in battle or amputated due to gangrene; if an accident cost him an eye, or even both eyes, the remaining parts of himself would be sufficient for him; he will be as happy with his body diminished as he was with it whole. Still, although he does not feel the want of the missing limbs, he would prefer that they not be missing.* 5 He is self-sufficient, not in that he wants to be without a friend, but in that he is able to—by which I mean that he bears the loss with equanimity. But in truth he will never be without a friend, for it rests with him how quickly he gets a replacement. Just as Phidias, if he should lose one of his statues, would immediately make another, so this artist at friend-making will substitute another in place of the one who is lost.*

6 Are you asking how he will make a friend so quickly? I will tell you, provided you agree that my debt is paid herewith, and the account is cleared as concerns this letter. Hecaton says,

I will show you a love charm without drugs, without herbs, without any witch's incantation: love, if you would be loved.*

Moreover, there is great pleasure to be had not only from the practice of an old and established friendship but also from the initiation and acquisition of a new one. 7 The difference between making a friend and having made one is the same as between sowing and reaping. The philosopher Attalus used to say that it is more pleasant to make a friend than to have a friend, "just as it is more pleasurable for an artist to paint a picture than to have painted one."* That focused concentration on one's work is deeply enjoyable in itself; the pleasure one has in the finished product after the work is done does not equal it. Now, the artist is enjoying the result of his art; while he was painting, he was enjoying the art itself. Children are more rewarding when fully grown, but sweeter in infancy.

8 Now let's return to our stated thesis. Even if the sage is self-sufficient, he still wants to have a friend. If for no other reason, he wants to keep such a great virtue from going unused. His motive is not what Epicurus says in this very letter, "to have someone to sit beside him in illness, or to assist him in imprisonment or in need."* Instead, it is to have someone whom he himself may sit beside in illness, whom he himself may liberate from an enemy's capture. He who looks to himself, and comes to friendship for that reason, thinks amiss. As he began, so will he end: he made the friend to gain his assistance in captivity, but he himself will be gone at the first clink of a chain. 9 These are what are commonly called fair-weather friendships. A friend taken on because of his utility will be pleasing only as long as he is useful. That is why those who are in prosperity have a crowd of friends hanging about, while those who have had a fall are deserted: friends run away just when they have the opportunity to prove their friendship. That is why there are so many terrible stories of people abandoning their friends, or even betraying them, through fear.

Beginnings and endings must agree. He who begins being a friend for the sake of expediency will also stop for the sake of expediency. Some amount of money will be chosen over the friendship if that friendship is valued for anything besides itself. 10 "Why make a friend?" To have someone I can die for, someone I can accompany into exile, someone whose life I can save, even by laying down my own. What you describe is a business deal, not a friendship, for it looks to its own advantage; it thinks in terms of results.

**11** No one doubts that the feelings of lovers bear some resemblance to friendship. One could even say that love is a friendship gone mad. So does anyone fall in love in order to make a profit? Or for the sake of ambition, or for glory? Love all by itself, caring nothing for other objectives, inflames the mind with desire for the other's beauty, and hopes the affection will be returned. What shall we conclude? Does a base emotion arise from a more honorable origin?*

**12** You say, "Our question is not whether friendship is choiceworthy in itself." On the contrary, that is the point that needs most of all to be established; for if friendship is choiceworthy in itself, then it is possible for one who is self-sufficient to pursue it. "In what way, then, does he pursue it?" As one does any deeply beautiful thing, not drawn by profit, and not cowed by the vagaries of fortune. The grandeur of friendship is diminished when one makes a friend just to better one's lot.

**13** "The wise person is self-sufficient." My dear Lucilius, many people misinterpret this. They pull the sage in on every side, driving him inside his own skin. The fact is, one has to make some distinctions as to what that assertion means and how far it extends. The wise person is self-sufficient as concerns living a good life, but not as concerns living in general. For the latter, there are many things he requires; for the former, only a sound and upright mind that rises superior to fortune.

**14** Let me tell you Chrysippus's distinction as well. He says that even though the wise man lacks nothing, he still has a use for many things. "By contrast, there is nothing the foolish person has a use for—since he does not know how to use things—and yet he lacks everything." The wise person has a use for hands and eyes and many other things that are needed for everyday living, and yet lacks nothing. For "lack" implies "need," and the wise person is not in need of anything.*

**15** Therefore, even though he is self-sufficient, he does have a use for friends, and wants to have as many as possible. But he does not want them in order to live a good life. He will do that even without friends, for the highest good does not look for instruments outside itself. It is raised in one's own home, and is complete all by itself. If you seek any part of it from outside, it begins to be subject to fortune.

**16** "But what sort of life will the wise man have if he is left without friends when in captivity, or stranded in some foreign country, or delayed on some long voyage, or cast away on a desert island?" The kind Jupiter has at that time when the world is dissolved and all gods are mingled into one, when nature ceases its operations for a while and he devotes himself to his own thoughts, and rests in himself. What the sage does is something like that: he retreats into himself and is his own company.*

**17** Still, as long as he has the option of arranging his affairs to suit his own preferences, he is self-sufficient, and yet takes a wife; self-sufficient, and yet raises children; self-sufficient, and yet would not live at all if it meant living without other people. What brings him to friendship is not his own expediency but a natural instinct. For just as we innately find certain other things appealing, so it is with friendship. Just as it is inherent in us to shun solitude and seek companionship—just as nature attaches human beings to one another—so also is there an innate prompting to pursue friendships.*

**18** All the same, even though the wise person loves his friends very deeply, putting them on a par with himself or, often, ahead of himself, he nonetheless considers every good to be bounded within himself, and will give the same opinion as Stilpo did—that Stilpo who is criticized in Epicurus's letter. Stilpo's homeland fell to invaders; his children were lost, his wife was lost, and he alone survived the destruction of his people. Yet he emerged happy; and when Demetrius, who was called Poliorcetes, or "City-Sacker," asked him whether he had lost anything, he replied, "All my goods are with me."* **19** Here is a brave man, and a tough one: he conquered even his enemy's conquest. "I have lost nothing," he said, and made Poliorcetes doubt whether he had really conquered at all. "All my goods are with me": justice, courage, prudence, and this in itself, the ability to think that nothing is good which can be taken away. We are amazed that some animals can pass through fire without damage to their bodies. How much more amazing is this man, who escaped fire, sword, and devastation, not only without injury but even without loss! You see how much easier it is to defeat an entire people than a single man? Stilpo's saying is shared by the Stoic: he too carries his goods intact through the devastation of cities, for he is self-sufficient. It is by that limit that he defines his prosperity.

**20** But you shouldn't think that we are the only ones to speak such noble words. Epicurus himself, for all his criticism of Stilpo, delivered a saying similar to his. Give me credit for it, even though I have already paid up for today. He says,

> Anyone who does not think that what he has is plenty, is miserable, even if he is ruler of the entire world.*

Or, if you think this a better way of expressing it (for our service should be given to thoughts, not words): "Wretched is he who does not believe himself supremely happy, though he rule the world."
**21** But to show you that these are widely shared opinions, no doubt dictated by nature, a comic poet supplies the following:

> No one is happy who does not believe himself to be.*

If you think your circumstances are bad, then does it matter what they are really like?

**22** "But look," you say. "What about So-and-So, with his tainted money, or So-and-So, master of many and slave of many more? If one of them claims to have a good life, does his opinion make it so?" It is not what he says that counts, but what he thinks—and not what he thinks on any one day, either, but what he thinks over time. Anyway, you need not worry about so great a prize being awarded to one who does not deserve it. Only the wise man is satisfied with what he has: all the foolish are disgusted with themselves, and suffer accordingly.

Farewell.

## Letter 10

*From Seneca to Lucilius*
*Greetings*

**1** So it is; I do not change my pronouncement. Flee the crowd; flee the company of a few; flee even a single companion. There is no one with whom I would be willing to share you. And see what opinion I have of you: I dare to entrust you to yourself.

It is said that Crates, a pupil of that Stilpo whom I mentioned in my last letter,* once saw a young man walking by himself and asked him what he was doing all alone.

"I am talking to myself," he replied.

"Be careful," said Crates. "Watch carefully, I beg you, for you are talking to a bad person."

2 When people are depressed or anxious, we keep an eye on them so that they do not use their time alone in some unfortunate way. There is not one of the senseless* who ought to be left alone. It is then that they set bad plans in motion; then, that they plot future perils for others or for themselves; then, that they marshal shameless desires. It is then that the mind brings out what it had concealed through fear or shame; then, that it heightens its daring, stimulates its lust, gives spur to its wrathfulness. The only advantage of solitude is that one is not confiding in anyone, there is no fear of informers. But the foolish person loses this advantage, for he betrays himself.

See, then, what my hope is concerning you—or rather, what I promise myself, since "hope" names a good of which one is unsure: I would rather you be by yourself than with with anyone else I can think of. 3 I remember how courageously you made a certain declaration, what strength there was in your words. I congratulated myself in that moment, saying, "*That* did not come off the top of his head; these remarks have some foundation. This man is not of the common sort; no, he looks toward his true healing." 4 This is how you should speak; this is how you should live. Take care that nothing makes you downcast. Even as you thank the gods for answering your former prayers, offer new and different ones. Ask for excellence of mind and for mental well-being, and only after that for bodily health. Is there any reason you should not offer such prayers over and over again? Be bold in your requests to God, for you are not going to ask for anything that does not belong to you.

5 But let me keep to my custom and send some little payment along with my letter. I have found something that rings true in the writings of Athenodorus:*

Here is when you may know that you are free of all desires: when you get to the point that you no longer ask God for anything except what you could ask for openly.

As it is, how crazy people are! When their prayers are quite disgraceful, they whisper them to the gods; if anyone is listening, they fall silent. It is something they are unwilling for humans to hear, and they say it to God! Consider whether the following may not be a healthful bit of advice: live with humans as if God may be watching; speak with God as if humans may be listening.

Farewell.

## Letter 11

*From Seneca to Lucilius*
*Greetings*

1 A conversation I had with your promising young friend immediately showed me how much intelligence and talent he has, and indeed how much progress he has already made. He has given us a sample of himself, and the rest of him will be like it, for what he said was not prepared in advance; he was caught off guard. When he began to collect himself, he blushed deeply, for he could not rid himself of that modesty which is such a good sign in a young person.

I suspect he is one who will retain this tendency even when he has fully grown up and has rid himself of every fault—even when he is wise. For natural flaws of body or mind are not removed by any amount of wisdom: what is innate and implanted may be mitigated by treatment but not overcome.* 2 There are people who, though utterly self-contained, still break out in a sweat when they appear in public, just as if they were tired and overheated. Others get weak in the knees when they are about to give a speech, or their teeth chatter, their lips clench, their tongue trips. These things are not eliminated either by training or by any amount of practice; no, nature exerts its force, using these flaws to remind even the strongest of what their nature is. 3 I am sure that blushing is one of these things; for even in the soberest of grown men it still arises, and suddenly too. True, it is seen more in the young, in whom the native heat is greater and the complexion more supple; but it also affects veteran soldiers and the elderly. Some people are more dangerous when blushing than at any other time; it is as if they had put all their shame into the blush. 4 Sulla was at his most violent when blood had risen to his cheeks. Nothing was softer than Pompey's face: every time he was in company, he blushed, and especially during his speeches.* I remember how Fabianus blushed when called to testify before the Senate; in him, this modesty was strangely becoming.*

5 This does not happen because of any mental weakness but only because of the newness of the situation. People who lack experience of something may be undismayed and yet still affected in this way, if their body's natural disposition tends toward blushing. For just as some people have sluggish° blood, so some have lively, energetic blood that rises swiftly to their faces. 6 As I said, such characteristics are not cast out by any amount of wisdom. If wisdom could erase *all* defects, it would have nature itself under its charge. All contributions made by the circumstances of one's birth and one's bodily temperament will remain with us after the mind has at length managed in large part to settle itself. None of these can be ordered down, any more than they can be summoned at will.

7 Actors imitate the emotions: they portray fear and trembling; they make a show of sadness; but when it comes to bashfulness, their means of indicating it are to tilt the head forward, lower the voice, and fix the eyes on the ground. They cannot make themselves blush, for that can neither be prevented nor induced. Against such things wisdom has no promise to give, no progress to make: they are under their own jurisdiction. They come unbidden and depart unbidden.

8 Now the letter is asking for its closing. Here it is, and a useful and salutary closing too, that I suggest you fix in mind.

We should develop a fondness for some good man and keep him always before our eyes, to live as though he were watching and act in all things as though he could see.*

9 Dear Lucilius, it was Epicurus who gave this instruction. He gave us a guardian and a tutor, and rightly so; for if a witness is present when people are about to commit a wrong, they usually desist. Let

the mind have someone it can respect, someone by whose authority it can make even its privacy more reverent.

Blessed is he who improves us not only when present but even when imagined! Blessed too is he who can revere some person so deeply as to bring order and composure to his existence just by remembering that person. One who is capable of such reverence will soon be worthy of reverence himself. 10 Choose Cato, then; or, if you think Cato too stern, choose Laelius, a man of milder temperament.* Choose anyone whom you admire for his actions, his words, even for his face, since the face reveals the mind within. Keep that person in view at all times as your guardian or your example. I repeat: we need a person who can set the standard for our conduct. You will never straighten what is crooked unless you have a ruler.

Farewell.

## Letter 12

*From Seneca to Lucilius*
*Greetings*

1 Everywhere I turn I see signs of my advancing age. Arriving at my villa near the city,* I began complaining about my expenditures on the building, which was falling apart. My property manager told me it was not his fault: he was doing everything he could, but the house was old. That villa was put up under my direction! What will become of me, if stonework that is my own age is that decrepit?

2 Annoyed with him, I seized on the nearest excuse to vent my anger. "Those plane trees," I said, "are obviously being neglected. They have no leaves; their branches are terribly gnarled and parched by the sun; their trunks are all discolored and the bark is flaking. This wouldn't be happening if they were kept fertilized and watered."

He swore to me by my ancestral spirit that he was doing all that, and taking care of them in every way, but the trees were getting old. Just between us—I was the one who planted them! When their first leaves came out, I was there to see them.

**3** Turning to the door, "Who's that?" I asked. "He's decrepit! You were right to station him by the door—he's on his way out! Where did you get him? Is it some whim of yours to take a corpse off someone's hands?"

But the man said, "Don't you recognize me? I'm Felicio! You used to bring your trinkets to show me.* I'm the property manager Philostitus's son, your playfellow."

"He's nuts!" said I. "Has he now turned into a little child, and also my playmate? Perhaps so! He's losing teeth enough!"

**4** My suburban villa has done me a service; it has brought my age before me at every turn. Let us embrace old age and love it. It is full of pleasure if you know what use to make of it. Fruit is sweetest just before it spoils, boyhood most attractive as it is departing; when one is devoted to wine, it is the last drink that brings the most pleasure—the one that puts you under, giving the final push to inebriation. **5** Every pleasure saves its greatest delights for its last moments. The most pleasurable time of life is on the downhill side, but before the drop-off. Even the time that stands at the very brink has its own pleasures, I believe. Or if not, then it has this instead: one no longer feels the need of any. How sweet it is to have worn out one's desires and left them behind!

**6** You say, "It is grievous to have death right before one's eyes." In the first place, death should be under the eyes of the young as well as the old, for we are not summoned according to the census.* Second, no one is so old as to be unjustified in hoping for one more day—and one day is a rung on the ladder of life.

One's entire life consists of parts, large circles enclosing smaller ones. One circle embraces all the rest; this corresponds to the span from birth to one's last day. A second encloses° the years of young adulthood; another binds one's entire childhood in its circuit. Further, a year contains within itself all the time periods which, multiplied, make up one's life. A month is bounded by a tighter circle, a day by the smallest; yet even a day moves from a beginning to an end, from sunrise to sunset. **7** That was why Heraclitus, who got his nickname from the obscurity of his sayings, said,

One day is equal to every day.*

This is interpreted in different ways. <One person>° says "equal" means "equal in number of hours"; this is true enough, for if a day is a period of twenty-four hours, all days are necessarily equal to each other, since night gains what is lost from daytime. Another says that one day is similar in nature to all other days, for even the longest stretch of time contains nothing that you do not also find in a single day: both light and darkness. The regular alternation of the heavens gives us more nights and more days, but does not change their nature, <although the day is>° sometimes briefer, sometimes more protracted. **8** Every day, then, should be treated as though it were bringing up the rear, as though it were the consummation and fulfillment of one's life.

Pacuvius, who made Syria his own by possession,* used to hold funeral ceremonies for himself, with wine and the ritual meal. After dinner he would have himself carried to bed as his catamites clapped their hands and chanted in Greek, to the accompaniment of instruments, "Life is done! Life is done!" **9** Each and every day he performed his own burial. Let us do the same, not for bad reasons, as he did, but for good. Glad and cheerful, let us say, as we go to our rest,

> I have done living; I have run the race
> that fortune set for me.*

If God gives us a tomorrow, let us be glad to receive it. The happiest person, the most untroubled possessor of himself, is the one who awaits the morrow without anxiety. Anyone who has said, "I have done living" rises profitably each morning, having gained one day.

**10** Now it is time for me to bring this letter to a close. "What?" you say. "Is it going to come to me without any payment?" Fear not: it does bring you a little something. But why do I say a little? It brings you a lot. What could be finer than this saying, which I now give to it to convey to you?

> It is bad to live under constraint, but nothing constrains us to live under constraint.*

How could it? The roads to freedom lie open on every side, many of them, and short and easy ones. Thanks be to God that no one can be made to remain alive. We can trample upon those very constraints. **11** "Epicurus said that," you say. "What business have you with another's property?" Whatever is true is my own. I shall persist in showering you with Epicurus, for the benefit of those people who repeat their oaths verbatim and regard not what is being said but who says it. By this they may know that the best sayings are held in common.

Farewell.

# BOOK TWO

# *Letter 13*

*From Seneca to Lucilius*
*Greetings*

**1** You have plenty of spirit, I know. Even before you began to equip yourself with the teachings that bring health and conquer adversity, you felt that you were doing quite well against fortune, and all the more after you came to grips with it and tested your strength. One can never be sure of one's strength until numerous difficulties have appeared on every side, or indeed until the moment when they have come quite close. That is the way for the true mind to prove itself, the mind that yields to no judgment but its own.

**2** Fortune tests the spirit's mettle. A boxer who has never suffered a beating cannot bring bold spirits to the match. It is the one who has seen his own blood—who has heard his teeth crunch under the fist—who has lost his footing and found himself spread-eagled beneath his opponent—the one who, though forced to yield, has never yielded in spirit, who after falling rises fiercer every time: *that* is the one who goes to the contest with vigorous hope. **3** Pursuing the analogy: just so has fortune often had the upper hand with you, and yet you have never surrendered: you have jumped up and stood still more boldly on your feet. For courage increases when it meets with a challenge. All the same, accept from me, if you will, some few words to help you strengthen your defenses.

**4** More things frighten us, Lucilius, than really affect us, and we are more often afflicted in thought than in fact. I mean this not in a Stoic sense but in a less exalted way. It is, of course, our doctrine that all those things that wring sighs and groans from people are minor matters and not worth thinking about.* But let's skip those great words—although, by all the gods, they are true. My advice to you is this, rather: don't be miserable before it is time. Those things you fear as if they were impending may never happen; certainly they have not happened yet. **5** Some things, then, torment us more than they should, some sooner than they should; and some torment us that should not do so at all: either we add to our pain, or we make it up, or we get ahead of it.

We are still at odds on that first question, and the case is contested. So let's put it off for the moment. Something I call minor will be quite serious in your estimation: I am well aware that some people laugh as they are beaten with whips, while others groan when merely slapped. We will investigate later on whether such things have power through their own strength or through our weakness. **6** What I am asking of you now is just this: whenever those around you begin to convince you that you are unhappy, consider what you actually feel rather than what you hear them say. Consult your own endurance; and since you are the best judge of your own affairs, ask yourself, "Why is it that these people are commiserating with me? On what grounds do they shrink from me, fearing even to come in contact with me, as though misfortune were contagious?" Is there really anything bad in your condition? Or is the reputation worse than the reality? Ask yourself, "Could it be that I am suffering and moaning for no reason? Am I making something bad that is not?"

**7** "How am I to know," you say, "whether the causes of my anxiety are real or empty?" Here is your measuring stick. We are tormented either by things past, or by things to come, or both. Concerning things present it is easy to make a judgment: if your body is at liberty, and healthy, if you are not in pain from any injury, then we can wait and see what is to come; today is not an issue.

**8** "Still, it is to come." First, find out whether there is firm evidence that trouble is on the way. For all too often we worry about what we merely suspect. Rumor plays tricks on us—rumor, that "brings down the battle,"* but brings down the individual even more. Yes, dear Lucilius, we are too quick to give way to opinion. We do not demand evidence of the things that frighten us, or check them out carefully; we quail, and take to our heels, like the army that breaks camp because of a dust cloud kicked up by a herd of cattle, or like people who are terrified by some item of anonymous gossip. **9** In a way, empty causes produce even more trepidation. Real dangers have an inherent limit; anything that arises from uncertainty, though, is given over to conjecture and to unrestrained anxiety.* Hence our most pernicious, our most uncontrollable fears are the crazy ones.

Our other fears are unreasonable; these are unreasoning. So let us look carefully at the facts.

10 Some evil is probable for the future; it is not proven right off. How many unexpected things have come to pass! How many of our expectations never happen at all! Even if it is to come, what good does it do to anticipate your grief? You will grieve soon enough, when it comes; in the meantime, allow yourself something better. What do you gain by that? Time.

11 Many things will happen that may avert the approaching danger, even if it is nearly at hand, or make it cease, or direct it toward someone else. The fire leaves an escape route; the collapsing building sets some people down gently; the sword is right at the throat, and then drawn back; the one condemned to death survives his executioner. Even bad fortune can be fickle. Perhaps it will happen, perhaps it won't; certainly it is not happening now. So keep the better things in view.

12 Often when no sign indicates that anything bad is on the way, the mind makes up its own false imaginings. Either it takes some ambiguous utterance and bends it toward the worse, or it supposes that someone is more gravely offended than he really is, thinking not how angry he is but how much he might be able to do in anger. But if fear goes to its fullest extent, then life is not worth living, and there is no end to our misery. Make use at one point of foresight; at another let mental toughness spurn even an evident danger. If not that, then drive out one fault with another: balance fear with hope.* Certain as it may be, no object of fear is more certain than this:

Panic subsides; hope derides.

13 Therefore give careful consideration to hope and fear alike; and whenever the situation remains uncertain, do yourself a favor and give credence to the thing you prefer. If the weight of opinion rests with fear, throw your support the other way.* Stop troubling yourself, and reflect often that the majority of human beings become upset and bothered even when nothing bad is either present or definite for the future. For no one resists his own movement, once begun; no one trims his fear to accord with reality. No one says, "My informant is of no account, an empty fellow; he either made it up, or believed someone who did." We let ourselves be blown about by the breeze, alarmed by

ambiguities as though they were confirmed facts. We lose our sense of proportion: the least cause of uneasiness turns right away into fear.

14 I am ashamed° to speak this way to you, coddling you with remedies so gentle. Another may say, "Perhaps it won't come"; for yourself say, "If it comes, so what? We will see which of us wins. Perhaps it is in my interests for it to come, and such a death will bring honor to my life." It was the hemlock that made Socrates great. Wrest from Cato his sword, his guarantor of liberty, and you take away the greater part of his glory.* 15 But I am urging you too much, when what you need is more reminding than urging. We are not pulling you in a different direction from your own nature. You were born to our doctrines. All the more, then: augment your own good; embellish it.

16 My letter will now be at an end if I just put the seal onto it, that is, if I entrust it with some grand saying to convey to you.

This too is one of the evils of foolishness: it is always beginning to live.*

Most excellent Lucilius, ponder the meaning of this saying, and you will understand how disgusting it is that people are so fickle, every day laying new foundations for life, starting on new projects even in the hour of death. 17 Cast your mind about to individual cases: you will think of old men who are preparing themselves more than ever before for a career, for travel, or for business. What is more shameful than an old man making a beginning on life?

I would not give the author of this saying if it were not one of the less well-known, uncirculated sayings of Epicurus, which I have allowed myself both to praise and to adopt.

Farewell.

## Letter 14

*From Seneca to Lucilius*
*Greetings*

1 I admit that a fondness for our body is innate in us; I admit that we are charged with the care of it. Nor do I hold that one ought not to

make any allowances for the body. What I do hold is that one ought not to be its slave. One who is a slave to the body—who is excessively fearful on account of it—who refers all things to it—will be a slave to many. **2** We should behave, not as if the body were the proper reason for our lives, but as if it were merely a necessity for life. Excessive love for it troubles us with fears, burdens us with worries, exposes us to criticism. Honor is cheap to one who holds the body too dear. Take scrupulous care of it, but on condition that when required by reason, or self-respect, or loyalty, it is to be thrown into the fire.*

**3** Even so, let us avoid not only danger but also discomfort, as much as we can, and retreat into safety, constantly devising ways of keeping away the objects of fear. If I am not mistaken, those objects are of three kinds. We fear poverty; we fear disease; and we fear the violent deeds of those more powerful than ourselves. **4** Among all these, the one that has most impact on us is the threat from another's power, for this arrives with a great deal of noise and activity. The natural evils I mentioned, poverty and disease, come on in silence; they have no terrors to strike our eyes or ears. But the evil of another makes a great show: it is encompassed with fire and sword, with chains, with packs of wild animals primed to leap upon our human vitals. **5** Imagine here the jail, the cross, the rack, the hook, the stake driven up through the middle of a person and coming out at the mouth, the limbs torn apart by chariots driven in different directions, the garment woven and smeared with flammable pitch, and everything else that savagery has devised. **6** It is no wonder, then, that our greatest fear is of this, since it comes in such great variety and with such frightening equipage. For just as the torturer is most effective when he sets many instruments of pain in view (for some who would have withstood the use of them are broken by the sight), so also among those things that subdue and dominate the mind, the greatest impact belongs to those that have something to display. Those other dangers are no less serious—hunger, I mean, and thirst; festering ulcers; fever burning right down in the gut—but they are unseen. Those have nothing to hold over our heads or before our eyes, while these overpower us, as great wars do, with their panoply and parade.

**7** Let us therefore make an effort to avoid giving offense. At one time it is the populace we have to fear; at another, if the state is ruled in such a way that the senate has charge of most matters, the men of most influence there; at another, individuals in whom is vested the power of the people and over the people. To have all these as friends would require much effort: it is enough if we do not have them as enemies. Thus the wise person will never provoke the anger of those in power, but will steer clear of it, just as one steers clear of a storm at sea. **8** When you were headed for Sicily,* you crossed the strait. The rash helmsman ignores the threatening South Wind (for it is the South Wind that whips up the Sicilian Sea into whitecaps) and does not set a course along the left-hand shore but along the other, where the eddy of Charybdis is quite near.* But the more cautious helmsman inquires of those who are familiar with that locale what the tides are and how to read cloud patterns, and steers well away from the stretch that is notorious for choppy water. The wise person does the same. He avoids the power that will do him harm, being cautious all along not to be seen avoiding it. For this too is part of safety, to be circumspect in pursuing it, since evasive action amounts to condemnation.

**9** So let us look about for ways to be safe from the common crowd. First of all, let us not desire the same objects: strife arises among those who are in competition. Then, let us not possess anything it would be very profitable to steal, and let there be very little on your person that is worth taking. No one goes after human blood on its own account, or very few do.* More act from calculation than from hatred. If a person is naked, the robber passes him by; the poor have peace, even where there is an ambush on the road.

**10** Next, we should keep in mind three things that are to be avoided, as the old proverb says: hatred, envy, and contempt.* Wisdom alone will show us how to do this. For it is difficult to balance one thing against another: in seeking to avoid resentment, we have to be careful not to incur contempt, lest while we refrain from trampling on others, we give the impression that we ourselves can be trampled upon. For many, the power to inspire fear in others has produced reasons to be afraid themselves. Let us refrain from both. Being considered superior is just as harmful as being despised.

**11** Therefore let us take refuge in philosophy. These studies, like the stoles of priests,* mark one as sacrosanct not only among the good but even among those who are bad in an ordinary way. For eloquence in the courts, or any other kind that stirs the multitude, produces rivals; but this quiet sort that is concerned only with its own business cannot be despised; in fact, it is honored above all arts, even among the worst people. Wickedness will never gain so much strength, nor conspire so much against the virtues, that the name of philosophy will cease to be revered as sacred.

Yet philosophy itself must be practiced calmly and with moderation. **12** "What?" you say. "Do you think Marcus Cato practiced it with moderation, he who stayed a civil war with his word? He who took his stand amid the weapons of furious generals? He who, when some were giving offense to Pompey, others to Caesar, challenged both at once?"* **13** One could at this point dispute whether the wise man was obliged to engage in politics in that situation:*

> What are you up to, Cato? The contest is not for freedom; that was lost long ago. The question is whether Caesar or Pompey will possess the state. What have you to do with such a controversy? It is no business of yours to take sides in it. It is a master that is being chosen: what difference does it make to you who wins? It is possible that the better man will win, but it's not possible to win without being the worse for it.

I have touched on Cato's final stand, but even in his earlier years the times were never such as permit the wise to join in that plundering of the state. What did Cato achieve other than raising his voice—and raising it in vain—when he was on one occasion lifted on the hands of the crowd and so ejected from the Forum, all covered with spit and scandalous abuse?° And on another occasion escorted out of the Senate and into a jail?*

**14** But we will investigate later on whether the wise person ought to devote any effort to public service. Meanwhile, I summon you to those Stoics who were cut out of politics and devoted themselves in retirement to the management of life and the establishment of laws for humankind, without offending any of the powerful.* The wise person will not disturb the customs of the public, and neither will he draw public attention by a strange manner of living.

**15** "What? Will one who adopts this plan be especially safe?" I cannot promise you that, any more than I can promise that a person of moderate habits will enjoy good health; and yet it is still the case that moderation promotes health. Ships have been known to sink in harbor—but what do you think happens in the middle of the ocean? How much more dangerous would it be to live a very busy and active life, if even a quiet life is not safe? Sometimes the innocent do perish—who denies it?—but more often the guilty. The skill remains, even when one is struck down through one's armaments.* <sup></sup>**16** In a word, the wise person considers intention, rather than outcome, in every situation. The beginnings are in our power; the results are judged by fortune, to which I grant no jurisdiction over myself. "But fortune will bring some trouble, some adversity." Death at the hands of a robber is not a condemnation.*

**17** Now you are stretching out your hand for the daily dole; I will fill you up with a golden one. And since I have mentioned gold, learn how the use and enjoyment of it may be made more pleasant for you:

He enjoys riches most who has least need of riches.

"Tell me the author," you say. Just to show you how generous I am, I am determined to praise another's material: it is Epicurus, or Metrodorus, or somebody from that shop.* **18** And what does it matter who said it? He said it for everyone.

He who feels the need of wealth also fears for his wealth. But no one has enjoyment from so vexed a good. He is eager to add to it; and while he is thinking about its increase, he is forgetting about its use. He is collecting on his accounts—pounding the pavement of the forum—flipping through his ledger. He is not master but factotum.

Farewell.

# Letter 15

*From Seneca to Lucilius*
*Greetings*

**1** It was a custom among our ancestors, practiced even into my own lifetime, to add to the opening words of a letter, "If you are doing well, that's good; I am doing well myself."* The right thing for us to say is, "If you are doing philosophy, that's good." For that is the only way one can really be doing well. Without that, the mind is sick; and the body too, even if it has great strength, is sound only as that of an insane or deranged person might be. 2 So care for the mind's health first and foremost, and for the other only secondarily: it will not cost you much, if you have resolved to be truly well.

It is foolish, dear Lucilius, and unbefitting an educated man, to busy oneself with exercising the muscles, broadening the shoulders, and strengthening the torso. You may have great success with your training diet and your bodybuilding, but never will you match the strength and weight of a prime ox. Besides, your mind is then weighed down by a more burdensome body, and is less agile as a result. Restrict your body, then, as much as you can, and give more latitude to the mind.

3 Those who are obsessed with such a regimen incur many discomforts. First, the exercises exhaust the spirit with the effort and leave it with less energy for concentration and intense study. Second, the expanded diet hampers its subtle nature.* Further, one has to take the worst sort of slave as one's master, persons who divide their time between oil and wine, who spend a day to their liking if they work up a good sweat and then make up for the loss of fluids by drink, which has more effect when one is depleted in that way.* Drinking and sweating—a life full of heartburn!

4 There are ways of exercising that are easy and quick, that give the body a workout without taking up too much time—for time is what we have to keep track of more than anything: running, and arm movements with various weights, and jumping, either the high jump or the long jump, or the dance jump, or (not to be class-conscious about it) the fuller's stomp.* Choose whichever you like, and make it easy by practice.° 5 But whatever you do, return quickly from the body to the mind and exercise that, night and day. A moderate effort is enough to nourish it, and its exercise is such as neither cold nor heat will hamper, nor even old age. Tend to the good that gets better with time.

6 I am not telling you to be always poring over a book or tablet: the mind should have some respite, but to relax, not to become lax. Getting out in the sedan chair limbers up the body, and does not preclude study: you could read, or dictate, or speak, or listen. In fact, even walking need not prevent you from doing any of these things.

7 Nor should you neglect to exercise your voice; but I forbid you

to practice in scales and rhythms, high notes and low. Why, you might then want to take walking lessons! Once you give an entry to those who earn their bread by inventing new devices, you will find yourself with someone to measure your stride, someone to watch you chew; and they will go boldly on with it for as long as you, in your patience and credulity, lead them on.* Well, then: are you going to start your voice off right away with shouting at the top of your lungs? The natural thing is to raise it by degrees; so much so, in fact, that even in lawsuits the speakers begin in a conversational tone and work their way up to full voice. No one starts out with "Loyalty, O Quirites!"* **8** So no matter how strongly your conviction urges you forward, let your attack on the vices be forceful at some moments, but at other times more gentle, as your voice and your diaphragm° feel inclined; and when you lower your voice again, don't let it drop off, but come down gradually through your in-between volume, not° cutting off with a fierce yelp like an untrained rustic. The point is not to give the voice a workout but for the voice to give the hearer a workout.

**9** I have relieved you of quite a bit of work. To that favor let me now add one little payment, one present° from Greece. Here you go, a fine precept:

> The foolish life is ungrateful and fearful; it looks wholly to the future.*

"Who said that?" you ask. The same as said the last. What life do you suppose it is that is being called foolish? That of Baba and Ision?* That's not it: it is our life that is meant. Blind avarice hurls us toward things that may harm and certainly will never satisfy us. If anything *could* satisfy us, it would have already. We do not think how pleasant it is to ask nothing, how great a thing not to depend on chance for fulfillment.

**10** So remind yourself often, Lucilius, how much you have achieved. When you see how many people are out ahead of you, think how many are behind. If you want to be thankful to the gods and to your own life, think how many people you have surpassed. But what does it matter about anyone else? You have surpassed yourself.

**11** Set a goal that you could not exceed even if you wanted to. Dismiss at last those treacherous goods that are more valuable in expectation than they are in attainment. If there were anything solid in them, we would eventually be sated with them; as it is, they make us thirsty even as we drink.* Get rid of the baggage; it is only for looks. As for the future, it is uncertain, at the behest of luck. Why should I beg fortune to give me things rather than demand them of myself? But why should I demand things at all? Just to make a big pile, forgetting how fragile a human being is? Why such labor? See, this day is my last—or if not the very last, still almost the last.

Farewell.

## Letter 16

*From Seneca to Lucilius*
*Greetings*

1 I'm sure you realize, Lucilius, that no one can live a truly happy life, or even a bearable life, without philosophy; also, that while it is complete wisdom that renders a life happy, even to begin that study makes life bearable. But this realization must be confirmed and fixed more deeply through daily rehearsal. It is more work to follow through on honorable aims than it is to conceive of them. One must persevere and add strength by constant study, until excellent intentions become excellence of mind.

2 So you don't need much verbiage or such lengthy protestations when you are with me. I understand that you have made a lot of progress. I know where these things you write are coming from. You are not making them up, or even touching them up. Still, I will tell you my opinion: I have hopes of you, but as yet no confidence. And if I have my way, you will adopt that same attitude toward yourself, and not be too quick to trust yourself without good reason. Shake yourself out; check yourself over; look at yourself in different ways. Above all, consider whether the progress you have made has been in philosophy, or in life itself. 3 Philosophy is not tricks before an audience, nor is it a thing set up for display. It consists not in words but in actions. One does not take it up just to have an amusing pastime, a remedy for boredom. It molds and shapes the mind, gives order to life and discipline to action, shows what to do and what not to do.

It sits at the helm and steers a course for us who are tossed in waves of uncertainty. Without it, there is no life that is not full of care and anxiety. For countless things happen every hour that need the advice philosophy alone can give.

4 Someone will say, "What use is philosophy to me if there is fate? What use is it if God is in charge? What use, if chance has the mastery? For what is certain cannot be changed, and against what is uncertain there is no way to prepare oneself. Either God has pre-empted my planning and decreed what I should do, or fortune has left nothing for my planning to achieve." 5 No matter which is true, Lucilius, or even if they all are, we must still practice philosophy. Perhaps the inexorable law of fate constrains us; perhaps God, the universal arbiter, governs all events; perhaps it is chance that drives human affairs, and disrupts them: all the same, it is philosophy that must preserve us.* Philosophy will urge us to give willing obedience to God, and but a grudging obedience to fortune. It will teach you to follow God; to cope with chance.

6 But this is not the time to begin a discourse on the question of what it is that is in our power if providence has dominion, or if a sequence of fated events drags us along in chains, or if spontaneous occurrences hold sway. Instead, I now return to where I was, advising you and exhorting you not to let your mind's endeavor dissipate and grow cold. Maintain it; settle it, so that what is now endeavor may become habit.

7 If I know you well, you have been peeking ahead ever since I began, to see what little gift this letter has brought along. Well, shake it out, and you'll see! But you need not marvel at my good graces, for I am still being generous with another's store. Yet why do I say "another's"? Whatever is said well by anyone belongs to me. This too was said by Epicurus:

> If you live according to nature, you will never be poor; if according to opinions, you will never be rich.*

8 Nature's demands are minimal; those of opinion are unbounded. Suppose all the belongings of many rich men were piled upon you. Suppose that fortune were to advance you beyond the means of any private individual, covering you with gold, clothing you with purple, endowing you with luxury and riches, so much that you could cover

the very ground with marble—wealth not only in your possession but even under your feet! Let there be statues too, and paintings, and everything any art has devised to indulge your expensive taste. What will you learn from these things? Only how to desire more. 9 Natural desires are limited; those born of false opinion have no stopping point, for falsehood is inherently unbounded. Those who travel by the road have some destination: wandering is limitless.

So pull back from empty things. When you want to know what it is that you are pursuing, whether it involves a natural desire or a blind one, consider whether there is any place where your desire can come to rest. If it goes far and yet always has further to go, you may be sure it is not natural.

Farewell.

## Letter 17

*From Seneca to Lucilius*
*Greetings*

1 Throw it all away if you are wise—or if you want to be. Press on toward excellence of mind with all your speed, with all your strength. If anything holds you back, untie the knot, or cut it!

"What stands in my way," you say, "is my family business. I want to get it set up in such a way that it will be able to provide for me while I am inactive, so that poverty will not be a burden to me nor I to anyone else." 2 When you say this, you seem not to realize the meaning and power of that good you have in view. You understand in a general way what great benefits philosophy confers, but you do not perceive the finer points: how much assistance it gives us in every endeavor, how it not only "facilitates" our great affairs, as Cicero says, but attends to even our smallest needs.* Trust me: you should make philosophy your advocate. It will persuade you not to linger over your balance sheet.

3 No doubt your aim, the purpose of all your delay, is to ensure that you need not fear poverty. But what if poverty is actually something to pursue? Many have found riches an obstacle to the philo-

sophical life: poverty is untrammeled, carefree. When the trumpet sounds, the poor know that they are not the ones who are under attack; when alarm of fire is raised, they look around for the exit, not for their belongings. When a poor person is about to embark, there is no tumult at the harbor, no bustling throng along the beach, attendants all of a single person; no pack of slaves standing around, to make one wish for the produce of foreign lands just to feed them all. 4 Feeding bellies is a simple matter when there are only a few of them, and when they are well trained, desiring only to be filled. Hunger is cheap; it is the palate that is expensive. Poverty is content to satisfy the immediate wants.

Why, then, do you refuse to take as your companion one whose habits it is sensible for the wealthy to imitate?* 5 If you want to have time for your mind, you must either be poor or resemble the poor. Study cannot be beneficial without some concern for frugality, and frugality is just voluntary poverty. So away with your excuses! "I don't yet have enough; once I reach that amount, I will devote my whole self to philosophy." Yet what is the very first thing you need to acquire? The very thing you are putting off; the lowest thing on your list. That is the place you need to begin. You say, "I want to get something ready for me to live on." While you are doing that, better learn to get yourself ready. Even if something prevents you from having a good living, nothing prevents you from having a good death.

6 Our practice of philosophy need not be hindered by poverty or even by extreme want. Those who are hastening in this direction should be ready to bear even hunger. People have borne hunger in time of siege, and what did they gain for their endurance besides not being left to the mercy of a conqueror? How much greater is this promise: freedom that lasts, and fear of no one, human or divine! Is that not worth going after, even while starving? 7 Armies have endured being deprived of everything: they have lived on the roots of plants; they have staved off hunger with things too foul to name; and all for domination—stranger still, for another person's domination! Who, then, will hesitate to put up with poverty when the aim is to liberate the mind from fits of madness? Therefore there is nothing you need to acquire beforehand. You may come to philosophy even without money for the journey.

**8** Is that how it is? Will you wish to have wisdom only after you have everything else as well? Is this to be your last piece of gear for living, your afterthought, as it were? Well, then: if you do own anything, turn now to philosophy; for how do you know you don't have too much already? Or if you own nothing, seek to gain this before anything else.

**9** "But I'll be without things I need." First of all, you can hardly be without such things, since nature demands very little, and the wise man adapts himself to nature. But if the final extremity should come upon him, he will very readily leave life behind and so cease to be a bother to himself. On the other hand, if what is required for the continuance of life is only a little bit, he will consider himself well off, and will give his belly and back what is due to them without anxiety or concern for anything beyond what is needed. Happy and carefree, he will laugh at the busy lives of the wealthy and at the hustle and bustle of those who compete for wealth, saying, **10** "Why do you postpone your own self? Will you wait for interest to accrue, for ventures to pay off, for some fat inheritance, when you could become rich right away? Wisdom pays off immediately: its wealth is bestowed on all to whom wealth has come to seem irrelevant."

This material applies to others, for *you* are more nearly among the wealthy. Change the century, and you have more than you need. But what is enough is the same in every age.

**11** I could have ended the letter here if I had not trained you badly. Parthian kings are not to be greeted without tribute, and you—one cannot bid you farewell without paying for it. What shall it be? I will get a loan from Epicurus:

> For many people, the acquisition of wealth is not the end of troubles but only a fresh set.*

**12** No surprise there: the fault is not in one's surroundings but in the mind itself. Whatever it was that made poverty a trial makes riches a trial as well. When a person is sick, it makes no difference whether you lay him on a wooden bed or a golden one: he'll take the disease along wherever you carry him. Even so, it matters not at all whether one sick in mind is placed in wealth or in poverty. The trouble is his own, and it follows him.

Farewell.

# Letter 18

*From Seneca to Lucilius*
*Greetings*

1 The month is December, and the city is sweating, more than ever. License has been granted to public self-indulgence, and everywhere is a great din of preparations, just as if there were some real difference between a day of Saturnalia and a business day.* But really there is not a bit of difference—so that I agree entirely with the one who said that what used to be the month of December is now the entire year! 2 If I had you here, I'd like to ask your opinion on what our behavior should be. Should we make no alteration at all in our daily routine? Or should we try not to appear at odds with the general custom, and so make our dinners more festive than usual, laying aside the toga? For what never used to happen except in some time of turmoil, some crisis of the state, we now do for pleasure because of the holiday: we alter our mode of dress.* 3 If I know you well, you would stand as intermediary. You would not want us to be exactly like the crowd with the party hats,* but neither would you want us to be completely different. And yet it may be that during these days, one ought more than ever to take charge of one's mind, ordering it to abstain from pleasures just when everyone else is indulging in them. For if it does not proceed and is not enticed into those luxuries which lead to dissipation, it gives a very sure proof of its own strength. 4 The latter is by far the bolder course, to remain cold sober when everyone else is drunk and vomiting. The former is more moderate: not to hold oneself apart or draw attention to oneself, while still not mingling in every respect—to do as others do, but not in the same manner. For one may celebrate the holiday without dissipation.

5 But I am determined to test how firm your mind really is. I will therefore give you the same instructions that great men have given. Set yourself a period of some days in which you will be content with very small amounts of food, and the cheapest kinds, and with coarse, uncomfortable clothing, and say to yourself, "Is this what I was afraid of?" 6 A time when the mind is free of anxieties is the very time

when it should prepare itself for adversity: amid the favors of fortune, one should strengthen oneself against the onslaughts of fortune. The soldier in time of peace goes for a run; he constructs a palisade even when no enemy is at hand, wearing himself out with extra effort so as to be strong enough when effort is required. If you want someone not to be alarmed in a crisis, train him ahead of time.

This was the practice of those who every month used to impose on themselves a time of poverty amounting almost to destitution. The point of it was that if they had schooled themselves in deprivation, they would never be frightened by it. 7 Don't suppose that I mean to recommend the "dinners of Timon," the "paupers' cells," and all the other things that self-indulgence plays at merely because it is bored with riches.* Let your pallet be a real one, your blanket really burlap, your bread actually hard and coarse. Endure it for three or four days, sometimes more, so that it won't be a game but really a trial. Believe me, Lucilius: you will find it exciting to be fed full for a couple of pence; and you will understand that you can be free of anxiety even without the aid of fortune. For even adverse fortune will give you enough to supply your needs. 8 Not that you therefore have reason to think you are doing some great thing. You will only be doing the same thing as many thousands of slaves and poor people. Think well of yourself only in that you are doing it without compulsion, and in that you will find it just as easy to endure this always as to try it occasionally. Let us try some practice bouts; let us make poverty our companion, so that fortune cannot catch us unawares. We will be less anxious in prosperity if we know how trivial a thing it is to be poor.

9 Even Epicurus, the expert on pleasure, used to have certain days on which he would barely satisfy his hunger, just to see whether that would do anything to reduce his complete and maximal pleasure; or if it did, how much, and whether the difference would be enough to justify anyone in making a great effort over it.* This is surely what he is saying in the letter he wrote to Polyaenus during the magistracy of Charinus.* In fact, he boasts that he can be fed for less than one bronze coin, while Metrodorus, who has not yet progressed to the same point, requires a whole coin.* 10 Do you think a person can be full after that sort of meal? In fact, there is pleasure in it, and not a trivial and fleeting pleasure either; not the kind that keeps having to

be refilled but a stable and sure pleasure. For although there is nothing delightful about water and barley gruel or a crust of bread, still it is a very great pleasure to be able to get pleasure even from these things, and to have brought oneself to that state which no adverse fortune can undo. 11 Meals in prison are more generous; the executioner is less stingy with those on death row. How great a spirit it is, then, that submits by choice to a harsher penalty than is assigned to the worst of convicts! That's a way to rob fortune of its shafts!

12 So make a start, dear Lucilius. Follow the custom of those men, and designate certain days when you part from your own property and make scarcity your companion. Begin to have dealings with poverty.

> Make bold, my guest, to rise above mere wealth;
> and shape yourself as well into a likeness
> worthy of God.*

13 No one is worthy of God unless he has risen above wealth. I do not forbid you to possess wealth; I only seek to make you fearless in possessing it. And the only way to achieve that is if you convince yourself that you will be happy even without it—if you look at it as something that might disappear at any moment.

14 Now let's begin rolling this letter up. "First, pay what you owe!" you say. I will refer you to Epicurus; payment is to be made by him.

> Anger beyond bounds begets insanity.*

You cannot but know how true this is, since you have had slaves— and enemies.* 15 This emotion flares up against people of every station, as much from love as from hatred, and as much in our business dealings as amid jokes and games. Nor does it matter whether the provocation is great or small: the only thing that makes any difference is the mind that is provoked. It is like fire: what matters is not the size of the flame but what is in its path. Where the material is solid, even the biggest blaze does not ignite it; dry and combustible stuff, though, catches even a spark and makes of it an inferno. That's how it is, dear Lucilius: the outcome of great anger is madness. Hence we should avoid anger, not to keep things in moderation, but to preserve our sanity.

Farewell.

# Letter 19

*From Seneca to Lucilius*
*Greetings*

1 I am thrilled every time I get one of your letters. For they fill me with great hope. No longer are they making promises on your behalf; now we have a solemn pledge. Do that, I beg—no, I beseech you, for what better request can I make of my friend than what I would ask on my friend's behalf? If you can, ease yourself out of that occupation of yours—and if you can't, then tear yourself away! We have wasted enough time. Old age is upon us: time to start getting our luggage together. 2 Surely no one can object to that. We have lived at sea; let us die in harbor.*

It's not that I would have you seek notoriety with your retirement. You should neither boast about it nor conceal it. I would never push you to the point where you would curse humanity's madness and hide yourself away in some den. Try to make your retirement such as will be noticeable but not conspicuous. 3 Then let those who are in the early stages of planning consider whether they wish to "spend life in obscurity."* You are not at liberty in the matter. Your vigorous talent, your elegant writings, your distinguished connections, brought you to the public's attention, and now fame has taken you over.* Even if you hide yourself away—even if you go completely underground—still your previous achievements will draw attention to you. 4 You cannot have the darkness: wherever you flee, much of your former light will attend you.

You can claim your rest without resentment from anyone, without missing anything, without a pang. For what could you possibly be sorry to leave behind? Your clients? It's not you they are following around, not any of them; it's what they might get from you. It used to be that clients were after one's friendship; now, they are in it for the spoils. Once the childless old man changes his will, they'll pay their visits to someone else's door. Great goods do not come at small prices. Count the cost: would you rather abandon some of your property, or abandon yourself?

5 If only it had been your lot to grow old in that station to which

you were born! If only fortune had not carried you out into the deep! The life of true health was in sight, and you have been driven far from it by your swift rise, your provincial governorship, and whatever promise these hold: higher offices await you, and one thing will lead to another. Where will it all end? **6** Why are you waiting until there is nothing more for you to want? That will never happen. We say there is a sequence of causes that constitutes the web of fate.* <You may be sure>° that there is a sequence of desires too: the end of one is the beginning of another.

The life you have sunk into is one of misery and servitude without end, and it will never release you on its own. Your neck is chafed by the yoke: draw it out. It would be better for it to be cut through at one stroke than to be oppressed forever. **7** If you curtail your resources to those of a private citizen, there will be less of everything, but ample for your needs, whereas now you have great piles of things and still are not satisfied. Which do you prefer: fulfillment in the midst of scarcity, or dearth in the midst of abundance? Prosperity is greedy, and exposed to the greed of others. As long as nothing is enough for you, you will not be enough for anyone else.

**8** "How shall I get out?" you say. However you can. Think how many risks you have taken for money, how many labors you have endured to gain fame. You should be just as bold in pursuit of leisure; otherwise you must grow old amid the cares of provincial governorships and then amid responsibilities in the city—amid the storm, amid waves ever renewed, which you cannot escape even with moderation and quiet living. You want to rest, but what of that? Your success wants otherwise. And you're still letting it grow! The more you achieve, the more you will have to fear.

**9** At this point I would like to draw your attention to a saying of Maecenas—for he spoke truth even on the rack.*

Lightens the peak itself on high.

If you ask which of his books contains this saying, it is written in the one entitled *Prometheus*. What he's trying to say is this: it is the high places that get struck by lightning. Tell me: would it be worth it to you to speak in such a garbled way, for any amount of power? He was a talented man, and would have provided a fine example of Roman rhetoric, if prosperity had not weakened him, or rather, castrated him. That's the end that is waiting for you if you don't trim your sails; if you don't steer closer to shore—as he wanted to do also, but for him it was too late.

10 I could have used that saying of Maecenas to square my account with you; but knowing you, you will raise an objection to that, and won't be willing to credit my remittance unless it comes from some stern and upright figure. As things are going I'll have to draw on Epicurus:

> Look to your dinner companions rather than your dinner, for feeding without a friend is the life of a lion or a wolf.*

11 That's not an option for you unless you have retired: otherwise you will be eating dinner with guests picked out by your secretary from among your troop of social callers.* It's a mistake to look for a friend in the reception hall and then test his worth at dinner. It's the worst part of a busy life, preoccupied with your own belongings: you think people are your friends when you are not a friend to them. You believe that the favors you are doing for people are winning them over to your side, when as far as some people are concerned, the more they owe, the greater is their hatred.* A small loan creates a debtor; a large one creates an enemy.

12 "What? Don't favors lead to friendships?" They do if one is able to exercise some choice as to who will receive them—if they are investments and not merely largesse. So, since you are just beginning to make your own decisions, take the philosophers' advice: what matters is not the favor but the person favored.

Farewell.

## Letter 20

*From Seneca to Lucilius*
*Greetings*

1 If you are doing well, and think yourself worthy of someday becoming your own person, I am glad of it. For it will be to my credit if I manage to extricate you from that place where you are now floun-

dering without hope of escape. But this I ask of you, this I urge you, dear Lucilius: let philosophy sink deep into your heart, and test your progress not by speech or writing but by strength of mind and by the lessening of your desires. Prove your words through your actions. **2** They have a different aim, those declaimers who seek to win the agreement of an audience; a different aim, those speakers of the present day, who merely set out to produce a prolix and varied rant for the entertainment of young men without enough to do. Philosophy teaches us to act, not to speak. Its demands are these: each person should live to the standard he himself has set; his manner of living should not be at odds either with itself or with his way of speaking; and all his actions should have a single tenor. This is the chief task of wisdom, and the best evidence of it too: that actions should be in accordance with words, that the person should be the same in all places, a match for himself. "Is there any such person?" Not many, but there are some. It is indeed difficult. And I don't mean, even, that the wise person always walks the same steps, but only that he walks a single road.

**3** So take stock of yourself. Is your manner of dress out of line with your house? Are you generous with yourself, but stingy with your family? Do you dine frugally, but spend extravagantly on your building projects? Adopt once and for all some single rule to live by, and make your whole life conform to it. Some people cut back at home only to extend themselves in public, and live large. This discrepancy is a fault, a sign that the mind is vacillating and does not yet hold to its own character.

**4** Moreover, I will tell you where that inconsistency comes from, that difference between action and intention. No one fixes his mind on what it is that he wants; or if he does, he fails to persevere and so falls away, not just altering his ways but actually regressing, returning to the very behavior he had forsworn. **5** Let me then set aside the old definitions of wisdom and give you one that takes in a whole method of human existence. Here's one I can be content with. What is wisdom? Always wanting the same thing, always rejecting the same thing. You do not even have to add the proviso that what you want should be right: only for the right can one have a consistent wish.

**6** Hence people don't know what it is they want except in the very moment when they want it. No one has made an all-round decision as to what he wants or does not want. Their judgment varies day by day, changing to its opposite. Many people live life as if it were a game. So press on with what you have begun. Perhaps it will take you to the top; or if not that, then to a point that you alone know is not yet the top.

7 You say, "What will happen to my flock of dependents if the family does not have an income?" Once you stop feeding that flock, it will feed itself. Or else poverty will teach you what you cannot teach yourself: your real, true friends will stay by you even then, while anyone who was not clinging to you but to something else will depart from you. Should we not love poverty for this if for nothing else? It will show you who your friends are. O, when will that day come when no one will lie to you for the sake of the office you hold!

8 Therefore leave every other prayer in God's hands, and direct your thoughts, your cares, your wishes, to this alone: contentment with yourself and with the goods that come from yourself. What prosperity could be nearer at hand? Trim yourself back to that small fortune that chance cannot take away.

And to make that easier for you to do, this letter's remittance will make reference to it. I'll deliver that immediately. 9 Although you may complain, my payments are still to be made, quite willingly, by Epicurus:

> Believe me, your speech will be more impressive on a pallet and in shabby clothing. Then, you won't only be speaking; you'll be proving what you say.*

I certainly hear the words of our friend Demetrius* differently after seeing how he slept: not only without a mattress but even without a blanket! He doesn't just preach the truth; he gives testimony to it.

10 "What's this? Can't one despise wealth while it is in one's pocket?" Why not? There is greatness of spirit also in the person who sees wealth heaped up around him and laughs long and loud for sheer amazement that it has come to him. Others tell him it is his; on his own he scarcely realizes it. It is a great thing not to be corrupted by living amid riches; great is the man who is a pauper in his wealth.

11 You say, "I do not know how such a man would bear poverty if he should come into it." Nor do I know, Epicurus, whether your boastful° pauper would scoff at wealth if he should come into it.

So we must evaluate the mind of each, and examine them to see whether the one relishes his poverty and whether the other declines to relish his wealth. Otherwise the pallet and shabby clothes are but little proof of good intent, if it is not also apparent that the person is enduring them by preference rather than of necessity. **12** But it is a promising sign when a person does not rush out to get them as if they were better clothes, yet still prepares himself for them as easy enough to bear. And it is easy, Lucilius; in fact, when you have rehearsed for it long before, it is enjoyable too. For there is something in such garments without which nothing else is enjoyable: there is tranquility.

**13** So I think it is really necessary to do what I told you in my letter great men have often done: set aside some days when by making a pretense of poverty we train ourselves for the real thing.* We should do it all the more since we are steeped in luxuries, and think everything harsh and difficult. Better to wake the mind from sleep; pinch it, and remind it of how little our nature actually requires. No one is born rich: everyone who comes forth into the light is ordered to be content with milk and a bit of cloth. From such beginnings do we come, and yet now whole kingdoms are not big enough for us!

Farewell.

## Letter 21

*From Seneca to Lucilius*
*Greetings*

**1** Do you think your business is with those people you wrote about? Your business is most of all with yourself: it is you that are the problem. You don't know what you want. You admire honorable conduct more than you imitate it; you see where happiness lies, but you dare not go after it.* So, since you have little insight into what it is that holds you back, I will tell you.

You suppose that the things you are about to leave behind are important; and just when you have set your eyes on that tranquility toward which you are headed, you linger over the gleam of this life you are leaving behind, like one who is to go down into mire and darkness. **2** You are mistaken, Lucilius. Passing from this life to that one means going up! You know the difference between a glow and a gleam, how one gives off light from its own sure origin, the other reflects light from something else. There is the same difference between this life and that. This life is suffused by a brightness that comes from outside itself, so that anyone who stands between will cast it into thick darkness; that life is radiant with a luster of its own.

Your studies will make you famous. I will report an example from Epicurus. **3** When he was writing to Idomeneus, calling him back from a life of fine appearance to a reliable and constant glory (though Idomeneus was at that time an aide to a powerful king, charged with great matters), he said,

> If glory matters to you, my letters will make you more famous than all those things you are attending to and that make others attend on you.*

**4** Was he not telling the truth? Who would have known about Idomeneus if Epicurus had not happened to write to him? All those potentates and satraps, even the king who granted Idomeneus his title, all are buried deep in oblivion. It is the letters of Cicero that prevent the name of Atticus from perishing. It would have profited him nothing that Agrippa married his daughter and Tiberius his granddaughter, or that Drusus Caesar was his great-grandson.* Among such great names, his own would no longer be spoken, had Cicero not made him an addressee.°* **5** Deep is the abyss of time that will close over us. A few talented minds will raise their heads above it, and although they too must eventually depart into silence, yet for long will they resist oblivion and assert their freedom.*

What Epicurus was able to promise his friend, I promise to you, Lucilius: I shall find favor with posterity, and I can bring others' names along with me, so that they will endure as well. Our poet Virgil promised eternal remembrance to two people, and gives it to them too:

> Fortunate pair! If there is anything
> that poems of mine can do, no future day

will ever erase you from the memory
of ages, while Aeneas's line shall dwell
on the unmoving rock, the Capitol,
and while the Roman father still holds sway.*

6 Those whom fortune has thrust into the midst of things, who have been the members and partakers of others' power, have great prestige and many visitors—while they are on their feet: the moment they are gone, they cease to be remembered. But minds of talent are held in growing esteem, and this extends not only to the authors themselves but to anything that is associated with their memory.

7 Now, I'm not going to let Idomeneus into my letter for free! He can make the payment for it himself. It was to him that Epicurus wrote that fine sentence urging him to enrich Pythocles in no common or ambivalent way. He says,

> If you want to make Pythocles rich, what you must do is not add to his money but subtract from his desires.*

8 This saying is too clear to need interpretation, and too well phrased to need improvement. My only addition is to remind you not to refer it only to wealth: its import will be the same wherever it is applied. If you want to make Pythocles honorable, what you must do is not add to his acccolades but subtract from his desires. If you wish to make Pythocles experience constant pleasure, what you must do is not add to his pleasure but subtract from his desires. If you wish to make Pythocles live a long and complete life, what you must do is not add to his years but subtract from his desires. 9 You need not regard these sayings as belonging to Epicurus: they are public property. I think philosophers should adopt senatorial practice. When someone has stated a judgment that pleases me in part, I ask him to divide his opinion, and I follow the part I approve.*

These splendid sayings of Epicurus also serve another purpose which makes me even more willing to mention them. They prove to those people who take refuge in him for base motives, thinking to find cover for their faults, that they need to live honorably no matter where they go.* 10 When you arrive at Epicurus's Gardens, and see° what is written there:

then the keeper of that house will be ready to receive you and, being hospitable and kind, will serve you a plate of porridge and a generous goblet of water and say to you, "Is this not a fine welcome?" "These gardens," he will say, "do not stimulate appetite; they appease it. They do not give drinks that make one thirstier, but quench thirst with its natural remedy, which comes free of charge. This is the pleasure in which I have lived to old age."

11 I am speaking to you now of those desires that are not allevi-ated by soothing speech, desires that must be given something to put an end to them. For about those superfluous desires that can be put off, rebuked, or suppressed, I remind you only of this: such pleasure is natural but not necessary. You do not owe it anything: anything you do devote to it is voluntary. The belly does not listen to instructions: it merely demands and solicits. Still, it is not a troublesome creditor. You can put it off with very little, if you just give it what you owe rather than what you can.

Farewell.

# BOOK THREE

# Letter 22

*From Seneca to Lucilius*
*Greetings*

**1** Now you understand that you have to get away from those seemingly important jobs that are so bad for you, but you ask how you can pull it off. Some things can only be pointed out in person. A doctor cannot appoint by letters the proper time for eating or bathing: he must feel the pulse. As the old saying goes, "The gladiator takes counsel in the ring": he gets his instructions from watching his adversary's expression, the movement of his hand, even a shift in his balance. **2** What is customarily done, what duty requires, can be dictated in the general case, and also written down: such advice is given not only to those who are away but even to posterity. But on the further question, when or in what way it should be done, no one can give advice at a distance: one must make the determination according to circumstances. **3** To note the occasion as it hastens by takes more than being there: you must also be vigilant. So keep an eye out for it, and if you see it, grab it, and act decisively and with all your strength to divest yourself of those responsibilities you have.

Here, in fact, is the advice I have to offer. Mark my words: you must get out—either out of that life or out of life itself! Yet at the same time I think you should walk softly, loosening this terrible knot you have tied rather than breaking the rope, with the proviso that if other means fail, you should indeed break it. No matter how timid you are, you surely would not choose to dangle forever over the cliff; it would be better to fall at once.

**4** Meanwhile, the first priority is to avoid further encumbrances. Content yourself with the tasks you have already taken on—or, as you would have it, the tasks that have come your way. Don't go out of your way to take on more, or you'll lose your excuse; it will be obvious that they didn't just come your way. Those things people are always saying are just not true: "I couldn't help it. I didn't want to, but what of that?

I had to." No one *has* to run after prosperity. There's something to be said for stopping. Even if you aren't actively resisting, you don't have to push on in the direction fortune is carrying you.

**5** Will you be annoyed if I bring in some experts to supplement my own advice? These are better counselors than I; indeed, I consult them myself when I am considering a course of action. Read the letter of Epicurus that concerns this issue.* It is one written to Idomeneus, telling him to get away, as much as he can, and to hurry, before some stronger power comes to interfere and he no longer has the freedom to retire. **6** He adds that nothing should be attempted except at an opportune time—but that when the long-anticipated moment does arrive, one should spring up at once. "If you are planning escape," he says, "you must never take naps"; and, "Even if circumstances are very difficult, I expect that retirement will be beneficial, provided we neither rush to it before it is time nor hang back from it when the time comes."

**7** I suppose you are now looking for a saying from the Stoics as well. Don't let anyone around you criticize them for being rash: they are more cautious than they are bold. You are perhaps expecting them to tell you, "It is shameful to bend beneath a burden. Come to grips with the responsibility you have assumed. A man who flees from labor, whose courage does not increase with the very difficulty of the situation, is not a brave and energetic person." **8** Those are the things they will say to you, but only as long as there is something gained by such perseverance, and as long as one does not have to do or undergo anything unworthy of a good man. Otherwise a person of character will not wear himself out with paltry and demeaning labor: he will not engage in business just for the sake of being busy. Neither will he do what you are expecting him to do, that is, continue to be caught up in an ambitious career, enduring its trials. When his involvement begins to seem burdensome—uncertain—perilous—he will retreat from it. It is not that he will turn his back; rather, he will withdraw by degrees toward safety.

**9** It is easy to escape from your job, dear Lucilius, if you have no regard for the rewards of the job. It is the rewards that hinder us and keep us at it. "What? Am I to abandon such great expectations? Am I to walk away just when the harvest is ripe? Shall I be stripped of my escort? Shall my sedan chair be unattended, my reception hall deserted?" These are the things people are unwilling to leave: they love the profits of misery even as they curse the miseries themselves. **10** They complain about their career in the same way as they complain about a girlfriend—which is to say that if you examine their true feelings, they don't hate it at all but only have a quarrel with it. Scrutinize those who are whining and threatening to flee, and you will see: their detention is voluntary. The things they say are making them miserable are the very things they wanted, the things they cannot do without.

**11** That's how it is, Lucilius: slavery holds on to a few; many hold on to slavery. But if you mean to lay aside your slavery—if your desire for freedom is genuine—if your sole purpose in asking for encouragement is to do what you have to do without being worried about it forever, then the entire troop of Stoics will cheer you on. Why shouldn't they? All the Zenos and Chrysippuses will urge you to choose the course that is moderate, that is honorable, that is your own.*

**12** But if the reason you are looking over your shoulder is to ascertain how much you will be able to take with you—that is, how large your retirement income will be—then you will never find release. As long as you hang on to the suitcase, you cannot swim to safety. Get your head above the water, and live a better life. May the gods bless you, but not in the way that they bless some people, with kindly visage according them great miseries. For such gifts—gifts that burn, that torture the receiver—they have but one excuse: they gave what was requested of them.

**13** I was just sealing up this letter, and now I must open it up again, to make sure that it doesn't leave here without its little ritual offering, but takes along some fine saying. One does occur to me; I hardly know whether it is more true or more eloquent. "Whose is it?" you ask. It belongs to Epicurus, for I am still drawing on other people's coffers.°

**14** Each of us leaves life as if he had just entered it.*

Take anyone you like, young, old, or somewhere in between: you will find them all equally fearful of death, equally ignorant of life. No one has any achievements: we put off for the future everything that belongs to us.

What pleases me most about this saying is that it reproaches the elderly for being infantile. **15** "Each of us leaves life just as he was born," he says. Wrong: we are worse when we die than when we are born. The fault rests with us, not with our nature. Nature should register a complaint against us, saying, "What's this? I brought you into the world with no desires, no fears, no superstitious credulity, no disloyalty, nor any of those other things that plague you. Just go out the way you came in!" **16** Anyone who dies with the same tranquility he had at birth has achieved wisdom. As it is, though, we tremble when danger approaches. The breathing grows labored—the face is drained of color—tears fall, and to no avail. We are at the very threshold of tranquility, and yet we worry. What could be more disgraceful?

**17** But here's why: because we are devoid of every good, we find the loss of life troublesome. For among us no part of life ever accrues to our benefit. We spend it all; it slips through our fingers. No one cares how well he lives but only how long—despite the fact that every one of us has the chance to live well, and no one can live long.

Farewell.

## Letter 23

*From Seneca to Lucilius*
*Greetings*

**1** Do you think I am going to write to you about how leniently the winter has dealt with us (and it *was* a short and mild winter), how harsh and unseasonably cold is the spring, and all the other nonsense people write when they are short of things to say? No, I'll write something that will benefit both you and me. What will that be? What else, but to exhort you toward excellence of mind? Would you like to know what it is that such excellence is founded upon? It is this: don't rejoice in empty things.*

**2** Did I say it was the foundation? The pinnacle, rather. Reaching the heights means knowing what to rejoice in—finding prosperity in that which no one else can control. Anyone who is enticed by hope is anxious and unsure of himself, even if hope is for something close at hand or not difficult to get, even if the things one hoped for never prove disappointing.

**3** Do this above all, dear Lucilius: learn how to experience joy.* Do you now suppose that because I am removing from you the things of fortune and think you should steer clear of hopes, those sweetest of beguilements, I am taking away many pleasures? Not at all: what I want is that gladness should never be absent from you. I want it to be born in your own home—and that is what will happen if it comes to be inside of you. Other delights do not fill the heart; they are trivial feelings that merely smooth the brow. Surely you don't think that every person who smiles is rejoicing! The mind must be energetic and confident; it must be upright, superior to every trial. **4** Believe me, real joy is a serious matter. Do you think that it is with a relaxed expression—or, as the self-indulgent say, *avec le sourire*—that one despises death, opens his home to poverty, reins in pleasure, and rehearses the endurance of pain? One who is pondering such things is experiencing a great joy, but hardly a soft or seductive one. This is the joy I want you to possess: you will never run out of it, once you learn where it is to be found. **5** Shallow mines yield but a little; the most precious lodes are hidden deep in the earth, and it is these that will repay the effort of digging with ever greater abundance. The pleasure that is in the amusements of the many is slight and superficial. And any joy lacks foundation when it has been imported from elsewhere. The joy of which I am speaking, to which I seek to direct you, is solid through and through, and has its widest scope within.

**6** There is only one course of action that can make you happy. I beg you, dearest Lucilius, to do it: cast aside those things that glitter on the outside, those things that are promised you by another or from another, and trample them underfoot. Look to your real good, and rejoice in what is yours. What is it that is yours? Yourself; the best part of you. As for your paltry body, it is true that nothing can be done without it, but think of it as a necessary thing rather than as something great.* The pleasures it accumulates are empty, short, and regrettable; besides, unless tempered with a good deal of self-control, they soon turn into pleasure's opposite. Yes, pleasure stands at the edge of a cliff, and tips toward pain if it does not keep within its bounds. But it is difficult to keep within bounds when you believe something to be good.

Greed for what is truly good is sure of satisfaction. **7** "What is that?" you ask, or "Where does it come from?" I will tell you: it comes from a good conscience, from honorable counsels, from right action, from despising the things of fortune, from a calm and steady mode of life that walks a single road. For how can people have anything sure, anything they can rely on, when they themselves jump around from one plan to another? Or if they don't even do that, but are merely blown about by every breeze of chance, hovering and flitting through life? **8** There are few who make deliberate arrangements for themselves and their possessions. The rest are like objects floating in a river: they are not advancing but only moving with the current. One ripple is gentler, and carries them easily along; another sweeps them away more roughly; one flows languidly and deposits them near the shore; yet another is a raging flood and hurls them out to sea. Let us decide, then, what it is that we want, and persevere in that.

**9** Here is the place for paying my debt. I can give you a saying of your dear Epicurus* in payment of this letter's bond:

It is wearisome to be always beginning one's life.*

Or, if this is a better way to express the thought,

They live badly who are always starting to live.

**10** "Why?" you ask. The saying requires an explanation. It is because for them, life is always unfinished: a person who has just begun to live cannot stand ready for death. We must endeavor to have enough of life, and no one achieves that when he is just at the point of laying out his life's project.

**11** Nor do you have cause to believe that such people are rare: practically everyone is like this. In fact, some people are just beginning right when it is time to quit. If you think this remarkable, I will add something to amaze you even more: some people quit living long before they begin.

Farewell.

# Letter 24

*From Seneca to Lucilius*
*Greetings*

**1** You write that you are worried about the outcome of a lawsuit that an enemy's rage has brought against you. You suppose that I will urge you to fix your thoughts on the best and to ease your mind with comforting expectations. After all, what need is there to take an advance on future troubles, ruining the present with fear of the future? When troubles come is time enough to bear them. Surely it is foolish to be miserable now just because you are going to be miserable later on!

**2** But what I will do is lead you down a different road to tranquility. If you want to be rid of worry, then fix your mind on whatever it is that you are afraid might happen as a thing that definitely will happen. Whatever bad event that might be, take the measure of it mentally and so assess your fear.* You will soon realize that what you fear is either no great matter or not long lasting.*

**3** Nor do I need to cast about very long for examples to strengthen you with. Every age supplies them. Wherever you direct your powers of recall, amid civic or external affairs, individuals will come to mind who were either morally advanced or exceptionally bold. Suppose you are convicted: can anything worse happen to you than being sent into exile, or being thrown in prison? Is there anything more terrifying than being burned—than dying? Take up each of these things in turn, and summon to mind those who have thought little of them. You will not have to conduct a search; rather, you have a number to choose from. **4** Rutilius endured his conviction as if the only thing that troubled him was being misjudged. Metellus endured exile bravely; Rutilius even gladly. While Metellus made sure that he would return for his country's sake, Rutilius refused to return in order to oppose Sulla, who at that time was meeting with no opposition.* Socrates lectured while in prison, and although there were people there to arrange an escape, he refused to leave; instead, he stayed, meaning to do away with humankind's two greatest fears: death and imprisonment.*

**5** Mucius put his hand in the flames.* It is a hard thing to be burned; how much harder when the burning comes about through your own agency! You see a man with no schooling, without benefit of any instructions concerning death or pain, equipped only with a soldier's toughness, exacting punishment from himself for vain endeavor. He witnessed his own right hand sizzling on the enemy's brazier. His flesh was peeling away from the bones, and yet he did not remove it until after the enemy had put out the fire beneath it. There are happier things he could have done in that camp, but no braver thing. Observe how much fiercer virtue is in confronting perils than cruelty in imposing them: Porsenna found it easier to pardon Mucius for trying to assassinate him than Mucius did to pardon himself for failing.

**6** "These stories," you say, "are the constant refrain in all the schools. I expect the minute you get to making light of death you'll tell me about Cato." Why shouldn't I tell you about Cato's last night, how he was reading a book by Plato with his sword right next to his head?* Those were the two things he had selected to equip himself against his final hour, the one so that he would be willing to die, the other so that he would be able. Once he had settled his affairs—insofar as such fractured and desperate affairs could be settled—he decided to take such action that no man would either have the privilege of killing Cato or the opportunity of saving him. **7** Drawing his sword, which up to that day he had preserved unstained with any act of violence, he said, "Fortune, you have achieved nothing by resisting all my endeavors. Until now I have fought for my country's freedom and not my own. My purpose in acting with such determination was not to live free but to live among the free. Now that hope is lost for humankind, let Cato be taken away to safety." **8** Then he struck the blow that meant death to his body; and when the doctors bound it up, with little left of blood, little of strength, but of spirit as much as before, and hostile now not only toward Caesar but also toward himself, he thrust his naked hands into the wound and did not release, but hurled from him, that noble spirit heedless of all domination.

**9** I am not piling up these examples just for literary exercise, but to exhort you not to fear those things that seem most alarming. It will be easier for me to do that if I show you that it is not only powerful men who have made light of this instant when the spirit is expelled:

some who are debased in other ways have shown themselves equal to the bravest in this regard. For instance, there was Scipio the father-in-law of Gnaeus Pompey.* Driven back to Africa by a contrary wind, and seeing his ship captured by the enemy, he impaled himself on his sword; and when people asked where the general was, he said, "All's well with the general." **10** This saying made him equal to his ancestors and kept up the glorious reputation preordained for the Scipios in Africa. It was a great thing to conquer Carthage; a greater thing to conquer death. "All's well with the general": how else should a general die? How else *Cato's* general?

**11** I am not sending you back to your history books, and neither am I going to collect examples from every age of men who made light of death, though there are many such. Look to our own times, times that we say are all too indolent and pampered: they will supply us with people of every station, every class, every time of life, who cut short their misfortunes by dying. Believe me, Lucilius, so little terror is there in death that by its good graces nothing else holds terror either. So listen unperturbed to your enemy's prosecution. **12** Your clear conscience gives reason to be confident; still, since many external factors have a bearing on the outcome, hope for the best but prepare yourself for the worst.

Remember above all to get rid of the commotion. Observe what each thing has inside, and you will learn: there is nothing to fear in your affairs but fear itself. **13** You see with children how people they love and know, people they play with, frighten them terribly if they see them wearing masks: well, the same thing happens with us, who are just slightly bigger children. In our case, though, the mask needs to be removed not only from people but from events as well, and their true face revealed.*

**14** "Why are you making me a show of swords and torches, of torturers clamoring in your train? Away with this façade you set before you, to terrify the fools! You are only death, whom recently my slave and even my serving maid despised. Why this great display of whips and racks spread out again before my eyes? Why the instruments of torture specially designed for every joint? Why a thousand more devices for dismembering a person bit by bit? Lay down your astonishing devices; bid the groans be silent, and the cries, the shrill vociferations extorted by the lash! You are only pain, whom that arthritic fellow there despises, whom the dyspeptic endures at fancy meals, whom the merest girl endures in childbirth. If I can bear you, you are slight; if I cannot, you are short."*

**15** Ponder these words in your mind. You have heard them many times, and said them too. But whether it was true what you have heard and said is true—that, you must prove by results. For the most shameful of the accusations against us is that we deal in the words of philosophy but not the actions. Well, then! Death, exile, pain loom over you: is this the first time you have realized it? You were born for this! Whatever *can* happen, let's think about as something that *will* happen.

**16** I know you are sure to have done already the things I am advising you to do. My further advice to you at this point is that you not allow your concern over this matter to overwhelm your mind, for that will deaden it, and you will have less energy when it is time to rouse yourself. Turn your thoughts away from your personal situation and toward that of people in general. Tell yourself that this paltry body is mortal, and that it is frail. It is not only unjust assaults or superior forces that threaten it with pain: its very pleasures turn into torments. Banquets cause it indigestion; drinking bouts cause tremors and dullness of the nerves; lusts bring on deformations of the hands and feet and all the joints.

**17** "I shall become poor." I will be one among many. "I shall be exiled." I'll think of myself as a native of my place of exile. "I shall be bound." What of it? Am I now unfettered? Nature has chained me to this heavy weight that is my body. "I shall die." What you are saying is this: I shall no longer be susceptible to illness, to imprisonment, to death.

**18** I am not so silly as to sing to you here the Epicurean song, about how fears of hell are empty, how Ixion is not spinning on his wheel nor Sisyphus shouldering his rock uphill, how no one's entrails can be devoured and regenerated daily.* No one is such a child as to be afraid of Cerberus and the dark and the skeleton figures of ghouls. Death either consumes us or sets us free. If we are released, then better things await us once our burden is removed; if we are consumed, then nothing is waiting for us at all: both goods and evils are gone.

**19** Allow me at this point to remind you of your own poem, advising you first to decide that you wrote it not just for other people but also for yourself. It is shameful to say one thing and mean another; how much more shameful to write one thing and mean another! I remember you once expanded on the theme, "We do not meet death all at once; we move toward it bit by bit." **20** We die every day, for every day some part of life is taken from us. Even when we are still growing, our life is shrinking. We lost our infancy, then childhood, then youth. All our time was lost in the moment of passage, right up to yesterday, and even today is divided with death as it goes by. As the water clock does not empty out its last drop only but also whatever dripped through it before, so our last hour of existence is not the only time we die but just the only time we finish dying. That is when we arrive at death, but we have been a long time coming there. **21** When you had explained all this in your usual ringing tones (you always were a great speaker, but never more intense than when giving voice to the truth), you said,

Death is not one event; the death that takes us is our last.*

I'd rather you read yourself than my letter! It will then be obvious to you that the death we fear is our last one, but not our only one.

**22** I see where you're looking! You are peeking to see what I have tucked into this letter, what spirited saying of some author or what useful precept. I'll send you something from the same material I just had in hand. Epicurus reproaches those who desire death as much as those who fear it, saying,

It is absurd to run after death out of disgust with life, when it is you, with your manner of living, who have made death something to run after.*

**23** Similarly in another passage he says,

What could be more absurd than to seek death when it is fear of death that has made your life unquiet?

To this may be added another saying of his, to the same effect:

So great is the foolishness, no, the madness of human beings, that some are driven toward their death by fear of death.

**24** By reflecting on any of these, you will strengthen your mind to endure either death or life. For we need to be admonished and strengthened both against excessive love of life and against excessive hatred of it. Even when reason advises one to make an end of oneself, the act should not be undertaken heedlessly or in haste. **25** A man of courage and wisdom should not flee life but merely depart from it.

Also, and especially, one must avoid that state which has come over many people: a craving for death. For just as there is for other things, dear Lucilius, so there is an ill-considered longing for death that frequently grips men who are noble and of an adventurous disposition, and frequently also those who are timid and shiftless. The first kind scorn life; the second kind are weighed down by it. **26** Others find that they have become satiated with seeing and doing the same things, and do not hate life so much as they are disgusted by it. We slip into it even at the instigation of philosophy, when we say, "How much more of the same things? I mean, how long will I wake and sleep, eat and grow hungry, grow cold and grow hot? Nothing has an ending: everything is connected to the rest of the world. Things chase each other in succession: night comes on the heels of day, day on the heels of night; summer yields to autumn, autumn is followed hard by winter, which then gives way to spring. Everything passes only to return. I do nothing that is new, see nothing that is new. Sometimes this too produces nausea." There are many who feel, not that life is hard, but that it is pointless.

Farewell.

## *Letter 25*

*From Seneca to Lucilius*
*Greetings*

**1** Concerning our two friends: we must proceed differently with each. One needs to have his faults removed, the other to have them broken.

I shall employ entire freedom of speech: if I do not offend him, I do not love him.*

"What?" you say. "Do you mean to take a forty-year-old pupil under your wing? Take thought for his age, which is now hardened and difficult to manage. He cannot be reshaped: one molds things while they are soft." **2** I don't know if I will succeed, but I would rather fail in my endeavor than in my duty to him. Nor should you give up hope: even long-term invalids can be cured if you take a stand against intemperance, and if you force them repeatedly to do things and put up with things against their will.

I don't have much confidence about the other one either, except for the fact that he still blushes for his wrongdoing. We must nurture that sense of shame: once it has solidified in his mind, there will be some room for hope. Because he is such a veteran, I think we must treat him more gently than the other, so that he won't give up on himself. **3** And there has never been a better time to approach him than right now, while he is in a quiet spell, while he has the look of a reformed character. This remission of his has deceived others, but it does not fool me: I expect his faults to return on a larger scale, for I know that they are not gone but only in abeyance. I shall spend some days on the matter and find out whether anything can be done or not.

**4** As for you, show us your courage—as indeed you do—and reduce your baggage. Not one of the things we have is necessary. Only let us return to the law of nature, and riches are ready and waiting. What we need is either free or cheap: bread and water are what nature demands. No one is too poor for those, and anyone who restricts his desire to them would compete with Jupiter in blessedness, as Epicurus says.* And speaking of Epicurus, I'll also enclose one of his aphorisms in this letter. He says,

**5** Do everything as though Epicurus were watching you.*

Assuredly it is beneficial to set a watch on yourself and to have someone to look up to, someone who you think will make a difference in your plans. To be sure, it is much grander if you live as if some good man were always present and held you in his gaze. But I am satisfied even with this: let everything you do be done as if watched by someone. Solitude encourages every fault in us. **6** Once you have progressed far enough to have some reverence even for yourself, then you may dismiss your tutor; meanwhile, put yourself under the guardianship of men of authority. Let it be Cato, or Scipio, or Laelius,* or someone else at whose coming even desperate characters would suppress their faults, while you go about making *yourself* the person in whose company you would not dare to do wrong.

When you have done that, and have begun to have some worth in your own eyes, I will begin to allow you to do what Epicurus also advises:

> The time to go off by yourself is especially when you are compelled to be in a crowd.*

7 You must differentiate yourself from numerous others, until such time as it is safe for you to go off by yourself. Look around at them individually: there is not one who would not be better off in anyone's company but his own. The time to go off by yourself is especially when you are compelled to be in a crowd—*if* you are a good man, a quiet man, a temperate man. Otherwise you had better retreat from yourself and into the crowd. Where you are, you are too close to a bad man.

Farewell.

## Letter 26

*From Seneca to Lucilius*
*Greetings*

1 Not long ago I was telling you that I had old age in sight; now I fear I have left old age behind. Now my years, and certainly my body, merit a different term. Since "old" is the word for advanced age, not for the age of disintegration, count me among those decrepit ones who are very near the end.

All the same, I give thanks to myself, in your presence, that I do not sense any impairment in my mind, even though I do in my body. 2 Only my faults have grown old, and those parts of me that pay service to my faults. My mind is vigorous and rejoices to have little to do with my body. It has shed a great deal of its burden; it is on a romp, and raises a dispute with me concerning old age, which it says is its time of flourishing. Let's believe it! And let it make use of the good that is proper to it.

**3** My mind tells me to ponder the matter and to discern what of my tranquility and moderate habits I owe to wisdom and what to my time of life; also, to distinguish carefully between things I cannot do and things I do not want to do. The purpose of this is that if there is something I am glad not to be able to do, I will regard it as something I don't want. What is there to complain about? Is it a problem if what needed to be over has come to an end?

**4** "It is a very big problem," you say, "for a person to wither and perish and—if I may speak accurately—to melt away. For we are not knocked flat all at once; rather, we waste away a little at a time, as each day erodes our strength." So our nature is slackening toward its resolution: is there some better way out? Not that a sudden blow, an immediate departure from life, is a bad thing; but this is the easy road, to just slip away.

As for me, I scrutinize myself as if the time of trial were drawing near, as if that day which is to pass judgment on all my years were at hand. **5** I say to myself, "My words and actions up to this point do not prove anything. Those are slight and deceptive pledges of courage, wrapped up in a great lot of blarney. Death will disclose to me what progress I have made." Thus I am unafraid as I prepare myself for that day when the artifices and disguises will be stripped away and I shall make judgment of myself. Is it just brave talk, or do I mean what I say? Were they for real, those defiant words I spoke against fortune, or were they just theater—just acting a part?

**6** "Away with the assessments of other people: they are always unreliable and contradictory. Away with lifelong programs of study: soon, now, death will pass its judgment on you. That's just what I mean. Lectures and learned seminars and sayings culled from the teachings of philosophers and educated conversation do not reveal the mind's real strength. For speech is bold even where the speaker is among the most timorous. What you have achieved will be revealed only when you breathe your last. I accept the terms; I do not quail before the judgment."

**7** Those are the things I say to myself; but imagine that I have said them to you as well. You are younger than I, but what does it matter? Years are not given out by quota. There's no way to know the point where death lies waiting for you, so you must wait for death at every point.

**8** Well, I wanted to stop here; my hand was preparing to sign off, but I must settle accounts and give this letter its travel money. Suppose I don't say where I will take out my loan—you know whose money box I use. Give me a little time, and the payment will come from home; meanwhile, Epicurus will provide. He says,

Rehearse for death.

Or if the thought can be conveyed better to us in a fuller expression:

It is a fine thing to learn death thoroughly.*

**9** Perhaps you think it is a waste of time to learn something you will need to use only once. But that is the very reason we ought to rehearse: if we cannot test whether we know it, we should be learning it always. **10** "Rehearse for death": he who says this is telling us to rehearse our freedom. One who has learned death has unlearned slavery, for death is above all powers, and certainly beyond all. What does death care for prison, for shackle and for cell? Its gate is ever at liberty. There is but one chain that binds us: the love of life. That, admittedly, we may not discard; yet we must lessen it, lest anything detain us when commanded by our situation, or hinder us from readiness to do at once what must be done someday.*

Farewell.

## Letter 27

*From Seneca to Lucilius*
*Greetings*

**1** "How is it that you are advising me?" you say. "Have you already advised yourself? Have you got yourself straightened out? Is that why you have the time to correct others?" I am not such a hypocrite as to offer cures while I am sick myself. No, I am lying in the same ward, as it were, conversing with you about our common ailment and sharing remedies. So listen to me as if I were talking to myself: I am letting you into my private room and giving myself instructions while you are standing by.

2 Loud and clear I tell myself: "Count your years, and you will be ashamed to have the same wishes and intentions you had as a child. Give yourself this gift as your day of death approaches: let your faults die before you. Dismiss those turbulent desires that cost you so much: they do harm both ahead of time and after the fact. Just as the worry over criminal acts does not depart, even if they are not discovered at the time, so also with wrongful desires: remorse remains when they themselves are gone. They are not solid, not dependable: even if they do no harm, they are fleeting. 3 Look about, rather, for some good that will remain. There is none but that which the mind discovers for itself from out of itself. Virtue alone yields lasting and untroubled joy.* Even if something does get in the way of that joy, it is interrupted only as daylight is by clouds, which pass beneath but do not ever overcome it." 4 When will it be your lot to attain to that joy? You have not been idle up to now—but pick up the pace. Much work remains to be done; and you must be the one to put in the attention and the toil if you want results. This is not something that can be delegated.

5 Another kind of literary activity allows for assistance. Within my memory there was Calvisius Sabinus, a wealthy man, who had both the inheritance and the character of a freedman—I never saw such a vulgarian with such a fortune.* So bad was his memory that he used to forget at one moment the name of Ulysses, at another that of Achilles or Priam, all of whom he knew just as well as we know our personal attendants from childhood. The aging nomenclator,* instead of recollecting names, simply makes them up—but no such person has ever addressed a constituency in as many wrong ways as Calvisius did the Trojans and the Achaeans. 6 Nonetheless, he wanted to appear learned. So he devised an expedient: he spent a great deal of money on slaves, one of whom was to know Homer by heart, another Hesiod, plus nine more, each assigned to one of the lyric poets. It is no wonder the cost was high, since any that were not to be found he paid to have instructed. Once he had assembled this staff, he began

to pester his dinner guests. He had the slaves right by his feet; and yet even though he regularly asked them for verses to quote, he often came to a halt in midsentence.

**7** Satellius Quadratus, who used to prey on the rich and stupid and (what goes with that) flatter them and (what goes with both) make fun of them too, had persuaded Sabinus that even his busboys should be literary scholars. When Sabinus pointed out that such slaves cost him a hundred thousand sesterces apiece, he said, "You could have bought as many libraries for less." Yet Sabinus was of the opinion that any knowledge possessed by anyone in his household was something he knew himself. **8** The same Satellius began to encourage him to take up wrestling, though he was physically slight, pale, and sickly. When Sabinus replied, "How can I? I'm barely alive!" he said, "Oh, please don't say that! Don't you see how many superhealthy slaves you have?" Excellence of mind cannot be borrowed or bought. I think too that if it were for sale, it would not find a buyer. Yet wickedness is purchased every day.

**9** But take what I owe you, and then farewell:

Poverty that adjusts to nature's restrictions is wealth.

Epicurus says this repeatedly in one passage and another,* but a thing is never said too much when it has not been well enough learned. Some people need to have remedies shown to them; others need them trodden in.

Farewell.

## Letter 28

*From Seneca to Lucilius*
*Greetings*

**1** Do you think you are the only one this has happened to? Are you amazed to find that even with such extensive travel, to so many varied locales, you have not managed to shake off gloom and heaviness from your mind? As if that were a new experience! You must change the mind, not the venue. Though you cross the sea, though "lands and cities drop away,"* as our poet Virgil says, still your faults will follow you wherever you go.

2 Here is what Socrates said to a person who had the same complaint as you: "Why are you surprised that traveling does you no good, when you travel in your own company? The thing that weighs on your mind is the same as drove you from home." What good will new countries do you? What use is touring cities and sites? All your dashing about is useless in the end. Do you ask why your flight is of no avail? You take yourself along.

You must shed the load that is on your mind: until you do that, no place will be pleasing to you. 3 Realize that your present condition is like that which Virgil depicts in the Sybil, in that moment when she is agitated and maddened, having inside her a vast spirit not her own:

The prophet bucks and thrashes, tries to shake
the god out of her heart.*

You go this way and that trying to shake off a load that becomes all the more cumbersome with movement. It's like a ship's cargo: properly stowed, it has little effect on the vessel; but if it slides around, it soon causes one side to go under. No matter how you act, you act against yourself. You harm yourself by your very movement, for you are jostling someone who is sick.

4 But once what is amiss is gotten rid of, then every change of place will become pleasurable. Even if you are exiled to the furthest corners of the earth, you will find that whatever barbaric spot you wind up in is a hospitable retreat for you. Where you go matters less than who you are when you go. Consequently, we ought not to consign the mind to any one place. We should live with this conviction: "I was not born in any one spot; my homeland is this entire world."

5 If that were clear to you, you would not be amazed to find that it does you no good to travel to various regions every time you grow weary of where you were before. If you believed that every region is your own, you would have been satisfied with the first.

As it is, you are not traveling so much as wandering, drifting, switching one place for another, when the object of your search—namely, to live well—is to be found in every place. 6 Can anything be as noisy as the forum? Yet one may live quietly there if need be. Still, if I am allowed to station myself at will, I will shun even the neighborhood within sight of the forum. For just as there are unhealthy places that put a strain on even the strongest constitution, so also for the mind that is good, but still gaining strength and not yet perfected, there are places that are not conducive to health.

**7** I disagree with those who plunge into the midst of the waves, who give approval to the life of tumult and struggle energetically every day against difficult surroundings. The wise person will endure those things, but will not choose them; he will choose a peaceful existence over the strife of battle. It is not of much use to have jettisoned your own faults if you have now to combat those of others. **8** "The Thirty Tyrants arrested Socrates," he says, "and yet they could not break his spirit.* What does it matter how many are the masters? Slavery is just one thing. If a person holds that one thing in contempt, he is free, no matter how large a crowd of oppressors is at hand."

**9** It is time to quit, but first I must pay my harbor tax:

Awareness of wrongdoing is the starting point for healing.*

Epicurus spoke very well here, I think, for he who does not know that he is doing wrong does not wish to be set right. Before you can reform yourself, you must realize your error. **10** Some people glory in their faults. Do you suppose they have any thought for the remedy? Surely not, since they count their bad habits as virtues!

Bring an accusation against yourself, as stringently as you can. Then conduct the investigation. Take the role of the accuser first, then the judge, and let that of the advocate come last. Offend yourself sometimes!

Farewell.

## Letter 29

*From Seneca to Lucilius*
*Greetings*

**1** You ask about our friend Marcellinus, wanting to know how he is getting along. His visits are infrequent, for no other reason than that he is afraid to hear the truth. But he is in no danger of that at the moment. For truth should be told only to those who will listen.

For that reason, people frequently express doubts about Diogenes and the other Cynics who employed wholesale freedom of speech and admonished everyone they encountered.* Were they right to do that? What if those being scolded were deaf and mute, either born that way or from some disease? **2** You say, "Why be economical with words? They cost nothing. I cannot know whether I will help the person I am admonishing, but if I admonish many, I know that I will help someone. I should scatter the seed broadly: if one makes many attempts, some of them are bound to succeed." **3** I think, dear Lucilius, that this is not what a great man should do. It dilutes his authority: if he makes his words too common, they do not have sufficient weight with the very people he could otherwise set straight. An archer ought not to hit the mark sometimes and miss it sometimes: anything that gets its results by chance is not a skill. Wisdom is a skill.* It should go after the sure thing, choosing those who will benefit and holding off from those who are beyond hope. Still, it should not abandon them too quickly: desperate cases call for desperate remedies.

**4** But I am not yet in despair about our Marcellinus. He can still be saved, but only if a hand is extended to him right away. Indeed, there is a danger that he will drag the rescuer down with him; for his intellect is very forceful, but tending just now toward ill. Nonetheless, I will go to meet this danger; I will dare to show him his faults. **5** He will do what he usually does: he will pass it off with jokes that would make even a mourner laugh; he'll make fun of himself first, and then make fun of me; he'll deflect everything I am about to say. He'll scrutinize our school and find objections to throw at our philosophers—payoffs, girlfriends, gluttony. **6** He'll show me one of them caught in adultery, another in a cook-shop, another in the palace.

He'll show me Aristo, the philosophical advisor of Marcus Lepidus,°* who used to lecture while riding in his sedan chair, for he made use of that time to get his works ready for circulation. When someone asked what school he belonged to, Scaurus quipped, "He's certainly not a Peripatetic!"* And when that illustrious man Julius Graecinus was asked what he thought of him, he answered, "I can't tell you—I don't know what he does on foot." Just as if he were being asked about a charioteer!

**7** All those charlatans who traffic in philosophy (and it would have been more to their credit to leave it alone) will be thrown in my face by Marcellinus. But I have made up my mind to bear with his insults. Let him move me to laughter; perhaps I shall move him to tears. Or, if he continues to laugh, I will rejoice, amid my sorrows as it were, that it is a cheerful form of madness that has come over him. But such cheerfulness does not last long. Watch closely, and you will see that the ones who laugh wildly are the same ones who are raving wildly a short while later.

**8** I am resolved to approach him and show him how much more he was worth back when many people thought he was worth less. Even if I don't prune away his faults, I will inhibit their growth. They won't be completely gone, but they will cease for a while. Or perhaps they really will be gone, if cessation becomes routine. That's not to be disdained. For, truly, when one is seriously ill, a good remission counts as health.

**9** While I am getting ready for him, here are my instructions for you. For you have the ability; you understand where you have been and where you are, and infer from that where it is you are headed. Settle your habits; lift your spirits; stand firm against every object of dread; take no account of those who put fear into you. A person would look stupid, wouldn't he, if he were afraid of a crowd in a spot where only one can pass at a time? It is the same with your death: although many people may be threatening you with it, they cannot all get to you at once. That's how nature has arranged the matter: a single person will deprive you of breath, just as a single person gave it to you.

**10** If you had any shame, you would excuse me the final payment. But since my debt is so nearly at an end, I won't be a cheapskate (no, not even I!), but will pay you what I owe.

Never have I wished to please the populace, for it does not approve of my knowledge, and I have no knowledge of what it does approve.*

**11** "Who said that?" you say, as if you did not know where I get my funds. Epicurus said it. But all of them, from every school, will cry out the same to you together, Peripatetics, Academics, Stoics, Cynics.* For what person that cherishes virtue can be cherished by the populace? It is by skill in wrongdoing that one cultivates popular acclaim. You must make yourself like them: they will not approve of you unless they recognize you. What matters, though, is not how you seem to others but how you seem to yourself. When people are base, you cannot win their love by any means that are not base.

12 What, then, will you gain from philosophy, which is so much admired and so far preferable to all other skills and all other possessions? Just this: that you would rather please yourself than please the people; that you take thought for the quality, not the number of judgments made about you; that you live without fear of gods or humans; that you either defeat your troubles or put an end to them. Otherwise, if I see you much acclaimed by the common crowd—if there is shouting and applause to greet your entrances, as at the pantomime shows—if women and boys sing your praises all over town—I will pity you. Why shouldn't I, when I know what road you took to reach such popularity?

Farewell.

# Letter 30

*From Seneca to Lucilius*
*Greetings*

**1** I have seen Aufidius Bassus,\* a fine man, who has had a stroke and is wrestling with the advance of years. He is fighting still, but this is a hold he will never break, for age has pressed its great weight on him at every point. You know that he has always been scrawny and weak in body. He has held it together for a long time—or rather, to put it more accurately, has kept it going. But suddenly his strength has failed.

**2** It's like when a boat takes on water: you stop up one leak, then another; but once it begins to open up and give way at many places, there's no way to fix it; it's just a leaky vessel. So it is with an aging body. Stopgap measures can sustain it for a while, but when every joint is giving way like the seams of a dilapidated house, when you cannot take care of one thing without something else giving out in the meanwhile, then it is time to look around for the exit.

**3** Yet our friend Bassus is as lively as ever in his mind. Philosophy does this: it enables a person to be cheerful within sight of death, and brave and cheerful no matter what condition his body is in, not giving up just because the body is giving out. A great captain sails on, even with his canvas in tatters; even if he has jettisoned the ship's equipment, he keeps the remnants of his vessel on course. That's what our Bassus is doing. He looks on his own end with such a calm expression that if he looked so on another's, you would think him uncaring. **4** It's a great thing, Lucilius, a lesson of many years—when the hour of no escape arrives, to depart in peace.

Other ways of dying have an admixture of hope. An illness abates; a fire is extinguished; a collapsing building lowers to the ground the people it might have crushed. Those swallowed up by the sea have been cast out unharmed just as forcibly as they were swept away; the soldier has withdrawn his sword from the very throat of the condemned. But he whom old age draws toward death has nothing to hope for; he alone cannot be rescued. It is the gentlest form of death, but also the slowest.

**5** It seemed to me that our Bassus was attending his own funeral—laying out his body for burial—living on after himself, and bearing his loss (that is, the loss of himself) as a philosopher should. For he speaks much about death, and tries hard to convince us that if there is anything unpleasant or frightening in this business, it is the fault of the person dying and not of death itself, and that there is no more discomfort in the moment of death than there is afterward. **6** A person would be crazy to fear something that's not going to happen to him, and it is equally crazy to fear something you won't feel. Or does anyone believe that he *will* feel death, when in fact it is through death that he ceases to feel anything else? "For that reason," he says, "death is so far removed from every evil that it is beyond every fear of evil."*

**7** All this, I know, has often been said, as indeed it should be; but it never did me as much good when I read it in books, or when I heard it from people who were not themselves in any danger. This time, though, the impact on me was very great, since the man was speaking about a death that was very near. **8** I will tell you my opinion: I think the person who is at the point of death is braver than one who is merely in the vicinity. For when death is at hand, it inspires even the untrained to face what cannot in any case be avoided. Thus the gladiator who has been terrified throughout the contest will offer his throat to his opponent and guide the wavering point home. But when death is only near at hand, though sure to come, it requires an unyielding mental strength. This is less often found, and can only really be exhibited by the wise person.

**9** So I was very glad to listen to him passing judgment, as it were, on death, and telling me what it is like when one has seen it close up. I imagine that if someone who had experienced death were to come to life again and tell you that death is not an evil, you would give him great credence and authority. In the same way, your best informants on the distress that accompanies the near approach of death will be those who have stood right next to it, who have not only seen it coming but even greeted it. **10** Among those you may count Bassus.

He did not want us to be deceived. Fearing death, he said, is as foolish as fearing old age; for just as age follows youth, so death follows age. "He who is unwilling to die never wanted to live, for life is given to us with death as a precondition. Death is where we are headed, and for that reason one would be mad to fear it. It is uncertainty that frightens us; when things are certain, we simply await them. 11 Death is a requirement that is imposed equitably and unavoidably. Who can complain about being under the same restrictions as everyone else? The first element in equity is equality.

"But I need not plead nature's case at this time. It is not nature's will that we should have any law but its own: what it has assembled, it breaks down; and what it breaks down, it assembles again. 12 If it should happen that old age releases a person gently, not tearing him suddenly away from life but letting him slip away gradually, then that person should give thanks to all the gods. He should indeed, for he had his fill before being taken to his rest, a rest that is necessary for mortal beings, and welcome to the weary.*

"You see some who long to die, who indeed insist on it more firmly than people usually ask to live. I don't know which ones I find more inspiring, those who ask for death or those who meet death with calm cheerfulness. For such requests sometimes come of madness or some sudden fit of outrage, while such tranquility comes of a settled judgment. There are people who come to death out of anger; there is no one who sees death coming to him and offers it a cheerful welcome, unless that person has been long resigned to it."

13 So I have to confess that although I had many reasons to visit Bassus often (he is after all a dear friend), I wanted in particular to see whether I would find him the same each time: would his mental energy diminish as his body grew weaker? But it kept growing, just as one often sees excitement building in a chariot team when it is in the seventh lap, with the palms of victory in sight. 14 In fact, he used to say, in conformity with Epicurus's teachings, "First of all, I hope there will be no pain in that last breath; but if there is, it will be short, and that itself is some comfort. For severe pain is never of long duration.* But if there is torment in the moment when mind separates from body, I will console myself thus: after that pain, I can no longer experience pain. For no doubt my aged breath is only barely clinging to my lips and needs no great force to draw it from my body. A fire that is well supplied with fuel needs water to put it

out and sometimes the collapse of the entire building; one that has exhausted its fuel gives out of its own accord."

**15** My dear Lucilius, I am glad to listen to these words. It's not as if they were new, but it is as if they have become a present reality to me. Why? Have I not watched many people reach their life's end? Yes, I have, but they make a greater impression on me when they come to death with no hatred for life, when they let death in rather than reaching for it.

**16** In fact, he used to say that the torment we feel comes about through our own agency, because we become alarmed when we believe that death is close at hand. But isn't it close to everyone, ready in every place and every moment? "Let us keep in mind," he said, "that in the moment when some cause of death seems to be drawing near, there are others, even nearer, that we don't fear. A man had received a death threat from an enemy—and a digestive ailment got there first. **17** If we are willing to draw some distinctions among the causes of our fear, we will find that some are real, others only apparent. It is not death we fear but the thought of death, for death itself is always the same distance away from us. So if death is ever to be feared, it is to be feared at all times. For what time is there that is not subject to death?"

**18** But I should be afraid that you will hate such long letters even *worse* than death! So I'll stop. As for you, if you want never to be afraid of death, think about it always.

Farewell.

## Letter 31

*From Seneca to Lucilius*
*Greetings*

**1** I recognize my Lucilius! He is beginning to make good on his promises. Keep it up! For you had the force of character to pursue every excellence, trampling underfoot the goods that are popularly esteemed. Great and good as I want you to be, it is no more than you were striving for. The foundations you have laid cover a wide area;

now make the result as grand as your endeavor. Bring your design to full completion!

2 In a word, you will be wise to close your ears. But wax will not be enough to stop them up; you need some tighter seal than what Ulysses is said to have used on his crew. That voice they feared was alluring, but it was not the voice of the public. This voice that you should fear does not sound from a single crag; it echoes around you from every direction and from every land. Sail on, then, not past a single spot where treacherous pleasures threaten, but past all the cities of the world. Turn a deaf ear to those who love you most: their intentions are good, but the things they are wishing for you are bad.* If you want to be truly prosperous, entreat the gods that none of the things they want for you may happen. 3 Those are not goods that they wish to see heaped upon you. There is but one good, and that is both the cause and the mainstay of happiness: trust in oneself.

But if you are ever to attain to it, you must think nothing of hard work, counting it as one of those objects that are neither good nor bad. For it cannot be that any one thing is bad at one time and good at another, or light and easy to bear at one time and terrifying at another. 4 Work is not a good. So what is? Not minding the work. For that reason, I am inclined to fault those who expend great effort over worthless things. On the other hand, when people strive toward honorable goals, I give them my approval, and all the more when they apply themselves strenuously and do not let themselves be defeated or thwarted. I cry, "Better so! Rise to the occasion! Take a deep breath, and climb that hill—at one bound, if you can do it!"

5 Noble spirits are nourished by hard work. Hence there is no reason for you to choose your wish, your aim, from among the things your parents prayed long ago for you to have. And in general it is shameful for a man who has achieved great things to be still bothering the gods. Why do you need prayers? Make your own prosperity! And you will do so if you have well understood that anything mingled with virtue is good, anything conjoined with bad conduct is shameful. Nothing shines unless it has some admixture of light; nothing is black unless it contains some darkness or has absorbed some kind of murk; nothing is hot without the assistance of fire, nothing cold without air.* In just the same way, it is association with virtue or vice that makes a thing honorable or shameful.

**6** What, then, is good? Knowledge of the facts. What is bad? Ignorance of the facts. The man who is truly wise and skilled will exercise avoidance or choice in accordance with circumstances; but he does not fear the things he avoids nor admire the things he chooses, not if he has a great and unconquerable spirit.*

I forbid you to abase yourself; I forbid you to be downcast. Not refusing labor is too little: ask for it. **7** "But what if the work is demeaning?" you say. "What if it is unnecessary or is demanded for frivolous reasons? Isn't such work bad?" No more so than labor expended on attractive objects. Your very endurance shows spirit, when you urge yourself on toward difficult tasks, saying, "Why the delay? A real man is not afraid of sweat."

**8** Besides, complete virtue consists in the evenness and steadiness of a life that is in harmony with itself through all events, which cannot come about unless one has knowledge and the skill of discerning things human and divine. This is the highest good; if you obtain it, you begin to be an associate of the gods and not a suppliant.*

**9** You ask, "How do I get there?" You need not scale the Alps, at either the Pennine or the Graian Pass, or navigate the Syrtaean shoals, or traverse the mountain fastness of Illyria; you need not approach the straits where Scylla and Charybdis are; and yet you passed through all of these for no more reward than your paltry governorship.* No, the road is both safe and pleasant, and is one for which you have been equipped by nature. Nature has given you certain gifts, and if you do not abandon them, you will mount up equal to a god.

**10** Money will not make you equal to a god: God owns nothing. A tunic bordered with purple will not do it; God is naked. Fame will not do it, and neither will self-display and spreading one's name far and wide: no one has personal acquaintance with God, and many think ill of him with impunity. Nor will a troop of slaves bearing your sedan chair through the streets, in the city and abroad: God, the greatest and most powerful god, is himself the bearer of everything. Not even beauty and strength can confer blessedness on you; neither endures the onset of age. **11** You must devote your efforts to that which does not deteriorate over time, and which no obstacle can bar. What is that? It is the mind—but specifically this mind, which is upright, great, and good. What else would you call it but God dwelling in a human body? This mind can be found just as well in a freedman or even a slave as in a Roman of equestrian status.* For what is a Roman equestrian, or a freedman, or a slave? Those are names born of ambition or of unfair treatment. One may leap up to heaven even from a chimney corner. Rise, then,

> and shape yourself as well into a likeness
> worthy of godhead.

But you will not make that likeness from gold or silver: from such materials no likeness can be made that truly resembles God. Bear in mind that in the days when the gods were well disposed, their images were of clay.*

Farewell.

## Letter 32

*From Seneca to Lucilius*
*Greetings*

1 I have been making inquiries about you. Every time someone comes through here from your vicinity, I ask what you are doing, and where you spend your time and with whom. You can't fool me! I am right with you. Live as if I were sure to hear about everything you do—no, to see it!

Are you wondering what pleases me the most out of everything I hear about you? It is that I hear nothing at all—that most of those whom I question do not know how you are doing. 2 This is beneficial, to have nothing to do with those who are unlike you, whose desires are different from yours. Indeed, I am confident that you cannot be turned aside and will persist in your intention, even if crowds of bothersome people surround you.

What, then, is the issue? I am not afraid that they will change you, but I am afraid that they will hinder you. Even he who delays you does great harm, especially since life is so short. And we make it even shorter by our inconsistency, when we make one fresh start after another. We tear it to bits; we shred it.

3 Make haste, then, dearest Lucilius, and think how much more

speed you would put on if an enemy were pursuing you from be-hind—if you saw mounted horsemen coming up from behind you, harrying your retreat. That is, in fact, what is happening; you are be-ing pursued. Put on speed! Make your escape; get yourself to safety. Remind yourself often how fine a thing it is to reach the summit of life before you die, and then to be in peace as you wait out the remainder of your time, relying only on yourself.° For once one pos-sesses happiness, duration does not make it any happier. 4 Ah, when will the day come when you will realize that time doesn't matter for you, and will be at peace, caring nothing for the future, completely satisfied with what you are! Would you like to know what it is that makes people greedy for the future? Not one of them yet belongs to himself.

There were other things your parents wished for you to have; what I wish is for you to have contempt for all their bountiful wishes. In their prayers, many are robbed to make you rich: whatever they trans-fer to you, they must take from someone else. 5 My wish is this: may you be your own master; may your mind, which is now driven this way and that by its concerns, come at last to a halt, sure and content in itself; may you come to understand those true goods that belong to you in the moment you understand them, and so feel no need of additional years. In order to rise above necessities, to gain one's discharge, to be free, one must live a life that is already complete.

Farewell.

## Letter 33

*From Seneca to Lucilius*
*Greetings*

1 You request that I should close these letters, as I did the earlier ones, with quotations, and that I should take them from the leaders of our own school. They did not busy themselves with flowery bits of speech: their entire fabric is masculine.* Where what is noteworthy stands out from the rest, you can be sure the quality is uneven. A single tree excites no wonder when the entire forest rises to the same height.

**2** Poems are stuffed with sayings of that sort, and historical writings too. So I do not want you to think of them as belonging to Epicurus: they are public property, and especially *our* property. But in him they attract more attention, just because they occur infrequently, because they are unexpected, because it is surprising that anything courageous should be said by a man who professed effeminacy. That, at least, is what most people think about him; to my mind, though, Epicurus is indeed brave, even if he did wear sleeves.* Courage, hard work, and a mind fit for war can be found among the Persians just as well as among those who wear a belt.

**3** And so you have no cause to demand excerpts and quotations. The kind of remark that is excerpted from other authors can be found without intermission in the writings of our school. Thus we do not have the eye-catchers you have in mind; with us, the buyers are not disappointed by entering the shop and finding nothing more than was hung up outside. We let them choose the display items from any point in the text they happen to prefer. **4** Just suppose we did want to separate a few individual sayings from the throng: To whom would we attribute them? To Zeno? To Cleanthes? To Chrysippus? To Posidonius? To Panaetius? We are not under a monarch. Each of us asserts his own freedom. Among the Epicureans, anything Hermarchus said, or Metrodorus, is attributed solely to one individual; in that camp everything anyone says is said under the guidance and auspices of one man.* We, however, have such a number of resources, all equally fine, that we cannot separate out just one, even if we try. I repeat, we cannot:

> only the pauper keeps count of his herd.*

Wherever you cast your eyes, you will read something that could have been outstanding if the remainder were not equally good. **5** For this reason, you must give up hope that you will ever be able to take just a quick sampling from the works of the greatest men. You must read them as wholes, come to grips with them as wholes. The subject matter is treated along the lines that are proper to it, and° an intellectual product is devised from which nothing can be removed without a collapse. Still, I have no objection to your studying the individual limbs, provided you retain the actual person. A beautiful woman is not the one whose ankle or shoulder is praised but the one whose overall appearance steals our admiration away from the individual parts.

**6** But if you insist, I will not be stingy with you, but will deal them out by the fistful. There are piles of them lying about; one only has to pick them up; there is no need to collect them. They come not by dribs and drabs but in a steady flow, all interconnected.

I'm sure these do a great deal for beginners and for listeners from outside the school. For individual sayings take hold more easily when they are isolated and rounded off like bits of verse. **7** That is why we give children proverbs to memorize, and what the Greeks call *chreiai*: they are what a child's mind is able to encompass, not yet having room for anything larger.* It is shameful, though, when a man who is making definite progress seizes on flowery bits or props himself up with a handful of commonplaces he has memorized. Let him stand on his own feet! Let him say these things for himself, not recall what he has memorized. For shame, that an old person, or one nearly old, should get his wisdom from a textbook! "This is what Zeno said": what do you say? "Cleanthes said this": what do you? How long will you march under another's command? Take charge: say something memorable on your own account; bring forth something from your own store.

**8** So I feel that all those people who are never authors but always interpreters, concealing themselves in the shadow of another, have nothing noble in them, for they have never dared to put into action what they have been so long in learning. They have trained their memories on other people's words; but remembering is one thing, knowing is something else. Remembering is keeping track of something you have committed to memory; knowing, by contrast, is making all those things your own, not having to depend on a model or to keep looking to your teacher for instructions. **9** "Zeno said this, and Cleanthes that." Let there be some distance between you and the book! How long will you be a pupil? Now, be a teacher as well. Why should I listen to things I can read? "It makes a big difference when things are spoken aloud," he says. Not when the speaker is only borrowing someone else's words, as a copyist might do!

**10** And there is another issue concerning these people who never take charge of their own lives: they begin by following their leaders on subjects where everyone else has declared independence; then they follow them in matters that are still subject to investigation. Nothing will ever be found out if we rest content with what has been found out already! Anyway, followers never find anything; no, they never even look for anything.

**11** How about it, then? Will I not walk in the footsteps of my predecessors? I will indeed use the ancient road—but if I find another route that is more direct and has fewer ups and downs, I will stake out that one. Those who advanced these doctrines before us are not our masters but our guides. The truth lies open to all; it has not yet been taken over. Much is left also for those yet to come.

Farewell.

## Letter 34

*From Seneca to Lucilius*
*Greetings*

**1** I swell—I exult—I shake off my years and feel again the heat of youth, each time I learn from your letters and from your actions how far you have surpassed even yourself. For you broke from the pack some time ago. If a farmer takes delight when a tree bears fruit, if a herdsman is pleased when his animals bear young, if one who sees a protégé reach adulthood always feels as if it were his own coming of age, then how do you think a person feels when he has been in charge of someone's intellectual development and sees that immature mind grown up all at once? **2** I claim you as my own; you are my handiwork. It was I who laid hands on you, having seen your potential, and encouraged you, got you going, and did not let you slow down but continued to spur you on—and I am doing that even now, but now I am cheering you in the race, and you in return are cheering for me.

**3** "Why say more?"° you ask. "I am willing all the time." That's most of it—and not only half, as in the saying "Well begun is half done." This is something that depends on the mind; so when one is willing to become good, goodness is in large part achieved.*

Do you know what I mean by a good person? One who is complete; one who has been perfected; one who would not be made to do wrong by any force, any stricture. **4** I foresee that you will be this good person, if you persevere, if you press on and make all your actions and words cohere and fit with one another, all struck from the same mold. If the actions are inconsistent, the mind has not been set to rights.

Farewell.

## *Letter 35*

*From Seneca to Lucilius*
*Greetings*

**1** When I urge you so strongly to study, I am serving my own ends. I want to have a friend, and this cannot happen for me unless you persevere in your program of self-improvement. For as it is, you love me, but you are not my friend.

"What do you mean? Is there any difference between the two?" Actually, they are quite dissimilar. A friend loves, but one who loves is not automatically a friend. That's why friendship is always beneficial, but love is sometimes even harmful. If nothing else, make your progress for this reason: to learn how to love.

**2** So make haste in your progress for my sake; otherwise your learning will have been for another. True, I am reaping the benefit even now, when I imagine how we two will be of one mind, and how the vigor you still have at your age will restore to me what I have lost—though the difference is not great between us. But I would like to be glad for real. **3** We get joy from those we love even in their absence, but it is light and fleeting. The sight of them, their presence, their conversation, has in it a kind of living pleasure, especially when you not only see the one you want, but see that one as you want him to be. Give me yourself, then: a great gift. And to make you work even harder, keep in mind that you are a mortal being—and that I am old.

**4** Hurry, then, to me; but first, hurry to yourself. As you progress, strive above all to be consistent with yourself. If ever you want to find out whether anything has been achieved, observe whether your intentions are the same today as they were yesterday. A change of intention shows that the mind is at sea, drifting here and there as carried by the wind.* A thing that is well grounded does not move about. That is how it is for the completely wise person, and also to some extent for the one who is making progress toward wisdom. What is the difference, then? The progressor moves, but does not shift position; he merely bobs in place. The wise person does not move at all.

Farewell.

## Letter 36

*From Seneca to Lucilius*
*Greetings*

1 Tell your friend that he should be bold enough to despise the criticism of those who say that he is seeking the shade and a life of leisure, abandoning his prestigious position, and that while he could achieve more, he has chosen quiet over everything. Let him show them, each and every day, how useful it is for him simply to mind his own business.

Those who attract the envy of others will always be moving along; some will be knocked aside; others will fall. Prosperity is a restless thing; it drives itself to distraction. It addles the brain, and not always in the same way, for it goads people in different directions—some toward power, others toward self-indulgence. Some are puffed up by it, others unmanned and made entirely feeble. 2 "But there are some who handle it well." Yes, there are, just as some handle wine well. But that should not convince you that the fortunate person is one surrounded by many hangers-on. They crowd around him as cattle crowd around a pond: they drink the water and stir up the mud.

"People are calling him a dilettante and a do-nothing." You know that some people have a perverse way of talking: they speak by opposites. 3 They used to call him a prosperous man; what of it? Was he one in fact? Neither do I care that some perceive him as excessively rough and grim. Aristo used to put it this way:

I would rather see a stern young man than one who is cheery and popular with a crowd. For the vintage that is to become a quality wine is harsh and bitter when just made; one that is palatable in the vat does not stand up to aging.*

So let them call him "stern" and "no friend to his own prospects." That sternness will turn out well with age, as long as he perseveres in attending on virtue and in imbibing the liberal studies. By which I do not mean those studies of which a smattering is enough; I mean *these* liberal studies.* In these, the mind needs a thorough steeping.

4 Now is the time to learn. "What do you mean? Is there any time that isn't the time to learn?" Not at all: it is honorable to learn at every time of life, but by the same token there is a time at which it is not honorable to be taking the introductory course. It is shameful, even ridiculous, for an old man to be still learning his letters. One should acquire an education in youth, and then in old age make use of it.

So if you make your friend the best he can be, you will be doing yourself a very great service. These, they say, are the favors one should ask; these the favors one should bestow. There can be no doubt that they are benefits of the highest order, as useful to give as to receive.

5 Anyway, he is no longer at liberty: he has given his pledge. Shameful as it is to default on a loan, it is still more shameful to default on one's own expectations. To pay the former sort of debt, the merchant needs a profitable voyage; the farmer needs fertile soil to till and kindly weather; but what your friend owes, he can pay by his willingness to do so, and in no other way.

6 Fortune has no jurisdiction over his conduct. Let him take charge of that himself, so that his mind may achieve its perfection in complete tranquility, not perceiving any loss or any gain, but retaining the same attitude no matter what befalls. If commonplace goods are piled around him, he towers over his possessions; if chance knocks down one of the piles, or all of them, he does not thereby become shorter.

7 If he had been born in Persia, he would have been drawing the bow from his infancy; if in Germany, he would have been casting a lightweight spear since childhood. If he had lived in the times of our ancestors, he would have learned riding and hand-to-hand combat. Each individual is encouraged and indeed required to learn

such skills by the training regimen of his own people. **8** So what is it that your friend needs to practice? A skill that will serve him well against all weapons and all kinds of enemies: that of caring nothing for death.

No one doubts that there is something frightening about death, something jarring not only to the body but to our rational nature, which has been designed for self-love. There would be no need to sharpen ourselves up in preparation for something that we were inclined to pursue willingly and instinctively in the same way that all creatures have a drive for self-preservation. **9** No one learns just so that he can lie down calmly in a bed of roses if the need should arise; rather, he toughens himself so as not to break faith under torture, so that if necessary he can stand guard throughout the night, even when he is wounded, without leaning on his spear. For those who rest against some support eventually fall asleep.

Death holds no disadvantage, for a disadvantage must be that of some existing person.°* **10** But if you are so desirous of longer life, keep in mind that things that vanish from our sight are not really spent; they are stored away in the natural world from which they came and are soon to come again. They cease to be, but they do not perish. And death, which we fear so deeply and refuse to meet, interrupts life, but does not abscond with it: the day will come again that will return us to the light. It is a day which many would refuse, except that we forget everything before returning.*

**11** Another day I will give you a fuller explanation of how all things that seem to perish are in fact transformed. He who departs with the expectation of returning ought to depart calmly. Consider cycles in the natural world: you will see nothing that is actually extinguished; rather, things descend and rise again by turns. Summer is over, but another year will bring it back; winter is gone but will return in its proper months. Night has buried the sun, but day in turn will soon drive out the night. The stars retrace their previous movements; one part of the sky is continually rising, the other setting.

**12** Well, I will bring this to an end, but let me add one word more. Neither young children nor those of wandering mind fear death; their state confers tranquility. It is most disgraceful if wisdom cannot do for us what foolishness does for them.

Farewell.

# Letter 37

*From Seneca to Lucilius*
*Greetings*

1 There is no better way of binding yourself to excellence of mind than the promise you have given, the oath of enlistment you have sworn: to be an excellent man. Only as a joke will anyone tell you that this is a soft and easy branch of service. I don't want you to be deceived. The words of this most honorable pledge are the same as that other most shameful one: "to be burned, to be bound, to be slain with the sword."* 2 Those who hire themselves out as gladiators, and pay in blood for their food and drink, are under contract to suffer those things even against their will; you are under contract to suffer them willingly and of your own volition. They have the option of lowering their weapons and testing the mercy of the crowd; you will not lower yours or beg for your life. You must die on your feet, unconquered. What is the use of winning yourself a few extra days or years? Once born, we have no possibility of reprieve.*

3 "How, then," you ask, "may I get my discharge?" You cannot escape the requirements, but you can conquer them. "Strength finds a way,"* and philosophy will give you that strength.° Deliver yourself to philosophy if you wish to be safe, to be tranquil, to be happy, and, what matters most, if you wish to be free. There is no other way you can gain your freedom.

4 Foolishness is low, despised, vile, slavish, subject to numerous violent emotions. These last are grievous masters, ruling you sometimes by turns, sometimes all together. Wisdom rids you of them; wisdom alone is liberty. There is but one road that leads to it, and that is a straight one. You will not go astray; go forward with confident step. If you wish to make all things subject to you, make yourself subject to reason. Once reason is your ruler, you will be ruler of many. From reason you will learn what to take on, and how; you will not just stumble upon things.

5 There is no one you can name who knows how he began to want what he now wants. People are not led by their intentions but jerked about by whims. Sometimes we make the best of fortune, but just as

often fortune gets the better of us. It is shameful to drift rather than to go forward; shameful to find oneself in the midst of a whirlwind of events and ask, astonished, "How did I get here?"

Farewell.

## *Letter 38*

*From Seneca to Lucilius*
*Greetings*

1 You are right to insist that we exchange these letters more frequently. The reason dialogue is highly beneficial is that it works its way into the mind bit by bit. Speeches prepared in advance and delivered before a crowd make for more noise, but less intimacy. Philosophy is good advice, and no one gives advice in ringing tones. There are times when one does need to deliver a campaign speech, if I may call it that, when someone is hesitating and needs a push. But when the aim is not to motivate learning but that the person should actually learn, then one has to revert to these less strident utterances. They get in more easily, and they stick; for one does not need a great number of words, but words that are effective.

2 They should be scattered like seeds.* A seed is just a little thing, and yet when it lands in the right spot, it unfolds its resources and expands into a great and growing plant. Reasoning does the same: when you examine it, it is of small extent; but when you put it into effect, it grows. Only a few words are said, but if the mind receives them well, they become tall and strong.

I say it again: words work like seeds. Though tiny, they achieve much. Only, as I said, the mind that receives them has to be suited to them, and has to absorb them. Then it will itself reproduce them, and many more than it received.

Farewell.

# Letter 39

*From Seneca to Lucilius*
*Greetings*

1 I will indeed put together the manuals you request, "carefully ordered and compressed to narrow scope." But it may be that you would benefit more from a regular course of study than from what is now commonly called a *breviarium*. (Back when we spoke real Latin, it was called a *summarium*.)* We need the one more while we are learning, the other when we already know; for the one teaches, the other reminds. But I will supply you with both.

Where you and I are concerned, there is no reason to request any particular author. Only the unknown man supplies a voucher.* 2 I shall write what you want me to, but in my own fashion. Meanwhile, you have plenty of others available whose writings will keep you in line well enough, I suppose. Just pick up an index of the philosophers; that itself will rouse you to exertion, once you see how many have labored on your behalf. You will yearn to be one of them yourself.

For this is the best trait of a noble nature: it is inspired by honorable examples. No man of exalted character takes pleasure in what is base and sordid; it is the sight of greatness that attracts and elevates him. 3 Just as a flame leaps upward and cannot be flattened, let alone made to rest, so our minds are always in motion, and the more vigorous ones are all the more lively and active. But it is a fortunate person who directs this energy toward the good. He will place himself outside the jurisdiction of fortune: he will moderate prosperity, minimize adversity, and scorn those things that others admire.

4 Greatness of spirit despises great wealth; it prefers moderate means to abundance. For moderation is useful and life-giving, while abundance harms a person through excess. It is like a yield of wheat that is so heavy it flattens the stalks; like a load of fruit that breaks the branches; like livestock that bear too many young for all to reach maturity. That happens with minds too when they are spoiled by immoderate prosperity, which they use to the detriment of others and even to their own.

5 What enemy has ever treated anyone as roughly as some people's

pleasures treat them? Their desires are uncontrolled—insane—and would be unforgivable, except that the damage is all to themselves. And it's not without reason that they are tormented with such frenzy. For desires that exceed the bounds of nature cannot but go on to infinity. Our nature has its own limit, but empty and perverse desires are inherently unbounded.* Our needs are measured by utility; beyond that, what line is there to draw?

**6** So they drown themselves in pleasures, having grown so accustomed to them that they can no longer do without them. They are especially miserable in that they have gotten to a point where what were once luxuries have become necessities. Rather than enjoying their pleasures, they are slaves to them; worst of all, they even love what is worst in themselves. The worst of their condition is when they not only enjoy their shameful behavior but even approve of it. Once vice becomes a code of conduct, there ceases to be any possibility of cure.

Farewell.

## Letter 40

*From Seneca to Lucilius*
*Greetings*

**1** I am grateful to you for writing so often, for you are showing me yourself, in the only way that you can. It never fails: I receive your letter, and right away we are together. If portraits of absent friends are a delight, refreshing our memory and easing the pain of separation with a kind of comfort, though false and empty, how much more delightful are letters, which bring us real traces, real news of an absent friend! For what is sweetest about seeing someone face to face is also to be found in a letter that bears the imprint of a friend's hand—a moment of recognition.

**2** You write that you heard the philosopher Serapio when he made a stop in your vicinity.* "It is his way to deliver a great onrush of words, not releasing them one at a time° but driving them on in stampede. For so many come that one voice is hardly enough!" I do not approve of this in a philosopher. A philosopher's manner of speaking should be well regulated, just as his life should be, but nothing is orderly if it is all in a rush. That is why, in Homer, the rapid and uninterrupted speech that is "like a snowstorm" is given to the younger orator,° while the gentle flow of speech "sweeter than honey" belongs to the elder.*

**3** Believe me, then, that the copious flow of words you told me about is more suited for the lecture circuit than for someone who has serious, important work to do and to teach. It's not that I want a slow drip and dribble of words, any more than I want a flood. A speaker should neither weary our waiting ears nor overwhelm them. For a meager, impoverished way of speaking makes the audience less attentive, since they grow bored with a slow and halting delivery; all the same, we learn more easily from what keeps us waiting than from what goes flying past us. Besides, we say that precepts are "imparted" to the pupil. Running away with something is not imparting it!

**4** Moreover, speech that aims at the truth should be unaffected and plain. This popular style of speaking has nothing to do with truth; it seeks to stir the crowd, to steal upon unguarded ears and carry them by storm. It does not expose itself to scrutiny, but is off at once. But how can speech supply us with discipline if it is itself undisciplined? Bear in mind that this kind of speech, which is intended to bring healing to the mind, has to get deep inside us. Remedies that do not stay in the system cannot be effective. **5** Anyway, the popular style is largely vacuous and inane, more sound than substance. I need the speech to calm my terrors, curb my temper, dispel my illusions, curtail my self-indulgence, and rebuke my greed. Which of these things can be done in a hurry? What doctor cures the sick while in transit?

Think of this: there is not even any pleasure to be had from such a tumult of words, hurtling on without any discimination. **6** In general when something has happened that you thought was impossible, you are satisfied to learn of it a single time. So also with these people who put words through their paces: a single hearing is plenty. For what is there in such speeches that anyone would want to learn or to imitate? What judgment is one to make about the speaker's mind when his speech is disorderly, out of control, unstoppable? **7** Just as people running downhill cannot stop where they meant to but are carried°

further than they intended by the momentum of their bodies, so this rapidity of speech is not in command of itself and not well suited to philosophy. Philosophy ought to place its words, not spew them out; it should go forward one step at a time.

**8** "What do you mean? Shouldn't it sometimes take wing?" Of course it should—but in such a way as to preserve its dignified character. Excessive vehemence strips that away. Philosophy should have great strength, but a strength that is under control; it should be an ever-flowing stream, not a flood.

I would scarcely permit even an advocate to use such a rapid rate of speech. For it forges ahead without discipline and cannot be called back. How is the juror to follow it? Especially since jurors are sometimes inexperienced and untrained. Even when the advocate is eager to show off or is carried away by his emotions, he should restrict his pace and his accumulation of ideas to what the ear can take in.

**9** You will be right, then, to disregard those who care about how much they say rather than how well, and to prefer, if you must, to speak haltingly, like Publius Vinicius.° When someone asked Asellius how Vinicius's speech went, he said, "Bit by bit." For as Geminius Varius said, "I don't know how you can call that man an orator; he can't string three words together."* Yet why should you not choose to speak as Vinicius does? **10** So what if some jokester comes your way like the one that heard Vinicius when he was groping for words as if he were dictating rather than speaking, and said to him, "Say, are you going to say something?"° For although Quintus Haterius was highly renowned as an orator in his day, his swift speaking is just what I would want the person of sense to avoid.* He never hesitated, never took a breath; he began but once, and left off only at the end.

**11** I suppose also that some things are either more or less suited to certain peoples. In Greeks you would put up with such license; we Romans make it a habit to put in the punctuation, even when we write.* Cicero too, the wellspring of our Roman eloquence, went forward one step at a time. Roman speech has more circumspection; it sets a value on itself, and lets others make their assessment as well. **12** Fabianus was a fine man both in his manner of living and in his depth of knowledge, and eloquent as well, although that is of lesser importance.* He used to lecture efficiently rather than energetically.

One could say that he exhibited a facility with language, but not that he had great speed of delivery. I allow that this may be a characteristic of the man of wisdom, though I do not make it a requirement. By all means, let his speech issue forth without impediment. But it is one thing to deliver, another to gush; I prefer delivery.

**13** Another reason I have to dissuade you from that contagion is that you cannot employ that style of speaking except by losing your sense of shame. You have to coarsen your sensibilities and never listen to yourself. That heedless dash will bring with it many expressions that you would wish to criticize. **14** I repeat: you cannot achieve it without losing your sense of propriety.

Besides that, you need to practice every day, and that means putting your energy into the words rather than the content. And even if a rapid flow of words comes easily to you, requiring no effort, still you should keep it in check. For just as a man of wisdom should be modest in his manner of walking, so should his speech be restrained, not impetuous.

The sum of all my summing up, and my command, is this: speak slowly.

Farewell.

## Letter 41

*From Seneca to Lucilius*
*Greetings*

**1** You are doing what is best and most beneficial for you if, as your letter says, you persevere in moving toward excellence of mind. How silly it is to pray for that! It is a wish you yourself can grant.

You need not raise your hands to heaven; you need not beg the temple keeper for privileged access, as if a near approach to the cult image would give us a better hearing. The god is near you—with you—inside you. **2** I mean it, Lucilius. A sacred spirit dwells within us, and is the observer and guardian of all our goods and ills. However we treat that spirit, so does the spirit treat us. In truth, no one is a good man without God. Or is there anyone who can rise superior to fortune without God's aid? It is God who supplies us with noble thoughts, with upright counsels. In each and every good man

resides a god: which god, remains unknown.*

**3** If you happen to be in a wood dense with ancient trees of unusual height, where interlocking branches exclude the light of day, the loftiness and seclusion of that forest spot, the wonder of finding above ground such a deep, unbroken shade, will convince you that divinity is there. If you behold some deeply eroded cavern, some vast chamber not made with hands but hollowed out by natural causes at the very roots of the mountain, it will impress upon your mind an intimation of religious awe. We venerate the sources of great rivers; we situate an altar wherever a rushing stream bursts suddenly from hiding; thermal springs are the site of ritual observance; and more than one lake has been held sacred for its darkness or its measureless depth. **4** So if you see a person undismayed by peril and untouched by desire, one cheerful in adversity and calm in the face of storms, someone who rises above all humankind and meets the gods at their own level, will you not be overcome with reverence before him?

Will you not say, "Something is there that is so great, so exalted, that we cannot possibly believe it to be of the same kind as that paltry body it inhabits. **5** A power divine has descended on him. That eminent and disciplined mind, passing through everything as lesser than itself, laughing at all our fears and all our longings, is driven by some celestial force. Such magnitude cannot stand upright without divinity to hold it up. In large part, then, its existence is in that place from which it has come down. Even as the sun's rays touch the earth and yet have their existence at their point of origin, so that great and sacred mind, that mind sent down to bring us nearer knowledge of the divine, dwells indeed with us and yet inheres within its source. Its reliance is there, and there are its aim and its objective: though it mingles in our affairs, it does so as our better."*

**6** So what mind is this? It is one that shines with a good that is its own. Do we praise a person for qualities belonging to someone else? What could be sillier than that? Do we marvel at possessions that can be transferred to another at a moment's notice? What could be more foolish? A golden bridle does not improve the horse. The tamed lion with his gold-encrusted mane, harried into submission and loaded down with trinkets, is goaded on by his handlers: how different is the spring of the wild lion, whose spirit is unbroken! Surely he, fierce in the attack, as nature intended—he, with his rugged splendor that has no ornament but in the terror of the beholder—is superior to that other languid, gilded creature!

7 No one should glory except in what is his own. We commend the vine only if its branches are laden with grapes, if it bears so heavily that the stakes cannot support it. Would anyone really prefer the vine that is hung with golden fruit and golden leaves? Fruitfulness is the distinctive excellence of the vine; similarly in a human being we should praise that which belongs to him. So what if he has attractive slaves, a lovely home, vast plantations, substantial investments? All these things surround him; they are not in him. 8 Praise in him that which nothing can take away and nothing can confer—that which is distinctive about the human being.*

Do you ask what that is? It is the mind, and rationality perfected within the mind. For a human being is a rational animal. Hence his good is complete if he fulfills that for which he is born. But what is it that this rationality requires of him? The easiest thing of all: to live in accordance with his own nature. It is our shared insanity that makes this difficult: we push one another into faults. And how can we be recalled to health, when all people drive us forward and no one holds us back?

Farewell.

# BOOK FIVE

# *Letter 42*

*From Seneca to Lucilius*
*Greetings*

1 He's convinced you already, has he, that he is a good man? In point of fact, it is not possible for a good man either to come into being or to be recognized in such a short time.

You realize what sort of good man I mean in the present context: one of the second rank, for that other one is born perhaps once every five hundred years, like the phoenix.* And it is not surprising that what is great should be produced at long intervals. Chance turns out the ordinary versions, the ones born into the crowd, with great frequency; but what is exceptional is rare, and that itself is a recommendation.

2 But the person to whom you refer is still very far from what he professes to be. If he knew what a good man is, he would not believe himself to be one yet—indeed, he might despair of ever becoming one.

"But he despises the wicked!" Yes, and so do even the wicked themselves. Wrongdoing has no harsher penalty than this: one offends oneself, and also one's family and friends.

3 "But he hates all those who use great power capriciously, through lack of power over themselves." Yes, and when he has that power himself, he will do just the same. There are many whose faults go undetected only because they are ineffectual: when these grow confident of their strength, they will act no less audaciously than those whose fortunes have already given them opportunity. They lack only the resources to display the full extent of their iniquity. 4 Even a poisonous snake is safe to handle in cold weather, when it is sluggish. Its venom is still there, but inactive. In the same way, there are many people whose cruelty, ambition, or self-indulgence fails to match the most outrageous cases only by the grace of fortune. Just give them the power to do what they want, and you will see: they want the same things as others do.

**5** Do you remember when you told me you had a certain person in your power, and I said he was fickle and prone to flee, and that you had him not by the foot but by the wing? I was wrong: it was only by a feather, and now he has escaped, leaving it behind. You know what tricks he later played on you—what twists and turns that in the end fooled no one but himself. He didn't see that he was moving rapidly through other people's perils toward his own. He didn't realize that the objects he was pursuing were superfluous—and that even if they weren't, they would still weigh him down.

**6** This indeed is a point we should keep in view. Those things we compete for—the things to which we devote so much effort—offer us either no advantage, or greater disadvantage. Some are superfluities; others are not worth the trouble, but we don't realize it. We think things come for free, when in fact their price is very steep. **7** Here is what makes our idiocy quite plain: we think the only things we pay for are those we spend our money on. The things we call free are those on which we spend our very selves. Things we wouldn't be willing to pay for if it meant giving up our house for them, or some pleasant or productive estate, we are quite ready to obtain at the cost of anxiety, of danger, of losing our freedom, our decency, our time. You see, we treat ourselves as if we were more worthless than anything else.

**8** So let's act in all situations and all our decisions as we do in the marketplace when a vendor has something we eagerly desire—let's ask how much it's going for. Often the price is very high even if you get it for nothing. I can show you many possessions that have cost us our liberty in the moment we acquired them. If those things did not belong to us, we would belong to ourselves.

**9** So think it over—and not only when you acquire something but when you lose something too.

"You'll never see that again." No, but it was only by chance that you got it; you will live without it as easily as you did before. If you had it a long time, you are losing it after you have had enough of it; if not, you are losing it before you get used to it.

"You won't have as much money." No, and you won't have as much trouble either.

**10** "You won't have as much influence." And neither will you incur as much resentment.

Take stock of all those things that drive us to distraction—those things we cry° the hardest to lose—and you'll see: it's not deprivation that troubles us but the thought of deprivation. One thinks a loss has occurred, but no one really feels that loss.

Once a person possesses himself, then nothing is ever lost to him. But those who have managed that are few and far between!

Farewell.

## Letter 43

*From Seneca to Lucilius*
*Greetings*

1 How did I find out, you ask? Who told me of your intentions, seeing that you hadn't told anyone yourself? The one who knows most things: gossip.

You say, "Since when am I of sufficient stature to attract gossip?" Don't measure yourself in relation to this locality, but in relation to your own place of residence. 2 Anything that stands out in its own surroundings is of stature there. Eminence is not of any one size: comparison raises or lowers it in one's estimation. A boat that is large on a river is quite a tiny vessel out at sea; and the same steering oar is big for one boat and small for another. 3 Since you are now in your province, you are a great man, no matter how little regard you have for yourself. Your activities, your dinner plans, even your sleeping arrangements are matters of interest and indeed of common knowledge.

Hence you must be all the more careful of your mode of life. Count yourself fortunate when you are able to live in a manner open to the public—when walls are there for shelter, not for concealment. For as a rule we think we have walls around us not to protect us but to afford greater privacy to our misdeeds. 4 I will tell you the measure of our degeneracy: you'll find hardly anyone who can live with his door open. It's not ostentation that puts a doorman in the vestibule; it's guilt. The way we live, an unannounced visit means getting caught.

But what's the use of hiding oneself away from sight, from hearing? **5** A good conscience welcomes a crowd; a bad one is racked with anxiety even in solitude. If your actions are honorable, let everyone know them; if shameful, what does it matter that nobody knows? *You* know. Alas for you, if you have no concern for *that* witness!

Farewell.

## Letter 44

*From Seneca to Lucilius*
*Greetings*

**1** You are running yourself down again. You tell me you had but a scant allowance first from birth and then from fortune, when all the while you could be separating yourself from the common crowd and rising to the summit of human prosperity.

If there is any good in philosophy, it is this: it has no regard for genealogies. If we trace our lineage back to the beginning, all humankind is of divine origins. **2** You are a Roman of equestrian status; your own hard work has advanced you to this rank.* But for heaven's sake, there are many who find themselves excluded from the priority seating;* some cannot gain entry to the Senate House; even the regiment is particular about the men it recruits for toil and danger. Meanwhile, excellence of mind is available to all: in this regard we are all nobly born.

Philosophy neither rejects anyone nor chooses anyone; it shines for all. **3** Socrates was no patrician; Cleanthes hauled water, and hired himself out to water people's gardens; Plato did not come to philosophy a nobleman but was ennobled by it.* Why should you not hope perhaps to become their equal? All of them are your ancestors if you prove yourself worthy of them. And you will do so if you persuade yourself, right now, that no one is superior to you merely by reason of noble birth.

**4** Everyone has the same number of ancestors. There is no one whose origins lie anywhere but in oblivion. Plato says that every king is of servile origin and every slave of kingly origin.* The changes and chances of time have mingled all things topsy-turvy. **5** Who has good breeding? The one whom nature has given a good disposition toward virtue. We must look to that alone. Otherwise, if you cast your mind back to ancient times, every person has an origin in that moment before which there was nothing. From the beginning of the world until now, our history is a constant succession of dignity and squalor.

An atrium full of smoke-stained images does not make one a nobleman.* No one lived his life just for us to brag about him: what happened before our time does not belong to us. It is the mind that confers nobility, for the mind has license, regardless of estate, to rise above the vagaries of chance. **6** Imagine that you are not a Roman of equestrian status but a freedman. You can still attain a condition in which you alone are free, even if those around you do not share your servile origins.

"How?" you ask. If you make your own distinctions of what is good and bad, without reference to popular notions. You should not consider where things come from but where they are headed. If something has the capacity to make your life happy, then that thing is a good in its own right, for it cannot be turned into a bad thing.*

**7** What, then, is the mistake people make, seeing that everyone wants a happy life? They take the instruments used by happiness to be happiness itself, and so abandon the very thing they are seeking.* For the chief point in a happy life is to be solidly secure and unshakably confident of that state;* and yet they gather up the causes of anxiety and haul, no, drag those burdens behind them on life's treacherous journey. For that reason they recede further and further from what they seek to attain, and the greater their efforts, the greater the hindrance they create for themselves. It is like hurrying in a maze: their very haste impedes them.

Farewell.

## Letter 45

*From Seneca to Lucilius*
*Greetings*

**1** You complain that there is an undersupply of books where you are. What matters is not how many you have but how good they are.

Varied reading gives pleasure; selective reading does real good. If a person wants to reach his destination, he should follow just one road, not wander around over many. What you are doing is traipsing around, not journeying.

2 "I wish you'd skip the advice," you say, "and just send the books!" I will send them, as many as I have; indeed, I am ready to "sweep out the barn" for you. I'd send myself over to you if I could. If it weren't for my hope that you will soon obtain leave to conclude your duties there, I would resolve on travel, elderly as I am. Even Scylla and Charybdis, the fabled straits, would not frighten me away.* I would not only cross them; I'd swim them, if it meant that I could embrace you again, and see for myself how much your mind has grown.

3 But as for your request that I send you my books, I don't think myself a cultured person on that account, any more than I would think myself handsome just because you had asked for my portrait. I realize it's not a judgment on your part but a matter of affection—or if a judgment is implied, it is a judgment swayed by affection. 4 Still, such as they are, read them as the books of one who does not know the truth but is still seeking it—and who is obdurate in the seeking. For I am nobody's freedman; I bear no one's name but my own.* I have great faith in the opinions of the great, but I make some claim for my own views as well. For even those great ones left us with questions, not answers.

Perhaps they would have found such answers as are needed if they had not also inquired into superfluities. 5 A great deal of their time was spent on verbal chicanery, riddling disputes that exercise the intellect to no avail. We tie knots; we knit ambiguous meanings into our words, and then we unravel them again.* Do we really have that much time? Do we know already how to live—how to die? We should hasten with all our mind to that point where it is the deceits of circumstance we have to look out for, not just deceitful words.

6 Why are you drawing distinctions for me between homonymous terms, terms that no one ever finds confusing except during the disputation itself? It is life that confuses us: draw your distinctions there! We embrace bad things rather than good; we choose one thing and then the opposite; our aims and intentions are all in conflict with one another. 7 Flattery looks very much like friendship, indeed not only resembles it but actually wins out against it. A person drinks

it in with eager ears and takes it deeply to heart, delighted by the very qualities that make it dangerous. Teach me to make distinctions there! A charming enemy comes to me as a friend; faults creep in calling themselves virtues; temerity cloaks itself with the name of courage; cowardice gets called moderation; and timidity passes itself off as caution. These are the perils that surround us: give us some pointers on these!

**8** But that person you are asking "whether he has horns"* is not so stupid as to feel his forehead for them! Nor is he such an idiot that he wouldn't know he had them unless you, with your fancy syllogism, convinced him of it! Those are just harmless tricks. They are like conjurors' shells and pebbles, which I find enjoyable just because I get fooled by them. The same can be said of those "riddles"—what better word can I use for *sophismata*?—they don't harm those who don't understand them, and they don't help those who do.*

**9** If you really want to draw distinctions among terms, explain to us the following: that the happy person is not the one ordinary people call happy, not the one who has been showered with money, but rather the one whose every good resides in the mind. That one is upright and exalted; he spurns underfoot the objects of wonder; he would not trade his life for any other that he sees. He assesses a person only by that part which makes him a human being. He takes nature for his teacher, regulates his life by nature's laws, lives as nature has directed. His goods are those no power can strip away; whatever is bad, he turns to good. He is sure in judgment, unshaken, undismayed. There are forces that move him, but none that alarm him. The sharpest, deadliest blows that fortune can inflict do not wound him: he feels but a sting, and that rarely. As for those other darts that assail the human race, those bounce off him like hail hitting a roof, that rattles and then melts without hurting the one inside.

**10** Why do you occupy my time with what even you call "the Lying Puzzle," about which so many books have been written?* Look here: my whole life is a lie; refute that! Turn its falsehood into truth, if you are so clever! It counts as necessities things that are merely superfluous, and even those that are not superfluous do not have any intrinsic significance as concerns a blessed and happy existence.

For the fact that something is necessary does not immediately make it a good. Otherwise we debase the good, if we apply that name to bread, and porridge, and the other things without which life cannot be sustained. **11** That which is good is by the same token necessary; that which is necessary is not by the same token a good, since, in fact, some things are necessary and yet very low on the scale of value. But no one is so oblivious to worth as to demote what is truly good to mere day-to-day utility.

**12** Well, then! Will you not redirect your efforts? Show us that much time is wasted pursuing what is superfluous, that many people miss out on life by going after life's equipment. Observe individuals, and study people in general, and you will find every one of us living for tomorrow.

**13** "Is there any harm in that?" you say. Yes, endless harm. For they are not living; they are only about to live. Everything is deferred. Even if we were paying attention, life would slip by us; as it is, we put off living, and our lives race past us as if they belonged to someone else—ending on the last day, yet lost to us every day.

But I don't want to exceed the proper length of a letter, which ought not to fill up the left hand of the reader.* So I'll put off for another day this quarrel I have with the excessively subtle dialecticians. It's one thing to have an interest in logic, quite another when they make logic their sole concern.

Farewell.

## Letter 46

*From Seneca to Lucilius*
*Greetings*

**1** Your book arrived as promised. I opened it, thinking to read it later at my convenience, and meaning for the moment only to take a taste; then the work itself seduced me to continue. How eloquent it was you may learn from this fact: it seemed light to me, though its bulk would seem at first glance to be that of Livy or Epicurus, not of your writings or mine.* Yet with such sweetness did it hold me and draw me on that I read it through without delay. The sunshine beckoned—

hunger nagged—a storm threatened—and still I read it through to the end. **2** It was not only delight that it gave me: it was joy.

What talent it showed—what spirit! I would have said, "What impact!" had there been in it any quiet stretches—had it roused itself only at intervals. But as it was, it was not impact but a steady state. The style is masculine and chaste; nonetheless, there came in from time to time that note of sweetness, that just-right gentle moment. You are tall, upright—this I would have you keep; this is how you should walk. The subject matter has also contributed something, which is why one should choose a fertile subject that will engage and motivate one's talent.

**3** I will write more about the book when I have been over it a second time; at present my judgment is hardly settled. It is as if I had heard these things rather than read them. Allow me to ask some questions as well. You have nothing to fear—I shall tell you the truth. Happy man! You have nothing that would give anyone cause to lie to you, even from so far away—except that nowadays we lie even when there is no cause, just out of habit.

Farewell.

## Letter 47

*From Seneca to Lucilius*
*Greetings*

**1** I am pleased to learn from those who have been with you that you live on familiar terms with your slaves. This is becoming in a person of your good sense and education.

"They are slaves." No, they are human beings.

"They are slaves." No, they are housemates.

"They are slaves." No, they are lowborn friends.

"They are slaves." Fellow slaves, rather, if you keep in mind that fortune has its way with you just as much as with them.

**2** For that reason, I laugh at those who think it is beneath them to share a meal with their slaves. Why not? There is but one reason: it's one of the traditions of arrogance for the master to eat his dinner with a crowd of slaves standing in a circle around him. He eats more than he can hold, immense greed loading his distended stomach—a stomach that has forgotten its proper function—merely so that he can expend more effort on vomiting than he did on ingestion. **3** Meanwhile, the poor slaves aren't allowed to move their lips even to speak—every murmur is curtailed by the rod. Not even a sneeze, not even a chance cough or a hiccup, is exempt from the lash; if the silence is broken by any sound of the voice, they pay a terrible price for it. All night they stand there, mute and famished. **4** The result is those same slaves who cannot speak in their master's presence are ready to speak about him to others.* But in the old days, when they not only spoke in the master's presence but actually conversed with him, slaves never had their lips sewn shut and yet were ready to risk their necks for him, to turn dangers that threatened him on their own heads. They spoke during dinner parties but were silent under torture. **5** It was later that the proverb began to go around, coming of that same arrogance: "Count your slaves and you count your enemies." They are not our enemies just by being there: we make them so.

I can hardly list all the cases of cruel and inhuman treatment such as would be abusive to beasts of burden, let alone human beings. While we recline at dinner, one is wiping up gobs of spit; another crawling under the couch to pick up the scraps the drunkards let fall. **6** A third carves the expensive fowl, his trained hand separating out perfect slices from the breast and from the thigh. Unhappy he, who lives for this alone—the proper carving of poultry! Or he would be if it were not worse to be the one who teaches him to do it. He learns because he has to; the other teaches at the behest of pleasure. **7** Another is the cupbearer, decked out like a woman and struggling against his years. He cannot escape boyhood—he is made to revert to it. Already he carries himself like a soldier, yet his cheeks are smooth, every hair shaved away or plucked out. He is on duty all night: his first shift is devoted to his master's drinking, his second to his lust—for he is a boy only at the party: in the bedroom he's the man. **8** Yet another has been assigned to evaluate the guests. It is his unhappy task to stand there and observe which ones are the flatterers, which cannot control their gluttony or keep a watch on their tongues. These are the ones who will be invited again the following day. In addition there are the arbiters of gourmandizing, who possess a fine-tuned awareness of the master's tastes: which foods stimulate his palate, which please his eye, which are new to him and may prove attractive even when he is queasy, which he has come to hate because they are served too often, and what he has a hankering for on that particular day. Such are the persons with whom he cannot bear to dine, thinking it beneath his dignity to come to the same table as his own slave. Heavens, no!

Yet how many masters might he have among them! **9** Once at the doorway of Callistus* I saw Callistus's own former master standing in attendance. He who had given up the man for sale, who had auctioned him off among the worn-out slaves, could not even gain admission, though others could. That was the thanks he got from the slave he had thrown in with the first lot, the ones the auctioneer warms up with. Turn and turn about: now it was Callistus's turn to write him down for exclusion—now it was Callistus who judged the man unworthy to cross his threshold. That master sold Callistus; now Callistus made him pay the price.

**10** Reflect, if you will: that man whom you call your slave was born of the same seeds as you—enjoys the same sky—breathes, lives, dies, just as you do. It is possible that you will see him a free man, and equally possible that he will see you enslaved. At the time of Varus's disaster, many highborn nobles were laid low, men who looked forward to a senatorial career after their military service. Luck made one of them a shepherd, another the guardian of a hut.* Go now and scoff! The fortunes of those you despise may come upon you at any time.

**11** I don't want to get carried away with some long speech about the treatment of slaves. We are indeed most haughty, cruel, and demeaning toward them. But all my instructions can be summed up in this: live with an inferior the same way you would want a superior to live with you. Each time you remember the extent of power over a slave, remember also that your own master has that same amount of power over you. **12** "But I have no master," you say. You're still young—perhaps someday you will. Don't you realize how old Hecuba was when she became a slave? Don't you realize how old Croesus was? The mother of Darius? Plato? Diogenes?*

**13** Live mercifully with your slave, amicably, even; and include him in your conversation, in your planning, and in your meals. At this point, the whole order of sybarites will cry out against me. "Nothing is more degrading than that! Nothing is more humiliating!" Yet I will catch these same men kissing the hands of other people's slaves.

**14** Don't you people know what our ancestors did to eliminate resentment toward masters and abuse toward slaves? They used the name "father of the household" for the master, and "household members" for the slaves—a term that still persists in stage mime. They instituted a holiday when masters would share a meal with their slaves—not that they did so only at that time, but that it was the custom on that day in particular. They allowed slaves to hold offices and pronounce judgments within the house, for they considered the house to be a polity in miniature.

**15** "What are you saying? Shall I admit all my slaves to my table?" No, no more than you admit all who are free. But you're wrong if you think I am going to exclude some on grounds that their work is less clean—the stable-hand, say, or the cowherd. I will evaluate them not by their jobs but by their character. Jobs are assigned by chance; character is something each person gives himself. Let some dine with you because they are worthy of that distinction, others to make them worthy. For if there is something slavish in them, owing to their life among the lowly, sharing meals with more honorable people will get rid of it.

**16** My dear Lucilius, you need not look for friends only in the Forum or in the Senate House. If you look closely, you will find them in your household also. Good materials often go to waste for lack of a skilled craftsman: try them out and you will see. Just as one would be foolish to consider buying a horse when one hasn't inspected the animal itself but only its saddle and bridle, so it is extremely foolish to judge a human being by his clothing and his position in life. For position is only one more garment that surrounds us.

**17** "He is a slave." But perhaps his mind is free. "He is a slave." Is that going to hurt his chances? Show me who isn't! One person is a slave to lust, another to greed, a third to ambition—and all are slaves to hope; all are slaves to fear. I will give you an ex-consul who is a slave to a little old lady, a wealthy man who is a slave to a servant girl. I will show you young men of the best families who are the vassals of pantomime dancers.* No servitude is more shameful than the kind we take on willingly.

So why be afraid of those snobs? Show your slaves a cheerful demeanor, above them and yet not haughty. Let them respect you rather than fear you. **18** At this point someone will say I am calling for emancipation and for knocking down masters from their exalted position, just because I said, "Let them respect you rather than fear you." "What's this?" he says. "Should they respect you as clients, as morning callers?"* He who says this has forgotten that what suffices for a god cannot be insufficient for slave owners. One who is respected is also loved, and love and fear do not mix. **19** Thus I think you are doing the right thing when you prefer not to be feared by your slaves and when you correct them only with words. Whips are for training speechless animals.

Not everything that offends us is harmful to us. It is our indulgences that make us go into a frenzy, becoming enraged at anything that doesn't suit our whim. We put on airs as if we were kings. **20** For kings too forget their own power and the weakness of others, and so become enraged, just as if they sustained some injury—from which experience they are quite safe, thanks to the magnitude of their fortunes. And they are well aware of that fact, and yet in their pettishness they grasp at any opportunity to hurt others. They consider themselves wronged just so they can do a wrong themselves.

**21** I don't wish to keep you any longer, for you need no encouragement. One thing about good character is that it is content with itself and so persists over time. A bad one is fickle: it changes frequently, not for the better but just for the sake of changing.

Farewell.

## Letter 48

*From Seneca to Lucilius*
*Greetings*

**1** To that letter you sent me from your trip abroad (a letter as long as the trip itself!) I shall reply later on. I need to go off by myself and figure out what advice to give you. For you also, in consulting me, took some time to think about it, and that was only to decide whether to consult. I have all the more reason to deliberate, since solving a puzzle takes more time than setting one. And this is especially the case since my interests here are different from yours.

2 Am I talking like an Epicurean again? In reality, my interests are the same as yours.* I wouldn't be your friend if everything that pertains to you were not my concern as well. Friendship creates between us a shared interest that includes everything. Neither good times nor bad affect just one of us; we live in common. And no one can have a happy life if he looks only to himself, turning everything to his own advantage. If you want to live for yourself, you must live for another. 3 This sense of companionship links all human beings to one another; it holds that there is a common law of humankind; and if carefully and reverently preserved, it contributes greatly also to the maintenance of that other companionship I was speaking of, the one within a friendship. For he who has much in common with a fellow human will have everything in common with his friend.*

4 That, most excellent Lucilius, is what I want those splitters of hairs to teach me—what I should do for a friend, or for a human being; not how many different ways the word "friend" is used or how many different things "human" can signify.* I see wisdom and foolishness headed in opposite directions: Which path shall I take? Which way are you sending me? One person treats every human being as his friend; another does not treat his friend like a human being; one makes a friend to serve his own interests; another makes himself ready to serve his friend's interests—and there *you* are, twisting words on the rack, pulling syllable from syllable. 5 As if I wouldn't be able to discern what ends I should or should not pursue unless I formulate sophistical arguments and string a false conclusion onto a true premise! For shame, that we who are mature men should play games with such serious matters!

6 "Mouse" is a syllable.

But a mouse eats cheese.

Therefore a syllable eats cheese.

Suppose I can't solve that one: what risk do I incur by not knowing how? What inconvenience even? Sure, I'd have to watch out—someday I might find myself catching syllables in mousetraps! Better be careful—my cheese might be eaten by a book!

But wait, maybe this is a smarter syllogism:

> Mouse is a syllable.
>
> But a syllable doesn't eat cheese.
>
> Therefore a mouse doesn't eat cheese.

7 What childish pranks! Is this what makes us knit our brows? Is this why we let our beards grow long? Are we pale and earnest in our teaching of *this*?

Would you like to know what philosophy has to offer the human race? Advice! One person is summoned by death, another burned up by poverty, another tormented by wealth—others' wealth or his own. This one shrinks from misfortune; that one wants to sneak away from his prosperity. This one is mistreated by other people; that one, by the gods. 8 Why are you making up little games? You have no time for joking around; you have been summoned to assist those in need. You have promised to aid the shipwrecked, the captive, the sick, the impoverished, and those who must stretch out their neck for the axe. Where are you wandering off to? What are you doing?

This person you are playing with is frightened: help him. He is in suspense: break through the snares that hold him.° All those around you are reaching their hands in your direction, imploring you for aid in lives that are ruined or are going to ruin. You are their hope, their succor. They are asking you to rescue them from turmoil; scattered and wandering, they need you to show them the bright light of truth. 9 Tell them what nature has made necessary, and what superfluous; how easy are the laws nature has established, and how pleasant and unencumbered life is for those who follow them, how bitter and heavy-laden for those who have placed their trust in opinion rather than in nature. But first, teach something° that will give relief to some of them. Which of your conundrums takes away desires? Which even mitigates them? They don't help, and that's not the worst of it—I only wish it were. They actually do harm. I'll prove to you very clearly, if you like, that a noble disposition is diminished and weakened when thrown amid such snares. 10 Here are soldiers who are to do battle against fortune, and how are they equipped? What weapons are supplied to them? I am ashamed to say.

Is this the way to the highest good? Through "if this" and "if that" and quibbles that would be shady and disreputable even for lawyers? When you interrogate a person and knowingly ensnare him in a falsehood, how different is that from causing him to lose a case on a technicality? But just as the praetor sets the defendant straight, so philosophy straightens out its pupils. **11** Why do you people walk away from your big promises? Such great things you said: that you would make me care no more for the glint of gold than I do for the flash of a sword; that I would be so tremendously consistent as to spurn underfoot the objects of both universal desire and universal fear! And you are now lowering yourselves to the most elementary of literary studies.* What is it that you say? "Thus mount we to the stars"?* This is what philosophy promises: to make me equal to the gods. This is what I was invited for; this is what I came for. Keep your promise!

**12** And so, dear Lucilius, withdraw as far as you can from such challenges and quibbles of philosophers. Honest, straightforward talk is better suited to real goodness. Even if you had a lot of life left to live, you would need to parcel out your time sparingly so as to have enough for necessities. As it is, with time in such short supply, what madness it is to learn things that are superfluous!

Farewell.

## Letter 49

*From Seneca to Lucilius*
*Greetings*

**1** Quite right, dear Lucilius: one is negligent and indeed remiss if one remembers a friend only when reminded by some particular locale. But sometimes familiar spots do awaken a yearning that has been hidden in our mind, not rekindling a memory that had gone out but stirring up one that was at rest. It's like the way a family's grief, though mitigated by the passage of time, is renewed by the sight of some slave child, or some garment or house, that was a favorite of the one who is gone.

Here's Campania—and it's incredible how this region, and above all Naples and your dear Pompeii, have made me wish for your presence all over again.* Every bit of you is before my eyes. I am leaving you even now. I see you blinking back tears—struggling in vain against emotions that cannot be suppressed. It seems only just now that I lost you.

**2** For remembrance makes everything "just now," doesn't it? Just now I was a boy, sitting in the house of Sotion the philosopher;* just now I began to argue cases; just now I stopped wanting to argue them; just now I ceased to be able. The rapidity of time is boundless—and is more evident when one looks back. For though it goes at breakneck speed, it glides by so smoothly that those who are intent on the present moment fail to notice it passing.

**3** Do you ask the reason for this? All the time that has passed is in the same place; we look on it all at once. All things are dropping into the same abyss. Besides, there cannot be long intervals within something that is brief overall. Our lifespan is a pinpoint—even less than a pinpoint. But nature has mocked even this infinitesimal point with a specious show of longer extent, making one element in it our infancy; another our childhood; another our youth; another a sloping course, as it were, between youth and age; another old age itself. That's a lot of steps for such a narrow span! **4** It was only just now that I saw you off, and yet that "just now" covers a fair portion of our lives. Let us keep in mind how brief those lives are, and how soon they will run out. Time never used to seem so swift; now its speed amazes me, whether because I perceive the finish line approaching, or because I have begun to pay attention and compute what I have lost.

**5** Thus I am all the more indignant that although even the most careful stewardship of time cannot make it last long enough for our needs, there are some who spend the better part of theirs on superfluities. Cicero says that twice his lifetime would not be time enough for him to read the lyric poets.* Well, I put the dialecticians in the same category, only they are more severe in their foolishness. The poets are frivolous by design; these logicians think they are accomplishing something. **6** I am not saying one should not give such things a look—but it should be only a look, a greeting from the doorway, just enough to make sure we are not taken in by them, thinking there is some deep and arcane value in what they do.

Why are you going to rack and ruin over that question? You would show more cleverness by scoffing at it than by solving it. Delving into minutiae is for one who has nothing to worry about—who travels by his own schedule. When the enemy is harrying your retreat, when the army is ordered to the march, then necessity discards what peace and leisure had collected. **7** I have no time to spare for chasing down ambiguous terms and exercising my ingenuity on them.

> Behold the assembled peoples, the high walls
> Sharpen their weapons, and the gates are shut.*

The clash and clatter of war are sounding all around me; I need courage to heed them. **8** Everyone would think I was crazy—and they would be right—if, in the midst of siege, while women and old men are carrying stones up to the battlements, while young men are massed inside the gates waiting, even begging for the signal to sortie, while enemy spears come flying within the gates and the ground beneath our feet quakes with tunneling and sapping, I should sit there, idly posing little conundrums like this:

> What you have not lost, you have.
>
> But you have not lost horns.
>
> Therefore you have horns.

That, or some other intellectual lunacy along the same lines!

**9** Yet you have my permission to think me just as crazy as they are if I spend time on such things. For in fact I am under siege at this moment. In the other case, it would have been an external danger threatening me; there would have been a wall between me and the enemy. As it is, deadly perils are right here with me. I have no time to waste on such foolishness: a great business is afoot.

What am I up to? Death is after me; life is on the retreat. Teach me something I can use against that! **10** Don't let me run from death any longer; don't let life run away from me! Encourage me to face what is difficult; give me the serenity° to accept what I cannot avoid. Expand the narrow confines of my remaining time. Teach me that the goodness of a life depends not on how long it is but on how it is used; and that it is possible—in fact quite common—for a person to have a long life that is scarcely a life at all. Say to me before I sleep, "It's possible you will not wake up," and when I rise, "It's possible you will never sleep again." Say to me when I go out, "It's possible you will not return," and when I return, "It's possible you will never leave. **11** You are wrong if you think it is only aboard ship that 'life is but an inch away from death.' The interval is the same wherever you go. There death is in full view, but everywhere it is just as close to us."

Dispel these shades for me, and you will find it easier to teach me the lessons I have been preparing myself to learn. Nature created us susceptible of instruction; it endowed us with reason, which, though imperfect, can yet be perfected. **12** Lecture to me on justice, on devotion, on frugality, on modesty—both kinds of modesty, the kind that keeps back from another person's body and the kind that takes care of one's own. Just don't sidetrack me, and I will get where I'm going much more easily. For as the tragic poet* says,

Straightforward is the speech of truth—

—and that is why we ought not to complicate things. Those are just verbal traps. Nothing could be less suitable for minds of great endeavor.

Farewell.

## Letter 50

*From Seneca to Lucilius*
*Greetings*

**1** Because I received your letter many months after you sent it, I did not think it worth my while to ask the bearer how you were doing. He would need a good memory to tell me that! But I hope that you are now living in such a way that I know how you are doing no matter where you are. What other endeavor do you have than to make yourself a better person each day—to lay aside some error, to come to understand that what you think are flaws in your situation are in fact flaws in yourself?

For we sometimes blame times and places for faults that in fact will travel with us wherever we go. **2** You know that my wife has a fool, Harpaste, who has long remained in my household as an inherited dependent. (I myself have a great aversion to these persons kept for show. If I ever want to be amused by a fool, I do not have to look far—I laugh at myself.) This woman, then, the fool, has suddenly lost her sight. It is scarcely credible what I am telling you, and yet it is true: she does not know she is blind, but asks her attendant over and over for a change of apartments, saying that her quarters are not well lit. **3** You should be well aware that what we laugh about in her case happens to every one of us. No one realizes he is grasping or avaricious. The blind at least request a guide; we wander about without one, and say, "It's not that I am ambitious; this is just how one has to live at Rome. It's not that I overspend; it's just that city living demands certain expenditures. It's not my fault that I am prone to anger, that I do not yet have any settled plan of life—this is just what a young person does." **4** Why do we deceive ourselves? Our trouble is not external to us: it is within, right down in the vital organs. The reason it is so difficult for us to be restored to health is that we do not realize we are sick. Our infirmities are very numerous, and very grave. Even when we do begin the healing process, how long might it take to rid ourselves of them? And as yet we are not even looking for a doctor!

Nor is the condition to be treated of recent onset. If it were, the matter would be relatively simple. The doctor would show the right way; and our minds, still young and impressionable, would follow. **5** If it is difficult to guide us back into our natural path, it is only because we have deserted it. We blush to learn excellence of mind. But for heaven's sake, is there any shame° in seeking instruction in so great a good? For there is no hope of the alternative—that it should arise in us by chance. One has to work at it! But the work is not hard, provided we start in time, as I said, and begin to shape and straighten the mind before its perversities become ingrained.*

**6** Yet I do not despair even when they are ingrained. Sustained, concentrated effort can overcome any resistance. Oaken beams can be straightened, no matter how warped they are; crooked tree trunks are unbent by heat, and altered from their native form to whatever shape we require. How much easier is it for the mind, a thing suppler and more yielding than any liquid, to assume a new form? For what else is the mind but breath disposed in a certain way?* And you see that breath, being lighter than any other material, is by the same token more adaptable.

7 It is true that we are now inhabited by vice, and have been so for a long time; but this does not mean, dear Lucilius, that you should give up hope. No one acquires an excellent mind without first having a bad one. All of us have been taken over already, and to learn virtue is to unlearn one's faults. 8 Yet we may be of good cheer as we tackle the job of self-correction; for once we do come into possession of the good, it is ours forever. One does not unlearn virtue.* For contrary properties, those that are where they do not belong, remain unsettled and thus can be dislodged and cast away, but whatever comes into its proper place abides steadfastly there. Virtue is in accordance with our nature; faults are inimical to it.*

9 But even as virtues once attained cannot depart from us and keeping them is easy, so also it is arduous to begin attaining them. For it is characteristic of a mind that is weak and ill to fear what it has not yet experienced, so that it has to be forced to make a start. After that, the medicine is not bitter; indeed, it gives delight even as it effects the cure.* With other sorts of treatments, pleasure comes after healing; philosophy, though, is at one and the same time both curative and sweet.

Farewell.

## Letter 51

*From Seneca to Lucilius*
*Greetings*

1 We make do with what we have, dear Lucilius. You have Etna there, tallest and° noblest mountain in Sicily—though why Messala calls it "unique," I cannot discover. Or was it Valgius? I have read it in both.*

Many places belch forth fire, and not only high places—though that happens more often, no doubt because fire tends upward—but level places too. And I content myself as best I can with Baiae.* Which I have now left, a day after arriving! Despite certain natural advantages, it is a place to avoid, and here's why: self-indulgence has adopted it as a party town.

**2** "What are you saying? Is there any place to which we should declare ourselves averse?" No, but just as some garments are more suitable than others for the wise and good man; just as he may not have an aversion to any one color but still regards some as less appropriate to a person who has expressed a commitment to frugality, so also there are places the man of wisdom, or the one making progress toward wisdom, will avoid as ill-adapted to excellence of character.

**3** Thus a person considering a retreat will never choose Canopus for it, although Canopus does not prevent one from living simply.* Neither will he choose Baiae: it has become a hostelry of vices. Self-indulgence allows itself more license there; it lets itself go there, as if by some privilege of the place.

**4** We should choose a healthful environment not only for our bodies but for our character as well. Just as I wouldn't want to live among torturers, so I wouldn't want to live among taverns. Why do I need to see drunks weaving their way along the beach, boatmen's revelries, lagoons echoing with band music, and all the other things that unrestricted self-indulgence not only commits but publicizes?

**5** We should endeavor to put as much distance as we can between ourselves and any incitements to vice; we should toughen our minds and keep them far away from the allures of pleasure. Hannibal was unstrung by a single winter there: the man whom the Alpine snows could not defeat was turned to jelly by the steam baths of Campania.* Though victor in arms, he was vanquished by vice. **6** We too must be soldiers on campaign, indeed on the kind of campaign that allows no rest, no leisure. Especially, we must take on the conquest of pleasures, which as you see have sometimes captivated even the most warlike temperaments. If we consider the magnitude of our undertaking, we will realize that fashionable dissipation cannot be our way. What are heated baths to me? What are saunas, those rooms full of steam just to drain the body of vigor? Let all our sweating be from work. **7** If we were to do what Hannibal did, interrupting our affairs, forgetting our war so as to put our efforts into coddling our bodies, everyone would reproach us, and rightly, for such ill-timed laziness. It would be dangerous even for a victor, let alone for one who is still on the way to victory. Less is allowed to us than to the warriors of Carthage: for us the danger is greater if we succumb; the effort is greater even if we persevere.

**8** Fortune is at war with me, yet I will not do its bidding; I will not bear its yoke. Indeed, I will do what takes even more courage: I will shake off that yoke. It will not do for my mind to be enfeebled. If I yield to pleasure, I must yield to pain, to toil, to poverty. Ambition will insist on the same rights over me, and so also will anger. With so many passions, I shall be pulled in one direction and another; indeed, I shall be torn to bits.

**9** Freedom is set before us; that is the prize we are working for. Do you ask what freedom is? It is this: not being a slave to anything—not to compulsion, not to chance events—making fortune meet us on a level field! The day I find fortune's power is too much for me is the day that power is annulled.* Why should I put up with fortune, when death is ready to hand?

**10** One who is serious about such reflections should choose settings that are conducive to sobriety and clean living. Too much comfort makes the spirit unmanly, and even mere location undoubtedly has some power to ruin one's strength. Draft animals whose hooves have been toughened by hard ground can travel on any road; those that have been fattened in soft meadows quickly go lame. The soldier who has been posted in steep places becomes ever stronger; the urbanite is a lazy fellow. Hands that go directly from plow handle to sword hilt can handle any kind of work, while those that gleam from manicure and massage give up the minute they have to get dirty.

**11** The harsher discipline of some places strengthens one's spirit and renders it fit for great endeavors. Scipio's exile was more honorable at Liternum than it would have been at Baiae: so great a fall should not have so soft a landing.* True, Gaius Marius, Gnaeus Pompey, and Caesar, those leaders on whom fortune bestowed the full resources of the Roman people, also built villas near Baiae, but they situated them on the tops of hills, feeling that as generals it would be more to their purpose to have a vantage point from which to view all the regions below. Just look at the sites they chose, and at the kinds of structures they built, and you will see: they are not villas but strongholds.

**12** Do you think Marcus Cato* would ever have lived there? Why? To count the adulterous ladies sailing by, the many kinds of pleasure boats painted in different colors, the roses floating all over the lagoon? To hear the musicians' nightly racket? Would he not have preferred to remain within some trench works dug by his own hand for a single night's use? What real man would not choose a bugler, rather than a symphony, to interrupt his slumbers?

**13** Well, that's enough of my quarrel with Baiae, though I can never quarrel long enough with the vices. Persecute those, I beg you, Lucilius, without limit and without end, for they themselves are limitless and endless. Cast out every fault that lacerates your heart. If you could not do so any other way, you should pluck out your heart itself with the faults attached. Most of all, banish pleasures; make them your worst enemies. They are like those robbers whom the Egyptians call "the Sweethearts": they embrace us just to throttle us.*

Farewell.

## Letter 52

*From Seneca to Lucilius*
*Greetings*

**1** What is it, Lucilius, that pulls us in the opposite direction from where we aim to go—that forces us back toward the very place we want to get away from? What is it that wrestles with our minds and doesn't allow us to want anything once and for all? We vacillate between different plans; there is nothing we want freely and unconditionally and for always. **2** "To make no determination," you say, "to have no lasting preference—that is folly." But how are we to tear ourselves away from that folly? And when? No one is strong enough to swim on his own to safety: someone has to extend a hand; someone has to give a pull.

**3** Epicurus says there are some who have escaped toward truth without assistance from anyone, forging their own path. His highest praise is reserved for these, whose impetus and advancement come from within. Others, he says, require aid from someone else: they would not get there if no one went before them, but they are good followers. Metrodorus, he says, is one of the latter sort—and that too is a fine intellect, but of the second tier.* We too are not of the first-rank distinction; we do well to be admitted to the second. And it's not as though you should look down on a person who is able to get to safety through the good graces of another. The willingness to be saved is very important as well.

4 Besides these you will find yet another kind of person, and these too are not to be despised: people who can be driven and compelled toward the right thing, who need not only a leader but a helper and, as it were, a drill sergeant. This is the third stripe. Would you like an example here as well? Epicurus says Hermarchus was such a person. For that reason, he has greater congratulations for the one, but more admiration for the other.* For although both arrived at the same destination, it is more praiseworthy to have achieved the same result with more difficult material.

5 Suppose two buildings have been erected that are both alike, equally tall and equally magnificent. For one,° the building site was on firm ground; the work there went on apace. The other's foundations were unstable because of loose, shifting soil, which required much work before it could be solidified. What one builder did <is in plain sight>;° for the other, the greater and more difficult part of his labor is hidden from the observer. 6 Some minds are easy and unencumbered in the making; others are "a labor of hands," as they say, and must busy themselves with their foundations. I would say, therefore, that although the person who has no difficulty with himself is indeed more fortunate, the more deserving on his own account is the one who has overcome the shortcomings of his own nature, not just making his way toward wisdom but actually dragging himself there.

7 Such a hard, unyielding intellect is ours to work on: you may as well recognize that fact. There are obstacles in our way. So let's put up a fight—and let's call in some reinforcements.

"Whom shall I call?" you ask. "This person here? That one there?" Really you should go back to our predecessors as well. They are not busy. It's not only the living who can assist us, but those who have passed away as well.

**8** Among the living, though, let's not choose those who spout a great onrush of words, spinning out all the clichés and talking for the crowd even when they are at home. Instead, let's call in those who teach by their manner of living. After saying what one ought to do, they prove it by doing so themselves; when they say one ought to avoid something, you don't catch them doing that same thing later on. Choose as your helper someone you admire more when you see him than when you listen to him.

**9** This is not to say that you should avoid those who customarily lecture before an audience. I don't forbid your listening to them as well, provided that they go amid the crowd not for the sake of ambition but only with the intention of improving both their hearers and themselves. For nothing could be more shameful than philosophy that hungers for applause. Does the patient praise the physician that operates on him?

> **10** Be still, then, all of you, and submit to your treatment in silence.* Even if you do cry out, I will listen to you only as to those who moan when touched on a sore spot. Do you want to give some indication that you are paying attention and are stirred by the greatness of the subject matter? You may do that, of course. Why shouldn't I allow it, as long you are registering an opinion in support of someone better than yourself?

Pythagoras's pupils were required to keep silence for five years. Surely you don't think, then, that when the privilege of speech was granted, that of uttering praise was given immediately as well? **11** But it is quite insane to go from the auditorium thrilled by the cheering of the uneducated. Why are you glad to be praised by people you are not able to praise in return? Fabianus used to lecture to an audience, but they listened to him with restraint.* Exclamations of praise did burst forth from them at times, but these were elicited by the subject matter, not by the mere sound of some fancy rhetorical polish. **12** Let there be a difference between the applause in a theater and applause in a lecture hall. There is such a thing as elegance even in giving praise.

All things are signs of everything else, if one pays heed to them. One can glean evidence of character from the most minute observations. The unchaste person is betrayed by his walk, his gesture, sometimes even a single reply—a finger touching the scalp—a roll of the eyes.* The immoral one is revealed by a laugh; the insane by his expression and bearing. All these things are open to view just by reading the signs. You can find out what sort of person each man is if you note how he praises others and how he himself is praised. **13** Listeners on every side are stretching out their hands toward the philosopher; a crowd of admirers clusters right in his face: you understand what is going on. That is no longer praise; it is only applause. All such fanfare should be left to those arts which make it their business to please the public; let philosophy be greeted with reverence.

**14** We will have to allow the young to yield to their impulsive minds—but only when they are indeed acting on impulse, when they cannot bid themselves be silent. Such praise conveys a kind of exhortation to the hearers themselves; it acts as a spur to the youthful spirit. But let them be stirred by the subject, not by affected phraseology. Otherwise eloquence is harmful to them, making them eager for itself rather than for its subject matter.

**15** I shall postpone further discussion of this, for it requires a lengthy treatment of its own: how one should lecture to the people, how much leeway to give yourself in their presence and how much to them in yours. There can be no doubt that philosophy has lost something by making a public spectacle of itself. Yet it is possible to lay open even its inner sanctum. For that, though, its representative must be a priest, not a huckster.

Farewell.

# BOOK SIX

# Letter 53

*From Seneca to Lucilius*
*Greetings*

1 What can I not be talked into? This time I was persuaded to take a trip by boat! The sea was calm when I set out. To be sure, the sky was heavy with mottled clouds, the kind that usually resolve themselves into rain or squalls; but I thought the mileage was so short from your town of Parthenope to Puteoli that I could get away with making the trip, even in uncertain and threatening weather.* So I tried to get done with it quickly by heading through the deep water directly toward the isle of Nesis, intending a shortcut past all the inlets.

2 The moment I got to where it made no difference whether I went on or turned back, the calm surface that had enticed me was no more. It was not yet a storm but sloping seas, with the waves ever more frequent. I began asking the helmsman to let me off somewhere on shore; he said, though, that the coastline was rugged and without anchorage, and that in a storm the land was the very thing he feared the most. 3 But I was in too bad a way to have any use for danger. I had that persistent seasickness that brings on nausea but does not relieve it by vomiting. So I forced the issue with the helmsman and required him to head for shore whether he wanted to or not.

As we drew near I did not wait for any of the instructions in Virgil to be carried out, for them to "turn the bow seaward" or "cast the anchor from the bow."* Remembering my abilities (for I have long been a swimmer), I threw myself into the sea as a cold-water enthusiast should, wearing my mantle. 4 Just imagine how I suffered as I staggered forward through the breakers, seeking a way, forcing a way. I understood then that sailors have reason to fear the land. It is unbelievable how much I endured just because I could not endure myself! Let me tell you, the reason Ulysses had shipwrecks everywhere was not so much that he was born to an angry sea; no, he was just prone to seasickness. I too will take twenty years to get wherever I am going if I have to get there by ship!

**5** As soon as I had settled my stomach—for you know it takes longer to escape from seasickness than from the sea—and as soon as I had applied some oil to refresh my body, I began to reflect on how easily we forget our imperfections. We forget even our obvious bodily defects, which give us constant reminders; but still more do we forget those that do not show on the outside—and the worse they are, the less we can see them. **6** A slight fever can deceive a person, but when it increases and becomes a genuine illness, even the toughest and most enduring are forced to admit it. There's pain in the feet, a prickling sensation in the joints; we pretend it isn't there, saying we've twisted an ankle or worn ourselves out by some exertion. As long as there is doubt, as long as the disease is in its early stages, we invent some specious name for it; but when it begins to cramp up the lower leg and cause distortion in both feet, we have no choice but to admit that it is arthritis. **7** It is the opposite with those infirmities that affect the mind.* With these, the worse one is afflicted, the less he is aware of it. There's nothing surprising in that, dear Lucilius. When one is just barely asleep, one has impressions in accordance with that state of rest and is sometimes even conscious of being asleep; deep sleep, though, blots out even our dreams, drowning the mind so deep that it has no awareness of itself at all. **8** Why do people not admit their faults? Because they are still in the midst of them. Dreams are told by those who are awake; admitting to one's faults is a sign of health.

Let us wake up, then, so that we will be able to recognize our mistakes. But philosophy is the only thing that will awaken us; the only thing that will rouse us from our deep sleep. Devote yourself entirely to philosophy. You are worthy of it, and it of you: embrace one another. Refuse every other claim on you, boldly and openly: there is no reason you need to do philosophy only in your spare time. **9** If you were ill, you would take a break from your responsibilities at home. Your career concerns would drop away; no one's defense case would be so important to you that you would go back down to the Forum while still anticipating a relapse. All your efforts would be devoted to freeing yourself from disease as soon as possible. What about it, then? Will you not do the same thing now? Get rid of everything that stands in your way; make time for excellence of mind. No one gets there while occupied with business.

Philosophy asserts its power. It grants us time; it does not merely accept what we give to it. Philosophy is a full-time job, not a hobby; it is our supervisor, and orders us to appear.° **10** Alexander once said to a town that promised him part of its arable land and half of all its production, "My purpose in coming to Asia was not to receive any gifts you might give, but to allow you to keep anything that I might leave."* Philosophy says the same thing, but in every situation. "I am not going to accept just the time you have left over; rather, you will have what I reject."

**11** Turn your entire mind to philosophy. Sit by philosophy and serve it, and you will be much above other people. Mortals will all be far behind you, and the gods not far ahead. Would you like to know what difference there will be between you and the gods? They will have a longer time of existence. But to encompass a complete whole in a miniature work of art—that is indeed the sign of a great craftsman. For the wise, a lifetime is as spacious as all of time is for God.* Indeed, there is a way the sage surpasses God. It is by gift of nature that God is without fear; the sage gives that same gift to himself. **12** Here indeed is a great achievement: to retain our human weakness and yet have the tranquility of God.

It is amazing what power there is in philosophy to beat back all the assaults of chance. No weapon lodges in its flesh; its defenses cannot be penetrated. When fortune's darts come in, it either ducks and lets them pass by, or stands its ground and lets them bounce back against the assailant.

Farewell.

## Letter 54

*From Seneca to Lucilius*
*Greetings*

**1** Ill health had given me a long respite; then suddenly it assailed me again. "What was the trouble?" you ask—and well you may, for there is no illness with which I am unacquainted. But there is one that has me in its charge, so to speak. Why should I use its Greek name?* I can call it wheezing; that fits well enough.

Its attack is quite brief, like a squall; it is usually over within the hour. No one can be at last gasp for very long! **2** Every bodily discomfort, every peril, has passed through me; and nothing, I think, is harder to bear. How could it not be? Anything else is just being sick; this is pushing out one's life breath. For this reason doctors call it "the rehearsal for death": the constriction sometimes achieves what it has so often attempted. **3** Do you think that I am glad to be writing these things to you, glad that I escaped? If I delight in this cessation as if it were a return to health, I am as laughable as the person who thinks he has won his case just because his hearing has been postponed.

Yet even as I was suffocating, I did not fail to find peace in cheerful and brave reflections. **4** "What is this?" said I. "Does death make trial of me so many times? Let it—I have made trial of it as well,° long ago. "When?" you ask. Before I was born. Death is just nonexistence. I know already what that is like: what will exist after me is the same as existed before me.* If there is any torment in this thing, then there must have been torment also before we saw the light of day. Yet we did not feel any discomfort at that time.

**5** I ask you this: wouldn't you say a person was quite stupid if he thought that a lamp was worse off after it was extinguished than before it was lighted? We too are extinguished; we too are lighted. Betweentimes there is something that we feel; on either side is complete lack of concern. Unless I am wrong, dear Lucilius, our mistake is that we think death comes after; in fact, it comes both before and after. Whatever was before us is death. What difference is there between ending and simply not beginning? Both have the same result: nonexistence.

**6** With these encouragements, and others in the same vein, I did not cease to encourage myself—without speaking, of course, since I had no breath to spare. Then, gradually, my wheezing, which had already given way to panting, began to come at greater intervals, then slowed and finally steadied. Even yet, though the attack is over, my breathing does not come naturally; I feel a kind of catch in it, a hesitation.

So be it, as long as I am not sighing on purpose! **7** Here is my pledge to you: I shall not tremble at the end; I am already prepared; I am not thinking at all about my overall span of life. The person you should praise—and imitate—is the one who enjoys living and yet is not reluctant to die. For what virtue is there in departing only when you are cast out? Yet there is virtue here too: I am indeed being cast out, and yet it is as if I am making my departure.

For that reason, the wise person too is never cast out, for being cast out is being driven away from a place you are unwilling to leave. The sage does nothing unwillingly: he escapes necessity in that he wishes to do what necessity will in any case require.

Farewell.

## Letter 55

1 I have just now come from a ride in a sedan chair, and I am as tired as if I had walked for just as long as I have been sitting. Even being carried for a long time is work, perhaps even harder work, since it is contrary to nature, which gave us feet so that we could walk for ourselves and eyes so that we could see for ourselves. Soft living punishes us with weakness: after refusing to do a thing for some time, we cease to be able to do it.

2 But it was really necessary for me to give this body a thorough shaking, to loosen any fluid that might have settled in my windpipe, or, if the problem was that my breathing was constricted for some reason, to allow the jostling to free it up, for I have learned that this does me some good. For this reason I stuck with it longer. The shoreline was beckoning that curves between Cumae and the villa of Servilius Vatia, bounded on one side by the sea and the other by the lake.* It is like a narrow roadway, and besides, it was solid because of a recent storm; for as you know, waves coming hard and fast pack the sand down, while an unusually long period of fair weather loosens it, when the moisture that binds it together drains away.

3 As is my custom, I began to look around to see whether I could find anything there that might be to my advantage. My eyes turned toward the villa that once belonged to Vatia. There he grew old, that wealthy ex-praetor, famous for nothing but repose, and for that rea-

son alone was considered fortunate. For every time someone went under, condemned by friendly relations with Asinius Gallus or by the hatred of Sejanus—or later by his love, since having been friends with Sejanus became as dangerous as having offended him—then people would exclaim, "O Vatia, you alone know how to live!"* 4 But what he knew was how to hide, not how to live. It matters a great deal whether your life is leisurely or cowardly. Never did I pass this villa during Vatia's lifetime without saying, "Here lies Vatia."

And yet, dear Lucilius, philosophy is so sacred, so deserving of respect, that anything that resembles it gives some satisfaction, even if it is only a sham. When a person is devoted to leisure, ordinary people tend to assume that he is on retreat, tranquil, self-sufficient, living for himself, when in fact these qualities pertain only to the wise person. He alone is the one who knows how to live for himself; for he knows how to live, and that has to come first. 5 Someone who runs away from the world and from people; who has gone into exile because his desires failed to prosper, and because he could not bear to see others more prosperous than he; who has gone to earth out of fear, like some idle and timorous animal—that person is living not for himself but (most shameful of all!) for the belly, for sleep, for lust. It does not follow that he is living for himself just because he is living for no one at all. Yet such a fine thing is consistency in action and perseverance in one's intent that even idleness is respected if one persists in it.

6 As for the villa itself, I can write nothing definite to you about it. I know only the façade and the other parts that are on display to passersby. There are two grottoes, handmade at great labor, as big as anyone's extended atrium. One admits no sunshine at all; in the other, the light lingers even until sunset. There is a grove of plane trees, through which a canal flows between Lake Acheron and the sea, like the Euripus.* It could provide a steady supply of fish even if drawn on regularly; however, it is not used when the sea is accessible: when a storm gives the sea fishermen a holiday, then it is ready to hand.

7 However, the big advantage of the villa is that it has the resort of Baiae right next door. It is free of the inconveniences of that town, yet partakes of its pleasures. Even I recognize that these are points in its favor. I think too that it is usable year round, for it catches the west wind; indeed, it blocks Baiae from catching it. Vatia was no fool to have chosen this site for the idle hours of his retirement.

**8** But location does not really contribute much to tranquility. What matters is a mind that accommodates all things to itself. I have seen people who are downcast in a pleasant, cheerful villa, and people in complete isolation who appear quite busy. Therefore you need not think yourself less well situated just because you are not in Campania. Still, why not be here? Turn your thoughts this way always. **9** One may converse with friends in their absence; in fact, you can do so as often as you wish, and for as long as you like. This pleasure—and a great pleasure it is—is something we actually enjoy more when we are apart. For we become spoiled by each other's presence: because we sometimes speak together, walk together, sit together, when we do separate we cease to think at all about those we have just seen.

**10** And here is another reason we should bear our separation calmly: everyone is much apart even from those who are close at hand. Think: first of all, they are separated at night; second, each has his different occupation; then there are periods of secluded study and excursions into the surrounding area. If you add these up, you will see that there is not much for long distance to take away from us. **11** One has to hold on to one's friend mentally, for the mind is never absent, and sees anyone it wants to every single day. So study with me! Dine with me! Walk with me! Nothing can be prohibited from our thoughts: if it could, then our lives would be cloistered indeed. I see you, dear Lucilius; I hear you, as much as ever. I am so much with you that I am on the verge of sending you notes of hand* rather than letters.

Farewell.

## Letter 56

*From Seneca to Lucilius*
*Greetings*

**1** I swear it—silence is not as necessary to a scholarly retreat as you might think. Here is cacophony sounding all about me—for I am living right upstairs from the bathhouse.*

Call to mind every sort of awful noise that grates on the ears.

When the stronger men do their exercises, swinging their hand weights about and straining with the effort (or pretending to), I hear the grunts each time they exhale, their rasping and gasping for breath. When I get some idle fellow who's happy with an ordinary man's massage, I hear the hands slapping his shoulders and the change of sound when they strike with the cupped hand or with the palm. Then if a ballplayer shows up and starts counting how many he catches, I'm done for! **2** Now add the quarrelsome type—and the one caught stealing—and the one who likes to hear himself sing in the bath chamber—and also the ones who jump into the swimming pool with a great splash. Besides all these, who are at least using their normal voices, imagine the tweezer man screeching over and over in his shrill falsetto, just to attract attention: he is never silent unless he is plucking someone's armpits and making him cry out instead. Now add the cries of the drink man, the sausage man, the bakery man, and all the different sellers of cooked foods, singing out their wares in their distinctive tones.

**3** "You must be made of steel," you say, "or deaf, to retain your concentration amid so many varied and discordant sounds! Why, our own Crispus° was driven to the point of death merely by a constant stream of visitors!"* Yet for me, in truth, the racket is of no more concern than waves or falling water. I've heard, though, of a race of people who relocated their city solely because they could not stand the tumult of one of the cataracts of the Nile.

**4** I think a voice is more distracting than any din; for the one engages our mental faculties, the other merely fills the ears with its reverberations. Among the noises that sound around me but do not distract me, I count passing carriages, a carpenter somewhere in the building, a nearby saw grinder, and that fellow who demonstrates flutes and trumpets near the Meta Sudans, not so much playing them as bellowing.* **5** Even now I find noises that recur at intervals more bothersome than a continuous drone. But I have inured myself to all such sounds to such an extent that I could even put up with hearing that horribly shrill cry that a coxswain uses to give the beat to his rowers. You see, I force my mind to pay attention to itself and not to be distracted by anything external. It does not matter what is making a noise outside, so long as there is no turmoil inside—as long as there is no wrangling between desire and fear, as long as greed is not at odds with self-indulgence, one carping at the other.

For how does it help to have silence in the neighborhood, when one's emotions are in tumult?

**6** All things were settled in night's restful calm.*

It's a lie: there is no restful calm but that which is settled by reason. Night doesn't take away our cares; rather, it exposes them to view, exchanging one anxiety for another. For even when we are asleep, our dreams may be as tumultuous as waking life. Only as the mind develops into excellence do we achieve any real tranquility.

**7** Look at a person who yearns for sleep in the quiet of a household laid to rest. Not one sound assails his ears: all his mob of slaves is hushed; they creep on tiptoe past his room. Yet all the same, he rolls to one side and the other, dozing fitfully amid his sorrows, and complains of sounds he did not really hear. **8** What do you suppose is the reason? His mind is noisy: he must put that to rest, must quell its insurrection. You need not think the mind is at rest just because the body is lying still. Sometimes quiet is itself unquiet. So when we are oppressed with idleness, let us rouse ourselves to action or busy ourselves with cultural pursuits. For idleness has no patience with itself. **9** Great generals, when they see the troops grow restive, assign them some labor and fill their time with marches: if they are kept busy, they find no leisure for insubordination. And nothing is more certain than that the faults of inactivity are dispelled by activity.

Many a time our weariness with affairs of state and second thoughts about an unrewarding and thankless job have induced us to go into retreat. Or so we thought; and yet, within that den where tiredness and fear have driven us, ambition all the while is festering anew. It has not been cut away; it has not ceased to trouble us; it was only fatigued or indeed only vexed that things did not go its way. **10** Of self-indulgence I say the same. It seems at times to be in remission; then, when we are pledged to modest living, it harries us again, and in the midst of our economy goes after pleasures we had not in fact renounced but only abandoned. And it pursues them all the more energetically the more they are kept under cover. For all our failings are milder in the open. Even the infirmities make the turn toward healing once they emerge from hiding and exhibit their full force.* Thus when greed, ambition, and other maladies of the human mind subside into apparent health, that is when you can tell they are at their deadliest.

**11** We seem to be at leisure, but we aren't. For if we truly are—if we have really sounded the retreat—if we have turned our back on things that merely glitter, then, as I was saying, nothing will distract us. No chatter of men, no song of birds will interrupt our thoughts— excellent thoughts, and now sure and solid too. **12** It is a lightweight mind and one not yet devoted to introspection that stirs at a voice or at chance occurrences. It has within some anxiety, some element of panic, that makes it uneasy. Our poet Virgil says,

> And I, who long endured the hurtling darts
> unmoved, the Achaeans massed in threatening ranks,
> now fear the wind, now start at every sound,
> trembling alike for my companion and my load.*

**13** The earlier case is that of the wise person, who is not alarmed by the hurtling arrows, the ranks of armed men in close formation, the clamor of a city under siege; the latter is the one without experience, who fears for his own affairs and trembles every time he hears a thump. Every voice seems to him a menacing roar; the slightest movement throws him into a panic. His baggage makes him fearful. **14** Choose any one of those prosperous persons, those who have much to carry and much in their train, and you will see him "trembling alike for his companion and his load."

Therefore you may be sure that your mind is settled only when no outcry reaches you, when no voice distracts you from yourself, whether with blandishments or with threats or just with meaningless noise.

**15** "What is it you're saying, then? Isn't it easier sometimes to be away from the racket?"

Yes, I grant that, and that's why I'm going to leave this place. I wanted to test myself, give myself a workout. But why should I be tormented any longer, when Ulysses found his companions such an easy solution?* That was effective even against the Sirens!

Farewell.

# Letter 57

*From Seneca to Lucilius*
*Greetings*

1 When I had to leave Baiae and head back to Naples, I did not attempt to go again by boat.* They said there was a storm, and I was
easy to convince! But there was so much mud all along the road
that you might think I had floated my way there after all. That day
I had the whole of the athletic regimen to put up with, for we went
right from the mud into the dust of the Naples tunnel.* 2 Nothing
is longer than that dungeon, nothing gloomier than those torches,
which only enabled us to see the darkness, not to see through it. Even
if there were any light in that place, the dust would have blocked it
out. Dust is a terrible annoyance even out in the open; what do you
suppose it was like there, where it billows up onto itself and, enclosed
in a space with no exchange of air, sinks back on those who stir it up?
Thus we endured two contrary discomforts at once: on the same road,
the same day, we struggled both with mud and with dust.

3 Still, the darkness did give me something to think about. For I
felt a kind of impact on my mind and, though without fear, a change,
brought about by the newness and unpleasantness of the unfamiliar
circumstance. And now I am not speaking about myself—for I am
far from being even a tolerable human being, let alone a perfect
one—but about that person over whom fortune no longer holds sway.
His mind too will be struck; his color will change.* 4 For there are
some things, dear Lucilius, that no virtue can escape: nature gives the
virtuous person a reminder of his own mortality. So he will change
expression at sad events, and shudder at sudden events, and grow
dizzy when looking down from a great height. This is not fear but
a natural reaction which cannot be assailed by reason. 5 Thus some
who are brave and very ready to shed their own blood cannot look
at that of others; some grow faint when handling and inspecting a
fresh wound, others at an old and infected wound; and there are yet
others who can bear the stroke of a sword more easily than the sight
of one. 6 What I felt, then, was, as I said, not an emotion but only

a change. As soon as I got back to the light of day, my cheerfulness returned without thought or bidding from me.

Then I began the old conversation with myself, about how foolish we are to fear some things more and some less, when all of them have the same ending. What difference does it make whether a person is crushed under a falling balcony* or under a rockslide? You'll find there is none. Yet some people fear the rockslide more, though both are equally fatal. For fear looks to the cause rather than the effect.

7 You think I am talking about the Stoics, who hold that the soul of one who is crushed by a great weight cannot persist through that event and, since it has no immediate egress, is scattered in an instant. But that's not what I am doing. In fact, I think those who say this are mistaken.* 8 Just as a flame cannot be crushed (for it escapes around whatever presses upon it) and just as air is not harmed by the punch of a fist or the crack of a whip, nor is it even split up, but merely swirls around whatever stirs it, so the mind, being made up of a very rarefied material, cannot be caught or broken up within the body, but owing to its fine texture passes through the very things that press upon it. As lightning strikes and flashes over a wide area yet finds its way back through a tiny opening, so the mind, which is even more thin-textured than fire, can escape through each and every body.*

9 Hence we should make some inquiry as to whether the mind can be immortal.* But of this, at least, you may be sure: if it does survive the body, it cannot by any means be crushed. For there is no sort of immortality that admits of exceptions, and there is nothing that can harm what is eternal.

Farewell.

## Letter 58

*From Seneca to Lucilius*
*Greetings*

1 The great poverty, indeed the destitution, of our language has never been more evident to me than it was today. We happened to be talking about Plato, and a thousand things came up for which we needed

a word but could not find one.* For some of them, in fact, a word did exist at one time but had been lost because of the fastidious standards we now uphold.

Destitute, and yet fastidious! It is intolerable. **2** What the Greeks call an *oestrus*—the stinging fly that drives herds pell-mell, scattering them all over the mountainside—used to be called in our language *asilus*. You may have Virgil for your authority on that:

> There is a fly, frequent in Alburnus
> and in the green oak grove near Silaris;
> *asilus* is its Roman name; the word in Greek
> is *oestrus*. Fierce it is, its high-pitched whine
> scatters the panicked herd all through the woods.*

**3** I believe one can conclude that the former term is no longer in use. But let me keep this brief. Some words that now have prefixes were at one time used without them. For instance, people used to say "termining with the sword" rather than "determining with the sword." Again, Virgil will demonstrate this to you:

> Tall men, born in all corners of the earth,
> meeting amongst themselves and termining with the sword.*

Nowadays the use of that word without a prefix has been lost. **4** The ancients used to say "if I order" for "if I will have ordered."* You need not believe me on that! Believe Virgil:

> The other troop should join with me to march
> wherever I order.

**5** My point in all this pedantry is not to show how much time I have wasted among literary scholars but to make clear to you how much of the vocabulary of Ennius and Accius has fallen into disuse, since even in Virgil, whom people read thoroughly every day, there are some terms that have been lost to us.*

**6** "What is the purpose of these preliminaries?" you ask. "What is your objective?" I won't conceal it from you. I want, if possible, to make your ears receptive to the word *essentia*—and I'll say it in any case, even if it offends your ears! I have Cicero as my guarantor for the term; his resources surely are ample. If you are looking for someone more recent, I can give you Fabianus, an author of great facility and elegance, whose speech was pure enough even for our current standards.*

What else can I do, dear Lucilius? How will I render *ousia*? For that is a necessary item: nature that comprises the basis of all things.* So I am asking your permission to use this word. Still, I will try to be as economical as I can in using the privilege you have granted. It may be that I will content myself with being allowed to use it.

7 You indulge me, but what's the use? There's no way I can express in Latin the concept that induced me to take our language to task. You will object to our Roman limitations even more than I do when you learn that the word I am incapable of rendering is just one syllable. Would you like to know what it is? It's *to on*.* You're thinking that I'm not very bright, and that a possible translation is right under my nose; namely, *quod est*, "that which is." But on my view, "that which is" differs considerably from *to on*. I am forced to use a verb in place of a noun; but if I must, I'll write "that which is."

8 Our friend, who is a very learned person, was saying today that *to on* is used by Plato in six ways.* I will explain all of them; first, though, I must state that there is such a thing as a genus and also a species. Now, at present we are looking for that primary genus on which all the remaining species depend, from which arises every division, and in which all things are included. We will find it if we take things one at a time and work backward, for in this way we will be led back to what is primary. 9 "Human being" is a species, as Aristotle says; "horse" is a species; "dog" is a species. Therefore we must look for some shared feature that is the link between all of them—something that encompasses them and has them subordinate to itself. What is that? It is "animate creature." Thus there begins to be a genus of all those items I just listed: "human being," "horse," "dog"—namely, "animate creature."

10 But some things have life° and yet are not animate creatures, for it is generally agreed that *anima*, the animating principle, inheres also in trees and bushes—which is why we say that they both live and die. Hence "living things" will occupy a higher place, since both animate creatures and plants are in this class.

But there are also things that are not living, for instance rocks; thus there will be something prior to living things, namely, "body."

I will divide this genus as follows: all bodies are either living or nonliving.

**11** Yet there is still something higher than "body," for we say that some things are corporeal and some incorporeal.* So what will that genus be from which these things are drawn? It will be the one to which we assigned the not entirely apposite name "that which is." This genus will be divided into species in this way: "that which is" is either corporeal or incorporeal. **12** This, then, is the first and primary genus, the generic genus, if I may call it that; all the others are genera, yes, but specific genera. For example, "human being" is a genus, since it has within itself species that are nations (Greeks, Romans, Parthians) or colors (white, black, yellow); it also has individuals—Cato, Cicero, Lucretius. Thus it counts as a genus in that it contains multiple things, but as a species in that it is subordinate to something else. "That which is," the generic genus, has nothing above it; it is the beginning of things; all others are subordinate to it.

**13** The Stoics want to place above this yet another, still more primary genus. I will say something about that in a moment, but first I want to point out that the genus I already described is rightly given pride of place, since it contains all things. **14** I divide "that which is" into species as follows: corporeal or incorporeal; there is no third species. How do I divide "body"? So as to say that bodies are either living or nonliving. Again, how do I divide "living things"? Like this: some have mind, some only life; or like this: some have the capacity for impulse—they walk and move from one place to another; some are implanted in the ground and are fed through their roots and grow. Again, into what species do I divide animate creatures? They are either mortal or immortal.*

**15** Some of the Stoics hold that the primary genus is the "something." I will include here their reason for holding this view. They say, "There are some things in the world's nature that are and some things that are not; but even the things that are not are included in the world—things that occur to the mind, such as centaurs, giants, and whatever else is devised by fictive thinking and begins to have some image, although it does not have substance."*

**16** Now I return to the topic I promised you: how Plato makes a sixfold division of the things that are.* The first "that which is" is not apprehended by sight or touch or any sense; it is the thinkable. "That which is by genus," for instance the generic human, does not present itself to the eye, but the specific does, such as Cicero and Cato. "Animate creature" is not seen, it is thought; what one sees are its species, horse and dog.

**17** What Plato posits as the second of the things that are is that which exceeds and surpasses all other things; this, he says, is "preeminent being." The word "poet" is used commonly, since this is the name for all who make verses; but among the Greeks, it has by now come to refer only to one: when you hear "poet," you understand "Homer." What is this, then? Obviously it is God, since it is greater and more powerful than everything else.*

**18** The third kind is of things that are said to be in the strict sense; these are innumerable, but are beyond our sight. Do you ask what these are? They are the distinctive accoutrements of Plato; he calls them Ideas (*ideas*).* From them everything we see comes into being, and everything is shaped in accordance with them. They are immortal, unchangeable, incorruptible. **19** As for what an Idea is—or rather, what Plato thinks an Idea is—listen: "An Idea is the eternal model of those things which come naturally into being."* To this definition I will add some interpretation so as to make the subject plainer to you. Suppose I want to make a portrait of you. I have you as a model for the picture: from that model, my mind receives a certain configuration to impart to its work. Hence that which instructs and informs me—your appearance, from which the imitation is derived—is an idea. The world's nature includes countless models of this sort: models of human beings, of the various fishes and trees. All things that must come into being by nature's agency are formed according to these models.

**20** The fourth position will be occupied by the *eidos*, or form.* As for what this *eidos* is, you must pay attention, and blame Plato, not me, for the difficulty of the subject. But without difficulty there is no fineness of distinction. A moment ago, I used the image of a painter. That painter, when he wanted to depict Virgil with his pigments, looked at the man himself. Virgil's appearance, the model for the work that was to be, was the Idea; that which the artist derived from it and imparted to his work is the *eidos*. **21** Do you ask the difference? One is the model, the other is the form derived from the model and imparted to the work. The artist imitates the one but makes the other. A statue has an appearance; this is the *eidos*. The model itself, the one the craftsman looked at when he made the statue, has an appearance; this is the Idea. Still another way of making the distinction, if you feel you need one, is that the *eidos* is in the work, the Idea outside the work, and not only outside the work but prior to the work.

**22** The fifth kind is of those things that exist commonly.* These begin to relate to us. Here are "everything," "people," "farm animals," "things."

The sixth kind is of those things that quasi-exist, like void and like time.

Everything we see or touch is excluded by Plato from those things which on his view "are" in the strict sense. For they are in flux and are constantly decreasing and increasing. Not one of us is the same in old age as he was in youth; not one of us is the same in the morning as he was the day before. Our bodies are carried away like rushing streams. Anything you see is passing as time passes; not one of the things we see stays put. I myself, even as I tell you of these changes, have changed.

**23** This is what Heraclitus means when he says, "We step into the same river twice and not at all."* The name of the river remains the same; the water has passed on. This is more evident in a river than in a human being; but a current sweeps us along as well, and it is no less swift. For that reason I am amazed that we are so far out of our minds as to love a thing that is so fleeting—the body—and that we are afraid ever to die, when every moment is the death of our previous condition. Why be afraid of something happening once when it is happening every day?

**24** I have spoken of how the human being is matter in flux, perishable and subject to every influence. The universe as well, though enduring and undefeated, changes and does not stay the same. For though it contains everything it had before, it contains those things in a different way; it changes their arrangement.

**25** "What have I to gain," you say, "from these fine distinctions of yours?" Nothing, if you ask me. But just as the engraver, tired from a long period of close work, turns his eyes away to rest and, as we say, to "nurture" them, so should we sometimes relax our minds and refresh them with some amusement. Still, even one's amusements should become worthwhile endeavors: if you put your mind to them, you will derive something potentially beneficial.

**26** That's my own custom, dear Lucilius: I take every thought, no matter how far removed from philosophy, and try to extract something from it and turn it to good use. What could be more distant from the reform of character than those matters I explained just now? How can the Platonic Ideas make me a better person? What am I going to get out of them to check my desires? Or is it just this: that all those things that minister to our senses, that entice and arouse us, are not accepted by Plato as things that truly exist? **27** Thus they are figments and present an appearance only for a time. None of them are stable or solid, and yet we desire them as if they were to exist forever, or as if we were to possess them forever.

Weak and fluid ourselves, we stand in the midst of illusions. So let us direct our minds toward things that are eternal. Let us fly upward and gaze in wonder at the forms of all things, and at God, who dwells among them. Since God could not make his created things immortal (for matter prevented it), in his providence he gives us this way to defend against death and through reason to overcome the deficiencies of the body.* **28** For all things last not because they are eternal but because they are defended by the concern of their ruler; if they were immortal, they would not need a guardian. The craftsman preserves them, by his power overcoming the fragility of the material. Let us spurn all those things which are so far from being valuable that it is in doubt whether they exist at all.

**29** At the same time, let us reflect on this: if providence preserves the universe itself from danger, which is just as mortal as we are,* then our own providence can also procure a somewhat longer lifespan for this paltry body of ours, as long as it enables us to govern and control those desires that are usually the cause of death. **30** Plato preserved himself into old age by careful management. True, he was strong of body and blessed with good fortune, and it was his broad chest that gave him his name.* But the perils of seafaring had reduced his strength greatly; still, by frugal living, taking good care of himself and limiting those things that arouse the appetites, he made it to old age despite many obstacles. **31** For I suppose you know that thanks to his careful management, Plato completed eighty-one years of life and died on his birthday, not a day short. For that reason, some

Persian soothsayers who happened to be in Athens made burnt offerings to him after his death, believing that since he had completed the most perfect number (which they get by multiplying nine times nine), his fate was of more than humankind. Well, I expect you would not mind giving up a few days from that total, and the sacrifice as well. **32** But frugal living *can* prolong old age; and although I don't think old age is something to hanker after, it's not to be turned down either. It's pleasant to be with yourself as long as you possibly can— provided you have made yourself worth being with.

So now I will give an opinion on the point you raise, whether it is appropriate to spurn extreme old age, not waiting for the end but making an end by one's own act. It's the next thing to cowardice when one merely waits in idleness for death to come, just as one must be excessively devoted to wine if he drains every drop from the vat and guzzles even the lees. **33** My question, though, is this: is the last part of life really the lees, or is it the finest, purest part? That is, provided the mind is without impairment, the senses intact and of use to the mind, and provided the body is not crippled and moribund before its time. For it matters a great deal whether one is prolonging life or prolonging death. **34** Yet if the body can no longer perform any service, why should it not be appropriate to release the suffering mind?

Perhaps what is called for is even to act a little before you must, lest when the time comes you should be unable. The risk of living in misery is worse than that of dying swiftly—and that being so, it's foolish not to use a small amount of time as coin to buy off a huge gamble. Rarely does a prolonged old age deliver anyone to death without impairment; on the contrary, people are frequently confined to their beds without use of their limbs. Do you think it is any more cruel to lose something of your life than it is to lose the privilege of ending it?

**35** Don't be unwilling to hear me, thinking that this opinion relates immediately to yourself. Assess what I'm saying on its own merits. I will not abandon old age as long as it allows me to keep my whole self—that is, the whole of my better part. But if it begins to attack my mind and lop off parts of it—if it keeps me alive without allowing me a life, then I will fling myself from the decayed and collapsing edifice.* **36** I will not die to escape sickness, provided it is curable and no impediment to the mind. I will not lay hands on myself because of pain: such a death is defeat. But if I know I will have to endure the pain without intermission, I will depart, not because of the pain itself, but because it will hinder me from everything that makes life worth living. He who dies merely because of pain is weak and lazy; he who lives merely for pain is a fool.

**37** But I am carrying on at length. There is material besides this, enough to make a day of it. But how will a man be able to end his life, when he cannot even end a letter? Farewell, then—a word you will be happier to read than this unremitting talk of death!

Farewell.

## Letter 59

*From Seneca to Lucilius*
*Greetings*

**1** From your letter I derived great pleasure—for you must allow me to use common parlance; you mustn't recall my words to their Stoic meanings. It is our doctrine that pleasure is a fault. Be that as it may, "pleasure" is the word we generally use to refer to a glad feeling of the mind. **2** I know, say I, that if we make words adhere to our statutes, then pleasure is discreditable, while joy pertains only to the wise person, for it is the elevation of a mind toward goods that are real and its own.* Nonetheless, in our ordinary speech we often say that we are overjoyed that one person was elected consul, or that another was married or that his wife has given birth, events which, far from being causes for joy, are frequently the beginnings of future sorrow. For it is an attribute of joy that it never ceases or turns into its opposite. **3** Thus when our poet Virgil says "and evil joys of mind,"* he speaks elegantly, but not properly, for no joy is evil. He merely applied that term to pleasures, and expressed his meaning in that way, for the people referred to are happy with what is bad for them.

**4** Still, I was not wrong to say that I derived great pleasure from your letter. For even though the untrained person may be rejoicing for an honorable reason, still I refer to his emotion as pleasure, because it is unruly and swift to revert to the opposite state, and because it is set in motion by belief in a false good and is uncontrolled and excessive.*

But let me get back to my intended topic, and tell you what it was that pleased me in your letter: you have your words under control. You are not carried away by your own eloquence; you don't let it go on longer than you intended. 5 Many people are drawn by the allure of some pleasing phrase into writing on some topic other than what they had set themselves. That doesn't happen to you: everything you write is concise and suitable to the subject. You say only as much as you wish, and convey more than you say. This indicates something even more important: it shows that your mind too contains nothing superfluous or overblown.

6 However, I do find some metaphors, not risky ones but ones that have ventured out before. I find imagery—and if anyone tells us not to use imagery, deeming it allowable only for poets, I think he must not have read even one of our older writers. For them, stylistic decorum was not yet the constant aim: they expressed themselves simply and in such a way as to get their point across. They are full of analogies, which to my mind are necessary, not for the reason poets use them, but to provide support for our weakness and to make the subject real to both speaker and hearer.

7 As it happens, I have just now been reading Sextius, a stern man.* The words of his philosophy are Greek, but the values are Roman. I was struck by an image he devised, of an army that marches in square formation, ready for battle, when it is anticipated that enemies might attack from any direction. "The wise man ought to do the same," he says. "He should station his virtues on every side so that whenever trouble arises, his garrison may be ready and may respond without disarray at a nod from their commander." We see in the armies of a great general how all the troops obey the leader's command at the same time, how the formation allows a signal given by one man to traverse the cavalry and the infantry simultaneously. We need that same alacrity, he says; in fact, we need it even more. 8 Armies often fear the enemy without reason; the march they thought most liable to attack is often the safest, but foolishness has no safety zone. It has something to fear from above and from below, and on either flank, up ahead and from the rear. Trembling at

everything, it is prepared for nothing, and takes fright even at those who come to bring aid. But the wise man is fortified against every incursion; he is determined, and will not retreat before the attack of poverty, of grief, of disrepute, or of pain. Undeterred, he will advance against them and even into their midst.

9 As for us, there are many things that bind us, many that sap our strength. We have languished a long time in our faults and cannot easily get free of them. It is not merely that we are tainted with them—we are steeped in them! But rather than slipping from one metaphor to the next, let me ask a question I often wonder about. Why does foolishness have such a tight hold on us? First, because we do not resist courageously; we do not work toward healing with all our strength. Second, because we do not sufficiently believe the things that men of wisdom have discovered; we do not take them into our hearts. We expend but little effort on such a great endeavor. 10 How can anyone learn an amount sufficient to combat his vices if he learns only in the spare time left over from cultivating those vices? Not one of us goes into any depth. We only hit the high points and think that a few minutes spent on philosophy is enough and more than enough for busy people.

11 What hinders us most of all is that we are quickly satisfied with ourselves. If we find someone willing to say that we are good men, sensible and chaste, we readily acknowledge the description. We are not content with a modicum of praise: whatever shameless flattery heaps onto us, we accept as if it were our due. When people insist that we are fine men, extremely wise men, we accept their account of us, even though we know them to be frequent and copious liars. We indulge ourselves to such a degree that we are willing to be praised for qualities that are the exact opposite of what we have just been doing. A man hears himself called "most merciful" even as he is exacting punishments, "most generous" in the midst of thieving, "most temperate" in the midst of drinking and debauchery. Consequently, we have no wish to change, just because we already believe we are the height of excellence.

12 Once, when Alexander* had taken to roaming about India, pillaging nations poorly known even to their neighbors, he was struck by an arrow. It was just as he was laying siege to some city, going about the walls to find the weak points. For a long time he

persevered, intent on finishing what he had begun; but once the flow of blood ceased and the wound crusted over, the pain increased, and he began to lose all feeling in the leg when he rode his horse. Forced to leave off, he remarked, "Everyone swears that I am a son of Jupiter, but this wound cries out that I am human." **13** We should do the same. Flattery makes a fool of every one of us, according to our station: let us say to them, "You call me sensible, but I myself see how many things I desire that are useless, how many I covet that are harmful. I do not even know what limits to observe in eating and drinking, something the very animals recognize by their feeling of fullness. To this day, I do not know the capacity of my own stomach."

**14** Now I will tell you how you may know that you are not wise. The wise person is filled with joy, cheerful and calm, unalarmed; he lives on equal terms with gods. Now look at yourself. If you are never downcast; if your mind is not bothered by any hopes concerning the future; if your mental state is even and consistent night and day, upright and content with itself, then you have indeed attained the fullness of the human good. But if you seek pleasure in every direction and of every kind, then be aware that you are as far removed from wisdom as you are from joy. Joy is your aim, but you are off course: you think that you will get there amid riches and accolades; in other words, you seek joy in the midst of anxiety! You go after those things on grounds that they will bestow happiness and pleasure, but in reality they are causes of pain.

**15** Everyone you see is in pursuit of joy, but they do not know where great and lasting joy is to be had. One tries to get it from dinner parties and self-indulgence; another from elections and crowds of supporters; another from his girlfriend; another from pointless display of education and literary studies that do not heal what is amiss. All of them are deceived by specious and short-lived enticements, like drunkenness, that pays for a single hour's cheery insanity with a long-lasting hangover, or like the applause and acclamation of a large following, that costs you great anxiety both to get and to retain.

**16** So ponder this: the result of wisdom is steadiness of joy. The wise mind is like the superlunary heaven: eternally serene. Thus you have reason to desire wisdom if wisdom is always accompanied by joy. But this joy has only one source: a consciousness of the virtues.

A person is not capable of joy unless he is brave, unless he is just, unless he is temperate.

**17** You say, "What do you mean? Don't foolish people rejoice?" No more than lions rejoice when they have caught their prey. When people have worn themselves out with wine and lust; when their vices outlast the night; when the pleasures they have consumed beyond the narrow limits of the body begin to suppurate; then in their misery they speak aloud that familiar line of Virgil:

> For you know how we spent that night, our last,
> amid deceiving joys.*

**18** Indulging themselves, they spend every night amid deceiving joys, as if it were indeed their last.

But the joy that attends on the gods and those who imitate the gods has no intermission and no end.* It would have an end if its source were from elsewhere; but it is not for anyone else to bestow, and for that reason it is not for anyone else to decide whether they shall have it. What fortune did not grant, fortune does not take away.

Farewell.

# BOOK SEVEN

# Letter 60

*From Seneca to Lucilius*
*Greetings*

**1** I am dissatisfied with you—at odds with you—angry at you. Do you still want the things your nursemaid wanted for you, or your tutor, or your mother? Do you still not understand how much of what they wanted for you is actually bad? O, how unfavorable to us are the prayers of our nearest and dearest! And all the more so when they turn out well. It's no wonder to me now that all kinds of troubles beset us from earliest childhood: we grow up amid the imprecations of our parents.* May the gods hear our prayer for ourselves as well, a prayer that costs nothing to fulfill.

**2** How long will we ask the gods for anything at all? Are we still not able to feed ourselves? Our planted fields occupy territory enough for large cities: how long? How long will a whole population do our reaping? How long will it take numerous ships—and more than one ocean—to provide the spread for a single dinner table? A bull is filled up by only a few acres of pasturage; a single wood suffices for more than one elephant; yet a human being feeds upon land and sea. **3** Why is that? Has nature given us such an insatiable maw that although the bodies we are given are of modest size, we yet surpass the largest, most ravenous eaters of the animal world? That is not the case, for how small are our natural requirements! It takes only a little to satisfy nature's demands. It is not bodily hunger that runs up the bill but ambition. **4** Therefore let us regard those who, as Sallust says, "heed the belly"* as belonging to the race of animals rather than of humans.

Indeed, there are some we should count not even as animate creatures but as corpses. A person is alive when he is of use to many; he is alive when he is of use to himself. Slackers who hide out at home might as well be in the tomb. Go ahead and write it in marble above their door:

PRECEDED IN DEATH BY
THEMSELVES.

Farewell.

## *Letter 61*

---

*From Seneca to Lucilius*
*Greetings*

**1** Let's stop wanting what we used to want. That's what I'm doing, for a fact: being an old man, I have stopped wanting the things I wanted as a boy. My sole endeavor, my one thought, both day and night, is this: to put an end to my prior ills. I strive to make a day count for a whole lifetime. It's not that I cling to it as if it were my last—not by any means, and yet I do look at it as if it could actually be my last. **2** I write you this letter in the same spirit, as if death were about to summon me in the very middle of writing. I'm ready to leave; the reason I enjoy life is that I am not too concerned about how long all this is going to last.

Before old age, I cared about living well; in old age, I care about dying well. But dying well is dying willingly. Make an effort never to do anything against your will. **3** That which you will be compelled to do if you are resistant is not compulsory if you do it willingly. This is what I mean: he who takes orders gladly escapes the bitterest part of servitude—doing what he would rather not. What makes people miserable is not acting under orders but acting against their will.

So let us arrange our minds in such a way that whatever circumstances require is what we want—and especially that we think about our own end without sadness. **4** We should prepare for death even before we prepare for life. Our life is well enough equipped. Yet we are greedy for life's equipment. We think we are missing something, and we always will think that. To have enough of life: neither days nor years can give us that, but only the mind. My life has been quite long enough, dearest Lucilius. Satisfied, I await my death.

Farewell.

## *Letter 62*

*From Seneca to Lucilius*
*Greetings*

1 They're lying, those people who want it to look as if the pressures of their jobs prevent them from engaging in liberal studies.* It is all pretense, for they themselves keep adding to their activities—if they are busy, it is their own fault. I have time, Lucilius, I do have time; and wherever I am, I am my own person. I do not give myself over to activities; I only lend myself, and I don't go looking for reasons to waste my time. When I come to a halt, no matter where I am, I sift through my thoughts and find some salutary reflection. 2 When I devote myself to friends, I do not even then withdraw from myself. And I don't linger with the people I am thrown in with merely by circumstance or by some reason arising from public service. Instead, I choose the very best company; and it is to them that I entrust my mind, in whatever place, in whatever age they have lived. 3 I carry about with me Demetrius, the best of men.* I abandon those clothed in Tyrian purple and converse with him, look up to him, who is barely clothed at all. Why shouldn't I look up to him? I have seen that he lacks nothing.

No one can have everything, but there is someone who can despise everything. The quickest way to wealth is to despise wealth. But our friend Demetrius lives not as one who despises all things but as one who has left those things for others to enjoy.

Farewell.

# Letter 63

*From Seneca to Lucilius*
*Greetings*

**1** I am sorry your friend Flaccus has passed away, but I want you not to grieve excessively.*

Not grieve at all? That I will not venture to ask of you, though I know it would be better. Such firmness of mind belongs only to the person who has risen high above misfortune. And even he will feel a twinge at something like this, but only a twinge. As for us, we may be forgiven our tears, if there are not too many, and if we do regain control. Having lost a friend, you should not be dry-eyed, but neither should you drown in weeping; you should cry, but not wail.

**2** Does my rule seem strict to you? And yet the greatest of the Greek poets allowed just one day for lawful mourning. And he says that even Niobe thought of food.*

Do you ask where lamentations come from? What is the source of weeping beyond measure? We are trying by our tears to prove our sense of loss: it is not that grief forces us but that we are exhibiting grief to others. People are not sad just for themselves. Hapless idiocy! Even in grief there is competition.

**3** "What then?" you ask. "Shall I forget my friend?" It's not very long that you are promising to remember him if your memory lasts only as long as your grief. The time is at hand when some chance thing will brighten your face with a laugh; very soon, I say, your pangs will subside, even the sharpest, and every feeling of loss will be eased. The minute you stop watching yourself, your look of sadness will be gone. Right now you are guarding your grief, but even so it is escaping. The more severe it is, the sooner it ends.

**4** Let us try to make the memory of those who are gone a pleasant one. If the thought brings torment, one does not willingly return to it, and so here: we are bound to feel a biting* when the names of loved ones come to mind. But even this has its own pleasure. **5** Our friend Attalus* used to say,

The memory of friends who have died gives a pleasure like that of apples that are both tart and sweet, or like the pleasing acidity of an old wine. After a time, though, all that pains us is extinguished, and only the pleasure remains.

**6** If we are to believe him,

Thinking of friends safe and sound is cakes and honey; remembering those who are gone is bittersweet. Yet who would deny that sharp and even bitter flavors are sometimes to our taste?

**7** My experience is different: to me, the thought of friends who have died is sweet, even comforting. For when I had friends, I had them as one who would lose them; now that I have lost them, I am as one who still has them.

And so, dear Lucilius, do what suits your sense of fairness. Stop misinterpreting what fortune has done for you. Fortune has taken something from you, but it was fortune that gave.

**8** Because we cannot be sure how long we will have our friends, let us eagerly enjoy them now. Let us consider how often we have gone on some long trip and left them behind, how often we failed to see them even when living in the same place: we will then understand that we lost more time with them while they were alive. Some people are careless about their friends while they have them, then grieve terribly for them when they are gone. **9** Will you put up with this? They have to lose people in order to love them! They are afraid there may be some doubt whether they really loved them, and this makes their grief even more effusive. They are looking for some delayed signs of their own affection.

**10** If we have other friends, we give them little credit and hardly merit their esteem if we do not find in them a valuable consolation for the one who has passed away. If, on the other hand, we have no other friends, then we are doing a worse injury to ourselves than fortune has done to us: fortune took one person from us, but we are taking from ourselves every person we do not make our friend. **11** Moreover, anyone who cannot make friends with more than one person does not love even that one very much. If someone who had lost his only tunic were to weep and wail, rather than look about for something to put over his shoulders to keep himself warm, wouldn't you think he was an idiot? The one you loved has passed away: find someone to love. Replacing the friend is better than crying.

**12** I know that what I am about to add is a well-worn saying, but I am not going to leave it out just because everyone else has said it.

Time puts an end to grief—

even if you did not choose to put an end to it yourself. One does become tired of grieving—but a thoughtful person should be deeply ashamed to let that be the means of healing. Better you should abandon your grief than it should abandon you. Given that you cannot continue very long even if you want to, you should stop as soon as you are able.

**13** Our forefathers established one year as the period of mourning for women, not that they should mourn that long, but that they should not mourn longer than that. For men there is no legal period, since no period is honorable.* Yet even among women, and those women who can hardly be dragged away from the bier—the ones we have to pry away from the corpse—even among them I defy you to show me one whose tears have lasted an entire month. Nothing becomes hateful as quickly as grief. When fresh, it brings sympathy and visits of consolation; once it grows old, it draws nothing but mockery. And rightly, for by then it is either stupid or feigned.

**14** And I am writing these things to you—I, who wept for my beloved Annaeus Serenus* so unrestrainedly that I myself may serve, most unwillingly, as an example of one conquered by grief. But today I censure my own behavior. I understand, now, that the main reason I felt such grief was that I had never thought it possible that his death should precede my own. I kept in mind only that he was younger than I, much younger. As if birth order determined our fate!

**15** So let us remember mortality, in ourselves as well as our loved ones. I ought to have said, back then, "My dear Serenus is younger than I, but what difference does that make? He ought to die after me, but he could die before." Because I did not do this, fortune struck me suddenly and unprepared. Now I keep in mind not only that everyone and everything must die, but that they die according to no determinate law. If it can happen at all, it can happen today.

**16** And so, most dear Lucilius, let us reflect that we too will soon be going where the one we mourn has gone. And perhaps the tales of philosophers are true, and there is a place that receives us.* If so, then the one we think is gone has only gone on ahead.

Farewell.

## Letter 64

*From Seneca to Lucilius*
*Greetings*

1 Yesterday you were with us. Now, that would be reason for complaint if yesterday were the only time. That's why I said "with us": for you are always with me. Some friends had come over so that my household would create some more smoke. Not like what billows out of fashionable kitchens, alarming the fire department, but just a modest plume, indicating that guests were in the house. 2 Our conversation ranged widely, as it does at a dinner party, not pursuing any topic to its conclusion but skipping around from one thing to another. Then there was a reading. It was a book by Quintus Sextius the Elder—a great man, you may be sure, and a Stoic, even if he denies it.* 3 By god, what vigor there is in the man—what spirit! That's not something you'll find in every philosopher. Some of them are widely renowned, and yet what they have written is dry and lifeless. They construct arguments, debate issues, and raise objections, yet they never rouse the spirit, because they are spiritless themselves. When you read Sextius, though, you will say, "He is alive—vigorous—free—he soars above humankind; he sends me away full of tremendous confidence."

4 I will tell you what is my own state of mind when I read him: I yearn to challenge every stroke of fortune—to shout, "Why let up, fortune? Do your worst! See, I am ready!" I gird myself with the mind of him who seeks a proving ground for himself, a place to demonstrate his courage:

> Amid the tamer herds he prays to meet
> the foaming boar, or else the tawny lion,
> come from the mountaintop.*

5 I yearn to have something to conquer—something I can endure as part of my training. For this is another of Sextius's outstanding qualities: he will show you the magnitude of true happiness, and yet not take away your hope of achieving it. You will realize that it is far above you, and yet know that one who wants to can attain that height.

6 This same attitude is inspired by virtue itself, namely, that you admire it and yet hope to achieve it. For me, at least, the very thought of wisdom absorbs much of my time. I am no less astonished when I gaze at it than I am sometimes by the heavens themselves, which I often see as if for the first time.

7 For that reason I hold in awe both the discoveries of philosophy and those who have made those discoveries; and I thrill to claim what is, as it were, an inheritance from many predecessors. Everything they collected, everything they labored over, was for me! But let us do what a good head of household does: let us add to our endowment. May it be a larger inheritance when it passes from me to posterity. Much work remains to be done, and always will: nothing prevents those born a thousand generations hence from making their contribution.

8 But even if the ancients did discover everything, here's something that will always be new: taking those discoveries made by others and applying them, understanding them, and organizing them. Suppose some medications had been handed down to us for healing the eye. I do not need to seek out any ointments other than these, and yet I still need to make use of them as suits the disease and the situation. One relieves inflammation of the eye itself, another decreases a swelling in the eyelid, another eases sudden pressure and watering, another improves vision—but only if you do your part, making up the powders and selecting the time and method of administration that is right for the individual. Remedies for the mind were discovered by the ancients; it is our job, though, to find out how to apply them and when. 9 Our predecessors achieved a great deal, but their work is still unfinished.

But we should admire them all the same; indeed, we should revere them as we do the gods. Why shouldn't I keep images of great men beside me, to stir my mind to action, and even celebrate their birthdays? Why shouldn't I address them by name each time, as a way to honor them? The same homage I render to my teachers, I owe also to the teachers of the human race, who are the source of so much good.

**10** If I see a consul or a praetor, I will honor their office in all the usual ways: I'll jump down from my horse; I'll uncover my head; I'll yield them the walkway. Well, then! Am I to give anything but the most respectful welcome to Marcus Cato, the elder and the younger? To Laelius the Wise?* To Socrates and Plato? To Zeno and Cleanthes? Truly I revere these men: when such great names are mentioned, I rise to my feet.

Farewell.

## *Letter 65*

*From Seneca to Lucilius*
*Greetings*

**1** Yesterday I shared the day with illness: it claimed the morning for itself but left me the afternoon.* At first I tested my breath with a little reading; when it stood up to that, I ventured to demand more of it—or rather to allow it more leeway. I did some writing; indeed, I wrote more intensely than usual, as I was contending with a difficult subject and did not want to be beaten by it. Finally some friends came by, so as to restrain me by force, like some unruly invalid. **2** Conversation took over from the pen, and out of that conversation I will convey to you the part that is still in contention. We have called on you to adjudicate the matter.

It's more work than you think: the case is threefold. As you know, the adherents of our Stoic school say that in the world's nature there are two things from which everything comes into being: cause and matter. Matter lies inert, a thing open to all possibilities, which will remain inactive unless moved by someone else. But cause—that is, reason—shapes matter and turns it in any direction it wants, producing from it various works.* Hence for any given thing there has to be something out of which it is made and something by which it is made: the latter is the cause, the former the matter.

**3** Every skill is an imitation of nature; so transfer what I was saying about things in general to those that have to be made by a human being. A statue has both material for the craftsman to work on and a craftsman to impose some appearance on the material. Thus in the case of the statue, the material is the bronze and the cause is the artisan. The same specification applies to all things: they consist of that which is made and that which makes.

4 The Stoics hold that there is just one cause, that which acts. Aristotle's view is that the word "cause" is used in three ways.* "The first cause," he says, "is the material itself, without which nothing can be created; the second is the artisan; the third is the form that is imposed upon each and every work, just as it is upon the statue." This is what Aristotle calls the *eidos*. "There is also a fourth cause," he says, "in addition to these, namely, the purpose of the work as a whole." 5 I will explain what that is. Bronze is the first cause of the statue, for it would never have been made if that from which it was cast or forged had not existed. The second cause is the craftsman, for the bronze could not have been worked into the shape of a statue if his skilled hand had not been added. The third cause is the form, for that statue would not be called a "spear bearer" or "youth tying a headband" if that appearance had not been imposed upon it.* The fourth cause is the purpose of making it; for if this had not been there, it would not have been made. 6 What is the purpose? It is what motivated the craftsman, what he was after in making it. Either it was money, if he crafted it to sell; or reputation, if he wanted to make a name for himself; or reverence, if he fashioned it as a gift for a temple. Therefore this too is a cause for its being made—or don't you agree that something without which a thing would not have been made should be counted as one of its causes?

7 To these causes Plato adds a fifth, the model, which he calls the Idea.* This is what the craftsman had in view when he made what he intended to make. It does not matter whether he has an external model to cast his eyes upon, or an internal one that he himself has conceived and set up within. These, the models of all things, God holds within himself, and encompasses in his mind the numbers and measures of everything that is to be achieved. He is full of those shapes that Plato calls Ideas—deathless, changeless, tireless. Thus while human beings indeed perish, humanity itself, according

to which a human being is molded, remains; and although human beings suffer and die, humanity is unaffected.

8 There are, then, five causes on Plato's account: that from which, that by which, that in which, that according to which, and that because of which. Last of all, there is that which comes of these. For instance, in a statue (to continue in my previous vein), that from which is the bronze, that by which is the craftsman, that in which is the form that is applied to it, that according to which is the model that the person who makes it is imitating, that because of which is the maker's purpose, and that which comes of these is the statue itself. 9 By Plato's account, the world too has all of these: the maker—this is God; that from which it is made—this is matter; the form—this is the condition and order of the world that we see; the model—which is to say, that according to which he made such a vast and supremely beautiful piece of work; the purpose—his aim in making it. What aim does God have, you ask? Goodness. That is definitely what Plato says: 10 "What was the cause of God's making the world? He is good; one who is good is not parsimonious with any good; he made it, then, to be the best world he could make."*

You be the judge, then, and make your ruling. Whose account seems to you most likely to be true? Not who gives the truest account, for that is as far above us as truth itself.

11 This host of causes posited by Aristotle and by Plato encompasses either too many things or too few. For if their view is that whenever the removal of something would make it impossible for some item to be made, that thing is a cause of its making, then they have named too few things. They should count time as a cause, for nothing can be made without time. They should count place: if there is nowhere in which a thing can be made, once more it will not be made. They should count motion: without motion, nothing is either made or destroyed; without it, there is no craftsmanship and indeed no changing.

12 We, however, are looking now for the primary and generic cause. This must be simple, for matter too is simple. Are we asking what this cause is? Unquestionably, it is productive reason, that is, God.* For all these things you have mentioned are not multiple individual causes but are dependent on one, the one that makes. 13 You

say that form is a cause? Form is what the craftsman imposes on his work; it is part of the cause but not the cause itself. The model is not the cause either but a necessary instrument of the cause. The model is necessary to the craftsman in the same way as the chisel and the pumice stone: without them his craft cannot go forward, and yet they are not parts of the craft, and neither are they causes. **14** Someone says, "The aim of the craftsman—the purpose for which he came to make something—is a cause." Even supposing it is a cause, it is not the efficient cause but a supervenient cause. And such causes are innumerable; what we are looking for is the generic cause. As for their claim that the entire world in all its fullness is a cause, there they speak with less than their usual sophistication. For there is a big difference between a work and the cause of that work.

**15** Either make your ruling, or do what is easier in this sort of case: say you find no clear solution and tell us to go home.

"What is the attraction for you in frittering away your time on these matters which do not eliminate any of your passions nor drive out any desires?" In fact I do go after those more important things;° I do engage in those studies by which the mind is calmed. I examine myself first, and then this world of ours. **16** Even now I am not wasting time, as you suppose. For as long as such studies are not beaten to death, nor dragged off down pointless pathways of scholarly sophistication, they do elevate the mind.* They lighten that burden under which it labors, longing to get free and to return to its origins. For this body is the weight and penalty of the mind: while thus oppressed, it is in chains, unless philosophy comes to its aid, bidding it gaze upon the world's nature and so draw breath, releasing it from earthly things to things divine. This is its freedom, its diversion: it gets away for a while from the prison-house where it is confined, and finds refreshment in the skies.* **17** Just as craftsmen, when they are engaged in some intricate task that strains the eyes and the light is indirect and poor, come out into the open and visit some place devoted to public recreation, there to refresh their eyes with the free light of day; even so does the mind, shut away in this somber, dark apartment, emerge whenever it can into the open and relax in the contemplation of the universe. **18** The wise person, and likewise the seeker after wisdom, abides indeed within his body, yet with his better part is absent, turning his thoughts to things above.

Like one sworn into the service,* he thinks himself well paid if he but remains alive, and due to his training has neither love of life nor hatred of it but endures this mortal time, though he knows of richer things to come.

**19** Do you forbid me to gaze upon the universe? Do you pull me back from the whole, and confine me to the part? Am I not to ask what are the beginnings of all things? Whose is the hand that shaped the world? When all things were merged into one and weltering in inactive matter, who separated them? Shall I not ask who is the craftsman of the universe itself? By what plan such vastness came to be ordered and regulated? Who collected what was scattered, separated what was mingled, apportioned visible form to all that lay in one vast and shapeless mass? What is the source of the mighty light that is shed on us? **20** Was it fire, or something brighter than fire? Shall I not ask these things? Am I not to know whence I have descended? Whether I shall see this world but once, or be born many times? Where I shall go when I depart? What abodes are waiting for my spirit when it is released from the slavery of human life? Do you deny me my share of heaven—which is to say, do you bid me live with eyes cast downward?

**21** Too great I am to be slave to my body; too great is that for which I was born. I regard the body as nothing but a shackle fastened around my freedom. Therefore I set it in the way of fortune as a hindrance, and do not allow any hurt to pass through it to me. This is the only thing in me that can suffer injury: in such vulnerable quarters does my free mind dwell. **22** Never will this flesh compel me to cowardice; never to pretenses unworthy of a good person; never will I tell a lie merely to honor this paltry body of mine. When I see fit, I will break off my alliance with it; and even now, while we adhere to one another, that alliance will not be of equal standing: the mind will draw every privilege to itself. Disregard for one's body is certain liberation.*

**23** But let me get back to my stated objective. This freedom is greatly abetted by that contemplation we were just talking about. It's like this. All things in the universe are made up of matter and God. God controls them, and they are his followers, ranged about him as their ruler and guide. But that which makes—which is God—is more powerful and valuable than matter, which is acted upon by him.

**24** Now in a human being, the mind performs the same role as God performs in the world, and what matter is in the world is in us the body. So let the inferior parts serve the better: let us be brave against the strokes of fortune; let us not tremble at injuries, or wounds, or fetters, or want.

What is death? Either an end or a crossing over. I am not afraid to come to an end (for that is the same as never having started), and neither am I afraid to cross over. For nowhere will I be as constricted as I am here.

Farewell.

## Letter 66

*From Seneca to Lucilius*
*Greetings*

**1** I have just seen Claranus, after a lapse of many years. He was a fellow student of mine—and, as I am sure you have figured out already, he is now elderly. But he is indeed youthful and lively in spirit, and is struggling against his paltry body.* Nature did not play fair when it placed a mind like his in such poor lodgings. Or perhaps that was exactly what nature wanted to show us: that no matter what the exterior, a very brave, very fine mind may lie within. Still, he has conquered every obstacle, and by not being concerned about himself has learned not to be concerned about other things. **2** I think the poet was mistaken when he said, "and virtue, more admired in comely figure."* For virtue needs nothing to ennoble it: it is its own great ornament, and makes sacred the body it inhabits.

Certainly I have begun to see our friend Claranus in a new way: he seems quite handsome to me, and as upright in stature as he is in spirit. **3** A great man may come out of a hovel; a great and handsome mind from a lowly and misshapen body.* I think nature must have made some people as they are just to prove that there is nowhere virtue cannot be born. If it could have produced minds with no clothing at all, it would have; but in fact it does something even better: it produces some people who are handicapped by their bodies and yet manage to break through everything that stands in their way. **4** Claranus was born as an example, I think, to help us realize that a misshapen body does not disfigure the mind; rather, a beautiful mind adorns the body. Anyway, although we spent only a very few days together, we did have many conversations, which I will now write out and send to you.

**5** On the first day, our topic for discussion was this: how can all goods be equal to one another if they are of threefold status? It is the position of our school that some goods are primary—for instance joy, peace, the safety of one's homeland—while others are secondary, manifested in unfortunate material, such as endurance under torture or self-control during serious illness. The former goods we choose for ourselves unconditionally, the latter if it becomes necessary. And there are still the tertiary goods, such as a modest walk, a calm and dignified facial expression, and gestures befitting an intelligent person.* **6** How can all these be equal to one another, when some are choiceworthy and others worthy of avoidance?*

If we want to sort these things out, let's go back to the principal good and consider what kind of thing it is. The spirit that gazes at what is real, that knows what to pursue and to avoid, that assigns value to things in accordance with nature and not by opinion—the spirit that injects itself into the cosmos as a whole and casts its contemplation over every action of the universe—the spirit that attends equally to thought and to action—that great and forceful spirit, not vanquished by adversity nor again by the blandishments of prosperity, that does not yield itself up to either but rises above all contingency, all accident—that most beautiful spirit, well marshaled in grace and likewise in strength, sound and sober, tranquil and undismayed—that spirit that no power can subdue, no chance event can either elevate or depress—that sort of spirit is what virtue is. **7** This is what it looks like if it displays the whole of itself at once, in a single viewing. But its specificities are many, for they are displayed in each change of life and in each activity, while virtue itself becomes neither less nor more.

For the supreme good cannot diminish, and neither is virtue permitted to retreat; rather, it is transformed first into one quality and then into another, shaped according to the condition of the things it is about to do.* **8** Whatever it touches, it attracts and tinctures with its own likeness; it adorns actions, friendships, sometimes entire households which it has entered and put in order. Whatever it handles, it makes lovable, remarkable, admirable. Its power, its magnitude, cannot increase any more, if only because that which is greatest has no augmentation. When a thing is right, you will find nothing more right, any more than a thing can be truer than what is true, or more temperate than what is temperate.* **9** Every virtue is in the limit, and a limit has a fixed measurement.* Consistency has no further to go, any more than confidence or truthfulness or loyalty. If a thing is perfect, what can be added to it? Nothing, or else that to which the addition is made was not perfect before. Hence nothing can be added to virtue either: if anything can be added to it, it was lacking before. Neither can any addition be made to that which is honorable: it is honorable for the very reasons I have given. And what else? Don't you agree that that which is seemly has the same form, bounded by definite endpoints? And likewise what is just and lawful? The possibility of increase shows that a thing is imperfect.

**10** Every good is subject to these same terms. Private utility is linked to public utility, indeed just as much as what is praiseworthy cannot be separated from what one ought to pursue. Thus it is that the virtues are equal to one another, as also are the deeds of virtue and all persons who possess the virtues. **11** When it comes to plants and animals, though, since they themselves are mortal, their virtues too are defeasible, transitory, and uncertain; they ebb and flow, and for that reason are not assigned the same value. Human virtues come under a single rule, for right reason itself is single and uniform. Nothing is more divine than the divine; nothing more celestial than the celestial.

**12** Mortal things rise° and fall; they dwindle and grow; they are emptied and filled; and for that reason they are as uneven as their lot is unstable. Things that are divine have but one nature. But reason is nothing other than a portion of the divine breath submerged in the human body.* If reason is divine, and there is no good without reason, then every good is divine. Furthermore, there is no distinction among things that are divine and so no distinction among goods either. Therefore there is equality between joy on the one hand and stouthearted endurance of torture, for there is the same greatness of spirit in both: relaxed and expansive in the one, concentrated and combative in the other. **13** Why not? Do you think the courage of one who bravely assails the enemy's fortifications is not equaled by the courage that sustains that assault with tremendous endurance? Do you think the greatness of Scipio, who laid siege to Numantia and forced those unconquered hands to turn to their own destruction, is not equaled by the greatness of the besieged, who knew that no one is surrounded as long as he has access to death, as long as he expires in the embrace of liberty?* In just the same way are the remaining goods equal to one another: calmness, forthrightness, generosity, consistency, serenity, endurance. For what underlies them all is the one thing, virtue, which supplies an upright and unwavering spirit.

14 "What do you mean? Is there no difference between joy and unbending endurance of pain?" None as concerns the virtues themselves; but there is a great deal of difference in the manner in which each is displayed, for in the one instance there is a natural relaxation and expansion of the mind; in the other pain, which is contrary to nature. For that reason, these things that admit of such vast differentiation are intermediates; yet the virtue that is in each is equal. 15 The material does not alter the virtue: difficult material does not make it worse, and cheerful, happy material does not make it better. Hence they are necessarily equal. For in both cases, what is done is done just as rightly, just as intelligently, just as honorably; therefore the goods are equal. Neither can this one person conduct himself any better in his joy, nor that one in his torments. But two things that cannot be made better must be equal to each other.

16 For if matters external to virtue can either diminish or augment it, then what is honorable ceases to be the sole good. If you concede that, then the honorable ceases to exist altogether.* Why? I'll tell you: because no action is honorable when performed by one who is unwilling or under compulsion. Everything that is honorable is voluntary. Mingle with it any reluctance, any complaint, any second thoughts, any fear, and it loses its best feature: it is no longer self-determined. Timorousness implies slavishness, and that which is unfree cannot be honorable. 17 Everything that is honorable is free of anxiety; it is tranquil. If a person refuses something, complains of it, thinks it is bad, then he is disturbed and welters in grievous conflict: on one side, rectitude appears and summons him; on the other, harm is suspected and causes him to withdraw. For this reason, one who is about to behave honorably does not consider what stands in his way

to be harmful, not even if he finds it uncomfortable; rather he wills it and performs it gladly. Everything that is honorable is unbidden, unforced; it is wholehearted; it has no association with anything bad.

**18** I know what response I may get at this point: "Are you trying to persuade us that it makes no difference whether someone feels joy or stays on the rack till he exhausts the torturer?"

To this my reply could have been as follows: "Even Epicurus says that the sage, if roasted in the bull of Phalaris, will say, 'It is pleasant; it does not matter to me at all.'* Why are you surprised, then, if I say there is equality in goods between one reclining at dinner and one standing up to torture, when Epicurus says what is even harder to believe, that it is pleasurable to be tortured?"

**19** But instead I make this reply: "There is a great difference between joy and pain. If I am asked to choose, I will pursue one and avoid the other; for the one is in accordance with nature, the other contrary to it. As long as they are evaluated in this way, they are very far apart; and yet when it comes to virtue, the two are equal; one virtue proceeds through happy circumstances, the other through sad ones. **20** Vexation and pain and anything else that is uncomfortable have no significance: they are overpowered by virtue. Just as the brightness of the sun causes our little lamps to grow dim, so it is with virtue: the sheer scale of it blots out all pains, discomforts, and hurts. Wherever it sheds its radiance, everything that appears in its absence is snuffed out; and when they encounter virtue, our discomforts play no larger part than does a rain shower in the ocean."*

**21** Here is how you may know that this is the case: if an action is fine, a good man will plunge into it without any hesitation. The executioner may be standing there, the torturer, the flame; yet he will persevere, his eyes being fixed on what he is to do, not what he will endure. He will entrust himself to the honorable deed as to a good man, and will regard it as useful—safe—profitable for himself. The action that is honorable, but harsh and difficult, will have the same standing with him as a good man has when he is poor or in exile, or thin and pale.

**22** Come, now, suppose that over here is a good man who has abundance of wealth; over there one who possesses nothing but himself, yet in himself possesses everything. Both are equally good, even if the fortunes allotted them are quite unequal. I repeat: the judgment we apply to persons is equally applicable to their circumstances.

**23** Virtue is just as praiseworthy when found in a body that is healthy and free as it is in one that is sick and in chains. So do not esteem your own virtue any more highly if fortune has provided it with a whole and sound body than you would if its body were disfigured in some way. That would be like judging the worth of a master by how his slaves are dressed. For all these things that belong to the domain of chance are servants: money, the body, reputation. They are weak, transitory, mortal, unstable in possession. By contrast, the works of virtue are free and unconquered. They are not more worthy of pursuit just because fortune deals kindly with them, nor are they less worthy of pursuit when circumstances are hostile.

**24** Pursuit in the circumstances of our lives works the same as friendship among people. If your friend is a good man, I don't suppose you would love him any more for being wealthy rather than poor, or for being tough and muscular rather than thin and feeble in body. In your circumstances too, then, you won't go after something more, or love it more, for being cheerful and peaceful than for being anxious and laborious. **25** Or if you would, then between two equally good men you would also be fonder of the one who has had a bath and a rubdown than the one who is covered with dust and needs a shave. Next, you would go so far as to feel more affection for one who is uninjured and in possession of all his limbs than one who is crippled or blind in one eye. Bit by bit, you would become so finicky that between two who are equally honorable and intelligent, you would choose the one with long, curly hair! When virtue is equal in both, their inequality in other respects does not count.* For all those other features are not parts of them but mere additions to them.

**26** Within the family, does any parent make such unfair estimations as to love a healthy child more than a sick one, or a fine, tall son more than a short or middle-sized child? Wild beasts do not draw distinctions among their cubs: when they lie down to nurse, they feed them all alike. Birds distribute equal shares of food to all their nestlings. Ulysses is in just as much of a hurry to get back to his rocky isle of Ithaca as Agamemnon is to return to the noble ramparts of Mycenae. No one loves his homeland because it is great, but only because it is his.

**27** What is the point of these comparisons? To show you that virtue looks on all its works with unbiased eyes as its own offspring, giving them all an equal measure of devotion. If anything, the more unstinting devotion is given to those in difficulties. Just as parental love inclines more toward the child who is the object of pity, so it is with virtue, which, when certain of its works appear to be in danger or trouble, does not love them more, but like a good parent gives them more attention and more nurturing.

**28** Why is no good greater than any other? Because nothing is more apt than what is apt, nothing more level than what is level. When one thing is equal to another, you cannot say that something else is more equal to it. Neither, then, is anything more honorable than what is honorable. **29** But if all the virtues are of an equal nature, then the three types of good are on a par. This is what I mean: rejoicing temperately is on a par with suffering temperately. Gladness there does not surpass firmness of mind here, that bites back its cries under the torturer. Those goods are desirable, these are worthy of admiration; nonetheless, both are equal, since the potency of the greater good is enough to defend against any discomfort there may be. **30** Anyone who thinks they are unequal is turning his eyes away from the virtues themselves and looking around at externals. True goods have the same weight, the same extent. Those false goods are largely hollow: they seem large and comely to the eye; but when they are summoned to the scales, they prove deceptive. **31** So it is, dear Lucilius: anything commended by true reasoning is solid and lasting; it strengthens the mind and lifts it to the skies, to remain there always.* Those things that are praised without good reason, that are goods according to the popular account, merely puff us up, causing us to delight in empty things. And again, those supposed evils that instill such terror alarm our minds in just the same way as animals do when they make a show of being dangerous. **32** On both sides, then, it is without cause that these things expand our minds and gnaw at them: the former are not worthy of joy, nor the latter of fear.*

Reason alone is unchangeable and steadfast in its judgment, for it is not the slave of the senses but their commander. Reason is equal to reason, just as right is equal to right. Thus virtue is likewise equal to virtue, for virtue is nothing other than right reason. All the virtues are reasoning processes:* if they are right, they are reasoning processes, and if they are right, they are also equal. **33** As reason is, so are the activities of reason; therefore they too are all equal. For since they resemble reason, they also resemble one another.

My claim is that the actions are equal to one another insofar as they are honorable and right. But there will still be big distinctions among them through differences in their material. The material is sometimes wider, sometimes narrower; sometimes of high rank, sometimes humble; sometimes pertaining to many, sometimes to only a few; still, what is best in all these actions is equal, for they are all honorable. **34** It is the same as with good men: they are all equal insofar as they are good, but they have differences in age (one is older, another younger); and in body (one is handsome, another ugly); and in fortune (one is rich, another poor; that one is well connected, powerful, known among cities and peoples, this one generally unknown and obscure). Yet as concerns their goodness, they are equal.

**35** Sensation makes no judgment concerning goods and evils; it does not know what is useful and what is not. It cannot render an opinion unless it is conveyed into the presence of its object. It is not such as to look ahead to the future or remember the past; it knows nothing of logical relations. Yet logical relations tie together the entire progression of time and the unity of a life that is to travel a straight path.* Reason, then, is the arbiter of what is good and bad, and reason holds cheap whatever is external and not its own. Those things which are neither good nor bad are in its judgment very small and trivial additions; for as far as reason is concerned, every good is in the mind. **36** But there are some goods that it regards as primary, goods that it approaches deliberately—for instance victory, good children, the welfare of one's homeland—others as secondary, goods that show up only in adverse circumstances—for instance bearing disease, fire, or exile with equanimity—and still others as intermediates, goods that are no more in accordance with nature than they are contrary to nature; for instance walking sensibly, sitting with composure. For sitting is not more in accordance with nature than standing or walking. **37** The first two types of good differ from one another. The primary goods are in accordance with nature: rejoicing in the devotion of one's children, in the safety of one's homeland. The secondary goods are contrary to nature: courageously standing up to torture and enduring thirst when one's vital organs are parched by disease.

**38** "What's that? Is anything contrary to nature a good?" No, but at times that in which the good is manifested is contrary to nature. Being wounded, or being roasted over a slow fire, or being afflicted with ill health is contrary to nature, but preserving an unflagging spirit amid such trials is in accordance with nature. **39** To put it briefly: the material of the good is sometimes contrary to nature; but the good never is, since there is no good without reason, and reason follows nature.

What, then, is reason? The imitation of nature. What is the highest good of the human being? Behaving as nature intended.

**40** "There can be no doubt that peace that never meets with strife is more fortunate than peace regained through much bloodshed. There can be no doubt that undisturbed health is a more fortunate thing than health achieved by main force and endurance out of serious and life-threatening illnesses. In the same way, there can be no doubt that joy is a greater good than a mind shored up to endure the torments of injury and the flame." **41** No, for those chance occurrences admit of tremendous differentiation: they are evaluated by the usefulness of those who take them on. One of the goods is a determination to be in agreement with nature; this is equal in all of them. When we vote in favor of someone in the Senate, it cannot be said that one senator was more in agreement than another. Everyone voted the same way. I say the same about the virtues: all of them are in agreement with nature. And I say the same about goods: all of them are in accordance with nature. **42** One person dies in his youth, another in old age, another right away in infancy, after having only a glimpse of life—all of them were equally mortal, even if death allowed some people's lives to last longer, cut off others in their bloom, and interrupted the very beginning of others.

**43** One man collapses at dinner; another dies as a continuation of sleep; another is done in by sexual intercourse. Compare with these the people who are run through by the sword or killed by snakebite or crushed by collapsing buildings—or tortured slowly to death by the gradual twisting and contracting of their sinews. Some of these can be said to have had a better ending, some a worse; but their deaths, in point of fact, are equal. What they have been through is different; what they have come to is one. No death is larger or smaller, for it has the same limit in every case—the end of a life. **44** I say the same to you about goods. This good is among unmitigated pleasures, that one amid bitter trials; the one has fortune's lavishness to govern, the other fortune's violence to subdue—and both are equally good, though one has walked a soft and level way, the other a rocky road. For all of them have the same end: they are goods; they are praiseworthy; they are the companions of virtue and reason. Virtue counts as equal all things it recognizes as good.

**45** Why should you be surprised to find this among our doctrines? In Epicurus there are two goods, the components of his highest and happiest good: that the body should be free of pain, the mind free of disturbance.* These goods do not increase if they are fulfilled: how is what is fulfilled going to increase? The body is free of pain; what can be added to this absence of pain? The mind is in agreement with itself and is calm, what can be added to this tranquility? **46** Just as a cloudless sky, washed with pure brightness from one side to the other, does not admit of any greater clarity, so when a person cares for both body and mind, and builds his good from both, his state is perfect. If there is no turmoil in his mind and no pain in his body, then his wish is fully achieved. If any further delights come his way, they do not augment his highest good but season it, as it were, and enhance it. For that ultimate good of human nature is restricted to peace of body and mind.

**47** I will show you a division of goods in Epicurus that is again very similar to this one of ours. In his works, there are some things which he prefers to have happen to him—such as "rest for the body, free from every discomfort, and relaxation for the mind as it rejoices in contemplating its own goods"—and other things which, although he prefers them not to happen, he nonetheless praises and regards with favor, including what I was talking about a little while ago: the endurance of ill health and of very severe pain. That is what Epicurus himself went through on that "last and most blessed day" of his life. For he said that the torments he was experiencing from his bladder and from stomach ulcers were "such as do not admit of any increase of pain," but that all the same that was a "blessed day" for him.* But one cannot spend a blessed day unless he is in possession of the highest good. **48** Thus even in Epicurus there are these goods that you would prefer not to experience, but that when they do occur are to be embraced—praised—considered equal with the very best goods. It's not possible to deny that this was a good equal to the very greatest goods when it is what brought a blessed life to its conclusion—what Epicurus gave thanks for with his dying breath.

49 Most excellent Lucilius, allow me to say something even more bold. If any goods could be greater than others, I would have given preference to these goods more than those others; I'd have said that the harsh ones are greater than the soft, luxurious kind. For beating down one's difficulties is greater than governing one's delights. 50 True, a person handles felicity well for the same reason as he deals bravely with disaster. The soldier who rests at ease outside the camp, since no enemy is on the attack, can be just as brave as the one who, though hamstrung, stays upright on his knees and does not let his weapons drop; still, the cry of "Well done, brave men!" is heard only by those who come back bloody from the front. So these are the goods I would praise: the courageous ones, the ones that have been tried and tested, the ones that have done battle with fortune.

51 Would I hesitate to praise Mucius's maimed and blistered hand above the unharmed hand of another, brave as that person might be?* There he stood, with nothing but scorn for a ring of enemies with their flames. He watched his own hand withering on his enemy's brazier, until Porsenna, whose efforts at punishment he was assisting, grew jealous of his glory and ordered that the fire be taken from him against his will. 52 Why shouldn't I list this as one of the primary goods? Why shouldn't I think it greater than those goods that are carefree, untested by fortune—just as much greater as it is less common to defeat an enemy with a missing hand than with a hand that wields a sword?

"What's that?" you say. "Is this a good you will choose for yourself?" Why shouldn't I? If such a deed cannot be chosen—yes, even chosen—then it cannot be done at all. 53 Should I choose rather to stretch out my hands for my catamites to massage the knuckles? For some courtesan, or some man turned courtesan, to stroke my fingertips? Why shouldn't I think Mucius more fortunate? He reached out to touch the flame just as if he were reaching out to be touched by the masseur! He put right whatever errors he had made; he won his war when weaponless and maimed. With that one mangled hand he conquered a pair of kings.

Farewell.

# Letter 67

*From Seneca to Lucilius*
*Greetings*

**1** Let me begin with commonplaces. Spring has begun to open out; but although it is tending already toward summer, with hot weather overdue, it has kept rather cool, and the weather is still unreliable. Often enough, it lapses back into winter. Would you like to know how doubtful it still is? I don't yet trust myself to a bath that is actually cold—I still take the edge off it. "That means enduring neither heat nor cold," you say. Quite true, dear Lucilius: my time of life is satisfied with its own chill. Even in midsummer I can hardly get warm, and rarely do I shed a garment.

**2** I am grateful to old age for keeping me to my bed. And why not be grateful on that account? Things that I ought not to have wanted to do, I now cannot do. My most abundant conversation is with books. Every time a letter arrives from you, it seems to me that I am with you. I feel as though I were actually answering you and not just writing back. So let's take up the subject you are asking about and scrutinize its nature as we would in conversation.

**3** You ask whether every good is desirable. "If it is a good to behave courageously while being tortured, bravely while being burned, patiently while ill, it follows that these things are desirable, but I do not see how any of them merits our wishes. Certainly I do not know of anyone whose wishes were fulfilled when he was cut by the lash, or twisted up by arthritis, or stretched on the rack."

**4** Make a distinction, dear Lucilius, and you will realize that there is something choiceworthy in these things. I would prefer to remain untouched by torture; but if I should ever have to endure it, I will wish to conduct myself courageously, honorably, boldly in that situation. I prefer—and why not?—that no war should come my way; but if it does, I will wish to endure with dignity the wounds, the hunger, and anything else that wars necessarily bring with them. I don't want to be ill—I'm not crazy!—but if I should ever have to be ill, I will wish my behavior to be neither intemperate nor unmanly. So it's not the discomforts that are desirable but the virtue with which you bear those discomforts.

**5** Some adherents of our school hold that the courageous endurance of all such things, while not to be shunned entirely, is nonetheless not desirable, because wishful pursuit should be directed toward what is thoroughly good, tranquil, and set beyond all annoyance. I disagree. Why? First, because it is impossible for anything to be good without being desirable. Second, if virtue is desirable, and there is no good without virtue, then every good is desirable. Third, even if <torture itself is not desirable>,° the courageous endurance of torture is desirable.

**6** Further, I inquire, is not courage desirable? Yet courage despises danger and even defies danger. That is the most beautiful, most admirable part of courage: refusing to yield to the flames, going to meet the wounds, sometimes not even ducking the arrows but taking them on the chest. If courage is desirable, then enduring torture patiently is desirable, for that is part of courage.

Make the distinction, as I said, and there will be nothing to lead you astray. For it is not suffering torture that is desirable but suffering it courageously. That is what I want, to act courageously—and that is virtue.

**7** "But who has ever wanted that for himself?" Some wishes are openly expressed, in that they concern particular items; some are latent, in that many things are included in a single wish.* For instance, I choose an honorable life for myself; but an honorable life consists in a variety of honorable actions. Contained within this wish are Regulus's crate; Cato's wound, torn open by his own hand; Rutilius's exile; the poisoned cup that carried Socrates from the prison to the skies.* So when I wanted an honorable life for myself, I also wanted these things without which, sometimes, life cannot be honorable.

**8** O three times, four times happy they
whose lot it was to fall beneath the high
ramparts of Troy, before their fathers' eyes!*

Is there any difference between wishing that for someone and granting that it was desirable?

**9** Decius sacrificed himself for his country: he rushed at full gallop into the midst of the enemy, seeking death.* Another Decius after him, emulating his father's virtue, swore the solemn and now familiar oath and dashed into the thick of the fray. He was anxious only that his offering be propitious, for he thought that a good death was something worth wishing for. Do you still doubt whether it is best* to die memorably, performing some act of virtue?

**10** When a person endures torture courageously, he employs all the virtues. Perhaps one of them is out front and most in evidence—namely, patience; still, courage is there, which is the basis of patience and perseverance and endurance; intelligence is there, without which no plan is put into action, and which urges you, when you cannot escape something, to bear it as bravely as you can; constancy is there, which cannot be dislodged from its post, which never lets go of its purpose whatever force be applied. The whole indivisible assembly of the virtues is there.* Whatever is honorably done is done by a single virtue, but in accordance with the counsels of the assemblage. But whatever is approved by all the virtues, even if it appears to be done by a single virtue, is desirable.

**11** What about it? Do you suppose that the only things that are desirable are those that come through pleasure and relaxation—things that take place behind fashionable doorways? There are goods of stern countenance; there are wishes whose fulfillment people celebrate not with congratulations but with admiration and reverence. **12** Do you really think Regulus did not choose to arrive at Carthage? Clothe yourself in the mind of a great man; stand aside for a while from the opinions of the common crowd. Form an impression of virtue that is as great as its merits—virtue at its greatest and most magnificent, virtue that we should honor not with incense and garlands but with sweat and blood. **13** Behold Marcus Cato as he turns his spotless hands against his own sacred breast, as he widens the wound that did not go deep enough. Tell me, are you going to say to him, "Oh, what a pity!" and "I'm so very sorry"? Will you not rather say, "I commend your achievement"?

**14** At this point, our own Demetrius comes to mind, he who calls the life free of care, without any assaults of fortune, "a dead sea."* To lie in undisturbed calm, with nothing to rouse yourself toward, nothing to strive after, nothing to denounce or contend against, testing the firmness of your mind: that is not tranquility; it is enfeeblement. **15** Attalus the Stoic used to say, "I would rather have fortune keep me in its encampments than in luxury. I am tortured, but courageously; it is well. I am slain, but courageously; it is well." Listen to Epicurus; he will say also "It is pleasant."* I, however, will never call such a stern and honorable deed by so soft a name. **16** I am burned, but undefeated: why should this not be desirable? Not because the fire burns me but because it does not defeat me.

Nothing is more excellent than virtue; nothing more beautiful. Whatever is done at its command is not only good but desirable as well.

Farewell.

## Letter 68

*From Seneca to Lucilius*
*Greetings*

**1** I support your plan: hide yourself away in leisure, but also hide the very fact that you are at leisure. Realize that in this you will be following the example of the Stoics, even if not their instructions. But you will be following their instructions too, for you will be justified in your own eyes, and really in anyone's. **2** When we enjoin service to the state, we do not mean to just any state, nor that one must serve at all times or without ending.* Besides, we assign to the wise man a state worthy of him, that is, the whole world. Thus he is not outside the state even if he does retire. Indeed, it may be that in abandoning this one little corner he is moving into a greater and more spacious realm—that he is taking up a seat in heaven, and realizes now what a lowly position he held when he used to mount to the tribunal or preside from the curule chair.* Bank this away in your mind: the sage is never more active than when things divine and human come into his view.

**3** I now return to my earlier exhortation, that you not let anyone know about your leisure. Don't put up a sign saying "Philosophy and Quiet." Give your plan some other name: call it ill health or weakness or laziness. Boasting of one's leisure is just an idle form of ambition.

**4** There are animals that keep from being found by disguising their tracks right around their lairs; you should do the same. Otherwise there will be those who will hunt you down. Many people pass by what is in full view but ferret out anything that is hidden away. To seal an entry is to challenge the thief. What is in plain sight seems to be of little value: leave it out in the open, and the burglar passes it by. That's the way of people generally—that is, of anyone who is ignorant: when something is secreted away, they want to break into it. **5** The best course, then, is not to boast of one's leisure. And to be too secluded, staying completely out of view, is itself a form of boasting. One person hides out at Tarentum; another buries himself away in Naples; another goes for many years without crossing the threshold of his own house. Anyone who makes his leisure somehow legendary is merely summoning an audience for it.

**6** When you retire, your object should not be for people to talk about you but for you to talk to yourself. And what will you say? Just what people are all too ready to say about others: the harsh assessment. Get used to speaking the truth, and to hearing it. Concentrate on those points where you feel you are weakest. **7** Each person knows his own bodily deficiencies. That's why one person lightens his digestion by vomiting, another supports it by frequent meals; another drains and cleanses his body by periods of fasting; and those who are troubled by gout abstain either from wine or from hot baths. People who are careless in other matters attend very closely to their own besetting problem. In the same way, there are diseased areas in our minds: these are what we must cure. **8** What am I doing in my leisure? I am tending to my wound. If I were to show you a swollen foot, a discolored hand, hamstrings so tight my legs could not unbend, you would allow me to lie in one place and coddle my infirmity. This is a greater ill, and one I cannot show to you: the infection, the abscess, is in my very heart.

No, don't praise me. Don't say, "What a great man! He has despised all things—has condemned the madness of human life and made his escape!" I have condemned nothing except myself. **9** Nor will you derive any benefit by coming to me for instruction. If you expect to find help here, you are mistaken. An invalid lives here, not a doctor. Better you should say, after you leave me, "I used to think that fellow was fortunate and a learned man; I was ready to listen to him with eager ears, but I was disappointed. I have seen nothing, heard nothing I would want to have. There's no reason for me to go back." If this is how you feel, if this is what you say, then you have gained something. I'd rather have your forgiveness for my leisure than your envy.

**10** "So, Seneca," you say, "are you recommending leisure to me? Are you lowering yourself to Epicurean maxims?"* I am indeed recommending leisure, but a leisure that will allow you to do greater and fairer deeds than what you leave behind. Knocking on the doors of the high and mighty, drawing up alphabetical lists of elderly persons without heirs, wielding great power in the forum—all such power is brief, invidious, and if truth be told, sordid. **11** One man will be far ahead of me in political influence, another in military service and the prestige that it confers, a third in the extent of his patronage. I cannot equal them; their influence is greater than mine—but I don't mind being beaten by everyone: it's worth it, as long as I am the victor over fortune.

**12** If only you had decided on this course of action a long time ago! If only we were not debating about happiness with death already in sight! Yet late as we are, we are now making no delay; for where once we had reason to teach us that many things are unnecessary or even harmful to us, we now have experience.

**13** So let us be like travelers late in their departure: let's add the spur, and so make up the time by greater speed. This time of life lends itself to such studies: its froth has subsided, and faults that the fervor of youth could not subdue succumb now to fatigue. Before long, they will be extinguished.

**14** "And when will lessons learned at the point of departure be of any use to you?" you say. "And for what?" For this: that I may depart a better man. You need not believe that any time of life is better suited for excellence of mind than when one has disciplined oneself through many trials and many lingering regrets, when one has tamed the emotions and come at last to what is healthful. This is the moment for achieving this good. He who comes to wisdom when old comes so many years the wiser.

Farewell.

# Letter 69

*From Seneca to Lucilius*
*Greetings*

1 I want you not to go traipsing about from place to place, and this for two reasons. First, such frequent travel is a sign of disquiet. The mind cannot find strength in its leisure unless it stops looking around and wandering around. To keep your mind within bounds, you must first stop your body from running away. 2 Second, it is the protracted cure that does the most good. You should rest without interruption and forget your former life. Let your eyes unlearn what they have seen; let your ears grow accustomed to more healthful words. Every time you go out, your old desires are stirred anew, even before you reach your destination. 3 It is like love. When one wants to rid oneself of that passion, one has to avoid all reminders of the body one's affections have chosen—for there is nothing that regains its raw power so easily—and so it is with every fervent desire: one must turn both eyes and ears away from what one has left behind.

4 Emotion is quick to fight back. Wherever it turns, it sees some immediate profit from its exertions. Every evil has something it can appeal to: greed promises you money; self-indulgence promises pleasures of many kinds; ambition promises you the purple,* the roar of the crowd, the power that comes of these and everything that power can do. 5 Your faults ply you with rewards; here, though, you must live unpaid.

Our faults have so long been left to grow that a whole life is hardly enough time to subdue them and bring them under the yoke. Our chances are even less if we divide up our brief span with interruptions. Even constant vigilance and effort can scarcely perfect some single element of our lives.

6 If you would hear my advice, then practice and train yourself in this: how to welcome death, or even summon it if circumstances so indicate.* It matters not whether death comes to us or we to death. Persuade yourself that it is wrong to say, as the ignorant often do, "It

is lovely to die by one's own death." No one dies by any death but his own. And you may ponder this as well: no one dies on any day but his own dying day. You are not losing any of your allotted time, for what you leave behind is not your own.

Farewell.

# BOOK EIGHT

# *Letter 70*

*From Seneca to Lucilius*
*Greetings*

1 After a long interval, I have seen Pompeii, your hometown. It took me back within sight of my youth. I felt as if I could still do the things I did there as a young man, and in fact as if it were only a short while since I did them. 2 Lucilius, we have skirted the shores of life. When one is at sea, as our poet Virgil says, "lands and cities drop away",* and it is just the same with us on this voyage of speeding time. First we lose sight of our childhood, then of our youth, then of the entire interval between youth and age, and then of the best years of old age as well. Finally there comes into view that ending shared by the entire human race. 3 We think it is a rock—but that's insane: it is the harbor. Sometimes we need to steer for it, but never away from it. One who has been carried there early in life should not complain any more than a sailor whose voyage has gone quickly. For as you know, one traveler is held back by lazy winds that play games with him and weary him with the boredom of a completely flat calm; another is driven swiftly on by an ungovernable gale. 4 Imagine the same thing happening to us. Life rushes some people toward where we are all headed, no matter how we try to delay; others it leaves to steep and simmer.

As you know, life is not always something to hang on to. Our good does not consist merely in living but in living well. Hence the wise person lives as long as he ought to, not as long as he can. He considers where he will be living, and how, and with whom, and what he will be doing. He is always thinking about the quality of his life, not the quantity. 5 If he encounters many hardships that banish tranquility, he releases himself.* Nor does he do so only in the extremity of need; rather, as soon as he begins to have doubts about his fortunes, he makes a careful assessment to determine whether it is time to quit. It is a matter of indifference to him whether he brings things to an end himself or only accepts the end that comes, and whether it happens later or sooner. He does not fear that end as if it were some terrible loss: no one can lose much when what he has is only a driblet. **6** Whether one dies sooner or later is not the issue; the issue is whether one dies well or badly. And dying well means that one escapes the risk of living badly.

For that reason I think it was quite unmanly what that fellow from Rhodes said, the one who had been thrown into a cage by a tyrant and was being fed like some wild animal.* When someone urged him to stop eating, he replied, "While life endures, all hopes remain." **7** Even if that is true, life is not worth buying at every price. Some things may be important—may even be certain of attainment—and yet I would not attain them through a base admission of weakness. Am I to think that fortune can do everything to a person as long as he remains alive? Rather, fortune can do nothing to a person as long as he knows how to die.

**8** And yet there are times when even if certain death awaits and he knows that his sentence has been predetermined, he still will not lend a hand in his own execution. Only if it were in his interests would he do so. It is foolish to die merely through fear of death. Someone is coming to kill you? Wait for him. Why the rush? Why are you the stand-in for someone else's cruelty? Do you begrudge your executioner his task? Are you sparing him the trouble? **9** Socrates could have starved himself to death, choosing lack of food over the poison. Yet he spent thirty days in prison waiting for death, not because he thought that anything might still happen (as if such a long time had room for many possible outcomes), but so that he might submit to the laws and give his friends the benefit of Socrates' last days.* To despise death but fear poison: what could be more foolish?

**10** Scribonia, a serious woman, was the aunt of Drusus Libo, a young man who was as stupid as he was wellborn.* He was very ambitious, more so than anyone could be in that period, and more than he should have been in any period. He was sick, and had been carried from the Senate in his litter. (Mind you, he was not well attended! All his relatives had shamelessly deserted him, for by that point he was the deceased rather than the defendant.) He then began to take counsel whether he should commit suicide or whether he should wait. Scribonia said to him, "Why does it please you to do another's business?" She did not persuade him; he laid hands on himself, and not without reason. For when one is bound to die in three or four days at an enemy's behest, then remaining alive *is* doing another's business. **11** Therefore you may not be able to make any overall pronouncement about what to do when death is predetermined by an external power, whether to go ahead with it or wait. For there are many considerations that could draw you in one direction or the other.

If one is a death with torture and the other easy and uncomplicated, why not put out your hand and take the latter? If I were getting ready to sail, I'd pick out a ship; if I were getting ready to move in somewhere, I'd pick out a house; just so, if I were about to die, I would choose my manner of death. **12** Besides, in the same way as long duration does not of itself make life better, so long duration does make death worse. In death, even more than in other things, we ought to make allowances for temperament. Let a person make his exit according to his own inclination. Whether he prefers the sword or the noose or some poison that spreads through the bloodstream, let him go forward with it and break the bonds of servitude.

A person's life should be pleasing not only to himself but also to others; his death need only please himself. The best death is the one he prefers. **13** It is foolish to think, "One person will say I did not act courageously enough; a second will say I was too rash; a third will say another kind of death was braver." Remember, if you will, that reputation has no bearing on the decision you now have in hand. There is only one consideration: to escape fortune's grasp as quickly as you can. Otherwise you will have people showing up to raise objections to your action.

**14** You will find some people, even some committed philosophers, who say that one should never take violent measures against one's own life, feeling that it is wrong to become one's own murderer. They say one should wait for the end that nature has decreed.* Those who say this do not realize that they are blocking the road to freedom. Of all the things the eternal law has done for us, this is the best: we have one way into life, but many ways out. **15** Am I to wait for the cruel action of disease, or of a person, when I could pass through the midst of my torments, shake off my adversities, and depart? This is the one reason why we cannot complain about life: life does not hold anyone by force. The human condition is well situated in that no one is miserable except by his own fault. If it suits you, live; if not, you are allowed to return to where you came from.

**16** You have often endured bloodletting in order to relieve a headache; people sometimes sever a vein as a way of losing weight. There is no need of a huge wound that splits open the chest. A lancet opens the way to that great freedom; a nick buys your tranquility. What is it, then, that makes us idle and reluctant? There is not one of us who thinks of the time when he must leave this apartment. We are like aging tenants, who even when mistreated still allow themselves to be detained by habit and by their fondness for the place. **17** Do you want to be free as concerns your body? Dwell in it as one who will move on. Keep in mind that you must someday be deprived of this habitation; you will then face your eviction more courageously.

But how can people take thought for their own end if they desire all things without end? **18** We need rehearsal for this more than anything else. With other things, we will perhaps turn out to have practiced them in vain. We have prepared our minds against poverty, and our wealth has remained. We have steeled ourselves to disregard pain and have been lucky enough to have sound and healthy bodies that never demanded any proof of our courage. We have taught ourselves to be brave in facing the loss of those we love, and fortune has kept our loved ones alive. Yet for this, and this alone, the day that will put our preparations into effect cannot fail to come.

**19** You need not suppose that only great men have been strong enough to break the bonds of our human slavery. You need not think that it can only be done by Cato, who extracted with his hand the breath that his dagger had not released.* People of the lowest rank have managed by extreme effort to escape to safety. When they were not accorded any convenient way of dying, and could not choose the means of death to suit them, they seized whatever was at hand, and by forcible endeavor made things into weapons that were not dangerous by nature. **20** Recently at the wild-animal games, one of the Germans went off to the latrine during the preparations for the morning show*—it was the only private moment he had without a guard—and there took the stick with a sponge attached that is put there for cleaning the unmentionables and stuffed the entire thing down his throat, closing off his airway. That was indeed offering insult to death. He went right ahead, unsanitary and indecent as it was: how stupid to be fussy about one's way of dying!

**21** What a brave man! He was worthy to be granted a choice in his fate. How boldly he would have used a sword; how courageously he would have thrown himself over some jagged cliff, or into the depths of the sea! With no resources from anywhere, he still found a way to provide his own death, his own weapon. From this you may know that there is but one thing that can delay our dying: the willingness. Each of us may decide for himself as to the merits of this ferocious man's deed—so long as we all agree that death, even the most disgusting, is preferable to slavery, even the cleanest slavery.

**22** Since I have started using unsavory examples, I'll keep on with it: each person will demand more of himself if he sees that even the most contemptible people could hold this thing in contempt. We think that the Catos, the Scipios, and the others whose deeds we habitually admire have been elevated beyond imitation; yet I will now demonstrate that such courage is exemplified just as often in the wild-animal games as in leaders of the Civil War.* **23** Not long ago, a man consigned to the morning spectacle was being conveyed there in a wagon surrounded by guards. Feigning sleepiness, he let his head sink lower and lower until he could get it between the spokes of the wheel, and then held himself down against his seat long enough for the wheel to come around and break his neck. Thus he used the very wagon that was carrying him to punishment as his means of escape.

**24** If what one wants is to break free and get away, there is nothing to prevent that. Nature keeps us in a prison without walls. If circumstances permit, we may look about for a gentle way out; if there are many instruments at hand with which to assert our claim to ourselves, we may ponder the matter and choose the best means of liberation. But if a person is in a difficult situation, let him seize on whatever is nearest and think that best, even if it is strange and unheard of. Ingenuity will not fail him if only determination does not. **25** Don't you see how even very watchful guards can be deceived by the meanest of chattel slaves, once pain goads them into action? The great man is not the one who merely commands his own death but the one who actually finds a death for himself.

But I promised you some more examples from the same offering.

**26** During the second staged naval battle, one of the barbarians took the lance he had been given to use against his opponent and sank the whole of it into his own throat. "Why did I not escape long ago," he cried, "from every torment, every ridicule? Why? Why am I waiting for death when I have a weapon?" It made the show more worth watching, since from it people learn that dying is more honorable than killing.

**27** Well, then. If desperate characters and criminals have such spirit, won't people also have it who have been prepared against misfortune by long practice and by reason, the ruler of all things? Reason teaches us that there are many ways of getting to our fate, but that the end is the same, and that since it is coming, it does not matter when it begins. **28** That same reasoning advises you to die in the way you prefer if you have that opportunity, but if not, to do so in whatever way you can, grasping any available means of doing violence to yourself. It is wrong to steal the means of living, but very fine to steal the means of dying.

Farewell.

## Letter 71

*From Seneca to Lucilius*
*Greetings*

**1** Over and over you consult me about specific matters, forgetting that you and I are separated by a wide and empty sea. Given that most advice depends on the situation, my response on some points is bound to reach you just when the opposite counsel would be more to your advantage. For advice is geared to events, and events are always moving—no, hurtling—along. So advice should be formulated on the day it is needed. And even that is too slow: let it be formulated "on the spot," as the saying goes.

How, then, is advice to be found? Let me explain. **2** Each time you want to know what to pursue or what to avoid, look to your highest good, the aim of your life as a whole. Everything we do ought to be in accordance with that aim. Only one who has the entirety of his life in view is in a position to arrange life's particulars. Even with paints all at the ready, no one can render a likeness until he has decided what he wants to paint. That's our mistake: everyone deliberates over the parts of life; no one over life as a whole. 3 If you want to shoot an arrow, you must know what you are trying to hit: only then can you direct the point and steady the shaft. Our counsels are all astray in that they have no mark to aim at. If one doesn't know what harbor to make for, there can be no favoring wind.

Chance has a great deal of power in our lives—necessarily so, since it is by chance that we are alive. 4 But sometimes people know things without knowing they know them. Just as we often look around for someone who is standing right next to us, so we generally fail to recognize life's goal and highest good even when it is before us. Lengthy explanations will not inform you what the highest good is: one must lay a finger on it, so to speak, and not let it be scattered about. How is it relevant for me to go into all the details, when one could simply say, "The highest good is that which is honorable."* Or, more surprisingly, "The sole good is that which is honorable; other supposed goods are counterfeit coin."

5 If you convince yourself of this, and fall deeply in love with virtue—for merely loving it is not enough!—then whatever virtue touches will be marvelously fortunate in your eyes, no matter how it appears to others. You will subdue even torture, if you bear it with no more concern than is felt by the torturer himself; even illness, if you do not curse fortune—that is, if you don't let the disease win. Indeed, everything others regard as bad will turn out to be a good if only you rise above it. Once you are clear on this point, that only what is honorable is good, then everything that is uncomfortable in itself will be counted as a good, as long as virtue renders it honorable. 6 Many people think that we Stoics promise more than the human condition is capable of, and with reason: they are looking to their bodies. Let them turn once again to the mind; then they will find in God the measure of humankind.*

Rouse yourself, most excellent Lucilius, and leave behind you that grammar school, those pedant philosophers who reduce this most amazing subject to words and syllables. By teaching the minutiae they debase the mind; they fritter it away. Be like those who made these discoveries, not like those who teach them with the aim of making philosophy seem difficult rather than great. 7 Socrates, he who summoned all philosophy back toward ethics, used to say that the very height of wisdom is in distinguishing between good and bad. He said,

> If I have any authority with you, then follow those, so that you may be happy; and if someone thinks you are a fool, let him. Whoever wants to may insult you or do you wrong: you will be unaffected, as long as virtue is on your side. If you want to be happy, if you truly want to be a good man, then let yourself be despised.*

In order to achieve this, one must oneself learn to despise all things. One must level the field among all things that are good; for there is no good apart from what is honorable, and what is honorable is equal in every instance.*

8 "What do you mean? Does it not matter whether Cato is elected praetor or rejected?* Does it make no difference at all whether he is defeated at Pharsalus or defeats his enemy? Is this good that he has in remaining unconquerable when his side is defeated really equal to the good he would have had if he had won the battle, returned to his homeland, and established peace?" Why not? Virtue while defeating adversity is just the same as it is while holding the line in the midst of prosperity; yet virtue cannot be made larger or smaller: it has but the one size.

9 "But Gnaeus Pompey will lose his army; the nobles, fairest ornament of the Republic, and the first line of Pompey's faction— senators in arms!—will be smashed in a single battle. The collapse of so great a power will cast remnants across the whole world: part of it will fall in Egypt, another part in Africa, a third in Spain. Our poor Republic will not even be granted to have just the one downfall." 10 All of that may happen: Juba may gain no advantage for his knowledge of home terrain, or from the stubborn courage of his commoners defending their king; the loyalty of the Uticans may fail, broken down by adversity; Scipio may fall short of the luck his name had hitherto enjoyed in Africa.* Yet provision was made long ago that Cato should take no harm. 11 "But he was defeated." Yes, another setback for Cato. He will accept the obstacle to his victory just as nobly as he accepted the obstacles to his praetorship. The day

he lost the election, he played a game; the night he was to die, he read a book.* It was all the same to him whether he lost the praetorship or lost his life; for he had convinced himself that whatever happened, he should endure it.

12 And really, why should he not endure the change in the Republic both courageously and calmly? What is exempt from the risk of change? Not the earth, not the sky, not the very fabric of the universe. Though woven by God's own agency, it will not keep to its present order forever: a day will come that will knock it off its course.* 13 All things proceed according to schedule: they must be born, grow, die. Everything you see passing above us, all that seems so solid beneath our feet, will crumble away; each thing has its own senescence. Nature sends them all away, after different spans yet to the same place. That which is, will not be.

Not that it perishes; rather it is dissolved. 14 For us, being dissolved is perishing, for we are looking at what is nearest to us. Our dull wits are pledged to the service of our bodies, and look no further than that. We would bear our own end and that of our loved ones with greater courage if we perceived that life and death, like everything else, come and go by turns. Compounds are dissolved, dissolute elements compounded, and in this way does the eternal craftsmanship of all-regulating God exert itself. 15 Thus like Marcus Cato our thoughts will speed through time and say,

"All humankind, now and in the future, is doomed to die; all cities that have ruled the world and all that have been trophies of some other power will someday disappear from sight, wiped out by varied forms of ruin. Wars will destroy some; others will be swallowed up by desuetude, and peace that turns to idleness, and that which is most ruinous to great resources—luxury. All these fertile plains will someday be covered up by some sudden incursion of the sea, or engulfed by subsidence of the earth into an unexpected cavern. Why, then, should I complain? Why should I be sad to go just a moment sooner than the end decreed for nations and peoples? 16 A great spirit should obey God, not hesitating to comply with every instruction of the world's law. Either it is being sent away to a better life, to dwell in greater and more tranquil light amid the things of God, or at least it will be free of discomfort, being mingled again with nature, returning to the universe."

So Cato's honorable life is not a greater good than his honorable death: virtue does not admit of augmentation. Socrates used to say that truth and virtue are the same thing. Just as truth does not increase, virtue does not increase either. It keeps its measures; it has its complement.*

17 You need not be surprised, then, that goods are equal to one another, not only those that one should make a point of pursuing but also those that one should take on if the situation warrants it. For if you accept that there is inequality, even such that you would consider the courageous endurance of torture to be one of the lesser goods, then you will also be regarding it as a bad thing.* You will be saying that Socrates was unfortunate in his prison, that Cato was unfortunate when he reopened his wounds even more bravely than he made them, that Regulus was more terribly afflicted than any of them, in that he kept a promise even to his enemies and paid the penalty for doing so. Yet no one, not even the most fainthearted, has dared to say that: they say that Regulus was not happy yet insist that he was not miserable either.* 18 The Old Academics admit that Regulus was happy even amid such torments, but not to the full and perfect extent of happiness.* This is completely unacceptable. If one is not happy, one cannot have attained the highest good. The highest good does not admit of any further degree of goodness, as long as there is virtue in it; as long as adversity does not diminish that virtue; as long as virtue remains intact even when the body is maimed. But it does remain intact, for I understand "virtue" to refer to that brave, exalted virtue which draws energy from whatever opposes it.

19 Young men of noble disposition, when struck by the beauty of some honorable deed, frequently adopt an attitude of not caring about any of the contingencies. But wisdom will confer that same way of thinking without further ado. Wisdom will shower us° with the conviction that what is honorable is the sole good, and that the honorable cannot be either reduced or heightened, any more than you can bend the straight line that is the accepted standard for straightness. Any change you make in it is detrimental to straightness. 20 Thus we will say the same about virtue: it too is straight; it

does not admit of curvature. Once a thing is vertical, what increase can be made in it?°* Virtue takes the measure of everything; nothing takes the measure of virtue. If virtue itself cannot be made any more straight and right, then no one of the things it does is more right than any other, for they necessarily conform to virtue's standard. Hence they are all equal.

21 "What's this?" you say. "Reclining at dinner is equal to being tortured?" Does this surprise you? Here is something that will amaze you even more: reclining at dinner is bad and lying on the rack is good if the one is done in a disgraceful manner and the other honorably. It is not the material that makes them good or bad but virtue: wherever that appears, everything is of the same measure and the same value.*

22 At this point, the person who judges everyone's spirit by his own waves his hands in my face because I say there is equality of goods between an honorable judge and an honorable defendant, and equality of goods between the returning general in his victory parade and the mentally unconquered captive that is trundled along in front of his chariot. Such people think that whatever they cannot do cannot be done; they form opinions about virtue based on their own weakness.

23 Why are you surprised that being burned, wounded, struck down, or shackled should be a source of satisfaction, sometimes even of gladness? When one is devoted to luxurious living, frugality is a punishment; when one is lazy, work is like a sentence; the fashionably effete person pities the industrious one; the idler finds study a torment. In just the same way, when we are all too weak for a task we think of it as harsh and intolerable. We forget there are many people who find it burdensome to go without wine or to be awakened at dawn. These things are not difficult by nature, but we ourselves are listless and feeble. 24 To take the measure of great challenges, one must have a great mind: otherwise one will think the fault lies with circumstances rather than with us. It is like certain objects which despite being quite straight still give the appearance of being bent or broken when lowered into the water.* It's not only what you see that matters; it's how you see. Our minds are too clouded to see things as they really are.

25 Give me a quick-witted youth who has not been corrupted;* he

will say that in his view, the more fortunate person is the one whose shoulders are unbowed as he bears every burden of adversity, the person who rises superior to fortune. Not to flinch in times of calm—there's nothing remarkable about that! What should excite wonder is when someone rises up while all are downcast; when someone stands while all are laid low.

**26** What is it that is bad about torture or other events we regard as unfavorable? Just this, I think: abasing one's mind, bowing down, yielding. None of these can happen to the man of wisdom: he stands upright under any load. Nothing diminishes him; nothing he has to endure displeases him. Among all the things that can happen to a human being, there is not one that he complains of just because it has happened to him. He knows his own strength; he knows that he exists for the bearing of burdens.

**27** I do not put the sage in a separate class from the rest of humankind, and neither do I eliminate pain and grief from him as if he were some sort of rock, not susceptible to any feeling. I keep in mind that he is made up of two parts. One is nonrational, and it is this that experiences the biting, the burning, the pain.* The other part is rational; it is this that holds unshakable opinions and that is fearless and unconquerable. In this latter resides the highest good of humankind. Before that good is filled out, the mind is uncertain and in turmoil; but when it has been perfected, the mind is stable and unmoved. **28** For this reason, the person who has made a start, the one who is committed to virtue but is still ascending the summit, who even if he is drawing near to perfect goodness has yet to apply the finishing touches, will sometimes slack off and allow his concentration to falter. For he has not yet gotten past the uncertainties; he is still on shaky ground. But the truly happy person, the person of accomplished virtue, loves himself most when he has met some challenge with exceptional courage. Trials that other people find frightening he not only endures but actually embraces, if they are the price of some honorable obligation. Rather than "What good fortune!" he would much prefer to hear "What good work!"

**29** I come now to the point you have been expecting me to address. Lest it should seem that this virtue of ours strays outside the natural order, the wise person will tremble and feel pain and grow pale. For all these are feelings of the body. Where, then, is the malady? Where is the real harm? I'll tell you: it is when those responses pull the mind down, when they induce it to confess itself a slave, when they make it regret its own nature.* **30** The wise person vanquishes misfortune through courage, but many who profess wisdom are terrified at times by the most trivial of threats. At this point the fault is ours, for demanding the same from one who is making progress as from the sage. I am still persuading myself of the principles I extol; I am not fully convinced. And even if I were, I would not have the lessons so well prepared, so well practiced, as to have them spring to my defense in every tribulation. **31** Just as some dyes are readily absorbed by the wool, others only after repeated soaking and simmering, so there are some studies that show up well in our minds as soon as we have learned them; this one, though, must permeate us thoroughly. It must soak in, giving not just a tinge of color but a real deep dye, or it cannot deliver on any of its promises.

**32** To tell it requires but a few quick words: that virtue is the sole good, and certainly that nothing is good without virtue; moreover, that virtue itself is located in our better part, namely, the rational part. What is this virtue? True and unshakable judgment, for from this come the impulses of the mind; by this, every impression that stimulates impulse is rendered perfectly clear.*

**33** It will be consonant with this judgment to regard all things that are associated with virtue as goods and as equal to one another. The goods of the body are indeed good for bodies, but overall they are not goods. They will indeed have some value, but no true worth; and they will differ widely from one another, some being of lesser degree and others greater. **34** Even among those who pursue wisdom, we must admit there are differences. One person's progress is such that he dares to face up to fortune, but not steadily; he lowers his gaze again when dazzled by the glare. Another has advanced to where he can confront fortune directly, or perhaps he has even mounted to the summit, his confidence complete. **35** What is imperfect cannot but stumble. Now they advance; now they slip backward or fall. But they will indeed slip backward if they do not persevere in their struggle and their progress: if they relax their efforts, their faithful determination, they necessarily lose ground. No one abandons the cause and then takes it up again at the same point.

**36** Let us press on, then; let us persevere. The challenges that lie ahead are greater than those we have overcome already. But most of progress consists in being willing to make progress.* This I recognize in myself: I am willing—with my entire mind, I am willing. And I see that you too are inspired; you are hurrying eagerly toward the most beautiful of ends. Let us both make haste! Only then is life worth living. Otherwise we are just marking time, and shamefully too, surrounded by ugliness. Let us strive to make every moment belong to us—but it never will belong to us until we belong to ourselves.

**37** How long till I despise both bad fortune and good? How long till I subdue every passion, subject them to my judgment, and cry, "Victory is mine!" Do you ask who it is that I have conquered? Not the Persians, not the most distant Medes, not some warlike tribe out beyond the furthest Parthians but avarice, and ambition, and that which conquers the conquerors of nations: the fear of death.

Farewell.

## Letter 72

*From Seneca to Lucilius*
*Greetings*

**1** The point you are inquiring about used to be plain as day to me; that's how thoroughly I knew the material. But it has been a long time since I tested my memory, and hence I cannot now recall it easily. You know what happens to papyrus rolls when they become stuck together with disuse; well, I feel as if that has happened to me: my mind needs to be unrolled occasionally and its contents brought to light if they are to be available when the need arises. So let's defer your question for the time being: it demands much effort and attention. As soon as I expect to stay in one place for a longer period, I will take it in hand. **2** For there are some subjects one can write about even in a traveling carriage; others demand a comfortable seat, some leisure time, and freedom from distraction.

Still, I should have some project to work on even in these busy days, entirely full though they are. For there will always be some new occupation to replace the one before it. We plant them like seeds, each producing many more. Besides, we keep giving ourselves postponements. "Once I finish this, I will devote my whole mind to it," and "As soon as I get through this troublesome task, I will give myself over to study." 3 We ought not to wait for our spare time to practice philosophy; rather, we should neglect other occupations to pursue this one task for which no amount of time would be sufficient, even if our lives were prolonged to the greatest extent of the human lifespan. You might as well not bother with philosophy if you are going to practice it intermittently. For it does not stay in one place during an interruption. No, it is like some object that springs back after being compressed: once you let up, you revert to where you were before. You have to take a stand against occupations. Rather than reducing your encumbrances, you should get rid of them altogether. There is no time that is not well suited to these healing studies, yet there are many who fail to study when caught up in the problems that give one reason to study.

4 "Some chance event will hinder me." But nothing hinders the one whose mind is cheerful and eager in every occupation. When one is imperfect, one's cheerfulness is still subject to interruption; but wise joy is seamless.* It is not interrupted by any cause, any chance event. The wise person is always and everywhere tranquil; for he does not depend on what belongs to another, and does not wait upon the favor of fortune or of any other person. His happiness lives at home. If it came into the mind from elsewhere, it would also depart—but it is born there. 5 He does occasionally experience a disturbance from outside to remind him of his mortality, but one that is too slight to do more than scratch the surface.* Yes, he feels the winds of adversity, but the greatest good is firmly in place. That is to say, there are some discomforts that are external to him, just as a strong, sound body might have a scratch or a pimple without there being any deep-seated affliction.

6 I mean that the difference between the man of perfect wisdom and another who is making progress toward wisdom is like the difference between a healthy person and one who is recovering from a long and serious illness, with whom it counts as health if he merely has a less serious episode of his disease. If this latter person does not pay attention, his progress becomes more and more difficult, with frequent backsliding, whereas the wise person cannot suffer a relapse

or indeed any sort of lapse at all. For health of body is a temporary condition, and one that no doctor can bestow, though he may restore it. Over and over he is roused from sleep to attend the same person who called him on some earlier occasion. But when the mind is healed, it is once and for all.

7 I will tell you what I mean by a mind that has been healed: one that is content in itself, that has confidence in itself; one that realizes that all those things we mortals wish to have, all the favors we give and ask in return, have no bearing whatever on happiness. For that to which any addition can be made is not complete, and that which can suffer diminution is not eternal. If cheerfulness is to endure, one must rejoice in one's own resources. All ordinary objects of longing are in flux, this way and that. Fortune's gifts are not ours to keep.

But even what we do receive from fortune brings satisfaction only when reason mixes it in due proportion. It is reason that makes things valuable to us, even external things: if we are greedy for them, we gain no satisfaction from them. 8 Attalus used to offer this analogy:

> Have you ever seen a dog snapping at morsels of bread or meat tossed by its master? Every time he catches one, he immediately gulps it down whole, his jaws always open, intent on the next one coming. It is the same with us. Everything fortune casts in our direction, we devour at once, ever intent on some dazzling prospect just beyond our grasp.*

This does not happen to the sage: he is fulfilled. If something comes his way, he picks it up without particular concern and then lays it aside the same way. His gladness is abundant, constant, and his own.

9 A person who has good intentions and is making progress, but who is still a long way from the summit, moves alternately upward and downward: now he mounts to the sky; now he is brought back down to earth. Novices devoid of training plummet downward without end; they fall into the chaos of Epicurus, a boundless void.* 10 There is yet a third contingent: those who are on the verge of wisdom. Although they have not yet reached it, they have it in sight— within striking distance, as it were. No longer are they buffeted by the waves; no longer do they even feel an undertow. Though not yet landed, they are already within the harbor.*

11 So, since there is so much distance between the highest and

lowest stages of progress, with even the middle stage subject to variation and the lowest at great risk of degeneracy, we ought not to succumb to occupations. They must be kept out: once they make it through the door, they will bring others in as well. Let's resist them from the beginning: the start will not be better than the finish.

Farewell.

## *Letter 73*

*From Seneca to Lucilius*
*Greetings*

1 People are wrong, I believe, when they suppose that devoted philosophers are headstrong and difficult to manage, having little regard for magistrates or kings or for anyone who governs the state. Quite the contrary: no one is more grateful to them, and with good reason, since no one benefits more from their administration than those who are enabled by it to enjoy the advantages of tranquil leisure.*

2 Therefore those whose project of living well has been greatly enhanced by the security of the state cannot but respect the one responsible for this good thing as if he were a parent, much more than do those restless characters who engage in business and politics. These latter owe much to their rulers, but they also make many demands on them. No amount of generosity can ever satisfy their desires: the more they are given, the more they want. One whose mind is on receiving forgets what he has already received. Of all the evils of acquisitiveness, the worst is ingratitude. 3 Moreover, those who are politically active never give a thought to how many people they have overtaken, but only to those who are out in front. The pleasure of seeing many behind them is nothing to the pain of seeing even one still ahead. All forms of ambition have this defect: they never look back. Nor is it only ambition that finds no rest, but every form of desire, for desire is always beginning afresh from its fulfillment.

4 But the pure, unblemished man, the one who has left the senate house and the forum for wider concerns, loves the people whose efforts enable him to do so in safety. He alone lends them disinterested

support, for he owes them a great debt of which they themselves are unaware. Just as he respects and admires his teachers, whose help has enabled him to escape the pathless waste, so he looks up to those under whose protection he devotes himself to cultural pursuits.

5 "But the king also protects others by his power." Does anyone deny it? But so does good weather affect all who sail, and yet the captain whose cargo is larger and more valuable feels a greater sense of obligation to Neptune; the merchant pays his vows more gladly than the owner of a common carrier; and even among merchants the one who was transporting spices and luxury textiles, items whose price is paid in gold, feels a deeper sense of obligation than the one who had taken on a cargo of cheap stuff destined to serve mainly as ballast. In just the same way, the benefits of this peace that we all enjoy are more deeply felt by those who make good use of it. 6 For there are many of our present-day toga wearers who find more to do in peacetime than in times of war. Do you suppose that people recognize the same obligation for peace when they squander it on drunkenness and lust or on other vices it would be worth a war to interrupt?

Surely you don't imagine that the wise person is so unfair as to disclaim any personal obligation for benefits that are held in common. I owe much to the sun and the moon, yet they do not rise for me alone; I am indebted on my own account to the seasons of the year and to God, who regulates them, even though <these things>° were not set up in my honor. 7 It is the foolish avarice of mortals that distinguishes between possession and ownership, counting nothing as one's own that belongs also to everyone else. The wise person realizes that nothing is more his own than what is allotted not to him alone but to the whole human race. For those would not be shared possessions if part of them did not belong to each individual. He thus holds joint possession of everything that is common property even in the least degree.

8 Besides, the truly great goods are not shared in the sense that a little bit of them is apportioned to each individual; rather, they belong entirely to each. From the money distribution, people take away the amount promised to each; the grain distribution and the meat distribution and other tangible forms of largesse are divided up and taken home; but these indivisible goods, peace and liberty, are given in their entirety not only to all but also to each.

**9** He reflects, then, on who it is that confers on him the use and enjoyment of these things; who it is that spares him from being summoned by public needs to arms, to guard duty, to patrolling the ramparts, and all the many other demands of war, and he renders thanks to his ruler. Philosophy's most important lesson is the proper way to owe a benefit and the proper way to repay one. But sometimes just acknowledging the debt is repayment enough. **10** So he will admit that he owes a great deal to the one whose intelligent management has blessed him with fertile hours of leisure, with control of his own time, with quietness untroubled by civic responsibilities.

> O Meliboeus, a god devised this peace for us;
> for in my mind that man will always be
> a god.*

**11** Much is owing to the governor even for those times of peace whose greatest gift is this:

> He bade my cattle browse, as now
> you see, and gave me license now to play
> the things I want upon my rural pipe.*

What value, then, shall we set on that time of peace which is spent among the gods—which makes us gods ourselves?

**12** Yes, Lucilius—gods! I am calling you to the heavens, and by the quickest route. Sextius used to say that the good man's power is as great as Jupiter's.* Jupiter has more to offer to humankind; but when two are wise, the wealth of one does not make him better than the other, any more than you would consider one skilled helmsman better than another just because his vessel was larger and more splendid. **13** In what way does Jupiter surpass the good man? He is good for longer. But the sage does not think himself less valuable just because his virtues are restricted to a smaller compass. Just as one wise man is not more blessed than another, even though one dies at a more advanced age and the other's virtue is limited to fewer years, so God does not surpass the wise human being in blessedness, even though he does in duration. Virtue is not greater just because it lasts longer.

**14** Jupiter has everything, yet he also gives everything to others for them to have. The use of those things is his only in the sense that he is the cause of others' using them.* The sage views others' possessions and despises them as calmly as Jupiter does; in fact, he thinks more highly of himself in that while Jupiter cannot use those things, he, being wise, does not want to.

**15** So let us believe Sextius when he shows us this most beautiful journey, when he cries, "This is the road by which one mounts to the stars: the road of frugality, the road of self-control, the road of courage." The gods are not scornful; they are not jealous of their own: they are welcoming; they lend a hand to those who would climb up. **16** Are you astounded that a human being can go to the gods? God comes to human beings. No, it is more intimate than that: God actually comes *into* human beings. For excellence of mind is never devoid of God. Seeds of divinity are scattered in human bodies: if a good gardener takes them in hand, the seedlings resemble their source and grow up equal to the parent plant. But poor cultivation, like sterile or boggy soil, kills the plants and produces only a crop of weeds.

Farewell.

## Letter 74

*From Seneca to Lucilius*
*Greetings*

**1** Your letter was a delight to me, dear Lucilius: it roused me, for I was growing faint; and it stirred my memory, which tends to be slow and feeble. You hold—and why shouldn't you!—that the best means toward happiness is this conviction of ours that honorable conduct is the only good. For he who regards other things as good is dominated by fortune and subject to another's whim; he who limits goodness to what is honorable is happy within himself.

**2** One person is grieved when his children die, worried when they are sick; another is sad when they are of base character and tinged with notoriety. This fellow is wracked with love for another's wife; that one with love for his own. You will find one man tormented by a lost election; for another, elected office yields its own frustrations. **3** But of all the suffering crowds of humankind, the greatest is of those who are troubled by the thought of death. That thought meets them at every turn, for death may come from any direction. Like troops passing through enemy territory, they must be looking around all the time, turning their heads at every sound. Unless this fear is driven from the breast, we live with quaking hearts.

**4** You will find some who have suffered exile and confiscation of property; others who endure the worst form of poverty, for they are bankrupt in the midst of wealth. You will find shipwrecked sailors and men who have undergone another kind of shipwreck, since the people's wrath or their envy—that dart most deadly to the upper class—has struck them carefree and unawares and has flattened them like one of those sudden storms that blow up from a cloudless sky, or like a thunderbolt that causes all the land around to tremble. Just as when someone is struck by lightning the bystanders are stunned as well, so in these chance disasters one is stricken by calamity, others by fear, as much alarmed by the sight of what can happen as those are to whom it has actually happened. **5** Everyone is made anxious by the sudden misfortunes of others. Like birds that are put to flight by the whir of the sling whether or not it is loaded, we are startled not only by the blow but even by the sound of the blow.

No one can be happy, then, who entrusts himself to this belief. For there is no happiness without tranquility: a life amid anxieties is a life of misery. **6** Everyone who is much devoted to the advantages of fortune inevitably sets himself up for great emotional turmoil. There is but one road that leads to safety: you must rise above external things and be content with what is honorable. For he who thinks there is something better than virtue, or that anything besides virtue is good at all, exposes his breast to everything fortune can throw at him and waits anxiously for the blows to land.

**7** Set before your mind the following image. Fortune is putting on a festival; elected office, wealth, and popularity are the largesse that it scatters amid this mortal crowd. Some of that largesse is torn to bits by many grasping hands; some shared out in faithless bargains; some carried off to the detriment of those who get it. Some of that falls to the inattentive; some is knocked away by those trying too eagerly to snatch it; but even when luck attends the catching, none of it brings anyone a joy that lasts even until tomorrow. The intelligent person therefore deserts the theater as soon as he sees the gifts brought in: he knows that small favors may come at a high price. No one grapples with him as he is leaving; no one throws a punch as he is headed for the door; the scuffle is around the loot. **8** The same thing happens with the gifts that fortune showers upon us. Poor things, we are all in a fever and a fret; we wish that we had many hands; we look this way and that. We think they are too slow in coming, these gifts that madden us with desire, that come to so few, though all expect them. **9** We want to be where they are falling; we rejoice if we catch a few where others have been disappointed. Either we pay a great price in anxiety for our cheap trinkets, or we get none° and are disappointed. Let us withdraw, then, from the show, yielding our places to those who are still snatching for the prizes. Let them be the ones to gaze at those goods suspended in midair—and let them be in greater suspense themselves.

**10** The person who is determined to be happy should make up his mind that the one good thing is honorable conduct. For if he imagines that there is any other good, first of all he thinks ill of providence, since many uncomfortable things happen to just men, and since whatever gifts we do receive are small and of brief duration compared with the age of the universe. **11** It is in consequence of this complaint that we are such thankless interpreters of the divine. We complain that our blessings are not ours forever, and that they are few, unreliable, and fleeting. Hence we are unwilling to live, unwilling to die; loathing life, we yet fear death. Every plan is adrift; no good fortune can satisfy us.

The reason, though, is that we have not attained that measureless and insurmountable good where all our wanting must come to an end, since beyond the summit there is nowhere more to go. **12** Do you ask why virtue lacks nothing? Virtue rejoices in present goods; has no longing for what is absent; finds nothing meager that will suffice. Abandon this attitude, and loyalty is lost; integrity is lost. For to preserve those values, one must endure many things that are regarded as bad and forgo many indulgences that are regarded as good. **13** Gone is courage, which requires risking oneself; gone is greatness of spirit, which cannot rise above its surroundings unless it holds in low esteem those objects which the common crowd prize most highly. Gratitude is lost, and readiness to return a favor, if we are afraid of hard work, if we treasure anything more than loyalty, if we do not turn our gaze toward what is best.

**14** But besides all that, either those so-called goods really are not good or human beings are more fortunate than God. For God makes no use of those things that are dear to us: lust means nothing to him, nor the delicacies of the table, nor wealth, nor any other of those tawdry pleasures that humans find so enticing. Either we must believe that there are goods that God does not have, or God's not having them is proof that they are not goods. **15** Moreover, many of these would-be goods belong to animals more abundantly than to human beings. Animals partake of food more eagerly, are less exhausted by sexual intercourse, have greater and more consistent strength. It follows that they are much happier than humans. For they live without wickedness or deceit; they have a greater and easier capacity for pleasure, and they enjoy those pleasures with no fear of shame or regret.

**16** Consider, then, whether that in which humanity surpasses the divine should be called good. Let us enclose the highest good within the mind: it loses its meaning if it passes from our best part to our worst, and is transferred to the senses, which are keener in speechless animals. Our supreme felicity ought not to be assigned to the flesh. The goods that reason gives are real; they are solid and eternal; they cannot fail; they cannot decrease or be diminished. **17** Those others are the goods of opinion: they share their name with real goods, but the distinctive property of the good is not in them. For this reason let them be termed "comforts," or, to use our school's terminology, "preferred things."* Let us realize that they are our possessions, not parts of ourselves; let them be with us only insofar as we remember that they are external to us. And even if they are with us, let them be counted as servants of the most humble kind, about which no one has reason to boast. What is more foolish than taking pride in something one did not personally perform?

**18** May all those things come to us, but may they not cling to us; so that if they should be taken away, their departure will not tear us apart. Let us use them, not glory in them; and let us use them sparingly, as loans that will someday be recalled. One who possesses them in an unreasoning manner does not keep them for long: in the absence of moderation, his very abundance is oppressive. If he trusts in these advantages that are so fleeting, they soon desert him; even if they do not,° they are still an affliction. Few people have been able to lay aside an abundance of goods gracefully. All the rest are brought down along with the fortunes that surrounded them in their eminence; they are weighed down by that which had exalted them.

**19** Therefore let intelligence come to our aid, imposing limits and careful management. For profligacy squanders its resources: the immoderate cannot last without moderating reason to keep it in check. You can see this in the fate of many cities that at the very height of their power have been laid low by self-indulgent regimes: everything courage has won, intemperance has destroyed. We must guard against such disasters. But there is no rampart fortune cannot storm. Our defenses must be arrayed within: if that part is safe, a person can be assailed but can never be captured. **20** Would you like to know what those defenses are? Taking no offense at anything that happens; knowing that what seems to harm you belongs to the preservation of the universe and fulfills the world's order and function; being pleased with whatever has been pleasing to God; taking pride in yourself and your own for one reason only: that you cannot be conquered, that you rise above your very ills, that by reason, the most powerful force there is, you overcome every misfortune, pain, and injury.

**21** Fall in love with reason! That love will arm you against the toughest trials. Love for her cubs hurls the lioness onto the javelin; savagery and impulsiveness make her indomitable. Hunger for glory moves many a young man's heart to despise both fire and sword. The semblance and shadow of courage drive some to willful death. As reason is braver and steadier than any of these, so does it issue forth more valiantly through every fear and danger.

**22** One might say, "It is futile to insist that there is no good but what is honorable. That armament will not make you safe from fortune and invulnerable. For among goods your school includes devoted children, good customs in one's homeland, and good parents. When those are endangered, you cannot look on without anxiety. You will be disturbed by an attack on your homeland, the death of your children, the enslavement of your parents."*

**23** In reply I will first set down the points that are customarily made on behalf of our school,* then add a further response that I think ought to be made.

The situation is different with those things whose loss means that they are replaced by some discomfort. For instance, when good health is ruined, it turns into ill health; when keen eyesight is extinguished, we are afflicted with blindness; when the tendons of the knee are cut, we not only lose the ability to run quickly but become lame as well. But with the objects I mentioned just now, there is no such risk. How so? If I have lost a good friend, I need not suffer disloyalty in his place; if my good children have died, neglectful ones do not succeed them.

**24** A further point is that in these cases, it is not the friends or the children that are lost but only their bodies. There is only one way the good perishes, namely, if it becomes bad; but nature does not permit that, since every virtue and every act of virtue remains unspoiled. Moreover, even if one's friends have indeed perished, and children of proven worth who were everything a parent could wish, we have something to fill the void. "What is that?" you ask. The same thing as made them good: virtue. **25** Virtue leaves no space empty; it occupies the entire mind, obviating all sense of loss. Virtue by itself is enough, for it has within it the strength and source of all good things. What does it matter if running water is intercepted or diverted, when the spring from which it flowed is undiminished? You will not say that a person's life is more just, more temperate, more intelligent, or more honorable when his children are alive than when they are lost; therefore it is not better either. Adding friends does not make one wiser; removing them does not make one more foolish; therefore friends do not make one happier or more miserable. As long as virtue is whole and sound, you will not feel any loss.

**26** "What are you saying? How can a person not be happier when surrounded by a crowd of friends and children?" Why should he be? The highest good neither decreases nor increases: it continues to fill out its own limit, no matter how fortune behaves. Regardless of whether he lives to a ripe old age or dies before growing old, the measure of the ultimate good is the same, even if its lifespan is different. **27** Whether you draw a large circle or a small one concerns the size, not the shape. One may last a long time; the other you may erase immediately, reducing it to the dust in which it was drawn, but both were the same with regard to their shape. Straightness is not a matter of size or number or duration; it cannot be either extended or reduced. Take an honorable life of a hundred years' duration and contract it to any length you wish, even to a single day: it is still equally honorable. **28** Sometimes virtue expands its scope; it rules kingdoms, cities, provinces, looks after friendships, performs various responsibilities among neighbors and children; at other times it is enclosed within a tight boundary of poverty, exile, or bereavement. Yet it is not made smaller when brought down to earth from a loftier pinnacle, from the estate of kings to that of the private citizen, from wide jurisdiction to the limitations of a single household or even a corner. **29** It is equally great even if it withdraws into itself, closed off on every side. For its spirit is no less great, no less upright, no less precise in intelligence, no less inflexible in justice. Therefore it is equally happy, for true happiness resides in just one place: the mind itself. The stability, the grandeur, the tranquility, of real happiness cannot be attained without knowledge of things divine and human.*

**30** Now, here is the reply I said I would give on my own account. The wise person is not afflicted by the loss of children or of friends, because he endures their death in the same spirit as he awaits his own. He does not fear the one any more than he grieves over the other. For virtue is made up of consistency: all its actions harmonize and agree with one another. This harmony is lost if the mind, which by rights should be elevated, is brought down by desire or grief. All anxiety and worry is dishonorable, all reluctance to act; for honorable conduct is sure and unhampered, undismayed, ever standing at the ready.

**31** "What do you mean? Doesn't the wise person experience something similar to emotion? Won't his color change, his expression show signs of alarm, his limbs grow cold, and everything else that does not come about at the mind's behest but by some unintentional impulse of nature?"* I grant that, but he will remain unchanged in his conviction that not one of the objects mentioned is bad or is such that a sound mind should quail at it. Everything that is to be done he will do promptly and boldly. **32** For it has been said that the distinctive property of foolishness is that all its actions are performed in a slothful and recalcitrant manner. The body goes in one direction, the mind in another; contrary impulses tear the person apart. The objects of its vanity and conceit are the very ones that render it despicable, and the actions in which it takes pride are not even willingly performed.

But when foolishness has something to fear, it is as tormented in its expectation as though the bad thing had already occurred: what it fears to endure, it endures already through fear. 33 Just as with bodily illness there are advance warnings that precede a seizure—a listless heaviness, unexplained fatigue, yawning, and a tingling that runs through the limbs—even so is the unhealthy mind shaken by misfortunes long before it is actually confronted with them: it anticipates them and is afflicted before its time. Yet what could be more senseless than suffering over what has not yet happened? Rather than awaiting future trials, you are summoning them to your side! Better you should delay them if you cannot dispel them altogether.

34 "Why," you ask, "should a person not be tormented by the future?" Suppose one were to hear that in fifty years' time he would be put to torture. The only way he would be alarmed would be if he were to bypass the intervening years and insert himself into the anxiety that is to come a lifespan later. The same thing happens with minds that deliberately make themselves ill by sorrowing over events long in the past. They are seeking out reasons for grief. Both the past and the future are absent; we have no sensation of either. And where you have no sensation, there is no source of pain.

Farewell.

# BOOK NINE

# Letter 75

*From Seneca to Lucilius*
*Greetings*

**1** You complain that I am expending less care on the letters I send you. So I am, for who expends care over a conversation? Only one who deliberately adopts an affected manner of speaking. I wish my letters to be like what my conversation would be if you and I were sitting or walking together: easy and unstudied. They have in them nothing forced, nothing feigned. **2** If it were possible, I would prefer to show you what I think rather than tell you. Even if I were delivering a speech, I would not stamp my foot or gesture with my hands, and I would not raise my voice. I would leave those things to the orators and be content to convey my thoughts to you in a manner that is neither ornate nor haphazard.

**3** The one impression I would want to make upon you is that I feel every one of the things I say; indeed, that I love them as well as feel them. People kiss a lover in one way and their children in another; yet even in that chaste and restrained caress there is a sufficient show of affection. It is not—by heaven—that I want what is said about such great themes to be jejune and arid (for there is a place for literary talent even in philosophy); still, it is not proper to expend a great deal of effort over the words. **4** Let this be the whole of our intention: let us say what we feel, and feel what we say; let the conversation be in harmony with how we live. What is it to fulfill one's promise? It is for the person we see and the person we hear to be one and the same. It is then that we see what sort of person it is who has promised, and how big a person he is; for then he is just one person.

**5** Our words should provide benefit rather than delight. Still, if eloquence can be achieved without effort, if it comes easily or costs but little, then let it come and attend on the most beautiful of subjects. But let it be such as will show off the subject rather than itself. Other arts are entirely concerned with one's talent; what is at issue here is the business of the mind. **6** The sick person does not go looking for an eloquent doctor, although if the person who has the ability to cure him also happens to be able to speak in a polished manner about the measures to be taken, he considers it a plus. Even so, he has no reason to congratulate himself on having found a doctor who is also an orator: it is of no more importance than when a skilled helmsman is also good-looking.

**7** Why are you tickling my ears? Why be so entertaining? There is other business at hand. What I need is to be cauterized, operated on, given a restricted diet. This is what you are summoned to do. Your responsibility is to cure a long-term illness which is both serious and widespread. It is as big a job as a physician's in an epidemic. Are you preoccupied with words? Be glad all along if you do not fail in the deed.

So many things to know: when will you learn them? When will you fix them in your mind so that they cannot be forgotten? When will you try them out? For these are not like other objects of study. With these, memorization is not enough: you must put them into effect. The happy person is not the one who knows them but the one who performs them.

**8** "But look: are there no levels below that person? Is it just wisdom and then a sudden drop-off?" No, I don't think that. The one who is making progress is indeed counted among the foolish, and yet he is separated from them by a considerable interval. And even among progressors there are important distinctions to be made.*

According to some, they are divided into three types. **9** First are those who do not yet possess wisdom but have set their feet in that vicinity, for being nearby is still being outside. Do you ask who these people are? They are those who have put aside their emotions and their faults, but whose loyalty is still untried. They do not yet possess their good in such a way as to use it; nonetheless, it is no longer possible for them to fall back into those things they have left behind. They are now in that place from which there is no backsliding, but they do not yet realize this about themselves. As I remember writing in one of my letters, "They do not know that they know."* Already it is their lot to enjoy their good, but not yet to be confident of it.

**10** Some authors delimit the aforementioned category of progressors in such a way as to assert that they have now rid themselves of the infirmities of mind* but not yet of the emotions, and that they are still in danger, since no one has gotten beyond peril of vice until he has shed it altogether, but no one has shed it altogether unless he has put on wisdom in its place. **11** The difference between infirmities of mind and emotions is something I have explained more than once. I will remind you now as well. The infirmities are faults that have become ingrained and hard, like greed and ambition. These are conditions that bind the mind much more tightly and have begun to be permanent afflictions. To give a brief definition, an infirmity is a persistent judgment in a corrupted person that certain things are very much worth pursuing that in fact are only slightly worth pursuing. Or, if you prefer, we can define it this way: it is being overly concerned with things that one ought to pursue either casually or not at all, or considering something to be of great value when in fact it is either of some lesser value or of no value at all. **12** The emotions are unjustifiable movements of the mind that are abrupt and agitated.* These, when they occur frequently and do not receive any treatment, cause the infirmity, just as a single cold in the head, if it is not protracted, brings on nothing more than a cough; but if it happens repeatedly for a long time, it brings on the wasting disease. Hence those who have made the most progress have gotten beyond the infirmities, but they still experience emotions, even though they are very near perfection.

**13** The second category comprises those who have put aside both the worst of the mind's failings and the emotions, but not in such a way as to have a secure grasp on their tranquility: they are still liable to relapse. **14** The third category is beyond many serious faults, but not all. They have escaped greed, but still experience anger; they are not troubled by lust, but are still subject to ambition. They no longer experience desire, but they still experience fear. Even in fear they are steadfast against some things but yield to others: they are unconcerned about death but still terrified of pain.

**15** Let us give some thought to this matter. It will be well for us if we can join the last group. By great natural gifts and constant studious application, one may attain to the second; the third stripe, however, is not to be despised. Think how many ills you see around you—how no wrong is unexampled, how much depravity advances each day, what misdeeds are committed both publicly and in private—and you will realize that it is sufficient achievement for us if we are not among the worst.

16 "I hope I can gain a higher rank," you say. That would be my wish for us; but it is a wish, not a promise. We have already been taken over: we are in the grip of faults even as we strive for virtue. I am ashamed to say it, but we seek honorable conduct only in our spare time. And yet if we make a clean break from the things that preoccupy us and from our faults that cling so closely, how great is the reward that awaits us! It will not be desire that drives us, nor fear. 17 Untroubled by any anxiety, undefiled by pleasure, we shall fear neither death nor the gods. For we shall know that death is not an evil, that the gods mean us no harm. That which does harm is as feeble as that which suffers harm: the best things have no capacity to harm at all.

18 What awaits us, if ever we emerge from this murky depth to the lofty regions above, is tranquility of mind and the freedom and independence that come when all error has been expelled. What is freedom, you ask? To fear no human being and no god, to want neither what is base nor what is excessive, to have absolute power over oneself. Just being one's own person is wealth beyond measure.

Farewell.

## Letter 76

*From Seneca to Lucilius*
*Greetings*

1 You swear you will become my enemy if I don't inform you about every one of my day's activities. See how forthright I am in my life with you. I will share even this: I am taking philosophy lessons! Today is the fifth day I have gone to school to hear the philosopher lecturing from two o'clock onward.

"What, at your age?" Why not? What could be more foolish than failing to learn a thing simply because you haven't learned it earlier?

2 "So I'm supposed to take after the youthful squires?"* I'm do-

ing quite well by my advancing years if I don't shame them any more than that. Here is a school that admits people at any age.

"Is this what old age is for—to go chasing after the young?" Shall I go to the theater in my old age; shall I ride in my sedan chair to the Circus, be present at every gladiatorial match, and yet blush to visit a philosopher? 3 You should keep learning as long as you lack knowledge; or, if we believe the proverb, as long as you live. And that is just what this learning is for: you should keep learning how to live for as long as you live. On that point I have something to teach as well. "What's that?" you ask. It is that even the old have something to learn.

4 But every time I enter the school, I am ashamed for the human race. As you know, I have to pass right by the theater of Naples on my way to the house of Metronax.* The theater is packed. A cheering crowd decides who is a good flutist; the trumpeter has a following, and so does the announcer. But in the place where the question is who is a good man, where one learns what a good man is, the seats are almost empty, and the general opinion is that those who are there have nothing better to do. People call them useless drones. Well, I don't mind that sort of ridicule: the criticism of ignorant people is not something to get upset about. One whose aims are honorable should scorn their very scorn.

5 Make haste, then, Lucilius. Move quickly, lest what happened to me should happen to you, and you become a pupil in your old age. But the real reason you should make haste is that the study you have embarked upon is one you can scarcely learn thoroughly even if you do become an elderly learner.

"How much progress can I make?" you say. As much as you attempt. 6 What are you waiting for? No one attains wisdom merely by chance. Money will come of its own accord; public office will be conferred on you; popularity and influence will perhaps be accorded you without any action on your part; virtue, though, will not just happen to you. The work it takes to recognize it is neither easy nor short; but the effort is worth making, for by it one will take possession of every good at once. For there is but one—the honorable. You will find nothing real, nothing sure, in those things that reputation favors.

7 I will now explain why the honorable is the sole good, since you judge that I failed in my earlier letter to achieve that end, praising

the thesis rather than proving it. Here, then, is a concise version of what has been said on the subject.*

**8** Each thing is so constituted as to have its own excellence. Fertility commends the vine; flavor the vintage; swiftness the stag. About a mule, you ask how strong its back is, for the only function of a mule is to carry burdens. In a dog, the chief quality is keenness of scent if it is to track the game; speed of foot if it is to chase the game down; and boldness if it is to dart in and harry. In each, its best quality ought to be that for which it is born and by which it is assessed. **9** What, then, is the distinctive property of a human being? Reason. It is by reason that the human surpasses animals and is second to the gods. Therefore perfected reason is the human's distinctive excellence; everything else is shared with animals and plants.

The human is strong; so are lions. He is beautiful; so are peacocks. He is swift; so are horses. I am not remarking that he is surpassed in all these attributes: my inquiry is not what attribute is greatest in humans but what it is that is particular to humans. The human has a body; so do trees. He has the capacity for impulse and voluntary movement; so do beasts, and worms too. He has a voice—but how much louder is the barking of dogs; how much higher the cry of the eagle; how much deeper the bellow of bulls; how much sweeter and more melodious the trilling of the lark! **10** What is special about a human being? Reason. When that is set straight and made complete, it achieves the blissful fulfillment of human nature.

Therefore if each thing is worthy of praise and arrives at the culmination of its own nature when it perfects its own particular good, and if the particular good for a human is reason, then if a person perfects his reason, he is worthy of praise and has attained the culmination of his own nature. This perfected reason is called virtue, and is also the same as the honorable.

**11** Hence the one thing that belongs solely to the human is the sole good of the human. For we are now asking not what the good is but what the human good is. If nothing but reason belongs solely to the human, this will be his sole good. But this good must be weighed in with all other attributes: if anyone proves to be bad, he will be blamed; if good, he will be approved.* Hence that by which a human being is approved and blamed is his primary and only distinctive attribute.

**12** You do not doubt that this is a good; you doubt whether it is his sole good. If someone should be found who has all other advantages—health, riches, a fine family tree, an entry hall crowded with visitors—but it is agreed that he is a bad person, you will criticize him. Conversely, if someone has none of those things I listed—neither money, nor throngs of clients, nor noble birth, nor a long line of ancestors—but it is agreed that he is a good person, you will approve of him. Hence this is indeed the sole good of the human, since one who has it is to be praised even if he is lacking in other advantages, while one who does not have it is condemned and rejected even if he is well supplied with other advantages.

**13** The situation is the same for humans as for things. What we call a good ship is not the one decorated with expensive paints, nor the one whose prow is tipped with gold or silver, nor the one whose hold is ornamented with ivory, nor the one laden with royal treasure and the bursaries of nations, but rather the steady vessel, stoutly made with joints that keep the water out, sturdy enough to withstand every assault of the sea, swift and unfazed by the wind. **14** What we call a good sword is not the one with a gilded baldric, nor the one whose sheath is studded with gems, but the one whose cutting edge is keen and whose point will slice through every kind of defensive armor. With a ruler, you do not ask how pretty it is but how straight it is. Everything is praised for that feature which is distinctive of it and for which it is obtained. **15** So in a human too, the pertinent consideration is not how much land he has under the plow, not how much capital he has to invest, not how many clients attend him, not how expensive a bed he lies in, not how transparent his drinking goblet is but how good a person he is. Yet he is good only if his reason is fully developed, straight and right, and adapted to the intent of his nature. **16** This is called virtue; this is the honorable and the sole good of the human being. For since only reason perfects a human, only reason makes him perfectly happy. But that by which alone he is made happy is his sole good.

We say too that those things which proceed from virtue and are connected with it—that is, all the activities of virtue—are themselves goods. Still, virtue is the sole good, because there is no good without it. **17** If every good inheres in the mind, then whatever strengthens, exalts, enlarges the mind is a good. But virtue makes the mind stronger, loftier, and more expansive. For other objects of our desire also lower the mind and weaken it, and when they seem to elevate us, they are actually puffing us up and deceiving us with empty wind. The sole good is therefore that by which the mind is made better.

**18** All the actions of an entire life are governed by consideration for what is honorable and what is base; reasoning about what to do or not do is guided accordingly. Let me explain. A good man will do what he believes is honorable, even if it is arduous, even if it is dangerous. Conversely, he will not do what he believes is base, even if it brings money, or pleasure, or power. Nothing will frighten him away from what is honorable; nothing will entice him toward what is base. **19** So it is only if there is no good other than virtue and nothing bad except what is shameful that he will pursue the honorable unconditionally and avoid the base unconditionally, and will look to those two in every action of life.

If virtue alone is unperverted and it alone maintains its own condition, then virtue is the one good that cannot turn out to be anything other than good. It escapes all risk of change. Foolishness creeps toward wisdom; wisdom does not relapse into foolishness.

**20** I have said (as perhaps you remember) that there are some who by unconsidered impulse have trodden beneath their feet those objects the common crowd either wants or dreads. Examples can be given of one who threw away his wealth, one who set his hand on fire, one whose smile did not abate under torture, one who shed not a tear at the funeral of his children, one who met death without dismay, all because love, anger, or desire drove them to court such dangers. If a brief steeling of the mind can do so much when roused by the spur of the moment, then virtue can achieve all the more, being rigorous not on some sudden impulse but equally on all occasions, constant in its strength. **21** It follows that those objects that are scorned quite often by the imprudent, and always by the wise, are neither good nor bad. Virtue itself, then, is the sole good, which walks proudly between opposite fortunes with lofty scorn for both.

**22** If you accept the view that something besides the honorable is a good, then every virtue will have a hard time. For no virtue can be maintained if it looks to anything beyond itself. If that is the case, it is contrary to reason,* on which the virtues depend, and to truth, which does not exist without reason. And any view that is contrary to truth is false.

**23** You admit that the good man must of necessity be supremely respectful toward the gods. For that reason he will calmly tolerate anything that happens to him, for he knows that it has happened through the divine law by which all events are regulated. If that is the case, then in his eyes honorable conduct will be the sole good; for that includes obedience to the gods, neither raging against the shocks of fortune nor complaining of one's own lot but accepting one's fate with patience and acting as commanded.* **24** If there is any good other than the honorable, then we will be dogged by lust for life and for life's equipment—and that is intolerable, unending, ill-defined. Thus the sole good is the honorable, which has a limit.

**25** We said that if things in which the gods have no share, like money and public office, are goods, then human life will be more blessed than the lives of the gods. Now add this consideration: if indeed our souls linger on when released from the body, a happier condition awaits them than while they are embodied. But if those things that we use through the body are goods, they will be worse off after their discharge, and that is contrary to our intuition that souls that are free and released into the universe are happier than souls locked up under siege. **26** I had also said that if those things are goods that pertain no more to humans than to animals devoid of speech, then animals too will partake of happiness, and that is impossible.

For the sake of the honorable, one ought to put up with absolutely anything; but if there were some good besides the honorable, there would be no such obligation.

**27** I pursued these topics at greater length in my earlier letter; here I have compressed them, giving a brief overview. But a view of this kind will never seem to you to be true unless you raise your mind to a higher level. Ask yourself this: if circumstances should require you to die for your country, purchasing the lives of all its citizens at the cost of your own, would you stretch out your neck not just willingly but even gladly? If you would, then there is no other good, for you are abandoning everything to have this.

See what great power there is in the honorable: you will die for the state, even if you realize the need only just before you are to do it. **28** Sometimes from an extremely beautiful object one experiences great joy even in a tiny space of time; and although no profit from the act performed accrues to the one who is deceased and removed from human life, still there is satisfaction in the very contemplation of the deed ahead. A just and courageous man, when he envisions the benefits of his death—the freedom of his homeland, the safety of all those for whom he lays down his life—is at the height of pleasure, and is gladdened by his own danger.* **29** But if one is deprived even of this joy that the doing of this greatest, last deed provides, even then one will still plunge down into death, finding satisfaction in acting correctly and with due devotion. Confront him with many reasons to be dissuaded; say to him, "Your act will soon be forgotten and will win hardly any gratitude or esteem from the populace." He will reply, "Everything you are saying is external to my task. My concern is with the task itself. I know that task is honorable, and so I follow wherever it summons me to go."

**30** This, then, is the sole good, as recognized not only by the perfect mind but also by the mind that is nobly born and of good natural disposition. Other things are fleeting and changeable. Possessing them is an anxious matter: even when a kindly fortune piles them on, they weigh heavily on their owners. Always they are a burden; sometimes they are even a mockery.

**31** Not one of those whom you see wearing the purple is fortunate, any more than actors are fortunate when assigned to bear the scepter and royal robes on stage, when they parade before the audience in wide garments and platform shoes, then immediately go off, remove their footgear, and resume their proper stature. Not one of those whom wealth and public office have taken to the top is truly great. Why does he appear great? You are including the pedestal in his measurement. A dwarf is not tall even if he stands on a mountain; a giant will keep his height even if he stands in a pit. **32** This is our mistake; this is how we are fooled: we do not assess people by what they are but add to them the trappings of their station. Yet when you want to make a true assessment of a person and know what he is like, strip him naked. Let him shed his inheritance, his offices, and all of fortune's other lies. Let him take off even his body. Contemplate his mind and see what is his quality and what his stature: is he great through his own store or someone else's? **33** If his gaze is steady as he looks upon the flashing swords, if he knows it makes no difference to him whether he breathes his last through his mouth or through his opened throat, then call him happy—if, when he hears of prison and exile and all the needless terrors of human thoughts, he feels no concern but says,

> "No aspect of these labors,
> Sibyl, arises new or unforeseen
> by me: I grasped it all before this day,
> and in my mind I faced and finished all.*

You, Aeneas, make such proclamations on this day only; I make them always to myself, and since I am human, prepare myself for human events."

**34** Misfortune's blow falls lightly when the mind is prepared for it. But the foolish and those who put their trust in fortune find that every aspect life presents is new and unexpected. For inexpert minds, a large portion of their misfortune lies in the novelty of it. **35** Evidence of this is that when they have grown used to the circumstances they had considered harsh, they endure them more patiently. For this reason the wise man accustoms himself to misfortunes that are yet to come: he takes what others make light through long endurance and makes it light through long reflection.* We sometimes hear the voices of the inexpert saying, "I knew this was waiting for me." The wise man knows that everything is waiting for him. No matter what happens, he says, "I knew it."

Farewell.

## Letter 77

*From Seneca to Lucilius*
*Greetings*

**1** Today all of a sudden the "ships of Alexandria" came into view. These are the ones that are customarily sent on ahead to announce the arrival of a fleet. People call them "mail-boats," and the sight of them is welcome in Campania. The whole populace stands on the docks of Puteoli and can pick out the Alexandrians amid the great traffic of shipping just by the design of their sails. For these boats alone are allowed to carry their topsails. **2** All vessels have topsails when out at sea, for nothing aids their progress as well as the upper portion of the canvas; that is what gives them their greatest speed. For this reason the yard is lowered when the wind becomes gusty and stronger than necessary, for the breeze lower down is not as forceful. Once they come in past Capri and the promontory from which

> Athena from the stormy heights
> stands guard supreme,*

the other boats are told to content themselves with their mainsails. Thus the topsail is the distinguishing mark of the Alexandrians.

**3** Amid this rush of people hurrying toward the shore, I took considerable pleasure in my own idleness, that is, in the fact that I did not hurry down to pick up letters from friends and family or to find out how my business was doing overseas and what profit it would yield. It has been a long time since I either lost or gained anything. This would have been the right attitude for me to take even if I were not old; it is even more right now. No matter how little I have, my travel money is still more than the road I have left to travel, especially as there is no need to finish this journey we are on. **4** A journey is unfinished if you stop in the middle, or anywhere short of your destination; but life is never cut short as long as one lives honorably. It is complete no matter where you end it, as long as you end it in a good way.

But it often happens that a person has to make a brave end for reasons that are not particularly weighty. For the reasons that keep us here are not weighty either. **5** Consider Tullius Marcellinus, whom you knew quite well.* He was a quiet young man, then quickly past his prime; then, beset by an illness that was not untreatable, but was lengthy, troublesome, and demanding, he began to make plans for his death. He called together a number of his friends. One after another they either advised the course they themselves would have adopted out of timidity, or turned to flattery and gave the advice they thought the one consulting them wanted to hear. **6** But our Stoic friend, who is an extraordinary person and—to speak the praises he deserves—a brave man and a man of action—gave him what I consider the best form of encouragement.* He began by speaking as follows:

"Don't torment yourself, Marcellinus, as though you were debating some momentous question. Being alive is not, in fact, of any great moment. Your slaves are alive; your animals also. What is great is to die honorably, sensibly, bravely. Think how long you have been doing the same thing over and over: food, sleep, sex, round and round in a circle. It is not only the sensible person, the brave person, and the miserable person who can conceive a wish to die: sheer disgust may wish for it as well."

7 What Marcellinus needed, though, was not encouragement so much as assistance, for his slaves would not obey him. The first thing the Stoic did was to allay their fear by explaining that household slaves would be at risk only if there were some doubt as to whether the master died of his own volition. If there were no such doubt, then thwarting his demise would be as bad an example as murdering him. 8 Next, he advised Marcellinus himself that just as when dinner is over one shares out the leftovers among the serving people, so when his life was over it would be natural for him to give something to those who had been his lifelong servants. Marcellinus was of a compliant disposition, and generous even when giving made a difference to him. He therefore distributed some small sums to his weeping slaves and actually spoke words of consolation to them.

9 He had no need of the knife or of any bloodshed. For three days he abstained from food, and he directed that a tent be set up right in his bedroom.* Then a tub was brought in. He lay in it for a long time, and by slipping repeatedly under the hot water he gradually gave way. From what he said, there was a kind of pleasure in it; a not infrequent occurrence when one is expiring without violence. Those of us who have had fainting spells have also experienced this.*

10 I have gone off on a tangent with this little story; but you will not mind learning that your friend's demise was neither difficult nor uncomfortable. For although he did commit suicide, his passing was exceedingly gentle; life just slipped away. But the anecdote will also be of use, for necessity often requires such things from us. There are times when we ought to die and do not want to, or when we are actually dying and do not want to. 11 No matter how naïve a person is, he knows he must die sometime, and yet when the time draws near he pulls back; he trembles; he begs to be excused.

Suppose someone were to burst into tears because he was not born a thousand years earlier; would you not think that ridiculously foolish? It is just as foolish for someone to weep that he will not be alive a thousand years in the future. The two are equal: your future nonexistence and your past. Both times are beyond our ken. **12** You have been cast into this moment of time; you might extend it, but for how long? Why are you crying? What is it you want? You're wasting your efforts.

> Stop hoping that your prayers will ever change
> what gods ordain.*

Your fate is fixed, determined by a vast, eternal necessity. You will go where all things go. Why is this news to you? It is the law to which you were born. It is what happened to your father, to your mother, to your ancestors, to all who came before you and to all who will come after you. A sequence that no power has ever defeated or changed constrains and compels all events.* **13** What multitudes will follow you, to die in their turn! What multitudes accompany you! You would be braver, no doubt, if many thousands would die along with you. But in fact, there are many thousands, people and animals alike, who do, yielding up their spirits in one way or another in this very moment when you hesitate to die. Did you think you would never reach the goal to which you have been headed all along? There is no journey without an ending.

**14** Do you expect me now to tell you exemplary tales about great men? I will tell you some about mere children. There is one about a Spartan who was captured when still very young. He kept shouting in his own Doric tongue, "I will not be a slave!" And he proved it, too: the first time he was ordered to do a slave's insulting task—for they told him to fetch the chamber pot—he dashed his head against a wall and burst his skull. **15** With freedom so near at hand, how is anyone a slave? Would you not wish for your own son to die in this way rather than grow old through fecklessness? Why, then, are you upset on your own behalf, when even a boy can die bravely? You may refuse to follow his lead and then be led there all the same. Let it be at your behest and not another's. Why not take on the spirit of that boy and say, "I am no slave"? Poor thing, you are a slave: a slave to others, a slave to property, a slave to life. For life itself is slavery when one lacks the courage to die.

**16** Do you in fact have anything worth waiting for? You linger, you tarry over your pleasures, but you have exhausted even those. Not one of them is new to you; not one is anything but loathsome to you from sheer surfeit. You know what wine tastes like, both with honey and without. It makes no difference whether a hundred gallons pass through your bladder or a thousand; either way you are nothing but a conduit. You know exactly what an oyster tastes like, and a mullet as well.* Self-indulgence has sampled everything; nothing remains for future years to try. And this is what you cannot tear yourself away from! **17** What else are you moping over? Can you not bear to let go of your friends? Do you even know how to be a friend? Your country? Do you value it even enough to allow dinner to be delayed for its sake? The sun? You would put it out like a lamp if you could; for what have you ever done that was worthy of its light? Be honest: it is not any longing for the Senate House or the Forum, or even for the world as a whole, that makes you reluctant to die. What you cannot part from is only your butcher shop—and thanks to you, there is nothing left in it. **18** You fear death, and yet when a platter of mushrooms is before you, how little you care!

You wish to live; do you know how? You fear to die; what of it? Isn't the life you are living a kind of death? Once when Gaius Caesar was traveling the Latium road, he was accosted by a prisoner on a chain gang, an aged fellow with a beard down to his chest, who begged for death.* "Are you alive now?" he said. That is the answer to give to those people who would be better off dead: "You fear to die; are you alive now?"

**19** "But what about me?" says another. "I want to live, and I am doing many honorable actions. I am reluctant to abandon the responsibilities of life, which I am working hard and faithfully to perform." Ah, but don't you know that dying is also one of life's responsibilities? You are not abandoning any responsibilities, for there is no set number you have to fulfill.

**20** There is no life that is not short. On a universal scale, even the lifespan of Nestor was short, and that of Sattia too, who ordered a tombstone saying she lived to ninety-nine.* You see how one person boasted of a long old age. Who could have put up with her if she had made it to a hundred?

Life is like a play: what matters is not how long the show goes on but how well it is acted. It makes no difference where you stop. Stop wherever you please; just make the ending a good one.

Farewell.

# Letter 78

*From Seneca to Lucilius*
*Greetings*

**1** So you are troubled with frequent sinus infections and with the bouts of fever that go with them when they are chronic and long lasting. I am sorry to hear it, and all the more as I have experienced this sort of illness.* At first I thought little of it; being young, I was able to put up with hardships and stubborn in dealing with ill health. Eventually I succumbed, and became so emaciated that my entire being seemed to be dripping out through my sinuses. **2** More than once I entertained an impulse to end my life; but my father was elderly, and that held me back. For although I thought that I could die bravely, I also thought that he, who was so kind to me, could not bravely bear the loss. So I commanded myself to live; for there are times when just continuing to live is a courageous action.

**3** I will tell you what consoled me then. But first I will say this: the thoughts that comforted me had medicinal powers. Honorable consolations are curative: what raises up the mind also benefits the body. It was my studies that saved me; it was philosophy that I had to thank when I rose from my bed and when I regained my strength. I owe it my life, and life is the least of what I owe to it. **4** Friends contributed greatly to my recovery: they encouraged me, sat up nights, talked to me, and so brought me comfort. O most excellent Lucilius, nothing strengthens an invalid as much as caring friends; nothing does as much to take away his thoughts of death, his fear. I felt that as long as they remained alive, I was not really dying. I mean, I kept thinking that I would live on, not among them but through them. It seemed to me I was not yielding up my spirit so much as passing it on.

These things gave me the will to help myself and to endure every torment. Without them it is a most wretched case: you have given over the intention to die but have no wish to live. **5** Therefore commit yourself to these remedies. The doctor will instruct you how far to walk, how long to exercise; he'll tell you not to indulge in idleness, which is the tendency when one lacks energy. He'll have you read aloud, exercising your breathing, since it is the passage and receptacle of the breath that is affected; and will bid you go out in a boat so that the gentle rocking will stimulate your digestive system. He'll advise you what foods to consume, when to order wine for the sake of strength, and when to skip the wine so as not to irritate your cough and make it worse. The advice I give is a remedy not for this illness only but for your whole life. It is this: despise death. Once we escape that fear, nothing is ever sad.

**6** Every illness involves three afflictions: fear of death, pain of body, interruption of life's pleasures. About death I've said enough. There's just one thing I have to add: it is the finish line, not for disease but for our nature. In many cases disease delays death, and looking ready to die has actually saved a person's life.* The reason you will die is not that you are sick but that you are alive. That fact will remain even after you get well; your recovery is an escape from sickness but not an escape from death.

**7** Let's turn now to the affliction that specifically characterizes illness. Illness includes periods of great pain, but these are made endurable by intermissions. For when pain is at its most extreme, it comes to an end. No one can experience terrible pain for very long: nature in its great love for us has designed us in such a way as to make pain either endurable or brief.* **8** The greatest pains belong to the slenderest parts of the body: the tendons, the finger joints, and all the other narrow parts feel the sharpest pangs as the malady is compacted into a tight space. But these parts also become numb quickly, the pain itself obliterating their sensation of pain. This may be because the native breath* is blocked in its flow and deteriorates, losing its invigorating and stimulating force; or it may be that contaminated fluid, having lost its means of drainage, creates pressure on itself and destroys sensation in the areas where it collects. **9** Hence gout, arthritis, and all painful conditions of the tendons and spine are intermittent when sensation is impaired at the pain site. With all of these, the onset is excruciating; then the attack is mitigated by the passage of time, until numbness brings an end to pain. Aches of the teeth, eyes, and ears are extremely acute just because they arise in a tiny area of the body—in fact, the same can be said of headaches— but when they are especially severe, one lapses into a stupor and then into sleep. **10** So we have this to console us when the pain is immense: if the sensation is excessive, it must end in lack of sensation.

The reason untrained persons are so troubled by bodily discomfort is that they have not been accustomed to content themselves with the mind; their dealings have largely been with the body. Hence the great and intelligent man abstracts mind from body, having much to do with the better, divine part of himself and only as much as necessary with the frail, complaining part.

**11** "But it is annoying to be deprived of the pleasures one is used to   to abstain from food, and to be thirsty and hungry." These things are hard to bear when one first begins to abstain; later, the longing subsides as the springs of our desire slacken and fail. The appetite then becomes peevish, and the food one previously desired is hateful. There is no bitterness in being deprived of what you no longer want.

**12** Moreover, there is no pain that does not cease periodically or at least decrease. Furthermore, one can take precautions and forestall its onset with medications. For every sort of pain gives some advance notice, especially those that occur on a regular basis. Coping with illness is tolerable if you scorn the worst threats illness can make.

**13** Don't make your own sufferings harder to bear by burdening yourself with complaints. Pain is a trivial matter when not augmented by belief. In fact, if you begin to encourage yourself, saying, "It's nothing, or at least it isn't much; let's put up with it until it is over," then as long as you think of it as trivial you will make it so. Everything depends on belief. It is not only ambition, self-indulgence, and avarice that look to opinion; we feel pain by it as well. Each person is as wretched as he believes himself to be.

**14** We should eliminate complaints about past sufferings, I believe, and such talk as this: "Nobody ever had it worse! Such torture—it was terrible! Nobody believed I would recover. My family was in despair over me; the doctors had all given up! Men broken on the rack are not as tormented as I was!" Even if those things are true, they are over now. What is the use in reliving past sufferings, being miserable now because you were miserable then? Besides, people always embellish their troubles, deceiving even themselves. Anyway, what is bitter to endure is pleasant when endurance is done. One naturally rejoices over troubles that are at an end.

There are two things, then, that one ought to cut back: fear of future troubles and memory of those that are past. One concerns me no longer, the other not yet. **15** When a person is in the midst of difficulties, let him say,

> Perhaps this too will someday bring us pleasure
> in memory.*

Let him contend against them° with all his might: if he yields, he will be beaten; if he exerts himself against his pain, he will defeat it. As it is, most people pull the building down on top of themselves when they ought to be holding it up. When something is leaning against you, hanging over you, crushing you with its weight, and you begin to back away from it, it topples toward you and lands all the more heavily on your head; but if you stand firm, you will be able to push it back.

**16** Boxers take many blows to the face and to the entire body; yet in their desire for glory they endure the pain, not only in competition but also in order to compete. Even their training inflicts pain. Let victory be our aim too in every contest. For us too there is a prize: not the garland, not the palm, not some trumpet heralding the announcement of our names, but excellence, firmness of mind, and the peace that is gained from then on once we make conquest of fortune in any trial of strength.

**17** "I feel great pain." What of it? If you bear it like a woman, do you feel it less? Just as enemies wreak more destruction in a rout, so does every stroke of misfortune fall more heavily on those who give up and turn their backs on it. "But it is a heavy load." What of it? Do we have our strength only for carrying light burdens?

Would you prefer your illness to be lengthy, or brief and intense? If lengthy, it gives some respite, some room to relax; it gives you plenty of time, for when there is a crisis° there is necessarily also a remission. A brief and acute illness has one of two outcomes: either it will come to an end, or it will bring the end. What difference does it make whether the disease is gone or I am? Either way, the pain is over.

**18** It will also be beneficial to depart mentally from the pain and turn your mind toward other thoughts.* Think of honorable deeds, brave deeds you have performed; reflect on what is good in your character. Let your memory range over everything you have most admired. Then bring to mind some great example of courage and victory over pain: the man who persevered in reading a book as he underwent surgery for varicose veins; the one who did not stop laughing while the torturers, angered by his defiance, tried out every implement of their cruelty on him. If pain has been defeated by laughter, can it not be defeated by reason? **19** Name anything you like: sinus infections, constant coughing so violent it brings up parts of your insides; fever that scalds you to the core; thirst; limbs twisted the wrong way by deformation of the joints; none of them are as bad as the flame—the rack—the branding iron—the force exerted on already aggravated wounds to make them deeper and more severe. Yet even among those there was one who did not groan. More than that: he did not even ask for mercy. More than that: he did not answer. More than that: he laughed, and he meant it! After that, don't you want to laugh down this pain you feel?

**20** "But illness prevents me from doing anything at all. It keeps me from meeting my responsibilities." Your body is impeded by it; your mind, however, is not. Ill health slows the legs of a runner; it weighs down the hands of a carpenter or tailor; but if your regular work is with your mind, you will continue to teach and exhort, to listen and learn, to inquire and reflect.

"And beyond that?" Do you think exercising self-control when you are sick is doing nothing? You will be showing everyone that illness can be defeated, or at least endured. **21** Believe me: there is a place for courage even on the sickbed. It is not only arms and battles that give evidence of a bold spirit unconquered by alarms: a brave man shows his quality even among the bedclothes. You have your task: wrestle well with illness! If it exercises no compulsion, no force of persuasion on you, then you offer a shining example. If only people observed us in sickness, how much material there would be for glory to celebrate! Be your own observer; celebrate yourself.

**22** Moreover, there are two types of pleasure. Illness inhibits bodily pleasures, but does not remove them entirely—in fact, if you make an accurate assessment, it is a stimulus to pleasure. A drink gives more enjoyment to one who is thirsty; food is more welcome to one who is hungry; and everything that comes after a period of privation is received with more delight. As for mental pleasures, no doctor orders his patient to abstain from them. And these are greater and more reliable pleasures. One who devotes himself to them with good understanding no longer cares for all those things that tickle the senses. **23** "Poor invalid!" Why? Because he does not strain his wine through snow? Because he does not use chips of ice to freshen his hefty schooners of strong drink? Because no one opens Campanian oysters for him right at the table? Because at his meals there is no hustle and bustle of chefs trundling braziers around with the roasts still on them? For self-indulgence has now come up with this device: the very kitchen comes out with the food, to make sure the dishes are not just warm but hot enough to scald the toughest palate. **24** "Poor invalid!" He will eat only as much as he can digest. The wild boar will not languish to one side as if it were a cheap meat banished from the table; his platter will not be piled high with the breasts of wildfowl because he cannot stand to see a bird served whole. What misfortune has befallen you? You will dine like an invalid—which is to say, in health and sanity.

**25** But as for the liquid diet, the warm water, and all the other things that seem intolerable to those fashionable characters (dissipated, that is—sick in mind rather than in body), we will have no difficulty in enduring them once we stop being frightened by death. And we will stop if we have learned the limits of goods and evils. Then at last will life no longer be tiresome to us, death no longer alarming. **26** For boredom cannot take over one's life when one ponders such a variety of exalted and divine themes: it is when one's leisure is spent in idleness that one is overcome by self-loathing. The mind that traverses all the universe will never weary of truth;* only falsehood will be tedious.

**27** Again, if death approaches and summons such a person—even a death many years before his time—he has already reaped all the benefits of a ripe old age. He has learned much of what there is to know in the world. He knows that when one's actions are honorable, they do not become more so by mere duration. But any life must appear short to those who measure it by pleasures that are empty and for that reason unlimited.*

**28** Create yourself anew with these thoughts; and meanwhile, save time for my letters. A day will come when we two will be reunited; indeed, commingled. Short it may be, but we will make it long by knowing how to use it. For as Posidonius says,

> A single day gives more time to the educated than the longest of lives for the untutored.*

In the meantime, latch on to this; hold fast to this: yield not to adversity; trust not to prosperity; fix your eyes on fortune's privilege, thinking that whatever can happen to you will indeed happen. What has been long expected is easier when it comes.

Farewell.

## Letter 79

*From Seneca to Lucilius*
*Greetings*

**1** I am looking forward to a letter from you describing what new information you have discovered on your sailing trip around Sicily; and in particular, some definite facts about Charybdis itself.* For I am well aware that Scylla is only a promontory, and not especially dangerous to navigation; Charybdis, though, I would like to have described to me in writing. Is it like the Charybdis of legend? If you happen to have made any observations—and it is well worth the trouble—then fill me in. Is there only one wind that makes it billow up, or does every squall stir up the sea in the same way? And is it true that anything that is drawn into the whirlpool there at the strait is carried many miles underwater until it surfaces near the beach at Taormina?

**2** If you write to me on these points, my next request will be a bold one: climb Etna too, in my honor. Some say that the summit of that mountain is being eaten away and is gradually diminishing in elevation. This is an inference from the fact that it used to be visible from further out at sea; but that might not be because the height of the peak is diminishing but because its fires are becoming fainter, spewing out less violently and in lesser amounts, as is the smoke during the day. Neither explanation is implausible. It could be that the mountain is shrinking, being consumed from within day by day; but it could also be that it remains the same, since the fire is not burning the mountain itself but welling up from some recess deep within the earth. In that case, the actual peak is not its source of supply but only a channel. 3 In Lycia there is a famous district, called by the inhabitants Hephaestion, where there are a number of holes in the ground surrounded by harmless flames that do no damage to the vegetation. The area is grassy and fertile, for the flames do not burn anything but merely flicker lazily in one place. 4 But let's save those inquiries until after you have written to me about the others. How far is it from the crater to the patches of snow? They are well sheltered from the heat—even in summer they do not melt.

No, don't charge this effort you are making to my account. In your fevered state, you'd have done it anyway, even if no one had requested it. 5 How much would I have to pay to keep you from touching on Mount Etna in your poem—Etna, the hallowed theme of every poet! Was Ovid prevented from writing about it just because Virgil had already covered it? Was Cornelius Severus deterred by either of them?* Anyway, it is fertile ground for everyone. The earlier writers have not, I think, exhausted the possibilities; rather, they have opened up the way. 6 It makes a big difference whether you take up a spent subject or one that has merely been treated before. A topic grows over time; invention does not preclude inventiveness. Besides, the last to come has the best of it: the words are all laid out for him, but a different arrangement lends them a fresh appearance. Not that he takes them up as belonging to someone else: they are public property. 7 If I know you at all, you are absolutely drooling over Etna, wishing to write something great to equal your predecessors. For modesty does not permit you to hope that you might surpass them. So great is your respect for those who have gone before that if the opportunity should arise for you to defeat them, I think you would rather curb your talent.

8 One of the good things about wisdom is that no one can be

beaten at it by another except during the ascent. Once you reach the heights, everything is on a level; there is no room for increase; it is a stopping point. Does the sun increase in size? Does the moon wax beyond the full? The level of the oceans does not rise; the world maintains its shape and its condition. 9 Whatever has attained its proper stature cannot exceed itself; everyone, therefore, who becomes wise will be on an equal footing. Each individual among them will have his own gifts: one will be more genial, another more quick-witted; one more fluent in his orations, another more elegant; but our concern is with the source of their happiness, and that is the same in all. 10 Whether Mount Etna could ever collapse onto itself, whether that lofty peak, visible far out at sea, is shrinking from the constant force of its fires, I do not know. What I do know is that no flame, no devastation will ever bring down the exalted nature of virtue. This is the one greatness that knows no diminishment. It can neither be heightened nor reduced; its magnitude is fixed, like that of the heavenly bodies.*

Let us endeavor to advance ourselves to that condition. 11 Much of the work has already been done. No, not much, if truth be told: merely being better than the worst is not goodness. Does a man boast of his eyesight just because he is able to tell that it is daytime? When the bright sun cuts through his fading vision, he is relieved to have escaped the darkness for a while, but he does not yet have the benefit of that light. 12 We will have no reason to congratulate ourselves until our weltering in the dark is over and our mind emerges not to squint at the brightness but to gaze full upon the light of day; to be restored to heaven from whence it came; to claim the place that is its birthright. Its origins summon it upward. It will be there even before it is released from this prison-house, as soon as it sheds its faults and flashes upward, pure and light, toward godlike contemplation.*

13 Dearest Lucilius, how glad I am that we are doing this—that we are pressing on in this direction with all our strength, even if few people ever know; even if no one knows. Glory is the shadow of virtue; it accompanies virtue even when it is not wanted.* But just as a shadow sometimes goes before, sometimes behind, so is it with glory: sometimes it is out ahead, presenting itself to view; sometimes it falls the other way and is all the greater for coming later, when envy has receded. 14 How long a time was Democritus thought to

be insane!* How narrowly Socrates escaped oblivion! How many years was Cato unknown to his country! It rejected him and did not understand him until it had lost him. The innocence and courage of Rutilius would never have come to light but for the injustice done to him; once wronged, he became a beacon.* Surely he must have been grateful for the chance to embrace his life in exile.

I have been speaking of those on whom adverse fortune conferred distinction; for many, though, their moral progress became known only after they were gone. And how many more have not been greeted by renown so much as exhumed by it! 15 Look at Epicurus: it is not only educated people who are amazed at him but even the ignorant masses; yet his existence was unknown even in Athens, in whose environs he had sequestered himself. Hence in one of his letters, after a hymn of gratitude remembering his friendship with Metrodorus (who had died many years before), he remarked at the end that amid such great blessings, it never did either of them any harm that Greece, that well-known land, not only failed to recognize them but scarcely even heard of them. 16 Surely, then, he must have been discovered only after he had ceased to exist; surely it was only then that his reputation became illustrious. Metrodorus too admits in one of his letters that he and Epicurus were not very well known, but says that those who were willing to follow in their footsteps would have a great name prepared for them.*

17 No instance of virtue lies hidden forever. If it has remained so for a time, it has lost nothing: though buried for a while in oblivion, suppressed by the resentment of its own generation, a day will come that will make it famous. One who thinks only of his contemporaries is born for but a few. There are many thousands of years to come, many thousands of peoples: look to them. Even if all those who live with you are silent because of jealousy, others will come who will judge your merits with neither malice nor favoritism. If fame is any reward for virtue, then that reward will never perish. To be sure, the speeches of posterity will be nothing to us; yet those speeches will attend us unawares.

18 In life or in death, the pursuit of virtue never goes unrewarded, as long as one has followed it in earnest, not with hairstyle and makeup but with a character that is the same on the surprise visit as on the planned occasion. Pretense is of no avail. Few are deceived by

the face that is just painted on: one's true identity goes right to the core. Deceits have nothing solid about them. A lie is a tenuous thing, and on close inspection, transparent.

Farewell.

## Letter 80

*From Seneca to Lucilius*
*Greetings*

**1** Today I am at leisure, not so much thanks to myself as to the games, which have called away all the bothersome people to watch the boxing. No one will burst in; no one will interrupt my train of thought, which goes forward more boldly in that it has this assurance. The door has ceased its constant creaking; my curtain will not be drawn aside; I have license to proceed in safety, as a person needs to do when he is striking out on his own and making a path for himself. Am I not following earlier thinkers, then? I am, but I also allow myself to discover new points, to change things, to abandon older views. I can agree with them without becoming subservient.

**2** But I spoke out of turn when I promised myself silence and uninterrupted privacy. Here comes a great roar from the stadium; and although it does not shake my resolution, it does distract me into wrestling with this very subject. I think to myself, "How many people exercise their bodies, and how few their minds! What a great confluence of people attend this fickle show merely for entertainment, and what solitude attends the pursuits of culture! How weak-minded are those whose strong arms and shoulders we admire!"

**3** Most of all, I ponder this. If the body can, with training, come to such a peak of endurance that it is able to sustain punches and kicks from more than one opponent, to bear the hottest glare of the sun, the most scorching heat of the dust, and to do this for an entire day while drenched with its own blood, then surely the mind can be strengthened far more easily to accept the blows of fortune, to be knocked down and trampled and yet get up again. For the body needs many things in order to thrive, but the mind grows by itself, feeds itself, trains itself. Athletes require a great deal of food and drink, much oil, and lengthy exercises; but virtue will be yours without any supplies or expenses. Anything that can make you a good person is already in your possession.

4 What do you need in order to be good? Willingness.* And what better aim could there be for your willingness than to wrest yourself from this slavery that oppresses everyone, this slavery that the lowliest chattel slaves, born in the dirt, strive in every way they can to escape? They cheat hunger to save up a pittance against their purchase price; and you, who think you were born free, will you not yearn to spend whatever it takes to gain your real freedom? 5 Why are you looking at your money box? It cannot be bought. It is pointless, then, to put an entry in your account book labeled "freedom." Freedom is not the possession of those who have bought or sold it. It is a good you must ask of yourself, must give yourself.

Free yourself first from the fear of death—the fear that is the yoke about our necks—and then from the fear of poverty. 6 If you want to know how little harm there is in poverty, compare the faces of the poor with those of the wealthy. The poor person laughs often and from the heart. None of his worries go deep: even if some care befalls him, it passes by like a wisp of cloud. But in those who are called well off we see a feigned cheerfulness under which runs a deep vein of gangrenous sorrow, made even deeper because as a rule they cannot be miserable in the sight of others but with pain gnawing at their very hearts must still act the part of happiness and success.

7 Here is an analogy (and I ought to use it more often, for it is the best way to express the point): human life is a play, assigning us roles we can scarcely fill. That man who parades onto the stage in sweeping robes, throws back his head, and says,

> Behold, I rule the Greeks as Pelops's heir;
> my realm extends from the Ionian Sea
> and Hellespont to the Isthmus of Corinth—

is a slave: he gets five measures of grain and five denarii for his performance.* 8 That haughty and intractable figure, puffed up with pride of his strength, who says,

Hold your tongue, Menelaus, or you die
by my right hand—

receives a daily wage and sleeps on a patchwork blanket. The same can be said of all those fashionable people carried in litters above the heads of the crowd: their happiness is just playing a part. If you strip them of their fine apparel, you will hold them in contempt.

9 When you are about to buy a horse, you order that the saddle be removed; you pull all the trappings off those that are for sale so that no bodily defects may escape your eye. Will you, then, assess the worth of a human being with clothes wrapped all about him? Slave dealers use the tricks of their trade to conceal anything that might be displeasing, and buyers for that reason are suspicious of every adornment. If you were to see an arm or a leg bound up in some way, you would demand that it be laid bare and the limb itself be shown to you. 10 Do you see that king of Scythia or of Sarmatia, with a splendid crown on his head? If you want to know his true worth, the entirety of his character, then take away his headdress: much that is bad lies hidden underneath.

But why do I speak of others? If you want to give yourself a thorough evaluation, set aside your money, your house, your rank, and look within yourself. Until you do that, you know what you are like only from what other people tell you.

Farewell.

# BOOK TEN

# Letter 81

*From Seneca to Lucilius*
*Greetings*

1 You complain that you have encountered someone who was ungrateful. If this is the first time, then you yourself should be grateful either to fortune or to your own efforts. But in this case, your efforts cannot achieve anything except to make yourself uncharitable. For if you are unwilling to risk the present situation, you won't confer any benefits at all. The result will be that instead of perishing with the recipient, the benefits will perish with you. Better there should be no response than no giving. Even after a bad harvest, one should still sow the seed: often, what was lost due to poor soil over a long period is regained in a single year when the soil is fertile. 2 It's worth dealing with some ungrateful types in order to find one who is grateful. No one has such a sure hand in conferring benefits that he is not frequently misled. Let some of them go astray so that others may hit the mark. After a shipwreck, men take to the seas again; a bad loan does not frighten the moneylender from the forum. Life will soon grind to a halt if one has to give up every activity that meets with resistance. But as for you, let what has happened make you all the more generous. For where the results of an action are uncertain, one should attempt it often in order to succeed now and then.

3 But I have said enough on this subject in my work entitled *On Benefits.** A more pressing inquiry, which has not to my mind been adequately discussed, concerns the person who has done us some service and then afterward harmed us. Has he made things even, canceling our debt of gratitude? If you like, you can compound the problem: the harm done at a later time was much greater than the service performed earlier.

4 If you ask the proverbially strict opinion of the inflexible judge, he will have the one action cancel the other, saying, "Even though there is a preponderance of injury, let's credit the difference to the

side of benefits." The harm was greater, but the service was done first, so let's take the factor of time into account. **5** There are additional considerations, which are so obvious that I need not remind you of them: how willing he was to perform the service, and how unwilling he was to commit the wrong, since both benefits and injuries depend on intent. "I did not wish to confer a benefit: I was shamed into it, or I was pestered to do it, or I hoped to gain by it." **6** Every benefit merits gratitude matching the attitude of the giver: one weighs not the size of the benefit but the willingness to bestow it. Now take the guesswork out of it: that previous action was a benefit, the subsequent action is an injury and is of greater magnitude than the other. A good man still does the reckoning in a way detrimental to himself: he adds to the benefit and subtracts from the injury.

The other, more lenient judge—the one I would prefer to be—will tell you to forget the injury but remember the favor. **7** You say, "Surely what accords with justice is to render to each his due: gratitude for a benefit, vengeance or at least resentment for an injury." That's true, when it is one person who commits the injury and another who confers the benefit; but when it is the same person, then the effect of the injury is negated by the benefit. For if a person ought to have been forgiven even without having done something meritorious beforehand, then when he does wrong after conferring benefits, what is owed is more than mere forgiveness. **8** I do not set the same price on the two: I consider a benefit to be worth more than an injury.

Not everyone knows how to be grateful. Even a thoughtless or untutored person or one from the common crowd can recognize an obligation, especially when it has not been long since he received the benefit; but he does not know the extent of his obligation. Only the wise person knows what value ought to be assigned to each thing. For the person I was just now speaking of, who is foolish even if well intentioned, repays the favor either less generously than he should or at the wrong time or place. Thus what ought to have been repaid is squandered and thrown away.

**9** It's amazing how apposite our language is in some cases, how the conventions of our ancient speech refer to certain things with expressions that not only work very well but also point out our responsibilities. For instance, surely we are in the habit of saying, "This person rendered thanks to that person" (*gratiam rettulit*). To "render" is to bring of your own accord what you owe. We don't say, "He gave back thanks" (*gratiam reddidit*). People give something back even when they do so unwillingly or at an inopportune time or by another's hand. We don't say, "He paid back the benefit" (*reposuit beneficium*) or "He reimbursed it" (*resolvit*). An expression that is suited to the repayment of debts doesn't seem right to us. 10 To "render" is to bring a thing back to the one you got it from. The word signifies that the act was voluntary: the one who brought it was answering his own summons.

The wise person will take stock in his mind of how much he has received and from whom, and when, where, why, and how. That's why we say that only the sage knows how to render thanks, just as only he knows how to confer a benefit. Naturally, this is the same wise person who finds more joy in giving than others do in receiving.

11 Some consider this to be one of those sayings of our school that run counter to everyone's expectations—the Greeks call them *paradoxa*. They say, "So only the sage knows how to render thanks? Nobody else knows how to repay what is owing to a creditor or to pay the amount due when he makes a purchase?" Lest there be resentment against our school, be aware that Epicurus holds the same opinion. At any rate, Metrodorus says that only the wise person knows how to render thanks.\* 12 Then the same Metrodorus expresses surprise when we say, "Only the wise person knows how to love; only the wise person is a friend." Yet rendering thanks is part of love and friendship. In fact, it is even more common and applicable to more people than true friendship is. Then that same Metrodorus is surprised that we say loyalty exists only in the sage—as if he himself did not say the same thing! Or do you think that a person exhibits loyalty when he does not know how to render thanks? 13 So let them stop charging us with saying what no one can believe!

They should realize that in the case of the wise person, what one sees is honorable conduct itself; in the case of the common person, a mere image and likeness of honorable conduct. No one *knows* how to render thanks except the sage. To be sure, the foolish person does also render thanks to the extent of his knowledge and ability. He is deficient in knowledge rather than in willingness, for willingness is not something that has to be learned. 14 One who is wise will assess all aspects of the situation relative to one another, for even when the act is the same, the obligation becomes greater or less according to the time, place, and reason. A thousand denarii, given at the right moment, will often achieve more in a household than showering a whole fortune upon it. It makes a great deal of difference whether you are making a gift or providing aid, whether your generosity rescues someone or merely furnishes him with something useful. Often the gift is small but its consequences are great. And don't you think it makes a great difference whether the gift is made from one's own resources or was passed on from some previous benefit?

**15** But let's not repeat points we have already covered sufficiently. In this comparative assessment of benefits and injuries, the good man will indeed judge what will be the fairest response, but he will incline toward benefits; he will lean in that direction. **16** In matters of this kind, there is a tendency to give much weight to social roles. "You did me a favor as concerns my slave; you injured me as concerns my father. You saved my son, but you took my father away from me." Every comparative assessment will take these and other similar matters into account; and if the difference is minimal, the wise person will let it go. Indeed, he will let it pass even if it is substantial but can be conceded without detriment to loyalty or devotion, that is, if the wrong pertains only to himself. **17** In sum, he will be easy to bargain with, generous in acknowledging an obligation, reluctant to make an injury cancel out a benefit. All his inclination, all his wishes, will tend toward gratitude and thanks.

It is a mistake to be more willing to receive a favor than to return one. Just as the person paying off a debt is more cheerful than the one who is borrowing, so should we be happier when unburdening ourselves of the great debt of a benefit received than when we are extremely obligated. **18** In this too, the ungrateful are mistaken: they pay their creditors with interest, but think that benefits can be held on to without repayment. In fact, our obligation for favors also increases with delay: the longer one waits, the more should be repaid. He who returns a benefit without interest is ungrateful. Therefore this too should be taken into account when one makes an assessment of receipts and expenditures.

**19** We should make every effort to show all the gratitude we can. For the good in it is our own. After all, gratitude is not justice (as is commonly believed), for justice pertains to others, but much of the good in gratitude redounds to oneself. Everyone who helps another person helps himself. I do not mean that one who has received aid will want to offer aid, or that one who has been protected will want to protect others. Nor do I mean that a good deed circles back by example to the doer. (Bad examples too revert to those who set them: no one wins any pity when the wrongs they suffer are just what they taught others how to do.) No, I mean that every virtue is its own reward. For one doesn't practice the virtues in order to receive a prize: the reward for right action is having acted rightly. **20** I do not show gratitude in order that my example will make someone else more generous in showing gratitude to me, but simply in order to perform a most pleasant and beautiful action. I show gratitude not because it is expedient but because it is agreeable. To prove this to you: if the only way I could show gratitude were by appearing to be ungrateful—if I could not return a benefit except by seeming to injure someone—I would be quite content to carry out an honorable intention in the midst of infamy. No one, I think, values virtue more or is more devoted to it than the man who has lost his good reputation in order to keep a good conscience.

**21** So as I said before, your gratitude is more for your good than for another's. The other person has gained a common, ordinary thing: receiving again what he had given. You have gained something wonderful, something that comes of the best possible state of mind: gratitude. For if vice makes people miserable and virtue makes them happy, and if gratitude is a virtue, then you have given what is commonplace and have obtained what is beyond price: a thankful heart, which only the divine, the blessed spirit can ever attain.

One who is in the opposite state experiences deep dissatisfaction. No one can be in his own good graces if he is not grateful to others. Do you think I am saying that the ingrate will eventually be miserable? I am not granting him any delay: he is miserable right now. **22** Therefore we should avoid ingratitude not for the sake of others but for our own sake. Only the smallest and lightest portion of one's wickedness overflows onto others; the worst of it—the thickest part, as it were—remains in the vessel to choke the possessor. As our friend Attalus used to say,

Vice drinks most of its own venom.*

This venom is not like the one that serpents make to poison others without detriment to themselves, for this kind is most deadly to those who possess it. **23** The ingrate torments himself, plagues himself: he hates the favors he has received, because he has to repay them; he makes them less than they are, while magnifying his injuries. And what could be more wretched than having all one's benefits drop away and only the injuries remain?

Wisdom, by contrast, adds luster to every benefit, commends them to itself, and takes delight in the constant recollection of them. **24** Bad people have just one pleasure, and a brief one, while they are receiving benefits; the wise person derives a steady and lasting joy. For his delight is not in receiving but in having received, and that is constant and undying. He thinks nothing of his injuries, forgetting them not out of carelessness but of his own volition. **25** He does not make the worst out of everything, nor does he go looking for someone to blame for his misfortune; rather, he attributes to fortune the misdeeds of other people. He does not find fault with people's words or facial expressions; he puts a kind interpretation on anything that happens and thus makes it easier to bear. He is not one to remember an offense rather than a service. Insofar as he can, he dwells on earlier and better memories of others, and does not change his attitude toward those who have deserved well of him unless their crimes are so greatly in excess that the difference is obvious, even to one who looks the other way. Even then he alters his attitude only to what it was before the previous benefit. For when the injury is equal to the benefit, some goodwill remains in his mind. **26** Just as a defendant is acquitted by a tie vote, and in every dubious case kindness inclines toward the better part, so, when good deeds are equal to the bad, the wise person ceases in his mind to be obliged but does not stop wanting to be obliged. He is like those who still pay up after a cancellation of debts.

**27** No one can be grateful unless he has little regard for the things that ordinary people lose their heads over. If you want to render thanks, you must be ready to go into exile, shed your own blood, face poverty, often even stain your own reputation and expose it to rumors you don't deserve. Gratitude comes at no small cost to oneself. **28** As long as we are seeking a benefit, there is nothing we value more highly; once we have obtained it, there is nothing we value less. What makes us forget the favors we have obtained? Our desire to obtain more: we don't think about what we have been granted already but only about our next request. We are drawn from what is right by wealth, honor, power, and everything else that is precious in our eyes, though cheap in actual worth. **29** We do not know how to set a value on things. We should not take public opinion as the basis for our deliberations; we should look to the nature of things. There is nothing wonderful in those objects, nothing to entice our minds, except our own habit of admiring them. For they are not held in high regard because they are desirable; rather, they are desired because people hold them in high regard. The errors of individuals cause a popular misconception, then the popular misconception causes individuals to err.

**30** But since we tend to believe the public, let us also believe them in this: that nothing is more honorable than gratitude. All nations, even the most barbarous, agree on this point; in this both good people and bad agree. **31** There are those who praise pleasure, and those who prefer hard work; there are those who say pain is the worst thing of all, while others will say that it is not even a bad thing. One person considers wealth the highest good; another says that money is the bane of human existence, and that there is no greater wealth than when fortune has nothing it can give you. Yet even amid such diversity of views, there is one point on which all of them speak with one voice, as they say: that when people have done us good service, we should render thanks. The whole discordant host agrees in this; yet even so, we sometimes give back injuries for favors, and the first reason some people are ungrateful is that they are unable to be grateful enough.

**32** The madness has reached such a pitch that it is now extremely dangerous to confer great benefits on anyone. For since the recipient is ashamed not to return them, he prefers that there be no one to return them to. Keep what you've been given! I don't ask for it back—I don't insist—I'd rather help you with impunity. No hatred is more deadly than that which comes from shame at having spoiled a benefit.

Farewell.

# Letter 82

*From Seneca to Lucilius*
*Greetings*

1 I've stopped worrying about you. You ask, "Which of the gods spoke up for me?" The one god that practices no deceit: a mind that loves what is right and good. Your better part is safe. Fortune can injure you, but what matters more is that I no longer fear you will injure yourself. Keep on the way you have begun, and let your calm manner become a settled disposition—calm, but not soft. 2 Better a hard life than a soft one! That is, if you take "a hard life" in the popular sense: a harsh life, full of labor and difficulty. We often hear people praise someone's life because they envy him. "He has a soft life," they say, but what they really mean is, "He is a soft fellow." For the mind becomes effeminate over time: reclining in idleness and leisure, it slackens to resemble the life it leads. What do you think? If one is a man, isn't it better to be stiff, even with the stiffness of death?° Besides, the effete have made their lives resemble the very thing they fear.* True leisure is very different from the bier!

3 You ask, "What are you saying? Isn't it better to rest, even in that way, than to get caught up in the whirlwind of business?" Yes, the strain is terrible, but so is lethargy. As far as I'm concerned, the corpse drenched with perfumed unguents is just as dead as the one dragged off by a hook.* Leisure without study is death; it's like being buried alive.

4 What's to be gained by getting away from it all? As if our worries won't follow us across the sea! What retreat is there where the fear of death cannot enter? What quiet spot, in the deepest mountain stronghold, that is not made fearsome by the thought of pain? No matter where you hide, you will be surrounded by the hue and cry of human misfortune.

All around us are external cares to deceive and oppress us; many more come boiling up from within, even in the midst of solitude. 5 We must surround ourselves with philosophy, the one rampart that can never be stormed, that the siege engines of fortune can never breach. The mind that has abandoned external goods, that asserts its freedom within its own citadel, has taken up an impregnable position. Sling-bullets and arrows fall harmlessly at its feet. We speak of the long arm of fortune, but fortune has no long arm: it catches nobody but those who hold on to it.

**6** So let's keep our distance from fortune as much as we can. But the only way we can do that is through an understanding of ourselves and of nature. Let us know where we are headed and where we come from; what is good for us and what is bad; what to pursue and what to avoid; what reason is, which distinguishes objects of pursuit and avoidance, soothes the madness of our desires, checks the savagery of our fears. **7** Some think they have overcome these forces even without philosophy; but when their tranquility is put to the test by some misfortune, the confession is wrung from them at last. The brave words die on their lips when the torturer says, "Stretch out your hand!" and death comes near. Then one can say to them, "It was easy for you to scoff at suffering before you had to face it. Here now is pain, which you said is endurable; here now is death, which you decried in such a fine long speech. The whips are cracking; the sword is flashing;

> Now is the time, Aeneas, for your courage;
> now is the time for your stout heart."*

**8** What will give you that stout heart is constant practice, rehearsing not your speeches but your mind and preparing yourself for death. He who has tried to use tricks of logic to persuade you that death is not an evil has neither encouraged you nor roused your spirit.

Most excellent Lucilius, we can but laugh at the perversity of the Greeks. I am amazed that I have not yet managed to shake them off. **9** Zeno, of our school, offers the following syllogism:

> Nothing bad is glorious.
>
> But death is glorious.
>
> Therefore death is not bad.

Now, that was a big help! You have freed me from fear; after that, I won't hesitate to offer my neck to the sword! Are you not willing to speak seriously? Do you mean to make me laugh, just when I'm about to die?

Indeed, it is hard for me to say who was more perverse—the one who believed this argument would eliminate the fear of death, or the one who tried to refute it as if it had some relevance.* **10** For he offered his own opposing argument, referring to our doctrine that death is one of the indifferents (or, as the Greeks say, *adiaphora*). He says,

> Nothing indifferent is glorious.
>
> But death is glorious.
>
> Therefore death is not indifferent.

You can see where this argument sneaks by a person. It is not death that is glorious but dying bravely. When you say, "Nothing indifferent is glorious," I concede the premise only with the stipulation that nothing is glorious that does not involve indifferents. For instance, I say that the following are indifferents (that is, that they are neither good nor bad): illness, pain, poverty, exile, death. **11** Not one of these is glorious in itself, yet nothing is glorious without them. For what we praise is not poverty but the person who is not humbled or bowed down by poverty; not exile but the person who went into exile with a braver face than he would have worn when sending another; not pain but the one over whom pain exercised no coercion. No one praises death; rather, we praise the spirit that death can carry off but cannot vanquish. **12** All such things are not in themselves either honorable or glorious, but any of them that virtue meets and handles is made honorable and glorious by it. In themselves, they are intermediate. What makes the difference is whether vice puts a hand to them or virtue. The same death that was glorious in Cato's case became immediately base and shameful in the case of Decimus Brutus.* For it was he who asked his executioners to wait a moment and went off to use the latrine. Then when they called him back and ordered him to stretch out his neck, he said, "I will if you let me live." What madness it is to run away when you cannot possibly escape! "I will if you let me live"—he might as well have added, "even under Antony!" Now there was a man who deserved to be spared!

**13** But as I was saying, it is evident that death in itself is neither bad nor good. The use Cato made of it was highly honorable; that made by Brutus was extremely shameful. Every object takes on a splendor not its own when virtue is added to it. We say that a room is well lighted even though the same room is quite dark during the night: daytime pours light into it, and night takes light away. **14** So it is with the things our school calls "indifferent" and "intermediate": wealth, strength, beauty, honors, power; and on the other hand death, exile, ill health, pain, and whatever else we fear in greater or lesser degree.* It is virtue or vice that gives them a good or bad name. A piece of iron is not in itself either hot or cold: thrust into the furnace, it glows red-hot; plunged into water, it cools down. Death is honorable only through that which is actually honorable, namely, virtue and the mind that cares nothing for externals.

**15** But even among these things, Lucilius, the ones we call intermediates, there is an important distinction to be made. For death is not indifferent in the same way as it is indifferent whether you have an odd or an even number of hairs on your head. Death is among those things that are not bad and yet have a semblance of badness. There is in us an innate love of self, an innate wish to survive and preserve ourselves, and an innate horror of disintegration,° because it seems to deprive us of many goods and to remove us from the surroundings we are used to.* Death is made alien to us also by the fact that we know this world already, but we do not know what the world toward which we are headed is like, and we have a horror of the unknown. Besides, we have a natural fear of darkness, and people believe that death will lead us into the dark. **16** So even if death is indifferent, it is not something one can easily ignore. The mind must be toughened by constant practice so as to endure the sight of it and its nearer approach.

We ought to care much less about death than we do. We have believed many scurrilous tales about it, and many have tried to outdo each other in inventing more. There are descriptions of a prison below the earth and regions of endless night, where

> The enormous guardian of hell
> rests on a bed of bones, and, snarling, gnaws
> them in the gory cavern, filling all
> the bloodless shades with fear.*

Even after you persuade people that those are just stories and that the deceased do not have anything left to be afraid of, there is another fear that crops up: their fear of Hades is equaled by their fear of being nowhere at all.

**17** Why shouldn't it be glorious to face death courageously, contending against those long-inculcated worries? Why shouldn't it be one of the greatest achievements of the human mind? A person will never mount up toward virtue if he believes death is an evil; but if he thinks it is indifferent, he will. Nature does not allow anyone to advance bravely toward what he believes to be bad; he will proceed slowly and reluctantly. But what one does against one's will, in a cowardly manner, is not glorious. Virtuous action is not done under duress. **18** Furthermore, no action can be honorable unless the mind is entirely set on its object, with no reluctance in any part of itself. When a person goes after something bad, either because he fears something worse or because he has other goods in view that make it worthwhile to absorb one bad thing, his judgments as an agent are at odds with each other. On one side is the judgment that bids him pursue his aims; on the other is the judgment that pulls him back and makes him shun whatever he suspects is dangerous. So he is torn in different directions; in which case glory is lost to him. For virtue acts on its decisions with harmony of mind; it is not afraid of what it is doing.

> And as for you, yield not to ills; oppose them
> more boldly than your fortune will allow.*

**19** You will not oppose them more boldly if you believe them to be bad. That belief must be driven from your heart; otherwise anxiety will make you hesitant in action. You will have to be pushed when you ought to charge ahead.

To be sure, our school would like Zeno's reasoning to be correct and the reasoning that runs counter to it to be fallacious and wrong. Speaking for myself, though, I do not reduce these matters to the rules of dialectic and those tired old conundrums of professional logicians. My view is that all that sort of thing ought to be thrown out. All it does is convince the interlocutor that he is being cheated. He may be forced to concede, but he will be saying something different from what he actually believes. Speeches on behalf of truth should be more straightforward; speeches against fear should be more courageous. **20** My preference would be to take this convoluted reasoning of theirs and lay it out straight so that I can persuade people, not put one over on them. When a commander is about to lead his army into battle to lay down their lives for their wives and children, how does he exhort them? Think of the Fabii, how their one household shouldered the whole burden of their country's war.* Think of the Spartans stationed at the narrows of Thermopylae. They expect neither victory nor homecoming: that place will be their tomb.* **21** How do you exhort them to put their own bodies in the way of an entire nation's destruction—to give up their lives before yielding their position? Will you say to them, "Nothing bad is glorious; but death is glorious; therefore death is not bad"? What an effective speech that would be! After hearing that, who would hesitate to hurl himself onto the spears—to die on his feet! On the contrary, how bravely Leonidas addressed them, saying, "Eat your breakfast, fellow soldiers; dinner will be in Hades." They had no trouble swallowing; the food did not stick in their throats or fall from their hands. They went readily to their breakfast—and their dinner. **22** And what about the Roman commander who, when his soldiers had been assigned to take over a certain position defended by a vast army of their enemies, addressed them thus: "Fellow soldiers, there is need for us to go; there is no need to return."* You see how straightforward, how imperious virtue is.

But as for your chicaneries, how can they possibly make anyone stand taller or more courageously? They crush the spirit; yet if there is ever a time when one's mind ought not to be constricted and forced into miniscule and thorny paths, it is when one is preparing for some great undertaking. **23** Our task is not to remove the fear of death from three hundred soldiers but to remove it from all who are mortal. How will you teach them that death is not a bad thing? How will you overcome the beliefs of a lifetime, instilled in earliest infancy? What help do you have to give to human weakness? What words of yours will set them on fire and send them into the midst of danger? What speech will break the covenant of fear; what force of composition will overturn the convictions of the human race arrayed against you? Do you offer me riddling words and snares of sneaky little questions? Great armaments for giant foes! **24** That savage African serpent was more frightening to the Roman legions than the war itself. In vain they shot at it with slings and arrows: not even the slayer of the Python could have wounded it.* After its massive bulk and impenetrable hide had resisted steel and every missile that human hands could fire, millstones beat it down at last. Will you then shoot such tiny darts, when your enemy is death? Will you take on a lion with a pin? Your arguments are sharp, but nothing is sharper than a blade of straw. Sometimes a thing is made useless and ineffective by its very fineness.

Farewell.

## Letter 83

*From Seneca to Lucilius*
*Greetings*

1 You tell me to describe every one of my days from start to finish. You must think well of me if you suppose there is nothing in them that I would hide from you. Our lives should indeed be like that, lived as if in the sight of others. Even our thoughts should be conducted as though some other person could gaze into our inmost breast. For there is someone who can. What use is there in keeping a secret from human beings? Nothing is hidden from God. God is in our minds; God enters into the midst of our thoughts. I say enters—as if he had ever left!

2 So I will do as you tell me, and write to you willingly of what I am doing, all in order. I will observe myself straightway, and conduct an inquiry of my day. It is a very useful practice. What makes us terrible people is that no one looks back over his life. We ponder what we are about to do (though not as often as we should); we do not ever reflect on what we have done. Yet plans for the future depend on the past.

3 Today has been a solid block of time. No one has taken any of it from me; the entire day has been split between resting and reading. Only a little has been devoted to bodily exercise, and on that account I am grateful to old age: it costs me but little. As soon as I stir myself, I am tired, but that is the aim of exercise even for the

strongest people. **4** Would you like to know about my regimen? A single trainer is enough for me. It is Pharius, a mere child, as you know, and a lovable one. But he will be replaced: I am now looking for someone even younger. To be sure, he says that we are at the same point in our lives—both losing our teeth! But already I can hardly keep up with him in running, and in a few days I won't be able to. You see what daily exercise is doing for me! The distance between two people increases quickly when they are moving in opposite directions. He is climbing even as I descend, and you know well how much more quickly the second happens. I misspoke: our time of life is not a descent but a free fall.

**5** But would you like to know the outcome of our race today? Something that rarely happens in running—a tie. After this flurry of activity (one can hardly call it a workout), I got down into a cold bath—for "cold" is the word I use when the water is just barely warm. And I used to be such a cold-water enthusiast! On the first of January, I used to pay my respects to the Canal. Just as I used to read or write or say something on that day, so also was it a ritual of mine to greet the new year with a dip in the Maiden.* But then I moved my encampment, first to the Tiber, and now to this tub, where—when I am at my bravest, and all indications are good—the water is warmed only by the sun. I can hardly manage a cold bath anymore.

**6** Next it is dry bread, a meal without a table, after which I need not wash my hands. I sleep hardly at all. You know my habits: I take just a very brief nap, a mule team's rest, as it were. It's enough for me if I doze off for a moment. Sometimes I know I have slept, and sometimes I only guess.

**7** Listen—you can hear the noise from the crowds at the races. Some sudden cry rises from every throat to assail my ears, but my thoughts carry on undisturbed, unbroken even. The roar does not bother me at all: many voices mingled into one are to me as waves on the shore or wind among the trees or any other meaningless sound.

**8** What, then, do I have to occupy my mind? I'll tell you. Yesterday's reflections have left me wondering what certain very intelligent men were thinking when they made their proofs of important points so trivial and confusing. Even if what they say is true, it seems more like falsehood. **9** Zeno, who is the greatest of men and the founder of our very brave, very chaste school of philosophy, wishes to dissuade us from drunkenness. Listen to how he proves that a good man will not become drunk:

> No one entrusts a secret to one who is drunk.
>
> But one does entrust a secret to a good man.
>
> Therefore a good man will not be drunk.*

In mockery of this, one could use similar reasoning to prove the exact opposite. Here's how—taking just one example:

> No one entrusts a secret to one who is asleep.
>
> But one does entrust a secret to a good man.
>
> Therefore a good man does not sleep.

10 Posidonius takes up the cause of our master Zeno in the one way he can, though even then the position seems to me untenable.* He says that "drunk" has two meanings: one is when a person is loaded with wine and not in control of himself, the other is when he is in the habit of becoming drunk and is susceptible to this fault. The latter, he says, is what Zeno has in mind—the one who is in the habit of becoming drunk, not the one who is drunk right now. This is the person to whom no one will entrust a secret, lest he blurt it out when he is drinking. 11 But that's false: the first syllogism posits one who is drunk, not one who will be so in the future. For you will grant that there is a big difference between a person who is drunk and a drunkard. A person who is drunk could be drunk for the very first time, without having acquired the habit. Conversely, the habitual drunkard can sometimes be free of drunkenness. For that reason, I understand the word in its usual signification, especially since it is employed by one who makes some claim to precision and who scrutinizes words. Besides, if Zeno understood the word one way but meant us to take it in another, then he made the ambiguity of a term the occasion for deceit, and one ought not to do that when truth is one's object. 12 But suppose he did mean that. What follows is false, that one does not entrust a secret to someone who has a habit of getting drunk. Think how many soldiers are entrusted with information that their commanders, tribunes, and centurions need to keep quiet. Yet soldiers are not models of sobriety. The plan to assassinate Caesar (I mean the Caesar who was in power after the defeat of Pompey) was disclosed

to Tillius Cimber* as well as to Cassius. Cassius drank water all his life; Tillius Cimber was besotted with wine and a troublemaker too. He himself told a joke about it. "How can I have any tolerance for people," he said, "when I don't have any for wine?"

**13** Each of us could name people who cannot be trusted with wine but can be trusted with a secret. I will recount just one example that occurs to me so that it won't be forgotten. Life should be well supplied with exemplary anecdotes so that we don't always have to go back to the old ones. Lucius Piso,* the commander of the city watch, got drunk once and was continually so thereafter. **14** He spent most of the night at parties, then slept until noon; noon was daybreak, as far as he was concerned. Still, he attended scrupulously to his responsibilities, on which depended the safety of Rome. The divine Augustus trusted this man with secret instructions when he appointed him to a command in Thrace, which he subdued; then Tiberius did the same as he was departing for Campania, since he was leaving much resentment and many causes for suspicion behind him in Rome. **15** I believe it was because Piso's drunkenness had yielded such good results that Tiberius later appointed Cossus as his urban prefect—a serious, well-disciplined man but positively soaked in wine, to the point that once when he had come directly to the Senate from a party, he had to be carried out because he had fallen asleep and could not be awakened. Nonetheless, Tiberius used to write to him with his own hand on matters he dared not confide even to his closest advisors. And Cossus never gave away a secret, either public or private.

**16** So let's get rid of the old commonplaces. "The mind impeded by drink is not under its own control. Just as clay storage jars filled with must tend to burst from the heat of fermentation, and everything inside comes shooting out, so is it when wine flows in intoxicating abundance: whatever lies hidden is cast forth in full view. Just as those who are overloaded with wine cannot keep their food down—for the wine washes it up—so is it with a secret: they spill it out, both their own and other people's." **17** Yes, this does often happen. But it also happens that when there is need, we do consult with people who we know drink freely. This disproves that platitude which is offered in Zeno's defense, that no one shares a secret with a habitual drunkard.

It is much better to attack drunkenness directly, exposing its faults. Even an ordinary decent person will avoid these, and still more the perfectly wise person. The latter is satisfied when thirst is quenched; and although he does sometimes let good cheer urge him to go somewhat further for another's sake, he stops short of drunkenness. **18** We can inquire some other time whether the wise person is mentally affected by an excess of wine and whether he then acts as people usually do when they are drunk. In the meantime, if what you want to establish is that a good man ought not to become inebriated, why do you resort to syllogisms? Just say how disgraceful it is for a person to imbibe more than he can hold, not knowing the size of his own stomach, and how many things people do when they are drunk that would embarrass them when sober. Say that drunkenness is nothing but voluntary insanity. Imagine the drunken state continuing for a number of days; would you hesitate to call that madness? So even as it is, it is not a lesser form of insanity but only a shorter one.

**19** Recount the example of Alexander of Macedon, who drove a spear through Clitus, his dearest and most loyal friend, during a dinner party. When he found out what he had done he wanted to die, and certainly that is what he deserved.* Drunkenness sets every vice aflame, and exposes them too, since it removes the sense of shame that sets constraints on our worst impulses. For more people are inhibited from wrongdoing by the disgrace of it than by their own good intentions. **20** When an excess of wine has possession of the mind, any fault that was hiding comes into the open. Drunkenness does not create faults—it brings out faults that already exist. It is then that the lustful person does not even wait for the bedroom but permits his desires to achieve everything they want without delay; it is then that the shameless person admits his infirmity* and even boasts of it; it is then that the quarrelsome fellow restrains neither his tongue nor his fist. In a rude person, arrogance becomes even more pronounced, as does cruelty in a savage temperament and malice in a spiteful one. Every vice has free rein; every vice is exposed to view.

**21** Mention too the loss of self-awareness, the slurred and indistinct speech, the blurred vision, the unsteady walk, the dizziness, the ceiling spinning around as if the entire house were caught in a whirlwind, the pains in the stomach when the wine seethes inwardly and causes bloat through the abdomen. It is endurable, nonetheless, while the effects of the drink still last. But what about afterward, when sleep has soured it and inebriation has turned into indigestion?

**22** Think what terrible events drunkenness has caused in human history. There are whole tribes of fierce warriors whom it has betrayed to their enemies; there are long-defended ramparts it has breached; peoples of fiercely independent spirit, who always refused to bear the yoke, have been forced by it to submit to foreign domination. Those who could never be defeated in battle have been vanquished by drink. **23** I spoke earlier about Alexander. He who had passed unharmed through so many campaigns, so many battles, so many winters, who defeated every challenge of climate and terrain, who crossed so many rivers descending from unknown wilds, so many distant seas, was vanquished at last by drinking without moderation from his "Beaker of Hercules"—for him, a beaker of death.*

**24** How is holding one's liquor a point of pride? When you have won the drinking bout, when the others are all retching or passing out and refuse your toasts, when you are the only one to survive the party, having defeated everyone by your marvelous prowess, your unmatched capacity for wine, even then you are outdone by a barrel.

**25** What was it that destroyed Mark Antony, a man of noble character and exceptional talent? Was it not drunkenness that drove him to foreign habits and the most un-Roman vices? That, and his love of Cleopatra, which was only increased by wine. It was this that made him an enemy to the state, that made him a lesser man than his enemies. It was this that made him cruel, when he used to have the heads of leading statesmen brought to him at dinner—when amid his elaborate feasts and the splendor of kings he would view the hands and faces of the proscribed. Even though he was loaded with wine, he thirsted for blood.* It would have been bad enough if he had been drinking as he did such things; that he did them when already drunk is still more intolerable.

**26** A devotion to drink generally does bring cruelty in its train, for one's soundness of mind then becomes flawed and uneven. Just as long illness causes people to become peevish and difficult and prone to take offense at the slightest thing, so continual drunkenness causes the mind to become brutish. For since they are frequently not themselves, the habit of insanity becomes ingrained, and faults acquired under the influence of wine thrive even without it.

**27** In your speech, then, tell us why the wise person ought not to become intoxicated. Show us by examples, not words, how ugly a thing it is, how unreasonable its demands. The easiest course is to prove that when our so-called pleasures get out of bounds, they become punishments instead. For if you attempt to argue that the wise man is not affected by large amounts of wine, that the upright character of his mind persists even through dissipation, then you might as well conclude that he would not be killed by drinking poison, would not be put to sleep by a sleeping draft, and would not vomit or expel the contents of his bowels after taking a dose of hellebore. But if his gait is unsteady and his speech is slurred, why should you consider him to be drunk in one part of himself and sober in another?

Farewell.

## Letter 84

*From Seneca to Lucilius*
*Greetings*

1 Those trips are shaking the laziness out of me. They have been beneficial, I believe, both to my health and to my studies. Why they should improve my health is plain to you: since my love of literature makes me lazy and neglectful of my body, I get some exercise through the labor of others.* Why they should aid my study I will explain: I have° withdrawn from readings. To be sure, reading is necessary, first that I may not be wrapped up in myself alone, and second that after finding out about the inquiries of others, I may judge concerning their discoveries and ponder what remains to be discovered. Reading nourishes one's talent and refreshes it when it is worn out with study, even though reading itself requires study. 2 We ought neither to write exclusively nor read exclusively: the first—writing, that is—will deaden and exhaust our powers; the second will weaken and dilute them. One must do both by turns, tempering one with the other, so that whatever is collected through reading may be assimilated into the body by writing.

3 We should be like bees, as the saying goes: first they fly about and choose the flowers best suited for making honey, then distribute what they have collected throughout the hive, and as our poet Virgil says,

> let the sweet nectar fill the swelling cells
> and lucent honey flow.*

4 Opinion is divided about bees. Do they merely extract liquid from flowers, which immediately becomes honey, or do they transform what they have collected into that sweet liquid by some intermingling of their own distinctive spirit?* For some hold that their expertise is not in making the honey but only in collecting it. They say that on the leaves of a certain reed in the land of India, one can

find a honey that is produced either by the dew of that atmosphere or by the exceptionally thick and sweet juice of the reed itself. Their view is that the same capacity resides in our own plants, though less noticeably, and is found and harvested by the creature that is born to this task. Others think that what the bees gather from flowers and tender grasses changes its character when stored away in the hive, by a process that includes some sort of fermentation, if I may use that term, during which the different flavors combine into one.

**5** But I digress from the matter at hand. We also must imitate these bees, and taking the things we have gathered from our diverse reading, first separate them (for things are better preserved when they are kept distinct), then, applying the care and ability of our own talent, conjoin those various samples into one savor, so that even if it is apparent where a thing has been taken from, it may yet appear to be different from that from which it was taken. **6** It is what we see nature do in our bodies through no effort of our own. The nutriments we have taken are burdensome for just so long as they retain their own character and swim as solids in the stomach; but when they have been changed from what they were, then at last they are added to our strength, passing into our bloodstream. Let us accomplish the same with these things that nourish the talent, not permitting the things we have consumed to remain whole but making them part of ourselves. **7** Let us digest them; otherwise they will pass into the memory, not into the talent. Let us faithfully adjust our thinking to theirs and make them our own, so that from the many there may come to be some sort of unity. It is like when a single problem in arithmetic involves various smaller sums: the many individual numbers become one total. Our minds should do the same: they should hide everything that has contributed and show forth only the results. **8** Even if you exhibit a resemblance to some admired author who has left a deep impression on you, I want you to resemble him as a son does, not as a statue does. A statue is a dead thing.

"What do you mean? Won't readers realize whose style, whose argumentation, whose well-turned remarks you are imitating?" It is possible they will not, I think, if a greatly talented man stamps his own form upon all the elements that he draws from his chosen model so that they all fit together into a unity.

**9** Do you not see how many voices combine to form a choir? Yet there is unity in the sound they produce. One is a high voice, another low, and another in the middle; women join the men, and flutes accompany them; yet one cannot make out the voices of individuals but only the one voice of them all. **10** The kind of chorus I mean is that known to the old philosophers, for in the shows we have now there are more people singing than there used to be in the audience. When the line of singers fills the aisles and the seating area is ringed with trumpeters and every kind of flute and water organ sounds together from the stage, then from the different sounds is produced a unison. This is what I want our mind to be like: in it are many skills, many precepts, examples from many ages, but all harmonized into one.

**11** "How is this to be done?" you ask. By constant concentration: if we do nothing except at the prompting of reason and avoid nothing except at the prompting of reason. If only you will listen, reason will speak to you, saying,

> "Give up those things that everyone always chases after. Give up on wealth: those who have it find it either a danger or a burden. Give up on bodily pleasures, and mental pleasures too: they make a person soft and flabby. Give up on ambition: it is a conceited thing, empty and inflated; it has no ending and is concerned only to get ahead and keep others from catching up. It suffers from envy—envy on both sides, in fact. And you see how unhappy it makes a person to be both the object and the subject of envy. **12** You see before you the homes of powerful men, the doorways thronged with well-wishers all pushing and shoving one another. Many an affront must you endure to get in; more, once you are inside. Pass them by, those staircases of the wealthy, those vestibules built up over our heads. To stand in them is to stand not just on a high ledge but on a slippery one too. Turn your steps, rather, toward wisdom. Seek out the largesse wisdom has to give: great serenity and also great abundance."

**13** What seems most eminent in human affairs, even though in reality it is puny and stands out only by comparison with what is the lowest, is reached nonetheless by steep and difficult paths. It is a rugged road that leads to the summit of prestige. But if you choose to scale *this* mountain, the one that rises above the things of fortune, you will see spread out beneath you everything that most people regard as heights. Yet the path to this summit lies on level ground.*

Farewell.

## Letter 85

*From Seneca to Lucilius*
*Greetings*

**1** I had intended to spare you by passing over the remaining complications, content with giving you just a taste of the arguments our school uses to prove that virtue is sufficient by itself to render our life completely happy. But you tell me to include everything, both our own dialectical arguments and the ones that have been worked out to make a laughingstock of us.* If I decide to do that, this won't be a letter; it will be a book!

I swear to you many times over that I take no pleasure in arguments of that kind. I'm embarrassed to march into battle for gods and men armed with nothing more than a pin:

**2** Anyone who is intelligent is also self-controlled.

But anyone who is self-controlled is also steady.

Anyone who is steady is also untroubled.

Anyone who is untroubled is without sadness.

Anyone who is without sadness is happy.

Therefore the intelligent person is happy, and intelligence is sufficient for happiness.*

**3** To this syllogism some of the Peripatetics reply that when people say of someone that he is "untroubled," "steady," and "without sadness," they mean that he is, for instance, troubled only very occasionally and in moderation, not that he is never troubled at all.* Similarly, they say that a person is said to be "without sadness" when he is not prone to sadness and when that fault is not frequent or excessive in him. They add that human nature does not allow anyone's mind to be immune to sadness, that the sage is not overcome by grief and yet is touched by it, and other similar points that accord with their doctrine. They do not eliminate the emotions; they only restrict them.

4 But how little credit we give the sage if he is merely to be stronger than weaklings, happier than those who are terribly depressed, more restrained than those who are out of control, greater than the lowest of the low! Suppose Ladas were to marvel at what a fast runner he was when those he saw behind him were only the crippled and the lame!*

> She'd skim the leaf tips of the growing grain
> and never bruise the tender blades in passing;
> she'd dart across the swelling sea uplifted
> and never wet her swift foot in the water.*

This is swiftness measured by its own standard, not the kind that is praised in comparison with the slowest runners there are. Suppose you were to call a person healthy when he had only a slight fever! A moderate amount of illness is not good health.

5 "The wise man is said to be untroubled in the same sense as some types of fruit are said to be seedless, ones in which hard seeds are less noticeable yet not completely lacking." That's wrong. What I take to be the case with the good man is not that faults are diminished but that they are absent. There should be none, not small ones; for if there are any, they will grow and eventually become an issue. An aggravated and serious eye infection causes blindness, but a minor infection is troubling as well.

6 If you attribute any emotions at all to the sage, reason will be outmatched by them and will be swept away as by a torrent, and all the more so since you attribute to him not just one emotion to contend with but all of them. A crowd of emotions, even moderate ones, is more powerful than any single emotion would be, even at full force. 7 He feels a desire for money, but a moderate desire; ambition, but not burning ambition; anger, but not unrelenting anger; restlessness, but not too nervous and uneasy a restlessness; lust, but not frenzied lust. It would be easier to deal with someone who had a single thoroughgoing fault than with one who has every fault, even though he has them in lesser degree.

8 Besides, the degree of emotion makes no difference: regardless

of degree, it knows nothing of obedience and heeds no advice. No animal, whether wild or tame and gentle, is swayed by reasoned argument: their nature is deaf to persuasion. In the same way, even the smallest emotions heed us not, hear us not. Lions and tigers never shed their savage nature: they may seem tame at times, but when you least expect it, their latent savagery is kindled again. We can never trust that our faults have been subdued.

9 Furthermore, if reason is of any use, then the emotions will not even begin: if they begin without the acquiescence of reason, they will continue without it. It is easier to forestall their beginnings than to govern the impulse.* Hence the notion of "moderation" is false and of no utility. We should treat it just as we would the suggestion that a person ought to go insane in moderation or get sick in moderation.

10 Only virtue exhibits restraint. The infirmities of the mind do not accept it: you will find it easier to get rid of them than to govern them. Surely it is not in doubt that established and ingrained faults of the human mind, like avarice, cruelty, and lack of self-control, are not subject to moderation. Therefore the emotions too are not, since it is from them that those faults arise.*

11 Besides, if you grant any scope to sadness, fear, desire, and the other depraved emotions, they will not be in our power. Why? Because the causes that trigger them are external to us. Hence they will increase in proportion to lesser or greater stimuli. Fear will be greater if what frightens it gets bigger or approaches nearer; desire will be keener, the larger the item one hopes to obtain. 12 If it is not in our power to determine whether emotions should occur at all, then neither is it in our power to determine their magnitude. If you allow them to begin, they will increase as their causes increase, and their magnitude will be whatever it becomes. Besides, even the smallest feelings may grow out of control. That which is destructive never observes a limit. The beginnings of diseases may be very slight, but they spread; and when one's body is sick, even the smallest addition will sometimes cause it to be overwhelmed.

13 But what madness it is to think that the beginnings of emotion are not subject to our will and yet believe that the endings are! How can I possibly have the power to restrict something that I had no power to prevent? Is it not easier to keep things out than to control them once they are let in?

**14** Some people draw the following distinction: "The intelligent and self-controlled person is tranquil in the disposition and character of his mind, but not in the event. For as concerns the character of his mind, he is untroubled and experiences neither grief nor fear, but many external causes act on him, and these bring turmoil upon him." **15** What they mean is something like this: he is not prone to anger and yet becomes angry at times; not fearful and yet feels fear at times—that is, he lacks the fault of fearfulness but not the emotion itself. If we allow that, then fear will turn by repeated experience into the corresponding fault; and anger, once admitted into the mind, will undo the fabric of that character which was once free of anger. **16** Anyway, suppose the wise man does not rise above external causes but has something that he fears. In that case, when the time comes for him to face battle and flame on behalf of country, laws, and liberty, he will go forth reluctantly, for his spirit will quail. But such mental inconsistency is not to be found in one who is wise.

**17** There is also another remark I believe I should make so that we won't confuse two proofs that ought to be kept separate. For there is reasoning to show that what is honorable is the only good, and then separate reasoning to show that virtue is sufficient for happiness. Everyone grants that if the honorable is the only good, then virtue suffices for happiness; they do not grant the converse, however, that if virtue alone makes a person happy, then the honorable is the only good. **18** Xenocrates and Speusippus hold that while a person can be made happy even by virtue alone, it is still not the case that what is honorable is the only good.* Epicurus too believes that one who has virtue is also happy; and yet it is his view that virtue itself is not sufficient for happiness, since it is the pleasure that arises from virtue that makes one happy, not virtue itself. The distinction is pointless, since he also says that virtue is never without pleasure.* So if the one is always joined to the other and cannot be separated from it, then virtue is also sufficient on its own. For even when it is alone it is never without pleasure.

**19** But the former view is absurd, the one that says that a person will indeed be happy through virtue alone and yet not completely happy. How that can come about is beyond my comprehension. The happy life contains a complete and insurmountable good; and if that is the case, then it is completely happy. If the life of the gods contains nothing greater or better, and if the happy life is divine, then there is no respect in which it could be raised to a higher degree. **20** Moreover, if the happy life lacks nothing, then every happy life is complete, and that same life is not only happy but the happiest there is. You do agree, surely, that the happy life is the supreme good? So if it contains the supreme good, it must be supremely happy. The ultimate good does not admit of any increase—for what will there be that is beyond the ultimate?—and it is the same with the happy life, since that implies the ultimate good. Again, if you posit that there is someone happier, you will also be positing that there is someone much happier.* You will be creating innumerable degrees of the ultimate good, while my own understanding of an ultimate good is that it does not admit of any further degree of goodness.

**21** If one happy person is less so than another, it follows that the one will desire the life of the happier person more than his own. But a happy person prefers his own life to any other. Neither assertion can be believed: that there is some further condition which the happy person would prefer to his own, or that he would not prefer that which is better than what he has. For surely the more intelligent one is, the more he will reach for what is best and want to obtain it in any way he can. And how is a person happy when there is something he is still able to want and indeed ought to want?

**22** I will tell you what lies behind this error: they do not realize that the happy life is just one life. It is quality, not quantity, that puts it in the position of being best. That's why its status is equal whether it is long or short, wide-ranging or more restricted, spread out over many places and many situations or collected into one. He who evaluates it by its number, its measure, its situation, deprives it of its chief excellence. What is the chief excellence of the happy life? Its fullness. **23** The aim of eating and drinking is, I think, satiety. One person eats more, another less; what difference does it make? Both are now satisfied. One drinks more, another less; what difference does it make? Neither of them is thirsty any longer. One has lived more years, another fewer; that doesn't matter if the many years and the few have made them equally happy. He whom you call "less happy" is not happy: that is not a word that can be scaled back.

**24** Anyone who is courageous is without fear.

Anyone who is without fear is without sadness.

Anyone who is without sadness is happy.

This line of reasoning belongs to our school. Those who try to refute it respond that the premise we take for granted, that anyone who is courageous is without fear, is actually false and controversial. "How's that? The brave person won't fear impending harm? You're talking about someone who is crazy and out of touch, not someone who is courageous. To be sure, the courageous person experiences a very moderate degree of fear, but he is not completely beyond fear."* **25** Those who say this wind up with the same view as before, in which they regard lesser faults as if they were virtues. For a person who is afraid less often and in lesser degree is not devoid of vice but only troubled by a less serious vice.

"But I think it's crazy not to be frightened by impending harm." What you say is true if those events really are harmful. But if one knows they are not, and instead holds that shameful conduct alone is bad, then he ought to look at dangers without concern, rising above what others regard as frightening. Otherwise, if not fearing harm makes one foolish and witless, then the more intelligent a person is, the more frightened he will be.

**26** "By your account, the courageous person will put himself in harm's way." No, he won't. He won't fear dangers, but he will avoid them.* It is fitting for him to exercise caution, but not for him to be afraid.

"What do you mean? Won't he be afraid of death, prison, fires, and all the other darts fortune may cast?" No, for he knows that they are not bad but only seem so. He thinks of them as only the hobgoblins of human life. **27** Talk to him of captivity, flogging, chains, starvation, the torments of disease and injury, anything else you might name: to him, they are only the delusions of a fevered mind. Leave them for cowards to fear! Or do you think that such things can be bad when there are situations in which we must come to them voluntarily? **28** Would you like to know what is bad? Yielding to supposed evils; giving up one's freedom to them—freedom, for whose sake we ought to endure all things! We lose our freedom if we do not rise above everything that puts a yoke on our necks.

They would not be wondering what is appropriate to a courageous person if they knew what courage is. It is neither rash bravado nor thrill-seeking nor love of danger. Rather, it is knowledge of how to distinguish between what is bad and what is not.* Courage is very careful of its own safety, yet it is also very well able to endure things whose bad appearance is false. **29** "How so? If a courageous man feels a knife pressed to his throat—if his body is gouged deeply, bit by bit—if he sees his entrails spill into his lap—if his torments are repeated after an interval to make them even more painful, and wounds that had just scabbed over are spurting fresh gouts of blood, will he not be afraid? Are you saying that he won't even feel the pain?" He will feel it, certainly, for virtue does not ever shed the sensations of a human being. Yet he is not afraid: undefeated, he looks down at his own pain from above. What is his state of mind in that moment, you ask? It is like those who encourage a friend in time of sickness.

**30** Whatever is bad does some harm.

Whatever harms a person makes him worse.

Pain and poverty do not make a person worse.

Therefore they are not bad.

One might say, "The premise you offer is false: it is not the case that whatever harms a person also makes him worse. Wind and storm harm the helmsman, but they do not make him worse."

**31** Some of the Stoics respond to this objection as follows: Wind and storm do make the helmsman worse, since he cannot achieve what he set out to do, that is, to hold his course. He is not made worse as concerns his skill, but he is made worse as concerns his activity.

To this the Peripatetic replies, "By that reasoning, even the wise person is made worse by poverty, pain, and everything else of that sort; for such things will impede his activities, even though they do not take away his virtue."*

**32** The objection would be right if it were not for a disanalogy between the helmsman's situation and that of the wise person. The latter's aim in life is not merely to complete the particular task he is attempting but to act rightly in all things; the helmsman's aim is merely to conduct the ship into harbor. The skills are subordinates

293

LETTER 85

and must deliver on what they promise to do; wisdom is the sovereign and director. The skills serve life; wisdom rules it.

**33** But I think we ought to respond in a different way. In my view, neither the skill of the helmsman nor the exercise of that skill is made worse by any storm. The helmsman has not promised you a favorable outcome; he has promised an effort to be of use and a knowledge of how to handle the ship. That knowledge is all the more in evidence when hindered by some blast of fortune. Anyone who can say, "Never this ship, Neptune, except upright!"* has satisfied the requirements of his skill. What the storm impedes is not the helmsman's activity but only the outcome.

**34** "What do you mean? Isn't the helmsman harmed by the gale that prevents him from reaching the harbor, makes his endeavors pointless, and either drives him back out to sea or knocks over the mast and so arrests his progress?" He is not harmed as a helmsman but only as one traveling by sea. Otherwise he is not a helmsman at all, for skill as a helmsman is not impeded by such circumstances; on the contrary, it is made manifest. As the saying goes, "In fair weather anyone can be a helmsman." The events you speak of are detrimental to the voyage, not to the helmsman as such. **35** The helmsman plays two roles. One is in common with everyone who embarks on the same ship: he too is a passenger. The other is his own role: he is the helmsman. The storm harms him in his role as passenger, not in his role as a helmsman.

**36** Then again, the skill of a helmsman is a good belonging to another: it pertains to his passengers, just as a doctor's skill is a good pertaining to his patients. By contrast, the skill of the wise person is a shared good: it belongs both to those he lives with and to himself. Thus even supposing that the helmsman is harmed when the service he promised to do for others is hindered by the storm, **37** the wise person is still not harmed by the storms of life—poverty, pain, and the rest. For not all his works are hindered but only those that pertain to others. He is himself, always, in his actions, and in the doing of them he is greatest when opposed by fortune. For it is then that he does the business of wisdom itself, which as we just said is his own good as well as that of others.

**38** Besides, he is not prevented from helping others just because he is constrained by circumstances. By reason of poverty he is prevented from teaching them how one ought to manage affairs of state, yet he does teach them how one ought to manage poverty. His work extends through the whole of his life. Thus no chance event precludes the wise man's activity, for what prevents him from other activities is now the very object of his efforts. He is well suited for either eventuality: prosperity he governs, adversity he vanquishes. **39** I repeat: his endeavor was to manifest his virtue both in prosperity and in adversity, keeping his gaze fixed on virtue itself and not on the material of virtue.* For that reason, he is undeterred by poverty or pain or anything else that causes untrained minds to turn and run away.

**40** You think he is constrained by misfortune? He makes use of it. It is not as though Phidias only knew how to make statues out of ivory; he made them in bronze as well.* If you had offered him marble or some other less expensive material, he would have made the best of that. In just the same way, the wise man will exhibit virtue in the midst of riches if he can, but if not, then in the midst of poverty; in his homeland if he can, but if not, then in exile; as a commander if he can, but if not, then as a soldier; in good health if he can, but if not, then in weakness. Whatever fortune comes his way, he will make something memorable of it.

**41** There are some sure-handed animal tamers who train the most savage and terrifying beasts not only to shed their ferocity and endure human contact but even to become gentle companions. The lion tamer slides his hand between the lion's jaws; the tiger's handler kisses his charge; the tiny Ethiopian bids the elephant to kneel and to walk the tightrope. The wise man is like that, a skillful master of misfortune. Pain, want, humiliation, prison, exile, are universally feared; but when they come to him, they are tame.

Farewell.

## Letter 86

*From Seneca to Lucilius*
*Greetings*

**1** I write this to you from lodgings right inside the villa of Scipio Africanus, having already paid my respects to the great man's shade and to the altar, which I suspect is also his tomb. His spirit has surely returned to heaven, from which it came. I believe that, not because he led great armies (for even Cambyses had those, and he was insane and took advantage of his insanity), but because of his exceptional self-control and his patriotism, which in my view was even more admirable after he left his homeland than while he was defending it.*

It had to be one or the other: Scipio at Rome, or Rome at liberty. **2** "I want nothing," he said, "that will detract from our laws and customs. Let all our citizens be equal under the law. O my homeland, make use of the service I have done you, but do so in my absence. I am the reason that you are free; I will also be the proof of it: I will depart, if I have grown greater than is in your interests." **3** How can I not admire the greatness of spirit with which he withdrew into voluntary exile and so removed the burden from the state? Things had reached a point where either freedom had to do Scipio a wrong, or Scipio had to do freedom a wrong. Neither would have been permissible; so he gave way to the laws and betook himself to Liternum, making the state his debtor not only for Hannibal's exile but for his own.*

**4** I have seen the villa built of squared masonry, the wall enclosing the grove, also the turrets rising in front, guarding the entrance on either side; the cistern below buildings and lawns, capacious enough even for the needs of an army; and the cramped bathing quarters. These last were dimly lit, as the old ones generally were, for our ancestors thought a bathhouse couldn't be hot unless it was dark. **5** So I took great pleasure in pondering the habits of Scipio—and our habits. In this little nook, the famous "terror of Carthage,"* the man who saved Rome from a second capture, would wash his body, worn out from working in the fields. For he took his exercise in the form of hard labor, tilling the soil himself as they did in olden times. This shabby roof was over his head; this cheap tile floor was under his feet.

But nowadays who could stand to bathe in such a style? **6** A man now thinks himself a shoddy pauper unless his walls gleam with large and costly mirrors, unless his Alexandrian marble has a contrasting inlay of Numidian and a mosaic border all around of many colors laid out like a painting, unless the chamber has a glass ceiling, unless Thasian dolomite—once a rare sight even in temples—rims the pools where we plunge our limbs drained by their heavy sweating, unless the water pours from spigots made of silver. **7** And those are just the plebeian fixtures! What shall I say of the bathhouses of freedmen? How many statues there are; how many columns that don't support anything but are put there only for decoration and for the sake of the expense! How many fountains babbling from tier to tier! We have reached such a pitch of luxury that we don't even want to walk unless we tread upon precious stones!

**8** In Scipio's bathhouse the windows are tiny, mere slits cut into the stone wall so as to admit light without making the building less defensible. But nowadays they refer to bath buildings as "moth holes" if they are not designed to take in the sunshine at all hours of the day through large windows, if one cannot get a suntan there along with one's bath, if one does not have a view from one's tub of the contryside and of the sea. For that reason, baths that drew admiring crowds at the time of their dedication are despised as outmoded the moment self-indulgence devises some new means of outdoing itself. **9** In the old days, there were only a few bathhouses, and they had no kind of décor: why decorate a building when the admission is only a farthing and the purpose is utility, not amusement? There were no water jets below the surface, no constant supply of fresh water as if from a hot spring, and no one cared whether the water that washed away dirt and grime was crystal clear. **10** And yet, in all truth, how delightful it is to enter those dark bathhouses with their plain stucco, when you know that the aedile who felt the water temperature with his own hand and adjusted it for you was Cato, or Fabius Maximus, or one of the Cornelii!* For aediles from the noblest families used to make it their business to enter the public establishments and ensure cleanliness and a serviceable and healthy temperature—not the temperature you find now, which is more like a furnace. It's so hot that a slave convicted of some crime should be sentenced to be *bathed* alive! As far as I can tell, there's no difference these days between going for a hot bath and entering a burning building!

**11** "How uncouth of Scipio," some people now say, "not to have broad panes of mica to let light into his steam room, not to brown in the sun before simmering in the tub! What a hopeless case! He didn't know how to live! His bathwater had not been filtered; it was often murky, and if there had been a lot of rain, it was almost like mud!" Nor did he mind that sort of bath, for he came there to wash off sweat from his body, not perfumed oil.

**12** What do you suppose some people will say about that? "I don't envy Scipio: he really did live in exile if he had that sort of bath!" As a matter of fact, he didn't even have that sort every day: accounts of life in old Rome indicate that they washed their arms and legs daily—the parts soiled by work, naturally—but their whole bodies only on market day.* At that someone will say, "Obviously they must have been very dirty! What do you suppose they smelled like?" Like military service; like work; like men. Now that fancy bathhouses have been invented, people are much filthier.

**13** When Horace set out to describe a notorious dandy, what did he say? "Bucillus smells of lozenges."* Nowadays you would speak of Bucillus as if he smelled of the goat—he'd take the place of Gargonius, whom Horace contrasted with Bucillus. It's not enough to put on perfume: you are supposed to reapply it two or three times a day so that it won't evaporate from your skin. And they actually take pride in that smell as if it were their own!

**14** If all this seems excessively severe, blame it on the villa. There I learned a lesson from Aegialus,* the hardworking head of household (for he now owns the farm): that even the most ancient tree can be transplanted. This is something we need to learn in our old age, for every one of us plants his olive grove for those who come after. For that matter, I've seen such a grove produce acceptable fruit in abundance in its third or fourth season.° **15** You too will enjoy the covering of the tree that

> grows later to make shade for your descendants,*

as our poet Virgil says—although Virgil was aiming to produce not an accurate description but an attractive one. What he wanted was not to teach farmers but to delight his readers. **16** To give just one example, here's something I couldn't help noticing today:

> In spring the beans are planted, and you too
> go in the crumbling furrows, rich lucerne,
> and at that time of year is millet tended.*

Should these crops be sown at the same time and both of them in spring? You be the judge: I'm writing to you in June, already getting toward July, and I've just seen them harvesting beans and sowing millet on the same day.

**17** Let me get back to that olive grove. I have seen it done by two methods. With the large trees, Aegialus cut back the limbs to one foot and transplanted the trunks with the taproot, trimming the roots and leaving just the central portion to which they were all attached. He coated this with manure, lowered it into the hole, and then instead of just filling it in with dirt he trampled and compressed it. **18** He says nothing else works as well as this—"compaction," he calls it. Presumably it keeps out the cold and wind; also, the tree doesn't move as much, and because of that, new roots are able to get started and to grasp the soil. For while they are still slender and not yet established, even a slight movement would surely dislodge them. He also scrapes the taproot before replanting, for he says that new roots emerge from all the exposed wood. The trunk should not stand more than three or four feet above the ground. In this way, it will sprout new foliage from near the ground, and there will not be a large portion of it that is dry and withered, as there is on old trees. **19** The other method of planting is like this: he took strong branches whose bark was still tender (such as you find on younger trees) and set them in the soil in the same manner. These are a bit slower in growing; but since they have come up as if from a scion, they have nothing gnarly or ill-favored about them.

**20** Still another thing I have observed is a grapevine being moved away from its elm at an advanced age.* In this case, one should gather up even the root hairs if possible, and then entrench a generous amount of the vine so that roots will sprout right from the stock. I have seen some that were planted not only in February but even at the end of March, and they are now gripping and embracing elms that were not originally their own. **21** Aegialus adds that all those trees that are large-boled, if I may use that expression, should be nurtured with water from the cistern. If that is beneficial to them, we are not dependent on the rain.

I don't intend to teach you anything more, for fear that I might turn you into a competitor, just as Aegialus did with me.

Farewell.

# Letter 87

*From Seneca to Lucilius*
*Greetings*

1 I was a shipwrecked sailor before ever I took ship. How it happened I refrain from mentioning, lest you think it counts as one of the Stoic paradoxes! Not one of them is false; not one is as strange as it seems at first. I'll prove it to you whenever you want me to; in fact, even if you don't want me to. Meanwhile, this trip has taught me how many of our possessions are superfluous and how easily we can lay them aside by choice, since when necessity deprives us of them we do not feel the loss.

2 With just a few slaves—what a single carriage has room for—and with no more gear than we carry on our persons, Maximus and I have been spending a very happy couple of days. My pallet lies on the ground and I on the pallet, with one of my two cloaks serving to cover it and the other to cover me. 3 Lunch was without extras and took no more than an hour° to prepare: dried figs go with me everywhere, and everywhere my writing tablets. If I have bread, the figs are my side dish; if not, they are my bread. They make every day the start of a new year; and I ensure that it is a happy new year too, with good thoughts and greatness of spirit.* For our spirit is never greater than when it lays aside everything not its own. By fearing nothing, it finds peace; by desiring nothing, it finds wealth.

4 The carriage I ride in is just a country wagon. The mules give no evidence of being alive except that they are walking; the drover has his boots off, and not because of the heat, either. I have a hard time persuading myself to let anyone see me in such a vehicle. It's perverse, but I'm still ashamed of doing what is right, and whenever we run across some more glamorous equipage I blush in spite of myself. That's proof that the habits I approve and admire are not yet firmly established. 5 He who blushes in a shabby carriage will boast of an expensive one. It's only a little progress that I have made so far. I don't yet dare to wear my frugality out in the open; I still care about the opinions of travelers, when I ought to have spoken out against the opinions of the whole human race, like this:

You are crazy; you are wrong; you gawk at superfluities; you don't judge anyone by what is truly his. When it's a matter of income, you size a man up carefully before you entrust him with a loan or even with a benefit (for you regard benefits too as expenditures).

**6** "His property is extensive, but so too are his debts."

"He has a lovely house, but he borrowed money to purchase it."

"No one turns out a more splendid retinue, but he does not pay his bills."

"If he satisfies his creditors, he will have nothing left."

You should do the same for the rest: figure out how much each person has that is truly his own.

**7** Do you think a fellow rich just because he eats from golden plates and cups even away from home; because he owns a plantation in every province; because his account book fills a fat scroll; because his estates just outside the city are so large that they would attract envy even if they were in thinly populated Apulia? He is a poor man all the same. Why? Because he is in debt. "How much does he owe?" you ask. Everything! Or do you perhaps think that owing one's goods to fortune is somehow different from owing a human creditor?

**8** Does it matter that one's mules are well fed and all the same color? Does it matter about the ornate carriage?

Swift steeds caparisoned with rich brocades;
the martingales are hung with gold; the bits
between their teeth are all of yellow gold.*

Such things improve neither the master nor the mule. **9** Cato the Censor,* whose life was as beneficial to the state as Scipio's—for one waged war against our enemies, the other against our vices—used to ride a packhorse; one laden with saddlebags, in fact, so as to carry various useful articles along with him. I only wish there could be a meeting on the road between him and one of our well-heeled young squires preceded by his runners, his Numidian slaves, and a great cloud of dust!* Such a one would appear to be a more elegant and better-attended traveler than Marcus Cato, no doubt! Yet in the midst of that fashionable getup, he is seriously considering whether to hire himself out as a gladiator or a wild-beast fighter. **10** What a credit it is to those times that a triumphant general, a censor—above all, a Cato—was satisfied with a single nag!* And he didn't even have it all to himself, for part of it was taken up by bundles hanging down on either side. Even so, would you not choose that one horse chafed by Cato's own legs over all those fat palfreys, those pacers and trotters?

**11** I see there will be no end to this topic unless I just make an end. So I'll stop now, at least as concerns bag and baggage. How well he foretold their present role who first called them *impedimenta!** I want now to share with you just a few of the investigations conducted by our school pertaining to virtue, which in our view is sufficient for happiness. **12**

That which is good makes people good, just as in musical skill that which is good makes one a musician.

Things depending on fortune do not make a person good.

Therefore such things are not goods.

Against this the Peripatetics* argue that our first premise is false. "People do not automatically become good from what is good. In music, there are things that are good, for instance a flute, a lyre, or an organ well suited for playing, but none of these makes a person a musician."

**13** Our reply to them will be this: "You do not understand our premise about what is good in music. We are not referring to the things that equip the musician but to the things that make him a musician. You are only considering the accoutrements of the skill; you don't look to the skill itself. That which is good in musicianship itself does automatically make one a musician."

**14** I would like to make the point still more clear. "Good" in the skill of music is said in two ways, one referring to what promotes the musician's results, the other to what promotes his skill. The instruments, flutes and organs and strings, have to do with the results, not with the skill itself. For he is a skilled musician even without them, though he may not be able to use his skill. Where the human being is concerned, we do not find the same duality, for the good of a human being is the same as the good of a life.

**15** That which can belong to the vilest and most despicable kinds of people is not a good.

But wealth can belong to the pimp and the manager of gladiators.*

Therefore wealth is not a good.

"Your premise is false," they say,* "for in the teaching of literature, in medicine, and in navigation, we see that the relevant goods belong to the humblest kinds of people." **16** But those skills make no claim to greatness of spirit; they do not soar to the heights, nor do they despise the things of fortune. Virtue elevates a person and places him above all that mortals hold dear. The things usually called good and bad are not for him the objects of any great desire or terror.

Chelidon, one of Cleopatra's eunuchs, owned a huge estate; more recently Natalis, a man whose tongue was as filthy as it was impudent (for women were cleansed in his mouth), was heir to many and had many heirs.* What are we to say? Did money render him unclean, or did he himself defile the money? There are those whom wealth befalls in the same way as silver coins fall in the sewer. **17** Virtue takes its stand above such things: it is assessed in its own currency. Things that can belong to just anybody do not count with it as goods. Medicine and navigation do not debar themselves and their practitioners from the admiration of such things. Someone who is not a good man can still be a doctor, a helmsman, a teacher of literature—for heaven's sakes, even a cook. When someone exhibits exceptional characteristics, you say he is an exceptional person: the person is of a kind with his characteristics.

**18** The value of a money bag is that of its contents; in fact, the bag is just an adjunct to its contents. Who sets any value on a full purse beyond the amount of money it contains? The same thing happens with the owners of large estates: they are adjuncts and appendages to their property. Why, then, is the wise man great? Because he has a great mind. So it is true that what belongs to the most contemptible kinds of people is not a good. **19** For that reason, I will never call freedom from pain a good: a cicada has that, and so does a flea. I will not even say that a quiet, untroubled existence is a good: what is more leisurely than a worm?* What makes a person wise, you ask? The same thing as makes one a god. There must be something divine—

exalted—great about him. The good does not belong to everyone; it does not abide just any possessor. **20** Consider:

> What every region yields; what each denies;
> here crops, there vines grow more abundantly;
> elsewhere the orchard fruits, and elsewhere grows
> green grass unbidden. Do you not perceive
> how Tmolus sends us fragrant saffron; how
> India sends us ivory; how the soft
> Sabaeans send their incense; how the naked
> Chalybs supply their iron?*

**21** These products have been assigned to different regions, so that mutual exchange was necessary if mortals wanted to obtain each other's merchandise. But the highest good has a region all its own. It is not produced where ivory is, or iron. What is its place, you ask? It is the mind. If the mind is not pure and chaste, it cannot have god within it.

**22** That which is good does not come of what is bad.

But wealth comes of avarice.

Therefore wealth is not a good.

One might say, "It is not true that good does not arise from what is bad, for money arises from temple robbery and theft.* Thus temple robbing and theft are indeed bad, but only because they produce more bad consequences than good; for they yield a profit, but they also produce fear, anxiety, torments of mind and of body."

**23** Whoever says this must admit that just as temple robbery is bad insofar as it produces many bad consequences, so also it is good insofar as it produces a good consequence. What could be more monstrous than that? Although nowadays we have convinced ourselves that temple robbery, theft, and adultery are good things. How many there are who are not ashamed of thieving; how many who boast of adultery! For minor acts of temple robbery are punished; great ones are carried in a triumphal parade. **24** Besides, if temple robbery is actually good in some respect, it will also be honorable and, since an honorable action is also a right action,° will be considered rightly done—something no one on earth can contemplate. Therefore goods cannot arise from what is bad. For if, as you say, temple robbery is bad only because it produces many bad consequences—if you excuse it from punishments and guarantee it safety, it will be good altogether. **25** Yet the greatest penalty for criminal acts is in the acts themselves. You are mistaken if you make them wait for the prison or the executioner: such acts are punished right away when performed, indeed in the very act of performing them. Therefore good does not arise from what is bad, any more than a fig from an olive tree: scion accords with seed. Goods cannot but run true to type. Just as what is honorable does not come of what is shameful, so the good does not come of the bad; for what is good and what is honorable are one and the same.

**26** Some members of our school answer the objection as follows: "Suppose that money is a good regardless of where it is obtained. Even so, and even if money is sometimes gained by temple robbing, it is not the case that the money actually came from one's robbing the temple. Think of it like this: a gold coin is in the same jar with a snake; if you take out the coin, you did not take it out by reason of a snake being there as well. That is to say, the jar does not supply me with gold because it also contains a snake; rather, it supplies gold in spite of the fact that it also contains a snake. In the same way, temple robbing produces a profit not because it is a despicable and criminal act, but because it contains profit as well. Just as the bad thing in the urn is the snake, not the gold that is in there with the snake, so in temple robbing the bad thing is the criminality, not the profit."

**27** I disagree; the two cases are not the same. In the one, I can take the gold out without the snake; in the other, I cannot have the profit without robbing the temple—that profit is not adjacent to the crime but combined with it.

> **28** If the pursuit of something brings many bad results, that thing is not a good.
>
> Our pursuit of wealth brings many bad results.
>
> Therefore wealth is not a good.

One might say, "Your premise has two meanings. One meaning is that our pursuit of wealth brings many bad results. But our pursuit of virtue also brings many bad results: a person takes ship for reasons of study and is shipwrecked, or in another case captured. **29** The second meaning is like this: that *through which* we get bad results is not a good. From such a premise, either it cannot be inferred that we get bad results through wealth or through pleasure, or else, if we do get many bad results through wealth, then wealth is not only not a good but actually a bad thing. But your school says only that wealth is not a good. Besides, you grant that wealth has its uses: you count it as one of the advantages of life. Yet by that same reasoning it will not even be an advantage, for through it we encounter many disadvantages."*

**30** Some respond to this as follows: "You are wrong to think that wealth is a disadvantage. Wealth does not harm anyone: what does the harm is one's own foolishness or the iniquity of another, just as a sword does not harm anyone but is only the tool of the slayer. Wealth does not hurt you just because you are harmed for the sake of your wealth." **31** A better response, in my view, is that of Posidonius, who says that wealth is a cause of evils not because wealth itself does anything bad but because it motivates those who will.* For there is a difference between the efficient cause, which of necessity harms something directly, and the antecedent cause. Wealth involves this latter sort of causality: it inflames the mind, gives birth to arrogance, attracts resentment, and sets the mind at odds with itself to such an extent that we delight to have a reputation for affluence, even though that reputation is likely to hurt us. **32** Good things ought properly to be blameless. Goods are pure: they do not corrupt the mind, do not cause anxiety; they elevate and expand the mind but without conceit. Goods inspire confidence, riches inspire audacity; goods produce greatness of spirit, riches produce extravagance, which is nothing but a false show of greatness.

**33** "If you go on that way," says my opponent, "wealth is not only not a good thing but is even a bad thing." Wealth would be a bad thing if it harmed us in itself—if, as I said, it involved efficient causality; but in fact it involves only antecedent causality. Even so, wealth is a cause that not only arouses our minds but even exerts a pull on them, for it generates a plausible impression of good that many people find convincing.* **34** Antecedent cause for resentment is found in virtue as well, for many people are resented because of their wisdom and many because of their justice. But this cause is not intrinsic to virtue, nor is it plausible; on the contrary, the more persuasive impression is the one that virtue makes on people's minds, inviting them to love and admire it.

**35** Posidonius says that one should reason like this:

> Those things which confer on the mind neither greatness nor confidence nor freedom from anxiety are not goods.
>
> But wealth, health, and similar things do not do any of those things.
>
> Therefore they are not goods.

He also expands the syllogism as follows:

> Those things which confer on the mind neither greatness nor confidence nor freedom from anxiety, but instead produce extravagance, conceit, and arrogance, are bad.
>
> Things dependent on fortune drive us to these latter.
>
> Therefore they are not goods.

**36** One might say, "By this reasoning they will not even be advantages." Advantages are of quite a different status from goods. An advantage is that in which there is more utility than annoyance; a good has to be a genuine good and innocent of any sort of harm. What is good is not that which is mostly beneficial but that which is entirely beneficial. **37** Moreover, an advantage belongs also to animals and to imperfect people and to the foolish. Thus it could have some disadvantage mixed in, but is called an advantage because it is evaluated by what is preponderant in it. A good belongs only to the wise person and is of necessity unadulterated.

**38** Be of good courage: you have only one enigma left. But it is a Herculean one:

> That which is good is not made up of things that are bad.
>
> But many instances of poverty make up one instance of wealth.
>
> Therefore wealth is not a good.

This syllogism is not recognized by our school; it is both devised and solved by the Peripatetics.* Posidonius says, however, that this sophism, which has been bandied about among dialecticians from every school, is refuted by Antipater as follows:

**39** The word "poverty" refers not to possession but to subtraction (or, as the ancients called it, "privation"; in Greek *kata sterēsin*). It refers not to what something has but to what it does not have. Thus it is not possible for anything to be filled up from many instances of emptiness. Wealth is made up of numerous resources, not of numerous instances of scarcity. You do not properly understand what poverty is. Poverty is not the condition of possessing a few things but that of not possessing many things: its meaning is derived not from what it has but from what it lacks.

**40** I could explain all this more easily if there were a Latin word that had the sense of the Greek *anuparxia*. Antipater applies this term to poverty; for myself, I don't see what poverty can be other than owning a small amount.*

Let's put off this inquiry into the substance of poverty and wealth to some other occasion, when we have a great deal of time to spare. And when that time comes, let's ask ourselves whether it might not be better to mitigate poverty and take down the arrogance of wealth, instead of quibbling over words as if we had already settled the facts of the case. **41** Imagine we have been summoned to a public meeting where the question is whether to pass a law to abolish wealth. Would these syllogisms win the debate for us? Would they persuade the Roman people to praise and yearn for poverty, the foundation and cause of their empire, and to fear their present wealth? Would such arguments make them realize that their wealth was derived from conquered peoples, and is the reason why ambition, bribery, and unrest have taken over a city of such great sanctity and restraint? That there is too much extravagance in displaying the spoils of conquest? That while one nation can despoil many, it is easier for the many to despoil the one? These are the points we need to carry. Rather than circumvent their greed, let us take it by storm! If we can, we should speak boldly; if not, then at least we should speak plainly.

Farewell.

# Letter 88

*From Seneca to Lucilius*
*Greetings*

1 You ask what I think of the liberal arts. I have no special regard for any of them, nor do I consider any study a good one if its aim is moneymaking. These are merely marketable skills, useful insofar as they prepare the mind but not as long-term occupations. One should stick with them only until the mind is capable of something more significant: they are our introductory curriculum, not our real work. 2 It's obvious why they are called "liberal" studies: because they are worthy of a free person. But there is only one study that is truly liberal, and that is the one that liberates a person, which is to say, the study of philosophy.* It alone is exalted—powerful—great in spirit; all others are trifling and childish. Or do you imagine there can be anything of value in a study when those who make a profession of it are utterly scandalous and despicable? Our aim should not be to learn them but to be done with learning them.

Some have held that the proper question about the liberal arts is whether they make one a good man. That is not something they claim to do, even—such knowledge is not their aim. 3 The literary studies are concerned with linguistic purity and, if carried further, with narratives; at most, they extend to the study of poetry. Which of these subjects paves a road toward virtue? The identification of syllables, the close attention to words and phrases, the memorization of stories, the rules of versification, the alteration of meters—which of these calms our fears, removes our greed, curbs our desire? 4 Let's pass on to geometry and music: there too, there is nothing that bids us refrain from fear or from desire. And if we don't know how to do that, it's no use knowing anything else.

‹The question is›° whether virtue is the subject these people are teaching. If it is not, then they are not imparting virtue to their pupils—and if it is, then they are philosophers. Would you like to know how far they are from making that their aim? Notice how different all their studies are from one another. If they were all teaching the same thing, there should be some similarity among them.

**5** Unless they manage to persuade you that Homer was a philosopher! But they invalidate their own arguments: at one moment they make him a Stoic, who gives his approval to virtue alone and will not shirk from what is honorable even to gain immortal life; at another an Epicurean, who praises civic repose while living amid songs and parties; at another a Peripatetic, who posits three types of goods; at another an Academic, who says there is no certainty about anything.* It just goes to show that not one of these philosophies is his, since they all are—for they are not compatible. But suppose we grant that Homer was a philosopher: surely he must have become one before he ever learned any poems. In that case, let's learn the things that made Homer wise.

**6** But for me to inquire into whether Homer or Hesiod came first is of no greater relevance than to know how it is that Hecuba grew old before her time, since she was in fact younger than Helen. What, I ask you, is the relevance of an inquiry into the relative ages of Patroclus and Achilles? **7** Do you seek to know the whereabouts of Ulysses' wanderings rather than how to rescue us from our own perpetual wandering? We haven't time to hear whether he was beset by a storm between Italy and Sicily or outside the bounds of the known world (since he couldn't have traveled so long in such a narrow strait). No, we ourselves are beset by storms of the mind every day of our lives, and our vices bring us all the troubles that Ulysses faced. They are all here: beauty that beguiles the eye, enemies, savage monsters that delight in human gore, on one side the Sirens' song, on the other shipwrecks and perils of every kind.* Teach me this: how to love my country, my wife, my father; teach me to reach that honorable destination, though I be shipwrecked along the way. **8** Why do you seek to know whether Penelope was unchaste; whether she deceived everyone around her; whether she suspected that the person she saw was Ulysses before she was told? Teach me what chastity is, how valuable it is, whether it belongs to the body or to the mind.

**9** I move on to music. You teach me how there can be harmony between high and low notes, how strings of different pitch can be concordant: teach me instead how there can be harmony within my own mind, how my intentions may not be discordant with one another. You show me which musical modes express sadness: show me instead how to keep from expressing sadness in the midst of adversity.

10 The geometrician teaches me to figure the size of a plantation, but he doesn't teach me how to figure what quantity of wealth is sufficient for a human being. He teaches me to do computations, adapting my fingers to the purposes of greed;* but he doesn't teach me that such computations are beside the point, that it doesn't make one any happier to have accountants wearing themselves out over one's income—indeed, that a man who would find it a misfortune to have to compute his own net worth possesses nothing but superfluities. 11 How does it help me to know how to divide up a field if I don't know how to divide it with my brother? How does it help me to figure out the precise size of a garden plot down to the tenth part of a foot if it upsets me that my unruly neighbor is shaving a little off my land? He teaches me how to keep from losing that strip near my property line, but what I want to know is how to lose all my property and yet remain cheerful. 12 "I'm being dispossessed of land that belonged to my father and my grandfather!" What of it? Who owned it before your grandfather? Can you even tell me what nation it belonged to, let alone what individual? You came to it not as a master but as a tyrant. Whose tenant are you? If you're lucky, you are the tenant of the man who will inherit it from you. The lawyers say that no one can establish *de facto* ownership of public land—but this that you inhabit and call your own belongs to the public; indeed, it belongs to the human race.* 13 What exceptional skill! You know how to measure curved shapes; you can make any figure you are given into a square; you can tell the distances between stars; there is in fact nothing you cannot measure. If you are such a skilled technician, measure the human mind! Tell how great it is—how puny it is. You know whether a line is at a right angle: what use is that to you if you do not know what is right in life?

14 I come now to the study that prides itself on its familiarity with the heavens:

where Saturn's frigid star betakes itself;
what orbits Mercury's wandering fire describes.*

What will I gain by knowing such things? Is it just so that I can worry when Saturn and Mars are in opposition, or when Mercury sets in the evening with Saturn looking on? I should learn instead that the planets are favorable no matter where they are, and that they cannot be changed. **15** Their movements are ordained by the continuous and inexorable workings of fate: they travel on fixed paths and either determine or signify all the world's events.* But if they cause everything to happen, how will it help you to know about what cannot be altered? And if they signify what will happen, what does it matter whether you foresee things you cannot avoid? They will happen whether you know about them or not. **16**

But if you look to the hurtling sun, the stars
that follow him in order, never will
tomorrow take you by surprise; you will
be safe from ambush by the cloudless night.*

In fact, I have already taken sufficient precautions against any such ambush.

**17** "Is it really true that tomorrow will never take me by surprise? Surely what happens to a person without his knowledge does take him by surprise." I do not know what *will* happen, but I do know what *can* happen. I exempt none of that from expectation: I expect it all; and if I am spared any of it, I count myself fortunate. Tomorrow does take me by surprise, if it lets me off. Yet even then it does not surprise me; for just as I know there is nothing that cannot happen to me, so also I know that none of it is certain to happen. Thus I expect the best, but prepare for the worst.*

**18** You must bear with me if I don't keep to the regular sequence: I can't bring myself to count painters among the practitioners of the liberal arts, any more than I count statue makers, marble workers, and all the other ministers of luxury. Likewise, I reject wrestlers and every sort of knowledge that consists merely of oil and dirt.* Otherwise I would have to count masseurs, cooks, and all those others who accommodate their talents to our pleasures. **19** What, pray tell, is the liberal art of those starving vomiters who keep the body at the feeding trough while the mind grows feeble for lack of nourishment? Shall we believe today's young people when they call *that* a liberal arts education? Our ancestors trained them to stand upright, to cast a spear, to hurl a javelin, to ride a horse, and to handle sword and shield. They taught their children nothing that had to be learned while reclining. Yet virtue is not taught or nurtured by any of these skills, either the old or the new. For what is to be gained by handling a horse, using the reins to restrain and guide its movements, while passions unrestrained and unbridled run away with the rider? What is to be gained by vanquishing many opponents in wrestling or boxing, when the victor is still a victim of anger?

**20** "What, then? Do the liberal studies have nothing to offer us?" Toward some ends they do contribute; but nothing toward virtue. For even the skills that consist in manual dexterity, which admit openly to their low status, furnish us with many of life's basic needs; yet they bear no relation to virtue. "Why, then, do we train our children in the liberal arts?" Not because they can ever impart virtue, but because they prepare the mind to receive virtue. Just as that initial "learning the letters" (as it used to be called), which imparts to children the rudiments of learning, does not teach them the liberal arts but does prepare a place for them, so the liberal arts themselves do not lead the mind all the way to virtue but do equip it for the journey.

**21** Posidonius says there are four kinds of arts: there are the common and base arts, the arts of the entertainer, the arts of childhood, and the liberal arts.* The common arts are those of workmen, which consist in manual dexterity and are devoted to furnishing life's basic needs. In these there is no attractiveness and no semblance of the honorable. **22** The arts of the entertainer are those concerned with the pleasures of eye and ear. Among them you may count the engineers who devise stage floors that rise into view unaided, platforms that soar into the sky without making a sound, and other such extraordinary contrivances: gaps that open up where there was level floor before, or that close of their own accord, or raised sections that gradually lower onto themselves. These things are impressive to the eyes of those who have no familiarity with such matters, who marvel at every unexpected occurrence since they do not know what causes it. **23** The arts of childhood have some similarity to the liberal arts. These are the ones the Greeks call "encyclical"; in our language, they are called "liberal." But the only arts that are truly liberal—indeed, to be frank, the only arts that are truly free—are those whose concern is virtue.

**24** One might say, "Philosophy has several parts: the study of nature is one, ethics is another, and logic is another. In the same way, the whole troop of liberal studies claims a place for itself within philosophy. When we come to investigate natural questions, we rely on evidence from geometry; so, being of assistance to philosophy, geometry must also be a part of philosophy." **25** There are many things that assist us without being part of us; indeed, if they were part of us, they would not be of assistance. Food is of assistance to the body and yet is not part of the body. Geometry does us a service; it is necessary to philosophy in the same way as the instrument maker is necessary to geometry itself. The latter is not part of geometry, and neither is geometry a part of philosophy. **26** Moreover, each of them has its own defined subject matter: the philosopher investigates and gains knowledge of natural phenomena, while the geometer collects figures and measurements and does calculations based on them. The rationale behind celestial phenomena, their efficacy and their nature: these are knowledge for the philosopher; their orbits, epicycles, and certain apparent movements in which they shift upward or downward or seem to stand still when in fact no heavenly body can stand still: these are problems for the mathematical astronomer. **27** The philosopher knows the reason for the images seen in mirrors; the geometer can tell you how far the object must be from its image and what shape of mirror produces images of a certain kind. The philosopher will prove that the sun is large; the astronomer will proceed by empirical methods to find out just how large it is. But in order to proceed in this way, he must have principles to go on. No art stands alone if its fundamentals are derived from elsewhere. **28** Philosophy asks nothing from any other study; it builds its entire edifice from the ground up. Mathematical astronomy is, as it were, an upper story, built on another's foundation: it takes its principles from elsewhere, and it is only with this aid that it gets any further. If it arrived at the truth on its own—if it were able to grasp the entire nature of the world—then I would grant that it has a great deal to offer us. For by dealing with celestial phenomena our minds increase in scope and gain in elevation.

There is just one way our minds attain their full stature, and that is by unalterable knowledge of what things are good and what are bad. But there is no other study that has anything to say on that subject. **29** Let us make a survey of the virtues, one by one. Courage is the one that scorns every object of fear: everything that frightens us, that drives our freedom beneath the yoke, is met with contempt—with a challenge—with conquest! Do the liberal studies do anything to strengthen this? Loyalty is the human heart's most sacred good, which no hardship drives toward deceit, no recompense toward treason. "Burn me," says loyalty; "cut me, kill me—I will not betray my own. The harder pain presses me for my secrets, the deeper I shall hide them." Can the liberal studies fashion such a spirit? Self-control takes command of our pleasures: some it despises and excludes, others it moderates, reducing them to healthy limits and never seeking them for their own sake; for it knows that the best limit on the objects of desire is to take what you need, not what you want. **30** Kindness forbids one to be arrogant or critical toward one's associates; it is gentle and approachable with everyone in word and deed and feeling; it thinks of every misfortune as its own, and welcomes every stroke of good fortune mainly to share it with another. Do the liberal studies teach such conduct? No, no more than they teach us honesty, temperance and moderation, frugality and thrift; no more than they teach clemency, which is as sparing of another's blood as of its own, knowing that no human being should ever forget the value of another.

**31** "You people say that one cannot attain virtue without the liberal arts; how is it, then, that you maintain they contribute nothing to virtue?" Like this: one cannot attain virtue without food either, yet food has nothing to do with virtue; just as timber does not contribute anything to a ship even though one cannot make a ship except out of timber. My point is that you have no reason to think that one thing contributes to another just because the other cannot come into being without it. **32** One might also observe that it is in fact possible to attain wisdom without the liberal studies, for although virtue does have to be learned, it is not through these that one learns it. What reason do I have for thinking that someone with no knowledge of letters will not become wise? Wisdom does not reside in letters. It imparts facts, not words—and perhaps the memory is more retentive when it has nothing but itself to rely on.

**33** Wisdom is vast and expansive; it needs room. One must learn about things human and divine, things past and yet to come, things transitory and things eternal.* One must learn about time—and see how many questions there are about that alone: first, whether it is a thing in itself; then, whether there is anything that precedes time, anything timeless. Did time begin along with the world, or, since something did exist before the world, did time also exist then? **34** There are countless questions to ask just about the mind: Where does it come from? What is it like? When does it begin to exist, and how long does it last? Does it migrate from place to place, changing its dwelling from one animate creature to another, or does it endure this slavery but once and upon release travel through the universe? Is it corporeal or incorporeal? What will it do once it has ceased to do anything through us? How will it use its freedom after it escapes this dungeon? Or does it forget its former life and begin to know itself at the moment it is taken from the body and passes on to the heights? **35** No matter what part of things human and divine you take hold of, you will find a vast number of subjects for inquiry and learning to wear yourself out with. With so many big questions waiting to occupy our minds, we must make room for them by evicting those others that are superfluous. Virtue will not take up residence within such narrow confines: so large a guest needs elbow room. So let everything be driven out, and let the whole heart be open to virtue.

**36** "Still, it is delightful to have familiarity with many different studies." In that case, let us keep only as much of them as we need. Or do you think reproach is justified when a person buys useless furnishings for his home and sets up a display of expensive objects, but not when someone busies himself with a superfluous array of literary studies? Wanting to know more than enough is a form of intemperance. **37** The fact is, that way of pursuing the liberal arts makes men annoying, long-winded, pompous, self-satisfied: because they have learned what they do not need to know, they fail to learn what they do need. The literary scholar Didymus wrote four thousand books.* I would pity him if he had only read that many needless volumes! In some, he tries to determine the birthplace of Homer; in others, who was Aeneas's real mother; in others, whether Anacreon was more prone to lust or to drunkenness; in others, whether Sappho was a whore; and he has other topics as well. If you knew the answers to such questions, you should try to unlearn them. And you tell me that life is too short! **38** But among our countrymen too, there are excesses it would take an axe to clear away. With what expenditure of time, with what annoyance to others' ears do we purchase that acclamation,

"Such an educated person!" Better we should content ourselves with a less cultivated title: "Such a good man!"

**39** How, then? Am I to scrutinize the histories of all peoples to find out who was the first to write poetry? Shall I compute how many years passed between Orpheus and Homer, seeing that there are no written records? Shall I familiarize myself with the editorial symbols by which Aristarchus marked up other people's poems, and spend my life on syllables?* Shall I linger over the dust of geometry?* Have I forgotten that salutary counsel, "Conserve your time"? Shall I learn these things—and what, then, shall I pass over? **40** During the principate of Gaius Caesar, the literary scholar Apion made a tour of Greece and was adopted by all those cities in the name of Homer.* He used to say that after Homer had completed his two themes, both the *Odyssey* and the *Iliad*, he added a preface to his work in which he took in the entire Trojan War. As proof of this, he alleged that the first two letters in the first line of the *Iliad* were put there on purpose to signify the number of volumes in the work. **41** That's the kind of thing a polymath has to know! Just think: how much of your time is taken up by illness, by your business both public and private, by your daily routines, by sleep? **42** Take the measure of your life: it does not have room for so many things.

I have been speaking of the liberal arts; but the philosophers have their own ways of wasting time, their own useless pursuits. They too descend to the marking out of syllables and the proper meanings of conjunctions and prepositions. Envying the literary scholars and the geometers, they have taken over all the superfluities of those studies, and in this way have come to know more about speaking properly than about living. **43** Let me tell you how much harm such excessive sophistication can do, and how far estranged it is from the truth. Protagoras claims to be able to speak with equal cogency on either side of any question—including the question of whether both sides of every question are capable of being defended!* Nausiphanes claims that none of the things that appear real are any more real than unreal.* **44** Parmenides says that none of the things that appear to us are differentiated from the One.° Zeno of Elea does away with the entire debate by declaring that nothing exists at all! The Pyrrhonists, the Megarians, the Eretrians, and the Academics are up to more or less the same thing: they have introduced that new form of knowledge which knows nothing at all.* **45** Cast them in, all of them, with the useless crowd of liberal studies! The first lot don't provide me with any beneficial form of knowledge; the others don't even leave me with any expectation of knowledge. It's better to learn superfluous things than nothing at all. One set does not lift any lamp to direct my gaze toward the truth; the other gouges out my very eyes! If I believe Protagoras, there is nothing in the world that is not ambiguous; if I believe Nausiphanes, the one thing that is certain is that there is no certainty; if I believe Parmenides, nothing exists but the One; if I believe Zeno, not even the One. **46** What are we, then? What are all these things that surround us, feed us, sustain us? The entire world is a shadow, either empty or deceptive. I can hardly say which group makes me angrier, those who wanted us to know nothing, or those who did not even leave us the ability to know nothing.

Farewell.

# BOOK FOURTEEN

# Letter 89

*From Seneca to Lucilius*
*Greetings*

**1** In asking for philosophy to be divided up and have its huge body dissected into its various limbs, you are requesting something useful, or rather essential, for anyone making haste toward wisdom. It's easier for us to reach an understanding of a whole by proceeding through its parts. If only we could encounter philosophy in its entirety, the way we view the entire heavens at a single glance! And indeed, it would be a sight very like the heavens. In that case, every mortal would be seized with wonder at it, and abandon those things we now believe to be great in our ignorance of true greatness. But since this cannot be, we must view philosophy in the same way as one studies different portions of the heavens.

**2** To be sure, the intellect of the wise embraces the entire mass of philosophy and surveys it as rapidly as our eye surveys the sky. For us, on the other hand, whose range of vision is limited by the mists we have to peer through, particular details are easier to register, since we are not yet capable of grasping the whole. So I will satisfy your demand and divide up philosophy, but into parts rather than little bits. Dividing it is useful; mincing it fine is not, because what's very small is just as difficult to grasp as what is very large. **3** A population is divided up by tribes, an army into units of a hundred men. Everything that has attained some magnitude is easier to apprehend when separated into parts, provided, as I said, that these are not too numerous and tiny. An extreme division is just as faulty as none at all: when anything is reduced to a powder, it ceases to have any structure at all.

**4** I will begin, then, if you don't mind, by stating the difference between wisdom and philosophy. Wisdom is the human mind's supreme good; philosophy is the love and aspiration for wisdom. The latter is proceeding toward the destination at which the former has arrived. What is the etymology of "philosophy"? That's obvious. In its very name it professes what it loves.* **5** Some have defined wisdom as the science of things human and divine, others as the knowledge of things human and divine and of their causes.* In my opinion, this last addition is superfluous, because the causes of things human and divine are part of the divine. There are also other definitions of philosophy. Some have called it commitment to virtue, others a commitment to rectifying the mind, and according to certain thinkers it is the effort to reason correctly. **6** What is generally agreed is that there is a difference between philosophy and wisdom, since the object of aspiration cannot be the same thing as the aspiration itself. Just as there is a great difference between avarice and money, with one desiring and the other being the object of desire, so too philosophy differs from wisdom. One is the outcome and reward of the other: philosophy is a progression, and wisdom is where it is headed. **7** *Sophia* is actually the Greek word for "wisdom." Romans too used to speak of *sophia*, just as we still use the Greek word *philosophia*. You have evidence for this in our old comedies and in the inscription on the tomb of Dossennus: "Stop, traveler, and read the *sophia* of Dossennus."*

**8** Even though philosophy is commitment to virtue, one being the pursuer and the other the object of pursuit, there are some in our school who have held that no distinction can be made, since there is no philosophy without virtue and no virtue without philosophy. Philosophy is indeed commitment to virtue, but by means of virtue itself. There can be no virtue without commitment to it, and neither can there be commitment to virtue without virtue itself. It is not like the archer who tries to hit a target from a distance: here, the target is not in some different place from the one aiming. Nor are the ways to virtue external to virtue, like roads to a city. One comes to virtue by means of itself; philosophy and virtue are inseparable.

**9** According to the major and most numerous authorities, philosophy has three parts: ethics, physics, and logic.* The first of these parts regulates the mind, the second studies the nature of things, and the third examines the meanings of words, the structure of sentences, and the forms of arguments, with a view to preventing falsehood from masquerading as truth. We also find schools that have either reduced or increased the divisions of philosophy. **10** Some among the Peripatetics have added politics as a fourth part, because they take it to require a specific training with its own subject matter; some have made the further addition of what they call "economics," meaning the science of running a household; and there are those who have made "kinds of life" a separate topic.* All these items can, however, be found in the ethical part of philosophy. **11** The Epicureans have supposed that there are just two parts of philosophy, physics and ethics, excluding logic. Then, when they found themselves forced to distinguish ambiguities and to expose falsehoods that lurk under the appearance of truth, they too introduced a topic they call "judgment and rule"—in other words, logic—but they regard it as only a supplement to physics.* **12** The Cyrenaics expunged physics as well as logic and limited themselves to ethics; yet they too reintroduce the excluded topics in another way.* They divide ethics into five parts, dealing respectively with (1) proper objects of pursuit and avoidance, (2) emotions, (3) actions, (4) causes, and (5) arguments. The causes of things in fact belong to physics and arguments to logic. **13** Aristo of Chios claimed that physics and logic are not only superfluous but also harmful, and he even pruned ethics, the one part that he had admitted.* He expunged the topic comprising admonitions, claiming that it was the job of a schoolteacher and not a philosopher—as if the philosopher were something other than humanity's schoolteacher!

**14** Since philosophy has three parts, let us begin by laying out its ethical part. Canonically, this is subdivided into three branches. The first assigns to each thing its proper value and determines what it is worth. This is an extremely useful investigation, for what is as needful as putting the price on things? The second deals with impulse, and the third with actions.* That is to say, the objectives of ethics are first, to enable you to judge what each thing is worth; second, to enable you to entertain a well-adjusted and controlled impulse with respect to them; and third, to enable you to achieve harmony between your impulse and your action so that you may be consistent in all your behavior.

**15** Any defect in one of these three areas also causes disturbance to the others. What good is it to have made a comparative assessment of everything if your impulses are ungoverned? What good is it to have restrained your impulses and have your desires under control if in your actions themselves you are insensitive to circumstances and don't know the proper time and place and manner of doing each thing? It is one thing to understand the worth and value of things; it is another to understand the demands of the moment, and something else again to restrain one's impulses and to proceed to what one has to do without rushing into things. A life is harmonious with itself only when action does not fall short of impulse and when impulse is generated on the basis of what each thing is worth, varying in its intensity according to the worth of its objective.

**16** The physical part of philosophy is divided into two subdivisions, namely, corporeal things and incorporeal things; and each of these has, as it were, its own levels. The topic of bodies is primarily divided into bodies that are causes and bodies that arise from causes—that is to say, the elements. As to the topic of elements, according to some, it has no subdivisions, but others divide it into matter, the cause that activates everything, and the elements.*

**17** It remains for me to divide the logical part of philosophy. All discourse is either continuous or split into questions and responses. The official term for the former is "rhetoric" and for the latter "dialectic." Rhetoric attends to expressions, thoughts, and organization. Dialectic is divided into two parts, words and meanings, that is, into the things that are said and the utterances through which they are said.* Then comes a huge subdivision of each of these topics. So at this point I will cut short my list and only "touch upon the tops of things."* Otherwise, were I to undertake to keep subdividing, you would get a technical treatise.

**18** You can read about these things, most excellent Lucilius. I don't mean to put you off, provided you immediately relate everything you read to your conduct. Discipline your conduct: arouse your flagging qualities, restrict those that are too free, tame the rebellious ones, and spare no effort in attacking your own passions and those of the world at large. To those who say, "Are you never going to stop?" give this response:

**19** "It is I who should be saying to you, 'When will *you* stop repeating your mistakes?' Do you want the cure to end sooner than the malady? I will go on about it all the more, and I will keep at it precisely because of your protests. Medicine applied to a benumbed limb only starts to be effective when a touch elicits pain.

The things I say will benefit you whether you like it or not. It's time for a candid voice to reach you. Since I cannot get a hearing from you one at a time, I will address you all in public.

**20** "When are you going to stop extending the boundaries of your property? Is land that held a whole people too limited for a single master? When are you going to stop spreading out your plantations? You are not even content to limit the size of your own estates by the area of whole provinces. Famous rivers flow entirely through private property. Mighty streams that constitute the frontiers of mighty nations belong to you, from their source to their mouth. You even find it too little if you have not made your landholdings the borders of the seas, if your overseer does not give orders beyond the Adriatic and the Ionian and the Aegean, if you don't consider islands that are homes to great leaders to be quite trivial possessions. Enlarge your property as much as you like, have as your estate what was once called an empire, take over everything you can—but let the property of others still exceed what belongs to you!

**21** "Now I turn to address you people whose self-indulgence extends as widely as those other people's greed. I ask you: how long will this go on? Every lake is overhung with your roofs! Every river is bordered by your buildings! Wherever one finds gushing streams of hot water, new pleasure houses will be started. Wherever a shore curves into a bay, you will instantly lay down foundations. Not satisfied with any ground that you have not altered, you will bring the sea into it! Your houses gleam everywhere, sometimes situated on mountains to give a great view of land and sea, sometimes built on flat land to the height of mountains. Yet when you have done so much enormous building, you still have only one body apiece, and that a puny one. What good are numerous bedrooms? You can only lie in one of them. Any place you do not occupy is not really yours.

**22** "Finally, I pass on to you whose endless and insatiable gluttony searches seas and lands in laborious pursuit of culinary fare, whether with hooks, or snares, or different kinds of nets. There is no peace for any animals unless you are bored with them. From those banquets of yours, procured through so many hands, how little you nibble with a mouth that is weary from its pleasures! Of that game, caught at such danger, how little is tasted by a master suffering from indigestion and nausea! Of all those shellfish imported from such distance, how little passes through your insatiable gut! Wretched people, don't you realize that your hunger is larger than your belly?"

**23** Tell all this to other people, but with the intention of listening to it yourself while you speak. Write it down, but with the intention of reading while you write, and relating everything to conduct and the abatement of frenzied passions. In your study, make it your aim not to know more, but to know better.

Farewell.

## Letter 90

*From Seneca to Lucilius*
*Greetings*

**1** Who can doubt, dear Lucilius, that our life is the gift of the immortal gods, but our living well is philosophy's gift? It would surely follow, then, that we owe more to philosophy than to the gods (since a good life is a greater benefit than mere life), were it not for the fact that philosophy itself has been bestowed on us by the gods. They have not granted knowledge of philosophy to anyone, but they have given everyone the capacity to acquire it.* **2** If they had made this knowledge common property, letting everyone be born with good sense, wisdom would have forfeited its greatest excellence—that it is not one of the things acquired by chance. Rather, its special value and splendor consist in the fact that it doesn't just happen, that we have ourselves to thank for it, that it is not to be solicited from anyone else. What would you have to admire in philosophy if it were simply a present?

**3** The sole task of philosophy is to discover the truth about matters human and divine. Philosophy is never unaccompanied by piety, reverence, and justice, and all the other assemblage of interrelated and connected virtues.* It teaches us to worship things divine and to love things human; it shows that power rests with the gods while sociability links human beings to one another. This last remained unsullied for a long time, until companionship was pulled apart by greed, which impoverished even those whom it had made wealthiest; for once people opted for private ownership, they ceased to hold everything in common.

**4** The first human beings, however, and those of their descendants who followed nature without straying,* took an exceptional individual as both their leader and their law, and entrusted themselves to his authority; for it is natural that the inferior should submit to the superior. Among groups of animals, the dominant ones are either the biggest or the fiercest. The bull that leads the herd is not a poor specimen; he is one that surpasses the other males in size and strength. The tallest elephant leads the herd. Among human beings, though, what matters is not size but excellence, and thus it was once the custom to choose leaders for their qualities of mind. For that reason the most fortunate peoples have been those that awarded power solely on the basis of merit. There is no need to restrict the power of someone who does not believe he has power to do more than he should.

**5** Accordingly, Posidonius holds that in the so-called Golden Age, government was in the hands of the wise.* They restrained aggression, protected the weaker from the stronger, dispensed policy, and indicated what was advantageous and what was not. Their good sense saw to it that their people did not run short of anything, their bravery warded off dangers, and their beneficence enhanced the prosperity of their subjects. They gave commands not to rule others but to serve them. They never used to test their strength against those who were the initial source of their power. They had neither the intent nor any reason to act unjustly; because their orders were properly given, they were properly obeyed. A king could utter no greater threat to his recalcitrant subjects than his own abdication.

**6** Yet once kingdoms were transformed into tyrannies with the infiltration of vices, there began to be a need for laws, and these too were first introduced by the wise. Solon, who founded Athens on the principle of equity, was one of the seven men made famous by their wisdom. If Lycurgus had lived at the same period, he would have added an eighth name to that blessed company.* We still revere the laws of Zaleucus and Charondas.* It was not in the forum or in lawyers' offices that these men acquired knowledge of the judicial principles they established in Sicily (still flourishing at that time), and throughout the Greek communities of Italy, but in the silent and holy retreat of Pythagoras.

**7** Thus far I agree with Posidonius. But I will not concede to him that philosophy invented the technologies we use in daily life; I will not claim for philosophy the renown that belongs to craftsmanship. According to him,

> When humans were scattered about, sheltering in huts or caves or hollow trees, philosophy taught them how to build houses.

In my opinion, it was not philosophy that devised the modern engineering of multistoried buildings and sprawling cities, any more than it was philosophy that invented cages for fish so that the gourmand would not have to risk a storm but could continue to fatten up all kinds of fish in the safety of the harbor, however wild the weather. **8** Are you going to say that philosophy taught human beings to keep things under lock and key? Wasn't that what gave the go-ahead to greed? Was it philosophy that piled up our towering buildings that are such a danger to their inhabitants? As if it were not enough for people to house themselves with whatever came to hand, discovering a natural shelter for themselves without artifice and difficulty.

**9** Take my word for it, the era that preceded architects and builders was truly happy. All those artifacts came along with self-indulgence: the squared timbers, the saw slicing through neat markings, the precise carpentry.

> For the first humans split soft wood with wedges.*

As well they might, for they were not preparing the roof of a future banquet hall. There were none of these long lines of wagons that make the streets shake, transporting pines or firs to support paneled ceilings laden with gold. **10** Their huts were propped up by forked poles positioned at each end. Bundles of branches and sloping piles of leaves allowed the heaviest rains to run off. Beneath these roofs they lived in security: their thatch let them be free. What dwells under marble and gold is servitude.

**11** I have a further disagreement with Posidonius over his claim

that iron tools were the invention of wise men. He could just as well
say that it was the wise who

> learned then to snare wild beasts, to trap the birds,
> and to set dogs all round the woodland glens.*

All that was discovered not by wisdom but by human ingenuity. **12** I
also disagree with his claim that it was the wise who discovered iron
and copper deposits at times when forest fires scorched the ground,
melting it and releasing a flow of metal from veins lying near the
surface. Such things are discovered by the kind of people who care
about them. **13** Again, unlike Posidonius, I don't consider it an interesting question whether hammers came into use before tongs. Both
of these implements were invented by someone whose intelligence
was keen and active but not great or inspired; and the same applies
to everything else that can only be discovered by one whose back is
bent, whose mind is focused on the ground.

The sage lived simply; he must have, for even in our modern age
he wants to be as unencumbered as possible.* **14** How, I ask, can
you consistently admire both Diogenes and Daedalus?* Which of
these is wise in your view? Is it the one who invented the saw, or
the one who, upon seeing a boy drinking water from his rounded
hand, immediately removed the cup from his knapsack and broke it,
criticizing himself in the following words: "What a fool I am to have
kept unnecessary baggage all this time!" Then he curled himself up in
his barrel and went to sleep! **15** Likewise, who do you think is wiser
today: the one who discovers how to make saffron perfume spurt to
a huge height from hidden pipes, who fills or empties channels with
a sudden gush of water, who constructs movable panels for dining-
room ceilings in such a way that the décor can be changed as quickly
as the courses; or, alternatively, the one who shows himself and other
people how nature has given us no commands that are harsh or difficult, that we can shelter ourselves without the marble worker and
the engineer, that we can clothe ourselves without the silk trade, that
we can have everything we need if we will just be content with what
the surface of the earth has provided. Once the human race becomes
willing to give this man a hearing, it will realize that cooks are as
unnecessary as soldiers.

**16** It was the wise, or at least people resembling the wise, who re-garded the body's security as something uncomplicated. The essential things are available with little effort; it is pampering that demands work. Follow nature, and you will not miss the artificer. Nature did not want us to be overtaxed in this regard, and has equipped us with the means to comply with all its requirements. "A naked body cannot bear to be cold." What, then? Aren't the skins of wild beasts and other animals quite capable of giving full protection against the cold? Are there not many peoples who use bark to cover their bodies, or make clothing out of feathers? Is it not the case even today that most of the Scythians clothe themselves in the pelts of foxes and martens, materials that are soft to the touch and impenetrable to winds? What, then? Who is there who can't weave a wicker frame, daub it with ordinary mud, cover it with straw or brush, and spend the winter safely with the rain running off down the sides? **17** "But we need denser shade to keep out the heat of the summer sun." What, then? Do there not remain from ancient times many hidden caves hollowed out by the passage of time or some other chance cause? What, then? Is it not a fact that the peoples of North Africa and others who live in excessively sunny climates take shelter in dug-outs, finding protection from the heat in the baked earth itself, when nothing else would have been adequate?

**18** Nature was not so unfair as to make life easy for all other creatures but impossible for human beings to live without numerous technical skills. No harsh demands have been made of us; nothing needed for our survival has been made difficult to find. We were born into a world where things were already prepared. We were the ones that made things difficult for ourselves by despising what was easy. Housing, clothing, the means of warming our bodies, food, and in fact everything that has now become a huge business was simply there, free for the taking and obtainable with little effort; for no one took more of anything than was needed. It is we who have made these things costly, strange, and only to be acquired by numerous and considerable technical skills.

**19** Nature provides what nature requires. Self-indulgence has abandoned nature, spurring itself on every day, growing through the centuries, and abetting vices by its own ingenuity. It lusted first for nonessentials, then for things that were harmful; now, finally, it has surrendered the mind to the body, bidding it serve the body's every whim. All the noisy occupations that hawk their wares to the community are in business for the body's sake. There was a time when all that the body got was rations, like a slave; but now, like a master, it has everything provided to it. This is why you find textile businesses here, craft workshops there; here the aromas produced by chefs, there the sensuous movements of dance teachers and sensuous and effeminate singing. The natural limit we once observed, restricting our wants to what is essential and within our resources, has vanished. Nowadays one is considered unrefined and poverty-stricken if one wants just what is enough.

**20** It's unbelievable, dear Lucilius, how easily even great men are diverted from the truth by the enjoyment of their own rhetoric. Take Posidonius, one of those, in my opinion, who have contributed the most to philosophy: wanting to describe, first, how some threads are twisted and others drawn out from loose bunches of wool, then how the hanging weights of the loom hold the warp straight up and down, and how, to soften the coarse warp threads that support the fabric, the weft is pressed tightly together by means of the batten, he has claimed that even the art of weaving was invented by the wise. He forgets that it was only later that this quite intricate procedure was discovered, whereby

> The warp is fixed upon the beam, the threads
> are separated by the cane, the weft
> slides through upon the shuttle, then is pressed
> by the broad comb's indented teeth.*

How would he have reacted if he had seen our modern looms, which produce clothing that is virtually transparent and gives no aid to the body or even to decency?

**21** He then moves on to farmers. He gives an equally eloquent account of how the ground is first turned by the plow and then given a second plowing to loosen the earth and facilitate the development of the roots, then how seeds are sown and weeds pulled by hand to prevent stray wild plants from growing up to damage the crops. This too, he says, was the work of the wise, as though agriculturalists were not making numerous discoveries even now for enhancing productivity. **22** Not content with these techniques, he proceeds to lower the sage into the flour mill, saying that it was he who first began to manufacture bread, in imitation of nature:

> When grain is taken into the mouth, it is crushed by the hardness of the teeth as they grind together, and anything that escapes is brought back to the teeth by the tongue, then mixed with saliva so that it will be moist and easy to swallow. Once it reaches the stomach, it is digested by the steady cooking action of that organ, and finally it is assimilated to the body. **23** Following this model, someone took two rough-textured stones and placed one on top of the other, to resemble the teeth: one part is fixed in place to let the other grind against it; then, by the friction of the two, the granules are crushed, then reground several times until they are reduced to very fine particles. He then sprinkled the flour with water, kneaded it, and shaped it into bread. At first it was baked in hot coals or in a clay pot; later came the gradual invention of ovens and other types of cookers whose heat can be controlled.

If he had gone just a little further, he would have claimed that it was the wise who invented shoe-making!

**24** It was certainly reason that figured out all these things, but not perfected reason. They are the inventions of humanity, not of a sage. And, in fact, the same is true of the boats we use to cross rivers and seas, with their sails equipped to catch the force of the winds and their rudders placed at the rear for steering the vessel this way and that. The idea was derived from fish, which regulate their movements by flicking their tails to one side or the other. **25** He says,

> It was actually a sage who invented all these things; but, because they were too trivial for him to tackle himself, he assigned them to menial assistants.

In reality, they were thought up by exactly the same people who make them their business today. We know for sure that certain products have only appeared in our own time; for instance, the use of windows that let in clear light by means of translucent glass, or bathhouses with vaulted floors and pipes set in the walls for spreading the heat and keeping the upper and lower parts of the room at an even temperature. What need for me to mention the marble that makes our temples and houses gleam, or the columns of rounded and polished stones that support porticoes and buildings large enough for crowds of people, or the shorthand signs that enable the most rapid talk to be taken down and the hand to keep up with the speed of the tongue? All these things have been produced by the lowliest slaves.

**26** Wisdom occupies a loftier seat. It does not train the hand; rather, it educates the mind. Do you want to know what it has unearthed and achieved? The answer is not graceful dance movements, nor is it the musical scales produced by trumpets and flutes, which release the air blown into them in one way or another and so transform it into sound. Wisdom does not labor over weapons or fortifications or implements of war. It fosters peace and summons the human race to live in harmony. **27** And it is not, I insist, a maker of tools for everyday needs. Why do you attribute such trivial things to wisdom? What you have before your eye is the technician of life itself. Indeed, it keeps the other crafts under its authority; for inasmuch as wisdom is master of life, it is master also of life's equipment. Wisdom, moreover, has happiness as its goal; it leads the way and opens the doors to that condition. **28** It indicates the things that are really bad and those that merely seem so. It purges our minds of illusion, giving them a substantive dignity while curtailing the sort of dignity that is all empty show, and insisting that we understand the difference between greatness and pomposity. It imparts to us a conception of nature as a whole and a conception of itself. It reveals the identity and attributes of the gods, including the spirits of the underworld, the household deities, and the tutelary spirits, and also those long-lasting° souls that have come to join the second rank of deities, together with their location, activities, powers, and intentions. When we become devotees of wisdom, we are given access not to some local shrine but to the mighty temple of all the gods, the vault of heaven itself, whose phenomena are brought before the mind's eye as they really are; for ordinary vision is inadequate to register so vast a spectacle.

**29** Next, wisdom takes us back to the world's origin, the everlasting rationality infused throughout the whole, and the power of all the generative principles to fashion individual things according to their kind. After this, it starts to investigate the mind, where it comes from, where it is located, how long it endures, how many parts it has. Then, turning from the corporeal* to the incorporeal, it scrutinizes truth and its criteria, and after that, the way to sort out ambiguities both in life and in utterance, for both involve confusions between truth and falsehood.*

**30** It is not the case, I maintain, that the sage detached himself, as Posidonius supposes, from technology; he never went near it at all. He would not have considered it worthwhile to invent something that he would not think worthy of continued use. He would not take up anything that had to be subsequently laid aside. **31** According to Posidonius, "Anacharsis invented the potter's wheel that fashions vases by its rotation." Then, because the potter's wheel is mentioned in Homer, he wants us to take this passage to be spurious rather than dismiss his own story.* For my part, I refuse to accept that Anacharsis invented this thing; or, if he did, then a sage did indeed invent it, but not by virtue of his being wise; for the wise do many things simply by virtue of being human. Suppose a sage is a superb runner: he will win a race by his speed and not by his wisdom.

I would like to show Posidonius a glassblower, whose breath forms the glass into many shapes that a careful hand could scarcely fashion. Here we have things that were discovered at a time when the sage himself was no longer to be found. **32** Posidonius tells us that Democritus is reputed to have invented the arch, a device that uses the keystone to secure the curve made by a set of gradually tilted stones. I must insist that this is untrue. Before Democritus there had to be bridges and doorways, the top of which is generally rounded.* **33** You are also forgetting that the very same Democritus discovered the means of softening ivory and of turning a pebble into an emerald by baking it, a procedure by which even today we color stones found to respond to it.* The sage may well have discovered these things, but not by virtue of his wisdom. In fact, he does many things that we observe quite unwise people doing just as well or even with greater skill and ease.

**34** Do you want to know what discoveries the philosopher has really brought to light? In the first place, the truths of nature, which he has pursued quite differently from other creatures, whose eyes are dim in relation to the divine. Second, the law of life, which he has brought into line with the universal order of things, teaching us not just to know the gods but to follow them and accept all that happens as their commands. He has told us not to give heed to false opinions and has weighed the value of everything by an authentic standard. He has condemned pleasures that are mixed with regret and praised the goods that will always give satisfaction. He has made known that the most fortunate person is the one who has no need of fortune, and the most powerful person is the one who has power over himself.

35 The philosophy I am describing is not the one that situates the citizen outside his community and the gods outside the world, making virtue the instrument of pleasure, but the philosophy that thinks nothing is good that is not honorable; the one that cannot be captivated by gifts from humans or from fortune; the one whose reward is this: that its followers cannot be swayed by rewards.*

I do not believe that this philosophy existed in that primitive era when technology was absent and the uses of things were still being learned by trial and error. 36 It came after° that happy epoch when nature's blessings were readily available for everyone's use, when greed and self-indulgence had not yet divided human beings against one another and they had not yet learned to abandon sociability for the sake of gain. The men living then were not wise, even if they were acting as the wise should act.

37 One could not imagine a better condition for the human race, not even if God were to grant one the opportunity to fashion earthly things and dispense rules of conduct to peoples. Nor could one prefer another way of life to that which existed among those of whom it is said,

> No plowmen tilled the fields; even to mark
> the land with boundaries was not allowed.
> Their work, their effort, served the common good,
> and earth itself, when no demands were made,
> gave all its gifts more gladly.*

38 What human race could have been more fortunate? Everyone had a share in the fruits of nature. Like a parent, nature provided for the maintenance of everyone: they were free of anxiety, for they used, but did not own, the resources of the community. Surely I may call that people supremely wealthy, for among them you could find no one who was poor.

This optimal state of things was disrupted by greed. In its passion to be acquisitive and turn things into private property, it succeeded in making everything belong to different people, and reduced itself to a mere fraction of its formerly huge stock. Greed introduced poverty, and by desiring much, it lost everything. 39 Nowadays it strives to recover its losses, piles one estate onto another by buying out or forcing out its neighbors, expands its lands into the area of whole provinces, takes a long journey through its own property and calls it ownership. Yet in spite of all this, no extension of boundaries will bring us back to our original condition. When we have completed this project, we shall possess a great deal—but we used to own the whole world.

40 The earth itself was more productive when it was untilled; it was abundant for the needs of peoples who were not plunderers. It was as great a pleasure to share with another what one had found amid nature's bounty as it was to find it in the first place. No one could possibly have either more or less than was needed. Things were shared in mutual harmony. The time had not yet come when the stronger began to lay hands on the weaker, the time when the greedy would conceal things as a supply for their own use and thereby remove the necessities of life from other people. Their concern for others was as great as for themselves. 41 Weapons were not constantly in use; hands unstained with human blood turned all their hostility against wild beasts. The people of that era found protection from the sun in some thick wood. Kept safe from the fierceness of rain and storms by a humble shelter of leaves, they passed their days quite safely, and at night they slept calmly without a sigh. We toss and turn with anxiety on our purple bedclothes, kept awake by the sting of our cares. How softly those people slept on the hard ground! 42 Rather than being overhung by coffered ceilings, they lay out of doors with the stars gliding above them and that magnificent nightly spectacle which is the motion of the celestial sphere, which carries on so great a work without a sound. By day as well as by night, views of this resplendent dwelling opened before them. They enjoyed the sight of constellations setting past the zenith and others rising again into visibility. 43 Must it not have been a delight to roam amid such a vast expanse of wonders?

You moderns, on the other hand, tremble at every sound your houses make. If something creaks, you flee in terror amid your fres-

coed walls. Those people did not dwell in homes resembling towns.
The free-flowing breath of the open air, the light shade given by
rock or tree, crystalline springs, freely running streams unspoiled
by industry, pipes, or any artificial watercourse, and meadows with a
natural beauty—these were the settings of their rural dwellings embellished only by the handicrafts of country folk. This was a home in
agreement with nature. It was a pleasure to live there, made anxious
neither by it nor for it. For houses nowadays make up a large part
of our fears.

**44** Splendid and innocent though their life was, they were not the
wise, for this word is only applicable to the greatest of undertakings.
Yet I would not deny that they were men of lofty spirit and, if I may
say so, but recently descended from the gods. Before the world was
exhausted, it certainly gave birth to superior beings. Their natural
disposition was in every case hardier and better suited to manual
labor, but it correspondingly fell short in perfection. Nature does not
bestow virtue: becoming good is a skill. **45** To be sure, those people
did not prospect for gold or silver or for gleaming gems to be found
in the dregs of the earth. At that time, far from having one human
being kill another merely for the pleasure of the spectacle, without
even the motive of anger or fear, they were merciful even to the
speechless animals. They were not yet wearing embroidered clothes,
or clothes interwoven with gold, for gold was still unmined.

**46** What is our conclusion, then? These people were innocent out
of ignorance. There is a great difference between refusing to do wrong
and not knowing how to do it. They lacked the virtues of justice, good
sense, moderation, and courage. Their unsophisticated life did possess
certain qualities resembling all these, but real virtue belongs only to
a mind that has been trained, thoroughly instructed, and brought to
the highest condition by constant practice. We are indeed born for
this, but not born with it. Until you provide some education, even the
best natures have only the raw material for virtue, not virtue itself.

Farewell.

# Letter 91

*From Seneca to Lucilius*
*Greetings*

1 Our friend Liberalis is quite upset at news of the fire that has completely consumed the municipality of Lyon.* This catastrophe could have shaken anyone, let alone a person deeply devoted to his native land. It has left him searching for the mental toughness with which he had undoubtedly armed himself against what he thought were possible objects of fear. I'm not surprised, though, that he had no advance fears of this disaster, so unforeseen and virtually unimaginable, because it was unprecedented. Fire has troubled many cities, but not to the point of completely annihilating them. Even when buildings have been set alight by enemy action, many places escape destruction; and it is rare for fires, even ones that are restarted several times, to consume everything to the point of leaving nothing for the tools of demolition. Even earthquakes have hardly ever been severe and deadly enough to flatten entire towns. In a word, this has never happened before: a fire of such determined ferocity that afterward there was nothing left to burn.

2 Such a range of splendid structures, any one of them capable of embellishing a city all by itself—and a single night has leveled them all! During such an extensive period of peace, we have suffered a greater loss than anything we might have feared from war. How is this credible? With military operations in abeyance everywhere, with security now extended throughout the civilized world, Lyon, which was the jewel of Gaul, is lost to view. In the past, people afflicted by a general disaster have at least had opportunity to fear such an eventuality before the fact; nothing of great importance has been wrecked in a mere instant. But here, a single night marked the difference between a mighty city and none at all. Its end took less time than I have taken in telling you of it.

3 Although our friend Liberalis is no weakling in facing his own troubles, he is quite depressed by all of this. It's no wonder he is downcast. When one is unprepared for a disaster, it has a greater effect: shock intensifies the blow. No mortal can fail to grieve more

deeply when amazement is added to the loss. 4 Accordingly, we should let nothing catch us unprepared. We should try to anticipate everything and reflect on what's possible rather than what usually happens.*

Absolutely anything can be overthrown in its finest hour by the caprice of fortune. The brighter it shines, the more it is liable to be attacked and shaken: for fortune, nothing is arduous, nothing difficult. 5 Not always does it come by a single road, not always by paths that are well worn. Sometimes it turns our hands against each other; at other times, relying on its own resources, it finds dangers for us that need no agent. No moment is exempt. In the midst of pleasure, things arise that cause us pain. In a time of peace, war breaks out, and all that one had relied on for security becomes an object of fear: friends turn into foes, allies into enemies. The calm of a summer day is suddenly transformed into storms greater than those of winter. Even without an enemy at hand, we suffer war's effects. If there are no other reasons for calamity, excessive prosperity finds its own reasons. The most careful people are attacked by illness; the sturdiest by physical decline; punishments affect those who are completely guiltless; riots those who live in total seclusion. People who have almost forgotten the power of chance find themselves picked out to experience some novel misfortune. 6 The achievements of a lifetime, put together with great effort and many answered prayers, are cast to ruin in a single day. But to speak of a day is to make our hastening calamities slower than they really are. An hour, a mere moment is enough to overturn an empire. It would be some relief to our frailty and our concerns if everything came to an end as slowly as it comes into existence. The reality is that it takes time for things to grow but little or no time for them to be lost.

7 Whether public or private, nothing stands still. People and cities alike are caught up in destiny's momentum. When all is quite calm, terror emerges; and with no disturbing factors on the horizon, trouble bursts out from where it is least expected. Regimes that have remained standing through civil and foreign wars collapse without anyone's intervention. How rare it is for a city to experience prosperity for long! Therefore we must think of everything and fortify our minds to face every possible contingency.

8 Exile, torture, war, shipwreck—keep rehearsing them in your

mind. You could be snatched away from your country, or your country from you; you could be driven out into the desert, or the place where you are now jostled by crowds of people could itself become a desert. We should set before our eyes the entire range of human fortunes, and calibrate our thoughts about the future not by the usual scale of events but by the magnitude of what could happen. If we wish not to be overwhelmed, stunned by rare occurrences as if they were unparalleled, we must take a comprehensive view of fortune. **9** How often have cities of Asia and Greece been leveled by a single earthquake! How many towns in Syria and Macedonia have been swallowed up! How often has this disaster devastated Cyprus! How often has Paphos collapsed onto itself! We have frequently had news that entire cities have been destroyed, and we are only a tiny fraction of the people who frequently hear about them.

So we should stand up to the hazards of fortune, knowing that rumor always exaggerates the importance of what has happened. **10** A wealthy city has burned, one that was in the provinces and yet not of them but rather an ornament to them; still, it was located on a single hill, and that not a very large one. But all those cities that enjoy a splendid and glorious reputation today will have even their traces removed by time. Do you not see how the most famous cities in Greece have now been demolished? Not even the foundations are left standing to show that they once existed. **11** Nor is it only the work of our hands that falls away, only human constructions that are overturned by the passage of time. Mountaintops crumble, entire regions have subsided, lands that were situated far from sight of the sea have been covered by the waves. Powerful volcanic fires have eroded the hills through which they used to glow, radically reducing the once-lofty peaks that were a comforting landmark to sailors. Since nature's own works are not unassailed, we should not complain about the destruction of cities. **12** They stand only to fall: this end is waiting for every one of them. Either subterranean wind pressure bursts its barriers and topples them, or floodwaters build up underground and burst out against them with shattering force,* or a volcanic eruption breaks the earth's crust, or age, from which nothing is safe, gradually overwhelms them, or an epidemic wipes out the population and the abandoned buildings crumble from neglect. It would take too long to count up all the ways by which misfortune may come. But I know one thing: whatever we mortals construct is condemned to be mortal. We live amid things that will die.

13 These, then, are the kinds of consolations I send to our friend Liberalis, burning as he is with an incredible love for his native land. Perhaps it has been consumed so that it may be rebuilt better than it was before. Damage has often made room for greater prosperity. Many things have fallen only to rise to greater heights. Timagenes, an opponent of our city's success, used to say that the only reason he was grieved by the fires at Rome was that he knew the rebuilt structures would be superior to those that had burned down.* 14 In the case of Lyon too, everyone will probably strive to rebuild even finer and taller buildings than those they have lost. Let us wish that their work may be more enduring and founded with happier prospects for a longer future. This municipality only dates back a hundred years, not even as old as the longest human life. Founded by Plancus, it grew into the densely populated center that we know, thanks to its favorable location.* Yet consider how many grievous disasters it has suffered within the lifespan of one elderly person!

15 Let us, therefore, shape our minds to be such as will understand and endure our lot, knowing that fortune shrinks from nothing, but exerts the same rights over empire and emperor alike, and the same powers over cities as over persons. We have no grounds to resent these things. We have come into a world where life is lived on such terms: accept them and comply, or reject them and leave by whatever route you like. You may resent any unfairness that is directed against you personally. But if it is a necessity that binds all social classes in its compass, make your peace with destiny, which brings everything to an end. 16 There is no reason for you to measure us by our tombs and by the monuments along the road, all of different heights. Once reduced to ashes, we are all the same size. Born unequal, we die equal. My point is the same for cities as for their inhabitants: Rome was captured just as Ardea was.* The one who established humanity's rights drew no distinction among us on the basis of birth or celebrity except for the duration of our lives. Once we arrive at the end of our mortal term, he says, "Away with ambition; let one law apply to everything that walks the earth." We are equal in that each of us is liable to every suffering: no one is more vulnerable than another; no one is more assured of surviving till tomorrow.

**17** Alexander the Great had begun to study geometry—a study that would make him wretched, when he learned how puny the earth is and how little of it he had captured.* I say it again: he was wretched, for he should have realized that his title was unjustified: who can be "great" in an area that is miniscule? The subjects he was studying were complicated and only to be learned with close attention—nothing that could be easily understood by a crazy person whose thoughts were flying far across the ocean. "Teach me the easy bits," he said; to which his teacher replied: "They are the same for everyone, and equally difficult." **18** Imagine the nature of things to be saying the same to you: "What you are complaining about is the same for everyone. I can't give anyone anything easier, but anyone who wants to can make them easier for himself." How so? By keeping himself serene.

You are obliged to feel pain and thirst and hunger and, if you happen to be granted a longer duration among humankind, old age; you are obliged to grow sick, experience loss, and finally die. Still, there's no reason for you to accept the views dinned into your ears by those around you. **19** There's nothing really harmful in these matters, nothing intolerable or harsh. Those people's fear has no basis except that they are all in agreement about it. It puts you in the position of treating death like the fear of a rumor, whereas nothing is more absurd than a person afraid of words. Our friend Demetrius has a witticism by which he indicates that the sayings of ignorant people mean no more to him than the rumblings of the digestive tract: "What is it to me," he says, "whether they make their sound from above or from below?"* **20** It's the height of madness to worry about being despised by the despicable. You had no good reason to fear what people say, and it's just the same with those things you would never fear if it were not for what people say. Could unfair gossip do any harm to a good man? Surely not, and neither should we listen to unfair gossip about death, for it too has a bad reputation. No one who brings charges against death has ever experienced it. Until that happens, it is rash to condemn what you don't know. But this much you do know—how many there are for whom it is a blessing, how many it liberates from torture, want, illness, suffering, and weariness. We are in no one's power when death is in our power.

Farewell.

# Letter 92

*From Seneca to Lucilius*
*Greetings*

1 You and I will agree, I think, that one pursues outward things for the body's sake, that one cares for the body in order to show respect for the mind, and that the mind includes subservient parts, responsible for our motor and nutritional functions, which are given to us on behalf of the directive faculty itself.\* This directive faculty includes both a nonrational and a rational component. The former is at the service of the latter, which is the one thing that does not look to anything else but rather refers everything else to itself. As you know, divine rationality is similarly at the head of all things, subordinate to none of them; and this rationality of ours, which derives from that divine rationality, is just the same.

2 Now, if we agree about this, it is only consistent that we should also agree on the other point; namely, that the happy life consists solely in perfecting our rationality; for perfected rationality is the one thing that keeps the spirit high and takes a stand against fortune.\* Whatever the situation may be, it keeps us free from anxiety.° Moreover, it is the one good thing that never fails. What I am saying is that a happy person is one who is not diminished by anything, who has a hold on all that matters, and relies on nothing but himself: one who depends on anything else for support is liable to fall. Otherwise things that are not our own will start to exercise much power over us. Who wants to rely on fortune, and what intelligent person flatters himself because of things that do not belong to him?

3 What is a happy life? It is security and lasting tranquility, the sources of which are a great spirit and a steady determination to abide by a good decision. How does one arrive at these things? By perceiving the truth in all its completeness, by maintaining orderliness, measure, and propriety in one's actions, by having a will that is always well intentioned and generous, focused on rationality and never deviating from it, as lovable as it is admirable. Let me sum it up for you like this: the man of wisdom should have the sort of mind that would befit a god. 4 What can a person be missing when

he possesses everything that is honorable? If other kinds of things are capable of making any contribution to the best condition, they will be necessary conditions of the happy life. But it would be utterly wrong and absurd to make the excellence of a rational spirit depend on nonrational things.

5 In spite of this, there are some who claim that the supreme good is such as to be increased, because it does not attain its greatest fullness when circumstances are unfavorable.* Even Antipater, one of the greatest Stoic authorities, says that he grants something to externals, albeit a tiny amount.* You get the idea—not being satisfied with daylight unless there is additional illumination from a little flame. But when you have the sun's brightness, what effect can a mere spark have? 6 If you are not satisfied with honorable conduct on its own, you are bound to want the addition of either absence of distress (which Greeks call *aochlēsia**) or pleasure. The former of these is admissible in any case, for the trouble-free mind is not impeded from studying the universe or distracted by anything from contemplating nature. But the latter, pleasure, is the good of a grazing animal: we are adding the nonrational to the rational, what is not honorable to what is honorable, and <the puny> to the great, <if a happy>° life is brought about by a mere tingling in the body.* 7 Why hesitate in that case to say that a human being is doing well if his palate is doing well? And are you going to consider one whose supreme good consists in flavors and colors and sounds to be even a human being, let alone a real man? Dismiss him, rather, from the ranks of the animal that is finest and second only to the divine! He should join the beasts, this animal who gets his gratification from the trough.

8 The mind's nonrational part has itself two parts—the one part spirited, ambitious, and wayward, consisting in emotions; the other base, idle, devoted to pleasures. Setting aside the former, which, though unruly, is at least superior, and certainly bolder and worthier of a man, these people have deemed the latter, which is spineless and abject, to be essential to the happy life. 9 By instructing rationality to be its slave, they have degraded and demoted the supreme good of the noblest of animals. Besides, they have created a monstrous amalgam from quite diverse and incongruent elements. As our poet Virgil says, describing Scylla:

Above, a human face,
that of a maiden beautifully breasted
down to the groin; below, a rank sea monster
with dolphin tails attached to a wolf's belly.*

Yet while Scylla's appendages are wild animals, fearsome and swift, consider the monstrosities from which those people have constructed wisdom! 10 The human being's frontal part is virtue itself. Attached to it is unserviceable and unstable flesh, a mere repository for food, as Posidonius calls it.* Virtue, that portion of divinity, terminates in a sticky mess: to its loftier and truly heavenly parts, which are worthy of worship, is adjoined a listless and unhealthy animal. Their other objective, freedom from distress, though incapable of provid ing the spirit with any positive benefit, would at least remove any impediments. Pleasure, on the other hand, actually undermines the spirit and softens all its strength. You could not discover such an ill-matched union of bodies. The most stalwart of things is connected with the utterly impotent, the most serious with the completely trivial, the holiest with the full range of immorality.

11 "Not so fast," says the opponent. "If good health, repose, and absence of pain are no impediment to virtue, will you not pursue them?" Well, I shall do so, of course—not because they are good but because they are in accordance with nature, and because my taking them will be an exercise of good judgment. What in that case will be good in them? Just this one thing—that they are well selected.* You see, when I put on decent clothing, or take a walk in the proper way, or dine as I should, it's not the dining or the walking or the clothing that is good but my intention in each case to maintain the measure that conforms to reason. 12 Let me elaborate: selecting clean cloth-ing is something a person ought to do, because a human is by nature a clean and seemly animal. Accordingly, while clean clothing is not in itself a good, the act of selecting it is, because goodness is present not in the thing but in the quality of the selection. It is the doing that is honorable, not the actual things we do. 13 Now suppose me to make the same point about one's body. This too is a sort of clothing in which nature has enveloped the spirit as its garment. But who has ever valued garments by their storage chest? A sheath does not make

a sword good or bad. So I give you the same answer about the body: if the possibility of making a selection is granted me, I shall take good health and strength, but what will be good will be my judgment about them and not the things themselves.

**14** "The wise person is happy, to be sure; yet he does not attain the supreme good unless he has some natural tools at his disposal. Thus while someone who has virtue cannot be miserable, one who lacks such natural goods as health and an unimpaired physical condition is still not perfectly happy." **15** You are granting the point that seems harder to believe when you admit that someone suffering very great and continuous pain is not only not miserable but even happy; yet you balk at the easier point, that such a person is perfectly happy. But if virtue has the power to prevent someone from being miserable, it will be easier for it to make him perfectly happy, since the distance from happy to perfectly happy is less than that from miserable to happy. Surely the thing that can snatch one out of disasters and situate one among the happy has the further power to make up the difference and make one perfectly happy? Does it give up just as it is reaching the summit? **16** Life includes advantages and disadvantages, both of them outside our control. If the good man is not miserable even though he is laden with every disadvantage, how is he not perfectly happy if he lacks some advantages? Just as the weight of disadvantages does not reduce him to misery, so the absence of advantages does not remove him from perfect happiness; he is as perfectly happy without advantages as he is free from misery under the weight of disadvantages. Otherwise, if the good belonging to him can be diminished it can be snatched away from him altogether. **17** As I was saying a bit ago, a spark makes no contribution to the light of the sun; for the sun's brightness obscures anything that might shine in its absence.

"But even the sun has its light blocked by certain things." Yet the sun is unimpaired, even when it is obstructed; and even if there is something in between that stops us from seeing it, it is still at work and still proceeding on its round. Every time it shines out between the clouds, it is no smaller or slower than when the sky is quite clear. There is a lot of difference between an impediment and a mere obstruction. **18** In the same way, nothing is subtracted from virtue by things that stand in its way; it is not diminished but is simply less illuminating. It may not strike us with equal brilliance, but in itself it is the same and deploys its force invisibly, just like the hidden sun. Thus disasters, losses, and unfair treatment have no more power against virtue than a cloud can exert against the sun.

**19** We know of the claim that a wise person who is physically impaired is neither miserable nor happy.* This too is a mistake. It treats chance events as equal in power to virtues and assigns the same value to honorable things as it accords to those that lack that quality. What could be more disgusting or more contemptible than equating the most admirable things with those that have no claim to our respect? Justice, piety, integrity, courage, and good sense are admirable. By contrast, strong legs, muscles, and teeth, all in peak condition, are quite ordinary, and frequently found in the most ordinary sort of people. **20** Moreover, if a wise person who is suffering in body is deemed neither miserable nor happy but left in an intermediate category, his life too will be neither desirable nor undesirable. Yet the proposition that the sage's life is not desirable is utterly ridiculous, and it is quite incredible to hold that any type of life exists that is neither desirable nor undesirable. Furthermore, if bodily losses do not make a person miserable, they allow a person to be happy; for things that lack the power to make a situation worse cannot stop it from being optimal either.

**21** The opponent says, "We are familiar with hot and cold, and between them comes lukewarm. Similarly, one person is happy, another is miserable, and a third person is neither of these." I want to undermine this analogy directed against us. If I pour more cold into the lukewarm, it will become cold; if I add more hot, it will eventually become hot. But in the case of the imagined person who is neither miserable nor happy, however much I increase the miseries, according to your own doctrine the person will not be miserable. So that analogy does not work. **22** Now I hand this imagined neither-miserable-nor-happy person over to you. I supply him with blindness; he doesn't become miserable. I add debility; he doesn't become miserable. I add constant and severe pains; and he still doesn't become miserable. **23** If such a supply of woes fails to make this person miserable, they could not dislodge him from a happy life either. If, as you admit, the sage cannot fall from happiness into misery, he cannot fall into a condition that is not happy. Why would anyone who begins to fall stop anywhere? The very thing that does not allow him to roll down to the bottom holds him at the top. Of course the happy life cannot be destroyed—it cannot even be reduced, and therefore virtue is a sufficient condition for it.

**24** "In that case, why isn't the wise person who has lived longer and has not had to cope with pain happier than the one who has always struggled with misfortune?" Tell me this: is he also a better and more honorable person? If not, he is certainly not happier. In order to live more happily, he needs to live more correctly: if there is no room for him to be more correct, there is no room for him to be happier. Virtue does not admit of degrees, and therefore happiness, which depends on virtue, does not admit of degrees either.* You see, virtue is such a great good that it does not experience any diminution when little things are added to it like premature death, pain, or various bodily ailments. As for pleasure, virtue does not deign to notice it. **25** The special quality of virtue is that it has no need of the future and does not count its own days. In a mere instant, it enjoys eternal blessings.

We find these things incredible and beyond human nature. That is because we measure virtue's grandeur by our own weakness and confer its name on our own failings. But wait—don't we find it equally incredible that someone undergoing extreme torment should say, "I am happy"? Yet those words have been heard within the very workshop of pleasure. "This final day of my life is the happiest," said Epicurus when he was experiencing the double torture of urinary blockage and an incurable ulcer of the stomach.* **26** Why, then, is such an attitude incredible in the case of those who cultivate virtue, seeing that it is also found in those who follow pleasure's commands? These people as well, base-minded degenerates that they are,* say that the sage will be neither miserable nor happy when experiencing the worst of pains and disasters. Yet this too is incredible, or rather, still more incredible; for I don't see how virtue, when thrust from its own pinnacle, fails to plunge to the bottom. Either it must make one happy or, if it has been dislodged from that, it will not stop one from being miserable. As long as it stands, it cannot be discharged: it must either conquer or be conquered.

**27** "It is only the immortal gods who possess virtue and a happy life; all we can get is a shadow and semblance of those goods. We approach, but we don't actually reach them." Not so. Gods and human beings have rationality in common; in them it has been perfected, in us it is perfectible.* **28** The problem is that our failings bring us to despair. For the person who takes second rank in that he is not sufficiently consistent to preserve the right in all situations—the one whose judgment is still fallible and weak—even he is near the mark. Imagine this person to lack vision and hearing, good health, a reasonable appearance, and a longish lifespan with all his faculties intact. **29** Notwithstanding these disadvantages, he can live a life he does not regret. But in the imperfect man there remains some tendency toward badness, because his mind is still capable of being motivated toward wrongdoing, although deeply ingrained and active badness° is gone from it. He is not yet good, only someone being fashioned in that direction; and one who lacks anything with respect to good, is bad.*

**30** But the one who, as the poet says, has "courage and manly spirit in his body"* is level with the gods and proceeds in their direction, mindful of his origin. There is nothing wrong in striving to climb up to the point one descended from. Indeed, there is no reason for you not to believe that there is something divine in one who is actually a part of God. This universe that houses us is a unity, and is God; we are God's companions, God's limbs.* Our mind has this capacity; it is transported thither unless it is weighed down by faults. Just as our bodily posture is erect, with its gaze toward the heavens, so our mind can stretch forth as far as it wishes, having been formed by the very nature of the world to want things on the divine scale. If it exerts the strength that belongs to it and grows to its fullest extent, it needs no route but its own to reach the summit.

**31** Getting to the heavens would be a mighty task, were it not that the mind is returning whence it came. Once it has found the way, it travels boldly, disdainful of everything else, heedless of money or gold or silver, which fully deserve the darkness in which they have lain. It estimates their value not by the gleam that dazzles the eyes of the ignorant, but by the dross from which our cupidity has unearthed and separated them. That is to say, the elevated spirit knows that genuine riches are found elsewhere than the treasure trove, and that what ought to be fully stocked is not one's money chest but oneself. **32** The mind is entitled to be master over everything, to be granted ownership of the world, to have its property extend from east to west, and like the gods to possess all things. From its high seat, it looks down on the wealthy amid their resources, all of them less happy with what they own than they are saddened by what belongs to others.

**33** Once the mind has raised itself to this sublime height, it treats the body too as only a necessary burden, to be looked after but not to be loved, and does not subject itself to that over which it is in authority. No one is free who is a slave to the body; for not to mention those other masters one finds when one is excessively concerned about it, the body is a grouchy and capricious master just on its own. **34** From it the spirit departs, sometimes in tranquility, sometimes with a great leap forth. Nor does it inquire what will then become of that which it has abandoned; but just as we care nothing for the hair that is cut from our beard or our head, so when the divine spirit is about to depart from the person, the future destination of its bodily frame— whether to be burned° or buried or torn apart by beasts—interests it no more than a newly delivered infant is interested in the afterbirth. Whether birds dismember the corpse or it is devoured "as prey given to sharks,"* what does it mean for the one who is no longer anything? **35** But as long as that spirit is still among the living, does it fear any threats after death from those who were not satisfied with death threats alone? "I am not terrified by the executioner's hook,"* it says, "or by disgusting mutilation inflicted as an insult to my corpse. I ask no one to give me the last rites, I leave my remains to no one. Nature has seen to it that nobody remains without a tomb. Time will bury anyone that cruelty has left exposed." Maecenas said it eloquently:

> I care not for a tomb, for nature buries those
> who are abandoned.*

You would think the speaker was a fully armed soldier. He certainly had a splendid and manly talent, or would have had, if prosperity had not ungirded it.

Farewell.

# BOOK FIFTEEN

# Letter 93

*From Seneca to Lucilius*
*Greetings*

1 The regrets you expressed when writing to me about the death of
the philosopher Metronax seemed to suggest that he could have lived
longer, and indeed should have.* I missed that sense of fairness that
you show in abundance when dealing with every person or business
matter, but lack at this one point—as does everyone else. In my experience, many people are fair in their attitudes toward human beings,
but no one is fair toward the gods. Every day we reproach fate, saying:
"Why was this man carried off in the middle of his career? Why not
that other person? Why is he prolonging an old age that is a burden
to himself as well as others?"

2 Look: Which do you think is fairer, for nature to obey you or for
you to obey nature? What does it matter how soon you leave a place
that you have to leave eventually? What we need to be concerned
about is not how long we live but whether we live sufficiently. For
a long life, you need the help of fate; but to live sufficiently, the essential thing is one's character.* A life is long if it is full, and it is full
only when the mind bestows on itself the goodness that is proper to
it, claiming for itself the authority over itself. 3 What help are eighty
years to a person who has spent his life in doing nothing? Such a
person has not lived; he has simply hung around in life. Rather than
dying in old age, he has spent a long time dying. You say, "He lived
eighty years." What matters is the date from which you count his
death.

4 "But that person died in his prime." Still, he performed the
functions of a good citizen, a good friend, and a good son. He did
not fall short in any role. Although his lifetime was incomplete, his
life actually was complete. "That other person lived eighty years." The
truth is, rather, that he existed that long—unless perhaps by "lived"
you mean that he lived in the sense we apply that word to trees. Look
here, Lucilius: let's try to make our lives valuable in the way that pre-

cious objects are valued, not by size but by weight. Let's measure our life by its performance, not by its duration.

Do you want to know the difference between the vigorous man, the one who scorns fortune, the veteran in all life's campaigns who has made it to life's ultimate good, and one who has merely had many years pass over him? The former is still there after death, while the latter was already dead before his death. 5 So we should praise and congratulate the person whose time has been well invested, no matter how short that time has been. He has seen the true light, has not been just one of the crowd, has lived and has thrived. There are times when he has enjoyed clear weather, and many more when he experienced only flashes of sunlight. Why do you ask how long he lived? He is still alive, having leapt across into posterity and entrusted himself to our memory.

6 Don't think, mind you, that I am going to refuse any addition of years. But if my life's span is cut short, I will not say that I have missed anything contributing to happiness. I have not prepared myself for living right up to the last day that I have greedily hoped for; rather, I have viewed every day as if it were my last. Why do you ask when I was born, or whether I am still enrolled on the young men's register? I have what belongs to me. 7 Just as one of small stature can be a complete human being, so too a life of less duration can be complete. Age is something external. How long I am to exist does not belong to me; what is mine is authentic existence. This you can demand of me—that I not measure out a humdrum age in obscurity; that I live my life, not pass it by.

8 You are asking about the length of the most abundant life. It's living until you have attained wisdom. Anyone who gets that far has achieved not the greatest length of life but the greatest goal of life. Boldly will he take pride in his achievement, thanking the gods—himself among them—and giving nature the credit for his existence. He will be quite right in his accounting, because he has given back to nature a better life than he received. He has established the model of a good man; he has indicated the quality and the magnitude of the good. If he had added a longer lifetime, it would have been like his own past.*

9 How long in fact should we live? We have achieved knowledge of the universe. We know the origins of nature's development, how

it organizes the world, through what changes it restores the year, and how it contains all that will ever be and makes itself its own goal. We know that the stars move by their own force, that nothing besides the earth is stationary, and that the remaining bodies proceed with unceasing speed. We know how the moon overtakes the sun and why, though it is slower, it leaves what is faster behind; we know how the moon receives or loses its light, and the causes that bring on night and restore day. You need to go to where you can get a nearer view of these things.

**10** "And yet," says the wise man, "I don't depart more bravely because I believe that I am traveling straight to my gods. I have earned admission to them; I have already been with them and dispatched my thoughts to them, and they have sent me theirs. But suppose that I am obliterated, with nothing of my humanity surviving my death. I am equally confident even if I depart with nowhere to go."*

**11** "He could have lived a lot longer." Yes, but a book can consist of just a few verses and still be admirable and useful. You know how voluminous the *Annals* of Tanusius are and what people say about them.* Some people live long lives with just the same result. **12** Do you judge the man who is slain on the final day of the games to be more fortunate than the one who dies during the middle? Do you think anyone is so stupidly eager for life that he prefers to be butchered in the stripping circle rather than in the arena?* One of us precedes the other by no larger an interval. Death visits everyone; the slayer follows close on the slain. This thing that is taken to be so troubling is a trifle. What does it matter how long you evade what you cannot escape?

Farewell.


## Letter 94

*From Seneca to Lucilius*
*Greetings*

**1** Some people have deemed only one part of philosophy legitimate—the part that, instead of instructing human beings in general, gives specific precepts* for each social role, such as advising a husband on how he should behave to his wife, a father on how to raise his children, or a master on how to regulate his slaves. They have rejected the other parts for straying beyond our actual needs. As if anyone could give advice about a part of life before having grasped life in its entirety!* 2 The Stoic Aristo, on the contrary, judges this part to be of little weight and incapable of sinking right into the mind, being nothing but advice from old women. In his view, the greatest help comes from the actual principles of philosophy and the structure of the ultimate good.*

Once someone has thoroughly understood and learned the structure of the ultimate good, he can prescribe to himself what should be done in each situation. 3 A person who is learning to throw the javelin aims at a fixed point and trains his hand to direct the missile. Once he has acquired the capacity through training and practice, he can apply it wherever he wants. What he learned was how to strike not this or that particular target but any target he likes. Similarly, one who has trained himself for life as a whole does not need to be advised on specifics. He has been taught comprehensively, not how to live with his wife or his son but how to live well, and that includes how to live with members of his family.

4 Cleanthes holds that even this part has its uses, but he takes it to be ineffective unless it is an outcome of the system as a whole, based on knowledge of the actual principles and main points of philosophy. Hence this topic is divided into two questions. First, is it useful or useless? And second, can it on its own create a good man? In other words, is it superfluous, or does it make all other parts superfluous?

5 Those who want to show that this part is superfluous* argue as follows: "If something affecting the eyes interferes with vision, it must be removed. As long as it is there, it's a waste of time for someone to advise the person, 'Walk like this!' or 'Stretch out your hand there!' Just so, when something is blinding the mind and preventing it from seeing its priorities and obligations, it is pointless for someone to advise, 'Live this way with your father, that way with your wife.' Precepts will be of no use as long as the mind is clouded by error. Once this cloud is dispelled, one's obligation in each in-

stance will become evident. Otherwise you are not curing the sick person but only telling him how a healthy person ought to behave. **6** You are showing a poor person how to act rich: how can he do so while his poverty persists? You're teaching a hungry person what he would do if he were well fed: instead, remove the hunger that gnaws at his vitals. My point is the same concerning all faults: you have to remove them, not offer precepts, which cannot be effective while the faults themselves remain. If you don't banish the false opinions that plague us, the miser will not heed your advice on the use of money, nor will the coward listen to what you say about rising above what threatens him. **7** You have to make the miser know that wealth is neither good nor bad; you have to show him wealthy people who are quite wretched. You have to make the coward know that whatever terrifies the general public is less frightful than it is rumored to be, that no one is in pain for ever,° or dies more than once; that the great consolation about dying, which we are bound by the law of nature to suffer, is that no one has to suffer it twice; that the cure for pain is toughness of mind, which stubbornly faces trials and so makes them easier; that an excellent thing about pain is that when prolonged, it cannot be severe, and when severe, it cannot be prolonged;* and finally that we must bravely accept everything necessity ordains.

**8** "When a person has been brought, by means of these principles, to a clear view of his condition, understanding that a happy life is one that conforms not to pleasure but to nature, falling in love with virtue as a human being's only good, avoiding shameful conduct as the only bad, and knowing that everything else—wealth, status, good health, strength, and high office—is intermediate and not to be counted as either good or bad, he will not need a preceptor for specifics, to say: 'Walk like this; dine like that,' or 'This is what suits a man, this a woman, this a husband, and this a bachelor.'

**9** "The people who are most painstaking in giving such advice are unable to act accordingly. These are the precepts a tutor gives a pupil, or a grandmother a grandson. The teacher who argues that one should never get angry is himself highly irascible. If you go into an elementary school, you will learn that these sayings gravely propounded by philosophers are in the children's exercise book.

**10** "Furthermore, will your precepts be straightforward or questionable? Things that are straightforward don't need a preceptor, while those that are questionable are not believed. Therefore giving precepts is superfluous. Look at it like this: if your advice is unclear or ambiguous, you will need to supplement it with proofs; if you are going to give proofs, then the grounds of your proof are more effective and are enough on their own. **11** Consider: 'This is the way you should treat a friend, this way a fellow citizen, and this way an ally.' Why? 'Because it is just.' I can learn all this from the topic that treats justice. There I find that fairness is desirable in itself; that we are not forced into it by fear or motivated by monetary gain; and that one who is pleased by anything in justice except the virtue itself is not just. Once I have convinced myself of this and absorbed it, what is the good of those precepts which instruct one who is already trained?

"Giving precepts to one who knows is superfluous; in the case of one who does not know, it is insufficient, because he ought to hear not only what is being prescribed to him but also why. **12** Again, are precepts necessary to one who has correct opinions concerning the good and the bad, or to one who lacks such opinions? The latter will not be helped by you; his ears are fully occupied by popular notions that conflict with your admonitions. The one who does have a precise judgment about the proper objects of pursuit and avoidance knows what he should do without your saying anything. Therefore this entire part of philosophy can be dispensed with.

**13** "There are two reasons for our shortcomings: either wrong opinions have imbued the mind with bad intentions or, even if it has not been taken over by errors, it is inclined to them and is swiftly ruined when some impression leads it astray. So we must either completely cure the sick mind and free it from its faults, or forestall the mind that is still free from error but headed in the wrong direction. The principles of philosophy do both; therefore the entire business of giving precepts is useless.

**14** "Furthermore, if we give precepts for specific situations, the task will be endless. The moneylender, the farmer, the businessman, the one who courts friendships with royalty, the one who loves above his station and the one who loves below—all will need to be given different precepts. **15** In the case of marriage, you will be prescribing how a man should live with a wife who was a virgin beforehand, how he should live with a previously married woman, or with a rich one, or with one who has no dowry. Don't you think there is some difference between a barren woman and a fertile one, between an older woman and a mere girl, between a mother and a stepmother? We cannot take in every type. Specific situations require specific treatment, whereas the laws of philosophy are concise and comprehensive.

**16** "Besides, the precepts of wisdom need to be definite and to have definite boundaries. What has no boundaries is beyond the scope of wisdom, which knows the limits of things. Therefore this prescriptive part of philosophy should be removed, since it cannot provide everyone with what it promises to a few. But wisdom encompasses everyone. **17** The only difference between the madness of people in general and the madness treated by doctors is that while the latter is an ailment due to disease, the former is due to false opinions.* One type is caused by illness; the other is the mind's poor health. Anyone who gives precepts to a madman about how he ought to speak or walk or behave in public and private would be crazier than the person he is advising. The person's atrabilious condition needs to be treated and the actual cause of his madness removed. Likewise in the other case, the insanity has to be dispelled; otherwise your words of advice will vanish into thin air."

**18** This is Aristo's argument. I will take up his points one by one. First, in response to his statement that if there is some impediment to vision, it must be removed, I admit that what the eye needs in order to see is not precepts but treatment to remove the impediment and clear the vision. Seeing is a natural process, so that in removing obstacles one is allowing nature to function as before. But nature does not teach us our obligation in particular cases. **19** Next, a person cured of cataract cannot, immediately on restoration of vision, restore other people's sight, but anyone freed from vice can also free other people. The eye does not need encouragement or advice in order to understand the distinctive properties of colors; it can distinguish black from white without any prompting. The mind, on the other hand, needs many precepts in order to see its obligations in life. Yet even those who treat diseases of the eye provide advice as well as the cure. **20** The doctor will say, "You should not immediately expose your weak vision to harsh light. Start by going from dark to shady areas, then venture further and gradually accustom yourself to full daylight. You should not study immediately after a meal or force your eyes while they are still swollen and inflamed. Avoid cold blasts hitting your face," and other admonitions of this sort, which are just as helpful as drugs. Medicine combines treatment with advice.

**21** "What causes wrongdoing is error," he* says. "Precepts do not remove that from us or vanquish our false opinions about what is good and bad." I grant that by themselves precepts do not succeed in overturning the mind's erroneous convictions, but that does not make them ineffective when they are combined with other means. First of all, they refresh the memory. Second, matters that appear too confusing when taken as a whole can be more carefully pondered when divided into parts. By his reasoning, you could say that consolations and exhortations are superfluous; but they are not superfluous; therefore neither are admonitions.

**22** He continues: "It is silly to tell the sick what to do as though they were healthy; what needs to be restored is health. Without that, precepts are useless." What about the fact that the healthy as well as the sick need to be reminded of certain things? For instance, not to eat greedily, to avoid getting tired. The rich and the poor have some precepts they share.

**23** "Cure their greed, and you will have nothing to prescribe to either the rich or the poor, once the desire of each has subsided." There is a difference between not lusting after money and knowing how to use it. Those who are greedy for it need to be taught about limits; even those who lack that fault need to learn how to use money.

"Remove their errors; then precepts are superfluous." That's wrong. Imagine a lessening of greed, a limit to extravagance, a curb on rashness, a stimulus to sloth—even when faults have been removed, we still need to learn what we ought to do and how to do it.

**24** "Prescriptions applied to serious faults will do no good." Nor does medicine overcome incurable ailments, but we still use it, in some cases as a remedy and in others as a relief. Even comprehensive philosophical reasoning, exerting all its force, will not remove the mind's infection when it has become ingrained and long lasting. But it does not follow that philosophy cures nothing because it does not cure everything.

**25** "What's the use of showing the obvious?" A great deal, because we sometimes do not apply our knowledge. A reminder does not teach, but it does call attention; it arouses us, focuses the memory and prevents it from slipping away. We overlook many things that are before our eyes; reminding is one form of exhortation. The mind often pretends not to notice things that are obvious, and so it must be forced to take note of even the most familiar matters. Calvus's statement about Vatinius is relevant here: "You all know that bribery has been going on, and everyone knows that you know it."* **26** You know that friendships involve binding obligations, but you do not maintain them. You know that a man who demands chastity from his wife, while seducing other men's wives, is a villain. You know that, just as she should have no dealings with an adulterer, you should have none with a mistress, but you don't act accordingly. Hence you need to have your attention called to these points over and over. These principles should not be stored away but readily at hand. We need to be frequently thinking about and dwelling on all such beneficial reminders so that we not only know them but also have them available. Besides, even points that are obvious to us can be made more so.

**27** He says, "If your precepts are not clear, you will have to add proofs; in which case, it is they and not the precepts that will help." Aren't you forgetting that the authority of the preceptor is beneficial even without proofs, just as the opinions of legal experts are valuable even if no reason for them is given? Besides, the actual precepts have great weight in themselves, especially if they are expressed in verse or packed into a memorable phrase in prose, like those sayings of Cato: "Don't buy what you can use but what you need; for what you cannot use, a penny is too high a price."* **28** Such are oracular responses and things of that kind. "Be sparing with time." "Know yourself." Will you demand an explanation when someone utters these lines to you?

When wrongs are done, forgetting is the cure.

Fortune favors the brave; the coward is his own enemy.*

Such sayings don't require a defense attorney. They have an immediate impact on our feelings, and are helpful because our nature is deploying its very own force. **29** Our minds contain the seeds of everything honorable, and these are activated by admonitions, just as a spark fanned by a slight breeze blossoms into flame.* Virtue is roused by a touch, a nudge. Besides, there are some things that are indeed present in the mind, but not accessible; these begin to be usable when they are put into words. Some things lie scattered over the mind's different compartments, and an untrained intellect cannot assemble them. Hence they need to be united and connected, so that they will be more effective and do more to elevate the mind. **30** If, on the other hand, precepts are of no help, we should get rid of all instruction, and be content just with nature. The proponents of this position fail to see that people differ, some having a quick and lively intellect, others being slow and dense, and in general showing a wide range of intelligence. Our intelligence is fostered and enhanced by precepts, and thus enabled to supplement our innate convictions and correct our errors.

**31** "If a person lacks correct principles, how will admonitions be of help to him, since he is still in bondage to his faults?" Quite simply to liberate him, because his natural disposition has not been obliterated but concealed and overwhelmed. Even so, it tries to emerge and struggle against the corrupting influences; with help and the assistance of precepts it can recover, provided it has not been fatally infected by a long-term malady. In that case, even the most complete and strenuous course of philosophy will be ineffective.

The only difference between the principles of philosophy and precepts is the generality of the former and the specificity of the latter. They are both prescriptive, the one universally and the other at the level of particulars.

**32** "But if a person has correct and honorable principles, admonition will be superfluous." Not at all. Such a person has indeed been taught what he should do, but he does not clearly perceive what that is. It is not only our emotions that stop us from acting according to our convictions but also our inexperience in discovering what each situation demands. Our minds are often quite calm, but too passive and untrained at discovering where our obligations lie, and admonition can point that out.

**33** "Banish false opinions concerning what is good and bad, replace them with true ones, and there will be nothing for admonition to do." This is certainly a way to set the mind in order, but not the only way. While reasoning can establish the nature of good and bad, precepts still have their own role to play. Justice and prudence consist of obligations, and obligations are organized by precepts. **34** Furthermore, our judgments concerning good and bad are validated by how we perform our obligations, and precepts guide our performance of these. There is complete consistency between them: the judgments cannot go first without precepts following, and the fact that the precepts follow in order proves that principles are taking the lead.

**35** "Precepts are unlimited in number." That's incorrect. They are not unlimited concerning the most important and essential things. They differ slightly according to the requirements of time, place, and person, but generic precepts are applied to these cases too.

**36** "Madness is not cured by precepts, and so vice is not cured by them either." The two cases are different. Once madness is removed, sanity is restored; but the elimination of false opinions is not immediately followed by a clear understanding of proper conduct—or if it is, admonition will still strengthen the correct opinion concerning good and bad. It is also incorrect to say that precepts are of no avail in the case of the insane. While they are of no help on their own, they do assist the cure. Criticism and rebuke can restrain the insane. (In speaking of the insane here, I mean those whose minds are disturbed but not totally lost.)

**37** "Laws do not make us behave as we should, and laws are merely precepts combined with threats." First of all, laws fail to persuade precisely because they contain an element of threat, whereas precepts exhort but do not compel. Second, while laws use fear to keep us away from criminal acts, precepts urge us toward our obligations. Moreover, laws too are conducive to good character, provided they instruct as well as command. **38** On this point I disagree with Posidonius, who says,

> I criticize Plato for supplying preambles to the laws. A law should be terse, to facilitate its grasp by ignorant people. It should be like the voice of divinity—ordering, not discussing. I find nothing more pedantic and silly than a law with a preamble. Advise me; tell me what you would have me do. I am not here to learn but to obey.*

But in fact such laws are helpful: that is why you will see bad character in states with bad laws.

**39** "They are not helpful in all cases." Philosophy is not, either, but that does not make it useless and incapable of shaping people's minds. What do you think? Isn't philosophy the law of life? And even if we deny that laws are helpful, it does not follow that admonitions are not helpful either. If that were the case, you would have to say that words of consolation are of no use, and likewise with words of warning, exhortation, praise, and blame. These are all types of admonition, avenues for arriving at a perfected state of mind.

**40** To instill a mind with honorable ideas, and to recall to rectitude those who are wavering and prone to do wrong, nothing is more effective than good men's company. When they are seen and heard frequently, their influence is gradually internalized and acquires the force of precepts. An actual encounter with the wise is, of course, beneficial, and one can get some benefit from a great man even if he is silent. **41** Just how this happens would be hard for me to tell you, but I am sure that it has happened. As Phaedo says,

> There are some tiny creatures whose attacks are so miniscule and insidious that we don't even feel them when they bite us. Their bite is marked by a swelling, but even the swelling itself shows no wound.*

The same will happen to you in associating with men who are wise. You will not realize how or when it helps you, but you will realize that it has.

**42** "What's the point of this?" you ask. I respond that good precepts, if they are often with you, will be as helpful as good role models. Pythagoras says that people's mental state changes when, upon entering a temple, they see images of the gods close up and experience some oracular voice. **43** No one will deny that even quite ignorant people are genuinely struck by certain precepts, like these very terse but weighty expressions: "Nothing in excess"; "A greedy mind is never satisfied"; "Expect others to treat you as you treat them." These sayings give us a jolt, they don't let anyone doubt them or ask why. That's how brightly truth shines, even without any reason being given. **44** If religious awe restrains people and controls their faults, why can't admonition do so too? If shame is instilled by rebukes, why can't admonition have this effect even if it uses unembellished precepts? Admittedly, a precept becomes more effective and penetrates more deeply when it includes some reasoning as to why particular things should be done and what advantage the agent can expect from obedience.

If orders are helpful, so too is admonition; orders are helpful;

therefore admonition is too. **45** There are two parts to virtue: one is the study of truth, and the other is action. Study is taught by instruction, action by admonition. Right action both trains us in virtue and makes virtue manifest. If one who is about to act is aided by persuasion, he will also be aided by admonition. Hence if right action is essential to virtue and admonition points out what actions are right, admonition also is essential. **46** Two things principally engender strength of mind: assurance of truth and confidence therein. Admonition produces both: it prompts true belief, and that in turn inspires the mind with great aspirations and fills it with confidence. Therefore admonition is not superfluous.

A truly great man, Marcus Agrippa—the only one of those made famous and powerful by the civil wars whose success benefited the state—used to say that he owed a lot to this maxim: "Concord makes small things great; discord saps the strength of the mightiest."* **47** He claimed that this made him an excellent brother and friend. If this kind of maxim, once lodged in the mind, can shape it, why couldn't this part of philosophy, which consists of such maxims, do the same? Virtue consists partly of learning and partly of practice. You have to learn, and you have to consolidate your lessons by action. In which case, not only are the doctrines of philosophy helpful but so also are the precepts, which keep our emotions in check, as if by force of law, and rule them out of order.

**48** The opponent says, "Philosophy is divided into the following parts: knowledge and mental disposition. A person who has learned and perceived what to do is not yet wise, not until his mind has been transformed into the things learned. Your third part, the one that consists of precepts, is merely derived from the other two—the cognitive principles and the mental disposition. Hence it is superfluous, since the other two parts are sufficient to instill virtue." **49** That line of reasoning would also make consolation superfluous (since it too is derived from the other two), and likewise admonition, persuasion, and even proof, since all these are products of a firmly established mental disposition. Yet while an excellent mental disposition is the source of these things, it also arises from them; it is both their creator and their product.

**50** Moreover, what you are describing is the condition of a man who is already perfect and has attained the full sum of human happiness. But getting there is a slow process. In the meantime, those who are imperfect but making progress need to be shown how to conduct themselves. Perhaps actual wisdom will bestow this on itself even without admonition, once it has already brought the mind to the point where it cannot be moved except in the right direction. But weaker characters need someone to go ahead of them and say: "This is what you should avoid; this is what you should do." 51 Besides, if a person waits for the time when he knows by himself the best thing to do, he will go wrong in the meanwhile and as a result will be prevented from reaching the stage where self-sufficiency is possible. Therefore he needs to be governed until he becomes capable of governing himself. Children learn by following a model. Their fingers are held and guided through the outlines of the letters by someone else's hand; then they are told to copy set pieces and follow them in forming their handwriting. Similarly, our mind is helped while being taught to follow a model.

52 These are the arguments that show that this part of philosophy is not superfluous. There is a further question as to whether this part is sufficient on its own to make a person wise. We shall treat this question in its own good time.* Meanwhile, proofs aside, it is surely clear that we need a counselor to give us precepts to counter those of the populace. 53 No word reaches our ears without doing us harm; we are harmed both by good wishes and by curses. For a curse plants false fears in us, while the affection of our friends teaches us badly even in wishing us well, by sending us off in pursuit of goods that are far away, uncertain and unstable, when we could produce our happiness at home. 54 We are not allowed, I tell you, to travel by the straight road. Our parents and even our slaves lead us astray. No one errs just at his own expense; our folly spreads to our neighbors, and theirs affects us in turn. That is why national failings are manifested in individuals; it is the populace that produces those faults. Each person becomes corrupt in corrupting others. He learns bad habits, then teaches them, and so the worst opinions of each are compounded by contact with the others into one vast pile of depravity.* 55 So we should have a guardian to pluck our ear repeatedly, dismiss what people say, and protest against the praises of the many. You are mistaken if you think that our faults originate with us: they are heaped onto us by transmission. That's

why the opinions that echo all around us should be driven away by frequent admonitions.

**56** Nature does not predispose us to any fault; it has begotten us whole and free. It has not placed anything in the open to provoke our greed. It has put gold and silver beneath our feet, and granted us to crush and trample upon everything for which we ourselves are often crushed and trampled. Nature raised our faces to the sky, and wanted us to look up to everything splendid and wonderful it has made: the rising and setting of the heavenly bodies, the swift turning of the firmament, which reveals to us the earth by day and the heavens at night; the movements of the planets, which are slow if you compare them with that of the firmament but tremendously rapid if you consider the orbits they traverse with uninterrupted speed; the eclipses of the sun and moon when they obstruct each other; and other phenomena that are worthy of awe, both those that proceed according to a regular cycle and those that leap forth when activated by sudden causes, such as trails of fire in the night or flashes of light in the cloudless sky with no stroke of lightning or thunder; or pillars, beams, and all kinds of fiery phenomena.* **57** All these things nature has positioned above us; but gold, and silver, and iron that for their sake never gives us peace, nature has hidden, as though it were bad for us to be entrusted with them. It is we who have brought them up into the light in order to fight over them; it is we who have unearthed both the causes and the instruments of our own dangers by excavating the heavy ground; it is we who have consigned our own misdeeds to fortune and who are not ashamed at setting the highest value on things that once lay in the depths of the earth. **58** Do you want to know how specious is the gleam that has deceived your eyes? There is nothing filthier or darker than these metals all the time they lie buried and encrusted with slag. Of course not. Once they are hauled out through interminable and murky tunnels, nothing is uglier than they are during the process of refinement and separation from their own dross. Next, have a look at the workmen whose hands clean off this barren subterranean soil. See how much soot defiles them. **59** But these metals befoul the mind more than the body, and there is greater filth in those who own them than in the artisan.

It is necessary, then, to be admonished, to have a counselor with integrity, and amid so much confusion, so much deceitful noise, to hear just one voice in the end. What voice will that be? That goes without saying: it is the voice that whispers healing words to you when you have been deafened by such a clamor of self-aggrandizement, the voice that says,

60 "There is no reason for you to envy those who are commonly called great and fortunate, no reason for applause to disturb your peace of mind and your sanity, no reason for a figure clad in purple and accompanied by armed attendants to make you hate your own peaceful existence, no reason for you to judge him more fortunate than yourself, just because the route is cleared for him and his officer forces you off the path. If you want to hold a position that is useful to yourself and burdensome to no one else, clear away your own faults. 61 Many men are available to set fire to cities, to bring down fortifications that have been impregnable for ages and secure for generations, to raise a mound as high as battlements and to shatter marvelously high walls with battering rams and siege engines. There are many to drive their forces forward, to put pressure on their enemies' rear, and to reach the ocean drenched with the blood of nations; but these men, in order to conquer their foe, have themselves been conquered by desire. Their advance met no resistance, but they did not resist their own ambition and cruelty. Just when they appeared to be harrying others, they themselves were being harried.

62 "A passion to ruin foreign lands possessed the unfortunate Alexander and dispatched him to unknown lands.* Do you regard as sane the man who begins with the destruction of Greece, where he was raised, the man who deprives each state of its excellence by telling the Spartans to be slaves and the Athenians to be silent? Not satisfied with the destruction of all the states that Philip had either conquered or purchased, he overthrows one here, another there, and infests the entire world with his armies. Like wild beasts that bite off more than their hunger demands, his cruelty is never satisfied.* 63 At one moment he is combining many kingdoms into just one; at another moment Greeks and Persians fear the same man; at another, even peoples left free by Darius are accepting the yoke. Yet he goes beyond the ocean and the sun, he thinks it shameful to turn his victorious progress away

from the tracks traveled by Hercules and Bacchus, he prepares to attack nature itself.* He doesn't want to be on the move but he can't stay still, just as weights thrown down a hill keep moving until they reach the bottom.

**64** "What motivated Gnaeus Pompey to engage in foreign and civil wars was neither virtue nor calculation but the crazed love of a delusive greatness.* At one time he attacked Spain and Sertorius, and at another time he sallied forth to enchain the pirates and bring peace to the seas—pretexts to conceal the extension of his power. **65** What drove him into Africa, into the north, against Mithridates, and Armenia, and all the corners of Asia? Only a boundless desire to become even greater, since he was the only person who did not find himself great enough. What impelled Caesar to combine his own destruction with that of the state? Pride, ambition, and limitless preeminence over others. He could not bear to have a single man ahead of him, although even the Republic tolerated a pair of men as its head. **66** Do you think that it was virtue that motivated Gaius Marius—who was consul only once, since it was only one consulship that he accepted legally; the others he stole—to seek out so many dangers, when he crushed the Teutons and the Cimbri and pursued Jugurtha through African deserts? No, Marius led armies, but ambition led Marius. **67** While these men were whirling down on the entire world, they themselves were in a whirl, just like tornadoes, which spin everything about because they themselves are already spinning, and rush on with greater force because they have no command over themselves. Hence, after bringing about a multitude of harm, they too feel the destructive force with which they have harmed so many. You should not believe that anyone becomes fortunate at the expense of another's misfortune."

**68** We need to counteract all these examples that crowd into our eyes and ears, and empty the load of harmful speech from our hearts. Virtue must be brought into the place that such talk has occupied, to root out the lies and false ideas, to set us apart from the populace that we too readily trust, and to bring us back to sound opinions. This, in fact, is wisdom: returning to nature and being restored to the condition from which the general errors have banished us. **69** Sanity consists largely in abandoning the advocates of insanity and getting far away from an association that is mutually harmful. To know that this is correct, you just need to notice how differently each person behaves in public from when he is by himself. Not that solitude as such teaches innocence any more than the countryside teaches plain living, but when witnesses and onlookers are absent, there is a reduction in those faults that profit from being displayed and seen. **70** What man dresses in purple raiment that will be shown to no one? Who feasts in secret on golden plates? Who lies down under the shade of some rural tree and displays his splendid luxury all alone? No one gets dressed up just for his own eyes, or even for a few close friends: he extends the trappings of his faults as the crowd of onlookers increases. **71** That's how things are. Every insane desire is exacerbated by people who admire it and are in on it. If you curb our display, you will curb our longings. Ambition, luxury, and caprice need a stage; you will cure them if you keep them from being viewed.

**72** Therefore if we are situated in the midst of a noisy city, let there be a preceptor at our side to contradict those who laud vast incomes and to praise instead the man who is wealthy on little and who measures wealth by how it is used. In opposition to those who extol influence and power, your preceptor should uphold a leisure devoted to study and a mind focused away from externals and back toward its own concerns. **73** He should point out persons who are happy by ordinary standards, but who in fact on their envied heights are trembling and disturbed and have an opinion about themselves far different from what others have of them. The place that looks lofty to others appears to them precarious. They lose heart and become fearful whenever they look down on the sheer drop from their greatness, thinking that all kinds of things can happen and that the highest points are the most slippery. **74** Then they become frightened of their gains, and the good fortune that made them oppress others now oppresses them. Then they praise calm leisure and independence, they hate glory, and try to escape from their estate while it is still intact. Only then do you see them practicing philosophy out of fear, seeking sound counsels for sick fortune. You see, it is as if good fortune and good character were opposite. We are wiser in adversity, for prosperity robs us of rectitude.

Farewell.

# Letter 95

*From Seneca to Lucilius*
*Greetings*

1 You ask me to make good on the topic I had said should be postponed, and to write to you about whether the part of philosophy the Greeks call *paraenetikē* and we call "prescriptive" is sufficient to perfect wisdom.* I know you will take it in good part if I refuse—and for that reason I agree all the more readily, making good on the proverb "Don't ask for what you would rather not get." 2 There are times when we beg hard for a thing that we would refuse if it were offered. Whether this is silliness or perversity, it ought to be punished with immediate compliance. There are many things we pretend to want when really we don't. A public lecturer comes in with a huge text in tiny writing and tightly rolled up. He reads a lot of it, then says, "I will stop if you like." "Keep going! keep going!" comes the shout, from an audience that really wants him to shut up immediately. Often, we want one thing, and pray for another, not telling the truth even to the gods—but the gods either don't listen, or they pity us. 3 In my case, though, pity is out of the question: I shall assert my freedom and inflict a huge letter on you. If it's more than you want to read, say, "I brought this on myself." Count yourself among the men who are tormented by a wife they schemed greatly to marry, or troubled by wealth that has cost them a vast amount of sweat, or tortured by the high positions they have sought by every means and effort, or otherwise responsible for their own miseries.

4 Enough of this preface. Let me get to the matter in hand. Some people say: "A happy life consists of right actions; precepts lead to right actions; therefore precepts are sufficient for a happy life." In fact, precepts are not always conducive to a happy life but only when they encounter a compliant disposition. Sometimes they are applied in vain, in cases when the mind is beset by wrong opinions. 5 Secondly, even if people act rightly, they may not know that they are doing so. Unless a person is well fashioned from the beginning and endowed with a completely rational disposition, it is impossible for him to fulfill all the measures so as to know when, how much, with

whom, how, and why a certain action is appropriate.* He cannot be whole-hearted in his endeavor to behave honorably, or even consistent and willing; instead, he will dither and hesitate.

**6** "If honorable action is an outcome of precepts, precepts are quite sufficient for a happy life; but the one is true, therefore the other is also true." Our response to this is that honorable actions do result from precepts, but not from precepts alone.

**7** "If the arts in general are satisfied with precepts, wisdom will be satisfied too, since it is the art of life. The way you make a pilot is by precepts: 'move the tiller this way, spread the sails like that, this is how to make use of a following wind, that's how to combat one blowing against you, here's the way to make the best of one that is gusty and variable.' Precepts train other kinds of craftsmen as well, and so they will also be able to train this craftsman in the art of living." **8** The arts you are talking about are concerned only with the tools of life, not with life as a whole. There is much from outside that can hinder and impede them, such as hope, desire, and fear. But nothing can prevent a person from exercising the skill that proclaims itself to be the art of life: it shakes off hindrances and tosses obstacles aside. This is how different it is from the other crafts: in their case, it is more excusable to err intentionally than by chance, but here the greatest fault is to go wrong deliberately. **9** Here is what I mean. A scholar will not blush if he makes a grammatical mistake deliberately, but will if he does so inadvertently. If a doctor does not realize that his patient is deteriorating, he is a worse practitioner than if he knows but pretends not to. But here in the art of living, voluntary faults are more blameworthy.

There is also the fact that many arts, including the most refined, have their own principles as well as their precepts. This is true, for instance, of medicine, where there are the different branches of Hippocrates, Asclepiades, and Themison.* **10** Moreover, no theoretical art is without its own principles, which the Greeks call *dogmata* and we may call "principles" (*decreta*) or "tenets" (*scita*) or "doctrines" (*placita*), as you will find in both geometry and astronomy. Philosophy is both theoretical and practical, observing at the same time as it acts. It would be a mistake for you to think that philosophy only looks after your mundane needs; it has loftier aspirations. Rather, it declares: "My focus is the entire universe; I don't confine myself to the mortal domain, content to give you positive or negative advice. I am summoned by things that are mighty and stationed above you, as Lucretius says:

11 I will begin to teach you now about
the larger scheme of heaven and of the gods;
I will unfold the basic elements from which
nature creates all things, augments and nurtures,
and in the end destroys them and dissolves them."*

It follows, then, that philosophy, by being theoretical, has its own principles. 12 Besides, no one will properly do what is incumbent on him without being endowed with the reasoning that enables him to fulfill all the measures of duty in every situation. He will not maintain those measures if he has acquired precepts that are applicable only to the situation at hand and not universally. The former are inherently weak and rootless, as it were, because they are merely partial. It is principles that can fortify us, maintain us in safety and tranquility, and simultaneously embrace the whole of our life and the whole of nature. The difference between philosophy's principles and its precepts is the same as that between the basic elements of something and its branches. The latter depend on the former, which are both their causes and the causes of everything.

13 The opponent says, "Ancient wisdom merely prescribed what to do and avoid, and yet those who lived in that time were much better men. Ever since scholars emerged, good people have been in short supply. Simple and obvious virtue changed into a difficult and devious science, teaching us how to debate instead of how to live." 14 The old-fashioned wisdom, as you say, was as unsophisticated in its origins as the other arts whose subtlety has evolved over time. Back then, though, there really was no need for elaborate cures. Wrongdoing had not reached so great a height or spread so widely: simple faults could be remedied by simple cures. Nowadays our defenses must be more elaborate, since the attacks against us are more powerful.

15 At one time medicine was the knowledge of a few herbs to check the flow of blood and help wounds to knit; then it gradually arrived at its present range of complexity. In the old days, not surprisingly, it had less work to do; for bodies were still firm and

strong, living on simple food that had not been corrupted by artifice and a desire to titillate. Once food started to be sought not to
relieve hunger but to arouse it, and countless seasonings had been
discovered to stimulate gluttony, what used to nourish the hungry
began to burden the overfed. **16** Thence came pallor and the tremor
of wine-sodden sinews, and the emaciation that comes of dyspepsia,
more pitiful even than that which comes of malnutrition. Thence
unsteady and tottering steps, and a constant reeling just like that of
actual intoxication. Thence fluid building up under all the skin, and
a belly distended from the habit of exceeding its capacity. Thence an
outbreak of jaundice, a discolored face, the ooze of decaying organs,°
fingers disfigured by arthritis, numb and dysfunctional muscles, or
the constant twitching of muscle spasms. **17** Need I talk of dizziness,
severe pains in the eye or the ear, raging headaches, and all the ulcer-
ated parts within our excretory organs? There are also countless types
of fever, some fierce in their attack, others creeping up with a gradual
infection, and others again that arrive accompanied by shivering and
violent shaking of our limbs. **18** What need for me to mention countless other ailments, the punishments of luxury?

These problems did not affect people in former times, when they
had not yet become soft by self-indulgence, when they were their
own masters and their own servants. They toughened their bodies by
genuine hard work, and exhausted themselves by running or hunting
or tilling the ground. The food that awaited them was such as could
only please people who were hungry. There was no need for such a
large supply of medicines or for so many surgical instruments and
pillboxes. Bad health was then a simple matter, and its causes were
simple: it is multiple courses that have caused multiple ailments.
**19** Take note of the quantity of things that luxury, ransacking land
and sea, mixes up for a single throat to swallow down. Inevitably,
such different items combine badly and are poorly digested, struggling against one another. It's not surprising that an irregular and
ill-assorted diet should cause illness, that vomiting takes place when
nutriments from opposite parts of nature are forced into the same
person. Our illnesses are as bizarre as our manner of living.

**20** The greatest of doctors and the founder of medicine said that
women do not lose their hair or have trouble with their feet.* But in
fact they *are* suffering hair loss and foot ailments. Female nature has

not changed, but it has been overcome. In matching men's licentiousness, women have also matched men's bodily discomforts. **21** They stay up just as late, drink just as much, and compete with men both in wrestling and in drinking bouts. No less than men, they disgorge food that their stomachs have reluctantly ingested, and they throw up all the wine they have drunk. Just like men, they gnaw ice as a palliative for their seething stomachs. They even match men at sex: though born to play the passive role, they practice an utterly perverted type of obscenity (may the gods and goddesses destroy them!) and straddle men. It's not surprising, then, that the greatest doctor and expert in physiology is proved wrong, since so many women suffer from hair loss and gout. As a result of their vices, they have lost the advantage of their sex; and by discarding their femininity, they have condemned themselves to men's ailments.

**22** The doctors of old had no idea about increasing the frequency of meals, fortifying the failing pulse with wine, bloodletting, and relieving long-term illness with hot baths. They did not know how to summon dormant and sluggish vitality to the extremities by means of ligatures on arms and legs. There was no need to mount a search for many other types of aid, since there were so few life-threatening conditions. **23** But today, how far health problems have advanced! This is the price we are paying for pleasures we have coveted beyond what is right and reasonable. You shouldn't wonder at the countless number of diseases—just add up the cooks! All academic life has stopped. Professors of the liberal arts have lost their audience and preside over remote crannies. All is quiet within the schools of rhetoric and philosophy. But how crammed the kitchens are, and how many young people crowd around the stoves of the wastrels! I refrain from describing the troops of wretched boys who are going to be sexually abused after the meals are over. **24** I pass over the regiments of catamites, ranked by their race and color but all with the same smooth skin, the same amount of down on their faces, the same hairstyle to ensure that straight hair is mingled with their curls. I exclude the throngs of bakers and waiters, who rush to bring in the dinner when the signal has been given.

**25** Ye gods, the number of people that just one belly keeps busy! In the case of those mushrooms, the gourmet poison, do you think that they are having no hidden effect on you, even if they have not yet done anything obvious? Do you really suppose that the ice you are eating during summer does not cause hardening of your liver? Do you really believe that those oysters, sluggish creatures fattened on mud, are not infecting you with any of their slimy heaviness? As regards imported garum, the costly rot of bad fish, do you really believe its salty decay will not give you heartburn?* Do you think that those festering foods that are taken almost straight from the fire into the mouth are harmlessly extinguished in your intestines? How foul and unhealthy the ensuing belches are! How disgusted people are with themselves when they breathe out last night's drunken binge! You can be sure that their intake is rotting rather than being digested.

**26** I remember there was once talk about a famous dish in which a restaurant rapidly approaching bankruptcy had piled up everything gourmets like to spend a whole day on—two kinds of mussels, oysters trimmed to their edible parts and marked off from one another by sea urchins, and the whole dish bestrewn with mullets neatly filleted and arranged° without the bones. **27** Single dishes are considered shameful nowadays; different flavors are combined into one. What should take place in the belly is occurring at the table. I expect soon to see dishes being served that have already been chewed. How close we are to that when the cook removes the shells and bones, leaving nothing for the teeth to do! People say: "It's a burden to indulge ourselves piecemeal. Let everything be served at the same time and blended into the same flavor. Why should I stretch out my hand for individual things? Let the various dishes all come together, with the tidbits of the many courses joined up and united." **28** Those who used to say that this was done to brag and boast should be immediately made aware that it is not showing off but rather deliberate gourmandizing. Let the foods we used to keep separate be combined, drenched in a single sauce! Make no distinction! Have oysters, sea urchins, mussels, and mullets cooked and served in a medley! No vomited food could be more jumbled up.

**29** Corresponding to this confusion of foods, diseases have arisen that are not single but complex, manifold, and multiform. To oppose them, medicine too has begun to arm itself with multiple diagnoses and multiple treatments. The same thing, I tell you, applies to philosophy. In days gone by, it was simpler; it dealt with lesser faults that were curable even with a mild treatment. To combat the huge wreckage of our moral condition, we need to try everything. I only wish that we could then defeat this corruption. **30** We are insane as a country, and not just as individuals. We reduce the incidence of individual killings, but what about wars and the splendid crime of genocide? There is no limit to our greed and cruelty. As long as these things are done in secret and confined to individuals, they are less destructive and less shocking, but savagery is also being committed on the authority of the Senate and popular mandate: acts that are forbidden to private citizens are required as a matter of public policy. **31** Offenses punishable by death when committed in secret we now praise, just because those who commit them are generals in full dress. Human beings are the gentlest species, but we are not ashamed to enjoy homicide, to wage war and pass it on to our children, although even wild animals devoid of speech maintain mutual peace.

**32** To combat such powerful and widespread madness, philosophy has become more energetic, and has acquired strength that is a match for the strength of its adversaries. It used to be easy to reprimand people who were keen on wine and finicky about food; they did not need a great effort to be restored to the simple life from which they had only slightly departed. **33** But "now is the need for your swift hands and master skill."* The hunt is on for pleasure from every quarter. No fault is self-contained. Luxury is rapacious. Honor has been forgotten. Nothing is shameful as long as it is profitable. The human being, an object of reverence for human beings, is now killed as a sport and entertainment. It used to be immoral for someone to be trained to inflict and receive wounds; but now unarmed and naked men are displayed, and the death of a human being is entertainment enough.

**34** At this perversion of morality, we need something unusually forceful to dispel the evils that have become ingrained. We need to muster the principles of philosophy so as to utterly root out these falsehoods that have become such deep convictions. By themselves such principles are useless, but they can be effective if we combine them with precepts, consolations, and exhortations. **35** If we want to hold people fast and tear them away from the bad things that possess them, they need to learn what good and bad really are, and to realize that everything except virtue changes its name, sometimes becoming bad and at other times good. Just as the first bonds of military service

are the soldier's oath of allegiance, love of the standard,* and a horror
of desertion, while other duties are easily required and imposed later
on those who have first taken the oath, so it is in the case of people
you want to bring to the happy life: one must first lay the foundations, then instill virtue. They need to be held in awe of virtue and
fall in love with virtue; they must want to live with virtue and refuse
to live without it.

**36** "Very well. But haven't some people managed to be decent
without elaborate training, and made great progress while simply
obeying bare precepts?" I agree, but they had a fortunate nature,
which picked up salutary habits along the way. Just as the immortal
gods did not learn any virtue, having been born with all of it, and
just as it is in their nature to be good, so there are human beings who
have been allotted a special disposition: without any long schooling,
they arrive at conclusions that normally have to be taught, embracing honorable principles as soon as they have heard them. That's why
we find these natures that are so receptive to virtue or so capable of
producing it themselves. But others, who are either slow and dense or
beset by bad habits, must have their mental rust laboriously rubbed
away.*

**37** Moreover, just as a philosophical education accelerates the
progress of those who are well inclined, so it will help those who
are weaker and remove their harmful opinions. You may see how
necessary such principles are in this way. Things lurk inside us that
make us lazy in relation to certain objectives and rash in regard to
others. This boldness can be checked and this indolence roused only
by removing their respective causes, which are mistaken fascination
and mistaken fear. As long as these things have hold of us, you may
say, "These are your duties to your father, those are what you owe to
your children, and these to your friends and your guests," but greed
will hold us back in the act of trying. Someone knows that he should
fight for his country, but fear will dissuade him. He knows that he
should exert himself to the utmost for his friends, but his pleasures
will stop him. He knows that a mistress is the most serious offense to
his wife, but his lust drives him in the opposite direction. **38** Therefore giving precepts will be of no help unless you first remove the
obstacles to them. It will be of no more use than putting weapons
near someone whose hands are tied. In order for the mind to be able

to proceed according to our precepts, it must first be released. **39** Even supposing that someone is acting properly, if he doesn't know why he is acting, he will not do it consistently and regularly. Some things will come out right by chance or by training, but without his having a rule in hand to which they conform and in which he can trust for the correctness of what he is doing. One who is good by chance will give no guarantee of being so forever.

**40** Furthermore, while precepts will perhaps ensure that a person does the right thing, they will not ensure that he does it in the right way. Without that, they are not conducive to virtue. I grant that someone will do the right thing when advised, but that's not enough, because the merit is not in the deed but in how it is done. **41** What is more outrageous than a banquet that costs as much as membership in the equestrian order? What is more deserving of official censure than spending this sum "on oneself and one's Genius," in the words of those who like to gorge themselves? Even quite frugal men have spent a million on their inaugural dinners.* The sum that would be disgraceful if it were merely spent to please the palate escapes criticism when spent on public office. In the latter case, it is not indulgence but an official expense.

**42** When Tiberius Caesar was sent a huge mullet (I don't mind mentioning, to water some people's mouths, that it supposedly weighed four and a half pounds), he ordered it to be taken to the market and sold, saying, "My friends, unless I am totally wrong, either Apicius or Publius Octavius will buy it."* His guess exceeded expectations. They placed their bids; Octavius won, and achieved huge fame among his friends for spending five thousand sesterces on the fish that Caesar had sold and that even Apicius had not managed to buy. To spend so much was shocking for Octavius, not so for the man who had bought the fish to send it to Tiberius. Yet I would criticize him too, since he was amazed by such a thing and thought it worthy of the emperor.

**43** When a person sits by a sick friend, we approve. But doing this for the sake of an inheritance makes one a vulture awaiting a corpse. The same acts may be either honorable or dishonorable: what counts is why or how they are done. Everything will be done honorably if we devote ourselves to what is honorable, and judge it and whatever depends on it to be the only good in human affairs. All the rest are goods just for the day. **44** Hence a conviction needs to be instilled that applies to one's life in its entirety. That is what I call a principle. As is the conviction, such will be one's actions and thoughts; as these are, such will be one's life. Advice on specifics is not enough for someone who is seeking to regulate the whole.

**45** In the book Marcus Brutus called *On Appropriate Action*, he gives many precepts to parents, children, and brothers, but no one will act as he should unless he has a point of reference.* We need to set forth the ultimate good to strive for, as the orientation for our every word and deed, just as sailors have to set their course by a particular star. **46** Without a goal, life drifts. But if a definitive goal needs to be set forth, principles begin to be necessary. I think you will accept that nothing is more reprehensible than wavering, indecision, and cowardly retreat. That will be our experience unless we remove the things that hold us back, give us pause, and stop us from advancing and wholeheartedly striving.

**47** It is customary to prescribe how the gods should be worshipped. Let us prohibit the lighting of lamps on the Sabbath, since gods have no need of light and even humans have no liking for soot. Let us stop the practice of the morning salutation and sitting at temple doors. Such services are pleasing to human ambition, but one worships God by acknowledging him. Let us ban bringing towels and scrapers to Jupiter* and holding a mirror for Juno. God does not require servants. How could he? He himself serves the human race; he is available everywhere for everyone. **48** You can teach people how to determine the amount of a sacrifice and how to refrain from burdensome ritual practices, but their progress will never be adequate unless they have acquired the right notion of God as one that has everything, gives everything, and is disinterestedly beneficent. **49** What is the reason for the gods' beneficence? It is their nature. It is a mistake to think that they are unwilling to do harm. They cannot do so. They cannot be injured, nor can they injure, since harming and being harmed are interconnected. The world's ultimate and supremely beautiful nature makes those who are immune to danger incapable of causing danger.

**50** The first step in worshipping the gods is believing in them, and the second is acknowledging their grandeur as well as their goodness, without which there is no grandeur—knowing that it is they who rule over the world, who control everything by their power, and who exercise guardianship over the human race, though they are sometimes inattentive to individuals. They do not dispense or contain anything bad; but they do reprove and restrain some people, impose penalties on them, and sometimes punish them while appearing to do them good.* If you want to please the gods, be good. Imitation is worship enough.

**51** Now we face a further question concerning the treatment of human beings. What is our aim? What precepts do we offer? That we should spare human blood? How small a thing it is to refrain from harming someone you ought to help! As if it were highly meritorious when one person avoids savagery in relation to another! Won't our precepts state that one should stretch out a hand to someone who has been shipwrecked, show the way to the wanderer, share one's bread with the starving? Why should I mention every service one should perform, every kind of harm one should avoid doing? Instead, I can pass on the following general rule concerning human duties. **52** This universe that you see, containing the human and the divine, is a unity; we are the limbs of a mighty body. Nature brought us to birth as kin, since it generated us all from the same materials and for the same purposes, endowing us with affection for one another and making us companionable. Nature established fairness and justice. According to nature's dispensation, it is worse to harm than to be harmed. On the basis of nature's command, let our hands be available to help whenever necessary. **53** Let this verse be in your heart and in your mouth:

I am a human being, I regard nothing human as foreign to me.*

Let us hold things in common, as we are born for the common good. Our companionship is just like an arch, which would collapse without the stones' mutual support to hold it up.

**54** After gods and human beings, let us consider how we should treat things. There is no point in tossing precepts about unless we preface them with the kind of judgment we need to have about each individual item, such as poverty, wealth, glory, disgrace, homeland, and exile. Setting popular opinion aside, let us assess these particulars and investigate what they are and not what they are called.

**55** We should turn next to the virtues. Precepts will take the form of telling us to value thoughtfulness highly, embrace courage, and if possible, wed ourselves to justice even more closely than to the other virtues. But such precepts will be useless if we do not know what virtue is, whether it is one thing or many, whether the virtues are interconnected or separate, whether the possession of one entails having all, and how they differ from one another.* **56** A builder has no more need to ask about the origin and use of his material than a pantomime performer has to investigate the art of dance. All these skills know their own principles; they are complete in themselves, since they don't have any bearing on life as a whole. But virtue is the understanding of both itself and of other things. We must learn all about virtue in order to learn virtue. **57** An action will not be right unless one's intention is right, since that is the source of the action. The intention will not be right, in its turn, unless the mental disposition is right, since that is the source of the intention. Further, the mental disposition will not be optimal unless the person has grasped the laws of life as a whole, has settled on the judgments needing to be made about each thing—unless he has brought the truth to bear on his situation. Peace of mind depends on securing an unchanging and definite judgment. Other people constantly lose and regain their footing, as they oscillate between letting things go and pursuing them.

**58** What is the reason for this instability? It is that nothing is certain for people who rely on popular opinion, the most unreliable of standards. If you want your choices to be consistent, you need to choose what's true. There is no route to truth without principles: they give a life its structure. Good and bad, honorable and disgraceful, just and unjust, scrupulous and unscrupulous, the virtues and their functions, material comforts, reputation and status, health, strength, beauty, keenness of perception—all these need to be evaluated. Let us know the value of every item on the list. **59** You see, you make mistakes and think some things are more valuable than they really are, to such an extent that things we prize most—wealth, influence, and power—should be valued at only a cent. You won't know this unless you have studied the actual structure that governs these relative values. Leaves cannot flourish by themselves; they need to be fixed in a branch from which to draw their sap. In the same way, precepts on their own wither; they need to be fixed in a philosophical system.

**60** Besides, those who do away with principles don't understand that the very argument that does away with them confirms them. Their claim is that life is adequately organized by precepts, making the principles of philosophy superfluous. But this very claim is a principle. For heaven's sake, it is just as if I were now to say that one should give up precepts on the grounds that they are superfluous, make use only of principles, and apply one's study just to them. In the act of denying the utility of precepts, I would be stating a precept. **61** Some things in philosophy need admonition; others need proof, a great deal of it, because they are complicated and scarcely revealed even with great care and precision. If proofs are necessary, so too are the principles that deduce the truth by arguments. Some things are self-evident, while others are obscure. The former are grasped by the senses and by memory; the latter are beyond these faculties. Reason is not entirely concerned with the self-evident; most of it, and the most beautiful part, is concerned with things that are hidden. What is hidden demands proof, and proof is impossible without principles; therefore principles are necessary.

**62** What generates and perfects fellow feeling with others is an assured conviction of facts.* Without that, when all mental contents are in flux, there is a need for principles that can provide the mind with a firm criterion of action. **63** Further, when we advise someone to place a friend in the same position as oneself or to realize that an enemy can become a friend, and to arouse love in the one and soften hatred in the other, we add the words "This is just and honorable." It is reason that secures the justice and honorableness of our principles. Therefore reason is necessary, since without it these principles do not exist.

**64** But let us connect precepts and principles. Branches without roots are useless, and the roots themselves are assisted by what they have produced. No one can fail to know how useful our hands are; their service is obvious. But the heart, the source of the hands' vitality, energy, and motion, is concealed. I can say the same about precepts. They are obvious, but the principles of philosophy are hidden. Just as the more sacred elements of a religion are known only to initiates, so in philosophy the inmost parts are revealed only to those who have been fully admitted and received into its mysteries. But precepts and the like are also shared with outsiders.

**65** Posidonius sees a need not only for "preception" (nothing stops me from using this term) but also for encouragement, consolation, and exhortation.* To these he adds the investigation of causes (I don't see why I should not call this "aetiology," since the scholars who keep guard over the Latin language arrogate the right to use this term). He says that it will also be useful to give an exemplification of each virtue: his term for this is *ethologia*, while others call it *characterismos*. This renders the features and marks of each virtue and vice, which enable similar things to be distinguished from one another. **66** This procedure has the same import as prescribing, since one who prescribes says, "Do this if you want to be temperate," while the person who exemplifies says, "One who does this and refrains from that is temperate." How do these differ? The one gives virtue's precepts, the other gives an instance.

These exemplifications, or "labels," to use the tax collectors' term, are useful, I admit.* Provide examples of praiseworthy conduct, and someone will be found to copy it. **67** Do you think it would be useful to be given criteria for recognizing a thoroughbred horse, to avoid being cheated as the purchaser and not waste time on a poor one? How much more useful to know the distinguishing marks of an outstanding mind! One can transfer them from another to oneself. **68**

> You'll know at once the foal of noble stock.
> He prances in the fields; he lightly plants
> his feet. He is the first who dares advance,
> dares risk the threatening floods, entrusts himself
> to the unknown bridge, not flinching at mere sounds.
> Long in the neck and with a shapely head,
> short flanks, a sturdy back; his chest is broad
> for breathing, and is richly muscled.
>                          If a distant clash of arms
> should reach him, he is on the move, his ears
> prick up, his limbs are quivering, and he snorts
> his nostrils, gathering his inward fire.*

**69** Our poet Virgil, while treating something else, has delineated the courageous man. I myself would employ no other image for a hero. If I had to describe Cato, fearless amid the clash of civil wars, the first to confront the armies already positioned at the Alps, and braving the perils of civil war himself, this is precisely the expression and demeanor I would give him.* **70** No one, in fact, could have "pranced" higher than he did when, simultaneously facing Caesar and Pompey, with everyone else supporting one side or the other, he challenged both leaders and showed that the Republic too had someone to back it. In Cato's case, it is obviously an understatement to say "not flinching at mere sounds." Why should he, when he does not flinch at real threats near at hand? In opposition to ten legions, Gallic auxiliaries, and a combined force of citizens and foreigners, he speaks his mind freely, urging the Republic not to fail in the cause of liberty but to try everything, since it is more honorable to fall into slavery than to enter into it. **71** What energy and spirit he displays, what confidence amid the general panic! He knows that he is the only one whose status is not at issue. The question is not whether Cato is free but whether he is among the free. Hence his contempt for dangers and swords. In admiration for the man's indomitable resolution, holding his ground while his country collapses, it is a pleasure to quote the words "his chest is broad for breathing, and is richly muscled."

**72** It will be helpful not only to state a good man's typical qualities, with a description of his character and features, but to give an account of what such men have been like—Cato's final and supremely courageous wound through which freedom dispatched his spirit; Laelius's wisdom and his amity with his friend Scipio; the splendid deeds of the other Cato at home and abroad; Tubero's wooden couches when he was spreading them out for public feast, with goatskins in place of coverlets and earthenware utensils laid out for the banquets in front of Jupiter's very shrine.* In a word, he gave poverty a sacred place on the Capitol. Although I know no other act by Tubero to rank him with the Catos, do we find this one insufficient? He was not throwing a party but practicing official parsimony. **73** People lusting for glory are so ignorant of what it really is or how it should be sought. On that day there were many whose furnishings were viewed by the Roman public, but only one at whom they marveled. The gold and silver of all the others has been broken up and melted down countless times, but Tubero's earthenware will last forever.

Farewell.

# BOOK SIXTEEN

# Letter 96

*From Seneca to Lucilius*
*Greetings*

1 You are still annoyed about something; you still complain. Don't
you realize that the only really bad thing here is your annoyance and
complaining? If you ask my opinion, nothing can be terrible for a
man unless there is something in the natural course of things that
he thinks is terrible. The day I can't stand something will be the day
I can no longer stand myself. "I am ill." That was bound to happen
to me. "My household staff have taken to their sickbeds, my income
has gone down, my house is creaking; I have been assailed by losses,
pains, work, and anxieties." That happens, or rather, it was bound to
happen. These things are predetermined, they are no accident.

2 Believe me, I am now disclosing my inmost feelings to you. In
everything that seems hostile and hard I have trained myself to be
like this: I don't obey God, I agree with him. I follow him by my own
choice, not because I must. Whatever happens to me I will accept
without getting sad or showing a gloomy face. I will willingly pay all
my taxes. All the things that make us groan and get frightened are
just life's taxes. You should not expect or seek exemption from them,
dear Lucilius.

3 You were troubled by pain in your bladder, you received worrying letters, your losses continued—let me get to the point, you feared
for your life. Well, didn't you know that in praying for old age, you
were praying for these things? A long life contains them all, just as
a long journey contains dust, mud, and rain. 4 "I did want to go on
living, but without all these problems." Such an effeminate tone is a
disgrace to a man. Take it as you will, but here is the prayer I make
for you—and I do it not only with all goodwill but also with all
seriousness: "May neither gods nor goddesses keep you in the lap
of luxury." Ask yourself: if some god gave you the choice, would you
rather live in the food market or in the military camp? Life, Lucilius,
is a campaign. That is why those who endure the trials, march uphill

and down through rough country, and put themselves into the most dangerous sorties are the heroes and leaders of the camp. The ones who are quietly rotting away at ease, while others do the hard work, are turtledoves: they are only safe because they are despised.

Farewell.

## Letter 97

*From Seneca to Lucilius*
*Greetings*

1 You are mistaken, dear Lucilius, if you think that our era is particularly culpable for self-indulgence and for neglect of high moral standards. One likes to blame such deficiencies on one's own times, but in reality it is not the times that are at fault but the people. No era has ever been free of blame. Indeed, if you begin to assess the iniquity of every age, I am ashamed to tell you that misconduct has never been more in evidence than it was in the time of Cato and in his very presence. 2 It's hard to believe, but money changed hands when Publius Clodius was tried for secret adultery with Caesar's wife.* Clodius had committed sacrilege against the ceremonial sacrifice which is said to be performed "for the people" and which is supposed to involve such an extreme exclusion of every male from the precinct that even pictures of male animals are covered up. And yet the jurors were bribed and—still more shocking—to sweeten the deal, married women and youths of noble birth were made to have sex with them. 3 The charge was less heinous than the acquittal. The one who had been accused of adultery instigated multiple adulteries, and only secured his own safety by making the jury as guilty as himself. This all took place at the proceedings where Cato gave evidence, though that was all he did. I will quote Cicero's words, because the facts would otherwise be incredible:

4 He invited the jurors over, made promises to them, pleaded with them, and bribed them. But by god! there was still worse to come: as the ultimate reward, some of the jury were offered

nights with specific women and assignations with youths of noble birth.*

5 The bribe was bad enough, but the extras were still more shocking. "That straitlaced fellow—would you like to have his wife? I will give her to you. That rich man, how about his? I'll see to it that she sleeps with you. If you don't get somebody's wife, then vote to convict me! That beauty you desire—she'll come to you. I promise you a night with her, and I'll be quick about it. My promise will be fulfilled within the two-day court recess." Arranging adulteries is more immoral than committing them, since it involves putting pressure on respectable married women. 6 Clodius's jury had sought protection from the Senate—which was necessary only if they were going to convict—and their request was granted. That's why, after the defendant was acquitted, Catulus amusingly told the jury: "Why did you ask us for protection? Was it so that your bribes would not be confiscated?"* Amid these jokes, a man got off who before his trial was an adulterer and during it a pimp. What he did to escape conviction was worse than what he did to deserve it.

7 Do you believe that anything has ever been more depraved than the moral standards of people impervious to restraint by religion or by courts of law, people who, in the special senatorial proceedings, committed a greater crime than the one being investigated? The question at stake was whether someone guilty of adultery could remain at liberty. What came out was the fact that such a person could not be acquitted without recourse to adultery. 8 This was negotiated in the presence of Pompey and Caesar, in the presence of Cicero and Cato. Mind you, this is the same Cato in whose presence the populace is said to have stopped asking for performances from the strippers at the festival of Flora.* If you can believe it, the audiences of that time had stricter standards than the juries!

Such things will be as they have been before; but while civic decadence will sometimes subside under pressure and fear, it will never do so of its own accord. 9 You should not suppose, then, that our time has yielded more to lust than any other, or less to the laws. The youth of today is much more disciplined than it was then, when an accused person denied an adultery charge before his jury, while the jury confessed to the same before him; when orgies were held to settle the case; when a Clodius, benefiting from the same vices that he was guilty of, arranged liaisons during the actual conduct of the case. Would anyone believe this—that a man undergoing trial for a single adultery could be acquitted by means of many adulteries?

10 The likes of Clodius are to be found in every age; the likes of Cato are not. We tend toward the worse, because there's always someone to lead the way and someone to follow. And even without them, the act goes on apace. We don't just incline toward wrongdoing, we dive right in. In other skills, mistakes are an embarrassment to the craftsman, who is upset by his errors; in life, wrongdoing is a source of positive delight. It's this that makes most people impossible to correct. 11 A helmsman doesn't get pleasure from an upturned vessel, or a physician from his patient's funeral, or an attorney if he loses the case for his defendant, but everyone enjoys his own immorality. One man takes delight in an adulterous affair, excited by the very difficulty of it; another gets a thrill out of forgery and theft and only reproaches himself when his luck fails. We have become accustomed to behaving badly, and this is the result.

12 On the other hand, all people do conceal their misdeeds. However well those things turn out, they hide the facts while they enjoy the profits. That tells you that even people who have gone utterly astray still have some sense of what's right; they are not ignorant of what's wrong, they just disregard it. But a good conscience wants to come into the open and be seen; wickedness fears even the dark. 13 That is why I think Epicurus put it well when he said: "A wrongdoer may happen to remain concealed, but he cannot be confident of concealment." A better way to express this thought would be "Wrongdoers gain nothing from concealment, because even if they have the good fortune to be concealed, they don't have the confidence of remaining so."* In other words, crimes cannot be safe. 14 This view is not inconsistent with our Stoic school, in my opinion, if we elucidate it in this way. How so? Because the first and greatest punishment for wrongdoers is the fact of having done wrong. No crime, even one embellished with the gifts of fortune or protected and safeguarded thereby, is free from punishment, since the penalty for crime lies in the crime. But even so, these secondary penalties—constant

fear, dread, and distrust of security—follow right on the heels of that primary one. Why should I free wickedness from this punishment? Why should I not leave it in perpetual suspense?

**15** We should disagree with Epicurus when he says that there is nothing that is just by nature, and that the reason one should refrain from misdeeds is that one cannot avoid the anxiety resulting from them; we should agree with him, though, that the wrongdoer is tormented by conscience and that his worst penalty is to bear the hounding and the lash of constant worry, because he cannot trust those who guarantee him security. This is proof in itself, Epicurus, that we have a natural horror of misdeeds: every criminal is afraid, even in a place of safety. **16** Fortune exempts many from punishment, but none from anxiety. Why, if not because we have an innate aversion to what nature has condemned? The reason one can never be sure that concealment will be successful is that conscience convicts people and reveals them to themselves. Wrongdoers are characteristically filled with dread. Since many crimes escape the retribution of the law and the designated penalties, we would be in a very bad way if it were not that such offenses are naturally and heavily penalized from our immediate resources, with fear taking the place of punishment.

Farewell.

## Letter 98

*From Seneca to Lucilius*
*Greetings*

**1** You should never take someone who depends on fortune to be fortunate. He who relies on happenstance has but a flimsy support for his gladness: a joy that has come in will go out. But the joy that arises from oneself is reliable and strong; it grows; it stays with us right to the end.* The other objects that are commonly admired are just goods for the day. "So can't they be both useful and pleasurable?" Of course they can, provided they depend on us, and not we on them.

**2** All the things that fortune favors become fruitful and pleasant only if those who possess them are also in possession of themselves and not in the power of their property. It is a mistake, Lucilius, to judge fortune responsible for anything that is good or bad for us. Fortune merely gives us the material for good and bad things—the preliminaries for what will turn out to be either good or bad within us.* For the mind is more powerful than every act of fortune: by itself the mind guides its affairs one way or the other, and is the cause of a happy or unhappy life for itself. 3 A bad mind turns everything into bad, even things that have arrived looking excellent. A mind that is upright and sound corrects fortune's wrongs, softens its hardness and roughness with the knowledge of how to endure, receives prosperity with gratitude and moderation, and shows firmness and fortitude in face of adversity. You could be sensible, do everything with good judgment and never exceed your strength, but you will not achieve the good that is sound and beyond threat unless you are secure in dealing with what is insecure.

4 Whether you want to look at other people (since we are more open in judging things that don't touch us personally) or take an unprejudiced look at yourself, you will perceive and admit that not one of your treasured possessions is useful unless you train yourself to resist the instability of chance and its consequences, unless you uncomplainingly repeat at each of your misfortunes,

The gods decided otherwise.*

5 Or rather, if you would like a braver and more appropriate formula to strengthen your mind, then whenever something turns out differently from what you were expecting, say, "The gods made a better decision." One who has such a disposition will find nothing amiss. That's the disposition a person will have if he considers the possible vicissitudes of the human condition before he feels any of them, if he does not regard his children, spouse, and property as permanent possessions or as a source of unhappiness if he should lose them in the future. 6 A mind that is anxious about the future and unhappy before misfortune even arrives is a disaster, concerned that the things it delights in should last forever. It will never be in repose, and in its anticipation of what is to come it will lose the present things that it could enjoy. The fear of losing something is equivalent to the pain of its loss.

**7** This does not mean that I am telling you to be negligent. By all means avoid what is frightening, guard against whatever you can by planning, watch out for anything that could do you harm, and avoid it long before it happens. Confidence and a mind steeled to endure everything will be your best recourse. He who can bear misfortune can also take precautions against it—and surely he will not be alarmed while the sea is still calm. Nothing is more wretched or more silly than premature fear. What madness it is to anticipate one's own trouble! **8** In short, to summarize my point and give you a characterization of those frenetic types who are a burden to themselves, they are just as upset before their troubles as they are when they experience them. Those who suffer before there is need suffer more than they need to.

The same weakness is responsible both for the failure to make a correct assessment of actual suffering and for the failure to anticipate it. The same lack of self-discipline causes people both to imagine that their good luck will last forever and to predict that their gains will not only last but increase. Forgetting this trampoline that bounces human affairs up and down, they suppose that for them alone, chance will be consistent.

**9** This is why I think Metrodorus spoke excellently in that letter he addressed to his sister on the loss of her very promising son: "Every good thing for mortal beings is likewise mortal."* He was referring to the goods that people flock to; for the true good, wisdom and virtue, does not perish but is secure and everlasting. This is the one immortal thing that can accrue to mortals. **10** Yet people are so flawed and so heedless of the destination to which the passage of each day is pushing them that they are caught by surprise when they lose something, even though on a single day they will lose everything. Those things you are considered to own are in your home, but they are not yours. Nothing is secure for the insecure, nothing is lasting and invincible for a person who is fragile. It is not only our property that has to go: it is ourselves too; and this very fact, if only we understand it, is consoling. Be calm when something goes: you must go as well.

**11** What help do we find, then, to counter these losses? Just this— that we hold what we have lost in our memory and don't allow the pleasure we have experienced from them to perish with them. We can be robbed of "having," but never of "having had." It is thoroughly ungrateful, after losing something, to have no sense of obligation for what one has received. Chance strips us of ownership, but lets us use things for a while; we lose even that enjoyment if we resort to wrongful longing.

**12** Tell yourself, "These things that seem so terrifying can all be overcome." Many people have overcome particular trials: Mucius overcame fire, Regulus torture, Socrates poison, Rutilius exile, and Cato death by the sword.* Let us too overcome something. **13** Conversely, things that commonly attract the crowd by their appearance of good fortune have often even been spurned by many people. Fabricius as a general refused wealth, and as a censor he gave it official disapproval.* Tubero judged poverty appropriate both to himself and to the Capitol: by using earthenware dishes at a public feast, he showed that a human being should be satisfied with what the gods were still using at that time. The elder Sextius rejected honors. By birth he should have held public office, but he refused the rank of senator when Julius Caesar offered it to him.* He knew that what can be given can also be taken away. Let us too, for our part, do something in a spirited way. Let us be included among the exemplary. **14** Why have we given up? Why have we lost hope? Whatever could be done in the past can still be done, provided that we cleanse our minds and follow nature. In straying from nature, one is bound to desire, to fear, and to become a slave to fortune. We can get back on track, we can recover a sound condition. Let us recover in order that we may endure whatever pains attack our body and say to fortune, "You're fighting with a man here! Go find somebody you can beat!"
 <. . .>*

**15** These and similar conversations are relieving the intensity of the ulcer. I sincerely hope that it is lessening and either being cured or else staying still and growing old with the patient himself. Actually, though, I am not worried about him. What concerns me is our loss in being robbed of an excellent old man. He himself has lived a full life. He doesn't want anything added to it for his own sake, but only for those to whom he is useful. **16** It is generous of him to go on living. Someone else would have put an end to these torments. But he thinks it is as shameful to take refuge in death as to flee from it.* "Very well, but will he not leave if the situation warrants that?"

Of course he would leave if no one could still make use of him, and if he had nothing to deal with except pain. **17** This, dear Lucilius, is learning philosophy on the job and practicing it for real: seeing what courage an intelligent man has in facing death and pain, when the one approaches and the other presses hard.

We must learn what to do from someone who is already doing it. Up to now we have been merely arguing about whether someone can withstand pain or whether the arrival of death can depress even the most courageous people. What need for more words? Let us proceed to the present case. Death does not make this man braver in facing pain, nor does pain make him braver in facing death. He relies on himself in both cases. The hope of death does not make his pain more bearable, and he does not die more gladly because he is tired of pain. He endures the one, and awaits the other.

Farewell.

## Letter 99

*From Seneca to Lucilius*
*Greetings*

**1** Enclosed is the letter I wrote to Marullus after he lost his infant son and I had word that he was taking it hard. In it I did not take the usual approach: I thought that I ought not to handle him gently, since he merited reproach rather than consolation.* For when a person has trouble dealing with some great affliction, one should make concessions for a little while, until grief expends itself or at least exhausts its initial force; but those who take it upon themselves to grieve should be reprimanded at the outset and should learn that even tears can sometimes be ridiculous.

**2** Do you expect solace? Here is chastisement. Are you so soft in bearing the death of your son? What would you be doing if you had lost a friend? The son who died was an uncertain hope, a tiny creature; only a little time died with him. **3** We go looking for reasons to grieve; we wish to complain of our lot even when it is unfair to do so, as if we were never to have just cause to complain. And yet, in truth, you had always seemed to me brave enough to handle even substantial misfortunes, let alone those illusory troubles at which people groan for the sake of custom. If you had suffered the greatest loss of all—that is, if you had lost a friend—even then your endeavor should have been to rejoice in having had a friend rather than grieve over having lost one.

4 But most people do not consider what great blessings they have received, what great joys they have experienced. This is one of the reasons why your grief is bad: not only is it pointless, but it is ungrateful too. Was it wasted effort, then, to have had such a friend? So many years together, so much that you had in common, such companionship in your shared pursuits; is that all for nothing? Do you bury the friendship along with the friend? And why do you mourn the loss if you have gained nothing by what you had? Believe me: the people we have loved remain with us in large part even after chance has taken them away. The time that is past is ours; nothing is more secure than what has already been. 5 Our hopes for the future make us ungrateful for what we have already received, forgetting that even if that hoped-for future ever comes, it too will swiftly become the past. He who takes pleasure only in the present moment puts too tight a restriction on his enjoyment of life. Both the future and the past have pleasure to give, the one in expectation, the other in memory; but the future is contingent and may never be, while the past cannot fail to have been. What madness it is, then, to allow the most secure of all your possessions to slip from your grasp! Let us find contentment in what we have already drawn from the well—provided our minds are not leaky sieves that let everything drain right through them.*

6 There are countless examples of people who have lost children in the flourishing time of youth and have come directly from the funeral into the Senate or some other public place and fulfilled their responsibilities immediately and without tears. And they were right: first of all, because there is no point in grieving if nothing is to be gained by it; second, because it is unreasonable to complain about what has happened to one person when the same end awaits us all; third, because it is foolish to object to a

loss when so little separates us from what we have lost. We should be all the more level-headed, because we ourselves are following the departed. **7** Consider how rapidly time speeds along; think how short the distance is that we traverse so quickly; look what a great assembly of humankind is headed in the same direction, with only short intervals between us, even when they seem long. The one you think of as lost has only gone on ahead. What could be more absurd than to weep for one who has traveled on along a road you too must take? **8** Does anyone weep over an event that he knew all along was going to happen? Or did he not realize that a human being is mortal? If he didn't, he was deceiving himself. Anyone who complains that a person has died is complaining that that person was human. We all live under the same condition: he who is born must eventually die. There are intervals between us, but the ending makes equals of us all.

**9** What comes between our first day and our last is variable and uncertain. If you measure it by our troubles, it is long even for a child; if by its rapidity, it is too short even for the old. Everything is dangerous and deceptive and more changeable than the weather; everything tumbles about and passes at fortune's behest into its opposite; and in all this tumult of human affairs there is nothing we can be sure of except death alone. Yet everyone complains of this, the one thing in which there is no deceit.

**10** "But he died when he was only a boy." I am not saying at this point that the person whose life ends quickly is better off. Instead, let us consider the person who has reached old age. How small an advantage he has over the infant! Just imagine the vast extent of time: embrace the universe in thought, and then compare that immeasurable span with what we call a human life, and you will see how small a thing it is that we yearn for and wish to prolong. And how much of that is taken up with tears and anxieties! **11** How much with wishing for death before it comes! How much with illness! How much with fear! How much belongs to helpless infancy or to useless old age! Why, half of it is spent in sleep. Add our sufferings, griefs, and dangers, and you will realize that even in the longest life we have only a little time to live.

**12** Is a person really worse off just because it is granted to him to die sooner? Who will concede that? His journey was over before fatigue set in. Life in itself is neither good nor bad; it is only the setting for good and bad. So he lost nothing but dice that were weighted against him. He might have turned out to be temperate and intelligent; he might have been shaped in a good way by your care; but the likelier expectation is that he would have turned out like most other people.* **13** Look: self-indulgence has taken young men from the noblest households and cast them out into the dust. Their own lust and that of others have involved them in immoral conduct. Not a day goes by for them without drunkenness or some egregious offense. It is evident that there was greater potential for fear than for hope.

So you ought not to go out of your way for reasons to grieve; and neither should you aggravate minor misfortunes by getting upset over them. **14** I am not urging you to strive for the heights: I do not have such a low opinion of you as to think you need summon all your courage against this event. What you feel is not grief but only a biting: it is you who are making it into grief.* A great lot of good philosophy has done you, if your strength of mind consists in missing a boy who was better known to his wet nurse than to his father!

**15** What's this? Am I now advocating harshness? Do I want your countenance to be frozen even at the funeral ceremony—do I forbid you even to experience a contraction of mind? Not at all. That is inhumanity, not virtue: looking on the bodies of your loved ones with the same expression as beheld them in life, failing to be moved at the first moment when your family is wrenched apart.* But suppose I did forbid it: some things are independent of our command. Tears fall even when we try to suppress them, and shedding them is a relief to the mind.

**16** What is it, then? Let's allow them to fall, but not summon them up. Let what flows be what emotion forces from us, not what is required to imitate others. Let's not add anything to our genuine mourning, increasing it to follow someone else's example. The show of grief demands more of us than grief itself requires. How often do you find someone who is sad on his own account? The sobs are louder when someone is looking. When people are by themselves, they make not a sound; then, when someone comes in, they burst afresh into paroxysms of grief. It is then that they strike themselves on the head (which they could have done more easily with no one grabbing their wrists); then that they invoke death on their own heads; then that they roll off the couch onto the floor. Without a spectator, grief comes to an end. **17** In this as in other matters we are beset with the vice of shaping our own conduct to the example of others, paying regard not to necessity but to custom. We depart from nature, giving ourselves over to the common crowd, which is never a good example and is hugely inconsistent in this as in everything else. When they see someone bearing his grief courageously, they call him unloving and a brute; when they see someone collapsed prostrate over the body, they say he is womanish and weak. All such things ought to be brought back to the standard of reason. **18** But nothing is more foolish than seeking a reputation for sorrow, giving one's approval to tears.

The wise man too sheds tears, I believe, sometimes when he allows them to flow and sometimes when they well up of their own accord.* I will explain the difference. When we are first assailed by the news of an untimely death, when we are holding the body that is soon to pass directly from our embrace into the flames, tears are squeezed out of us by a necessity of nature: just as the breath, when struck by grief's blow, shakes the entire body, so does it press upon and expel the moisture in the vicinity of the eyes. **19** These tears are shed due to internal pressure and involuntarily. There are others, though, to which we give egress when we revisit the memory of those we have lost and find an element of sweetness in our sorrow—when we think of their pleasant conversation, their cheerful company, their devoted service. At that time, the eyes release their tears, just as in joy. These we indulge; the others conquer us. **20** So you need not hold back your tears because another person is standing near, or sitting at your side; nor should you make yourself cry because of them: neither tears nor the lack of tears is ever as shameful as when tears are feigned. Let them come of their own accord.

One can be tranquil and composed even in the midst of tears. The wise have often shed tears without detriment to their moral standing and with such restraint as to maintain both dignity and humanity. **21** I repeat: one can be obedient to nature and still maintain one's decorum. I have seen people who command respect even at the funeral of a family member, when love showed on their faces without any false semblance of grieving, and all that was there was stirred by genuine emotion. There is seemliness even in grief, and that is something the wise person must preserve. Enough is enough, in tears as in everything else. Excessive griefs, like excessive joys, belong to the foolish.

**22** Accept calmly whatever you must. What has happened that is unbelievable or new? How many funerals are being arranged at this very moment! How many grave wrappings are being purchased! How many people are still grieving after you have finished! Every time you remember that he was a child, remember also that he was a human being, and hence without definite prospects. Fortune does not necessarily escort us all the way to old age, but dismisses us when it sees fit.

**23** Speak of him often, however, and celebrate his memory as much as you can: it will return to you more frequently if it comes without bitterness, for no one is eager to spend time with a sad person, let alone with sadness itself. If there were any little things he used to say, any babyish jokes that gave you pleasure, repeat them often. Insist boldly that he could have fulfilled the expectations that you as a father had conceived for him. **24** Forgetting one's own, burying their memory with their bodies, weeping profusely but remembering them hardly at all, is evidence of inhumanity. That is how birds and beasts of the wild love their young: their affection is agitated and almost rabid; but when the object of it dies, it too perishes utterly. Such behavior is not appropriate in a sensible man. Let him cease grieving but persevere in remembering.

**25** I do not by any means approve of what Metrodorus says, that there is a pleasure that is akin to sorrow, and that in situations like this one should try to catch hold of that pleasure.* Metrodorus's exact words are as follows: "From Metrodorus's letters to his sister. 'For there is a pleasure akin to grief that one ought to go hunting for in this situation.'" **26** I am not in any doubt as to what view you will take of these words. For what could be more shameful than to try to catch pleasure in the very midst of grief—indeed, through grief—and to go looking for something delightful even amid one's tears? And these are the people who reproach us for excessive rigor and complain that our teachings are harsh, just because we say one should either not admit grief into the mind or else cast it out quickly. Which, pray tell, is harder to believe, and which is less human: not to feel grief when one loses a friend, or to try to snare a pleasure right in the midst of grief?

**27** What we teach is honorable: that after emotion has wrung some tears from us and is, as it were, off the boil, one should not give the mind over to grief.* Really, are you serious in saying that pleasure should be mixed right in with grief? That's how we comfort children, by giving them a cookie, or quiet a crying baby with a drink of milk!

Will you not allow pleasure to cease even in the moment when a son is burning on the pyre, when a friend is breathing his last? Are we to be titillated even by our mourning? Which is more honorable: to eliminate grief from the mind, or to let pleasure in to the very midst of grief? Did I say "let pleasure in"? He actually tries to snatch pleasure from out of grief itself. **28** He says, "There is a pleasure akin to grief." That is something we Stoics are allowed to say; you are not. You acknowledge only one form of good, namely pleasure, and only one thing that is bad, namely pain. How can there be any kinship between good and bad? But suppose there is: is this a fit moment to dig it out? Do we scrutinize grief itself to see if there is something sweet and pleasant about it? **29** There are medical treatments that are beneficial for some parts of the body but cannot be used on others because they are considered ugly and embarrassing. What might be helpful in one spot becomes shameful merely because of where the wound is located. Are you not ashamed to use pleasure as a remedy for grief? That laceration needs a more rigorous treatment.

Remind us instead how one who has perished has no awareness of anything bad; for if he has awareness, he has not perished.* **30** I repeat: one who is no more is not hurt by anything, for if he is being hurt, he is alive. Which do you think bothers him: his nonexistence, or some continued existence? But nonexistence can hardly be a torment to him: how can one be aware of nothing? Nor can he be tormented by a continued existence, for then he has escaped the worst disadvantage of death, which is that one ceases to exist.

**31** To the person who is weeping and longing for one who was snatched away in youth, let's say this as well: young or old, every life is equally short when compared with that of the universe. For any possible lifespan is less even than what one would call a tiny bit. A tiny bit is at least something, but this life of ours is practically nothing. And yet we share it with all and sundry. What fools we are!

**32** In writing this for you, I did not suppose that you were looking to me for a belated remedy, for I am sure you have already said all these things to yourself. My purpose was, rather, to chide you for having forgotten yourself for a short time, and to encourage you to be bold against fortune hereafter. You should regard all its blows not as possibilities but as eventual certainties.

Farewell.

## Letter 100

*From Seneca to Lucilius*
*Greetings*

**1** In your letter you tell me that you found Papirius Fabianus's book *On Politics* an absorbing read but ultimately disappointing.* Then, forgetting that it is a work of philosophy, you criticize its composition.

Suppose you are right—that he lets the words gush out without arranging them. For a start, that has its own charm; it's a style appropriate to a smoothly running discourse. There is a big difference, I think, between careless writing and fluent writing. **2** And there is yet a further distinction to be made, a very important one: Fabianus, as I see it, lets his discourse flow, but he doesn't release a flood: his language is copious, but it moves right along without ever losing control. From the outset, it gives the impression of not having been worked over or revised to death. But even if we go by your assessment, his objective was to set our conduct in order, not our words; he wrote this work for the mind, not the ear. 3 Besides, if he had been speaking in person, you would not have had time to study the details, for you would have been captivated by the speech as a whole. Material that we like because of the speaker's energy is generally less attractive when we read it. Still, it is quite something to catch a person's eye at first glance, even if careful scrutiny will find some faults. 4 In my opinion, the speaker who reaches out and grabs our approval is greater than the one who has to earn it. But I realize that the latter is a surer bet and gives a more confident promise of future achievement.

Meticulous discourse does not suit a philosopher. If someone is timid in his words, when will he be brave and resolute or put his own person at risk? 5 Fabianus was not careless in his manner of speaking; rather, he was unconcerned. That is why you will find nothing uncouth in his style: his expressions are well chosen but never strained. Contrary to current fashion, he does not invert the natural word order, but his phrasing, though taken from everyday speech, is very fine. You get noble and splendid ideas from him; they have not been forced into aphorisms, but are expansively worded. We can find things that are not sufficiently concise or that are poorly constructed or inelegant by today's standards. But all in all, there is no sign of any meaningless refinement. 6 To be sure, one may miss the many different colors of marble, the plumbing that sends a supply of water into the bedrooms, the pauper's cell, and everything else that our luxurious tastes supply because we are dissatisfied with simple attractiveness.* But, as the saying goes, it's a well-built house.

There is the further point that opinions about style differ. Some people want style to be stripped of all roughness, others like it to be so rugged that they even deliberately disrupt sentences that happen to have been expressed more smoothly, and break off concluding phrases so that they don't accord with one's expectations. 7 Read Cicero: his style is all of a piece. When at length he rounds off a sentence, the manner is gentle and yet not effeminate. By contrast, the style of Asinius Pollio is jerky and abrupt, stopping when you least expect it. In Cicero there is always closure, but in Pollio things just break off, except in the very few cases that conform to a definite rhythm and a uniform pattern.*

8 You also say that you find his entire work flat and insufficiently elevated, but I don't find this blemish in him. His style is not flat but

temperate, fashioned to suit his mind's calm and orderly disposition; it is level, not low. It does lack rhetorical intensity, the provocations you are looking for, and the sudden impact of aphorisms. But taken as a whole, the work, whatever you think of its artistry, is noble. His style does not possess distinction, but will bestow it.

9 What writer can you name that you find preferable to Fabianus? Mention Cicero, whose books on philosophy are almost as numerous as those of Fabianus. I will concede, but something is not immediately puny because it is below the greatest. Mention Asinius Pollio: I will concede, and simply reply that in so great a field, it is quite something to come out third. You may also adduce Livy: his writings include dialogues (works that are as historical as they are philosophical) and books that deal specifically with philosophy.* I will make room for him too. Yet observe how many Fabianus outstrips in being surpassed by just three writers, the three great masters of style.

10 Still, he does not exhibit every quality. Though his style is lofty, it is not bold, and while it is capacious, it lacks impetuosity and force; it is clear rather than brilliant. "One misses," you say, "a harsh denunciation of vices, a spirited response to dangers, a proud retort to fortune, and a scornful attack on ambition. I want luxury to be reprimanded, debauchery pilloried, and aggression crushed. Let us have something of oratory's sting, tragedy's grandeur, and comedy's plainness." You want him to focus on words, which are a puny thing. He has allied himself with the greatness of his topic; rather than advertising his eloquence, he draws it after him like a shadow. 11 To be sure, there will be gaps in what he covers, loosely written passages and words that fail to arouse and provoke us. I admit all this. Many sentences will go by without striking us, and sometimes his style will be sloppy and too discursive. But there will be lots of light throughout and large stretches free from tedium. Finally, he will succeed in showing you that he really believes what he has written. You will realize that his aim is for you to know his views, not for him to please you. All his work has progress as its goal, and excellence of mind. It does not look for applause.

12 I have no doubt that his writings are like this, although I do not recall them in great detail. What sticks with me is a general impression of their tone, as when one has known someone a long time but has not recently had a close conversation with him. Certainly

when I heard him, that's how I found his work, not flawless but rich, such as might inspire a promising young man to imitate him while hoping also to surpass him. This I find the most effective type of encouragement. It is disheartening when one is moved to imitate an author but despairs of doing so. In any case, Fabianus was abundantly expressive, and though open to criticism at some passages, overall he was splendid.

Farewell.

# BOOK SEVENTEEN

# *Letter 101*

*From Seneca to Lucilius*
*Greetings*

**1** Every day and every hour reveals how negligible we are, reminding us, with some fresh proof, that we have forgotten our fragility. The passage of time compels us to think about death just as we are reflecting on eternity.

What is this preamble getting at, you wonder? Cornelius Senecio, a prominent and conscientious Roman equestrian—you knew him.* From a humble beginning he had risen high by his own efforts. His future success was going to be an easy ride, because prestige is easier to increase than it is to acquire in the first place. **2** Money too is very slow to accumulate from poverty: until it creeps out of that condition, it doesn't grow. But Senecio was at the point of achieving wealth, assisted by two very effective qualities he possessed: he knew how to get money and he knew how to keep it. Either of those could have made him rich. **3** Here was a person who lived very simply, as careful with his estate as he was with his health. He had visited me in the morning, as he generally did, and then spent the whole day up till evening at the bedside of a friend who was seriously ill. After being quite cheerful at dinner, Senecio had a sudden attack of angina that left him with a swollen throat and scarcely able to breathe until dawn. So he died, only a very few hours after performing all the duties of a sound and healthy man. **4** While privately investing at home and abroad, and engaging in every type of public business in pursuit of profit, just at the moment when everything was going his way and with money flooding in, he was carried off.

Now is the time to plant your pears, O Meliboeus;
  now is the time to put your vines in order.*

How foolish it is to plan out one's life when one is not even master of tomorrow! What madness it is to undertake lengthy projects, saying:

"I will buy and build, I will make loans and demand them back, I will hold public offices, and then I will retire to enjoy a long and leisurely old age." 5 Everything is uncertain, believe me, even for those who are fortunate. No one should make himself any promises concerning the future. The very thing we are grasping can slip through our hands, and the moment that we are seizing can be cut short by chance. There is a regularity to the flow of time, but we ourselves are left in the dark. What can I make of nature's certainty if my own affairs are uncertain? 6 We plan distant voyages and delayed homecomings after traveling beside foreign shores, we plan a military career and the long-awaited payments earned by tough campaigning, we plan provincial governorships and advancement through the ranks. Meanwhile, death is at our side, but we never think of it except when it is someone else's; we meet with instances of mortality all the time, but they stick in our minds only as long as they surprise us. 7 What is more foolish than being surprised that an event that could happen on every day has happened on a particular day? There is an absolute termination to human life at the point fixed by our fate's implacable necessity, but not one of us knows how close he is getting to that termination. Let us, then, compose our minds as if we have reached the end. Let us not put anything off: let us settle our accounts with life each and every day.

8 The biggest problem with our lives is that they are always unfinished, that some part of them is always being postponed. By putting the final touch on one's life every day, you don't lack time. It is this lack that generates fear and gnawing desire for the future. Nothing is more wretched than worrying about how things are going to turn out. We are constantly in the grip of panic as to how much is left or what the future holds. 9 How shall we escape this turmoil? There is only one way—by not allowing our life to look to the future but gathering it into itself. People hang on the future because they are frustrated by the present. But once my debt to myself has been paid and my mind has firmly accepted the fact that there is no difference between a day and an era, it can take a long view of all the days and things that are to come, and merrily contemplate the whole extent of time. If one is firm in one's attitude to uncertainty, why should one be disturbed by the fluctuation and instability of fortune?

10 And so, dear Lucilius, make haste to live, and treat each day as

a life in itself. A person who prepares himself like this, making the daily round his entire life, is quite secure. Those who live on hope find every present moment slipping away; they are taken over by greed and the fear of death, a most miserable state that makes everything else quite miserable. This was the basis for Maecenas's utterly shocking prayer in which he accepts infirmity, deformity, and ultimately a piercing crucifixion,* provided that amid these sufferings he can extend his life:

> 11 Make me feeble of hand,
> make me feeble of foot;
> put a hump on my back
> make me lose all my teeth—
> while there's life in my body, I'm fine.
> Let me live, let me live,
> though I sit on the point of the cross;
> let me live.*

12 Here is a prayer that would have been most dreadful if it had been fulfilled, a request to protract suffering as if that were life. I would have thought him completely worthless if he had really been willing to continue up to crucifixion. Listen to what he says: "You can weaken me as long as some breath remains in my broken and useless body; you can deform me as long as I get some extra time in my monstrous and twisted condition; you can hang me up and impale me on a cross." Is it worth so much to press on one's own wound—to hang spread out on a cross while delaying the best thing about suffering, namely, the end of the torment? Is it so valuable to preserve life just to breathe one's last? 13 All you could wish for this man is heaven's indulgence! What is he getting at with this shameful and womanish verse, this bargaining with the most abject fear, this foul begging for life? I don't think he could have heard Virgil reciting,

> Is death so miserable?*

Maecenas prays for suffering at its worst, and makes it still more unendurable by wanting it prolonged and endured. What does he get for that? A longer life, of course! But what kind of life is protracted dying? 14 Can we find anyone who would waste away amid sufferings, dying limb by limb and repeatedly gasping for breath, rather than expire once and for all? Can we find anyone already enfeebled, deformed, ballooning out into ugly swellings on his shoulders and chest, with many reasons for dying quite apart from crucifixion, who would even so be willing to be attached to the horrible gibbet and draw breath that is to bring with it so many tortures?

You should now admit that nature is very kind in making our death inevitable. **15** Yet many people have been ready to make much worse bargains than Maecenas—even betraying a friend, in order to prolong life, or voluntarily giving up their children into prostitution, to have the chance of seeing a daylight that is cognizant of their many crimes. We have to shake off this passion for life. We need to learn that it makes no difference when you suffer, because you are bound to suffer sooner or later. What matters is not how long you live but how well. And often, living well consists in not living long.

Farewell.

## Letter 102

*From Seneca to Lucilius*
*Greetings*

**1** It's annoying to be aroused from a pleasant dream—for the pleasure one loses, even though it's imaginary, has a genuine effect—and your letter has done me a similarly bad turn: it interrupted me when I was absorbed in the kind of musing that I find congenial and would have prolonged if given the chance. **2** I was taking delight in an inquiry into the soul's immortality; more than that, I was ready to believe in it. I was sympathizing with the opinions of those great men* who endorse this most pleasing state of affairs, though they hardly manage to prove it. I was surrendering myself to this mighty hope. Already I was beginning to hate my present existence; already I was fed up with the remnants of my feeble life. I had the prospect of passing over into that boundless time and possession of eternity—when suddenly I was awakened by the arrival of your letter, and lost this lovely dream. But if I can get rid of you, I shall look for it and get it back.

**3** The beginning of your letter insists° that I did not complete the investigation in which I was trying to prove the Stoic doctrine that posthumous renown is something good.* I failed, so you say, to resolve our opponents' objection: "No good can consist of things that are separated from each other; but this does consist of things that are separated."* **4** Your difficulty, dear Lucilius, pertains to another topic within the same investigation, so I held back not only from responding to it but also from discussing other relevant issues as well; for as you know, ethics involves some matters of logic. For this reason, I have up to now addressed the subject matter most directly relevant to ethics: whether it is foolish and unnecessary to extend one's concern beyond one's last day; or whether our goods die with us and there is nothing that belongs to one who is no more, or whether any profit can be felt or sought beforehand from that which, when it occurs, we shall not exist to perceive. **5** All these questions have a bearing on ethics, and so I have put them in their own proper place. The objections of logicians to this Stoic doctrine had to be kept apart, and so I put them aside. But now, because you are demanding the whole lot, I shall run through all the objections and then rebut them one by one.

**6** To make my rebuttals intelligible, I need to make some prefatory remarks. What do I mean? Some bodies are continuous, such as a human being. Others are composite, like a ship or a house or everything that is unified by the joining of different parts. And yet others are composed of separated parts, each of which remains a discrete member, such as an army, a population, a senate. The elements of which these latter bodies are composed are cohesive by law or by function, but by nature they are separate individuals. **7** What further prefatory remarks should I make? Our Stoic doctrine is that no good can consist of things that are separated. This is because a single good thing must be controlled and governed by a single spirit, which is to say that the directive faculty of a single good thing must itself be single.* This is intrinsically demonstrable, should you ever want proof. Meanwhile, I have had to assume it as a premise, since our own weapons are being fired against us.

**8** Thus the opponent says, "You claim that no thing that is good is composed of things that are separated. But the renown you are talking about is the favorable opinion of good men. Reputation is not one person's statement, nor is notoriety one person's negative assessment; and renown, likewise, is not a case of pleasing just one good person. In order for renown to exist, a number of distinguished and notable men must agree. Renown results from the judgments of a plurality, that is, from persons who are separated. Therefore it is not a good thing."

9 Further: "Renown is praise awarded to a good man by good men. Praise is speech, that is, a meaningful utterance. But utterance, even if it is from good men, is not itself a good thing. Even though everything about the good man is admirable and praiseworthy, it is not the case that everything done by a good man is a good. He applauds and he hisses, but no one calls the applause or the hissing a good thing, any more than they call his sneeze or his cough a good thing. Therefore renown is not a good thing.

10 "Finally, tell us whether the good belongs to the one praising or the one praised. If you say that it is the good of the one praised, you are acting as absurdly as if you declared another person's good health to be mine. But praising those who merit praise is an honorable act. Hence the good belongs to the one praising, whose action it is, and not to us who are being praised. This was the question at issue."

11 I will now run through these points one by one. To begin, there is the question of whether any good can consist of things that are separated. This is an issue that is still being investigated, and each side has its supporters. Next, does renown require a plurality of votes? No, it can even be satisfied with the judgment of a single good man: it is the good man who decides that we are good.

12 "How so?" says our opponent. "Will reputation be the esteem of a single person and notoriety the slander of one individual? Glory too I take to be more widely extended and requiring many people's agreement." But the case of reputation and notoriety is different from that of glory. Why? Because if a good man has a good opinion of me, I am in the same position as if all good men had the same view. In fact, they would all have the same view if they knew me. Their judgment is one and the same, equally marked by the truth. They cannot disagree with one another, and so it is as if they all had the same view, since it is not possible for them to take a different view. 13 When it comes to glory—that is, to reputation—one person's opinion does

not suffice.* In the one case, a single judgment can stand for all; because if all good men were asked, their judgment would be unanimous. In the other case, different people make different judgments. Agreements will be difficult to find, and the entire situation will be rife with doubt, uncertainty, and suspicion. Do you suppose that everyone can be of one mind? That does not even hold for the single individual. What decides in the case of the good man is what is true; truth has a single force and a single face. With these others, what they accept are falsehoods, which are never consistent but always subject to change and disagreement.

14 "But praise is merely an utterance, and an utterance is not something good." When those Stoics say that renown is praise awarded to the good by the good, they are referring not to an utterance but to a belief. In fact, a good man may say nothing; but if he judges someone to be praiseworthy, that person has been praised. 15 Besides, praise is not the same as eulogy, which requires utterance. Hence no one speaks of a "funeral praise" but says "eulogy," for the service performed by a eulogy consists in speaking it aloud. When we say that someone is praiseworthy, we are not promising him people's kindly words but their favorable judgments. Therefore there is praise even when someone thinks well of a good man without speaking, and praises him just to himself.

16 Further, as I have said, praise refers to an attitude of mind, not to the words that express and bring into public notice the praise one has conceived of. To praise is to judge that someone should be praised. When our tragedian says that it is splendid "to be praised by one who has been praised," he means "by one who is praiseworthy."* And when an equally ancient poet says "praise nourishes the arts," he is not speaking of eulogy, which ruins the arts. Nothing, in fact, has done as much as popular approval to corrupt rhetoric and every other practice intended for the ear. 17 A reputation certainly needs to be voiced, but renown can occur without being uttered; all that it needs is a judgment. Renown is complete not only in the company of people who are silent but even among those who shout it down. Let me tell you the difference between renown and glory: glory comes from the judgment of the masses, whereas the basis of renown is the judgment of people who are good.

18 "Whose good is renown, meaning the praise awarded by the

good to someone good? Is it the good of the one praised or of the one who praises?" It is both. It is mine, when I am praised, because I am by nature loving toward all people,* and because I am happy to have acted well and pleased to have encountered grateful communicators of my virtues. Their gratitude makes this a good pertaining to many; but it is also mine because my disposition is such that I regard the good of others as mine, at least in the case of those to whom I myself have been the cause of good. **19** The very same good also belongs to those who award the praise, since it is conducted virtuously, and every virtuous act is something good. This could not have accrued to them if I myself had not been virtuous. Thus merited praise is a good for both parties, just as good judgment is a good both for the one judging and the one who has the benefit of the judgment. Surely you agree that justice is a good both for the one who has it and for the one who is paid what is due. To praise a deserving person is justice. Therefore the good belongs to both parties.

**20** Let this be enough of a response to these quibblers. It should not be our project to discuss minutiae and drag philosophy down from its majesty into these petty matters. How much more satisfying it is to travel the straight and open road than to design detours for yourself, which you have to retrace with great trouble! Arguments of this type are nothing more than the diversions of clever debaters.

**21** Tell me, rather, how natural it is to extend one's mind into the infinite. The human mind is a great and noble thing. It allows no limits to be set to itself except those that it also shares with the divine. In the first place, it refuses any lowly homeland, such as Ephesus or Alexandria or even some more populous and well-built city. Its true homeland is one that encompasses the heights and the entirety of the world—the vault of heaven itself; within which lie both seas and lands; within which the lower air separates the human from the divine, yet also unites them; and in which so many divine powers have their fixed position and vigilantly attend to their specific functions.* **22** Secondly, the mind refuses a restricted lifetime for itself. "All the years," it says, "are mine. No epoch is closed to great intellects, no time is unavailable for reflection. When the day arrives that is to separate this mixture of divine and human, I shall leave this body here where I found it and surrender myself to the gods. Even now I am not apart from them, but I am held back by the weight of earth."

**23** All our mortal life is but a time of waiting, a prelude for that better and longer life. Our mothers' womb contains us for ten months, preparing us not for itself but for that place into which we emerge into view once we are able to draw breath and survive in the open; in the same way, during the interval that extends from infancy to old age, we are developing toward a different birth. A different beginning awaits us, a different state of affairs. **24** As yet we cannot endure the heavens except from a distance. Therefore look forward fearlessly to that critical hour. It is not the final moment of the mind, but only of the body. Regard everything that lies around you like the luggage in a hotel room. You must move on. You came in at nature's behest, and you are going back the same way. **25** You are not allowed to take out more than you brought in, or rather, the main part of what you brought with you into life must be laid aside. You will be stripped of this covering of skin, your closest garment; stripped of your flesh and of the blood that is diffused throughout your body; stripped of the bones and sinews that support your soft and fluid parts.

**26** The day that you dread as your last is the birthday of your eternity. Set down your burden. Why do you delay? Did you not once before abandon a body in which you were hiding and come out? You linger; you resist. But at that time too you were pushed out, by your mother's mighty efforts. You weep and wail. This very thing, weeping, is what one does at birth, but then one had to forgive you; you had arrived completely untrained and inexperienced. When you were sent forth from the warm and soft poultice of your mother's womb, a freer air breathed upon you, and then you encountered a hard hand's touch. Being still delicate and completely ignorant, you were bewildered by this unfamiliar environment. **27** But now it is no novelty for you to be separated from what you were previously a part of. Calmly dismiss your now unneeded limbs, and lay aside this body that you have so long inhabited. It will be torn apart, crushed, and destroyed. Why are you sad? This is the way things are. The afterbirth always perishes. Why do you love it as though it were your own? It was just your covering. The day will come that will tear you forth and take you away from association with this foul and evil-smelling belly.

**28** As much as you can, withdraw from it now and from all plea-sure except that which is linked to the necessities° of embodied life.* Estrange yourself even now from the body, and contemplate something higher and more sublime. In due course, nature's secrets will be revealed to you, the present fog will disappear, and a clear light will fall upon you from every side. Picture to yourself the magnitude of that brilliance when so many stars combine their light. No shadow will disturb this serenity. Every side of the sky will be equally luminous. The interchange of day and night belongs to the lower atmosphere. After you have gazed with your entire being on the fullness of light, you will admit that you have lived in the dark. Now you see it dimly through those narrow openings that are your eyes, but already you wonder at it from afar. How will the divine light look to you when you see it in its own region? **29** These thoughts allow nothing paltry, trivial, or degrading to settle in the mind. They declare that the gods are witnesses of everything. They tell us to win their approval, to prepare ourselves for them in the time to come, and to set our sights on immortality. No one who has this idea will fear any armies, or shrink at the trumpet's sound, or be scared by any threats. **30** Why shouldn't he be unafraid, given that he actually looks forward to death?

But even he° who judges that the mind lasts only as long as it is held by the body's chain, and that once released it is immediately dissipated, still strives to make himself useful after death.* Even though he is snatched from our eyes, still,

> His valor and the glory of his race
> come often to our minds.*

Think of how much we benefit from good examples. You will then realize that the memory of great men is no less useful than their presence.

Farewell.

# Letter 103

*From Seneca to Lucilius*
*Greetings*

**1** Why are you keeping a lookout for things that may possibly happen to you, but may very well not happen? I am talking about fires, collapse of buildings, and other things that do come our way but are not intended to do us harm. Keep an eye, rather, on things that do have it in for us and lay traps for us, and avoid those. Although accidents like shipwreck and being thrown from a carriage are serious enough, they are infrequent. It's the danger that one human can do to another that is a daily occurrence.

Equip yourself against this and focus on this. No calamity is more common, none more persistent, none more insidious. **2** Storms threaten before they surge, buildings creak before they collapse, and smoke gives warning of fire; but damage caused by human beings is immediate, and the closer it comes the more carefully it is hidden. It's a mistake to trust the faces of the people you meet: they have the appearance of human beings but the character of wild animals, except that with animals it is the first attack that is the most dangerous. They don't pass people by and then turn and pursue them. They are never provoked to do injury except under compulsion, when hunger or fear forces them to fight. One human being, on the other hand, positively likes to destroy another.

**3** Still, when you consider what dangers you may be in from other people, you should also be thinking about people's responsibilities to one another. Keep an eye on one person to avoid being hurt by him, on another to avoid hurting him. You should show pleasure at everyone's successes, feel for them when their affairs go wrong, remembering when you should be forthcoming and when you should be wary instead.

**4** By living like this, what will you gain? You will not necessarily escape harm, but you will avoid being caught unawares. Withdraw into philosophy as much as you can. Philosophy will protect you; you will be safe, or at least safer, in philosophy's sanctuary. People only knock into one another when they are walking on the same path.

**5** But you should not brag about your philosophy. Many people have been put in danger by crassly boasting about it. You should use philosophy to remove your faults, not to criticize other people's. You should not distance philosophy from the general way of the world, nor let it seem to be condemning everything that it refrains from doing itself. It's possible to practice wisdom without parade and without incurring resentment.

Farewell.

# Letter 104

*From Seneca to Lucilius*
*Greetings*

**1** I have run away to my villa at Nomentum.* Why, do you think? To escape the city? No, I wanted to avoid a fever that was creeping up and had already cast its hold on me. My doctor was saying that it had started with a rapid and irregular pulse. So I gave orders for my carriage to be made ready at once. I insisted on leaving in spite of my dear Paulina's attempts to stop me. All I could say was what my mentor Gallio had said when he was on the point of starting to have a fever in Greece.* He immediately boarded a ship, and kept insisting that his sickness was due to the location and not to his body. **2** I told this to Paulina.* She is very anxious about my health. In fact, realizing that her soul is completely bound up with mine, I am beginning, in my concern for her, to be concerned about myself. Getting on in years has made me more resolute in facing lots of things, but here I am losing the benefit of age. I have come to think that within this old man there's a young person who needs indulgence. Since I can't prevail on her to show more courage in loving me, she prevails on me to love myself more carefully.

**3** One has to give in, you see, to honorable feelings. There are times when, to honor a family member, one has to summon back one's dying breath, however painfully, and actually hold it in one's mouth. A good man should live not as long as it pleases him but as long as he ought to. The person who does not think enough of his wife or his friend to prolong his life—who insists on dying—is thoroughly self-indulgent. When the interest of loved ones demands it, the mind should require even this of itself: even if one not only wants to die but has actually begun to do so, one should interrupt the process and give oneself over to their needs. **4** Returning to life for another's sake is the mark of a lofty spirit, as great men have often done. But, in addition, I think it is supremely kind to be especially careful of your old age if you are aware that such behavior is pleasing, useful, and desirable to any of your loved ones, highly enjoyable though it is at that time to be more relaxed about one's survival and more daring in one's manner of living. **5** Besides, such self-care brings with it great joy and rewards, for what can be more delightful than being so dear to your wife that you consequently become dearer to yourself? And so my Paulina succeeds in burdening me not only with her fears but also with my own.

**6** I suppose you are curious to know how my travel project has worked out. As soon as I got away from the city's heavy atmosphere and the smell that smoking kitchens make when they discharge their accumulation of noxious fumes and dust, I felt an immediate change in my health. Can you imagine how much my strength increased once I reached my vineyards? Like an animal let out to pasture, I really attacked my food. The result is that I am fully myself again now, without a trace of physical unsteadiness and mental weakness. I'm beginning to concentrate completely on my studies.

**7** For that, location is of no avail unless the mind makes time for itself, keeping a place of retreat even amid busy moments. On the contrary, if you're always choosing remote spots in a quest for leisure, you'll find something to distract you everywhere. We are told that Socrates gave the following response to someone who complained that travel had done him no good: "It serves you right—you've been traveling with yourself!"* **8** How well some people would be doing if they could get away from themselves! Their pressures and anxieties and failings and terrors are all due to themselves. What good is it to cross the sea and move to a new city? If you want to escape from your troubles, what you need is not to be in a different place but to be a different person. Imagine you have come to Athens or Rhodes. Choose any city you like. Does the character of the place make any difference? You'll be taking your own character with you. **9** You'll still regard wealth as a good, and be tortured by what you falsely and most unhappily believe to be your poverty. No matter how much you own, the mere fact that someone has more will make you think that your resources are insufficient by exactly the amount that his are greater. You will go on regarding public office as a good, and be upset when one fellow is elected consul and another even reelected. You will be jealous whenever you read someone's name a number of times in the official records. Your craze for success will still be so great that you think no one is behind you if anyone is ahead of you.

**10** You'll go on regarding death as the worst of all things, even though the worst thing about death is what precedes it—the fear. You'll be terrified by mere apprehensions as well as by real dangers, constantly troubled by phantoms. How will it help you

> to have eluded
> so many Argive towns, and steered your flight
> right through the enemy's midst?*

Peace itself will supply you with fears. Once your mind has yielded to alarm, your confidence will not hold even in situations that are safe: having acquired the habit of thoughtless anxiety, it lacks the capacity to secure its own safety. It does not shun danger but rather takes flight, even though we are more exposed to dangers when we don't face them.

**11** You'll continue to regard the loss of anyone you love as a most grievous blow, though all the while this will be as silly as weeping because leaves are falling from the lovely trees that adorn your home. Look on everything that pleases you the same way as you look at verdant leaves:° enjoy them while they last. One or another of them will fall as the days pass, but their loss is easy to bear, because leaves grow again. It's no different with the loss of those you love and think of as your life's delight. They can be replaced, even though they are not reborn.

**12** "But they will not be the same." Even you yourself will not be the same. Every day changes you, and every hour; but when other people are snatched away the change is quite obvious, whereas in your own case this escapes notice, because it is not happening on the outside. Other people are taken from us, but at the same time *we* are being stolen imperceptibly from ourselves. You will not be conscious of these changes, nor will you be able to remedy the afflictions, but you will nonetheless make trouble for yourself by hoping for some things and despairing of others. Wisdom lies in combining the two: you should neither hope without doubting nor doubt without hoping.

**13** What has travel as such been able to do for anyone? It doesn't control pleasures, curb desires, check outbursts of temper, or mitigate love's wild assaults: in a word, it removes no troubles from the mind. It does not bestow judgment or shake off error; all it does is provide a change of scene to hold our attention for a moment, as some new trinket might entertain a child. **14** Apart from that, travel exacerbates the instability of a mind that is already unhealthy. Indeed, the very movement of the carriage makes us more restless and irritable. The result is that people who had been passionate to visit some spot are even more eager to leave it, just like birds that fly from one perch to another and are gone more swiftly than they arrived. **15** Travel will acquaint you with other races, it will show you mountains of strange shape, unfamiliar plains, and valleys watered by inexhaustible streams. It will enable you to observe the peculiarities of certain rivers—how the Nile rises in its summer flood, how the Tigris vanishes and then reappears in full force after traveling some distance underground, or how the Meander repeatedly winds around (a theme that poets love to embellish) and often loops back nearly into its own channel before flowing on—yet it will not improve you, either in body or in mind.

**16** We need to spend our time on study and on the authorities of wisdom in order to learn what has already been investigated and to investigate what has not yet been discovered. This is the way for the mind to be emancipated from its miserable enslavement and claimed for freedom. But as long as you are ignorant of what to avoid and what to pursue, and remain ignorant of the just, the unjust, the honorable, and the dishonorable, you will not really be traveling but only wandering. **17** Your rushing around will bring you no benefit, since you are traveling in company with your emotions, and your troubles follow along. Indeed, I wish they *were* following you, because then they would be further away! As it is, you are not staying ahead of them but carrying them on your back: wherever you go, you are burdened with the same burning discomforts.

A sick person does not need a place; he needs medical treatment. **18** If someone has broken a leg or dislocated a joint, he doesn't get on a carriage or a ship; he calls a doctor to set the fracture or relocate the limb. Do you get the point? When the mind has been broken and sprained in so many places, do you think it can be restored by changing places? Your trouble is too grave to be cured by moving around. **19** Travel does not make one a doctor or an orator. One does not learn a skill from one's location. Do you suppose that wisdom, the greatest of all skills, can be assembled on a journey? Believe me, there is no journey that could deposit you beyond desires, beyond outbursts of temper, beyond your fears. If that were so, the human race would have headed there in droves. So long as you carry around the reasons for your troubles, wandering all over the world, those troubles will continue to harass and torment you. **20** Are you puzzled that running away is not helping you? What you are running from is with you. You need to correct your flaws, unload your burdens, and keep your desires within a healthy limit. Expel all iniquity from your mind.

If you want to have pleasant travels, look to the company you keep. Greed will cling to you as long as the people you spend time with are greedy or mean. Conceit will stick to you as long as you spend your time with arrogant types. You will not rid yourself of cruelty if you make a torturer a close friend, and the company of adulterers will only inflame your lusts. **21** If you really want to be rid of your vices, you must stay away from the patterns of those vices. If a miser, or seducer, or sadist, or cheat were close to you, they would do you a lot of harm—but in fact, these are already inside you! Make a conversion to better models. Live with either of the Catos, or with Laelius, or Tubero; or, if you prefer to cohabit with Greeks, spend your time with Socrates or Zeno.* The former will teach you, if it is necessary, how to die; the latter, how to die before it is necessary. **22** Live with Chrysippus or Posidonius. They will educate you in the knowledge of things human and divine; they will tell you to work not so much at speaking charmingly and captivating an audience with your words but at toughening your mind and hardening it in the face of challenges.

There is only one haven for this stormy and turbulent life of ours: to rise above future events, to stand firm, ready to receive the blows of fortune head-on, out in the open and unflinching. **23** Nature brought us forth to be resolute. It made some creatures fierce, others cunning, and others timid, but its gift to us was a proud and lofty spirit that seeks where it may live most honorably rather than most safely; a spirit that closely resembles that of the universe, which it follows and strives to match, as far as that is permissible to the steps of mortal beings.* This spirit advances itself, it is confident of being praised and highly regarded. **24** It is master of everything and superior to everything. Consequently, it should not submit to anything or find anything heavy enough to weigh a man down:

Death and distress: shapes fearsome in appearance.*

Not in the least fearsome, if one can fully face them and break through the darkness. Many things that seem terrifying at night turn out to be amusing in the daylight. "Death and distress: shapes fearsome in appearance": our poet Virgil put it very well when he called them terrible not in fact but "in appearance," meaning that they seem terrible, but are not. **25** I repeat: what is as dreadful about these things as is commonly attributed to them? I beg you, Lucilius, to tell me: Why fear hard work, when one is a man? Why fear death, when one is a human being? I frequently encounter people who think that what they themselves cannot do is impossible, and who say that our Stoic theories are beyond the capacities of human nature. **26** I myself have a much higher opinion of human beings: they are actually capable of doing these things, but they are unwilling. Has anyone who really made the effort ever found the task beyond him? Hasn't it always been found easier in the doing? It is not the difficulty of things that saps our confidence, but our lack of confidence that creates the difficulty.

**27** If you need a model, take Socrates, a very patient old man.* He suffered all kinds of hardships, but he was overwhelmed neither by poverty (which his domestic troubles made more onerous) nor by the physical work he had to endure, including military service. He was hard pressed at home, whether we think of his ill-mannered wife with her shrewish tongue or his ineducable children, resembling their mother rather than their father. Outside the home,° he lived either in war or under tyranny or in a freedom that was more cruel than war and tyrants.* **28** The war lasted for twenty-seven years. After it ended, the state was subjected to the harm caused by the Thirty Tyrants, many of whom were personally hostile to Socrates. Finally, he was charged with the most serious offenses. He was accused of undermining religion and corrupting the youth by inciting them against the gods, their fathers, and the state. After this came prison and the hemlock. All this had so little effect on Socrates' mind that it did not even alter his facial expression.* What remarkable and unique distinction! Right up to the end, no one ever saw Socrates any more or less cheerful than usual. Amid the extreme changes of fortune, he was always unchanged.

**29** Would you like a second model? Take the younger Cato, against whom fortune's assaults were more violent and more persistent.* At every juncture, and finally at his death, Cato showed that a brave man can both live and die in defiance of fortune. He spent his entire life either as a soldier in the civil wars or in the peace° that was already breeding civil war. You may say that he, just like Socrates, pledged himself to liberty in the midst of slaves°—unless you happen to think that Pompey, Caesar, and Crassus were the allies of freedom. **30** No matter how often the political world changed, no one ever observed any change in Cato. He maintained the same character in every circumstance, whether elected to office or defeated, as a prosecutor or in the province;* in his political speeches, in the army, in death. In sum, at the moment of national crisis, with Caesar on one side equipped with ten legions in peak condition and the support of entire foreign nations, and with Pompey on the other, Cato was ready to stand alone against them all. When one faction was leaning to Caesar, and the other to Pompey, Cato was the only one who took the part of the Republic. **31** If you would like to form a mental image of that time, picture, on one side, the general populace—the common people, all keyed up for revolution; on the other side, the highest nobility and equestrians, all that were of the highest rank in the state; and in between two remnants, the Republic, and Cato. You will be amazed, I tell you, when you catch sight of

Atreus's son and Priam, and the scourge of both, Achilles.*

**32** Both sides meet with reproof, and both are stripped of their weapons, when Cato states his view of both: namely, "If Caesar wins, I will choose death; but if Pompey wins, I will go into exile." What did Cato have to fear? He had appointed for himself, whether in defeat or in victory, outcomes as stern as his enemies could have appointed at their most hostile. He died, then, by his own decree.

**33** You see that human beings are able to endure toil: Cato led an army on foot through the middle of the African deserts. You see that they can put up with thirst: Cato dragging the remains of his ill-equipped and defeated force over arid hills did not moisten his lips while dressed in full armor, and whenever water was available he was the last to drink.* You see that one can rise above status and distinction: Cato played ball on the same day that he lost his election.* You see that it is possible not to fear those with superior power: Cato challenged Pompey and Caesar at the same time, though no one else dared to offend the one without gaining the favor of the other. You see that one can rise above death as well as exile: Cato condemned himself both to exile and to death, and in between to war.

**34** Once we remove our necks from the yoke, we are capable of facing these troubles with the same degree of fortitude. We must begin by spurning pleasures; they weaken and emasculate us with their many demands, and they make us demand much of fortune. Next, we must spurn wealth: it is the recompense of slavery. We should give up gold and silver and everything else that weighs down prosperous houses. Liberty does not come for free. If you value it highly, you must devalue everything else.

Farewell.

## Letter 105

*From Seneca to Lucilius*
*Greetings*

**1** I am going to tell you what you need to watch out for in order to have a safer life. But please regard these precepts as comparable to the advice I might give you on how to stay healthy in the region of Ardea.* Put your mind to the factors that prompt one person to injure another. You will come across hope, envy, hatred, fear, and disrespect.

**2** The least significant of all these is disrespect, so much so that many people resort to it as a remedy. Being disrespected is certainly crushing, but the hurt doesn't last. It is something done casually and without premeditation. Even in war no one fights with the opponent who is down but only with the one who is on his feet. **3** As for the hopes of the unscrupulous, you can avoid them if you own nothing that might encourage them to covet what is not theirs, and if you possess nothing that stands out. People crave even little things if they catch the eye and are rare.° Envy you will escape if you don't force yourself on people's attention, if you don't brag about your possessions, and if you learn to take pleasure in private. **4** Hatred comes either from causing offense, which you can avoid by not provoking anyone, or else it is unprovoked, in which case a genial manner will protect you. Many people have incurred this risk; in fact, some have had to deal with hatred even though they have never had a single enemy. To avoid being feared, what you need are moderate circumstances and mildness of character. Let people know you are the sort of person they can offend without danger to themselves. Ensure that they can make up with you easily. To be feared is as troublesome at home as it is in public, whether you are feared by your slaves or by free men. Everyone has enough strength to do you harm. Besides, those who are feared are themselves fearful: no one has ever managed to instill fear in others while remaining free of anxiety. 5 That still leaves disrespect; but it is within anyone's power to keep disrespect within bounds by taking it over and making it something he incurs of his own free will, and not because it is deserved. Cultural pursuits help to mitigate its negative effects, and so do connections with those who have influence with someone powerful. It will be useful for you to associate with them, but don't get closely involved; otherwise the solution could be worse than the problem.

6 What will be most helpful in general is to stay calm, talk very little with other people but a great deal with yourself. Conversation has a subtle and seductive charm; just like drinking or sex, it elicits our secrets. No one will conceal what he has heard, or tell only as much as he has heard, or tell a story without naming the source. Each person has someone to whom he entrusts exactly what he has been entrusted with. Even if he restrains his own garrulity and is content with just one pair of ears, he will generate a multitude of others, and so what was recently a secret becomes matter for gossip.

7 Security consists largely in doing no wrong. People who lack self-control have lives that are frantic and disturbed. Their fears are exactly commensurate with their misdeeds; they are never at rest. After acting, they are agitated and unable to go on. Their conscience does not allow them to proceed with something else and keeps forcing them to confront themselves. Anyone expecting punishment undergoes punishment, and anyone who deserves it expects it. 8 Safety is compatible with a bad conscience, but tranquility is not. The guilty person thinks that he could be caught, even if he isn't caught. In his

sleep he is restless. Whenever he talks of someone's crime, he thinks of his own, taking it to be insufficiently covered up and concealed. The wrongdoer sometimes has the chance of concealment, but never the confidence of it.*

Farewell.

## Letter 106

*From Seneca to Lucilius*
*Greetings*

1 The reason I am rather late in answering your letters has nothing to do with being too busy. Don't listen to this excuse! I have plenty of time, and so has everyone who wants it. No one is pursued by business. It's people themselves who go after it and regard being busy as proof that they are well off. What was it, then, that stopped me from writing back at once? The question you were asking fits into my larger project. 2 As you know, my plan is to compose a comprehensive study of ethics, with a detailed account of all the relevant questions.* So I wondered whether I should put you off until I reached the appropriate topic, or give you my decision out of order. Since you have come from so far away, I didn't think I should make you wait any longer. 3 So I shall extract this point from its sequence in the overall structure, and without your requesting it I will also send anything else that is germane.

4 Are you wondering what that might be? The sort of thing that is pleasing, rather than beneficial, to know, like the answer to your question: is a good thing a body?*

A good thing, inasmuch as it benefits, acts; what acts is a body.

A good thing activates the mind, and in a certain way shapes and structures it; shaping and structuring are distinctive of body.

The goods of the body are corporeal; therefore, since the mind too is a body, the goods of the mind are also corporeal.

**5** Since a human being is corporeal, the good of a human being must be a body: undeniably, the things that nourish a human being and that maintain or restore his health are bodies; therefore the human being's good is also a body.

I don't suppose you are in any doubt that emotions are bodies, including anger, love, and sadness (just to put in something else that falls outside your question), since you admit, surely, that they alter our expression, furrow our brow, relax our face, evoke a blush, or turn us pale. Well, then, do you suppose that such clear marks of the body are stamped onto it by anything except a body? **6** If emotions are bodies, so too are mental infirmities such as greed, cruelty, and faults that have become ingrained and incurable.* So vice too is a body, and so are all its species such as malice, envy, and pride. **7** Therefore good qualities are also bodies, first because they are the opposites of these other things, and second because they will give you similar indications. You can see in a person's eyes the energy produced by courage, the concentration that comes of prudence, the moderation and repose that reverence generates, the calm produced by joy, the steeliness that comes with severity, and the easiness that attends a mild disposition. The things that change the color and look of bodies are bodies; it is on bodies that they wield their power. But all the virtues that I have mentioned are good things, as is everything that depends on them.

**8** Surely you don't doubt that anything that can touch is a body, as Lucretius says?

Nothing can touch and be touched except a body.*

None of the things I have mentioned would cause a body to change without touching it. Therefore they are bodies. **9** In addition, anything that has the power to drive or enforce or stop or restrain is a body. What follows, then? Aren't we stopped by fear, driven by boldness, and spurred on by courage? Doesn't moderation restrain us and call us back? Aren't we exalted by joy and depressed by sadness? **10** In sum, whatever we do we execute under the command of virtue or vice. What commands a body is a body, just as the thing that applies force to a body is a body. The good of a body is corporeal, and the good of a human being is also the good of a body. Therefore the human being's good is corporeal.

**11** Now that I have done what you asked of me, it is time for me to anticipate the remark that I see you making: "We are just playing checkers here." We are wasting our minds on trivialities, things that make people clever rather than good. To be wise is something more obvious, or rather, more straightforward. **12** You don't need a lot of scholarly study to achieve mental excellence. Yet we are squandering philosophy itself, just as we squander our other resources on what is trivial. In scholarly study, as in everything else, we suffer from excess. We are learning not for life but for the classroom.

Farewell.

## *Letter 107*

*From Seneca to Lucilius*
*Greetings*

**1** Where are your good sense and your powers of discernment? What's happened to your strength of character? Are you bothered about something so very trivial? Your slaves saw that you were busy and took that as an opportunity to escape. If it had been your friends cheating you—let's go ahead and use that conventional but erroneous term,* to make it more shameful when they do not behave as friends—anyway, if it had been your "friends," all your affairs <would> lose by it. As it is,>° you lose nothing but people who were giving you poor service and who regarded you as a difficult person.

**2** There's nothing unusual or unexpected in this event. To be upset about such things is as absurd as complaining about being splashed in the bathhouse or jostled in a public place or soiled on a muddy road. Life imposes the same conditions on us as we encounter in the bathhouse, in a crowd, or on a journey. Some things will be deliberate acts of aggression, others will just be accidents. Life is not a bed of roses. You have set out on a long road. You are bound to trip up, collide, fall down, get tired, and exclaim, "I'm ready to die"—which will be a lie. At one spot you will leave a companion behind, at another you will bury one, and somewhere else you will be frightened by one. These are the sorts of mishaps you have to negotiate on this rugged journey.

**3** Does he really wish to die? Let him prepare himself for all that lies ahead, knowing that he has come to the place where thunder resounds, where

> wails and avenging cares have made their beds,
> where wan diseases dwell and grim old age.*

This is the company in which you have to spend your life. You cannot escape these things, but you can rise above them, and you will succeed in doing so if you frequently reflect on and anticipate the future. **4** Everyone has greater fortitude in arriving at a situation for which he has long prepared himself, and hardships that have been anticipated can also be withstood.* In contrast, utterly trivial things can terrify people who are not prepared for them. We must see to it that we have not overlooked anything. Because everything is more serious when it is new, constant reflection will ensure that you do not face any trouble as a raw recruit.

**5** "My slaves have abandoned me." Yes, and another man's slaves have robbed him, accused him of crimes, killed him, betrayed him, trampled on him, made designs against him with poison or criminal charges. Many people have experienced your litany of woes, and many <will experience>° them again. Many different weapons are directed against us. Some of them have already stuck into us, others are hurtling toward us and about to arrive, while some that were intended for others strike us a glancing blow. **6** We should not be surprised about any of the things that we are born to face, things that no one should complain about because they are the same for everyone. I mean it: they are the same, because even the things people escape are things they could have suffered. A law is fair not when everyone has experience of it but when it is applicable to everyone. Tell your mind to be fair, and let us pay the taxes of our mortality without complaining.

**7** Winter brings cold, and we have to shiver. Summer restores the heat, and we have to perspire. Irregular weather puts a strain on health, and we have to become ill. There are places where we shall encounter wild beasts and human beings who are more dangerous than any wild beast. We shall suffer damage from water and from fire. We cannot change this state of affairs. What we can do is adopt a resolute character, as befits a good man, in order to endure the chances of life with bravery and be in agreement with nature. 8 Nature controls this visible realm by means of changes. Clear skies follow after cloudy weather, seas become turbulent after a calm; winds blow in turn; day follows night; one part of the sky rises, and another sets. It is the world's contrarieties that give rise to its longevity. 9 We must adapt our minds to this law, following it and obeying it. No matter what happens, we should think that it had to happen and not wish to reproach nature. It is best to endure what you cannot correct, and to go along uncomplainingly with the divinity who is in charge of the entire course of events. It is a poor soldier who groans as he follows his commander.

10 Let us, then, tirelessly and vigorously accept our orders. Let us not desert the course taken by this most beautiful of worlds, with which all our future experience is interwoven. Let us address Jupiter, the steersman of this great mass, in those eloquent lines of our own Cleanthes, which on the model of Cicero, that master of eloquence, I allow myself to translate.* If you like them, credit them to my account; and if you don't like them, you will know that I have just been following Cicero's example:

11 Guide me, o father, lord of the lofty firmament,
wherever you decide; I hasten to obey;
I am here and ready. But if I be reluctant,
groaning, I still must go; in wretchedness must suffer,
what might have been my own act, were I virtuous.
Fate guides the man who's willing, drags the unwilling.

12 That's how we should live and speak, with fate finding us ready and prepared. This is the strong character that has surrendered himself to fate. In contrast we have the puny degenerate, struggling, thinking ill of the world order, and preferring to correct the gods rather than himself.

Farewell.

# Letter 108

*From Seneca to Lucilius*
*Greetings*

**1** Your inquiry is on a matter there is no point knowing about except just to know; and still, with no other point than that, you are in a hurry to find out and aren't willing to wait for the books I'm now putting together covering the entire domain of ethics.* I'll get to it right away, but first I'll write about how you ought to hold off on your desire for learning—a burning desire, I see—so that it doesn't become counterproductive. **2** You ought not to take up every subject you encounter, nor should you delve greedily into every topic in its entirety: pieces of it will give you a sense of the whole. We should adjust the burden to our strength, not taking on more than we can handle. Don't drink as much as you want, but as much as you can hold. Just keep the right attitude, though, and the time will come when you can hold as much as you want. The more the mind takes in, the larger it becomes.

**3** I remember how Attalus used to teach us when we were constantly in attendance at his lectures, being the first to come and last to leave, and asking him to expound on various topics even when he was out walking—for he did not just receive pupils; he went out and found them. "Teacher and learner should have the same purpose," he used to say, "the one to enable progress, the other to make progress."* **4** One who studies with a philosopher should have some benefit to take home with him every day, either better health or a mind more open to healing. But he will, for the power of philosophy is so great that it aids not only students but even casual bystanders. People who are out in the sun get a tan, even if they didn't go out for that purpose; people who sit around for a while in a perfume-shop carry the aroma of the place away with them; and those who have been around a philosopher necessarily take away something beneficial, even if they don't make any effort. Observe: I say "even if they don't make any effort," not "even if they resist."

**5** "What do you mean? Don't we know people who have studied with a philosopher for many years and have not gained even a tinge of color?" Of course I do, and very persistent people too, but I would describe them as hangers-on rather than as students of philosophy. **6** Some people come not to learn but only to listen. It is like when we are enticed into the theater to delight our ears with speech or song or story. You can see that the majority of this audience regards a philosophical lecture as a mere diversion. They are not seeking to lay aside any of their faults or to adopt any rule of life by which to regulate their habits, but only to find enjoyment in the pleasures of the ear. Some even come with notebooks, not to record the content but to take down phrases that they can then repeat, with no more benefit to others than they have derived themselves. **7** Some are stirred by fine-sounding speeches and take on the emotion of the speakers. Their expressions are eager; their spirits are aroused; they are as excited as Phrygian eunuchs,° half-men raving on command at the sound of the flute.* What sweeps them away is the beauty of the subject matter, not the sound of empty words. Whenever someone speaks fiercely against the fear of death, or boldly against the vagaries of fortune, they are ready to act immediately on what they have heard. They are very responsive; they are just what they are told to be—if the mood stays with them, if their fine resolve is not assailed by the people, that great discourager of honorable conduct. Few are able to take home with them the intention they have formed.

**8** It is easy to rouse a listener and make him desire what is right, for nature has given everyone the foundations and seeds of the virtues.* We are all born for such things; and when someone provides a stimulus, the good awakens in our minds as if from sleep. Have you not observed how applause echoes in the theater when certain lines are spoken which we, the public, recognize and affirm as true?

**9** Penury is deprived of much, but avarice of all.

The greedy man is good to none, but worst to his own self.*

The vilest criminal applauds these lines, rejoicing to hear an attack on his own vices. Just imagine the effect when the lines are spoken by a philosopher, when healthful precepts are imbued with poetic rhythms to drive them deeper into the minds of the uneducated. **10** For, as Cleanthes used to say,

Just as the sound of our breath is amplified when driven through a trumpet with its narrow windings, flared at the end, so our thoughts are amplified by the stringent requirements of verse.*

The same points are attended to less carefully and make less of an impact when expressed in plain speech. When meter with its specified pattern of long and short syllables is added to an excellent idea, that same sentiment is hurled, as it were, by a stronger arm. 11 Much is said about not caring for money; long speeches advise people that riches are found in the mind, not in the bank account, and that the wealthy person is the one who adjusts to his poverty and makes himself rich with little. But our minds are struck much more when we hear verses like these:

That mortal man needs least whose wants are least.

He who can want what is enough, has what he wants.*

12 When we hear such things we feel compelled to admit that they are true, for even people who are never satisfied with what they have admire them and cheer for them and cry aloud how they hate money. When you see this reaction, press your advantage: load everything onto them, and leave behind all those subtleties, those syllogisms and sophisms and other clever but pointless tricks. Speak against avarice; speak against self-indulgence; and when you see that you are making progress and having an effect on your audience, press harder still: you will be amazed how beneficial such a speech can be when it is intent on the cure and entirely devoted to the good of its audience. It is easy to turn the hearts of young people toward the love of what is honorable and right. When people can still be taught—that is, when they are only lightly corrupted—truth lays its hand upon them if only it finds a suitable advocate.*

13 In my own case, when I used to hear Attalus at the climax of a speech against faults, against errors, against everything bad in life, I often felt pity for the human race and thought that Attalus was an exalted being, above the pinnacle of human affairs. He said himself that he was a king; but I thought he was more than that, for here was a man who could censure kings. 14 And when he started recommending poverty, arguing that any possessions in excess of our basic

needs are only a burden to weigh us down, I often wanted to walk out of the lecture a poor man. When he began to castigate our pleasures, praising a chaste body, an abstemious diet, and a pure mind—pure not only of illicit pleasures but even of unnecessary ones—then I wanted to put a check on my gluttonous belly.

**15** Some of the resolutions I made at that time are still with me, Lucilius. For I went at it all with great enthusiasm; and even after I resumed a more urbane manner of living, I kept a few of those good habits. All my life since then, I have refrained from eating oysters and mushrooms. These are not food; they are only tidbits meant to entice those who are full to eat some more (which is what the glutton wants, to stuff himself beyond capacity), for they go down easily, and come back up easily too. **16** All my life since then, I have abstained from perfumed oil: the best smell for the body is no smell at all. Since then I have kept my stomach free of wine, and all my life I have avoided the baths. Boiling one's body and then draining it by sweating seems to me both pointless and decadent. Other practices I had given up have since returned; but though I have ceased to abstain from them, I observe very strict limits. Such restrictions are near to abstinence and in fact may even be more difficult, because some habits are easier to break than to reduce.

**17** Since I have started telling you how much more eagerly I went after philosophy as a young man than I hurry after it now that I am old, I won't be embarrassed to admit how smitten I was with love for Pythagoras. Sotion explained to me why Pythagoras abstained from animal foods, and why Sextius later did the same.* Their reasons were different, but impressive in both cases. **18** Sextius held that a person could get enough to eat without resorting to butchery; and that when bloodshed is adapted to the purposes of pleasure, one develops a habit of cruelty.* He also used to say that one should pare away the resources of self-indulgence, and he offered reasoning to show that variety in food is alien to our bodies and detrimental to health. **19** Pythagoras, for his part, spoke of a relationship among all things and of an interchange of minds passing from one form to another. If you believe him, no soul ever dies, or even ceases its activity except for the brief instant when it transfers to another body. Eventually, we will find out how many ages must pass, how many times it must travel from one lodging to the next before it returns into a human being. In the meantime, Pythagoras instilled in humankind a fear of wrongdoing—more specifically, of parricide. For if some spirit related to them happened to be dwelling in a given body, they might, without realizing it, assault the soul of their parent with the knife or with their teeth. **20** After Sotion had explained all this, filling it out with his own arguments, he added,

> Do you not believe that souls are allotted to one body after another, and that what we call death is really transmigration? Do you not believe that in these cattle, these wild animals or sea creatures, there lives a mind that was once that of a human? Do you not believe that things in this world do not perish, but only change their location—that not only do the heavenly bodies revolve in definite orbits, but animate creatures also cycle through the ages, their minds coming round to where they started? Great men have believed these things. **21** Therefore refrain from judgment, if you will, but be open-minded about it. If these things are true, then abstaining from animal foods means not harming anyone; if they are false, it is a matter of economy. How much of a loss is it for you to refrain from savagery?° I am only depriving you of the food of lions and of vultures.

**22** Inspired by these words, I began to abstain from animal foods, and a year later the habit was both easy and pleasant for me. I thought my mind was livelier, and even today I suspect it might have been. Would you like to know why I gave it up? The time when I was a young man was in the early years of Tiberius's principate. Religions of foreign origin were then being eliminated, and abstinence from animal foods was considered proof of adherence. So at the request of my father (who did not fear opprobrium but had a hatred of philosophy), I returned to my former habits; he had no trouble, really, in persuading me to dine in better style. **23** Attalus used to recommend a mattress that would not yield to the body. I use such a mattress even in my old age, the kind that does not hold an imprint.

My purpose in telling you all this has been to show how excited brand-new recruits can become about every form of good behavior when they have someone to exhort and encourage them. But there is also some wrongdoing, both on the part of instructors, when they teach us how to argue a point and not how to live, and on the part of students, when their purpose in attending is not to improve their minds but to develop their rhetorical talent. Hence what used to be philosophy has now become mere philology.

**24** It matters a great deal what one's purpose is in approaching any field of study. When the prospective literary scholar examines his copy of Virgil, and reads that exceptional line,

> time flies on irretrievable,*

his thought is not "We must take care—if we do not make haste, we will be left behind—the fleeting moment hurries on, and hurries us—heedlessly are we swept along—we are always procrastinating—opportunity hurtles by and still we make delays." No, he reads it just so that he can observe that every time Virgil speaks about the rapid movement of time, he uses the word "flies" (*fugit*), as follows:

> The best times of our lives, poor mortal creatures,
> fly first away, and in their place come illness
> and sad old age and suffering and pain,
> until hard pitiless death takes us away.*

**25** The person who looks to philosophy takes these same lines and applies them as he ought. "The reason Virgil never says that time 'passes,' but always that it 'flies,' is that flying is the quickest kind of movement, and his point is that the best people are the first to be taken away. Why not quicken our own steps to match the pace of that swiftest of all runners? Our better days are hastening on; worse days will follow. **26** Our life is like a storage jar: the purest of its contents are decanted first; all the sediment and turbid matter sink to the bottom. Are we going to let the best of our lives be siphoned off for others, and keep only the dregs for ourselves? Keep these lines always in mind; let them be to you as an oracular response:

> The best times of our lives, poor mortal creatures,
> fly first away.

**27** Why the best? Because what remains is uncertain. Why the best? Because when we are young, we are able to learn, since our minds are still flexible and can be turned toward better things; because this is the time of life that is suited to strenuous effort, to exercising the mind with study and the body with work. What remains is slower, wearier, nearer to the end. Let us therefore forget all our diversions and aim for this one thing with all our mind, lest we come too late to understand the rapidity of fleeting time, which we cannot detain. Let us be pleased with each new day as the best that life will give us, and so add it to our store. Life is flying away; we must catch it."

**28** The one who reads with the eye of a literary scholar does not consider why the best times of our lives come first—that in their place comes illness, that old age looms over us even while we are still intent on our youth. Instead, he says that Virgil always uses the words "illness" and "old age" together. So he does, and with good reason! For old age is an illness that has no cure. **29** "Moreover," he says, "Virgil employs a fixed epithet for old age: he calls it 'sad':

> and in their place come illness
> and sad old age . . .

Elsewhere he says,

> where wan diseases dwell and grim old age."*

Each person finds in the same material reflections suited to his own pursuits. And no wonder: in one and the same meadow the ox looks for grass, the dog for a hare, and the stork for a lizard. **30** When three people, one an antiquarian, one a literary scholar, and one a philosopher, pick up Cicero's treatise *On the Republic*, each directs his attention to something different. The philosopher is amazed that so many points could have been made against justice.* The antiquarian, reading the same passage, takes note of the fact that there were two Roman kings, one of whom had no father and the other no mother. For there are no clear reports about Servius's mother, and Ancus is not said to have had a father but only to have been the grandson of Numa.* **31** He remarks also that the official whom we call a "dictator" was in ancient times called "master of the populace." That information can be found today in the augurs' record book, and there is further evidence in the fact that the dictator's appointee is called "master of horse." He points out, furthermore, that Romulus died during an eclipse of the sun, and that there was such a thing as the appeal to the people even during the monarchy. This is also in the pontifical record, and Fenestella and a few others° share this view.* **32** When the literary scholar expounds these same scrolls, the first thing he puts into his commentary is the fact that Cicero uses the word *reapse* for *re ipsa* ("in reality"), and likewise *sepse* for *se ipse* ("himself"). Then he moves on to changes in linguistic usage over time. For instance, Cicero writes, "Since his interruption has called us back from the very lime line," that is, the finish line. What we now call the chalk line (*creta*) at the races, the old writers called a lime line (*calx*). **33** Then he collects various lines of Ennius, especially the ones about Scipio Africanus,

> whom neither citizen nor foe
> could ever repay the price of his assistance.*

From these lines, he concludes that in the old writers the word "assistance" (*ops*) meant not just "aid" but also "endeavor." For Ennius's point is that no one, neither citizen nor foe, could ever repay Scipio the price of his endeavor. **34** Next, he congratulates himself for finding out the source of Virgil's line,

> Above whom heaven's massive portal thunders.*

He says that Ennius stole the line from Homer, and Virgil took it from Ennius; for Cicero, in the same work *On the Republic*, quotes this couplet of Ennius:

> If it be right for anyone to mount the skies,
> for me alone does heaven's great portal open.

**35** But I don't mean to turn into an antiquarian or literary scholar on my own account. My business is elsewhere. I am only advising that when we read and listen to the philosophers, we should direct our attention toward our goal, which is happiness. We should not be trying to track down archaic words, neologisms, peculiar metaphors, and figures of speech, but to seek out beneficial precepts and courageous and inspiring utterances that will soon find application in our lives. Let us learn them so thoroughly that words turn into actions.

**36** But of all those who have done humankind a bad turn, the worst are those who teach philosophy for money, as if it were some tradesman's craft, and then live their lives in a manner very different from their precepts. For, being prime examples of the very faults they criticize in others, they provide a fine demonstration of how useless their teaching is. **37** Such instruction cannot do me any good, any more than a helmsman who is prone to seasickness during a storm. When the waves are coming fast and a hand is needed to grip the tiller, to wrestle with the sea itself, to take down the sail in a high wind, what is the use of a helmsman who is panicking and throwing up? And life is beset by worse storms than any ship. I don't need someone to talk at me; I need someone to steer!

**38** Everything they say, all their fine speeches before crowds of listeners, are taken over from someone else. The words are those of Plato, or of Zeno, or of Chrysippus or Posidonius or one of the many other great names in philosophy. How can they prove that those ideas are their own? I'll tell you: they must practice what they preach.

**39** Since I have finished saying what I wanted to convey to you, I shall now comply with your request. I'll put your inquiry into a fresh letter so that you won't be fatigued when taking up a thorny subject that needs a thoughtful and attentive hearing.

Farewell.

## Letter 109

*From Seneca to Lucilius*
*Greetings*

**1** You want to know whether one wise person can help another. We say that a wise person is one who is replete with every good thing and has attained the summit.* How, then, the question goes, is it possible to help anyone who possesses the ultimate good?

Good people are helpful to each other because each gives exercise to the other's virtues, keeping his wisdom in the stance proper to it.* Each of them needs someone to compare and investigate with. **2** Practice is the training for proficient wrestlers, and musicians are stimulated by those who are as expert as themselves. The sage too needs his virtues to be activated: just as he makes himself active, so also he is made active by another person who is wise. **3** How exactly will the one help the other? By giving him a prod and demonstrating opportunities for honorable actions. Apart from this, the wise man will give utterance to some of his own reflections and let the other learn his discoveries; even he will always have something to discover, something to extend his mind with.

**4** A bad man harms a bad man and makes him worse by arousing his anger, approving his gloom, and praising his pleasures. Bad men are at their worst when they combine their faults to the greatest extent, and a single aggregate of wrongdoing is the result. Conversely, one good man will help another.

**5** "But how?" you say. He will bring him joy and strengthen his confidence, and each one's delight will grow from the sight of their mutual tranquility. Apart from that, they will pass on to each other the knowledge of certain things, since the sage does not know everything. Even if he did have such knowledge, someone might be able to figure out shorter ways to get to the facts and point those out to him, making it easier to encompass the entire matter. **6** One wise person will help another, not only with his own strength (that goes without saying) but also with the strength of the one he helps. Of course, the latter can fully develop his own capacities even when left to himself: the runner's speed is his own. Yet even so, he is helped by being cheered on.

"One wise person does not really help another; each helps himself. To grasp this, just remove the distinctive ability from one of them, and the other will have nothing to activate."* **7** If you talk that way, you could say also that there is no sweetness in honey. Consider a person who feels compelled to eat honey: he is captivated by that sort of taste because his tongue and palate are adjusted to it, but if they should happen not to be, he will find it disagreeable; in fact, there are some people who because of illness find honey bitter. Both wise men need to be in good form so that the one will be able to help and the other will be suitable material to receive help.

**8** "But it is superfluous to apply heat to something that is already extremely hot, and it is equally superfluous for someone to help the man who has attained the highest good. Does a fully equipped farmer ask someone else for equipment? Does a soldier who is adequately armed for the front line need any additional weapons? So too the wise man has no needs: he is sufficiently equipped and armed for life." **9** To these challenges I respond as follows: even something extremely hot needs a supply of heat to maintain that degree of temperature.

"But heat as such is essentially hot."* For a start, you are comparing things that are much too different: heat is a single thing, whereas help comes in many forms. Next, heat does not need additional heat in order to be hot; but the sage cannot maintain his mental disposition without taking others like himself into his friendship, so as to share his virtues with them.* **10** Furthermore, you should note that there is mutual friendship among all the virtues. Therefore help is provided by one who loves the virtues of a person like himself and who in return supplies his own virtues to be loved. Things that are alike give pleasure, especially when they are honorable and their recipients know how to be mutual in approving them.

**11** And again, the mind of one who is wise can be activated in an expert manner only by another wise person, just as only a human being can activate another human being in a rational way. Therefore, just as reason is needed to motivate reason, so perfect reason is needed to activate perfect reason.

**12** The word "help" is also used when people provide us with intermediate things, such as income, influence, safety, and other things that are appreciated or needed in our lives. As concerns these, the wise person will get help even from the fool. But genuine help consists of activating a mind in accordance with nature, both by means of the helper's own virtue and by the virtue of the one who is activated. This will not happen without benefit accruing to the helper as well; for by activating another's virtue, one must also activate one's own.

**13** But even if you set aside the ultimate goods and the things that produce them, the wise can still help one another.* For one of them to find another one is something choiceworthy in itself, because every good thing is naturally dear to every other, and so each of them is as much attached to a good person as he is to himself. **14** To prove my point, I need to leave this topic and turn to another one—the question whether the wise person will deliberate on his own or appeal to someone else for advice. He has to do the latter in the course of ordinary public and private business, what we may call the human condition. In these matters, he needs advice from other people, just as the doctor, the helmsman, the lawyer, and the magistrate need advice from others. And so one wise person will help another by suggesting a course of action; but he will also be useful in weighty and elevated matters, as I have said, by sharing his views about honorable things and contributing his thoughts and reflections. **15** But even beyond that, it is in accordance with nature to embrace one's friends and to take as much pleasure in their advancement as if it were one's own. Indeed, if we fail to do this, virtue will not remain with us for long, for virtue thrives by the active exercise of our sentiments.

Virtue enjoins us to make the best of our present circumstances, to take thought for the future, to deliberate and concentrate. Concentration and effectiveness will be facilitated by taking a partner. For this reason, a virtuous person will seek out either a man who is already perfect or one whose progress is close to perfection. The help he will get from a perfect man consists in his own plans being assisted by the wisdom that they share. **16** It is said that people are more perceptive in the business of others than they are in their own.° This affects those who are blinded by self-love and those who are too frightened in dangerous situations to observe their own advantage. People will start to be wise when they are freer from anxiety and beyond fear. But there are some things that even the wise see more accurately in cases that are not their own. Besides, they give one another that sweetest and most honorable gift of "having the same wishes and the same aversions."* By working together, they will produce an excellent result.

**17** I have dealt with your demand, although its place was in the set of topics I am covering in my books on ethics.* As I keep telling you, please realize that all we are doing with such questions is exercising the intellect. All the time, I keep coming back to thought, "How does this topic help me? Make me more brave, more just, more self-controlled. I am not yet ready for action. I still need the doctor. **18** Why do you ask me for useless knowledge? You promised me great things; the results I see are minimal.° You said that I would be fearless even if swords were flashing around me, even if the blade were pressed to my throat. You said that I would be safe even if fires were blazing around me, even if a sudden hurricane were to hurl my boat all over the sea. Provide me with a course of treatment such that I spurn pleasure and glory. Later on you will teach me how to solve complex questions, clarify ambiguities, and see through obscurities. For now, teach me what is indispensable."

Farewell.

# BOOK NINETEEN

438

# *Letter 110*

*From Seneca to Lucilius*
*Greetings*

**1** I send you greetings from my villa at Nomentum, wishing you excellence of mind—and that is a wish for divine favor as well, since anyone who truly shows favor to himself also has the goodwill and support of all the gods. Set aside for the moment the idea of some people that each one of us has been given a tutelary god—not a god of high rank but one of lower status, the ones that Ovid calls "commoner gods."* In setting this aside, however, I want you to remember that our ancestors, who did believe in them, must have been Stoics, because they assigned a personal Genius or Juno to each individual.* **2** On another occasion, we shall see whether the gods have enough spare time to look after ordinary people's business. Meanwhile, be assured that regardless of whether we are assigned such guardians or are neglected and given over to fortune, the worst curse you can utter against anyone is to pray that he be his own enemy.

But there is no reason why you should pray for the gods to be hostile to anyone who seems deserving of punishment. They are already hostile to such a person, I insist, even if he seems to enjoy their favor. **3** If you carefully study human circumstances as they really are rather than as they are described, you will realize that more often than not, our troubles do us no real harm. How many times has so-called disaster been both the cause and the beginning of happiness! How often has a person been elevated in rank amid great applause, mounting higher and higher up toward the edge of a cliff, when in fact even his previous position was so high as to risk a dangerous fall! **4** But the actual fall contains nothing inherently bad if you look to the end beyond which nature casts no one down. The finality of all our affairs is near at hand—near at hand, I repeat, are the fortunate person's downfall and the unfortunate person's release. It is we who stretch things out, extending them by our hopes and our fears. The wise policy is to measure everything by our mortality. You should limit your enjoyment and at the same time your fear. It's worth not enjoying anything for long so as to avoid fearing anything for long.

**5** But why do I restrict this failing? There is no reason for you to regard anything as fearful. The things that fill us with alarm and panic are mere phantoms. Not one of us has unearthed the truth; we transmit our fears to one another. No one dares to go right up to the things that upset people and get to know the nature of fear and indeed its value. The falsehood and groundlessness of fear still have credence because they are not refuted. Let's recognize the importance of looking hard at the facts. **6** Then we shall see that the things people fear are brief, uncertain, and harmless. Our mental confusion is the way it appeared to Lucretius:

> Like children in the dark, afraid and trembling
> at all they cannot see, so we fear in the daylight.*

What, then? Aren't we, with our fear in daylight, more foolish than any child? **7** But actually, Lucretius, you are wrong. It's not that we are afraid in daylight, but that we have turned everything that affects us into darkness. We see nothing, neither what harms us nor what is expedient: all our lives we rush into things, but that does not make us hold back or step more cautiously. You can see how crazy it is to be impetuous in the dark. Our behavior means that it takes us longer to retrace our steps; but although we don't know where we are going, we keep speeding along in the direction we are bent on.

**8** Light can break, if we are willing. But there is only one way this can happen—if one gains knowledge of things human and divine, not in a superficial way but indelibly, going over one's knowledge and applying it repeatedly to oneself, investigating what things are good, what are bad, and what are erroneously so described; what things are honorable and shameful; what is the nature of divine providence.* **9** Nor does the human intellect have to stay within these limits: we are at liberty to look out even beyond the vault of heaven to see where it is going, whence it arose, and to what final state it is moving at so great a speed. Removing our minds from such divine contemplation, we have applied them to mean and lowly things, enslaving them to greed. We have abandoned the vault of heaven, its boundaries, its masters who control all things, in order to probe into the earth and investigate what trouble we can excavate, not content with what was on offer. **10** Our divine progenitor had made everything available that would be beneficial to us, not waiting for us to seek it out but giving it freely; everything that would be harmful he buried very deeply. The only thing we can complain about is ourselves: we have brought forth the means of our destruction against the will of nature that keeps them hidden. We have devoted our minds to pleasure (indulging in which is the beginning of all troubles), and surrendered ourselves to ambition, fame, and equally worthless and useless things.

**11** What, then, do I recommend? Not that you do anything new (since these are not fresh maladies we are seeking to cure) but first of all to consider by yourself what is needed and what is superfluous. What is needed can be found anywhere; it is the superfluities that one has to devote all one's time and effort to find. **12** I am not telling you to give yourself airs if you look down on golden couches and bejeweled cups. What is the virtue in scorning superfluities? Admire yourself when you look down on necessities! It is nothing much to dispense with royal show, to feel no longing for thousand-pound boars or flamingoes' tongues and all the other excesses of the luxurious taste that can no longer stand to eat the entire creature and instead chooses bits of different ones. I shall not admire you until you care nothing even for ordinary bread, and convince yourself that grass grows not only for grazing animals but when necessary for human beings as well; if you realize that our belly (which we stuff with costly fare as if were a safe) can be filled with the leaves of trees. We should satisfy our hunger without being particular. Why should it matter what goes into the stomach? It won't be there long. **13** You like a table set with the catch from land and sea, some items more pleasing because they are brought fresh, while others, after forced feeding and fattening, are spilling out of themselves and scarcely able to hold their shape. You like these delicacies with their artfully arranged elegance. Yet in fact, though they have been acquired with difficulty and subtly seasoned, once they have gone down into the belly they will be subjected to one and the same filth. Do you want to look down on the pleasures of eating? Think of where your food ends up.

**14** I remember how much everyone admired Attalus when he said the following:

"For a long time I was deceived by wealth. Seeing it glitter in one place and another, I was agog, thinking that it was the same deep down as it appeared on the surface. Then in some procession I saw the wealth of a whole city: vessels embossed in silver and gold and other materials even more costly; vestments dyed with pigments imported not only from beyond our own borders but even from beyond the boundaries of our enemies; on either side male and female slaves of exceptional elegance and beauty; and whatever else the fortunes of imperial power had put on display from its resources. **15** I said to myself, 'This is just a way to stir up desires that were active enough already! What is this parade of money all about? Are we come together just to have lessons in greed?' In fact, I left there with less acquisitiveness than I had brought with me. **16** I ceased to care about wealth, not because it is superfluous but because it is trivial. Did you not see how that parade, though carefully orchestrated and moving slowly, was over within a few hours? Has something that could not last a whole day filled our entire life? **17** This thought occurred as well: all those riches seemed to me as superfluous to their owners as they were to the observers.

"For this reason, whenever my eyes are smitten by this kind of thing, or whenever I encounter a splendid house with a well-trained regiment of slaves and a litter on the shoulders of handsome bearers, I say to myself, 'Why are you impressed and all agape? It's just a show.' People don't own these things, they display them; and in the very moment they give us pleasure, they are also passing away. **18** Turn yourself instead toward real riches. Learn to be satisfied with little, and loudly and spiritedly proclaim:

> We have water, we have porridge, let us compete for happiness with Jupiter himself.*

Let us, I beg you, make the same challenge even without these things. It's shameful to base a happy life on gold and silver, and equally shameful to base it on water and porridge.

**19** "'What am I to do if even these things are not available?' Are you asking what is the cure for penury? Starvation sets the limit to starvation: if not so, then what difference does it make whether you are a slave to vast resources or to a pittance? What does it matter how small something is if fortune can refuse it to you? **20** This very water and porridge are liable to be controlled by someone else. The free person is not the one over whom fortune has little power, but the one against whom fortune is powerless. This is the truth—if you want to challenge Jupiter, who has no wants, you must want nothing."

This is what Attalus told us, and what nature has told everyone. If you make the effort to reflect frequently on these things, you will strive to be happy, not seem happy—that is, to seem happy to yourself and not to others.

Farewell.

## Letter 111

*From Seneca to Lucilius*
*Greetings*

**1** You asked me what is the Latin for *sophismata*? There have been lots of attempts to find a word for them, but no single term has stuck. We don't, of course, like actual sophisms or make use of them, and we don't like the word either. I think Cicero's word "quibbles" (*cavillationes*) is the most apt.* **2** People who get absorbed in them do concoct real teasers, but it doesn't help them to live better by making them braver or more self-controlled or more high-minded.

In contrast, when a person has taken up philosophy as a treatment for himself, he enlarges his mind and exudes confidence. His superiority becomes more impressive the closer you get to him. **3** It's what happens with lofty mountains. From a distance their height is less apparent, but when you are near them their true elevation becomes quite clear. That, dear Lucilius, is what the authentic philosopher is like, the one who philosophizes in reality and not by tricks. He stands on a peak, marvelous, tall, truly great. He doesn't stretch right up or walk on tiptoe like people who improve their height by cheating, wanting to look taller than they really are. He is content with his actual size. 4 Why should he not be content to have grown to a point that the hand of fortune cannot reach? He is therefore above ordinary human events and equal to himself in every situation, whether his life moves ahead smoothly or is tossed around and passes through obstacles and difficulties. This steadfastness cannot be assured by the quibbles I was discussing a while ago. The mind plays with them but gets no benefit; it actually pulls philosophy down from its height to the flat ground.

5 I wouldn't forbid you from sometimes engaging in this activity, but only when you want to do nothing. There is, though, something very bad about them, the way they make us find them attractive, and by their specious subtlety hold our attention and delay us just when we are summoned by such weighty things, with scarcely an entire life being long enough for you to learn this one thing—not to think life itself important. "What about taking command of your life?" you say. That's the second task. No one has ever taken full command of his life without first ceasing to care about it.

Farewell.

## Letter 112

*From Seneca to Lucilius*
*Greetings*

1 I really do want your friend to be fashioned according to your desire, and I have made a start, but he proves to be a hard case. No, it's worse than that: he is a very soft case, a man depraved by a bad habit that has been long established.

2 Let me give you an analogy drawn from a hobby of mine.* It is not every vine that takes a graft: if it is old and gnarled, or weak and spindly, it either will not accept the scion or will not nourish it; it won't be joined with it and take on its quality and nature. For that reason, we usually make the initial cut above the soil so that if the

vine doesn't respond, we can try again, grafting a second time below the soil.

**3** This fellow you are writing to me about with all these instructions has no strength in him; he has indulged his faults. He is at one and the same time both enervated and hardened: he can neither accept reasoning nor provide it with nourishment. "But he himself wants this." Don't believe it. I don't mean that he is lying to you: he thinks that he wants it. He is fed up with self-indulgence; soon he will be reconciled to it again.

**4** "But he says he is tired of his way of life." No denying that; who isn't? People love their faults and hate them at the same time. So let's reserve judgment about him until he supplies us with proof that he and self-indulgence have become enemies. Right now, it is just that they are not getting along.

Farewell.

## Letter 113

*From Seneca to Lucilius*
*Greetings*

**1** You want me to send you my opinion on the question our school has bandied about, as to whether justice, courage, prudence, and the other virtues are animate creatures.* Minutiae of this kind, dearest Lucilius, have made people think that we train our minds on trivialities and waste our free time on discussions that will do us no good. I will comply with your request and expound our school's doctrine, but I warn you that I am of a different opinion. My view is that some topics are only right for people who go in for Greek shoes and cloaks.

So I will tell you what arguments moved our predecessors, or rather, what arguments they themselves set in motion:

**2** The mind is an animate creature; that is uncontroversial, since the mind makes us animate creatures and the expression "animate creatures" (*animalia*) is derived from it.*

But virtue is just the mind disposed in a certain way.

Therefore virtue is an animate creature.

Again:

> Virtue does something.
>
> But nothing can be done without an impulse.
>
> So, since it has an impulse, and only an animate creature has an impulse, virtue is an animate creature.

3 One might say, "If virtue is an animate creature, virtue itself possesses virtue." Why shouldn't it possess itself? In the way that the wise person does everything by means of virtue, so virtue acts by means of itself.

"In that case, all crafts are animate creatures, and likewise everything we consider and have in our minds. It follows that many thousands of animate creatures are dwelling in the narrow confines of our breast, and that each of us individuals is a multitude of animate creatures or possesses such a multitude." Do you wonder how to respond to this challenge? Although each one of these will be an animate creature, they will not be a multitude of animate creatures. How so? I will tell you, if you give me your close and undivided attention.

4 Individual animate creatures must have individual substances. The animate creatures you are speaking of have only one mind each; therefore it is only possible for each of them to be one animate creature, not multiple animate creatures. I myself am both an animate creature and a human being, yet you will not say that there are two of us. 5 Why not? Because the two would have to be separate. I mean that the one would have to be disjoined from the other, to constitute two. Anything that is multiple in a single entity falls under a single nature. Hence it is single. My mind is an animate creature, and so am I, but we are not two. Why not? Because my mind is a part of me. Something will only be counted by itself when it stands on its own. As long as it is a component of something else, it cannot be regarded as a different thing. Why not? Because that which is a different thing must be a thing in its own right, having its own distinctive property and being complete in itself.*

6 I warned you that I myself have a different opinion. If this doctrine is accepted, not only the virtues will be animate creatures but their opposing vices will be too, and also the emotions like anger, fear, grief, and mistrust. The matter will go on and on. All opinions

and all thoughts will be animate creatures. That is completely unacceptable. Not everything done by a human being is itself a human being. 7 "What is justice?" one asks. The mind disposed in a certain way. "So if the mind is an animate creature, justice is as well?" Not at all. Justice is a condition of the mind, a particular capacity. One and the same mind undergoes a variety of configurations, but it is not a different animate creature every time it does something different. Neither is everything done by the mind an animate creature.

8 If justice is an animate creature, and likewise courage and the other virtues, do they cease to be animate creatures from time to time and begin again, or are they always so? Virtues cannot come to an end. In that case many, or rather innumerable, animate creatures are circulating in this one mind.

9 One might say, "They are not many, because they are connected to a single thing, by virtue of being the parts and the components of a single thing." So we are giving our mind a shape like that of the hydra, any one of whose heads fights just by itself and causes harm just by itself. Yet not one of those heads is an animate creature; it is the head of an animate creature, while the hydra itself is a single animate creature. No one has said that the lion or the dragon in a Chimaera is an animate creature. These are its parts, and parts are not animate creatures.

10 Why do you deduce that justice is an animate creature? "It does something; that is, it benefits; anything that acts and benefits has an impulse; and what has an impulse is an animate creature." This is true if it has its own impulse, but in the case of justice the impulse belongs to the mind.

11 Every animate creature retains its original identity until it dies. A human being is a human being until he dies, a horse is a horse, and a dog is a dog. They cannot turn into something else. Suppose that justice—that is, the mind disposed in a certain way—is an animate creature. If we believe that, then courage is an animate creature because it is the mind disposed in a certain way. What mind? The mind that just now was justice? That mind is housed in the earlier animate creature; it cannot cross over into a different one. It must persist in the animate creature where it began its existence.

12 Besides, a single mind cannot belong to two animate creatures, much less a larger number. If justice, courage, self-control, and the

other virtues are animate creatures, how will they have a single mind? They must each have minds of their own; otherwise they are not animate creatures. **13** A plurality of animate creatures cannot have a single body. This our opponents themselves admit. What is the body of justice? "The mind." And what is the body of courage? "The same mind." Yet two animate creatures cannot have a single body. **14** "But that same mind clothes itself in the garb of justice, of courage, of self-control." That's how it would work if the mind were not courage at the time it is justice, and were not self-control at the time it is courage. But in fact all the virtues are present at the same time. How, then, will the individual virtues be animate creatures, seeing that a mind is single and cannot make more than a single animate creature?*

**15** Finally, no animate creature is a part of another animate creature; but justice is a part of the mind; therefore it is not an animate creature.

I think I am wasting effort on something obvious, something to be annoyed about rather than to debate. No animate creature is a part of something else. Look around at the bodies of everything. Not one of them is without its characteristic color, shape, and size. **16** There are many reasons for marveling at the divine creator's intellect, and they include, in my opinion, the fact that in the vast supply of things nothing ever turns out to be just the same. Even things that seem alike are different when you compare them. The creator has made numerous kinds of leaves, each one with its own distinctive property—numerous animate creatures, yet not one of them is exactly the same size as another, or without at least some difference. The creator imposed a requirement on himself that things that were different should be dissimilar and unequal. The virtues, as you Stoics say, are equal. Therefore they are not animate creatures.

**17** No animate creature fails to do things by itself; yet virtue does nothing by itself but acts only in conjunction with a human being. All animate creatures are either rational, like human beings, or nonrational, like beasts and cattle; virtues are certainly rational, but they are neither human nor divine; therefore they are not animate creatures.

**18** No animate creature endowed with reason does anything unless, first, it has been prompted by the impression of some particular thing; next, it has entertained an impulse; and finally, assent has confirmed this impulse. Let me tell you what assent is. "It is fitting for me to walk": I walk only after I have told myself this and have approved my judgment. "It is fitting for me to sit": then only do I sit.* This assent is not found in virtue. **19** Imagine that it is prudence: how will prudence assent to the judgment "It is fitting for me to walk"? This is not within its nature. Prudence looks to the interests of the thing it belongs to, not to itself, since it is incapable of walking or sitting. Therefore prudence does not possess assent, and what does not possess assent is not an animate creature endowed with reason. If virtue is an animate creature, it is something rational; but it is not something rational; therefore it is not an animate creature. **20** If virtue is an animate creature and every good is virtue, every good is an animate creature. Our school grants this. Saving one's father is a good, prudently stating one's opinion in the senate is a good, and so too is justly rendering judgment. Therefore saving one's father is an animate creature, and likewise prudently stating one's opinion. The point will go° so far that you cannot stop laughing. Prudently holding your tongue is a good, <and so too is dining well>°; therefore holding your tongue and dining are animate creatures. **21** Indeed, I will not stop playing around and amusing myself with these pedantic absurdities. If justice and courage are animate creatures, they are certainly earthly. Every earthly animate creature gets sick, and hungry, and thirsty. Therefore justice gets sick, courage gets hungry, and mercy gets thirsty.

**22** What next? Won't I ask them what shape these animate creatures have? Is it a human being's or a horse's or a wild beast's? If they give them a round shape like that of a god, I will ask whether greed, luxury, and madness are equally round. For they too are animate creatures.* If they make them round too, I will even ask whether prudent walking is an animate creature. They have to grant that, and go on to say that walking is an animate creature—and in fact a round one.

**23** You shouldn't think that I am the first member of our school to extemporize and have my own opinion. Cleanthes and Chrysippus did not agree about what walking is. Cleanthes says that it is the vital breath stretching from the directive faculty all the way to the feet, whereas Chrysippus says that it is the directive faculty itself.* Why, then, following the example of Chrysippus, shouldn't each man assert his own freedom and make fun of these animate creatures that are so numerous that the world itself cannot contain them?

**24** The opponent says, "The virtues are not a multitude of animate creatures, and yet they are animate creatures. Just as someone can be both a poet and an orator while remaining a single person, so these virtues are animate creatures but not a multitude of animate creatures. One and the same mind is also a just mind, and a sensible mind, a brave mind, being disposed in a certain way relative to each of the virtues." **25** <The controversy is>° settled; we are in agreement. For I too grant for the moment that the mind is an animate creature, deferring my final judgment on the matter to a later date. However, I deny that the mind's actions are animate creatures. Otherwise all words will be animate creatures, and so will all lines of verse. For if prudent speech is a good, and every good is an animate creature, speech is an animate creature. A prudent line of verse is a good, and every good is an animate creature, therefore a line of verse is an animate creature. In that case, "Arms and the man I sing" is an animate creature—but they cannot call it a round one, since it has six feet!*

**26** "For heaven's sake!" you say. "What a web you are weaving at this point!" I burst out laughing when I envision that solecisms, barbarisms, and syllogisms are animate creatures, and like a painter, I give them suitable faces. Is this what we are discussing with bent brow and knotted forehead? Can I not quote Caecilius* and say, "What solemn idiocy!" It's simply ludicrous. So let's instead turn to something that is useful and salutary for us, and ask how we can arrive at the virtues and what route will bring us to them.

**27** Don't teach me whether courage is an animate creature but that no animate creature is happy without courage, that is, unless it has acquired the strength to resist chance occurrences, and by pondering every contingency has mastered them before they happen. What is courage? It is the impregnable fortification for human weakness. By encircling himself with it, a person can calmly endure throughout this life's siege, because he uses his own strength and his own weapons. **28** At this point, I want to tell you the view of our Stoic philosopher Posidonius:

You should never think that the weapons of fortune will make you safe: fight with your own! Fortune does not arm us against fortune itself. Hence men who are equipped to resist the enemy are unarmed to resist fortune.*

**29** Alexander, it's true, destroyed and routed the Persians, the Hyrcanians, the Indians, and all the nations stretching from east to west; but he himself lay in darkness after killing one friend and again after losing another, alternately grieving over his crime and his loss. The conqueror of so many kings and peoples was felled by anger and gloom. He endeavored to control everything except his passions.*

**30** How terribly those people go astray who long to extend their imperial authority beyond the seas and deem themselves supremely fortunate if they hold many provinces with their armies and add new ones to the old, ignorant of that realm which is of equal greatness to the divine—self-mastery, the greatest command of all. **31** Teach° me the sanctity of the justice that looks to another's good, seeking nothing for itself except opportunities to be active. May it have nothing in common with self-seeking and reputation, but be content with itself!

Above all else, each person should convince himself of the following principle: "I should be just without reward." No, that is too little: he should persuade himself to enjoy spending unstintingly on this most lovely virtue. All his thoughts should be as distant as possible from personal advantages. You should not look around for the reward from a just action: there is a greater reward in simply doing the just thing.

**32** Keep concentrating on what I told you a while ago, that the number of people who are familiar with your fair-mindedness is completely irrelevant. People who want their virtue to be advertised are working for renown rather than virtue. Aren't you willing to be just without renown? In fact, of course, you will often have to combine being just with being disgraced. And then if you are wise, you should take delight in the bad reputation you have won by your good behavior.

Farewell.

# Letter 114

*From Seneca to Lucilius*
*Greetings*

1 What is the reason, you ask, why some ages foster a debased style of eloquence? Why are there tendencies among writers toward one vice or another, so that at one moment everything is long-winded bombast, at another effeminate mannerisms and singsong affectation? Why is there sometimes a fashion for forceful expressions—too forceful for what they convey—and at other times for unfinished sentences and innuendo, implying more than has been said? Why was one age unabashed in its use of metaphors? It's the familiar saying, proverbial among the Greeks: as we live, so do we speak. 2 Just as each individual's actions resemble his manner of speaking,° so does the style of speaking in a certain period resemble the conduct of the citizenry if discipline is in abeyance and dissipation has taken its place. Decadence in language is a sure sign of widespread self-indulgence if it is not found in just one or two but meets with general approval. 3 The condition of the talent cannot be different from that of the mind. If the mind is healthy, well put together, serious, self-controlled, the talent is likewise completely sober; if the mind is flawed, the talent is likewise inflamed. Do you not see that if the mind has lost its vigor, the limbs trail along and the feet shuffle? If the mind is effeminate, the softness is seen even in the walk; if it is energetic and fierce, the stride is quick; if it raves or is angry (a condition similar to raving), the movement of the body is disturbed and goes hurtling along instead of walking. Must not this be all the more true of the talent, since the talent is completely mixed with the mind and receives from it its shape, direction, and principle?

4 Maecenas's manner of life is so well known that there is no need for me to describe how he walked, how decadent he was, how he loved to be looked at and made no effort to hide his faults. What shall we say, then? Is not his prose style just as loose as his ungirded tunic? Is not his diction just as flamboyant as are his dress, his attendants, his house, his wife?* He might have been an extremely talented man if he had kept to the straight path, if he had not gone out of his

way to avoid being understood, if he had not been dissolute even in his language. That's what you will see in his discourse: the style of a drunkard—convoluted, wandering, full of liberties. 5

Along the rill, the strand, the forests foliage-clad.*

For shame! Try this:

They plow the deep with skiffs, leave gardens in the curling wake.

What's that again? Or these:

He curls his lady-hair and pigeons with his lips, sighing begins to speak, like woodland lords that chapel themselves with drooping neck.

An unregenerate crew, they test men at a party; with the wine cup they harrow houses and set a lure toward death.

Genius that scarce attests to his own festal day.

Filaments of yellow candle and the clatterish mill.

A hearth clad by a mother or a wife.

6 When you read these examples, does it not occur to you at once that this is the man who always went about the city in a loose tunic? For when he took command in Caesar's absence, he was without a belt even when he was giving the watchword. This is the man who appeared on the tribunal, the speakers' platform, and in every public gathering with a shawl draped over his head, ears sticking out on either side, just like the rich man's runaway slaves in a comic play. This is the man who at the height of civil wars, with the city armed and in turmoil, came among the people escorted by a pair of eunuchs—who were more masculine than he was. This is the man who married his wife a thousand times, though he had but one. 7 These words, so wantonly combined, so carelessly thrown about, so far from normal usage in their positioning, demonstrate that his character was equally outlandish, equally depraved, equally perverse. He gets great praise for his clemency, since he spared the sword and refrained from bloody deeds, displaying his power only in his licentious behavior. 8 Yet he spoils this very praise with the affectations of his contorted prose, which make it clear that he was not gentle but soft. Anyone

can see as much from the circuitous word order, the peculiar diction, the bizarre ideas—great ideas, often, but spineless in the manner of expression. Here is a head that was turned by too much prosperity.

**9** In some instances the fault lies with the individual; in others with the times. When prosperity brings on widespread self-indulgence, the first thing that happens is that more care is given to dress and grooming; next, there is a great fuss over household furnishings; then attention turns to the houses themselves: a new wing makes a house into a villa; inner walls gleam with imported marble; roof tiles are embellished with gold; coffered ceilings are reflected in the polished tiles of the flooring. Next, opulence finds its way to the table. Novelty and changes in the accustomed order become the fashion: what once was dessert becomes an appetizer; what used to be served while guests were arriving now follows them out the door. **10** Once the mind has taken on the habit of rejecting what is customary and holding all traditional usage in contempt, it seeks novelty also in its manner of speech. Sometimes it recalls archaic and outmoded words and brings them back into use; sometimes it skews normal usage and even invents new words that have never been heard before.° Sometimes—what is all the rage just now—a spate of striking metaphors is considered the height of elegance. **11** Some speakers cut short the thought, thinking they will be well received if the sentence is left hanging as a mere hint to the listener of what is meant. Others cannot let go of a thought but draw it out further and further. Others carry things to a fault—which one has to do sometimes, in a grand endeavor—but then don't stop, and instead fall in love with the fault for its own sake. So wherever you see a debased rhetorical style come into fashion, you may be sure that other forms of conduct have also gone astray. Just as luxury in dress and dinner parties is a symptom of sickness within the society, so an unrestrained style of eloquence, when commonly practiced, demonstrates that the mind from which the words proceed has fallen into decline.

**12** Debased usages are taken up not only by the lower elements in the audience but also by the more educated crowd. You need not be surprised at that: their togas are different; their tastes are the same. What might surprise you more is that praise is accorded not only to a faulty performance but even to the faults themselves. This is what always happens: no talent has ever become popular without being forgiven for some faults. Give me any great name you like, and I will tell you what his contemporaries forgave in him, what they chose to ignore. I can give you many examples of men whose faults were not held against them, and some whose faults were even to their advantage. Again, I can give you examples of very famous men, men held up as models for admiration, who would be ruined if one were to correct their mistakes—their faults are so closely intermingled with their excellences that removing one would remove the other. 13 Moreover, there is no set rule for rhetorical style: it changes with the convention of the community, and that never remains the same for very long.

Many of our current orators seek out words from an earlier time, so that they sound like the Twelve Tables. Gracchus, Crassus, and Curio are too recent and too civilized for their taste: they go all the way back to Appius and Coruncanius.* Others do the opposite: they don't want to employ any expression that is not in current usage, and so end up sounding trite and banal. 14 Both approaches are quite mistaken, just as it is a mistake to use only expressions that stand out or that have a poetical ring, avoiding everything ordinary and commonplace. As far as I am concerned, both are equally at fault. One grooms himself more than he ought, the other less; one plucks the hair from his legs, the other neglects even his armpits.

15 Let's move on to the question of word order. How many kinds of error can I describe for you there? Some people favor a harsh, jerky style: they deliberately rearrange a phrase if it runs along too smoothly, wanting every juxtaposition to be abrupt. They think there is a rugged masculinity in anything that strikes the ear as uneven. Others glide along so softly and melodiously as to create not a rhetorical composition but a musical one. 16 Need I mention the ones who postpone certain words and make us wait a long time for them to appear at long last at the end of the sentence? How about the nicely turned Ciceronian period, that holds us gently in suspense until it resolves, never deviating from the prescribed rhythm? Nor does the fault consist only° in the form of the sentences, but also if the thoughts expressed are either feeble and childish or undisciplined, daring more than modesty permits; or if they are flowery and overly sweet; or if they are fine-sounding but empty, having no real import.

17 Such faults are made popular by a single speaker who domi-

nates oratory in his times; the rest imitate him and also influence one another. For example, when Sallust was writing, half-finished thoughts, abrupt ends to phrases, and mystifying brevity were considered the height of elegance. Lucius Arruntius, an exceptionally frugal man and a historian of the Punic War, was a follower of Sallust and excelled at writing in that manner. Sallust has the phrase, "He effected an army with silver"; that is, he bought one. Arruntius fell in love with that expression* and used it on every page. In one place he says, "They effected a rout for our men"; in another, "Hiero, king of the Syracusans, effected a war"; in another, "This news effected the surrender of Panhormus to the Romans." 18 And that's only a sampling of such expressions—the whole book is full of them. Locutions found occasionally in Sallust are frequent in his pages; indeed, they occur almost continually, and there's a reason for that: the one slipped into them by accident, the other went looking for them. 19 You see what happens when someone takes a fault as a model for imitation. Sallust spoke of "wintering waters"; Arruntius in Book 1 of the *Punic War* says, "The season wintered suddenly," and in another passage, meaning to say that it had been a cold year, "The whole year wintered"; and in another, "Then he sent sixty cargo vessels unladen but for the troops and necessary crew, for the north wind was wintering." He shoves the word in everywhere he can. Sallust says in one passage, "In the midst of civil strife he seeks the reputes of goodness and of fairness." Arruntius could not resist saying right away in book 1 that the "reputes" concerning Regulus were tremendous. 20 These faults and others like them that are acquired through imitation are not signs of self-indulgence or a debased mind. You can infer a person's disposition only from his own faults, those arising from himself. When he is angry, his language is likewise angry; when he is upset, his language is excessively vehement; when he is a fop, his language is languid and loose-limbed.

21 Consider what you see in men who pluck out all or most of their facial hair, or shave a small area around the lips and let the rest grow, or wear capes of outrageous colors or togas of loose weave. They don't want to do anything that might be overlooked. They seek to catch the eye and draw attention to themselves, not minding criticism as long as they are noticed. Such is the prose of Maecenas and of every writer who errs not by mistake but consciously and deliberately.

This comes of a serious mental fault. **22** Just as when one drinks wine the speech does not begin to falter until the mind, overwhelmed by its burden, has swayed or succumbed, so also that drunkenness of his prose (what else can I call it?) does not affect a person unless his mind is already slipping. Let us therefore care for the mind; for from it proceed meaning and words, demeanor, facial expression, and walk. If the mind is healthy and sound, its language is likewise sturdy, strong, and virile; if the mind stumbles, the rest collapses as well. **23**

> Preserve their king, and all are of one mind;
> if he is lost, they break their faith.*

The mind is our king: while it is unharmed, our other parts all do their duty, maintaining their obedience and their subservience; but if it falters, they hesitate, and if it yields to pleasure, then its skills and activities wilt, its every endeavor is suggestive of laxity and languor.

**24** Since I've made the comparison, I'll continue it. Our mind is sometimes a king, sometimes a tyrant. It is a king when it looks toward what is honorable, concerns itself with the well-being of the body entrusted to it, and commands no ugly or shameful action; but when it is undisciplined, greedy, and lascivious, it passes over to the terrible, hateful name and becomes a tyrant. Then undisciplined emotions take it over and weigh upon it. At first, to be sure, it rejoices, as does the populace when it receives largesse to its own detriment and is fed full to no purpose, pawing at what it cannot consume. **25** But when this tyrant's sickness erodes its strength more and more, when the indulgences work their way down into the bones and tendons, then it finds enjoyment in the sight of those to whom it has made itself useless through excessive greed: it takes vicarious pleasure in observing the pleasures of others, becoming an accomplice and a witness to their lusts, since in surfeit it has robbed itself of the use of its own. Though it has an abundance of gratifications at hand, it derives from them more bitterness than satisfaction, because it cannot send the entire parade of them through the throat and stomach, because it cannot tussle with the entire mob of catamites and women: it grieves, in fact, that the greater part of its felicity is inaccessible because of the narrow confines of the body.

**26** Dear Lucilius, is this not madness? Not one among us thinks of himself as mortal; not one as weak; indeed, not one of us thinks of himself as just one person! Look at our kitchens, with so many ovens, and cooks running this way and that between them: can you believe it is just one belly, when all this commotion is preparing a meal for it? Look at our wine cellars, our warehouses filled with many generations of vintages: can you believe it is just one belly, when the wines of so many years and regions are laid by for its use? Look how many places the soil is tilled, how many thousands of peasants are at work plowing and hoeing: can you believe it is just one belly, when fields are sown for it both in Sicily and in North Africa? **27** When will we be whole and sound? When will we moderate our desires? When each one of us takes a count of himself and a measure of his own body, and realizes how little he can really contain and for how short a time. But nothing will do as much to help you toward self-control in all things as the reflection that life is short, and the little we have of it is uncertain. In every act, keep your eyes on death.

Farewell.

# Letter 115

*From Seneca to Lucilius*
*Greetings*

**1** I prefer that you not be too anxious about words and sentence structure, dear Lucilius. I have more important things for you to worry about. Ask yourself what you are writing, not how; and even for the content your aim should be not to write it but to feel it, and to take those thoughts and impress them more deeply upon yourself, like a seal.

**2** When someone's rhetorical style exhibits great care and polish, you may be sure that his mind is likewise occupied with trivial matters. The great man speaks more casually than that: his words are heartfelt, not carefully arranged. You know those prettified youths with their hairstyles and beard styles, straight from the salon: you don't expect anything brave, anything solid from them! Speech is the dress and grooming of the mind: if our style is all trimmed about and made up and fussed over, it shows that the mind does not ring true either, that something is amiss. Melodiousness is no masculine ornament.

**3** If we could examine the mind of a good man, O what a beautiful, what a sacred sight we would see! What grandeur, what calm would shine forth in it, and what constellations of the virtues: justice on one side, courage on the other, moderation and prudence over there. Besides these, frugality, self-control, endurance, generosity, and cheerfulness would shed their light upon it, and human kindness, which (hard as it is to believe) is in fact a rarity among human beings. Foresight too, and refinement, and most outstanding of all, greatness of spirit: what grace, and, by god, what dignity would these bestow! How great its authority would be, and how much appreciated: beloved it would be, yet at the same time revered. **4** If one could only behold this countenance, more lofty and more radiant than anything in human life is wont to be, would he not stop, astonished as by the advent of a deity, and utter a voiceless prayer of propitiation for the sight, then summoned by the benevolence of that visage, step forward into adoration and worship? Then after gazing for a long time at that aspect, so high exalted above anything in our experience, at those eyes beaming with a gentle light yet also with living fire, he would at last, in fear and wonder, exclaim in the words of our poet Virgil:

> **5** Maiden, how shall I name you? For your face
> is not that of a mortal, and your voice
> has not a human sound. Be kindly, then,
> and lighten all my labors.*

This deity will be manifest to us; it will lighten our labors, if we choose to worship it. But such worship does not consist in slaughtering the fattened carcasses of bulls, or in dedicating objects of gold and silver or pouring donations into some treasury, but only in a pure and righteous will. **6** Let me say it again: there is not one of us who would not be on fire with love for it, if only we could see it. As it is, there are many obstacles that either dazzle us with excessive brightness or plunge us into darkness. But just as medicines can cleanse our eyes and sharpen our vision, so also, if only we are willing, we can free our minds of every impediment to their vision. Virtue will then be visible to us, even buried in the body, even with poverty in the way, even with low estate and poor reputation crowding in around it. I repeat: we will see that beautiful sight, even though it may be covered with dirt. **7** And we will perceive just as well the nastiness and grime of the mind that is full of distress even when it is surrounded by the glitter and gleam of wealth, when the false glare of high repute and great power assails the eyes from every side.

**8** Only then will we be in a position to understand what worthless items we admire. We are just like children, who set great store by their playthings and care more about any cheap trinket than they do about a sibling or even a parent. As Aristo says, how are we different from them, except that we with our statues and paintings have a more expensive form of silliness? They delight in smooth pebbles found on the beach with specks of different colors; we delight in patterned marbles imported from the deserts of Egypt or the wilds of Africa, broad columns supporting some hall or dining pavilion large enough for an entire town. **9** We marvel at rooms with marble walls, even though we know it is only a thin veneer. We deceive our own eyes: when we gild a ceiling, are we not rejoicing in a lie? For we know that some unattractive wood is hidden under the gold. And the pretense of ornamentation is not only in paneling and coffering. Look at all those who strut about in high places: their prosperity is nothing but gilding. Examine it closely and you will see how much rottenness is hidden beneath that thin coating of status. **10** One thing has a lock on every magistracy, every judgeship; one thing makes the magistrate or the judge: money! From the moment when money began to be held in honor, true honor has fallen by the wayside. Merchants and merchandise by turns, we ask not what a thing is but what it costs. We are loyal at a price, and disloyal at a price: we behave honorably as long as we expect to get something for it, and will do the opposite if criminality has more to offer us.

**11** We learned from our parents to gaze with admiration at silver and gold.* Greed instilled at a tender age has settled in deep and has grown with us. Next come the people at large: on every other point they are at odds with one another, but on this they agree. This they admire, this they want for themselves and their families; this they consecrate to the gods when they want to appear grateful, as if it were the greatest of all human possessions. Then our character becomes so debased that poverty is held accursed, despised by the rich and loathed by the paupers themselves. **12** The works of the poets come in as well, inflaming our passions: wealth is praised in them as if it were the sole glory and adornment of life. As far as the poets are concerned, the immortal gods have nothing better to give or to possess for themselves.

> The palace of the Sun was high on lofty columns,
> splendid with shining gold.*

13 And look at his chariot:

> The axle was of gold; the shaft was gold;
> the curving wheels were rimmed about with gold;
> and silver were their radiating spokes.*

They also speak of the "Golden Age," meaning to portray that as the best era.

14 Even in Greek tragedy there are those who for a profit would give up their innocence, their health, even their good name.*

> Let me be called a scoundrel, but a rich one.

> We all ask if he's rich, not if he's good.

> Not why you have it, not the place you got it,
> but just how much—that's what they want to know.

> In all the world, a man's worth what he owns.

> What should one be ashamed of? Having nothing.

> Let me live rich, or let me die a pauper.

> To die while making money; that's a blessing.

> Money's the vast good of the human race.
> It is more pleasant than a mother's love,
> a baby's touch, the reverence due a father.
> If Venus's face can match this lovely sparkle,
> she well deserves the loves of gods and men.

15 When this last speech was delivered in Euripides' tragedy,* the entire populace leapt to its feet with the single aim of driving both actor and play from the theater, until Euripides himself jumped up on the stage and begged the audience to wait and see how that ad-

mirer of gold would come out. Bellerophon got his just deserts in that story, and so does every person in his own. **16** For greed never goes unpunished. Yet greed in itself is punishment enough. What tears, what pain it costs us! How it suffers over what it lacks—and how it suffers over what it has acquired! There are the day-to-day worries too: the more a person has, the more anxiety he feels. Money is even more of a torment to those who have it than to those who are trying to get it. How they lament each loss! For they lose large sums, and think them even larger than they are. Even if fortune takes nothing away from them, whatever they fail to acquire seems like a loss.

**17** "But people call him a prosperous man, a wealthy man, and wish to have as much as he does." I grant you that. What of it? So they incur both misery and envy; can you think of a worse state? If only those who wish for other people's riches would consult first with the rich themselves! And if only those who run for office would consult first with previous candidates who have been elected to the most prestigious positions in the state! They would change their wishes quickly enough. Yet those who complain of their own success are still eager for more of it. People are never satisfied with their own prosperity, even when it comes to them all at once. They complain of their own plans, their own advancements, and say always that what they left behind was preferable.

**18** So this is what philosophy will do for you—and indeed, I think it is the greatest gift of all: you will never regret what you have done. This is the solid ground of happiness, which no tempest can shake. But you will not get there on the winds of rhetoric, the easy flow of words. Let that go as it will; but let the mind have its own consistency, its own composure. Let it be great, secure in its beliefs, and content where others are discontent. Let it judge of its own progress by its manner of living, realizing that it has knowledge only to the extent that it is free of desire and fear.

Farewell.

# Letter 116

*From Seneca to Lucilius*
*Greetings*

**1** The question has often been raised whether it is better to have moderate emotions or none at all. Philosophers of our school exclude them altogether, whereas the Peripatetics restrain them. I myself don't see how it can be healthy or useful to have even a moderate amount of an illness.*

Don't be afraid, I am not going to rob you of anything that you don't want to be refused. I will be accommodating and compliant to your own tendencies and to the things you regard as life's necessities, utilities, and joys; I will merely remove what's faulty. After I have banned desire, I will allow for wanting,* so that you will do the same things without anxiety and with firmer resolve, and will experience even your pleasures with greater intensity. Why shouldn't pleasures come your way even more easily if you are their master rather than their slave?

**2** You respond, "It's natural for me to suffer torment at the loss of a friend. Allow my justified tears the right to fall! It's natural to be affected by people's opinions and to be saddened when they are negative. Why won't you let me have such an honorable fear of being badly thought of?" No fault lacks its advocate. At the start they are all bashful and persuadable, but then they grow and grow. You won't succeed in stopping them once you allow them to begin. **3** All emotions are feeble at first; then they arouse themselves and gather strength as they advance. It's easier to refuse them entry than to drive them out.

No one is denying that all emotions stem from a source that is, in a sense, natural. Nature has endowed us with a concern for ourselves; but once we indulge this concern excessively, it becomes a fault. Nature infused the necessities of life with pleasure, not so that we would pursue pleasure, but so that the supervening pleasure would make what is indispensable more welcome to us. If the pleasure is pursued for its own sake, it becomes self-indulgence. Let us, then, resist emotions as soon as they start to come in, since, as I said, it's easier to refuse them admission than to get them to leave.

**4** I hear you say, "Let me grieve to some extent, and feel apprehension to some extent." But this "some extent" of yours goes on and on, and it refuses to stop when you want it to. The wise person can safely restrain himself without getting upset, and can put a halt to his tears and pleasures when he wants to. We others have difficulty in withdrawing, and so it's best for us not to go on at all. **5** I think Panaetius gave a neat response to the youth who asked whether the wise man would fall in love. "As regards the wise man," he said, "we shall see; but as for you and me, who are a long way from achieving wisdom, we had better refrain so as to avoid a condition that is frantic, out of control, enslaved to another, and lacking in self-worth. If our advances are accepted, we are excited by the other person's favor; if not, we are set on fire by the disdain. An easy love affair is as harmful as one fraught with difficulty; we are drawn in by ease, and we struggle against difficulty. Knowing our weakness, then, we do better to stay calm. Let us not entrust our feeble disposition to wine or beauty or flattery or any other temptation."*

**6** My point is that Panaetius's response to the question about love applies to all emotions. Let's stay off the slippery ground as far as possible, since it's hard for us to stand firm even on dry land. **7** You will confront me on this issue with the standard objection to the Stoics: "Your promises are too great; your demands are too exacting. We are merely little folk; we can't deny ourselves everything. We are going to feel sorrow, but just a bit; we are going to long for things, but in moderation; we shall get angry, but not implacably so." **8** Do you know why we aren't capable of such things? We don't believe that we have that capability.

In fact, though, there's something else involved: our love for our own faults. We defend them and we would rather make excuses for them than shake them off. Human nature has been endowed with sufficient strength if only we use it. We have only to assemble our resources and get them all to fight on our behalf rather than against us. Inability is just an excuse; the real reason is unwillingness.

Farewell.

# Letter 117

*From Seneca to Lucilius*
*Greetings*

**1** By posing such trifling questions to me, you will keep me very busy, and without realizing it, you will involve me in a lot of argument and trouble. I cannot in good faith disagree with our school on these points, and yet I cannot in good conscience agree with them. You are asking about the truth of the Stoic doctrine that wisdom is something good, but *being wise* is not.* First I will explain the Stoics' thinking; then I will venture to state my own opinion.

**2** Our school holds that what is good is a body, because what is good acts, and whatever acts is a body.* What is good benefits; but in order for something to benefit, it has to act; if it acts, it is a body. Stoics also say that wisdom is something good. It follows that they have to say that it is corporeal. **3** But they do not think that *being wise* has the same status: it is incorporeal and supervenient on something else, namely, wisdom.* Hence it neither acts upon nor benefits anything. "What's that? Don't we say that *being wise* is something good?" We do say it, but with reference to what it depends on, that is, with reference to wisdom itself.

**4** In opposition to them, listen to the response made by others before I begin to go my own way and align myself with a different viewpoint. "In that way," these others say, "*living happily* is not something good either. Like it or not, your school has to respond that a happy life is something good and *living happily* is not something good." **5** The following objection is also made: "You want to be wise; therefore *being wise* is a choiceworthy thing; if it is choiceworthy, it is something good." Our school is forced to twist words and insert one more syllable into the expression "choiceworthy," which our language does not allow to be inserted. If you permit me, I will make the insertion. "What is good," they say, "is 'choiceworthy'; what accrues to us when we have obtained the good thing is 'choosable.'* The latter is not sought as something good, but is an addition to the good that has been sought."

**6** I am not of the same view, and I judge that members of our school fall into this trap because they are already shackled by the first link in the chain and do not have the freedom to alter their formula. We are in the habit of granting a lot to the preconception of all people, and we take the fact that everyone agrees on something to be evidence for its truth.* For instance, we infer that gods exist (among other reasons) because everyone has this opinion implanted in them and no nation anywhere is so remote from laws and customs that it does not believe in some gods. When we discuss the immortality of souls, it weighs heavily with us that people generally agree on this point and either fear or worship the shades of the underworld. I make use of this general conviction: you will find no one who does not think that both wisdom and *being wise* are good things.

**7** I shall not do what defeated gladiators do and appeal to the public. Let us join battle with our own weapons. Is what supervenes on a thing external or internal to it? If it is internal to it, it is as much a body as that thing. For nothing can supervene on something without touching it, and what touches something is a body; nothing can supervene without activity, and what is active is a body. If it is external, it must have withdrawn after it supervened. If it withdrew, it is capable of motion, and what is capable of motion is a body.

**8** You are expecting me to deny that a race is different from *racing*, heat from *heating*, and light from *lighting*. I grant that these are different but not that they are of a different status. If health is an indifferent, the same goes for *being in good health*. And if beauty is an indifferent, the same goes for *being beautiful*. If justice is something good, so also is *being just*; if shameful behavior is something bad, so also is *behaving shamefully*, just as much as, if eye soreness is something bad, the same goes for *having sore eyes*. As proof of this, consider: neither can exist without the other. One who has wisdom is wise, and one who is wise has wisdom. It is indubitable that the one is exactly like the other; in fact, some people find them to be one and the same.

**9** But I would like to ask them this: since all things are either good or bad or indifferent, in which category should we place *being wise*? In their view, it is not a good, and it is certainly not something bad. It follows that it is intermediate. But the intermediate is also what we call indifferent, meaning something like money, beauty, and high status, which can befall the bad person as much as the good. But this thing, *to be wise*, cannot befall anyone who is not good. Therefore it is not indifferent. And it is certainly not a bad thing, because it cannot befall anyone bad. Therefore it is a good. That which only the good person can have is a good. Only the good person can have *being wise*. Therefore it is a good.

**10** One might say, "It is something that supervenes on wisdom." In that case, I ask whether what you call *being wise* activates wisdom or is activated by wisdom. Either way, whether it acts or is acted upon, it is a body. That is because everything that acts or is acted upon is a body.* If it is a body, it is a good; for the only thing that kept it from being a good was that it was incorporeal.

**11** The Peripatetics hold that there is no difference between wisdom and *being wise*, because each of them implies the other. You cannot really believe, can you, that anyone can *be wise* without possessing wisdom, or that anyone who *is wise* does not possess wisdom? **12** But the old logicians make a distinction between these two things, and from them this distinction has come right down to the Stoics.* Let me explain it. There is a difference, is there not, between "a field" and "possessing a field," because the latter pertains to the possessor but not to the field as such. In the same way, there is a difference between wisdom and *being wise*. You will grant, I presume, that there are two items here: what is possessed, and the one who possesses it. Wisdom is what is possessed, and the one who *is wise* possesses it. Wisdom is a perfected mind, or a mind brought to its ultimate and best condition; that is to say, wisdom is the art of life. What is *being wise*? I cannot describe *it* as a perfected mind, but as that which befalls one who possesses a perfected mind. Thus a good mind is one thing, and possessing, as it were, a good mind is something else.

**13** My opponent says, "There are different kinds of bodies: for instance, this one is a human being, and that one is a horse. They are accompanied by movements of thought that make predications about bodies. These movements have their own distinctive property, apart from the bodies. For example, I see Cato walking: sense perception has revealed this, and my mind has believed it. What I see is a body, and it is to a body that I have directed my eyes and my mind. Then I say, 'Cato is walking.' What I now say is not a body but something predicated of a body, which some call a 'proposition,' others a 'predication,' and others 'what is said.'* Similarly, when we say 'wisdom,' we understand something corporeal; when we say '*is wise*,' we are saying something about a body. There is a very great difference between referring to something and saying something about that thing."

**14** Let us suppose for now that we are dealing here with *two* things. (I am not yet stating my own opinion.) What is to stop one of them from being different but still good? Just now I was drawing a distinction between "a field" and "possessing a field." Obviously, the one who possesses has a different nature from the thing that is possessed. One is land, and the other is a person. But in the matter that is under discussion, each thing is of the same nature, both the one who possesses wisdom and wisdom itself. **15** Besides, in the former case that which is possessed and its possessor are quite distinct, but here, possessor and thing possessed are inherent in the same item. While land is possessed legally, wisdom is possessed naturally. Land can be sold and passed on to someone else, but wisdom cannot depart from its owner. Hence you should not draw comparisons between things that are intrinsically different.

I had started to say that the things we are discussing could be two in number and yet in both cases good. For instance, wisdom and the wise person are two in number, but you concede that both of them are good. Just as nothing prevents both wisdom and the possessor of wisdom from being good, so nothing prevents wisdom and *having wisdom*, that is, *being wise*, from being good. **16** I want to be a wise person just for this reason: so that I may *be wise*. Well, then! Mustn't the latter be a good, given that without it, the former isn't a good either? It is your doctrine, surely, that wisdom should not be accepted if it is not to be used. What is the use of wisdom? *To be wise.* This is what makes wisdom supremely valuable. Remove its use, and wisdom becomes superfluous. If tortures are bad, *being tortured* is bad; in fact, if you eliminate the consequent, then tortures would not be bad. Wisdom is the disposition of a perfected mind, and *being wise* is the use of a perfected mind. How can the use of something not be good if the thing itself is not good without its use?

**17** I ask you whether wisdom is choiceworthy. You answer that it is. I ask you whether the use of wisdom is choiceworthy. You say again that it is. In fact, you say that you would not accept it if you were prevented from using it. That which is choiceworthy is good. *Being wise* is the use of wisdom, in exactly the way that speaking eloquently is the use of eloquence and seeing is the use of eyes. Therefore *being wise* is the use of wisdom; but the use of wisdom is choiceworthy; therefore *being wise* is choiceworthy. If it is choiceworthy, it is good.

18 All this time, I have been reproaching myself for imitating the people I accuse and for wasting words on an open-and-shut case. Can there be any doubt that if heat is bad, it is also bad to be hot? That if cold is bad, it is bad to be cold? That if life is good, living is good too? While all these points are germane to wisdom, they are not internal to it. We need to spend time within wisdom itself.

19 Supposing we want to take the discussion in a different direction, philosophy offers plenty of diversions. Let's investigate the nature of the gods, or the nutriment of the stars and their various orbits, or whether human affairs develop in correspondence to their motions, or whether they are the origin of movement for terrestrial bodies and minds, or whether even so-called chance occurrences are bound by a fixed law and nothing ever happens spontaneously or outside the world's order. These topics are remote from moral education, but they elevate the mind and raise it to the magnitude of its subject matter.* What I was talking about a while ago lowers and diminishes us; it does not sharpen the mind, as you people suppose, but merely narrows it. 20 Are we, I beg you, going to waste our effort on something that may be false and is certainly useless? We need that effort—we owe it to greater and better things! How am I going to be better off from knowing whether wisdom and *being wise* are different, or from knowing that the former is a good but the latter is not? I'll risk this one. Let's roll the dice: you get wisdom and I get *being wise*. We shall come out even.

21 I would rather you show me the way to achieve these things. Tell me what I ought to avoid and what I ought to aim for, what practices will enable me to strengthen my flagging mind, how I may ward off things that catch me by surprise and upset me, how I can be a match for any number of misfortunes, how I may dispel the troubles that have come upon me and the ones that I have brought upon myself. Teach me how to bear sorrow without groaning and success without making others groan, and how not to await the final and inevitable moment passively but to decide for myself when to make my escape. 22 Nothing seems to me more shameful than to pray for death. If you want to live, why do you pray to die? If you do

not want to, why do you ask the gods for what they gave you when you were born? Just as it has been settled that you will die at some time, whether you want to or not, so it is in your power to die whenever you wish. The one is necessary for you, the other is an option.

**23** I just read a most shocking opening of a supposedly eminent rhetorician's speech: "If only I could die as soon as possible!" Madman, you are praying for what is already yours. "If only I could die as soon as possible!" Have you perhaps grown old as you were talking? If not, why wait? No one is stopping you. Slip off however you like. Choose any part of the natural world, and tell it to provide you with an exit. Consider the elements through which the world is governed, water, earth, and air: these are no more causes of living than they are ways to die. **24** "If only I could die as soon as possible"? What do you mean by "as soon as possible"? Why set a date? Death can happen faster than you are praying for. Your words belong to a feeble mind, one that uses this curse just to gain pity. A person who prays for death does not really want to die. Ask the gods for life and health. But if what you want is to die, death has this benefit: you no longer need to pray.

**25** These should be our reflections, dear Lucilius, these are the ways to shape our minds. This is wisdom and this is *being wise*: not engaging in pointless debates over the most futile technicalities. When fortune has presented you with so many problems that you have not yet solved, are you still quibbling? How foolish it is to be still brandishing your weapons after you have heard the signal for battle! Away with these practice weapons! You need the real things. Tell me the means of keeping my mind undisturbed by any gloom or dread, the means of shedding this load of unacknowledged desires. Get something done!

**26** "Wisdom is a good, but *being wise* is not." This is the way for us to be told that we are not wise, and for our entire philosophy to be mocked as a waste of time. Suppose I were to tell you that there is also a debate about whether future wisdom is a good. Tell me: would it make you wonder whether granaries already feel the future harvest? Whether children have some strength or solidity that enables them to feel their future maturity? While people are sick, they derive no more benefit from health that is to come than a runner or a wrestler is refreshed by a vacation that is still many months away. **27** No one is ignorant of the fact that what is in the future is not good, precisely because it is in the future. Anything good is necessarily beneficial, and only present things can benefit. Something that does not benefit is not good, while if it does benefit, it is already so. I am to be wise in the future. That will be a good for me when I am wise, but meanwhile it is not. Something must exist before it can take on a certain quality.

**28** How, I ask you, can something that is still nothing be a good already? If I say about something, "It is in the future," isn't that the best possible proof that it does not exist? What is still to come has clearly not yet arrived. "Spring will come": I know that it is now winter. "Summer will come": I know that it is not summer. My strongest argument for something's not being present is that it is future. **29** I will be wise, I hope, but meanwhile I am not wise. If I had that good, I would already be free of my present bad condition. My being wise is in the future. Thence you can realize that I am not yet wise. I cannot be in that good condition and in this bad condition at the same time. The two do not coexist: good and bad are not together in the same person.

**30** Let's speed past these intricate trifles and hasten to what is going to bring us real help. No one who has anxiously summoned a midwife for his daughter in labor peruses the announcement and program for the games. No one who is running to a fire at his house studies the checkerboard to see how the trapped piece can escape. **31** But, for heaven's sake, such news is coming at you from all sides: the house in flames, your children in danger, your country under siege, your goods being ransacked. Pile on shipwrecks, earthquakes, and anything else that is fearful. When you are surrounded by all these things, do you only have time for amusements? Are you investigating the difference between wisdom and *being wise*? Are you tying and untying knots, when such a huge weight hangs over your head?

**32** Nature has not been so kind and generous in the time it has given us that we can afford to waste any. Take a look at how many moments the most careful people lose. Each person loses some time to illness, either his own or in his family; some time goes to essential business, some to civic duties; and sleep takes up a part of our life. When our time is so compressed and rushed and fleeting, what good is it to waste the greater part of it on trivialities? **33** Consider too that the mind prefers to amuse itself rather than restore its health, making philosophy into entertainment when it is really a cure. I don't know the difference between wisdom and *being wise*. I do know that it makes no difference whether I know this or not. Tell me: when I have learned what the difference is, will I then be wise? Why, then, do you keep me busy with the terminology of wisdom rather than with the acts of wisdom? Make me braver, make me more confident, make me fortune's equal or superior. And I can be superior if I direct all that I learn toward this goal.

Farewell.

# BOOK TWENTY

## *Letter 118*

*From Seneca to Lucilius*
*Greetings*

1 You are pressing me to write more often. Let's do the accounts, then, and you will not find yourself in the black. We had agreed that you would take the initiative by writing first and I would write back. Still, I will not be stringent with you. I know that you are trustworthy, so I will give you something on credit. But I will not do what Cicero, that master of eloquence, tells Atticus to do: even if he has nothing to say, to write whatever comes into his head.* 2 I can never lack for something to write, even setting aside all the stuff that fills Cicero's letters, like what candidate is in difficulties; who is campaigning on borrowed means and who is using his own; who has Caesar's support for the consulship, or Pompey's, or that of his own money box; or "what a harsh financier Caecilius is, who won't lend a penny even to his relatives at less than one percent a month."* Instead of treating other people's problems, it is better to address one's own—to examine oneself, see all the things one is a candidate for, and then not campaign for any of them.

3 The fine thing to do, my dear Lucilius, the course of safety and freedom, is to seek no office at all, to bypass all fortune's elections. When the constituencies have assembled and the candidates wait in suspense on their platforms, some offering bribes, others doing business through an agent, and yet others kissing the hands of people they will not deign to touch once elected, and everyone is all agog waiting for the herald's proclamation, how enjoyable it would be, don't you think, to stand there idly watching this market with nothing to sell or to buy? 4 But how much greater is the joy one feels when one gazes without concern not at the elections for praetors or consuls but at the mighty efforts people expend in seeking offices that are renewed annually, or permanent positions of power, or successful results of war and triumphal celebrations, or wealth, or

marriages and children, or their own safety and that of their families!
What a mental achievement it is to be the only person who seeks
nothing, asks no favors from anyone, and says, "Fortune, you and I
have nothing to do with each other. I grant you no power over me.
I know that men like Cato are rejected by you, while you create the
likes of Vatinius.* I do not ask you for anything." This is the way to
remove fortune from office.

5 So we can write to each other about these things, pouring forth
material that will be constantly renewed as we survey so many restless thousands who go from bad to worse in their quest for some
ruinous acquisition, pursuing things that they will soon need to
avoid or to despise. 6 Who was ever satisfied to gain what seemed
at first too much to expect? Prosperity is not some greedy prize, as
people suppose; it is a paltry thing, and therefore satisfies no one.
You believe your wants to be on a high level, because you are far
away from them. But the man who has attained them finds them
insignificant. If I am not mistaken, he is still seeking to climb. The
point that you regard as the summit is merely a step on the way
for him. 7 Everyone suffers from not knowing the truth. Misled by
talk, they are drawn toward things they take to be good; and then,
after achieving them and suffering greatly, they discover them to be
bad or worthless or less than they had expected. Most people are
impressed by things that deceive them from a distance, and "good"
is commonly equated with "big."

8 To prevent this happening to us too, let's inquire into what is
good. It has been explained in different ways and given different
definitions.* One definition runs thus: "A good thing is one that
attracts the mind and draws it to itself." To this the immediate response is: what if it attracts us, but to our detriment? You know how
many bad things are enticing. There is a difference between what is
true and what seems true. Hence that which is good is joined with
"true," since it is not good if it is not a true good. But what attracts
and entices us to itself seems true: it creeps up on us, appeals to us,
seduces us. 9 Another definition goes like this: "A good thing is one
that arouses desire for itself, or what stirs the impulse of a mind that
moves toward it." But this evokes the same objection: many things
stir the mind's impulse that are bad for those who pursue them.

A better definition runs thus: "A good thing is one that arouses the mind's impulse toward itself in accordance with nature, and is only to be sought when it has begun to be choiceworthy." At this point it is also honorable, which is to say, completely worthy of pursuit.

10 This topic prompts me to state the difference between the good and the honorable. They both have something in common and inseparable: nothing can be good unless it contains something honorable, and the honorable is certainly good. What, then, is the difference between them? The honorable is that which is completely good, namely, that by which the happy life is brought to fulfillment and by association with which other things become good as well. 11 What I mean is the following. Some things are neither good nor bad, things like military or diplomatic service or judicial authority. When these activities are performed honorably, they begin to be good and pass from the status of ambivalent to that of good. It is association with the honorable that makes such things good; the honorable is good in itself. Goodness derives from honorableness; honorableness depends on itself. What is good could have been bad; what is honorable could never have been anything but good.

12 There is a definition that runs thus: "The good is what is in accordance with nature." Now watch my words. What is good is in accordance with nature, but what is in accordance with nature is not immediately good as well. Many things, in fact, agree with nature but are too paltry for the term "good" to befit them. They are trivial and contemptible. There is no tiny and contemptible good. As long as something is insignificant, it is not good. When it begins to be good, it is not insignificant. How can one recognize something as good? When it is *completely* in accordance with nature.

13 "You acknowledge," you say, "that what is good is in accordance with nature, that being its distinctive property.* You also acknowledge that some things that are not good are in accordance with nature. How, then, can the former be good but the latter not? When both things share the special quality of being in accordance with nature, how does it come about that they have a different distinctive property?" By the very size of them. 14 There is nothing novel in the fact that some things change by growing. The former child becomes a youth. His distinctive property becomes different. The child is incapable of reason, but the youth possesses rationality. When some

things grow, they not only change into something larger but into something different.

**15** One might say, "Becoming larger is not a change into something different. It does not matter whether you fill a flask or a vat with wine; the distinctive property of wine is present in either case. A small amount of honey does not differ in taste from a large amount." The examples you adduce are different; they are cases in which the same quality persists, however much they are enlarged. **16** Some things do continue in their kind and in their distinctive property when they are made bigger. But there are other cases where, after many increments of size, the final addition works at last a change: it imparts to them a new state of being, different from before. It is a single stone that makes an arch—the keystone, which is slotted in between the sloping sides and by its coming binds them together. Why does the final addition accomplish so much, though small in itself? Because it is not only an addition but also a completion.

**17** Some things, as they develop, shed their previous form and pass into a new one. When the mind has spent a long time extending something and has grown tired from pursuing its magnitude, the thing begins to be called "infinite." It becomes very different from what it was when it seemed to be large but finite. In the same way, we have thought of something that was difficult to divide. Finally, as the difficulty increased, the thing was found to be "indivisible." Likewise, we arrived at "the immobile" from what could scarcely or hardly be moved. By the same reasoning, something was merely in accordance with nature, then because of its magnitude it passed over into a different distinctive property and became a good.

Farewell.

## Letter 119

*From Seneca to Lucilius*
*Greetings*

**1** Each time I make a discovery, I don't wait for you to say, "Share!" I say it to myself. Do you want to know what it is I have discovered?

Get out your wallet—it's a terrific deal: I am going to teach you how to get rich in the fastest way possible. You can't wait to hear this, can you? You're quite right: I will show you a shortcut to fantastic wealth. But you are going to need a financial backer. In order to do business, you must take out a loan, only not, please, through an agent; I don't want the brokers gossiping about you. **2** I have a backer ready and waiting to give you, the one Cato* recommends in his dictum: "You should borrow from yourself."

No matter how small the amount, it will be enough if only we get what we need from ourselves. Dear Lucilius, not wanting is just as good as having. The result is the same in both cases: either way, you will avoid anxiety. It's not that I am advising you to deny your nature—for nature is obdurate: it cannot be conquered; it demands its due. You should understand, rather, that everything that goes beyond nature is a favor and not a necessity. **3** I am hungry, so I have to eat. Nature does not care whether the bread is coarse or of the finest flour: its interest is not in pleasing the stomach but merely in filling it. I am thirsty, but nature does not care whether I take water from the nearest pool or whether it is water I have chilled in a pile of snow. All that nature commands is quenching the thirst. It does not matter whether my cup is made of gold, crystal, or agate or whether it is just a Tibur cup or even the hollow of my hand.* **4** Look to the ultimate point of everything, and then you will let go of the extras. Hunger summons me, my hand should reach for the nearest food. Hunger will make anything I find acceptable. There's nothing a starving person will reject.

**5** Are you still wondering what it is that I am so pleased about? It was finding this splendid saying:

The wise person is the keenest investigator of natural wealth.*

You come back at me saying: "That's a real let-down. Are you serious? I had the cash on hand. I was looking into where I might set sail to do business, or what public contract I might secure, or what merchandise I might obtain. This is cheating, teaching me poverty after promising me riches." So you think that someone who lacks nothing is poor? "No," you reply, "but that's thanks to himself and acceptance of his situation, not thanks to fortune." You don't, then, judge someone to be wealthy precisely because he cannot lose his wealth? **6** Would you rather have a large amount, or enough? Those who have a large amount want more, which is a proof that they do not yet have enough. The one who has enough has attained the one thing the rich can never get: a stopping point. Or do you think it isn't really wealth just because no one has been proscribed* on account of it? Just because no one has been poisoned for it by his son or by his wife? Just because it is safe in a war, and tranquil during peace? Just because it is neither dangerous to own nor troublesome to manage?

**7** "But it's a meager possession merely not to be cold, not to be hungry, not to be thirsty."* Jupiter has nothing more. What is sufficient is never too little, and what is insufficient is never a lot. Alexander is still poor after conquering Darius and India. Isn't that the truth? Still searching for realms to make his own, he explores unknown seas, he sends new fleets onto the ocean, and as it were, bursts through the very ramparts of the world.* **8** What satisfies nature does not satisfy man. Here is one who has gained everything and yet lusts for something more. So blind are our minds: once a person begins to advance, he forgets where he began. He started out by contending for possession of an obscure corner and reached the very ends of the earth, yet now he is depressed because he has to return through a world that is his alone.

**9** Money never made anyone rich: all it does is infect everyone who touches it with a lust for more of itself. Are you asking about the reason for this? The more one has, the more one becomes able to have. In sum, take anyone you like from those whose names are listed alongside Crassus and Licinus:* set him before us, if you please, and let him state his total wealth, counting whatever he has in hand and all that he is hoping for. In my view, if you will accept it, the man is poor; even in your view, he could become poor. **10** But one who has aligned himself with nature's demands is not only free of any awareness of poverty, he is beyond the fear of poverty. In fact, though, it is quite difficult to restrict one's possessions to nature's limit. Even the person we are cutting down to size, the one whom you call poor, has something in excess of what he needs.

**11** But the eyes of the people are blinded and captivated by wealth, as when stacks of coins are carried in procession from the house, when even the roof is inlaid heavily with gold, when the domestic staff have either been selected for their natural good looks or are dressed to catch the eye. All such success aims only at being noticed. The one whom we have removed from the public and from fortune is happy on the inside. 12 As for those in whose minds an overworked poverty masquerades as wealth, they have wealth in the same way that we are said to have a fever, when actually it has us. We often put it the other way round, saying, "The fever has hold of him": in the same way, we should say, "Wealth has hold of him."

There is no advice I would rather give you than this, which no one can hear too often: you should measure everything by your natural desires, which can be satisfied either at no cost or only a little. Just don't mingle those desires with vices. 13 Are you asking about the quality of the table your food is being laid on, the quality of the silver plate, the matched pairs of waiters with their smooth skin? Nature desires nothing except a meal.

> Your throat is parched with thirst: do you demand
> A golden cup? You're starved: do you despise
> All food except the peacock and the turbot?*

14 Hunger is not ambitious. It is satisfied to stop, and it does not much care what makes it stop. After that are only the torments of a wretched self-indulgence that looks for ways to stimulate hunger after it is sated, to stuff the stomach rather than fill it, to rouse a thirst that was relieved by the first drink. That's why Horace gets it just right when he says that thirst cares neither for the cup nor for the elegance of the server. If you think it matters to you whether the slave boy has curly hair and the cup is of some translucent material, you are not thirsty.

15 Of all the gifts nature has given us, this is the finest: real need is not particular. What is superfluous admits of choice: "This isn't nice enough, that is too commonplace, this hurts my eyes." The world's creator, the author of our laws of life, established the conditions for us to be well cared for without being pampered. Everything we need for our welfare is ready and available, but luxuries come only at the cost of misery and trouble. 16 Let us, then, enjoy this benefit of nature, regarding it as one of the best. Let us believe that nature deserves our gratitude, and chiefly in this: that when we desire something out of need, we are not particular about taking it.

Farewell.

# Letter 120

*From Seneca to Lucilius*
*Greetings*

**1** Your letter wandered over several little questions, but eventually it settled on just one, asking me to explain how we ever arrived at a conception of the good and the honorable. According to some philosophers, the good and the honorable are different things, but we Stoics take them to be merely distinct.*

**2** Here's what I mean by that. The good, for some people, is just what is useful, and thus they apply the term to wealth, to a horse, to a wine, to a shoe—so little do they value the good, and so far does it descend among menial things. The honorable, they think, is what accords with the reasoning of a fully appropriate action, such as caring devotedly for an elderly father, assisting a poverty-stricken friend, campaigning bravely, delivering a sensible and well-balanced policy statement.* **3** We too make a distinction, but we take the two to be essentially one. Nothing is good unless it is honorable, and what is honorable is necessarily good. I judge it to be superfluous for me to add what is the difference between these conceptions, because I have mentioned it frequently. The one point I will state is that in our view, nothing is good that can be used badly. You can see how many people make bad use of wealth, social rank, and physical strength.

Now I return to the point you want me to discuss, how we first acquired a conception of the good and the honorable. **4** Nature could not teach us this: what nature has given us is not knowledge but only seeds of knowledge.* Some people say that we merely happened upon the conception, but it is beyond belief that anyone should have stumbled upon a notion of virtue by chance. Our own view is that the honorable and the good are inferred through observation and comparison of repeated actions; in the judgment of our school, they are understood "by analogy."

Since this term 'analogy' has been naturalized by Latin scholars, rather than rejecting it, I think it should be fully accepted into the Roman community.* So I will use it not only as legitimate but as fully established. **5** Let me explain what this analogy is. We knew about bodily health; from this we figured out that there also exists a health of the mind. We knew about bodily strength; from this we inferred that there also exists a strength of the mind. Certain acts of generosity or humanity or courage had amazed us. We began to admire them as though they were perfect. There were many flaws in them, hidden by the brilliant appearance of some splendid deed; these we overlooked. Nature tells us to magnify praiseworthy actions, and everyone always carries glorification beyond the facts. Thus it was from these acts that we derived the notion of a mighty good.

**6** Fabricius rejected Pyrrhus's gold, believing that the ability to scorn a king's money was a greater thing than having a kingdom.* Later, when Pyrrhus's doctor undertook to poison him, that same Fabricius warned the king to beware of the plot. Both actions showed the same strength of character: not to be won over by gold, and not to win by poison. We admired a great man, one who was swayed neither by the offers of the king nor by offers made against the king, a man who stuck by his own good example, who did what is hardest of all in that he maintained his integrity even in war, believing that even an enemy can be wronged. Even in extreme poverty, which was with him a point of pride, he rejected wealth in the same way that he rejected the use of poison. "Live, Pyrrhus," he said, "thanks to me, and be glad of what once pained you: that Fabricius is incorruptible."

**7** Horatius Cocles blocked the narrow bridge all alone. He ordered that his own retreat be cut off to remove a route for the enemy, and kept the assailants at bay until he heard the collapsing timbers resound with a huge crash.* When he looked back and saw that his own peril had put his country out of danger, he cried: "Come on, if anyone wants to pursue me the way I am going!" He then plunged headlong, and as he made his way out of the rushing river was as heedful of his arms as of the safety of his person. With the honor of his victorious weapons intact, he returned as safely as if he had crossed the bridge.

**8** These and similar deeds gave us a picture of virtue. Let me add something you may find amazing. We sometimes gained a notion of the honorable from things that are bad, and excellence has been made clear from its opposite. Some virtues and vices, as you know, border on one another, and in people who are depraved and dishonorable there is some likeness to rectitude. Thus a spendthrift gives the false impression of being generous, even though there is a huge difference between knowing how to give and not knowing how to save. Let me tell you, Lucilius, there are many people who don't donate their wealth but throw it away. I refuse to call someone generous who has no respect for money. Carelessness can look like good nature, and temerity like courage. **9** This similarity compelled us to take thought and distinguish things that are close in appearance but immensely different in fact. In observing those who had become famous for doing an outstanding deed, we began to notice the sort of person who did do something with nobility and great zeal, but once only. We saw him brave in war but timorous in the forum, enduring poverty with spirit but abject in handling disgrace. We praised the deed, but despised the man. **10** Another whom we saw was kindly to his friends, forbearing to his enemies, dutiful and respectful in his public and private behavior. We observed with what patience he bore his troubles, with what foresight he managed his responsibilities. We saw that when monetary contributions were required, he gave freely; when exertion was demanded, he labored tirelessly, relieving his fatigue with strength of character. Moreover, he was always the same, consistent in every action, good no longer from policy but under the guidance of a habit that made him not only able to act rightly but unable to act other than rightly. In him we understood that virtue had been perfected.

**11** We divided this virtue into parts. It was right that desires should be curbed, fears checked, actions performed intelligently, and each person rendered his due; and so we grasped moderation, bravery, prudence, and justice, and assigned to each its own proper function.* From what, then, did we gain the understanding of virtue? That man's orderliness revealed it to us, his seemliness and consistency, the harmony among all his actions, and his greatness in surmounting everything. It was thus that we came to understand happiness, the life that flows smoothly and is completely under its own control.

**12** How, then, did this very point* become evident to us? Let me tell you. The perfect man, the one in possession of virtue, never cursed his luck and never reacted to circumstances with a grim face. Believing himself to be a citizen and soldier of the world, he took on each labor as though it were a command. He treated no incident as an annoying nuisance and misfortune but as a task assigned to himself. "Whatever it is," he says, "this is mine to do. It is rough and tough, so let's get busy!" **13** Hence there was no mistaking the evident greatness of the man who never groaned about troubles and never complained about his fate. He gave many people an understanding of himself. He shone like a light in the dark, drawing attention to himself, because he was calm and gentle, equally resigned to human affairs and to acts of God. **14** He had a mind that was perfect and at the peak of its condition.

The only mind that could be superior is the divine intellect from which a part has passed down into this mortal heart of ours. That heart is at its most divine when it reflects on its own mortality. Then it knows that a human being is born in order to complete life's term with a body that is not a home but a sort of short-term guesthouse—something you have to leave when you see that you are being bothersome to your host.* **15** Let me assure you, Lucilius, that when the mind recognizes the lowliness and limitations of its present environment and is unafraid of leaving it, it gives a very strong indication that it has a loftier source. When we remember where we have come from, we know where we are headed. Don't we notice how many inconveniences trouble us and how little satisfied we are with our bodies? **16** Now it is our head we are complaining about, now our stomach, and now our chest and throat. Sometimes the problem is sore muscles, at other times aching feet; now diarrhea and now a drippy nose. We have too much blood or too little. We are harassed on all sides and driven from home: that is what happens to those who live in other people's houses. **17** Yet even though we are allotted such decaying bodies, we nonetheless make plans for eternity. In our hopes we seize on the maximum possible extent for a human life, not content with any finite sum of money or influence. What can be more shameless and more stupid than this? Nothing is enough for us, soon to die though we are. Indeed, we are already dying. Every day we stand closer to our last, and every hour thrusts us toward the place from which we are bound to fall. **18** See what blindness afflicts our minds. What I call the future is happening right now, and a large part of it is already past. For the time we have lived is already where it was before we were alive. We are wrong to fear our last day: each day contributes the same amount to death.* The faltering footstep does not weary us; it only shows that we are weary. Our last day arrives at death, but every one of our days approaches it. Death does not grab us, it picks away at us.

So a great mind, cognizant of its better nature, makes a real effort to behave honorably and assiduously in the position where it has been placed, but it does not regard any of its surroundings as its own. It uses them as things it has been lent, like a traveler who is moving on. **19** When we saw a person with this strength of character, how could we not get a notion of a remarkable disposition, especially if its consistency, as I said, showed it to be genuine greatness? Truth is stable and consistent; false things do not last. Some people are Vatinius and Cato by turns. Sometimes they find Curius insufficiently austere, Fabricius not poor enough, and Tubero lacking in frugality and modest living; at other times they compete with Licinus in wealth, Apicius in gourmet dining, and Maecenas in refinement.* **20** The best evidence of a bad character is variability and constant shifting between pretense of virtues and love of vices:

> Sometimes he had two hundred slaves, and sometimes ten;
> now he would talk of great affairs, of kings and princes;
> now, "Just a three-legged table, just a dish of salt;
> a homespun toga, good enough to keep me warm."
> Yet if you gave this modest man, content with little,
> a million sesterces, in five days they'd be gone.*

**21** There are many people like the one Horatius Flaccus describes, this man who is never the same, who goes off in so many directions that he doesn't even resemble himself. Did I say "many"? I meant practically everyone. Every man changes his plans and aspirations by the day. One day he wants to have a wife, the next only a girlfriend. Now he wants to lord it over people, but another time he is more obsequious than a slave in his behavior. Now he is so self-aggrandizing as to attract resentment, but on another occasion he is more self-effacing than those of lowest degree. First he scatters largesse to the crowd, then dives for it himself.

**22** This is the clearest indication of a mind that lacks good sense. It goes around with no stable identity, and (what I find most dishonorable) it is inconsistent with itself. Realize that it is a great thing to act as just one person. But only the wise person does that; the rest of us take on many different forms. At one time you find us thrifty and serious, at another time extravagant and silly. We keep changing our masks, taking one off and putting on another that is its opposite. This, then, you should demand of yourself: keep up the part you have begun to play, right until you leave the stage. See to it that you can be praised; or if not that, at least make sure you can be recognized. Of the person you saw just yesterday, it could fairly be said: "Who is he?" That's how much he has changed.

Farewell.

## Letter 121

*From Seneca to Lucilius*
*Greetings*

**1** You will sue me, I'm sure, when I set today's little problem before you, the one we have been stuck on for long enough already. You're going to shout out again: "What's this got to do with ethics?" Start shouting; but meanwhile, let me first find you some other opponents to sue, namely, Posidonius and Archedemus: it's these men who will go to court.* Next, let me say that what pertains to ethics does not necessarily make for ethical conduct. **2** One study pertains to the nutrition of human beings, others to our physical training, our clothing, our learning, or our entertainment: all of them are concerned with human beings, even if not all of them make people better. As for ethics, one inquiry has to do with conduct in one way, another in another: some correct and regulate it, while others investigate its nature and origin. **3** When I ask why nature produced human beings and why it made them superior to other animals, do you conclude that I have abandoned the field of ethics? That would be incorrect. I mean, how will you know what conduct should be adopted unless you have discovered what is best for a human being and have studied human nature? You will not understand what you should do and what you should avoid until you have learned what you owe to your own nature.

**4** "I want," you say, "to learn how to reduce my desires and my fears. Shake me out of my superstition. Teach me that so-called happiness is a trivial and empty thing, which very easily takes on the additional syllable and becomes *un*happiness." I will satisfy your desire: I will encourage your virtues and flog your vices. Even if someone finds me excessive and intemperate in this role, I will not cease to persecute wickedness, to curb the fiercest passions, to check the advance of pleasures that turn into pain, and to protest against our prayers. I mean it; for our prayers are for the very things that are worst for us, and when they are gratified we get everything for which we need consolation.*

5 Meanwhile, allow me to thrash out topics that seem a bit more distant from our present concern. We were discussing whether all animals have a perception of their own constitution.* The principal evidence that they do is how suitably and adroitly they move their limbs, just as though they were trained to do so. No creature lacks agility in managing its own parts. A skilled craftsman handles his tools with ease; a navigator knows how to steer his ship; a portrait painter is very quick in selecting from his copious supply of colors and moves with ready eye and hand between his palette and his work of art. An animal is equally agile in all the use it makes of itself. 6 We often admire skillful pantomime dancers, because their hands are ready to convey all the meaning of the subject matter and its emotions, and their gestures keep up with the rapidity of the spoken word.* What art gives to artists, nature gives to animals. Not one of them has difficulty in handling its limbs; not one falters in making use of itself. They do this from the moment they come into the world—the knowledge is with them from the beginning. They are born trained.

7 One might say, "The reason why animals are adept at moving their limbs is that they would feel pain if they moved them in any other way. Thus it is under compulsion that they do as people of your school say; and what causes them to move in the right way is fear, not volition." This is wrong. Things that are driven by necessity are slow; agility is the mark of spontaneous movement. Indeed, instead of being compelled to move by fear of pain, they actually strive for their natural movement even when pain hinders them. 8 Consider a baby that would like to stand up and is just getting used to supporting itself: as soon as it begins to test its strength, it falls down; but it keeps getting up again, crying all the time, until it has painfully

trained itself to do what its nature demands. When certain animals with hard shells are turned upside down, they keep twisting and digging with their feet and moving sideways until they get back into their proper position. An inverted tortoise feels no pain, but it is disturbed by missing its natural condition and keeps rocking itself until it stands on its feet. **9** Thus all animals have a perception of their own constitution, and this explains why they are so dexterous in managing their limbs. Indeed, this is our best evidence that they are born with this awareness: no animal is unskilled in making use of itself.

**10** "According to the members of your school," says the opponent, "constitution is 'the mind's directive faculty disposed in a certain way relative to the body.'* How could a baby understand something so intricate and refined, which even you yourselves are scarcely capable of describing? All animals would have to be born logicians in order to understand a definition that is obscure to the majority of Romans." **11** That objection would be valid if I said that animals understood the definition of constitution, as distinct from their constitution as such. It is easier to understand nature than it is to describe it. So the baby does not know what constitution is, but it does know its own constitution. It does not know what an animal is, but it perceives that it is an animal.

**12** Furthermore, its understanding of its own constitution is vague, rudimentary, and unclear. We, likewise, know that we have a mind and yet do not know what the mind is, where it is located, what it is like, or where it comes from. We are aware of our mind, even though we do not know its nature and location. Such is the case with all animals' awareness of their own constitution. Animals necessarily have a perception of that through which they also perceive other things; they necessarily perceive that which they obey, that by which they are governed. **13** Every one of us understands that there is something that activates one's impulses, but we do not know what it is. One knows that one has a motivating principle, but one does not know what it is or where it comes from. In the same way, even babies and animals have a perception of their directive part, but that perception is not properly clear and distinct.

**14** "You say that every animal from the outset is attached to its own constitution, but also that the human constitution is a rational one. Therefore the human being is attached to itself not as an animate creature but as a rational creature, for the human being is dear to itself by virtue of that part that makes it human. How, then, can a baby be attached to a rational constitution when it is not yet rational?"

15 Each stage of life has its own constitution: one for the baby, another for the child, another for the young person, and another for the mature. Each is attached to the constitution it is in. A baby has no teeth; it is attached to this, its present constitution. The teeth emerge; it is attached to this constitution. For even a blade of wheat, which will eventually yield a crop, has one constitution when it is young and scarcely taller than the furrow, another when it has gained strength and stands on a stalk which, though soft, can bear its weight, and yet another when it grows golden and the grain hardens in the ear, forecasting harvest time. Whatever constitution the plant arrives at, it retains and adapts to. 16 The stages of life are different—infancy, childhood, youth, and maturity. Yet I, who have been a baby, a boy, and a youth, remain the same person. So, although each thing's constitution changes, it is attached to its constitution in the same way. My natural attachment is not to the boy or the youth or the mature man but to myself. Therefore a baby is attached to its own constitution, the one it has as a baby, and not to the one it will have as a youth. Even though it will later mature into a greater condition, that does not imply that the condition in which it is born is not also in accordance with nature.

17 An animal is attached first to its very self; for there must be something to which everything else may be referred. I seek pleasure. For whom? For myself. So I am looking after myself. I try to avoid pain. For whom? For myself. So I am looking after myself. If I do everything for the sake of looking after myself, my concern for myself is prior to everything else. This concern is present in all animals; it is not grafted onto them but innate. 18 Nature raises its own offspring and does not reject them. And because the most reliable guardian is the closest, each individual has been entrusted to itself. Hence, as I have said in earlier letters,* even young animals, when just born or hatched, know at once by themselves what is harmful and avoid things that could cause their death. They even display fearful reactions at the shadow of things flying overhead, vulnerable as they are to birds of prey. No animal enters life without fear of death.

19 "How can an animal at birth have understanding of what ei-

ther promotes its safety or could cause its death?" First of all, our question is whether it can understand these things, not how it does so. That animals have this understanding is evident from the fact that if they were now to gain such understanding, they would not do anything beyond what they do already. Why is it that a hen does not shun a peacock or a goose, but flees a hawk, which is much smaller than those birds and not even something it is acquainted with? Why are chickens afraid of a weasel but not of a dog? It is evident that they have within them a knowledge, not derived from experience, of what will injure them; for they avoid something before they can have experience of it. 20 Secondly, to prevent you from thinking that this happens by chance, they do not fear things other than those that they should, and they never forget this precaution and attentiveness. They are consistent in their avoidance of danger. In addition, they do not become more timorous in the course of their lives. This shows that they arrive at this condition not by experience but as a result of a natural instinct toward self-preservation. What experience teaches is late in coming and unevenly distributed; everything that nature transmits is immediate and consistent in all cases.

21 If, however, you press me, I will tell you how every animal cannot help but understand what is dangerous. It is aware that it consists of flesh; and so it is aware of what can cut flesh or burn or crush flesh, and of which animals are equipped with the means of doing it harm. It acquires an impression of these as dangerous and inimical. These tendencies are interconnected: at the same time as each animal is attached to its own preservation, it both seeks out what will be beneficial and avoids what will be harmful. Impulses toward useful things are natural, aversions to their opposites are also natural.

Whatever nature prescribes takes place without any reflection to prompt it, without any premeditation. 22 Don't you see how clever bees are in constructing their cells, how harmonious in performing their respective tasks? Don't you see how a spider's web is beyond human capacity to imitate, and what a task it is to arrange the threads, some of them in straight lines as support, with others running in a circle at increasing intervals, so that the smaller creatures the web is made to catch may be entangled and held as in a net? 23 This art is innate, not learned. That is why no animal has more learning than another. You will see that spiders' webs are all the same, and that in a hive all the angles of a honeycomb are equal. Whatever training imparts is variable and uneven; capacities that come from nature are distributed equally.

Nature has conferred nothing beyond the instinct to preserve oneself and a facility in doing so, which is why animals begin to learn at the moment they begin to live. **24** And it is not surprising that they are born with exactly the abilities without which their birth would be fruitless. This is the first equipment nature conferred on them for their continuing existence—attachment to self and love of self. They would not have the power to survive unless they desired to do so. This desire just by itself was not enough to help them, but without it nothing else would have done so. In no animal will you find a low regard for self, or even a neglect of self. Mute creatures, though dull-witted in other respects, are clever at living. You will see that creatures which are useless to others are not deficient when it comes to themselves.

Farewell.

## Letter 122

*From Seneca to Lucilius*
*Greetings*

**1** The day has already experienced a decline. It has shrunk back a bit, but still affords plenty of time to those who rise, as it were, with the sun. We are better and more capable of meeting our social duties if we even anticipate the dawn, gaining the early light. It's a disgrace to lie half-asleep when the sun is already high in the sky, and only start the day at the noon hour. For many people, even noon counts as predawn! **2** Others invert the functions of day and night: their eyes are still sodden with yesterday's drinking bout, and they don't open them until evening approaches. They are like those people described by Virgil, whom nature has hidden directly beneath our feet:

> when Dawn, with snorting steeds, approaches us,
> the sunset-star is kindled red for them.*

In this case, though, it is not their part of the globe that is opposite to ours but their manner of living.

**3** In this very city there are Antipodeans—people who, as Marcus Cato says, have never seen either a sunrise or a sunset. Do you suppose they know how to live? They don't even know *when* to live! Do they too fear death, now that they have buried themselves alive? They are as sinister as birds of the night. Though they pass their dark hours amid wines and perfumes, though they devote all their topsy-turvy wakefulness to a succession of dinners with multiple courses, they are not partying but celebrating their own funerals. Except that obsequies for the real dead take place during the day! But really, no day is long enough for an active person. Let's extend our life: action is both life's function and the proof that one is alive. It's night that one ought to shorten, transferring part of it into the day.

**4** Fowl that are purchased for dinner parties are kept in a dark place so that they remain inactive and fatten easily. As they lie about without moving, their lazy bodies swell; in their shaded confinement,° useless bloat comes over them. But the bodies of these people who have devoted themselves to the dark are actually disgusting. Their color is more alarming than the pallor of invalids: feebleness and decrepitude have whitened their complexion, and their flesh, even in life, has begun to putrefy. Yet I would call this the least of their troubles. How much more darkness is in their minds! Such people are dazed within—completely befogged—worse than blind. Who ever had eyes just to see in the dark?

**5** Would you like to know the origin of this bizarre habit of avoiding the day and transferring one's entire life into the night? All our faults contend against nature, they all abandon due order. Self-indulgence makes it a goal to delight in perversity, not just to depart from the straight path but to get as distant from it as possible, and finally take up exactly the opposite position. **6** You surely agree that it is against nature to drink before a meal, taking wine without food into the bloodstream and arriving for dinner already drunk. Yet this fault is common among our young men, who go for a workout just so they can have a drink the moment they exit the baths, still surrounded by naked men. Worse yet, they drink while bathing, removing over and over the sweat they have generated by glass after glass of heated wine. Drinking after lunch or after dinner is crude, they think, the choice of country bumpkins who know nothing of sophisticated pleasure: neat wine gives delight only when it does not mingle with food and can go straight to the brain. Getting drunk is best on an empty stomach!

**7** You surely agree that it is against nature for men to adopt women's clothing. Aren't they living against nature when they aim to look young and beautiful at an advanced age? What could be more cruel or more pitiful? Never to become a man, just so that one can keep receiving sex from a man! If his gender fails to rescue him from abuse, will not maturity do so? **8** You surely agree that it is contrary to nature to yearn for roses in winter, to force lilies to bloom in cold weather by bathing them in warm water and moving their pots at just the right moment. What about people who plant fruit trees on the tops of houses? Their roofs and gables are festooned with foliage, with roots higher than where the treetops ought to reach; is that not contrary to nature? Is it not contrary to nature to lay the foundations for hot baths in the sea and to think one cannot have an elegant swim unless the heated pool is lashed by waves and storms?

**9** After making it their rule to want everything to be contrary to nature, people finally abandon nature completely. "It's daytime," they say, "time to go to sleep. The town is hushed: now we should do our exercises, go for a drive, and have lunch. It's almost dawn: time for dinner. Let's not behave like ordinary folk; it's demeaning to live in the usual boring way. Away with the public day, let us have a special morning just for us!" **10** As far as I'm concerned, people like this are already in the morgue. How far are they from a funeral, and an untimely one at that, seeing that they already live by the light of torches and candles?

Many people, as I recall, were living this way at one time, including Acilius Buta, a former praetor.* He ran through an enormous inheritance. When he admitted his losses to Tiberius, the emperor said: "You're a bit late to wake up." **11** Julius Montanus, an acceptable poet, known both for his friendship with Tiberius and for their falling out, was giving a reading one day.* Now Montanus liked to fill his work with sunrises and sunsets. Annoyed at having to spend all day listening to him recite, someone remarked that no one should attend his declamations—at which point Pinarius Natta* said: "Can I not be more generous than that? I am ready to listen to him from

sunrise to sunset." **12** Then, when Montanus had spoken the following lines:

> Phoebus begins to spread his blazing fires,
> the rosy day gleams forth; the mournful swallow
> commences patient feeding of her young;
> her gentle beak attends each screeching throat—

Varus cried out: "It's Buta's bedtime." (This Varus was a Roman of
equestrian status, a companion of Marcus Vinicius* and a constant
presence at high-class dinners, which he paid for with his witty remarks.) **13** Next, after Montanus had recited:

> Now shepherds pen their flocks within the folds;
> now restful night begins to soothe the land . . .

Varus said: "What do you mean? Is it night already? I will go and
pay my morning respects to Buta." Nothing was more notorious than
this man's inverted lifestyle, though, as I said, it was fashionable at
the time.

**14** The reason some people live this way is not that they think that
night itself has any greater pleasure to offer but because they don't
like anything that is normal. Light is a burden to a guilty conscience,
and the fact that it is free makes it of no value to those whose sole
basis for desiring and despising anything is how much it costs. Moreover, extravagant people want their life to be talked about as long as
they live, for if it goes quiet they think they are wasting their efforts.
And so they keep doing something to arouse gossip. Many people are
big spenders, and many keep mistresses. In order to make a name in
this company, you need to go in for notoriety as well as luxury. It's a
busy town: common vices get no attention at all.

**15** I once heard Albinovanus Pedo* (he was a most delightful
storyteller) telling how he had lived above the house of Sextus Papinius, who was one of this tribe of light-shunners. "Around the third
hour of the night," he said, "I hear the sound of whips. I ask what
the master is doing. The answer is that he is reckoning up.* Around
the sixth hour of the night, I hear some vigorous shouting. I ask
what is happening. I am told that he is practicing his vocal exercises.
Around the eighth hour of the night, I ask what the sound of wheels
means. I am told that he is out for a drive. **16** Around dawn people

are running around, slaves are being summoned, stewards and cooks are in an uproar. I ask what is up. The answer is that he has asked for honey-wine and polenta, coming out of his bath. Someone said: "His dinner must have lasted all day." Certainly not. He lived a very frugal life, consuming nothing except the night. So when some people called Sextus miserly and mean, Pedo said: "You could say he lives on lamplight."*

17 You should not be surprised at finding so many individual forms of vice. There are many different vices, too many for you to count their manifestations or to grasp all their kinds. Concern for what is right takes but one form; depravity is manifold, always taking some new direction. The same applies to character. When people follow nature, they are straightforward, unencumbered, and largely similar. The perverted ones are very much at odds with others and with themselves.

18 But the principal cause of this malady, in my opinion, is a hatred of ordinary life. Just as such people distinguish themselves from others by their manner of dress, the stylishness of their dinner parties, and the refinement of their carriages, they also want to be a separate class in the way they manage their time. People whose reward for wrongdoing is notoriety don't want to commit ordinary offenses. 19 That is the aim of everyone who lives backwards, so to speak. And so, dear Lucilius, we should stick to the path that nature has prescribed for us, and we should not deviate from it. Follow nature, and everything is easy and accessible; strain against it, and you will live like a rower pulling against the current.

Farewell.

## Letter 123

*From Seneca to Lucilius*
*Greetings*

1 Late at night I have reached my Alban villa,* exhausted from a journey that was uncomfortable rather than long. I find nothing in readiness except myself. So I have settled my weary self down now

in my study, and get this much good from the fact that my cook and baker are delayed. In fact, this is the very thing I am discussing with myself, how nothing is serious if one takes it lightly, nothing needs to be annoying, provided that one doesn't add one's own annoyance to it. **2** My baker has no bread, but my manager has some, and so do my head slave and my tenants. "Bad bread," you say. But wait! It will become good. Hunger will soon make it into a soft loaf of the finest flour. That is why one ought not to eat before hunger gives the command. I will delay my meal, then, until I have good bread again or else until I don't mind having bread that is bad.

**3** It is essential to get accustomed to lean fare. Difficulties of time and place confront even those who are wealthy and well equipped for pleasure,° thwarting their intentions. No one can have everything he wants. What a person can do is give up wanting what he doesn't have and use cheerfully the things that are available. A big part of independence is a well-disciplined stomach, one that can put up with rough treatment. **4** It's beyond all estimates how much pleasure I get from the fact that my weariness is at peace with itself. I am not looking for a massage or a bath, just the healing effects of time. Rest removes the accretions of toil. The coming dinner, whatever it is, will be more delightful than an inaugural feast.* **5** In short,° I have instantly put my mind to a sort of test, and a particularly straightforward and accurate test at that. For when the mind has prepared itself and made a resolution to be patient, we have no clear indication of its true resolve. The most reliable proofs are those that come on the spur of the moment, if the mind views troubles not only dispassionately but serenely, without resentment and without complaint, and if it makes up for whatever is missing by not wishing for it, and reflects that while something may be lacking in its routine, in itself it lacks nothing.

**6** With many things, we only realize how superfluous they are when they begin to run short. We were using them not because we had to but because they were available. How many things we acquire only because other people have bought them or because they are in other people's homes! Many of our problems stem from the fact that we live by conforming to other people's standards, following fashion instead of taking reason as our guide. If only a few people did something, we would refuse to copy them; yet as soon as more people take up the practice, we adopt it as well, as if mere frequency somehow made it more honorable. Once a misconception becomes widespread, we let it stand in for rectitude.

7 Nowadays everyone travels with an escort of Numidian horse and a troop of runners leading the way. It is a disgrace to have no attendants to push oncoming travelers off the road, to indicate the coming of a dignitary by a great cloud of dust.* Everyone nowadays has a mule train to carry their collection of crystal and agate cups and fine-wrought silver vessels. It is a disgrace to give the impression that the sum total of your baggage is stuff that could be jostled along without breaking. Everyone has a retinue of pages who slather their faces with lotion when they travel so that the sun or the cold won't harm their tender skin. It is a disgrace to have youthful attendants with healthy skin who need no pharmaceutical products!

8 We should avoid conversation with all these people. They are the sort who pass on their faults and trade them with one another. We used to think it was terrible when people would show off in words; today, though, there are people who make a show of their faults. Conversation with them does a lot of harm. For even if it has no immediate effect, it leaves seeds in the mind; it stays with us even after we have left their company, a bad effect that will rise up again later on. 9 After listening to a concert, people's ears are still full of the melody and of the sweet singing that restricts their ability to think and makes them unable to focus on serious matters. In the same way, the talk of flatterers and those who encourage vice lingers long after it is heard. It is not easy to shake the mind free from a sweet sound. It keeps on; it persists; it comes back at intervals. For this reason, our ears need to be closed to harmful voices from the outset. Once those voices have made a start and gained admission, they are all the more audacious.

10 Next, we come among such sayings as the following:*

"Virtue, philosophy, and justice are just the noise of meaningless words! The only happiness is to do well in life. Eating, drinking, spending one's fortune: this is living, this is remembering that one is mortal. The days flow by; life moves on irretrievable. What are we waiting for? What's the good of cultivating philosophy? We can't have pleasure when we are old, so why impose austerity on our life now, when we are still capable and still want things?

So° get ahead of death, and let everything that it will steal from you be spent now on yourself.° You don't have a girlfriend, and neither do you have a catamite to make your girlfriend jealous. You never get drunk, and your dinners give the impression that you are waiting for your father to approve your daily expenses. This is not living, it's attending to someone else's life! 11 It is totally crazy to deny yourself everything, devoting your attention to property that will just go to your heir. That way, the size of your estate will turn your friend into an enemy: the greater his inheritance, the more he will rejoice at your death. As for those prigs, those stern critics of other people's lives and enemies of their own, who like to lecture the public—don't give them a second thought; don't hesitate to prefer a good life to a good name."

12 Voices like these are as much to be shunned as those that Ulysses refused to pass until he was tied to the mast.* They have the same power: they alienate you from your country, your parents, your friends, and your virtues, and lure you into a life of shame with promises that make you unhappy, even if they were not shameful.° How much better it is to follow a straight path and let it finally guide you to the point where only what is honorable gives you pleasure!

13 We shall be able to reach that point if we understand that there are two kinds of things that can either entice or repel us. The enticing ones are wealth, pleasures, beauty, ambition, and everything else that is seductive and pleasing. We are repelled by hard physical work, death, pain, public disapproval, and an austere diet. Hence we should train ourselves neither to fear the latter things nor to desire the former. We should contend against our inclinations, resisting the attractive things and advancing against those that assail us.*

14 Don't you notice how much people's posture differs when they are climbing a hill from when they are descending? While going down they lean their bodies back, but when climbing they lean forward. It is a deliberate error, when descending, to let your weight go forward, and similarly, to let it go backward when ascending. We descend into pleasures, Lucilius, but to face difficulties and hardships we have to climb. In the latter case, we should push our bodies forward, but in the former case we should hold them back.

15 Do you suppose that my point right now is that the only people

who are dangerous to our ears are those who praise pleasure and who alarm us with the thought of pain, a thing that is fearsome enough on its own? No, I think we are also harmed by those who, under the guise of the Stoic school, urge us into vices. For instance, they insist that only a person who is wise and highly educated is a lover.*

> "The wise man is the only one with expertise in this area. Likewise, he has the greatest skill at engaging in symposia and dinner parties. Let us investigate the following question: up to what age should young men be objects of love?"

16 Consigning these points to Greek custom, we should lend our ears rather to the following:

> "No one is good by accident; virtue has to be learned. Pleasure is a poor and pathetic thing, of no value. Even speechless animals have a share in pleasure; the smallest and most trivial species of animal fly after it. Glory is an empty thing, more fleeting and volatile than air. Poverty is only a problem for those who don't accept it. Death is no evil. What is it, then, you ask? It is the one right that belongs in equal measure to all humankind. Superstition is a crazy mistake. It fears those who should be loved and trespasses against those it worships. If you are going to malign the gods, you might as well deny that they exist."

17 These are the lessons you need to learn or, rather, take to heart. Philosophy should not supply excuses for vice. The sick have no hope of healing when their doctor recommends intemperance.

Farewell.


## Letter 124

*From Seneca to Lucilius*
*Greetings*

> 1 I can convey the wisdom of the ancients
> to you unless you balk at it, unless
> you find it hard to learn their subtle thinking.*

But you do not balk; you are not put off by any technicality. Your mind is of high quality and is not concerned only with big issues. Yet I also applaud how you relate everything to some self-improvement: the only time you lose patience is when the highest degree of technicality achieves nothing. I will try to ensure that that does not happen now.

The question here is about whether the good is grasped by the sensory faculty or by the intellect. This inquiry is related to the thesis that the good is not present in animals devoid of speech and in infants.* 2 All those who put pleasure in the highest position judge the good to be an object of the senses. We, on the other hand, who assign the good to the mind, take it to be an object of the understanding.

If the senses were what ascertain the good, we would not reject any pleasure, since there is no pleasure that does not entice and please us.* Conversely, we would never willingly undergo any pain, because there is no pain that is not an unwelcome sensation. 3 Moreover, people who are too fond of pleasure and who have an extreme fear of pain would not deserve criticism. Yet we disapprove of gluttons and people addicted to sex, and we despise those who are dissuaded from every manly undertaking by fear of pain. If the senses were the criteria of good and bad, how would these people do wrong by obeying them? For you have ceded to the senses the authority to decide what to pursue and what to avoid. 4 But obviously it is reason that has charge of that. Reason settles questions about the happy life, virtue, and the honorable, and likewise about the good and the bad. By letting the senses make pronouncements about the good, our opponents allow the least valuable part to pass judgment on the superior; for sense perception is dull and imprecise, and is less acute in human beings than in other creatures. 5 Suppose someone wanted to distinguish tiny things by touch instead of by sight! We have no further sense, more precise and focused than vision, that would enable us to distinguish the good and the bad. So you can see that someone for whom touch constitutes the criterion of the ultimate good and bad is wallowing in the depths of ignorance and has thrown the sublime and the divine down to the ground.*

6 The opponent says, "Every branch of knowledge and every skill must have some basis in what is evident and available to the senses, and grow and develop from there. In the same way, the happy life

has its foundation and point of origin in what is evident and what is available to the senses. Surely it is your view as well that the happy life has its origin in things that are evident."

7 Our view is that to be happy is to be in accordance with nature, and that whether something is in accordance with nature is just as obviously and directly apparent as whether something is intact and whole. Even a newborn has a share in what is in accordance with nature, but this I call not the good but only the beginning of the good. You accord the ultimate good, pleasure, to the stage of infancy, with the consequence that one who is just being born starts out at the place to which the perfected person arrives. You are placing the top of the tree where the root belongs! 8 It would be patently wrong to say that a fetus, a frail, incomplete, and still unformed thing, with even its gender undetermined, is already in a state that is good. Yet how much difference is there, really, between a newborn infant and one that is still a heavy weight hidden in the mother's womb? Both are equally immature as concerns the understanding of good and bad. An infant is not yet capable of grasping the good, any more than a tree is, or some animal devoid of speech. So why is the good not present in a tree or an animal? Because reason is not there either. In the same way, the good is not present in the infant: the infant too lacks reason. Only when it gets to reason will it get to the good.

9 Some animals are devoid of reason, some are not yet rational, and some are rational but only imperfectly. The good is not present in any of these creatures; only with the advent of reason does it come. What, then, is the difference between the animals I just mentioned? In the one that is devoid of reason the good will never be present. In the one not yet rational it is not possible for the good to be present at this time. In the one that is rational but only imperfectly, it is possible for the good to be present, but it is not in fact present. 10 This is what I mean, Lucilius: the good is not found in just any body nor at just any stage of life; it is as distant from infancy as the last is from the first or as the complete is from what is just beginning. Hence the good is not in a little body that is soft and just beginning its development. Not at all—no more than in a seed.

11 You could state the matter thus. We do acknowledge a kind of good for trees and plants. This is not present in the first shoots at the moment when they break through the ground. There is a kind

of good for wheat. It is not present in the tender stalk or when the soft ear detaches itself from the husk but only when the wheat has been ripened by summer heat and proper maturity.* No nature brings forth its own good unless it has achieved fulfillment. Thus the good of human beings is only to be found in one in whom reason has been perfected. 12 What is this good? Let me tell you: it is a mind that is free and upright, puts other things beneath itself but itself beneath none. This good is so far beyond the grasp of infancy that it is not to be expected in a child, or even properly in a young adult. Old age is doing well if it arrives there after long and concentrated study. If this is the good, it is also an object of the understanding.

13 "You have said that there is a kind of good for trees and for plants. So infants too can have a good." The truly good does not exist in trees or in animals devoid of speech; what is good in these beings is called good by indulgence. "What is it, then?" you say. It is what accords with the nature of each. To be sure, the good cannot possibly befall a speechless animal; rather, it belongs to a more fortunate and superior nature. There is no good where there is no place for reason. 14 There are four natures to be considered here, those of trees, animals, humans, and gods. The latter two are of the same nature insofar° as they are rational, but they also differ in that one of them is mortal and the other one immortal. The good of one of them—that would be the god, of course—is perfected just by nature; in the other, namely, the human, it is perfected by effort. The rest, which lack reason, are only perfect in their own nature, not truly perfect. This is because unqualified perfection means perfection in accordance with universal nature, and universal nature is rational. Other things can be perfect in their own kind. 15 A creature that lacks the capacity for happiness also lacks the capacity for that which produces happiness; but it is goods that produce happiness. A speechless animal has neither the capacity for happiness nor the capacity for what produces happiness; hence a speechless animal does not have a good.

16 An animal grasps the present by means of its sensory faculty. It recalls the past only when this faculty is prompted by some event. For example, a horse recalls a road when it is brought to where the road starts; in the stable, however, it has no memory of the road, no matter how often it has passed that way. The third division of time, the future, has no significance for animals. 17 How, then, can we sup-

pose that a perfect nature is possible for creatures whose experience of time is imperfect? Time consists of three parts, past, present, and future. Animals are granted only the part that is most fleeting and transitory, the present. Their memory of the past is only occasional and never brought back except by contact with something in the present.* **18** Therefore the good of a perfect nature cannot exist in a nature that is imperfect; if that were the case, even plants would have it. I am not denying that speechless animals are endowed with very strong impulses to pursue things that appear to accord with their nature, but such impulses are unorganized and sporadic. The good, on the other hand, is never unorganized and sporadic.*

**19** "How is this?" you are saying. "Do animals move in a sporadic and unsystematic manner?" I would describe their movements in this way if their nature were capable of order, but the truth is that they move in accordance with their own nature. Something is disorganized if and only if it is capable of being organized, just as the anxious is what could be free of anxiety. There is no vice in anyone who lacks the possibility of virtue. The movements of animals result from their nature. **20** Not to belabor the point, there will be a kind of good in an animal, a kind of virtue, a kind of perfection, but it will not be unconditionally a good or a virtue or perfect. All these are found only in rational beings who have the privilege of understanding the cause, the extent, and the procedure.

**21** Are you wondering where this discussion is heading and how it will be of benefit to your mind? I respond: by training and sharpening the mind, and by keeping it on the right track in all its future activities. It is even beneficial in that it delays us from running off into some course of depravity. I have this too to say. There is no greater benefit I can do you than by showing you your own good, by distinguishing you from the speechless animals and situating you with the divine.

**22** Why, may I say, do you nurture and train your bodily strength? Nature has granted greater power to domestic and wild animals. Why do you cultivate your appearance? When you have done everything you can, you will still not be as beautiful as animals are. Why do you spend huge efforts on your hair? Whether you let it down in the Parthian fashion or tie it up as the Germans do or let it go wild in the Scythian way, any horse will have a thicker mane to toss; the mane that bristles on any lion's neck will be more handsome. After practicing for speed, you will still be no match for a hare. **23** Why not abandon all the points on which you are bound to be surpassed, cease to strive after what is foreign to your nature, and return to the good that is your own?

What is this good? Just this: a mind made flawless, a mind that rivals the divine, that elevates itself above the human sphere and places nothing beyond itself.* You are a reasoning animal. What, then, is the good in you? It is perfect reason. Take your reason from where it is now to its own ultimate achievement, let it grow to its fullest possible extent. **24** Do not judge yourself to be happy until all your joys arise from yourself,* until, after viewing the objects of human competition, covetousness, and possessiveness, you find— I will not say nothing to prefer, but nothing to set your heart on. I will give you a brief rule by which to measure yourself, to gauge when you have achieved perfection: you will possess your own good when you understand that the fortunate are really the least fortunate of all.

Farewell.

## A. Quoted by Aulus Gellius, 12.2.11, 12.2.2–10, from Book 22 of the *Letters on Ethics to Lucilius*

Some of Ennius's thoughts are so fine that even though they were written amid the unwashed, they might well be found pleasing among those who wear perfume.[1] <But his verses are sometimes quite ridiculous, for instance> the following lines about Cethegus:

> Of him, the commoners, the ones who lived
> and spent their lives in those days, said he was
> the people's choicest flower, Persuasion's marrow.[2]

You may be sure that those who like verses of this kind would admire even the couches of Sotericus.[3] . . .

It amazes me that men who are themselves highly eloquent and who are devoted to Ennius have praised his laughable verses rather than his best ones. Cicero, for one, among the excellent lines of Ennius that he quotes, includes these as well. I am not surprised that someone was capable of writing these lines, considering that there was someone capable of praising them. Unless it was that Cicero, the great orator, was pleading his own case, meaning to make his own poetry look good by comparison! And in Cicero's own work you will find passages, even in his prose, from which you can infer that he derived some benefit from his reading of Ennius, <as for instance when he writes,> in his books *On the Republic,* "since Menelaus of Sparta had a kind of sweet-speaking complaisance," <and elsewhere,> "he cultivates brief-speaking in his oratory."[4] . . . The fault lay not with Cicero but with the time: one could not help but speak that way, when such was one's reading material. <But Cicero had reason to insert some bits of Ennius into his writing, for in so doing he evaded criticism of his style as overly elaborate and polished. . . .>

Our poet Virgil too inserted into his work some awkward and ungainly lines and some hypermetric lines, just so that Ennius's compatriots would recognize an element of archaism in the new poem.

## B. Quoted by Aulus Gellius, 12.1.13, without indication of the exact source

What does it matter how much you have? There is much more that you do not have.[5]

# Notes

## Abbreviations

LS     Long, A. A., and D. N. Sedley, eds., *The Hellenistic Philosophers*, 2 vols. Cambridge: Cambridge University Press, 1987.

*SVF*    *Stoicorum Veterum Fragmenta*, ed. H. von Arnim, 4 vols. Leipzig: Teubner, 1903–24.

**1.1**    The most common legal procedure for manumission of a slave required a third party to assert the freedom of the former slave. Compare 8.7 and *On the Shortness of Life* 4.2; and, for the expression, 33.4, 113.23.

**1.2**    The thought is elucidated by comparison with 24.19–20.

**1.5**    A Greek version of the proverb appears in Hesiod, *Works and Days* 369. For the thought, compare 108.26.

**2.5**    Epicurus was the founder in Athens of the Garden, a school of philosophy based on natural science and on hedonism in ethics. For Epicurus, pleasure is the only rational motivation for human action; but the most pleasurable existence overall for a human being consists in mental tranquility, and an unambitious life of frugality is the best way to achieve this. Seneca, like Cicero, sees Epicureanism as the direct rival to Stoicism, and his remarks about it are often sharply polemical: see 9.8–10, 88.5, 90.35, 99.25–26, and in the essays *On Leisure* 7.1, *On Benefits* 4.2–3, *On the Happy Life* 7.1–3, 12.5. Nonetheless, he is quite knowledgeable about Epicurean principles and major figures in the school, and expresses warm appreciation for some aspects of Epicurus's character and writings. Here, as often in the early letters, he quotes from a work of Epicurus that has not otherwise survived, perhaps the letter collection implied in 9.1 or the collection of maxims mentioned in 13.17. See Graver 2015.

**3.2**    Theophrastus was an associate of Aristotle and succeeded him as head of the Lyceum in 322 BCE. The saying alluded to here must have been "Judge first, then love."

**3.6**    Either L. Pomponius, a writer of *fabula togata* (comedy) and farce in the early first century BCE; or P. Pomponius Secundus, a contemporary of Seneca, mentioned in Tacitus and Quintilian as a talented tragedian who resisted oppression under Tiberius. Seneca's quotation is not in verse.

**4.1** For this form of pleasure, see the note on 23.3.

**4.3** The Epicurean argument; see the note on 30.6.

**4.7** Pompey was ambushed and beheaded in 48 BCE at the command of the youthful Ptolemy XIII; the eunuch Potheinos and others of his advisors played an important part in the decision. Seneca mentions the event also in *On Anger* 2.2, and it is described in detail by his nephew Lucan (*Civil War* 8.482–535). Marcus Licinius Crassus, one of the most powerful political leaders of the 50s BCE and the wealthiest man in Rome, was ignominiously killed in a disastrous campaign against the Parthians in Mesopotamia.

Marcus Aemilius Lepidus was the friend and brother-in-law of the emperor Gaius Caesar (Caligula) and was for a time recognized as his heir; he was executed on suspicion of insurrection in 39 CE. Caligula himself was assassinated only two years later by his praetorian guard under the leadership of Cassius Chaerea.

**4.10** I.e., from the writings of Epicurus; see the note on 2.5, and compare 16.7. The saying (which Seneca quotes again in 27.9) is extant in Greek as part of *Vatican Sayings* 25 and is also quoted in Porphyry's *Letter to Marcella* 27 (frag. 202 Usener).

This remark is also from Epicurus, and may be from the same context, since we have it in the *Vatican Sayings* (33) and again in Porphyry's *Letter to Marcella* 30 (frag. 200 Usener). Compare 25.4, 119.7.

**5.7** Hecaton was a Stoic philosopher (hence "our own") of the early first century BCE, a pupil of Panaetius and an associate of the Quintus Aelius Tubero mentioned in 95.72. He was the author of several treatises on ethics.

**5.8** In calling foresight (*providentia*) the greatest good for a human being, Seneca takes it to be equivalent to intelligence or practical wisdom (*prudentia*), one of the four cardinal virtues. But foresight may also be thought of simply as our capacity to anticipate future events. If events outside our control are improperly regarded as goods or evils, then such foresight sets us up for emotional disturbance. See also the notes on 8.3 and 9.3.

**6.3** Both companionship (*societas*) and commonality (Gk. *koinōnia*) were important elements in the Stoic conception of friendship. See 9.3–18, with the second note on 9.3, and compare 48.3, 109.13–16.

**6.6** Zeno founded the Stoic school in Athens around 300 BCE; Cleanthes succeeded him as its head in 262. Seneca knows some details about their lives and philosophical views; see, for instance, 44.3, 82.9, 83.9, 94.4, 107.10–11; *Consolation to Helvia* 12.4.

Metrodorus, Hermarchus, and Polyaenus were close friends and colleagues of Epicurus.

**6.7** See the note on 5.7.

**7.5** Cruelty is injurious to oneself, because the example teaches others to be cruel as well. The thought seems to be proverbial; compare 81.19, and see Plato, *Apology* 25e. In this case, though, the gladiator at whom the people are shouting can hardly become any worse.

**7.6** All three are mentioned repeatedly by Seneca as examples of moral rectitude: Socrates, for instance, at 28.8 and 104.27–28, Laelius (the friend of Scipio Aemilianus) at 95.72, Cato at 51.12 and 87.9–10. It is probably the elder Cato that Seneca has in mind here (cf. 11.10), but Seneca sometimes mentions the younger Cato as well in such lists: compare 64.10 and 95.72, and see the note on 14.12.

**7.10** Democritus, a contemporary of Socrates, was as much renowned for moral philosophy as for his views on atoms and void.

**7.11** The statement is not otherwise recorded; see the note on 2.5.

**8.1** Stoic ethics favored active service to society, including political action, unless prevented by adverse circumstances. See the note on 68.2.

**8.3** The speech that follows gives an initial statement of the core message of Stoic ethics, that what is truly valuable in human life is to be found not in the fortuitous advantages most people think of as good but in the human mind; i.e., in one's own character and conduct. The same idea will be expressed later on in terms more characteristic of Stoicism; see the note on 31.6.

**8.7** The saying is not otherwise recorded; see the note on 2.5.

Part of the manumission ceremony required the former master to turn the freed slave around in a circle.

**8.8** The *fabulae togatae* were comic (or seriocomic) plays not based on Greek models.

**8.9** Publilius Syrus (1st c. BCE) produced scripts for a popular form of drama known as "mime," i.e., light comedy or farce. Publilius was especially known for his aphorisms, a collection of which was still being read in schools in the time of Jerome (Jerome, *Letter* 107.8). The line Seneca quotes here appears at the beginning of the surviving collection as edited by Friedrich 1964.

**8.10**  Both quotations are in verse, in the same meter as the preceding quotation from Publilius Syrus. Seneca refers to Lucilius's talents as a writer a number of times in the collection, notably in 24.19–21, 46, and 79.4–7.

**9.1**  Epicurus's letter is known only from what Seneca says about it here and below (9.8, 9.18).

It was common in the Hellenistic period for discussions of ethical issues to be framed in terms of the character and experience of the wise person or sage. In effect, the wise person is the intellectual and moral exemplar who functions as an ideal for ordinary people to imitate.

Stilpo practiced philosophy in Megara during the late fourth and early third centuries BCE. He was an associate of Crates the Cynic (see the note on 10.1), with whom he shared an emphasis on personal virtue and self-reliance, and a teacher of Zeno of Citium. See Diogenes Laertius 2.113–20.

**9.2**  *Impatientia* ("non-sufferance") is the closest Latin equivalent for the Greek *apatheia* ("impassivity") in terms of its derivation but does not have the required meaning.

**9.3**  Seneca is fully in agreement with the usual Stoic position on ordinary emotions like grief, fear, and desire, namely that they are causally dependent on false notions of value and should be eliminated altogether (see especially letters 85 and 116). At the same time, he is quick to point out that the Stoics do not aim for an unnatural lack of feeling: they agree with everyone else that the emotions have a basis in human nature, and they hold that even a morally perfect person would experience certain kinds of feelings (for which see further the notes on 11.1 and 23.3, and compare 99.15). The more extreme position that eliminates all feelings from the wise person is associated in his mind with the Cynic philosophers; compare *On the Shortness of Life* 14.2 ("to conquer human nature with the Stoics; to abandon it with the Cynics").

Like Aristotle in *Nicomachean Ethics* 1.7, the Stoics posited that one who seeks to live the best possible life must be self-sufficient; i.e., not dependent on anyone else for happiness. Nonetheless, they held that because we are social beings by nature, a person of good character will want to have friends. They explained this position by appealing to the notion of a shared existence (companionship and commonality, as in 6.3) and by pointing out that friendship provides opportunities for virtuous activity (9.8, cf. 109.3–6). For the Stoic background, see Cicero,

On Ends 3.65–70; Diogenes Laertius 7.123–24; Stobaeus 2.7.5l (73W = SVF 3.112) and 2.7.11i, 101–2W (SVF 3.626).

**9.4** The analogy between a deceased friend and a missing part of one's own body may owe something to Stilpo: compare the report in Stobaeus 4.44.83, where Stilpo argues that the correct response when a friend or relative dies is to care more tenderly for one's other connections, just as a farmer would take better care of other branches of a tree that lost one branch, or a person would take better care of other parts of his own body after losing one.

**9.5** The thought belongs to the consolatory tradition; compare 63.10–11, and for Phidias see the note on 85.40.

**9.6** See the note on 5.7.

**9.7** Attalus is mentioned by Seneca the Elder (*Suasoriae* 2.12) as a Stoic philosopher, "the subtlest and most eloquent of our age," who lost his property under Sejanus. Seneca was deeply impressed by him as a young man (108.13–16) and quotes several of his sayings; see 67.15, 72.8, 81.22, 108.3.

**9.8** For the Epicurean doctrine, compare *Principal Doctrine* 28 and the first of the three Epicurean positions reported by Cicero in *On Ends* 1.66–70: friendship provides the intelligent hedonist with security against future misfortune, a necessary element in happiness (*Vatican Sayings* 33; Cicero, *Tusculan Disputations* 3.38; Plutarch, *That a Follower of Epicurus Cannot Live Pleasantly* 1089d [frag. 68 Usener]).

**9.11** The argument is *a fortiori*. Even though romantic love is a base emotion, it arises from disinterested motives: no one falls in love merely to make a profit or for the sake of ambition. But the basis of friendship can hardly be *less* honorable than that of a base emotion, and so friendship must arise from disinterested motives as well.

**9.14** Chrysippus of Soli was the most widely influential of the early Stoic philosophers and the leader of the school from 232 BCE until his death ca. 206 BCE. Seneca knows at least some of his writings, and greatly admires his intellect (*On Benefits* 1.3.8). The remark quoted here is known also to Plutarch, who quotes it in Greek (*On Common Conceptions* 1068a). In his Latin rendering of it, Seneca plays on two senses of the expression *opus esse*, either "have need of" or "have a use for."

**9.16** In Stoic cosmology, the entire universe is at intervals dissolved into fire and then regenerated by Zeus, who is equated with the designing fire that structures all things. During the periods of conflagration, Zeus is alone with his own thoughts and does not mind the absence of other gods (Epictetus, *Discourses* 3.13.4–8; cf. Plutarch, *On Common Conceptions* 1077d = *SVF* 2.396). For the wise person's retreat, compare 74.28–29.

**9.17**   In Stoic thought, "attachment" (*conciliatio*; Gk. *oikeiōsis*) is the instinctual process by which human beings come to recognize some objects as akin to themselves and therefore to prefer them over their opposites: physical preservation over destruction, understanding over ignorance, human contact over solitude. This last preference supplies the basis for friendship and familial love. See also 109.13 and 121.14, and compare Cicero, *On Ends* 3.16–21, 3.62.

**9.18**   For Stilpo see the note on 9.1. Demetrius Poliorcetes' sack of Megara occurred in 307 BCE. The anecdote recounted here is told also in Diogenes Laertius 2.115 (where Stilpo goes on to explain that he retains his eloquence and his knowledge); see also Stobaeus 3.40.8 (738–39W).

**9.20**   The statement (frag. 474 Usener) is not otherwise recorded; see the note on 2.5.

**9.21**   The source of the line is unknown.

**10.1**   Crates of Thebes was a Cynic philosopher of the fourth through early third centuries BCE and the first teacher of Zeno of Citium. He had a reputation for caustic humor.

**10.2**   "The senseless" are the general run of people who lack the virtue of intelligence or good sense (*prudentia*).

**10.5**   This Athenodorus may be either Athenodorus Cordylion, who was for a time the house philosopher of Cato the Younger; or perhaps more likely the scholar Athenodorus Calvus, a teacher of Octavian. Both were associated with Tarsus in Asia Minor.

**11.1**   The Stoics held that a person who possessed a full understanding of the world would not experience ordinary emotions like shame or fear; see the note on 9.3. However, such a person would still be subject to involuntary reactions like blushing and stage fright, which are not dependent on false beliefs about value and in no way morally culpable. Compare 57.3–6, 71.29, 74.31, 99.18–19; *On Anger* 2.3–4.

**11.4**   Lucius Cornelius Sulla held absolute power in Rome from 82 BCE to 80 BCE, during which time he ordered several thousand executions. Gnaeus Pompey "the Great," though not an accomplished speaker, achieved extensive military victories and a political career rivaling Julius Caesar's.

Papirius Fabianus was one of Seneca's personal models in rhetoric and philosophy. Described by the elder Seneca as a *philosophus*, he is admired by both Senecas especially for his probity of life and his elegant oratory (40.12, 52.11, 58.6; *On the Shortness of Life* 10.1; Seneca the Elder *Controversiae* 2 pref.). His rhetorical style is treated at length in letter 100.

**11.8** The statement (frag. 210 Usener) is not otherwise recorded; see the note on 2.5.

**11.10** It was the elder Cato who was known for his severity; see 51.12 and 87.9–10, and compare 95.72, where the two Catos are named together. The elder was known for moral maxims of the kind cited in 94.27 and 119.2. For Laelius see the note on 95.72.

**12.1** This estate must be the one mentioned in Tacitus, *Annals* 15.60.4, as the scene of Seneca's death. Seneca also mentions two other villas, one in Nomentum (104.1, 110.1) and one in the Alban Hills (123.1).

**12.3** Gifts of clay figurines (*sigillaria*) were made especially at the festival of Saturnalia, which masters celebrated jointly with their slaves. But children might have played with such things at any time.

**12.6** I.e., according to our year of birth. The Roman censors kept a register of citizens according to age.

**12.7** Heraclitus of Ephesus (ca. 535–475 BCE), called "the Obscure" for his riddling aphorisms (Cicero, *On Ends* 2.15).

**12.8** This Pacuvius governed Syria during the 20s CE as proxy for Aelius Lamia, who was detained in Rome by Tiberius. "By possession" is humorous exaggeration: in Roman law one could acquire title to a tract of land by possessing it for two years, but governors did not own their provinces.

**12.9** Virgil, *Aeneid* 4.653. The same verse is quoted in *On the Happy Life* 19.1 by an Epicurean as he commits suicide.

**12.10** The statement (frag. 487 Usener) is identified just below as by Epicurus; it is not otherwise recorded (see the note on 2.5), but compare *Letter to Menoeceus* 127.

**13.4** See the note on 8.3.

**13.8** The expression seems to be proverbial; compare Livy 27.45, where the point is that little things may have a great psychological impact on an army.

**13.9** The thought here is probably influenced by Epicurus; see the note on 39.5.

**13.12** Hope is here a "fault" because the hopeful person expects circumstances to improve, even when there is no rational basis for the expectation.

Nonetheless, it may be expedient to make use of hope as a corrective to fears we find difficult to control. Compare 5.8.

**13.13** The metaphor is drawn from political debate in the Roman Senate.

**13.14** A guarantor of liberty was a person who could attest to an ex-slave's free status in case of legal challenge. Seneca means that when Caesar and his army tried to force Cato (the Younger; see the note on 14.12) to capitulate, he proved himself a free man by committing suicide.

**13.16** The statement (frag. 494 Usener) is identified just below as by Epicurus; it is not otherwise recorded (see the note on 2.5).

**14.2** Seneca consistently maintains that we have an innate inclination to preserve our physical selves and under normal circumstances a responsibility to do so. In some unusual situations, however, we may have a responsibility to do the opposite, sometimes even to commit suicide. All this is in keeping with Stoic thought: see the notes on 31.6 and 82.15, and for suicide in particular the note on 70.5.

**14.8** An oblique reference to Lucilius's position within the imperial administration as procurator (civil governor) of Sicily. Seneca alludes to his addressee's position chiefly as an opportunity for sightseeing; compare 19.5–8, where it seems a burden, with 31.9, 45.2, 51.1, 79.1–4. In the preface to *Natural Questions* 4A, the post is called a "leisurely" one, such as would afford plenty of time for study and writing.

The treacherous currents of the Straits of Messina, between the Italian peninsula and the island of Sicily, were thought by Romans to have been the originals of Scylla and Charybdis in *Odyssey* book 9. Navigating the passage safely required an exact knowledge of its dangers.

**14.9** For this uncommon type of cruelty, see the note on 83.25.

**14.10** The proverb is not otherwise known.

**14.11** These "stoles" were long strips of carded wool called *infulae*, worn by priests in token of purity during a sacrifice.

**14.12** Marcus Porcius Cato Uticensis (Cato the Younger) was a major political figure of the Late Republic. Championing the interests of the optimate class, he resisted the increasing power of Caesar and Pompey during the 50s BCE, but in the civil war of the 40s gave his support to Pompey, who commanded the legions of the Senate. Seneca mentions Cato frequently, treating him as an especially prominent example of Roman virtue: compare especially 24.6–8, 71.8–16, and 104.29–33, and see the notes on all three passages.

**14.13** The paragraph that follows provides a sample of the kind of arguments that were sometimes made in the course of rhetorical training, where Cato was a stock figure: compare *On Tranquility of Mind* 19; Persius, *Satires* 3.45–48; Seneca the Elder, *Controversiae* 9.6.7 (cf. 10.1.8), 6.8, *Suasoriae* 6.2, 4, 10. The attitude expressed toward Cato's decision is quite different from what Seneca says elsewhere; see Griffin 1968. For Seneca's actual position on retirement from political action, compare his essay *On Leisure*, and see further letters 68 and 105.

Cato had opposed legislation proposed by Caesar during his consulship in 59 BCE that would have made grants of public lands to Pompey's returning soldiers. Caesar stopped Cato's speech by having him dragged from the Forum. In a later incident, Cato spoke so insistently against a measure assigning powerful military commands to Pompey and Crassus that he was jailed by the presiding tribune (Plutarch, *Cato the Younger* 43).

**14.14** "Laws for humankind" are moral principles as opposed to political laws. Seneca gives extensive discussion to such principles in letters 94 and 95.

**14.15** Seneca uses this odd expression also in *Natural Questions* 4a pref. 5, where the point seems again to be that even the most careful and skilled efforts may not always suffice to defend oneself.

**14.16** The robber represents chance misfortune, as in 4.8. There is no shame in losing one's life to random events.

**14.17** Metrodorus belonged to the school ("shop") of Epicurus; compare 6.6. Seneca is familiar with some of his writings, which include personal letters like those of Epicurus (quoted by Seneca in 79.16, 98.9, 99.25–26) and some work, perhaps also a letter, touching on gratitude (81.11–12). For the thought here, compare Epicurus, *Letter to Menoeceus* 130.

**15.1** The formula is only five words in Latin (*si vales, bene est, valeo*) and was standard enough to be abbreviated to *SVBEV.*

**15.3** In Stoic philosophy, the mind or spirit is a fine-textured material substance called "breath" (*pneuma*). See also the note on 50.6.

Oil was used to massage the muscles before exercise. These complaints against exercise combined with drinking on an empty stomach are expanded in 122.6.

**15.4** The fuller performed the distasteful work of laundering woolens by trampling or jumping on them in a vat of water mixed with urine.

**15.7** Members of the upper classes sometimes engaged specialists in dietetics to monitor and improve their eating habits and exercise routines.

"Quirites" is an elevated expression for "Roman citizens."

**15.9**   The author is Epicurean, as in 14.17, but the statement (frag. 491 Usener) is not otherwise recorded; see the note on 2.5. Compare *Letter to Menoeceus* 127, "the future is neither wholly ours nor wholly not ours."

Baba and Ision appear to be names (or stage names) of jesters; compare *Pumpkinification* 11, where Augurinus and Baba make appropriately foolish parallels for Claudius.

**15.11**   Again, the thought is Epicurean in coloring; see the note on 39.5, and compare Lucretius 4.1097–1100.

**16.5**   Of the three views listed, only the second would be accepted by a Stoic; see the note on 76.23.

**16.7**   The saying (frag. 201 Usener) is not otherwise recorded but is close in thought to the one quoted in 4.10; see also 27.9, and compare Epicurus, *Principal Doctrines* 15 and 21.

**17.2**   The word "facilitate" (*opitulari*) is used by Cicero in a number of his extant letters and speeches, but not with "philosophy" as the subject. It is possible that Seneca has in mind a passage in the lost dialogue *Hortensius*.

**17.4**   The one whose habits Seneca recommends imitating is poverty; i.e., the poor person. The theme is developed in 18.5–6.

**17.11**   The statement (frag. 479 Usener) also quoted in Porphyry's *Letter to Marcella* 28; compare 4.10.

**18.1**   The Saturnalia during the third week of December was Rome's carnival season, celebrated with parties and gift exchange and with a playful exchange of roles between masters and slaves.

**18.2**   The toga was the attire of business and government, too formal as well as too heavy for a convivial occasion. Looser and more colorful garments would be made of silk or cotton.

**18.3**   During the Saturnalia, slave owners might for fun put on the *pilleus*, a tall felt hat usually worn by freedmen.

**18.7**   Seneca speaks of some fashionable practices of mock asceticism. The name of Timon, of the fifth century BCE in Athens, was associated with misanthropy and suggests simple meals without guests; "paupers' cells" must be small unfurnished rooms used by the wealthy for periods of retreat or perhaps only for show. Compare 5.1–2, 100.6.

**18.9**   Epicureans practiced abstemious living even on ordinary days: see 21.10, and compare Diogenes Laertius 10.11; Epicurus, *Letter to Menoeceus* 130–31.

Polyaenus was one of Epicurus's principal colleagues; compare 6.6. The archonship of Charinus is datable to 308/7 BCE.

Epicurus probably wrote in terms of the obol, the small silver penny of Athens; Seneca translates to the *as*, the bronze coin of Rome. For Metrodorus see the note on 14.17, and compare 52.3–4.

**18.12**  Virgil, *Aeneid* 8.364–65. In the *Aeneid*, these words are spoken by Evander as Aeneas enters his cottage, reminding the hero that Hercules, later to be deified, had also stayed in that house.

**18.14**  The management of anger was an important topic for Epicureans as well as Stoics. The connection with insanity was a commonplace; it may be understood either metaphorically or literally; compare *On Anger* 1.1, 2.5. The statement quoted here (frag. 484 Usener) is not otherwise recorded for Epicurus; see the note on 2.5.

Anger at slaves features in a number of the anecdotes in Seneca's treatise *On Anger*, e.g., at 1.15.3.

**19.2**  The metaphor is similarly used by Seneca the Elder, addressing his youngest son, Annaeus Mela: "I will keep you in harbor," meaning that he should not go into politics but should stick with rhetoric and philosophy (*Controversiae* 2 pref.).

**19.3**  A Latin equivalent for the Epicurean precept "live unknown." The advice to live a quiet life, not participating in politics or seeking any kind of fame, was especially characteristic of the Epicurean school, but was offered by philosophers of other schools as well. Stoics usually argued for the opposite view; compare 8.1, and see further on 68.2.

For Lucilius's advancement, compare 44.2, where his equestrian status is attributed to his own efforts, and see also *Natural Questions* 4a pref.

**19.6**  See the note on 76.23.

**19.9**  The wealthy Gaius Maecenas was a trusted advisor to Octavian who served as his vice-regent in Italy during the civil wars and occasionally later in his principate; his writings survive only in fragments. Seneca quotes from his poetry also in 92.35 and 101.11 and from his prose writings in 114.4–8, 22. He presents Maecenas as a man of strong abilities who was ruined by soft living and by a difficult relationship with his wife (see further on 114.4). The phrase "on the rack" suggests that the line given here is spoken by the character Prometheus, who was tortured by Zeus for the theft of fire. (As a Roman citizen, Maecenas could not himself have been subjected to torture.)

**19.10** The statement (frag. 542 Usener) is not otherwise recorded; see the note on 2.5.

**19.11** The social secretary (*nomenclator*) was a slave whose job it was to keep track of a nobleman's acquaintances.

The conferring of benefits or favors (*beneficia*) was an important mechanism for business and social relations at Rome. Seneca explores the issue further in letter 81 and in his treatise *On Benefits*.

**20.9** This saying of Epicurus (frag. 206 Usener) is not otherwise recorded (see the note on 2.5); for the asceticism, compare 18.9, 21.10.

Demetrius, a personal acquaintance of Seneca, practiced philosophy in the manner of the Cynics, renouncing not only material possessions but even the desire of possessions (*On the Happy Life* 18.3). Seneca mentions his asceticism also in 62.3 and his earthy sayings in 67.14 and 91.19.

**20.13** Compare 18.5–7.

**21.1** The fundamental axiom of Stoic ethics is that honorable conduct (*honestum*, Gk. *to kalon*) is the sole human good and thus the only source of happiness (see further the notes on 66.16 and 76.7). Lucilius is thus represented as sympathetic to Stoicism but not yet able to put his convictions into practice.

**21.3** Idomeneus was a close associate of Epicurus and a writer of history, biography, and philosophy, in addition to the political achievements mentioned here. Epicurus's letter urging him to retire from politics (frag. 132 Usener) is quoted again in 22.5–6 (frag. 133 Usener); compare Plutarch, *Against Colotes* 1127d (frag. 134 Usener).

**21.4** Titus Pomponius Atticus was Cicero's closest friend and the recipient of most of his extant correspondence. Though interested in historical research, he did not seek fame on his own account (Cicero, *Letters to Atticus* 17.17.5). Marcus Vipsanius Agrippa, Octavian's friend and most important military commander, married Atticus's daughter Caecilia. Their daughter Vipsania was Tiberius's first wife and mother of Drusus the Younger.

Seneca's verb *adplicuisset* refers specifically to Cicero's writing Atticus's name after his own in the salutations of his letters.

**21.5** The survival of which Seneca speaks here is the survival of one's reputation through literature; compare Ennius's epitaph: "Living I roll / through mouths of men," and Horace, *Odes* 3.31; Ovid, *Metamorphoses* 15, 875–79.

Virgil, *Aeneid* 9.446–49. The two people addressed are Nisus and Euryalus, young soldiers, adventurous but not especially intelligent, who lose their lives on a nighttime spying mission. Virgil's apostrophe to them implies a strong claim for the efficacy of his own poetic narrative.

**21.7** Pythocles was another colleague of Epicurus and the recipient of one of his three extant letters. The fragment is extant in Greek in Stobaeus 3.17.23, 495W (frag. 135 Usener).

**21.9** The procedures of the Roman Senate allowed senators to reject one portion of a proposed piece of legislation but endorse another. Seneca is in general strongly opposed to Epicurean hedonism; see the note on 2.5.

Epicurus held that virtuous behavior as conventionally understood is an essential means to a tranquil and therefore pleasurable existence (*Principal Doctrine* 5, *Letter to Menoeceus* 10.131–32). An Epicurean allegiance thus did not provide an excuse for dissolute living. For the thought here, compare *On the Happy Life* 13.3; for Epicurean asceticism, compare 18.9, 20.9.

**22.5** See the note on 21.3.

**22.11** Zeno and Chrysippus were early leaders of the Stoic school; see the notes on 6.6 and 9.14.

**22.14** Compare Epicurus, *Vatican Sayings* 60.

**23.1** To "rejoice" (*gaudere*) is to experience joy (*gaudium*). In normal Latin usage, "joy" might refer to any form of delight, regardless of what occasioned it. Seneca now restricts joy to the feeling of gladness that, according to Stoicism, accompanies a virtuous disposition.

**23.3** Unlike the ordinary flawed person who delights wrongly in empty things, the wise person who is the Stoic ideal (see the note on 9.1) would experience joy in his own character and good deeds or those of virtuous friends. This joy is a strong feeling; it is called "exhilaration" (*On the Happy Life* 4.4) and, in Stoic terminology, an "elevation of mind" (59.2). To experience it, Lucilius must perfect his character, since only a fully virtuous and wise person possesses the genuine goods that are the proper object of joy. For the Stoic background, see Cicero, *Tusculan Disputations* 4.13; Diogenes Laertius 7.116; Graver 2007.

**23.6** Seneca regularly belittles the body, with its pleasures and pains, in contrast to the grandeur of the mind. Compare 24.16, 41.4, 58.29, 65.22, 66.1, *On the Happy Life* 4.4, *Consolation to Helvia* 11.7.

**23.9**   Epicurus is "your dear Epicurus" in that Lucilius is represented as having a proprietary interest in the maxim enclosed at the end of each letter. Compare 20.9, and see note 3 in the introduction to this book.

The saying (frag. 493 Usener) is not otherwise recorded; see the note on 2.5.

**24.2**   The advice to reflect on all possible misfortunes is not meant to license groundless worry (cf. 13.8–12) but rather to afford an accurate assessment of what a human life is likely to include, thus mitigating the psychological impact of inevitable misfortune. Compare 76.35, 88.16–17, 91.4, 107.4. Cicero, in describing the same practice in *Tusculan Disputations* 3.28–31, supplies the term "prerehearsal of future ills" (*praemeditatio futurorum malorum*). Though not originating with the Stoics, the technique was favored by them: see *Tusculan Disputations* 3.52; Galen, *Precepts of Hippocrates and Plato* 4.7.7–11.

The words "either no great matter or not long lasting" recall Epicurus's position on the fear of pain; see the note on 30.14. Epicurus, however, had recommended *against* the prerehearsal of future ills (Cicero, *Tusculan Disputations* 3.32).

**24.4**   P. Rutilius Rufus, an associate of the younger Scipio, was exiled on a trumped-up charge in 92 BCE, but bore it in a principled manner and subsequently declined to return (*On Benefits* 6.37; Cicero, *De Oratore* 1.227–30). He is compared with Q. Caecilius Metellus Numidicus, who went into voluntary exile for political reasons a few years earlier. For Sulla see the note on 11.4.

Socrates' situation is as described in Plato's *Crito*, except that in Plato's account his motivation for remaining in the prison is obedience to the laws. Compare 70.9.

**24.5**   According to legend, Gaius Mucius Scaevola attempted in 507 BCE to assassinate the Etruscan Lars Porsenna, who was besieging Rome. Captured, he thrust his right hand into a brazier of coals to demonstrate his indifference to pain or, in some accounts, to show defiance by punishing his hand for its failure. Compare 66.51; *On Providence* 3.5; Livy 2.12–13.5.

**24.6**   For Cato see the note on 14.12. The story of his suicide is told with additional details (and a different speech) in *On Providence* 2.9–12. The book was Plato's *Phaedo*, which recounts the death of Socrates together with philosophical arguments justifying belief in an immortal soul. The *Phaedo* does not, however, condone suicide, except in exceptional circumstances (when "God sends some necessity," 62c). Cato presumably feels that his situation qualifies for the exception.

**24.9** Caecilius Metellus Scipio was the commander of the Republican forces at the battle of Thapsus in North Africa in 46 BCE; Cato was his second in command. Unlike his illustrious ancestors P. Cornelius Scipio Africanus, who defeated the Carthaginians at Zama in 202, and P. Cornelius Scipio Aemilianus, who razed the city in 146, Metellus was utterly defeated and later committed suicide.

**24.13** The speech that follows is Seneca's example of the kind of internal discourse one should practice.

**24.14** This sentence again adapts the Epicurean slogan; compare 30.14.

**24.18** Seneca may be thinking specifically of the poem of Lucretius, which argues at some length against fears of Hades and reinterprets the myths of Ixion, Sisyphus, and others supposed to have been punished in the underworld (3.965ff). Compare also Cicero, *Tusculan Disputations* 1.10–11. Seneca's personal views on survival after death are optimistic, but he makes no claim to certainty: compare 57.8, 58.27, 63.16, 79.12, 92.30–34.

**24.21** Unlike the two quoted at 8.10, the Latin line given here is a hexameter verse. Seneca remarks in *Natural Questions* 4a pref. 14 that Lucilius's poems were not of the sort that could be expected to make money; this is perhaps an indication that the entire content was philosophical.

**24.22** This saying (frag. 496 Usener) and the two that follow (frags. 498 and 497 Usener) should be compared with the similar assertion of Lucretius in 3.79–82. For Epicurus's position on suicide, see *Letter to Menoeceus* 125–27; for Seneca's Stoic position, the note on 70.5.

**25.1** Seneca will speak frankly to the second friend, the one who needs to be broken of his faults rather than merely cleansed of them. Frankness or freedom of speech (*libertas*, Gk. *parrhēsia*) was a mark of friendship (Cicero, *On Friendship* 44). It was also recognized as a technique in philosophical instruction, as in the treatise on the subject by the Epicurean Philodemus.

**25.4** The remark is extant in Greek in *Vatican Sayings* 33; Stobaeus 3.17.30 (frag. 602 Usener); it is quoted also by Cicero (*On Ends* 2.88). Stoics made the same claim, but for different reasons; see the note on 31.8, and compare 73.12–14, 110.18–20, 119.5–7.

**25.5** This second saying (frag. 211 Usener) is not otherwise recorded; see the note on 2.5, and compare 11.8.

**25.6** All are typical examples of moral rectitude from the Roman Republic; compare 95.72. (Cato is probably Cato the Elder, as at 11.10.) In speaking of Scipio, Seneca may be thinking either of Metellus Scipio, just mentioned in 24.9 (and compare 70.22), or of Scipio Africanus, whose character he admires in 86.1–5.

The saying of Epicurus is not otherwise recorded; see the note on 2.5.

**26.8**   This exact statement is not otherwise reported for Epicurus; but compare *Letter to Menoeceus* 124–25, and see the note on 30.6.

**26.10**   I.e., to die; compare 58.34–36, and see the note on 70.5.

**27.3**   See the note on 23.3.

**27.5**   Since the freedman Calvisius Sabinus bears the name of an important consular family, he (or his father) must have been manumitted by a member of that family.

The nomenclator or social secretary was responsible for helping the nobleman to remember names; compare 19.11.

**27.9**   See the note on 4.10.

**28.1**   I.e., beneath the horizon; Virgil, *Aeneid* 3.72.

**28.3**   Virgil, *Aeneid* 6.78–79.

**28.8**   The Thirty Tyrants were oligarchs installed at Athens after the city was defeated by Sparta in 404 BCE; Socrates (according to Plato's *Apology* 32c–e) refused to cooperate in their program of juridical murder.

**28.9**   Awareness of wrongdoing was an important theme in Epicureanism (cf. 97.13); however, this particular remark (frag. 522 Usener) is not otherwise recorded.

**29.1**   Diogenes of Sinope was the best known of the Cynic philosophers of the fourth century BCE. Like other Cynics, he made a practice of delivering moral exhortation in the marketplace rather than in a school setting or to individuals. For freedom of speech, see the note on 25.1.

**29.3**   By "wisdom" (*sapientia*), Seneca here means the practice of delivering moral admonition.

**29.6**   The translation reflects the reading *M. Lepidi philosophum* as reported by Erasmus from a now-lost manuscript; for Marcus Lepidus, see the note on 4.7. Extant manuscripts read *lepidum philosophum*, "an elegant philosopher"; but since there was another important philosopher named Aristo (Aristo of Chios, first mentioned in 36.3), it seems likely that Seneca would have included a phrase to clarify the identity of the philosopher about whom these anecdotes are told.

Lepidus was a contemporary of both Mamercus Scaurus (d. 34 CE) and Julius Graecinus, a man of learning and integrity who was executed under Caligula (*On Benefits* 2.21.5–6). In his remark about the Peripatetics, Scaurus is making a pun: the Peripatetics were followers of Aristotle, but *peripatetikos* also means "inclined to walk."

**29.10** This is the "final payment," because the end of the third scroll is at hand; in book 4, the quotations from Epicurus will be discontinued. The saying is extant in Greek in the Paris Gnomologion (frag. 187 Usener); for the thought, see the note on 19.3.

**29.11** The list covers most of the main options for philosophical allegiance from the Hellenistic period through Seneca's day. The Peripatetics were a loosely organized school of philosophers who claimed to follow Aristotle in ethics; Academics similarly considered themselves followers of Plato; the Cynics emphasized the renunciation of conventional values.

**30.1** Aufidius Bassus is mentioned in Quintilian 10.1.103 as a writer of histories, including a history of the wars in Germany.

**30.6** Bassus gives the Epicurean reasoning, as in Epicurus, *Letter to Menoeceus* 125 and Lucretius 3.830–42: it is irrational to fear death because when death arrives, one is no longer alive to experience it. The allegiance is made explicit in 30.14. For the Epicurean, a rational approach to death means recognizing that it is logically impossible for those who have died to experience death as painful.

**30.12** This paragraph recalls the address of Nature in Lucretius, especially in the claim that death disassembles materials that will be reassembled to make a new life (3.964–71) and in the analogy to satisfaction with an ample meal (3.960).

**30.14** Bassus's remarks on pain (frag. 503 Usener) suggest familiarity with Epicurus, *Principal Doctrine* 4 [LS 21C], which states that severe pain lasts only a short time, while chronic illnesses involve a preponderance of pleasure over pain. Seneca sometimes makes the same remark on his own account: see 24.2, 24.14, 94.7.

**31.2** In Stoic thought, the human being is designed by nature for development toward the human good, which is perfected reason. In nearly all cases, however, we are corrupted, sometimes by the intrinsic plausibility of certain kinds of error (e.g., that wealth is a good thing in itself, as at 87.33), but most often by the influence of other people (Diogenes Laertius 7.89; Galen, *Precepts of Hippocrates and Plato* 5.5.13–20 [*SVF* 3.229a]; Calcidius, *On the Timaeus of Plato* 165–66 [= *SVF* 3.229]). The corrupting influences of the surrounding culture, including even the prayers of our parents on our behalf, are a frequent theme: compare 60.1, 94.53–55, 115.11, 121.4. The imagery here incorporates both the Sirens' song (cf. especially 123.12) and the echo of voices from the rocks as in Plato, *Republic* 6.492c.

**31.5** In Stoic physics, heat and cold are properties imparted to substances by the admixture of elemental fire and elemental air respectively; see, for instance, Galen, *Precepts of Hippocrates and Plato* 5.3.8 [LS 47H].

**31.6** The Stoic doctrine on preferred and dispreferred indifferents supplies a basis for reasonable pursuit of such objects as health, financial security, life, and good repute, and for avoidance of their opposites. But the wise person pursues and avoids the indifferents without either desiring them as genuinely good things or fearing them as genuinely bad. They are only the tools or material with which virtue has to work; and although our preferences in regard to them are grounded in human nature, there will be situations in which it is appropriate to set aside those preferences. Compare 82.14–15, 92.11–12, 123.13; and for the Stoic background, see Diogenes Laertius 7.102–5 [LS 58A–B]; Sextus Empiricus, *Against the Mathematicians* 11.64–67 [LS 58F]; Epictetus, *Discourses* 2.6.9 [LS 58J]; Plutarch, *On Common Conceptions* 1069e [LS 59A].

**31.8** The standard Stoic definition of "wisdom" is "knowledge of things divine and human" (see further on 89.5). The mind of the wise person is equal to the divine in that its perfected rationality reflects the coherent organization of the cosmos. It is not inferior to God in blessedness, although it lacks immortality. Compare Cicero, *On the Nature of the Gods* 2.153; Plutarch, *On Common Conceptions* 1061f [LS 63I]. Seneca returns to the point often, notably at 53.11–12, 73.13 (where he attributes it to Sextius); also at *On Providence* 1.5, *On the Constancy of the Wise Person* 8.2, *Natural Questions* 1 pref. 11–17). See further the note on 59.18.

**31.9** It is unclear why Lucilius's work as governor of the province of Sicily in 63–64 CE would have required him to face the Pennine and the Graian Passes (Alpine passes now known as the Little St. Bernard Pass and Great St. Bernard Pass) or the mountains of Illyria on the Balkan Peninsula. It is more plausible that he would have had to voyage past Scylla and Charybdis (i.e., the Straits of Messina) and the Syrtaean shoals just north of modern Libya.

**31.11** Both Seneca and Lucilius belonged to the equestrian order, membership in which required substantial wealth.

The quotation is from Virgil, *Aeneid* 8.364–65; the imagery concerns figurines of the gods in terra-cotta. In *Consolation to Helvia* 10, Seneca more explicitly associates such figurines with the simplicity and probity of earlier generations of Romans, who kept the oaths they swore by them.

**33.1** These "flowery bits" (*flosculi*) are aphorisms expressed with some rhetorical flourish; compare 33.7. For the use of philosophical maxims, especially maxims drawn from Epicurus, compare 2.4–5.

**33.2** Men's garments usually did not have sleeves.

**33.4** Zeno, Cleanthes, Chrysippus, Posidonius, and Panaetius were all important Stoic authors; see the notes on 6.6, 9.14, 78.28, 116.5. For the Epicurean names, compare 6.6, 14.17, 52.4–5. As concerns Metrodorus, the statement is an exaggeration, for Seneca sometimes quotes him as a philosopher in his own right; see the note on 14.17.

The quotation is from Ovid, *Metamorphoses* 13.824.

**33.7** A *chreia*, or "set piece," was a pithy remark attributed to a named individual. Boys were required to memorize such remarks as an early stage of their training in oratory.

**34.3** Seneca speaks in several passages of an attitude of willingness (*velle* or *voluntas*) as a key factor in moral progress; see especially 16.1, 52.3, 71.36, 72.9, 80.4. Elsewhere, the same Latin words sometimes refer to actions that are performed by choice; i.e., that originate with oneself and are performed for one's own reasons; examples include 61.3, 66.16, 76.9, 77.7, 81.24, 95.9, 121.7. In most passages, we translate as "wish," "intention," or "volition."

**35.4** Both the foolish and the wise person act voluntarily; i.e., according to their intentions (*voluntates*). In the foolish person, however, these intentions are inadequately grounded and thus inconsistent. For the Stoic background, see the note on 71.32.

**36.3** This Aristo must be the Stoic philosopher Aristo of Chios; see the note on 89.13.

For "liberal studies" meaning "philosophy," compare 88.2.

**36.9** The argument is Epicurean; see the note on 30.6, and compare 99.29.

**36.10** In the mythological narrative of Virgil, *Aeneid* 6.703–51, souls preparing for reincarnation drink from Lethe, the river of forgetfulness.

**37.1** Quoted from the oath sworn by gladiators; compare Petronius, *Satyricon* 117. Service as a gladiator was regarded as shameful; compare 7.4–5.

**37.2** Once alive, we have no way to escape death. The word "reprieve" (*missio*) can refer either to the release of a wounded gladiator from the arena or to the discharge of a soldier from duty.

**37.3** Virgil, *Aeneid* 2.494.

**38.2** The image is Platonic; compare *Phaedrus* 276b–277a.

**39.1** The word *breviarium* was apparently just coming into use for the kind of volume Lucilius is supposed to have requested.

A person who had no means of proving his identity might ask an acquaintance to vouch for him in some transaction. Seneca means that he can write the requested summaries himself and on his own authority rather than supplying something in the form of excerpts from famous authors.

**39.5** The thought here is strongly reminiscent of Epicurus; see especially *Letter to Menoeceus* 127–28, *Principal Doctrine* 21.

**40.2** The philosopher Serapio is unknown except for what Seneca says here.

The younger orator is Odysseus (*Iliad* 3.221–23); the elder is Nestor as in *Iliad* 1.248–49. Cicero had similarly contrasted the two in *Brutus* 40; see also Plato, *Phaedrus* 261b.

**40.9** These anecdotes belong to the Augustan period. Publius Vinicius (consul in 2 CE) is mentioned by the elder Seneca as a talented speaker who did not put up with foolishness (*Controversiae* 7.5.11). "Asellius" is identified by Préchac with Arellius Fuscus, a well-known orator (Seneca the Elder, *Controversiae* 10, pref. 13) and the teacher of Fabianus (see 40.12, 11.4). Quintus Varius Geminius held important magistracies under Augustus (*Prosopographia Imperii Romani pars III* 385.187); he had a reputation for turning a phrase (e.g., Seneca the Elder, *Controversiae* 6.8).

**40.10** Quintus Haterius (consul in 5 BCE) had a political career under Augustus and Tiberius; his public speaking is described by Seneca the Elder as rapid to a fault (*Controversiae* 4.7), and by Tacitus (*Annals* 4.61) as dependent more on excited delivery than on content.

**40.11** The few samples we have of Roman handwriting suggest that punctuation consisted primarily of dots separating the words.

**40.12** For Fabianus see the note on 11.4.

**41.2** Virgil, *Aeneid* 8.352.

**41.5** For the divinity of the wise person's mind within Stoicism, see the note on 31.8. But the imagery throughout this passage also recalls the Platonic image of the body as an earthly prison for a mind or soul that is of divine origin. See also the note on 58.27, and compare Plato, *Phaedo* 82d–83b; Cicero, *Tusculan Disputations* 1.74–75.

**41.8** A fuller version of the same argument is given in 76.7–12.

**42.1** Moral perfection or wisdom is a possible attainment, according to Stoicism, but taken to be so rare that no certain instances of it could be attested by Stoic authorities. Hence Seneca's comparison to the mythical phoenix, an image exploited by the school's critics; see Alexander of Aphrodisias, *On Fate* 199 [LS 61N]. Compare 71.8.

**44.2** Compare 19.3.

Fourteen rows in the theater were reserved for those who met the property qualification for equestrian status.

**44.3** Tradition made Socrates the son of a stoneworker (Diogenes Laertius 2.18). For Cleanthes see the note on 6.6; his nighttime work as a water carrier is also reported in Diogenes Laertius 7.2. Plato was actually born of an aristocratic Athenian family.

**44.4** Seneca is perhaps thinking of Socrates' observation at *Theaetetus* 175a, that everyone has both kings and slaves among his ancestors.

**44.5** The atrium or front room of an elite family at Rome would have a display of wax masks representing noble ancestors.

**44.6** The Stoics argued that good things are ones that benefit the possessor not just in some situations but always: benefit is the essential property of the good in the same way as heat is the essential property of fire or sweetness of honey. Compare 118.13–16, and for the Stoic background Diogenes Laertius 7.102–3 [LS 58A]; Cicero, *On Ends* 3.33–34 [LS 60D]; see also the note on 113.5.

**44.7** Objects conventionally regarded as goods should be counted as preferred indifferents, sometimes called the "instruments" or "material" of happiness. See the note on 31.6.

For the claim that happiness entails an unshakable confidence that the good condition will last, see Cicero, *Tusculan Disputations* 5.40–41 [LS 63L], and compare 92.2–3. Such confidence is inherent in virtuous knowledge: see the note on 50.8.

**45.2** See the note on 14.8.

**45.4** Freed slaves took the names of their former masters.

**45.5** The study of logic, including semantics, syntax, and forms of argumentation, was a major concern of the Stoic founders, especially Chrysippus; see LS chaps. 31, 36, 37. Seneca has no objection to the study of ethical arguments in the form of syllogisms (see 82.9–10, 85.1–35, 87.14–40), but he objects to logic as an end in itself (45.6–13, 49.5). In particular, he is concerned that the logical puzzles called *sophismata* may displace serious work in ethics. See Barnes 1997, 12–23.

**45.8** The "horned man" sophism is quoted in full in 49.8. Additional examples of such puzzles include the "liar" sophism mentioned just below in 45.10 and the two "mouse" syllogisms in 48.6. These did not originate with the Stoa; they were propounded by earlier dialecticians, but were of interest to the Stoic founders as well (Cicero, *Prior Academics* 2.75; Plutarch, *On Stoic Self-Contradictions* 1034f).

For the term *sophismata*, see the note on 111.1.

**45.10** The ancient "liar" sophism had a number of variations; in its most basic form, however, it asks, "If you say you are lying, are you lying or telling the truth?" Chrysippus studied it extensively; see Diogenes Laertius 7.197–98 [LS 37B]; Cicero, *Prior Academics* 2.95–96 [LS 37H]. Related puzzles are still of interest to logicians.

**45.13** Long documents were written on papyrus scrolls, which would be rolled up in the left hand as one proceeded through the text.

**46.1** Livy and Epicurus were both voluminous writers; see further on 2.5 and 100.9. Seneca contrasts the modest proportions of Lucilius's literary production to date (his *corpus*, or body of work) with the length of his newest composition.

**47.4** This would include giving evidence against him in court.

**47.9** The freedman Gaius Julius Callistus was one of Caligula's most powerful advisors and was later implicated in his death. Universally feared, he kept his power intact through the change of regime and amassed great wealth under Claudius. From what Seneca says here, it appears he was originally purchased by Caligula at open auction and subsequently freed. The name of the former master is unknown.

**47.10** Three legions under the command of Publius Quinctilius Varus were defeated by German tribes in 9 CE; nearly all were killed, but some military personnel in the area were instead captured and enslaved.

**47.12** Three examples from mythology and history are followed by two from the biographies of philosophers. Hecuba, the elderly queen of Troy, was enslaved after the city fell; Croesus, king of Lydia, was defeated by the Persians and became the servant of Cyrus; the aged mother of the Persian king Darius III was captured by Alexander in 333 BCE. The story that Plato was once sold as a slave in Sicily is told in Diogenes Laertius 3.19–21; that of Diogenes of Sinope, in Diogenes Laertius 6.29–30.

**47.17** Pantomime dancers, both male and female, used singing and movement to enact episodes from mythology. Highly popular as entertainers, they were either slaves or freed persons.

**47.18** Freed slaves became clients of their former masters and were expected to call on them every morning.

**48.2** For the Epicurean view here criticized, see the note on 9.8.

**48.3** For companionship within Stoic friendship, compare 6.3, and see the second note on 9.3.

**48.4** See the note on 45.5.

**48.11** Literary scholars (*grammatici*) were concerned with various aspects of semantics as well as with literary history. Compare 88.3, 88.42, 108.32–34.

The quotation is from Virgil, *Aeneid* 9.641.

**49.1** Campania is the coastal region around the Bay of Naples, where Pompeii and a number of other towns were located. For Lucilius's association with Pompeii, compare 70.1, but also "your town of Parthenope" (which can only be Naples) in 53.1.

**49.2** Sotion was an associate or pupil of Quintus Sextius (108.17; see the note on 59.7), but nothing is known of Sotion's own teaching beyond the sample Seneca provides in 108.17–21.

**49.5** The remark of Cicero is not found in his extant works; it is sometimes assigned to the *Hortensius*. For Seneca's complaint against the dialecticians, see the note on 45.5.

**49.7** Virgil, *Aeneid* 8.385–86.

**49.12** Euripides, *Phoenician Women* 469.

**50.5** In order to develop toward the human good, people must first overcome the effects of moral corruption that have acted upon them since childhood (see the note on 31.2), inducing them to adopt incorrect notions of value. Such errors become ingrained through repetition in the absence of rational reflection, at which point they become the stable traits of character termed "sicknesses" or "infirmities." Typical examples include greed, irascibility, and ambition. The acquisition of virtue thus depends on continuous self-scrutiny and training. Compare 75.10–12; also Cicero, *Tusculan Disputations* 4.24–25; Stobaeus 2.7.10e, 93W; Epictetus, *Discourses* 2.8–10.

**50.6** For Stoics, the human mind or spirit is composed entirely of *pneuma* ("breath"), a fine-textured material in which the coolness of air is blended with the warmth of the designing fire (Alexander of Aphrodisias, *On Mixture and Increase* 224 [LS 47I]; see the note on 9.16). *Pneuma* is mingled with all components of the body and endows the entire body with its life functions. It resides especially in the heart, where it serves as the directive faculty (*hēgemonikon*) of the person as a whole and provides the capacity to form mental impressions and impulses and the special attribute of reason (Diogenes Laertius 7.85–86 [LS 57A]; Stobaeus 1.49.33, 368W [LS 53K]). In Stoic terminology, a qualified substance—in this case, breath—is "disposed in a certain way" when it takes on a further attribute. See also the note on 66.7, together with LS chap. 29; and compare 92.1.

**50.8**    Virtue in Stoicism is equivalent to an absolutely correct and unshakable understanding of how to behave; and this, once gained, is normally impervious to change (Diogenes Laertius 7.127 [LS 61I]).

By "contrary properties," Seneca means properties contrary to the nature of the substance in which they are found. The false beliefs that are the vices are contrary to the nature of the rational mind, because they are erroneous and because they will not stand up to reflective scrutiny.

**50.9**    The metaphor is as in Lucretius 1.936–42, but the claim that virtue brings pleasure along as a by-product is entirely Stoic; see Diogenes Laertius 7.86 [LS 57A], and compare *On the Happy Life* 9.1–2.

**51.1**    Marcus Valerius Messala Corvinus (consul in 31 BCE) was the author of various prose works and an important literary patron. Valgius Rufus (consul in 12 BCE) was an author in both poetry and prose and a member of Maecenas's literary circle (Horace, *Satires* 1.10.82).

Baiae, on the Bay of Naples, was a fashionable resort town known especially for luxury bathing establishments supplied by mineral springs and heated by the subterranean magma of the Phlegraean Fields. Seneca shows interest in the hydrothermal activity of the region in *Natural Questions* 3.24.

**51.3**    The Egyptian town of Canopus was on the coast near Alexandria; it was famed as a resort for pleasure seekers (Strabo 17.1.7).

**51.5**    Livy's account makes it Hannibal's army that succumbed to the pleasures of Campania rather than Hannibal himself (Livy 23.18.10–18).

**51.9**    The power to end one's own life guarantees that one need never be subject to the whims of fortune; compare 13.14, and see the note on 70.5.

**51.11**    P. Cornelius Scipio Africanus, one of Rome's most successful generals and political leaders, fell into legal difficulties in 184 BCE and chose to retire to his estate at Liternum in Campania, where he died a year later. The marshy environs of Liternum made it less comfortable than the pleasure grounds at Baiae. Seneca gives a detailed description of Scipio's villa in 86.4–11.

**51.12**  This must be Marcus Porcius Cato the Elder (consul in 195 BCE), a contemporary of Scipio Africanus. Cato was remembered by Romans especially for his strict opposition to all forms of luxurious living (a program he pursued during his term as censor in 184) and for rigid military discipline. Compare 87.9–10, and see also the note on 11.10. Roman armies traveling on active duty regularly dug trenches around even their temporary camps.

**51.13**  There is a play on words: the Greek word *philētēs*, "sweetheart," resembles *phēlētēs*, "robber," which is also Greek, but presumably in use in Greek-speaking Egypt (Gummere).

**52.3**  Metrodorus was an especially close associate of Epicurus; see 6.6, and compare 79.15–16.

**52.4**  Hermarchus too was a close associate of Epicurus; see 6.6. Epicurus regards him as more admirable than Metrodorus, because he too managed to achieve a blessed life by Epicurean standards, even though his intellectual gifts were less impressive.

**52.10**  Seneca here switches to the second-person plural and gives an imaginary rendering of how a philosopher might properly exhort an audience.

**52.11**  For Fabianus see the note on 11.4.

**52.12**  Touching the scalp with one finger was understood as a signal of sexual availability to other men (Seneca the Elder, *Controversiae* 3.19; Plutarch, *Pompey* 48).

**53.1**  Parthenope was an ancient name for the city of Naples; Puteoli is now Pozzuoli, about ten miles west along the coast. The isle of Nesis, now called Nisida, lies along the sea route from one to the other.

**53.3**  Virgil, *Aeneid* 6.3 and 3.277.

**53.7**  Compare 50.5–6, and see the note on 50.5.

**53.10**  For Seneca's use of Alexander the Great, see the note on 59.12. This particular anecdote is not paralleled in our other sources for Alexander.

**53.11**  See the note on 31.8.

**54.1**  The Greek word Seneca has in mind is presumably *asthma* ("gasping"). Concerning his illness, see Griffin 1992, 42–43, and compare 65.1, 77.9, 78.1–2.

**54.4**  This symmetry argument against the fear of death appears also in Lucretius 3.832–43 and 972–77. Compare 77.11.

**55.2**  The ancient settlement of Cumae was just on the other side of Cape Misenum from the resort of Baiae. The lake is Lake Acheron; see the note on 55.6. Servilius Vatia was a member of a distinguished patrician family, but is not known as an individual beyond what Seneca says about him in this letter.

**55.3**  Asinius Gallus (consul in 8 BCE) was a high-ranking senator who fell into disfavor with Tiberius and was eventually imprisoned in 30 CE (Tacitus, *Annals* 1.12, 2.36, 3.71; Dio Cassius 58.3). Aelius Sejanus was praetorian prefect under Tiberius; he used his power ruthlessly but fell out of favor in 31 CE and was himself executed, whereupon many of his supporters were also tried and convicted.

**55.6**  Lake Acheron, now called Lake Fusaro, is a saltwater pond separated from the sea by a narrow spit of land. Ruins on the high ground at Torregaveta, just south of the lake, are identified locally as those of Vatia's villa. The Euripus is the narrow channel that divides the long island of Euboea from the mainland in Greece.

**55.11**  Seneca's word is *codecilli*, referring to the wooden tablets on which brief informal notes were typically written. Longer letters and serious literary compositions were written on sheets or rolls of papyrus.

**56.1**  Seneca now represents himself as having taken temporary lodgings above one of the numerous bathing establishments at Baiae (see the note on 51.1).

**56.3**  The translation reflects the reading *Crispum*, an easy correction for *Crisipum* or *Chrysippum* in the MSS. (As Gummere notes, the reference to the constant stream of visitors [*adsidua salutatio*] suggests Roman customs not pertinent to the Stoic philosopher Chrysippus of Soli.) Seneca's friend Passienus Crispus was a wealthy and prominent orator and statesman and a stepfather to Nero; he is mentioned also in *On Benefits* 1.15.5 and *Natural Questions* 4a pref. 6. The supposed death by visitation is not to be taken literally; it must be a *bon mot* by Crispus, who was noted for his acerbic wit.

**56.4**  The Meta Sudans was a street fountain, no doubt similar in design to the fountain of that name built in Rome under Augustus.

**56.6**  The line is by Varro of Atax; it is cited by Seneca the Elder (*Controversiae* 7.1.27), who remarks that it was also known to Ovid.

**56.10**  For the negative traits of character termed "infirmities," see the note on 50.5.

**56.12**  Virgil, *Aeneid* 2.726–29.

**56.15**  He sealed their ears with wax, as in 31.2.

**57.1**  Compare 53.1. Baiae is some fifteen miles from Naples overland; the sea route was longer, but less time-consuming in fair weather.

A typical athletic regimen involved wrestling, which would take place in an area made soft with mud, or ball playing and other exercises on a packed-earth surface. Athletes might also use dust on their hands for a better grip. The Naples tunnel (whose entrance can still be seen today) connected that city with Baiae.

**57.3**  For these involuntary reactions, see the note on 11.1.

**57.6**  "Balcony" is our conjecture for the nonce usage *vigiliarium*.

**57.7**  The Stoic claim against which Seneca is arguing is not otherwise recorded; however, it is only a special case for the more general Stoic position, which was that the human mind or spirit, being composed of a light and fiery substance (see the note on 50.6), can survive death for a limited period—in the case of a wise person, until the next world conflagration (see the note on 9.16, with Diogenes Laertius 7.157; Eusebius, *Evangelical Preparation* 15.20.6 [LS 53W]). Seneca's own view in the remainder of the paragraph is thus in accordance with Stoic physics.

**57.8**  For the ability of lightning to pass through narrow openings, compare *Natural Questions* 2.52; Lucretius 6.225–30, 348–49. Seneca assumes that lightning returns to its source after striking; compare *Natural Questions* 2.40.

**57.9**  See the note on 58.27.

**58.1**  Seneca will devote several paragraphs to the issue of terminology before reporting the conversation itself, beginning in 58.8. The poverty of the Latin language, i.e., its lack of resources for rendering the Greek philosophical lexicon, is similarly a complaint of Lucretius (1.136–39).

**58.2**  Virgil, *Georgics* 3.146–50.

**58.3**  Virgil, *Aeneid* 12.708–9.

**58.4**  The verb form *iusso* was archaic; first-century-BCE speakers regularized it to *iussero*. The quotation is from Virgil, *Aeneid* 11.467.

**58.5**  Ennius (ca. 239–169 BCE) and Accius (ca. 170–86 BCE) were at one time the most respected Latin poets, but had been superseded by Virgil and other writers of more recent date. For the activity of literary scholars in Seneca's time, compare 88.3, 88.37, 88.40, 108.24–32.

**58.6** The Latin word *essentia* ("is-ness," the noun derived from *esse*, "to be") was not in common usage at this date. Quintilian, who attributes it to one Sergius Plautius, calls it "very harsh" (8.3.33). If, as Seneca asserts, the term was used by Cicero, the work in question does not survive. For Fabianus see the note on 11.4. Although Seneca requests permission to use the word, he does not in fact make use of it either here or elsewhere.

Seneca's phrase "a necessary item" (*res necessaria*) seems to be a play on words. Not only is it necessary that he find some equivalent for the Greek word *ousia*, but *ousia* ("being" or "substance") is a necessary principle in metaphysics. Our translation assumes that *natura* is in the nominative case renaming *ousia*.

**58.7** Greek for "the existent" or "the thing that is."

**58.8** Although the discussion that follows has clear antecedents in the Platonic dialogues themselves (see especially *Sophist* 243d–49d, *Timaeus* 27e–29d), the listing of six "ways" (*modi*) in which Plato speaks of "the existent" is an interpretation by Seneca's friend or perhaps by Seneca himself, or one found in some book he has read. His approach, combining an enumeration of the "ways in which a thing is said" with a division of existent things by species, genera, and then "higher" or more fundamental genera, suggests both Aristotelian and Stoic influences.

**58.11** Another standard Stoic division; compare 89.16. A "body" or corporeal thing was anything that could act or be acted upon. Among the things Stoics counted as incorporeals are propositions or "things said" (for which see 117.10–13), time, place, and void (Sextus Empiricus, *Against the Mathematicians* 10.218 [LS 27D]).

**58.14** Seneca's word "animate creatures" (*animalia*) refers to all creatures that have "mind" (*animum*) or the capacity for impulse, including not only animals in our sense but also human beings and gods.

**58.15** Although centaurs and the like do not exist, they are still *something*, since we have an image of them in our minds and can speak coherently about them. For Stoic thought on this topic, see Alexander of Aphrodisias, *On Aristotle's Topics* 301.19–25 [LS 27B].

**58.16** What was said in 58.8 was that Plato has six ways of using the expression *to on*, not that those different ways of speaking neatly divide up everything that exists. Either way, the division is not made by Plato himself.

**58.17** In Plato, *Laws* 716a, God is "the beginning, middle, and end of the things that are"; in 716c, "the measure of all things."

**58.18** In a Platonic context, the word *idea* does not refer only to a thought or concept, as in modern English, but is closer in meaning to *eidos* (usually translated as "form"); the two words are etymologically related. Plato himself does not always distinguish the terms as clearly as Seneca does here. See also the note on 65.7.

**58.19** Compare Plato, *Timaeus* 48e.

**58.20** Compare 65.4 on Aristotle's use of the same term.

**58.22** The things that exist "commonly" are usually taken to be sensible particulars or individual members of various genera, e.g., Cato or the particular table one is looking at. On this interpretation, "commonly" means "in the ordinary sense of the word," and "begin to relate to us" means "belong to sense experience." These would then be the very items that Seneca says just below are *not* counted by Plato as things that are. Another possibility is that the things that exist "commonly" are various sorts of collections; compare 102.6–7. This reading takes "commonly" to mean "in common" (cf. 58.17) and "begin to relate to us" to mean "begin to resemble Stoic thought."

**58.23** For Heraclitus see the note on 12.7. His dictum about the river is quoted by Plato in *Cratylus* 402a.

**58.27** Here and in 65.16–18, Seneca is clearly attracted to the thought that the mind is inherently divine, that it is imprisoned within the body as form or cause within matter (cf. also 41.5–6), and that when it contemplates abstract ideas it finds release and some form of immortality. All this is strongly Platonic in coloring: compare *Phaedo* 82d–83b, and note the emphasis on the resistance of matter and the question whether concrete objects truly exist. But at least some of these notions can also be given a Stoic interpretation, for Stoics likewise spoke of a creator god who acts within the universe and who provides reason to human beings as our means of becoming godlike. See also the note on 31.8, and compare 102.2.

**58.29** In Stoic thought, the universe itself is a living being, with its own impulses and appropriate actions; it is mortal in that it is periodically consumed and regenerated by its own designing fire (see the note on 9.16). The providence or foresight of the universe is analogous to the mind of a human being; compare Cicero, *On the Nature of the Gods* 2.58. For the denigration of the body, see the note on 23.6.

**58.30** Ancient tradition associated the name Plato with the Greek word *platus*, meaning "broad" or "flat." For all these biographical details, compare Diogenes Laertius 3.1–45.

**58.35**  A life (*vita*) includes the use of one's mental faculties; merely being alive might include only the basic life functions such as respiration (*anima*). For the position on suicide stated here, see the note on 70.5.

**59.2**  See the note on 23.3.

**59.3**  Virgil, *Aeneid* 6.278–79.

**59.4**  The object of the ordinary person's delight may be a false good even if it is something conventionally regarded as honorable, such as winning an election or, as here, receiving a letter from a friend.

**59.7**  This is either the same Quintus Sextius the Elder whom Seneca mentions at 64.2–5 or his son, also called Sextius, who shared his positions in ethics (*Natural Questions* 7.32). Sextius's philosophy is described by Seneca as fully compatible with Stoicism (64.2) but with an emphasis on practical ethics, extolling frugality, self-control, and courage (73.12–16) and recommending vegetarianism (108.17–18) along with such practical expedients as looking in a mirror to control anger (*On Anger* 2.36) and mentally reviewing each day's conduct at bedtime (*On Anger* 3.36). Concerning the elder Sextius, Seneca reports in 98.13 that though nobly born, he declined a magistracy offered by Julius Caesar.

**59.12**  Seneca is interested in Alexander the Great chiefly as an example of unrestrained and insatiable passions, especially pride and lust for conquest (53.10, 91.17, 94.62–63, 119.7), but also excessive drinking, anger, and grief (83.19, 83.23, 113.29). The present anecdote (which is given in similar form in Quintus Curtius Rufus 8.10) is an exception: pain forces Alexander to admit limitations he otherwise seeks to transcend.

**59.17**  Virgil, *Aeneid* 6.513–14.

**59.18**  The wise resemble God in perfect rationality and in blessedness; see the note on 31.8. That they consciously imitate God is a further idea which Seneca expresses also in 92.30, 104.23, and 124.23–24, and in *On Providence* 1.5. The theme is characteristic of the Platonic tradition, under the influence of Plato, *Theaetetus* 176b, but it is also fully compatible with Stoic thought; see, for instance, Epictetus, *Discourses* 2.14.11–13.

**60.1**  See the note on 31.2.

**60.4**  The phrase is from the first sentence of Sallust's *Catilinarian War*.

**62.1**  I.e., in philosophy; compare 36.3, 88.2.

**62.3**  See the note on 20.9.

**63.1**  Educated Greeks and Romans regularly composed letters or treatises of consolation, meant to comfort friends or relatives who had suffered bereavement or some other major affliction. Such works generally sounded familiar themes such as the sweetness of memory, the healing effects of time, and the inevitability of death for all human beings; often too they included examples from literature or history of individuals who rose above similar misfortunes. Compare Cicero, *Ad Familiares* 5.16.2, *Letters to Atticus* 12.11, *Tusculan Disputations* 3.55–64, 4.75–79. In the present letter, as in his earlier *Consolation to Marcia* and more extensively in letter 99, Seneca discusses the experience of grief in conjunction with Stoic views on the emotions and on friendship.

**63.2** In *Iliad* 19.226–29, Odysseus advises Achilles to abandon his grief for Patroclus on grounds that in wartime a single day is all that can be allowed for mourning. Later, in 24.602–17, Achilles reminds the grieving Priam that even Niobe, whose grief for her twelve children was proverbial, stopped on the tenth day to eat a meal.

**63.4** For "biting" (*morsus*) referring to the sensation of mental pain, see the note on 99.14. The reference to pleasure is explained in more detail in 99.3: rather than grieve at the death of a friend, one should rejoice in having had a friend. Seneca does not, however, approve the similar claim of Metrodorus in 99.25–26.

**63.5** See the note on 9.7.

**63.13** Roman law imposed on widows a one-year period of mourning before remarriage (Cassius Dio 56.43; Ovid, *Fasti* 1.33–36). There was no corresponding law for widowers.

**63.14** Seneca's relative Annaeus Serenus had died suddenly of poison after having risen to some prominence in the imperial administration (Pliny the Elder 22.96; Tacitus, *Annals* 13.13; Griffin 1992, 447–48). Three of Seneca's shorter philosophical dialogues are addressed to him.

**63.16** Seneca may be thinking especially of Plato, *Apology* 40e-41c, *Phaedo* 67ab. For the thought, compare 93.10, and see also the note on 24.18.

**64.2** See the note on 59.7.

**64.4** Virgil, *Aeneid* 4.158–59.

**64.10** For the elder Cato, see the notes on 11.10 and 51.12; for the younger, the note on 14.12; for Laelius, the note on 95.72.

**65.1** For Seneca's history of respiratory difficulties, see the note on 54.1.

**65.2** The word Seneca uses for matter (*materia*) is also his regular word for the material from which something is made. In Stoic thought, cause and matter are the two primary components of the universe. Matter (or "material") is featureless and inert, capable of taking on whatever shapes, qualities, and motions are imparted to it by cause, which is also called "reason" and "God." See Diogenes Laertius 7.134 [LS 44B]; Sextus Empiricus, *Against the Mathematicians* 9.75–76 [LS 44C]; and Calcidius 292–93 [LS 44D–E], and compare 58.28–29.

**65.4** Seneca provides a summary version of Aristotle's theory of causality laid out in *Physics* 2.3 and *Metaphysics* 5.2. For the term *eidos*, compare 58.20–22, where a similar understanding of it is attributed to Plato.

**65.5** The "spear bearer" (*doryphoros*) and "youth tying a headband" (*diadumenos*) were statue types that would have been familiar to Seneca's readers. Both were believed to have been copied from originals by the Greek sculptor Polyclitus (Pliny the Elder 34.55).

**65.7** Although Plato obviously does not "add" to Aristotle's later account, his discussion of the patterns (*paradeigmata*) used by the demiurge in *Timaeus* 27d–28d gives "cause" a distinctly different signification from anything in Aristotle. For the term *idea*, compare 58.18. The account of Plato's position that follows resembles teachings by Platonists of Seneca's time and later; see Dillon 1996, 135–39; Inwood 2007c, 136–55; Sedley 2005.

**65.10** Compare Plato, *Timaeus* 29d.

**65.12** Seneca satisfies his demand for "the primary and generic cause" by specifying the Stoics' active principle, the "designing fire" or God (see the note on 9.16). This cause is "the one that makes," since for Stoics it is the active principle that makes everything what it is by acting upon prime matter, called the "passive principle." In saying that matter and cause are "simple" (unitary and undifferentiated), he is referring not to the bronze of the statue and the human craftsman but to matter and cause as such, taken generically.

**65.16** Seneca remarks elsewhere that the study of astronomy and other abstract subjects elevates the mind and reminds it of its divine origin (88.33–35, *On Leisure* 5.5–6, *Natural Questions* 1 pref.).

The imagery of the prison-house is Platonic; see the note on 41.5.

**65.18** Either military service or service as a gladiator; compare 37.1–2.

**65.22** See the note on 23.6.

**66.1** For the thought, compare 65.22, and see the note on 23.6.

**66.2** Virgil, *Aeneid* 5.344.

**66.3** Compare 18.12 and Virgil, *Aeneid* 8.362–69 (Aeneas, like Hercules, stays in Evander's hut).

**66.5** The threefold classification is explained more clearly in 66.36–37. The basis of it is the "preferred," "dispreferred," or "absolutely indifferent" status of the circumstances, which Seneca terms the "material" of the good (cf. 66.15, 66.33, 71.21, 85.39; and see Chrysippus in Plutarch, *On Common Conceptions* 1069e [LS 59A]). In treating peace and national welfare or endurance under torture as "goods," Seneca means that they are goods exclusively for virtuous agents. Taken by themselves, peace and so forth are indifferent (see the note on 31.6). For the Stoic background, see Diogenes Laertius 7.101 [LS 60O]. Similar threefold classifications (though not this particular one) are to be found in Stobaeus 2.7.5e, 70W [LS 60L] and in Diogenes Laertius 7.94–95.

**66.6** Strictly speaking, there are no goods that are worthy of avoidance. However, the goods here called "secondary," like self-control during serious illness, take place in circumstances it is usually appropriate to avoid.

**66.7** The mind or spirit is "breath disposed in a certain way" (see the note on 50.6); but that generic disposition is always subject to further particularizations: a certain stretch of *pneuma* can be arranged into a mind, and further into a virtuous mind, and further yet into a virtuous mind engaged in a certain action. Compare 113.2, and for the Stoic background see Sextus Empiricus, *Outlines of Pyrrhonism* 2.81–82 [LS 33P]; Alexander of Aphrodisias, *On Soul* 118 [LS 29A].

**66.8** The same word in Latin means both "right" and "straight," either in the geometric or in the moral sense. For the distinction between scalar properties (those that can be either increased or decreased) and nonscalar properties (those that achieve some absolute standard), compare Cicero, *On Ends* 3.48; Plutarch, *On Common Conceptions* 1063ab; Simplicius, *On Aristotle's Categories* 237.25–238.20 [LS 47S]. Straightness appears as an example in all three.

**66.9** Seneca's word is *modus*, apparently in a sense equivalent to Greek *horos*: virtue, like straightness, is a limit in that it does not merely approach the standard but achieves it. In the same way, temperance is a limit in that it is an absolute and consistent control of one's impulses, and similarly with the other virtues.

**66.12** For the kinship of human reason with the divine, see the note on 58.27.

**66.13** The town of Numantia on the Iberian peninsula was subjected to siege by P. Cornelius Scipio Aemilianus in 133–132 BCE. Rather than surrender, the inhabitants submitted to starvation and eventually to mutual suicide.

**66.16** One of the Stoics' preliminary arguments in favor of their most distinctive axiom, "only what is honorable is good," was that if anything else is considered good, then the honorable (i.e., virtue) loses its special character. Compare Cicero, *On Ends* 3.10.

**66.18** Phalaris, the sixth-century-BCE Sicilian tyrant, was supposed to have tortured people by enclosing them in a bronze bull to which flames were applied. The same saying of Epicurus is reported in Diogenes Laertius 10.118 and in Cicero, *On Ends* 2.88, *Tusculan Disputations* 2.17 (frag. 601 Usener).

**66.20** Very similar comparisons are made by Cicero's Stoic speaker in *On Ends* 3.45.

**66.25** *Non comparet* ("does not count") puns on *par* ("equal") and *comparat* ("is equivalent").

**66.31** I.e., in continuous contemplation; see 58.27 and note.

**66.32** In Stoic terminology, the sensation of joy or gladness is related to an expansion or elevation of the mind's pneumatic material. Compare 59.2, and see Cicero, *Tusculan Disputations* 4.15; Galen, *Precepts of Hippocrates and Plato* 4.2.4–6 [LS 65D], 4.3.2 [LS 65K]. For the expression "gnaw at them" (*mordet*) referring to mental pain, see the note on 99.14.

The cardinal virtues are defined by Stoics as various forms of knowledge: courage is the knowledge of what one ought to endure, justice is the knowledge of what one should distribute to others, and so forth (Stobaeus 2.7.5b5, 63W [LS 61D]). See also the note on 67.10.

**66.35** Or "the right path"; see the note on 66.8.

**66.45** For this account of the highest good, see Epicurus, *Letter to Menoeceus* 128; on the limits of blessedness in Epicurus, also *Principal Doctrines* 18–20.

**66.47** For these remarks of Epicurus, compare 92.25, and see Diogenes Laertius 10.22; Cicero, *On Ends* 2.96.

**66.51** Mucius Scaevola; see the note on 24.5.

**67.7** If every wish were considered separately, as directed at a single proposition, then no one would ever wish to be tortured. But there are also generic or second-order wishes, such as the wish to live an honorable life. In such cases, the fulfillment of the generic wish will entail various subordinate wishes, one of which might be to behave honorably under torture.

M. Atilius Regulus was one of the Roman commanders against Carthage during the First Punic War (264–241 BCE). According to Livy (*perioche* 18) and Horace (*Odes* 3.5), he was captured by the Carthaginians and later sent to Rome on parole to negotiate a settlement, but instead urged the senate to continue the war. Then, honoring the terms of his parole, he returned to Carthage and allowed himself to be executed by being enclosed in a spiked crate. For Rutilius see the note on 24.4; for Cato, on 14.12.

**67.8**   Virgil, *Aeneid* 1.94–96.

**67.9**   The solo charge of Publius Decius Mus was a ritual act of self-sacrifice that turned the tide of battle against the Latini in 340 BCE (Livy 8.9–10). His son by the same name sacrificed himself in a similar manner against the Gauls in 295 (Livy 10.26–29).

In view of his argument, we might have expected Seneca to write not "whether it is best" (*optimum*) but "whether it is choiceworthy" (*optabile*).

**67.10**   Stoic theory held that any person who possesses one of the virtues necessarily possesses them all, and further, that any action done on the basis of one virtue is simultaneously, though secondarily, done on the basis of every other virtue as well. Nonetheless, the virtues are not merely different names for a single condition, for each virtue has its own distinctive sphere of application: temperance regulates our impulses, justice makes fair distributions, and so on. Compare 113.14 and 120.11, and for the Stoic background, Diogenes Laertius 7.126; Stobaeus 2.7.5b5, 63W [LS 61D]. In his account of this doctrine, Seneca includes not only the cardinal virtues of courage and intelligence but also the minor virtues of patience, perseverance, endurance, and constancy; compare Diogenes Laertius 7.92; Stobaeus 2.7.5b2, 60W [LS 61H].

**67.14**   Seneca's word *malacia* ("enfeeblement") is a bilingual pun: in Greek, as he well knew, it denotes moral weakness and often also effeminacy; but *malacia* is also used in Latin in the sense of a flat calm at sea, a near-synonym for *tranquillitas* (Caesar, *Gallic War* 3.15.3). For Demetrius see the note on 20.9.

**67.15**   For Attalus see the note on 9.7; for this saying of Epicurus, compare 66.18.

**68.2**   The Stoic position (as Seneca states it in his brief treatise *On Leisure*) is that one should engage in some form of public service throughout life, but that retirement is permissible if circumstances prevent one from being effective—for instance, if one is in poor health or lacks sufficient power and influence, or if the state is hopelessly corrupt. (Cf. Diogenes Laertius 7.121.) The exemptions are broad in scope, however, and Seneca also insists that philosophical study and writing is itself a legitimate form of public service.

The curule chair was an ornate folding stool whose use was restricted to high-level magistrates.

**68.10**  See the note on 19.3.

**69.4**  A toga bordered with purple was worn by Roman senators.

**69.6**  See the note on 70.5.

**70.2**  Virgil, *Aeneid* 3.72.

**70.5**  Life in itself—its mere duration—is of no intrinsic value in Stoic thought: it is one of the preferred indifferents (see the note on 31.6); but there are situations in which suicide is appropriate, when dispreferred circumstances prevail without possibility of improvement. See Cicero, *On Ends* 3.60–61 [LS 66G]; Diogenes Laertius 7.130 [LS 66H]. In his presentation of the doctrine, Seneca stresses that while no hard and fast rule can be given, and while the motivating circumstances need not be immediate or extreme (58.32–36, 77.4–6), it is important to take into consideration not only one's own comfort but also one's responsibilities to other people (98.16, 104.3). See further Griffin 1992, 372–83.

**70.6**  Telesphorus of Rhodes, held captive by the tyrant Lysimachus. His suffering is described in detail in *On Anger* 3.17.

**70.9**  The situation is as described in Plato's *Crito*; compare 24.4.

**70.10**  Scribonia was Octavian's second wife; Marcus Scribonius Libo Drusus, her great-nephew, was brought to trial in 15 CE on a charge of conspiring against Tiberius (Tacitus, *Annals* 2.27–32).

**70.14**  This is the position expressed by Plato's Socrates in *Phaedo* 62a–c.

**70.19**  See the note on 24.6.

**70.20**  Seneca's description in 7.3–4 indicates that the morning fights with wild animals were actually just a painful means of execution.

**70.22**  The Scipio who was a leader in the Civil War was Metellus Scipio, whose suicide is described alongside that of Cato in 24.9.

**71.4**  For the arguments that support this distinctively Stoic axiom, see 76.7–26.

**71.6**  See the notes on 31.8. and 58.17.

**71.7**  The speech is a loose paraphrase of the words of Socrates in Plato, *Gorgias* 527c. "Follow those" might mean either "follow those men" (the ones to whom Seneca has just referred) or "stick with ethics"; the latter is more appropriately attributed to Socrates.

The arguments that follow resemble those already given in 66.5–44. For the equality of goods, see especially the notes on 66.8 and 66.9.

**71.8**  For Cato see the note on 14.12. Seneca's treatment of him here recalls that of his essay *On the Constancy of the Wise Person* 2.1–3 and 7.1, where Cato appears as one of those rare historical figures who have attained the Stoic ideal of wisdom. Cato was defeated for the praetorship in 55 BCE. Later, he was on the losing side at the battle of Pharsalus in 48 BCE, at which Caesar's legions decisively defeated the forces of the Roman Republic led by Pompey.

**71.10**  After Pharsalus, Pompey escaped with a few retainers to Egypt, where he was assassinated on the orders of Ptolemy XIII. The remainder of the Republican forces sailed under the command of Metellus Scipio (see the note on 24.9) to Africa, where they were assisted by King Juba until their defeat at Thapsus and the subsequent suicide of Cato at Utica. Some then made their way to Spain under the command of Pompey's two sons, but were again defeated at the battle of Munda in 45.

**71.11**  For Cato's suicide, see the note on 24.6.

**71.12**  See the note on 9.16.

**71.16**  Virtue "keeps its measures" (*habet numeros suos*) because it exhibits perfect internal consistency (a nonscalar property; see the note on 66.8) and because virtuous actions are completely right. See the note on 95.5.

**71.17**  Seneca assumes that a good can only be diminished by the admixture of something bad. He speaks loosely, however: according to the terms of his argument, the badness in this case would be not the courageous endurance but the fact that one is enduring torture at all.

That one in Regulus's position would be neither happy nor miserable was a view held by the Peripatetics, who followed Aristotle (*Nicomachean Ethics* 1.10, 1101a8–11) in thinking that one who is virtuous but encompassed by grave misfortunes would be in an intermediate condition (Stobaeus 2.8.18, 133W). See further the note on 85.31, and compare 92.19.

**71.18**  In 85.18–20, Seneca cites Plato's earliest followers for the view that while virtue is both necessary and sufficient for happiness, complete happiness requires the addition of some external goods. Compare 92.5–7, 14–18. The same view is articulated by Cicero in *On Ends* 5 and *Tusculan Disputations* 5 on behalf of Antiochus of Ascalon, who likewise attributes it to the Old Academy. In *Natural Questions* 7.32, Seneca remarks that the Old Academy had no prominent adherents in his own day.

**71.20** For the metaphor, see the note on 66.8.

**71.21** The "material" consists in preferred or dispreferred indifferents (see the note on 66.5). The last part of the sentence is somewhat illogical: Seneca means, of course, that virtue makes anything good and vice makes anything bad.

**71.24** The oar that appears bent where it enters the water was a standard example of sensory illusion; see, for instance, Lucretius 4.436–42.

**71.25** Although our judgments are, in general, corrupted by the surrounding culture (see the note on 50.5), a young person of good natural abilities may have more accurate intuitions about value. For such fortunate natures, see the note on 95.36.

**72.27** The nonrational part here is the body, with its sensitivity to pain.

**71.29** For such involuntary reactions, see the note on 11.1. Harmless in themselves, these reactions could be misinterpreted as indications that one is incapable of responding appropriately to misfortune.

**71.32** The imagery is of a liquid that is without turbidity or sediment; compare *On Clemency* 2.6. In Stoic terminology, all voluntary behavior is analyzed in terms of mental events called "impulses," each of which takes the form of an assent to some mental impression. (See the note on 113.18.) In the wise person, a fully correct and coherent understanding of the world guarantees that assent will be given only to impressions of particular clarity.

**71.36** For willingness in this sense, see the note on 34.3.

**72.4** See the note on 23.3.

**72.5** These light and superficial disturbances would seem to be the same involuntary reactions as in 71.29. See also the note on 11.1.

**72.8** For Attalus see the note on 9.7.

**72.9** In Epicurean physics, uncompounded atoms travel continually through a limitless void (Epicurus, *Letter to Herodotus* 41–42; Cicero, *On the Nature of the Gods* 1.54). Seneca may be alluding satirically to the Epicurean argument that if it were not for the random atomic swerve (*klinamen*), which is also responsible for volitional action in humans and animals, the atoms would fall downward forever without ever colliding to produce a world (Lucretius 2.216–50; Cicero *On Ends* 1.18–20).

**72.10**  Compare 75.8–14, and see the note on 75.8.

**73.1**  Seneca's attitude has a basis in Stoic doctrines about our obligations to the state and about gratitude for favors received: compare Cicero, *On Ends* 3.63–64; Seneca, *On Benefits* 6.18–24; and see Griffin 1992, 208 and 360–66.

**73.10**  Virgil, *Eclogues* 1.6–7. These and the following lines refer allegorically to the future emperor Augustus.

**73.11**  Virgil, *Eclogues* 1.9–10.

**73.12**  For Sextius see the note on 59.7. Compare the Stoic doctrines in 9.16 and 31.8 and the Epicurean in 25.4 and 110.18–20.

**73.14**  The capacities that enable a human being to act are ultimately to be attributed to God as universal cause; see the note on 65.12.

**74.17**  For the distinctive property of the good, see the note on 44.6; for preferred indifferents, on 31.6.

**74.22**  The unnamed opponent exploits some of the fine points of the Stoics' elaborate theory of value. A virtuous person could happen to have a virtuous child or parent, or be part of a virtuous community: in these cases, the relationship to the family member or community would count as an "external" or "mixed" good; see Diogenes Laertius 7.95; Stobaeus 2.7.5m, 74W, and 11.q, 114W. The opponent's own position must be that of either the Old Academics or the Peripatetics; for these views, see the notes on 71.18 and 85.31 respectively.

**74.23**  The arguments given in the following paragraphs resemble Stoic views explained in 66.8–10.

**74.29**  The self-sufficiency of the human mind thus resembles that of Zeus during the conflagration; compare 9.14–16. "Knowledge of things divine and human" is the usual Stoic definition of "wisdom" (see further on 89.5).

**74.31**  For these involuntary reactions, see the note on 11.1, and compare 71.29.

**75.8**  Because Stoic doctrine takes virtue and vice to be absolute and mutually exclusive conditions, anyone who has not attained virtue is necessarily flawed (Cicero, *On Ends* 3.48; Plutarch, *On Common Conceptions* 1063ab). But one can still progress toward virtue (Diogenes Laertius

7.91); for while all imperfect conditions are equally imperfect, they are not alike in other respects. Compare 92.27–29, together with the remark by Chrysippus that even when one is performing all the appropriate actions, one is not virtuous until one's performance is entirely secure and consistent (Stobaeus 4.39, 906W [LS 59I]; also Cicero, *On Ends* 3.20).

**75.9** The reference is to 71.4.

**75.10** Many negative traits of character were described by Stoics as tendencies to experience certain emotions especially often or for trivial cause. For these "infirmities," see the note on 50.5.

**75.12** Seneca (or his source) combines two standard Stoic definitions of "emotion": "a movement of mind contrary to reason" and an "overly vehement impulse"; see, for instance, Diogenes Laertius 7.110; Stobaeus 2.7.10, 88–90W [LS 65A]; Cicero, *Tusculan Disputations* 4.11; Galen, *Precepts of Hippocrates and Plato* 4.2.10–18 [LS 65J]. Like other Stoics, he holds that emotions as defined can and should be eliminated altogether. See further the notes on 9.3 and 85.9.

**76.2** See the note on 87.9.

**76.4** The philosopher Metronax is known only from Seneca's mention of him here and in 93.1, where he has recently died.

**76.7** The point was addressed earlier at 71.4–21 and 74.1–29. The proof attempted in the following paragraphs is closely related to arguments given by Plato (*Republic* 1.352d–354a) and Aristotle (*Nicomachean Ethics* 1.7) for believing that happiness (*eudaimonia*) consists essentially in virtuous character and conduct. However, neither of those philosophers deemed perfected reason to be the *only* human good. The Stoic version of the argument is found also in Epictetus, *Discourses* 1.6 [LS 63E].

**76.11** I.e., if a person's *reasoning* is bad or good, the person will be criticized or praised accordingly.

**76.22** If the essence of the honorable and of the virtues is reason, then it would be contradictory to suppose that there could be any nonrational goods.

**76.23** The Stoics held that all events depend on antecedent causes, with nothing at all occurring by chance in the sense of occurring randomly and without reason. Considered collectively, antecedent causes constitute fate; i.e., a sequence or web of causes which is also the immutable and providential will of Zeus. Our actions are nonetheless in our power, since it is our own acts of assent that bring them about, even though those acts of assent are themselves part of the fated sequence. The virtuous attitude is to acquiesce in the divine governance of events and to perform willingly whatever one perceives as incumbent on a rational being. Compare the hymn of Cleanthes quoted in 107.10–12, and for the Stoic background, Alexander of Aphrodisias, *On Fate* 191–92 [LS 55N]; Cicero, *On Divination* 1.125–26 [LS 55L]; Cicero, *On Fate* 39–43 [LS 62C].

**76.28** See the note on 23.3.

**76.33** Virgil, *Aeneid* 6.103–5.

**76.35** For the technique of prerehearsal, see the note on 24.2.

**77.2** The source of the quotation is unknown.

**77.5** Nothing is known of Tullius Marcellinus beyond what Seneca says here.

**77.6** Seneca speaks as if he has a specific person in mind, but does not give a name. For the Stoic position on suicide, see the note on 70.5.

**77.9** The purpose of the tent seems to be to speed the intended drowning by concentrating steam near the water's surface.

For Seneca's own history of respiratory difficulties, see the note on 54.1.

**77.12** Virgil, *Aeneid* 6.376.

For the Stoic view of fate, which Seneca reflects here, see the note on 76.23.

**77.16** The Mediterranean fish called a red mullet (*mullus*) was highly valued by the Romans, who appreciated both its color and its oyster-like flavor; see *Natural Questions* 3.18; Pliny the Elder 9.64–66; and for the high prices paid for these fish, see the note on 95.42.

**77.18** The anecdote about Gaius Caesar (Caligula) is not otherwise attested.

**77.20** Sattia (or Statilia) is mentioned in Pliny the Elder 7.158 as a noble-woman from the time of Claudius who lived to the age of ninety-nine. The "tombstone of Sattia" also appears in Martial 3.93.20 as a metaphor for longevity. Nestor appears in the *Iliad* and *Odyssey* as a man aged beyond the usual human lifespan.

**78.1** See the note on 54.1.

**78.6** In cases involving a high fever, for instance (*On Anger* 1.12.6; Griffin 1992, 54).

**78.7** This sentence combines a familiar Epicurean slogan (see the note on 30.14) with the Stoic emphasis on providential design.

**78.8** See the note on 50.6.

**78.15** Virgil, *Aeneid* 1.223.

**78.18** Again, the language recalls an Epicurean expedient for coping with pain; compare Cicero, *Tusculan Disputations* 3.33.

**78.26** Compare 65.16–18, and see the note on 58.27.

**78.27** Because virtue is a nonscalar property (see the note on 66.8), Stoics held that the happiness of the wise does not increase with the duration of life: see Cicero, *On Ends* 3.45–48; Plutarch, *On Common Conceptions* 1062A; and compare 92.25. But the thought here is influenced by Epicurus as well; see the note on 39.5.

**78.28** The Stoic philosopher Posidonius, a pupil of Panaetius (see the note on 116.5), taught at Rhodes in the first half of the first century BCE. Seneca is well acquainted with a number of his works (see especially 87.31–40, 88.21, 89.5–33) and regards him as one of the most important names in philosophy. His various remarks about Posidonius are treated in detail in Kidd 1988.

**79.1** Lucilius was genuinely interested in the geography of Sicily; see the note on 14.8. In *Natural Questions* 3.1.1, Seneca quotes a hexameter line from a poem of Lucilius concerning another feature of the island, the fountain of Arethusa, which was said to come from an underground river originating in the Peloponnese ("from springs of Sicily there leaps an Elian stream").

**79.5** Ovid's description is in *Metamorphoses* 15.340–55; Virgil's, in *Aeneid* 3.571–82. Cornelius Severus was an epic poet, a friend of Ovid (*Letters from Pontus* 4.16.9), whose poem on the Sicilian War is mentioned in Quintilian 10.1.89.

**79.10** See the note on 66.8. The magnitude of stars is constant as opposed to that of comets and other variable phenomena of the night sky (*Natural Questions* 1.1.10).

**79.12** The imagery is Platonic; see the note on 41.5.

**79.13** Compare Cicero, *Tusculan Disputations* 1.91.

**79.14** A popular legend held that the people of Abdera, Democritus's hometown, supposing him to be insane, requested help from the physician Hippocrates, who told them they were mistaken.

For Cato see the note on 14.12; for Rutilius, on 24.4.

**79.16** Metrodorus was one of the chief colleagues of Epicurus; however, the two letters Seneca mentions are not otherwise known. For Metrodorus's own writings, see the note on 14.17.

**80.4** For willingness in this sense, see the note on 34.3.

**80.7** We have no other information about this play except that it was known also to Quintilian (9.4.140). The speaker is Atreus, perhaps beginning Accius's tragedy by that name. The quotation that follows could conceivably come from the same play.

**81.3** Seneca's seven-book treatise *On Benefits* explores the ethics of conferring benefits, i.e., doing favors for other people, and the implications for gratitude and obligation. For analysis see Griffin 2013, which includes a discussion of this letter.

**81.11** Metrodorus was a close associate of Epicurus. For his writings, see the note on 14.17.

**81.22** For Attalus see the note on 9.7.

**82.2** The "effete," i.e., those who live lives of fashionable dissipation, are so idle and achieve so little that their lives resemble death.

**82.3** At public executions, a hook was used to remove the cadaver from view.

**82.7** Virgil, *Aeneid* 6.261.

**82.9** Seneca's objection is not to the argument itself but to anyone's thinking that it might be effective against the fear of death. See the note on 45.5. Seneca does not name the opponent who attempts refutation. It is possible that the argument is his own (as in 83.9) or that of an Academic or Peripatetic rival (cf. 87.38).

**82.12** Decimus Iunius Brutus Albinus in 43 BCE took up the command of the senatorial armies resisting Mark Antony in Gaul, but was defeated without battle. Deserted by his troops, he was captured and executed on Antony's orders. For the anecdote here, compare Valerius Maximus 9.13.3.

**82.14** In Greek Stoicism, the two terms "indifferent" (*adiaphora*; cf. 82.10) and "intermediate" (*mesa*) are used interchangeably for the kinds of objects that do not in themselves contribute to happiness or unhappiness. For the doctrine, see the note on 31.6; and for the statement of it here, compare especially Diogenes Laertius 7.104–5 [LS 58B].

**82.15** The instinct for self-preservation arises from the orientation all creatures naturally have toward their own constitution. Compare Cicero, *On Laws* 1.31–33. Seneca explains these issues in more detail in 121.17–18.

**82.16** Seneca here combines two passages of Virgil: the description of Cerberus in *Aeneid* 6.400–401 and that of the monster Cacus in *Aeneid* 8.296–97.

**82.18** Virgil, *Aeneid* 6.95–96.

**82.20** In 479 BCE, the powerful Fabian clan undertook to fight Rome's war with the Etruscan town of Veii as a private obligation (Livy 2.48–50).

In 480 BCE, a small Greek force including three hundred Spartan foot soldiers under the command of Leonidas made a desperate stand to halt the advance of the Persian army at the mountain pass of Thermopylae (Herodotus 7.222–28).

**82.22** During the First Punic War, the military tribune Marcus Calpurnius Flamma led a detachment of volunteers to create a diversion, giving the main body of the army a chance to escape. Livy (22.60) gives the number of volunteers as three hundred; Aulus Gellius (3.7) says four hundred.

**82.24** A fantastic serpent, 120 feet in length, was supposed to have been killed during the First Punic War by Roman troops under M. Atilius Regulus. Seneca's account follows that of Livy (*perioche* 18) as preserved in Valerius Maximus 1.8.*ext.* 19. The god Apollo used arrows to kill the massive Python of Delphi.

**83.5** The Canal was in the Campus Martius in the middle of Rome. The Maiden was one of the aqueducts that supplied Rome and was known for particularly cold water; compare Ovid, *Ars Amatoria* 3.385.

**83.9** For the form of the argument, compare 82.9, also mentioning Zeno, and see the note on 45.5.

**83.10** For Posidonius see the note on 78.28.

**83.12** Lucius Tillius Cimber had held the praetorship under Caesar in 46 BCE; at the time of Caesar's murder, he had just been appointed to an important governorship. It was he who gave the signal for the assassination to begin. See also *On Anger* 3.31.5.

**83.13** Although he has promised just one example, Seneca provides two. Lucius Calpurnius Piso (consul in 15 BCE) held the office of city prefect from 14 CE to 32 CE; Cossus Cornelius Lentulus (consul in 1 BCE) later assumed the same office. Both are mentioned in Suetonius as drinking companions of Tiberius (*Tiberius* 42).

**83.19** See the note on 59.12.

**83.20** Shamelessness is called an infirmity in the sense of a negative trait of character; see the notes on 50.5 and 75.10. The term would be equally applicable to the other faults listed here.

**83.23** Among the conflicting accounts of Alexander's death, one (preserved in Diodorus Siculus 17.117) connects it with his draining a wine goblet of twelve pints' capacity in honor of Heracles.

**83.25** The Latin word *crudelitas* ("cruelty") is etymologically connected with *crudus* ("raw") and is often associated by Seneca with the eating of raw flesh: compare 94.62, 108.18, *On Clemency* 1.25, *On Anger* 2.5; and see *On Clemency* 2.4, where such bloodthirstiness is distinguished from the ordinary vice of cruelty (i.e., excessive severity). Antony's devotion to wine was part of his public image; compare Pliny the Elder 14.28.

**84.1** His slaves; Seneca uses a sedan chair for his excursions. Compare 15.6, 55.1–2.

**84.3** Virgil, *Aeneid* 1.432–33.

**84.4** In Stoic thought, the abilities characteristic of a species are imparted by the particular kind of "spirit" or "breath" (*pneuma*) present in each. See also the note on 50.6.

**84.13** The thought is made clearer by comparison with *On Anger* 2.13. Although progress toward virtue is exalted and is challenging in itself (it requires "constant concentration" [84.11]), it is level ground in comparison to the toil and danger of moneymaking and political ambition.

**85.1** At least some of the Stoics' opponents agreed with them that virtue is sufficient for happiness; i.e., that anyone who is virtuous is also happy (see 85.17–18). They did not concede, however, that virtue is sufficient by itself to render a life completely happy; i.e., that no other sort of good is needed to make one's life the best it can possibly be. Although ambivalent about the concise forms of argumentation favored by his Stoic predecessors (cf. 82.9–10), Seneca is fully in agreement with the substance of their position.

**85.2** Cicero is familiar with a similar Stoic syllogism; compare *Tusculan Disputations* 3.18.

**85.3** As Seneca understands them, Aristotle's later followers hold that emotions are part of human nature and should be moderated (i.e., experienced in moderate amounts) but not eliminated altogether. Reserving for later the claim about human nature (see letter 116), he deals here with the question of "moderate amounts," arguing in accordance with Stoic precedents that the moderation approach is logically flawed and is in any case doomed to failure. Compare *On Anger* 1.9–17; Cicero, *Tusculan Disputations* 3.22, 3.71, 4.38–42; Galen, *Precepts of Hippocrates and Plato* 4.2.14–18 [LS 65J].

**85.4**  Ladas was a proverbially swift runner; he was commemorated in a famous statue by the Athenian sculptor Myron (*Greek Anthology* 16.54; Pausanias 8.12.5).

The quotation is from Virgil, *Aeneid* 7.808–11. "She" is the huntress Camilla.

**85.9**  The Stoics held that emotions are a form of voluntary behavior: they are defined as impulses, which means that they are dependent on the rational mind's assent to certain value-laden impressions. (See the note on 75.12, and compare 113.18.) Once that assent has been given, however, the excessive vehemence of the emotive impulse makes it ungovernable. The only way to control an emotion is therefore to withhold assent in the first place. Compare 116.1–6, *On Anger* 1.7–8, 2.35, and for the Stoic background, see Cicero, *Tusculan Disputations* 4.42; Galen, *Precepts of Hippocrates and Plato* 4.7.16–17.

**85.10**  For the Stoic background on these faults, compare 75.10–12, and see also the note on 50.5.

**85.18**  Speusippus was Plato's nephew and became head of the Academy after Plato died in 347 BCE; Xenocrates succeeded him. For their position (which will be taken up again in the following paragraph), see the note on 71.18, and see further the arguments against it in 92.5–7, 14–18.

For the Epicureans, virtuous behavior is a necessary condition for a pleasurable life, and is also sufficient for it: one lives pleasurably if and only if one also behaves virtuously (Epicurus, *Principal Doctrine* 5). Yet virtue is not what makes one happy, since virtuous behavior is not pleasurable in itself. Compare 21.9.

**85.20**  There would be an infinite regress: one could just keep on positing a slightly happier person.

**85.24**  This is again the Peripatetic view; compare 85.3.

**85.26**  For the Stoic position on rational avoidance, see the note on 31.6.

**85.28**  Compare Stoic definitions of "courage" as "knowledge of what one ought to do and avoid" or "knowledge of what one ought to endure" (see the note on 66.32).

**85.31**  Like Aristotle himself in *Nicomachean Ethics* 1.9, the Peripatetic holds that bodily health and some financial resources are necessary to happiness, because without them the good person would not be able to put the virtues into action. But the Peripatetics also maintain that there are three distinct types of goods: goods of the mind, such as courage and intelligence; goods of the body, such as health and freedom from pain; and external goods, such as money and reputation (see Sharples 2010, 165–68). To Seneca's way of thinking, they thus "extend the boundaries of human happiness far and wide" (*On Benefits* 5.13).

**85.33** What is essential to the helmsman's skill is a determination to keep the ship upright at all costs. The omission of the verb (sc., "shall you drown") suggests that the saying was proverbial.

**85.39** The material of virtue consists in preferred or dispreferred indifferents (see the note on 31.6).

**85.40** The Athenian sculptor Phidias, a contemporary and friend of Pericles, was especially known for his works in ivory and bronze.

**86.1** For Scipio's voluntary exile to Liternum, see the note on 51.11, and see Livy 38.53, which confirms that his tomb was there. Cambyses was king of Persia 530–522 BCE; the account of his madness is in Herodotus 3.25, 29.

**86.3** Scipio's campaign against Carthage caused Hannibal to withdraw his forces from Italian soil.

**86.5** Lucretius 3.1034.

**86.10** An aedile was a high-ranking official who held responsibility for the construction and oversight of public buildings, including baths, and for the enforcement of sumptuary laws. Cato (the Elder; see the note on 51.12) held the office in 199 BCE; Publius Cornelius Scipio Africanus, in 193. Quintus Fabius Maximus Verrucosus was one of the most illustrious political and military leaders of the generation preceding Cato and Scipio.

**86.12** Market day in the Roman Republic was every ninth day.

**86.13** Horace, *Satires* 1.2.27, where the name is Rufillus. Horace's full line reads, "Rufillus smells of lozenges; Gargonius of the goat." "The goat" was Roman slang for body odor.

**86.14** The freedman Aegialus, according to Pliny the Elder 14.49, earned much respect for his skill in cultivating the villa at Liternum. In the same context, Pliny reports that Seneca was sufficiently interested in farming to spend a large sum on an estate in Nomentum owned by a rival, the literary scholar Palaemon; there the vineyards had been cultivated with renowned success by one Acilius Sthenelus.

**86.15** Virgil, *Georgics* 2.58.

**86.16** Virgil, *Georgics* 1.215–16.

**86.20** Grapevines were planted at the roots of elm trees, which normally served as their lifelong supports.

**87.3** Specially prepared figs were a traditional New Year's Day gift among the Romans. The ones referred to here are more ordinary fare, but Seneca celebrates anyway.

**87.8** Virgil, *Aeneid* 7.277–79.

**87.9** For Cato see the notes on 11.10 and 51.12.

The squires (*trossuli*), mentioned also in 76.2, are fashionable young men given to lavish expenditure on horses (Varro, *Menippean Satires* 480; Persius 1.82). For their lavish entourage, compare 123.7.

**87.10** As part of his triumph (a victory parade awarded by the Senate), Cato had ridden in a chariot pulled by four horses.

**87.11** *Impedimenta* ("hindrances") is the normal Latin word for "luggage."

**87.12** As in 74.22 and 85.31, the Peripatetics argue for a more inclusive notion of goods than a Stoic would allow.

**87.15** The manager (*lanista*) was one who trained a troop of gladiators and subsequently profited from their expertise.

Although not named as such, the persons raising objections to this and the subsequent arguments must still be Peripatetic philosophers.

**87.16** Because Seneca speaks of this Natalis in the past tense, he is probably not to be identified with the equestrian Antonius Natalis, who, according to Tacitus (*Annals* 15.50–60), was one of the principal informers against the Pisonian conspirators.

**87.19** Freedom from bodily pain and freedom from mental distress are the two components of the human good in Epicureanism; compare 66.45–46, and for Seneca's contempt, *On Benefits* 4.13.1.

**87.20** Virgil, *Georgics* 1.53–58.

**87.22** Temples were often the repositories of large sums of money.

**87.29** For the Stoic position on such advantages and disadvantages, see the note on 31.6.

**87.31** For Posidonius see the note on 78.28.

**87.33** Such intrinsically persuasive impressions play an important role in the Stoic explanation for moral corruption. See the note on 31.2.

**87.38** The argument is one that needs to be "solved" by the Peripatetics, because it purports to show that wealth is not a good, whereas they hold that it is (see the note on 85.31). At the same time, however, it works from the assumption that poverty is an evil, which Stoics would not accept.

**87.40** The Greek word means "lack of property," but also "nonexistence" and in logical contexts "nonpredication." Antipater of Tarsus was head of the Stoic school in the mid-second century BCE. His argument must have been that the very word for "poverty" ("lack of property") denotes what does not exist rather than what does, what cannot be predicated of a person rather than what can. Hence poverty is *not* a matter of owning a small amount—and Seneca is being deliberately obtuse.

**88.2** The Latin word *liberalis* means "characteristic of a free person"; i.e., not of a slave. In claiming the term "liberal studies" for philosophy alone, Seneca aligns himself with Posidonius, as reported in 88.21–23. For most of the letter, however, he reverts to common usage, making "liberal studies" refer to a standard program of literary studies, geometry, music, and astronomy.

**88.5** The practice of interpreting Homeric epic to accord with one's own philosophical views was indeed common in the period. For some examples of Stoic practice, see Long 1992. For Seneca's polemic against Epicureanism here, compare *On Benefits* 4.2.1; for the Peripatetics, see the note on 85.31; for Academic skepticism, the note on 88.44.

**88.7** The Sirens' song suggests corrupting influences from the culture; compare 31.2, 123.12.

**88.10** The Romans used systems of finger computation to calculate even large sums.

**88.12** Under Roman law, one could under certain conditions acquire title to a piece of land by continuous possession for a certain length of time; this was not possible, however, if the land was publicly owned. For the Stoic idea that the world is the shared possession of all creatures, compare *On Benefits* 6.3, 7.1.

**88.14** Virgil, *Georgics* 1.336–37.

**88.15** The view that the planets actually cause events on earth is associated in *Natural Questions* 2.32 with the astrologers called "Chaldeans." The Stoic view was that the planets merely signify what is to happen; see Cicero, *On Divination* 1.82–83, 117–18 [LS 42D–E].

**88.16** Virgil, *Georgics* 1.424–26.

**88.17** See the note on 24.2.

**88.18**  Ancient athletes rubbed themselves with oil and then with dust to provide a better grip for wrestling and other sports.

**88.21**  For Posidonius see the note on 78.28.

**88.33**  See the note on 65.16. The usual Stoic definition of "wisdom" is "knowledge of things divine and human" (see further on 89.5). For the questions that follow concerning time, see LS chap. 51; for those concerning the nature of the mind, see the notes on 50.6 and 58.27 and LS chap. 53.

**88.37**  The Greek scholar Didymus, working in Alexandria in the second half of the first century BCE, established texts and compiled commentaries for virtually the entirety of earlier Greek literature.

**88.39**  Aristarchus of Samothrace lived during the second century BCE in Alexandria, where he worked especially on the texts of the *Iliad* and *Odyssey* and other Greek poems. His system of editorial marks (including, among others, the asterisk) made possible the first systematic work in textual criticism.

Mathematicians sketched geometrical figures on a board sprinkled with dust or sand.

**88.40**  The principate of Gaius Caesar (Caligula) was during the years 37–41 BCE. Apion was a pupil of Didymus known for anti-Jewish polemic and for scholarly work on the Homeric poems. From what Seneca says here, he seems to have claimed that the first two letters of the *Iliad* (*mu* and *ēta*) refer to the number forty-eight, which is the number of books in the two epics combined.

**88.43**  Protagoras of Abdera was active in Athens in the fifth century BCE; he is more often described as a sophist than as a philosopher. His claim about opposing arguments (cf. Diogenes Laertius 9.51), together with his well-known assertion that "man is the measure of all things," was sometimes taken to imply skepticism about the possibility of knowledge (Aristotle, *Metaphysics* 11.6).

Nausiphanes was a fourth-century-BCE atomist, with connections to Democritus and the skeptic Pyrrho. The claim Seneca mentions can be compared with Democritus's assertion that perceived properties like sweet, sour, hot, and cold are only "by convention" (Sextus Empiricus, *Against the Mathematicians* 7.136).

**88.44**  Parmenides and Zeno of Elea were among the most eminent early Greek philosophers; they are mentioned here as having held views that will seem peculiar to the average person. The Pyrrhonists, Megarians, Eretrians, and Academics all belong to the Hellenistic period. The

Pyrrhonists, followers of Pyrrho of Elis, were skeptical philosophers, questioning whether anything can be known. The "New" or later Academics were likewise skeptical; they are to be distinguished from the Old Academics, whom Seneca mentions elsewhere (see the note on 71.18, and compare *Natural Questions* 7.32).

**89.4** The word *philosophia* in Greek signifies "love of wisdom," as will be explained in 89.7.

**89.5** The former of these definitions is standard Stoicism; compare Cicero, *Tusculan Disputations* 4.57; Sextus Empiricus, *Against the Mathematicians* 9.11 (*SVF* 2.36); Aetius 1, pref. 2 [LS 26A]. The latter, adding "knowledge of causes," is also attested by Cicero (*On Duties* 2.5).

**89.7** Dossennus was a family name as well as the name of a stock character of Atellan farce. It is unclear whether the inscription (which is not otherwise attested) has anything to do with the latter.

**89.9** This tripartite division of philosophy probably preceded the foundation of the Stoic school, but it was most strongly associated with Stoics: see Diogenes Laertius 7.39–41 [LS 26B].

**89.10** The topic of "kinds of life" (which Seneca himself treats separately in the short treatise *On Leisure*) concerned whether one ought to devote one's life primarily to the pursuit of pleasure, to study, or to political action.

**89.11** Epicurus rejected formal logic, but wrote a short treatise called *Kanōn* dealing with scientific methodology and the criteria of truth. The Greek word *kanōn* means "ruler" or "standard of judgment."

**89.12** The Cyrenaics were a group of hedonist philosophers whose founder was Aristippus, an associate of Socrates. What Seneca says here about their views closely resembles a later account by Sextus Empiricus, *Against the Mathematicians* 7.11.

**89.13** Aristo of Chios studied with Zeno of Citium and was later viewed as a dissident from the mainstream Stoic tradition. Restricting philosophy to ethics, he rejected the distinction between "preferred" and "dispreferred" indifferents (see note on 31.6), holding that "circumstance" rather than nature is the only rational basis for discriminating between them. See Sextus Empiricus, *Against the Mathematicians* 11.64–67 [LS 58F]. His arguments concerning admonitions are treated at length in letter 94.

**89.14** Seneca's partitioning of ethics may be compared with the scheme in Cicero, *On Duties* 2.18, and with the one used later by Epictetus (*Discourses* 3.2 [LS 56C]). A more elaborate partitioning is reported as standard by Diogenes Laertius (7.84 [LS 56A]). Determinations concerning the proper value (*axia*) of externals are made on the basis of what accords with our nature, as in Stobaeus 2.7.7f, 83W [LS 58D]. See also the notes on 31.6 and 92.11. For impulse and action, see the notes on 71.32 and 113.18.

**89.16** For the division into corporeal and incorporeal things, see 58.11–14 and the note on 58.11; for causes, the note on 65.2; for the four elements, Stobaeus 1.10.16c, 129–30W [LS 47A].

**89.17** Diogenes Laertius 7.41–44 [LS 31A] provides a fuller account of the Stoic partitioning of rhetoric and dialectic, including the division of the latter into significations and utterances.

The quotation is from Virgil, *Aeneid* 1.342.

**90.1** Like other Stoics, Seneca emphasizes that the human capacity for reason gives us not wisdom itself but the possibility of developing wisdom; see the note on 94.29. Further specification is needed, however, as to the nature of wisdom itself. Does the standard definition "matters human and divine" (see 89.5) pertain only to the virtues of individuals and the government of human communities, or does it extend to all kinds of inventions and acquired skills? Seneca will argue for the former, taking issue with a historical work by Posidonius.

**90.3** See the note on 67.10.

**90.4** These would be persons who had not yet become subject to moral corruption (see the note on 31.2).

**90.5** For Posidonius see the note on 78.28. The material cited in this letter must derive from his historical writings.

**90.6** A list of "seven sages" was traditional among the Greeks as early as Plato (*Protagoras* 343a); all were intellectual and/or political leaders of the sixth or fifth century BCE. Solon, who wrote a law code for Athens, was among them; Lycurgus, traditionally named as the lawgiver of Sparta, lived too early.

Zaleucus and Charondas were remembered as lawgivers for the Sicilian cities of Locri and Catania respectively; both in fact predated Pythagoras, but by Seneca's date a lack of concern for chronology in speaking about Pythagoras was itself traditional.

**90.9** Virgil, *Georgics* 1.144.

**90.11** Virgil, *Georgics* 1.139–40.

**90.13** Seneca's word for "sage" (i.e., for an inventor or teacher of long ago, as described by Posidonius) is the same as his word for "wise person" (the intellectual and moral exemplar; see the note on 9.1).

**90.14** For Diogenes (of Sinope), see the note on 29.1. Daedalus, the legendary inventor (his name means "ingenious"), is credited by Pliny the Elder (7.80) with the invention of carpentry and of such carpenter's tools as the saw, drill, and plumb line.

**90.20** Ovid, *Metamorphoses* 6.55–58, but the version Seneca gives differs significantly from our texts of Ovid.

**90.29** In Stoic thought, the mind was considered corporeal in nature. See the note on 50.6.

For the list of topics, compare Seneca's explication of the parts of the philosophical curriculum in 89.9–17.

**90.31** Anacharsis of Scythia (sixth century BCE) was sometimes listed as one of the Seven Sages; the potter's wheel, which is mentioned already in *Iliad* 18.600–601, is of course much older.

**90.32** In addition to his writings on physics and ethics, Democritus of Abdera was credited with treatises on a wide range of technical subjects (Diogenes Laertius 9.48); he did not, however, invent the arch.

**90.33** The Romans were familiar with techniques for producing colored enamels and for softening ivory for carving by soaking it in an acidic solution.

**90.35** The philosophy criticized is Epicureanism. For Seneca's attitude to the school, see the note on 2.5.

**90.37** Virgil, *Georgics* 1.125–28.

**91.1** This Liberalis is probably the Aebutius Liberalis who is the addressee of Seneca's treatise *On Benefits*; see Griffin 1992, 455–56. According to 91.13, the present letter summarizes a letter of consolation previously sent to Liberalis. The Roman colony of Lugdunum, modern Lyon, was the empire's most important administrative center north of the Alps. If this fire is the disaster mentioned in Tacitus, *Annals* 16.13, it must have taken place shortly after the great fire at Rome in the summer of 64 CE.

**91.4** The technique of prerehearsal; see the note on 24.2. This must be the method by which Liberalis has "armed himself" in 91.1.

**91.12** For earthquakes caused by subterranean wind or water, see *Natural Questions* 6.7 and 6.12–13.

**91.13** Timagenes of Alexandria came to Rome as a prisoner of war in 55 BCE and later worked as a historian under Augustus and Asinius Pollio. Both Senecas tell of him that he had an acid wit and that after falling into disfavor with Augustus, he had his record of the princeps's achievements publicly burned (Seneca the Elder, *Controversiae* 10.5.22; Seneca, *On Anger* 3.23).

**91.14** The founding of Lugdunum by L. Munatius Plancus is confirmed by his funerary inscription; *Corpus Inscriptionum Latinarum* 10.6087. As the colony was founded in 43 BCE, it was in fact somewhat more than a hundred years old.

**91.16** Rome was captured and sacked by a Gallic tribe in 390 BCE; Ardea, a small hill town nearby, was devastated by the Samnites later in the same century.

**91.17** See the note on 59.12.

**91.19** For Demetrius see the note on 20.9.

**92.1** Like the Academic and Peripatetic philosophers whose positions on value he means to contend, Seneca here allows for different "parts" of the mind that are responsible for movement and nourishment, emotion and impulse, and rational thought. He holds, however, that it is only the rational part that directs the person as a whole, and that our understanding of value must accordingly refer only to our rational nature. For the Academic and Peripatetic background, see Plutarch, *On Moral Virtue* 441d–442e and Stobaeus 2.7.13, 117–18W, together with Plato, *Republic* 4.435c–443e; Aristotle, *Nicomachean Ethics* 1.13.

**92.2** This Stoic account of happiness is defended by an appeal to the natural function of the human being; see the note on 76.7. For the emphasis on security and confidence, see the note on 44.7.

**92.5** The view that virtue is sufficient for happiness, but that happiness will still be increased by the addition of external goods, is attributed in 85.18–20 to Plato's early followers Xenocrates and Speusippus; it is a close relative of the Peripatetic position Seneca is about to criticize. See the notes on 71.18 and 85.31.

The Stoic Antipater of Tarsus in fact argued *against* Peripatetic notions of value (87.39–40). The "selective value" he himself assigned to externals (Stobaeus 2.7.7f, 83W) is quite a different matter. The comparison of the value of externals to a tiny flame as against the light of day was used by orthodox Stoics as well; compare Cicero, *On Ends* 3.45 with 5.71, 90–91.

**92.6** The term *aochlēsia* was used by philosophers of several different schools, including Speusippus (Clement, *Stromata* 2.22.133), the Peripatetics (Stobaeus 2.7.3c, 47W and 2.7.19, 137W), and Epicurus (*Letter to Menoeceus* 127). The Peripatetics' use of it was similarly criticized by Chrysippus: Galen, *Precepts of Hippocrates and Plato* 5.6 = *SVF* 3.12.

Typical objections to hedonist accounts of the highest good (that pleasure is "a mere tingling in the body" or "the good of a grazing animal") are here deployed against the Peripatetics; compare *On the Happy Life* 5.4 against the Epicureans, Cicero, *On Ends* 2.40 against the Cyrenaics.

**92.9** Virgil, *Aeneid* 3.426–28.

**92.10** For Posidonius see the note on 78.28.

**92.11** In Stoic terminology, "selection" (*eklogē*) is impulse directed toward a preferred or dispreferred indifferent as such (Stobaeus 2.7.7g, 84–85W [LS 8E]; Cicero, *On Ends* 3.20). See the notes on 31.6 and 89.14. In the virtuous person, such an impulse is itself a good, since it is an activity of virtue.

**92.19** A Peripatetic claim; see the note on 71.17.

**92.24** Virtue does not admit of degrees because it is a nonscalar property, like straightness; see the note on 66.8.

**92.25** For the deathbed saying of Epicurus, see the note on 66.47.

**92.26** The appeal to Epicurus's last day makes an *a fortiori* case against those who insist that pain has real disvalue: if even a hedonist can be happy in circumstances of extreme pain, the Peripatetic opponents are "base-minded degenerates" to think otherwise.

**92.27** See the note on 82.15, and compare 90.1.

**92.29** Compare 75.8–14, and see the note on 75.8.

**92.30** Virgil, *Aeneid* 5.363, but our manuscripts of Virgil read *in pectore* ("in his chest") rather than *in corpore* ("in his body").

In Stoic cosmology, all portions of the universe are infused with the divine spirit (*pneuma*), a portion of which is present in human beings and endows us with our rational nature. For the wise person's resemblance to God, see the notes on 58.27 and 59.18.

**92.34** Seneca quotes a half-line of Virgil, *Aeneid* 9.485, but his version differs from our manuscripts of Virgil, which have *canibus Latinis* ("dogs of Latium") rather than *canibus marinis* ("dogs of the sea," i.e., sharks).

**92.35** A hook was used to drag away the bodies of those who had been executed.

For Maecenas see the note on 19.9, and compare especially 114.4–8. The source of the quotation is unknown.

**93.1** Metronax is mentioned in 76.4 as a resident of Naples; he is not otherwise known.

**93.2** For the Stoic position on fate, see the note on 76.23.

**93.8** Increased duration cannot make the wise person any happier. For the Stoic background, see the note on 78.27.

**93.10** The wise man takes the attitude of Socrates in Plato, *Apology* 40e–41c; compare 63.16.

**93.11** Tanusius Geminus was a writer of history; little else is known of him.

**93.12** The stripping circle (*spoliarium*) was an area of the amphitheater where dead gladiators were stripped of their equipment.

**94.1** This and the following letter consider and contrast the relative merits of two modes of philosophical discourse that Seneca calls respectively "precepts" (*praecepta*) and "principles" (*decreta*). The precept-giving or prescriptive mode offers nontechnical instructions for every station in life; this is contrasted with the mode that establishes the underlying rationale for understanding and achieving the human good. See especially Schafer 2009.

**94.2** For Aristo of Chios, see the note on 89.13.

**94.5** The arguments that follow are identified in 94.18 as coming from Aristo.

**94.7** This is Epicurus's *Principal Doctrine* 4 [LS 21C]; see the note on 30.14.

**94.17** The Stoics held that all the nonwise are insane, on the grounds that they lack the virtue of self-control and are thus subject to instability of impulse (Diogenes Laertius 7.124; Stobaeus 2.7.5b13, 68W).

**94.21** "He" is Aristo, as indicated in 94.18.

**94.25** Publius Vatinius was repeatedly accused of bribery and corruption. In 54 BCE, after he defeated Cato in the elections for praetor, he was prosecuted by Licinius Calvus, but was acquitted through the influence of Caesar. The same fragment of Calvus's speech is quoted by Quintilian (6.1.13). Seneca treats Vatinius as an egregious case of moral depravity, contrasting him with Cato in 118.4 and 120.19.

**94.27** Cato the Elder; see the note on 11.10.

**94.28** The first of these two aphorisms appears in the collection attributed to Publilius Syrus (Friedrich 1964, 51); see the note on 8.9.

**94.29** Our innate tendencies to prefer certain kinds of objects serve as the starting points for our development toward perfected rationality; hence they are sometimes referred to as the "seeds" or "sparks" of the virtues. These tendencies would include our instinct for self-preservation (121.17–18) and for the companionship of others (9.17). Compare 108.8 and 120.4, and for the Stoic background see Stobaeus 2.7.5b3, 62W and 2.7.5b8, 65W [LS 61L]; Cicero, *On Duties* 1.11–17, *On Ends* 3.16–21 [LS 59D].

**94.38** For Posidonius see the note on 78.28. The preambles he is criticizing are those Plato attaches to the laws in his dialogue *The Laws*.

**94.41** Socrates' friend and disciple Phaedo established a school at Elis in the Peloponnese and became the author of several philosophical dialogues.

**94.46** For Agrippa see the note on 21.4. The proverb is also in Sallust, *Jugurthine War* 10.

**94.52** Seneca gives his response in letter 95.

**94.54** See the note on 31.2.

**94.56** Sun pillars, "beams" (parhelia), and related phenomena are treated extensively in *Natural Questions* 1.1, 7.4–5, 7.20.

**94.62** Alexander was popularly known as fortunate (*felix*) because of his extraordinary conquests; here, his uncontrolled passion for conquest makes him instead unfortunate (*infelix*). See the note on 59.12.

For this sense of the word "cruelty," see the note on 83.25.

**94.63** The defeat of the powerful Darius III of Persia was essential to Alexander's campaign. Alexander "challenges nature" in that he passes beyond the boundaries of the known world, here represented by the travels of Hercules to the west and Bacchus to the east. Compare 119.7.

**94.64** Seneca plays on Pompey's honorific title as "great" (*magnus*).

**95.1** Having argued in letter 94 that *paraenetikē*, i.e., the sort of philosophical discourse that provides precepts for various situations, has some utility (see the note on 94.1), Seneca now considers a related question: can it provide sufficient training to equip a person for happiness, or do we also need to teach basic principles?

**95.5** "All the measures" (*omnes numeros*) is the Stoics' technical expression for the completeness required of "right actions" (*katorthōmata*). Compare 71.16, and see Diogenes Laertius 7.100; Stobaeus 2.7.11a, 93W [LS 59K]; Cicero, *On Ends* 3.25 [LS 64H]; and LS vol. 1, p. 367. The requirements are spelled out in 95.12 and 95.57.

**95.9** Medicine was a theoretical as well as a practical science. Some physicians proceeded on the assumption that diseases have "hidden causes," which must be discovered, citing Hippocrates of Cos; others, like Asclepiades of Bithynia, spoke of "particles" and bodily "pores," or like Themison of Laodicea of a particular "method" that the physician should follow.

**95.11** Lucretius 1.54.

**95.20** Compare Hippocrates, *Aphorisms* 6.28–29.

**95.25** Garum was a condiment, the preparation of which involved the brining and fermentation of certain fish.

**95.33** Virgil, *Aeneid* 8.442.

**95.35** The standard carried by each Roman legion took the form of a bronze eagle affixed to a staff. Standards were objects of veneration and might be guarded at great personal risk.

**95.36** For persons fortunate by nature, see Stobaeus 2.7.11m, 107–8 W (*SVF* 3.366); for the image of mental rust, compare also Cicero, *Tusculan Disputations* 4.32.

**95.41** In order to qualify for the equestrian order, one had to possess property worth four hundred thousand sesterces, a fantastic sum to imagine spending on a single meal. A person's Genius (*genius*) was the divine spirit thought to accompany a Roman throughout life and celebrated annually on that person's birthday (Horace, *Epistle* 2.2.187–89). Men taking up official positions were expected to spend lavishly on an inaugural dinner for their new colleagues in office.

**95.42** The red mullet; see the note on 77.16. Apicius appears also in *On the Happy Life* 11.4 and *Consolation to Helvia* 10 as a gourmand willing to spend any sum for a delicacy. Similar stories about the prices paid for unusually large mullets are told by Pliny the Elder in 9.66–67 (where Apicius is again mentioned) and by numerous other authors.

**95.45** Marcus Iunius Brutus, who was later to join the conspiracy against Caesar, had endorsed Antiochus's version of the Academic school (Cicero, *On Ends* 5.8). He was also the author of a treatise, *On Virtue* (Cicero, *On Ends* 1.8). As Brutus wrote in Latin (Quintilian 10.1.123), it is puzzling that Seneca gives the title in Greek (*Peri Kathēkontos* rather than the Latin *De Officio*). See Rawson 1985, 285–86; Sedley 1997.

**95.47** Towels and scrapers (strigils) were used in the Roman bath to remove dirt and perspiration from the body. Offerings of such objects might be taken to imply anthropomorphic gods.

**95.50** The meaning is clarified by comparison with 110.2–3.

**95.53** Terence, *The Self-Tormentor* 77.

**95.55** See the note on 67.10.

**95.62** "Fellow feeling" is the usual meaning in Latin of Seneca's expression *sensus communis* (cf. 5.4, and see *OLD* s.v. *communis* 5c). However, some interpreters connect the term with the Stoic *koinē ennoia* ("shared concept"), and link the sentence to what precedes rather than with what follows.

**95.65** For Posidonius see the note on 78.28, and compare his position on unexplained laws in 94.38.

**95.66** A "label" (*eikonismos*) was a detailed description of an individual used as identification for tax purposes.

**95.68** Virgil, *Georgics* 3.75–81, 83–85.

**95.69** See the note on 14.12, and compare 104.31–32.

**95.72** Gaius Laelius, called "the Wise," was remembered for his political restraint and for his close friendship with Scipio Aemilianus. For Cato the Elder, see the note on 51.12. Quintus Aelius Tubero was the nephew of Scipio Aemilianus and a student of the Stoic Panaetius. Upon Scipio's death in 129 BC, Tubero arranged the traditional funeral banquet on goatskins and earthenware vessels, a gesture associating him with the old Roman virtues of frugality and self-control (Cicero, *Pro Murena* 75).

**97.2** The trial of Clodius in July of 61 BC for violating the ritual of the Bona Dea is described by Cicero, who prosecuted the case on behalf of the Senate, in a letter to Atticus (*Letters to Atticus* 1.16).

**97.4** Cicero, *Letters to Atticus* 1.16.5.

**97.6** Catulus was a prominent member of the senate; his witticism appears in the same words in *Letters to Atticus* 1.16.6.

**97.8** Cato was said to have been so revered by the plebeians that in his presence they would not call for that part of the festival of Flora which involved ribald joking and public nudity (Valerius Maximus 2.10.8).

**97.13** Compare Epicurus, *Principal Doctrine* 35. Seneca will return to the point at 105.8.

**98.1** For wise joy, see the note on 23.3.

**98.2** See the note on 31.6.

**98.4** Virgil, *Aeneid* 2.428.

**98.9** Metrodorus was a close associate of Epicurus. For his writings, see the note on 14.17.

**98.12** For Mucius Scaevola, see the note on 24.5; for Regulus, on 67.7; for Rutilius, on 24.4; for Cato's suicide, on 24.6.

**98.13** Gaius Fabricius Luscinus, negotiating with Pyrrhus of Epirus for the release of prisoners in 279 BCE, refused a bribe that would have enriched him for life; later, as censor, he was unusually strict in enforcing limitations on personal wealth. His experiences with Pyrrhus are described in some detail in 120.6.

For Tubero see the note on 95.72; for Sextius, on 59.7.

**98.14** At this point, our manuscripts appear to have omitted a transitional section of this letter in which Seneca described how an elderly friend has been coping with pain and the approach of death.

**98.16** His decision is in accordance with the Stoic position on suicide; see the note on 70.5.

**99.1** Consolatory letters and treatises were expected to make some allowance for grief. Seneca's own consolatory essays had done so; compare 63.1. In the present case, however, he feels that the bereavement is a relatively minor affliction. Marullus is undoubtedly a relative of the rhetorician who taught Seneca's father (*Contr.* 1 pref. 22).

**99.5** The imagery is reminiscent of Lucretius 3.1003–10, where ingratitude for past blessings is compared to the daughters of Danaus in Hades, who are perpetually drawing water in a sieve.

**99.12** This unusual consolatory gambit is closely tied to Stoic views on value (see the note on 31.6) and the rarity of genuine goodness (42.1, 71.25).

**99.14** "Bite" or "biting" (*morsus*, Gk. *daknos*) is often used in Stoic contexts to refer to the sensation of mental pain as distinct from emotional distress itself. As here, it is often paired with "contraction" (*contractio* or *contrahi*, Gk. *sustolē*). See Galen, *Precepts of Hippocrates and Plato* 4.2.4–6, 4.3.2; Cicero, *Tusculan Disputations* 3.83, 4.15; Seneca, *Consolation to Marcia* 7.1.

**99.15** For this defense, see the note on 9.3.

**99.18** The involuntary tears are an indication of the wise person's humanity; see the note on 11.1. The voluntary tears are more surprising: these turn out to be akin to (or perhaps actually) the wise person's distinctive response of joy (see the note on 23.3), here occasioned by the memory of the deceased person's good qualities.

**99.25** Metrodorus was a close associate of Epicurus and shared his philosophical views. For his writings, see further on 14.17. In quoting from his letter, Seneca supplies both the Greek original (not included here) and his own translation into Latin.

**99.27** For the Stoic position, see the note on 85.9, and compare 116.2–3.

**99.29** Despite the polemic against Metrodorus, this is exactly the Epicurean argument against the fear of death (or, generally, against regarding death as an evil).

**100.1** For Fabianus see the note on 11.4.

**100.6** As also in 18.7, the "pauper's cell" seems to be an affectation of extensive households making a show of their surplus wealth by maintaining a chamber in which one might escape from it.

**100.7** Rhythmical "concluding phrases" (*clausulae*) were a requirement of good prose style at the time of Cicero. Asinius Pollio, the patron of Virgil, was considered an important orator and historian as well as a poet; his writings are now lost.

**100.9** We have no other evidence regarding these works of Livy, who is known to us only as a historian. It may be relevant, however, that Seneca mentions him in 46.1 in conjunction with Epicurus and Lucilius himself, both of whom he regards as writers of moral philosophy. Livy was highly regarded as a stylist; see *On Anger* 1.20.6; Quintilian 8.1.3.

**101.1** Cornelius Senecio is unknown except for what Seneca says here.

**101.4** Virgil, *Eclogues* 1.73.

**101.10** One particularly torturous form of crucifixion involved a spike positioned on the cross in such a way as to pierce the victim's genitals (Seneca, *Consolation to Marcia* 20.3).

**101.11** For Maecenas see the note on 19.9. The meter in Latin is the unusual Priapean.

**101.13** Virgil, *Aeneid* 12.646.

**102.2** For these philosophical views, compare 58.27 and 65.16–18, both with Platonic antecedents; perhaps also the Pythagorean view explained in 108.19–21.

**102.3** The question raised concerns a technicality within the Stoics' elaborate theory of value, not unlike the problem posed at 74.22. Although fame of the ordinary kind is merely a preferred indifferent, there were at least some Stoics who argued that praise coming from wise observers counts as a good, no doubt because such praise depends on genuinely good conduct (Cicero, *On Ends* 3.57; also *SVF* 3.161, 162). From what Seneca says here, it appears that some Stoics were prepared to assert, further, that this good persists after the death of the agent.

In their objection, the unnamed opponents point to the Stoic axiom "No thing that is good can consist of things that are separated" (Stobaeus 2.7.11c, 94W = *SVF* 3.98), arguing that because renown depends on the praise of many individuals, it necessarily consists of things that are separated.

**102.7** For the terminology, see the note on 50.6.

**102.13** For the sake of clarity, Seneca substitutes the word *fama* ("reputation") for *gloria* ("glory"), since in his usage *gloria* often refers to the praise of the wise, which he also calls *claritas* ("renown").

**102.16** The tragedian is Naevius, in his play *Hector's Departure* (Warmington 2:118). The poet referred to in the next line is undoubtedly Ennius (Skutsch 1985, 715), but the context is lost.

**102.18** In Stoic thought, human beings are naturally inclined toward sociability, for which see the note on 9.17.

**102.21** The stars are also deities with tasks to perform; compare 88.15.

**102.28** For Stoic thought on this natural pleasure, compare Diogenes Laertius 7.86 [LS 57A].

**102.30** "Once released it is immediately dissipated" looks like a reference to Epicurean beliefs (cf. Epicurus, *Letter to Herodotus* 65 [LS 14A]; Lucretius 3.538–39). However, Seneca sometimes expresses similar beliefs in his own voice: see, for instance, 71.13–16. The textual problem in this sentence, and the structure of thought throughout the letter, are discussed in Leeman 1951.

The quotation is from Virgil, *Aeneid* 4.3–4.

**104.1** Both this letter and letter 110 are written from Seneca's villa at Nomentum, about eighteen miles northeast of Rome.

Following Roman custom, Seneca's father had allowed a close friend, the senator Lucius Iunius Gallio, to adopt Seneca's older brother Novatus. It is the brother, now known as Lucius Iunius Gallio Annaeanus, who is referred to here. He is Seneca's mentor (*dominus*) in that he is the head of the family, the elder Seneca having died in 39 or 40 CE. Gallio Annaeanus also served as governor of the province of Greece (Achaea) in 51–52; he is mentioned in Acts 18:12–17 for dismissing the charges brought against the apostle Paul.

**104.2** Seneca's wife Pompeia Paulina was a member of a prominent senatorial family. Her devotion to her husband figures prominently in the account of his death in Tacitus, *Annals* 15.63–64.

**104.7** Compare 28.2.

**104.10** Virgil, *Aeneid* 3.282–83.

**104.21** The first group are typical examples of moral rectitude from the Roman Republic; compare 25.6, 95.72. Zeno of Citium, Chrysippus, and Posidonius were important Stoic philosophers. For Zeno's suicide, see Diogenes Laertius 7.28, and compare 58.34–36.

**104.23** See the note on 59.18.

**104.24** Virgil, *Aeneid* 6.277.

**104.27** Seneca now brings together a number of biographical details about Socrates, most of which have already been mentioned; compare especially 24.4, 28.8, and 70.9. The tradition concerning Socrates' wife goes back to Xenophon, *Symposium* 2.10.

The word "freedom" (*libertas*) refers to the Athenian democracy, since it was after the democracy was restored that Socrates was tried and sentenced to death.

**104.28** This claim about Socrates is made also by Cicero, *Tusculan Disputations* 3.31, and by Seneca in *On Anger* 2.7.

**104.29** The biographical sketch that follows recapitulates points that have already been made (cf. especially 14.12–13, 24.6–8, 71.8–11) but also provides further details. Seneca's knowledge of Cato's life may owe something to the biography written at around this time by Thrasea Paetus (mentioned by Plutarch, *Cato the Younger* 25.1).

**104.30** The prosecution Seneca has in mind is probably that of Murena in 63 BC, described as especially stern in Cicero's speech for the defense. The province is Cyprus, which Cato administered on special commission in 58 BC with scrupulous honesty.

**104.31** Virgil, *Aeneid* 1.458.

**104.33** These events are vividly described by Lucan, *Civil War* 9.371–618.

The story of Cato's playing ball after losing the election for the consulship of 51 BC is told also by Plutarch, *Cato the Younger* 49–50.

**105.1** The region of Ardea was notorious for being malaria-ridden (Strabo 5.3.5), so Seneca must be wittily cautioning Lucilius against assuming that what follows will guarantee success.

**105.8** Seneca here states as his own view the Epicurean principle quoted in 97.13.

**106.2** This plan is mentioned again in 108.1 and 109.17; see Leeman 1953. The Christian author Lactantius quotes several times from what he calls Seneca's *Books on Ethics* (*libri moralis philosophiae*); see Vottero 1998, 204–9, 340–54.

**106.4** For the Stoic doctrine on body, see the note on 58.11, and for the arguments Seneca supplies here, compare 117.2. Note that in the first two the conclusion (i.e., that the good is a body) remains unstated.

**106.6** For the negative traits of character called "infirmities," compare 75.10–12, and see the note on 50.5.

**106.8** Lucretius 1.304.

**107.1** Freed slaves became clients of their former masters and were often employed by them in business; in that role, they were conventionally referred to as "friends" (*amici*).

**107.3** Virgil, *Aeneid* 6, 274–75. Compare 108.29.

**107.4** "Anticipated" (*praemeditata*) refers to the prerehearsal of future ills; see the note on 24.2. The theme is frequent in consolations; compare, for instance, 91.3–4.

**107.10** For Cleanthes see the note on 6.6, and compare 108.10 on the use of poetry in philosophical teaching. The hymn is quoted in its original Greek by Epictetus, *Manual* 53 [LS 62B]; for its philosophical content, see the note on 76.23, and compare the longer hymn quoted in Stobaeus 1.1.12, 23–27W [LS 54I]. Cicero in his philosophical treatises frequently translates bits of Greek poetry into Latin verse.

**108.1** See the note on 106.2.

**108.3** For Attalus see the note on 9.7.

**108.7** Certain festivals of the goddess Cybele, thought to be of Near Eastern origin, involved ecstatic dancing to the music of flutes, cymbals, and tambourines, with some worshippers practicing self-castration.

**108.8** See the note on 94.29.

**108.9** The two lines appear consecutively in the collection attributed to Publilius Syrus (Friedrich 1964, 49); see the note on 8.9.

**108.10** For Cleanthes see the note on 6.6; for Cleanthes' own use of poetry, see the prayer to Zeus quoted in 107.11.

**108.11** The source of these lines is unknown.

**108.12** Faults of character, such as avarice and ambition (see the note on 50.5), are less deeply ingrained in the young than in older persons.

**108.17** Seneca mentions studying with Sotion also in 49.2, indicating that this was at an age when he had not yet begun to argue cases; i.e., in his early teens. From the passage here, it appears that Sotion offered the Pythagorean rather than the Sextian justification for vegetarianism. For Sextius's other views, see the note on 59.7.

**108.18** For this sense of the word "cruelty," see the note on 83.25.

**108.24** Virgil, *Georgics* 3.284.

Virgil, *Georgics* 3.66–68.

**108.29** Virgil, *Aeneid* 6.275.

**108.30** Cicero's *On the Republic*, which survives only in part, combines theoretical issues in political philosophy with much anecdotal information on the historical development of the Roman government. In book 3 of that work, the skeptical philosopher Philus speaks as a devil's advocate "against justice"; i.e., against there being any natural basis for ethics.

According to both Cicero (*On the Republic* 2.33) and Livy (1.32), Ancus Marcius, the grandson of Numa Pompilius through the maternal line, was made Rome's fourth king by popular acclamation. Servius Tullius, the sixth king, is said in *On the Republic* 2.37 to have been the child of a slave woman of the Tarquins and an unknown father.

**108.31** For these historical details, compare Cicero, *On the Republic* 1.25, 63. Fenestella wrote a lengthy chronicle of Roman history through the Late Republic.

**108.33** These and the following lines concern Scipio Africanus, who was Ennius's patron late in life; compare 86.1, and see also Lactantius 1.18.10. If, as seems likely, both quotations derive from the same passage in Ennius, we might venture with the aid of Vahlen 1903, 215–16, to combine these fragments from *On the Republic* with Cicero's Ennian quotations in *On Laws* 2.57 and *Tusculan Disputations* 5.49 into an epitaph similar in meter and style to the one Ennius composed for himself:

> Here lies a man whom neither citizen nor foe
> could ever repay the price of his assistance.
> "From the Maeotian sea, from furthest east

there is no one to rival my achievements.
If it be right for anyone to mount the skies,
for me alone does heaven's great portal open."

**108.34** Virgil, *Georgics* 3.260–61.

**109.1** "We" means "we Stoics."

It was standard doctrine that the wise benefit one another (*SVF* 3.626), but in what does this benefit consist? The answer given here develops further the view articulated in 9.4–19 and especially in 9.8: while the wise are indeed self-sufficient, friendship provides them with an important opportunity for the activation of the virtues. This view has much in common with Aristotle's argument in *Nicomachean Ethics* 9.9.

**109.6** The objector proposes a thought experiment: take away the wisdom from one of two wise persons, and the other will no longer be able to benefit him, since benefit here entails activating the other's wisdom. The objection fails, because the thought experiment is impossible to carry out. You can no more remove a wise person's distinctive property of wisdom than you can remove from honey its distinctive property of sweetness.

**109.9** Heat is the essential property of fire, which is the most active of the four elements posited in Stoic physics. Heat also figures prominently in a standard explanation for the intrinsic nature of goodness (see the note on 44.6).

Seneca's language here suggests that friendship between the wise is actually a necessary condition for the exercise of virtue. There is some inconsistency with 9.15–16, where the wise person is able to have a good life even without friends. Earlier Stoics had pointed out that direct contact between persons (which *would* be dependent on circumstances) is not strictly necessary for the conferring of a benefit: in theory, anything the wise person does is beneficial in some way (Plutarch, *On Common Conceptions* 1068f = *SVF* 3.627).

**109.13** It was standard doctrine that friends are "productive" goods (*SVF* 3.107–8). For instinctual attachment, see the note on 9.17.

**109.16** The phrase was proverbial of close friendship; compare Sallust, *Catilinian Conspiracy* 20.

**109.17** See the note on 106.2.

**110.1** Ovid, *Metamorphoses* 1.595.

In line with popular belief, the Stoics accepted the existence of *daimones* (lesser deities), who are in sympathy with human beings and watch over human affairs (Diogenes Laertius 7.151); see further Algra 2003, 171–72.

**110.6**  Lucretius 3.55–56.

**110.8**  See the note on 89.5.

**110.18**  For the Epicurean associations of this remark, see the note on 25.4.

**111.1**  For examples of these puzzles, compare 48.5–6 and 49.8, and see the note on 45.5. For the Latin rendering of *sophismata*, compare 45.8, where Seneca claims that *captiones* ("riddles") is the best translation. In fact, Cicero never uses *cavillationes* or any related word in the sense indicated here: at *Prior Academics* 2.75, he uses *fallaces conclusiunculae* ("deceitful syllogisms"), and at *Prior Academics* 2.45–46 he seems to favor *captiones*. Seneca perhaps misremembers which of his own preferred renderings was derived from Cicero, for he himself uses *cavillationes* and related words quite frequently; e.g., at 45.5, 64.3, 82.8, 102.20.

**112.2**  Seneca was strongly interested in viticulture; compare *Natural Questions* 3.7.1 (where he calls himself "a meticulous digger of vines"), and see the note on 86.14.

**113.1**  The virtues in Stoicism are corporeal in nature, since they are dispositions of the corporeal mind (see the note on 50.6 and 66.7). From this it might seem to follow that the virtues are animate beings in their own right. For the doctrine, see also Stobaeus 2.7.5b7, 65W.

**113.2**  I.e., from the word *animus* ("mind").

**113.5**  Here and in 113.16, the argument appeals to the Stoic metaphysical doctrine that each numerically distinct entity has its own distinctive property (*proprium* or *proprietas*; Gk. *idiōs poion*), which persists though many kinds of change (Simplicius, *On Aristotle's Treatise On Soul* 217–18 = LS 28I). Because the virtues are not individuated in this way, they cannot be considered animate beings in their own right.

**113.14**  The Stoics held that while each virtue is a distinct disposition, anyone who possesses one virtue necessarily possesses them all. (See the note on 67.10.) On this basis, Seneca rejects the view of his opponent that a person could take on the virtues successively, like different suits of clothing.

**113.18**  An impression whose content is "it is fitting for me to walk" is what the parallel text in Stobaeus calls an "impulsory impression of what is appropriate in that moment" (Stobaeus 2.7.9, 86W [LS 53Q]). When

Seneca speaks of the creature's having "entertained an impulse" (*impetum cepit*), he means that it must have generated such an impulsory impression before giving assent to it. Compare his use of the same phrase in 78.2, 89.14, and *Consolation to Helvia* 1.1, and for the doctrine, see also 71.32.

**113.22** Chrysippus held that the human soul when separated from the body assumes a spherical form (scholiast on *Iliad* 23.65 [*SVF* 2.815]); compare Jerome, *Letter* 109.23 (*SVF* 2.816). Seneca is also familiar with a Stoic claim that the gods themselves are round, for which he cites Varro (*Pumpkinification* 8); compare Cicero, *On the Nature of the Gods* 1.18, 2.46–48.

**113.23** For the early Stoics Cleanthes and Chrysippus, see the notes on 6.6 and 9.14. For vital breath and the directive faculty, see the note on 50.6.

**113.25** "Arms and the man I sing" begins the opening line of Virgil's *Aeneid*, each (complete) line of which has six metrical feet.

**113.26** Caecilius Statius was a comic playwright of the second century BCE.

**113.28** For Posidonius see the note on 78.28.

**113.29** See the note on 59.12.

**114.4** For Maecenas see the note on 19.9. The attendants mentioned presumably include his freedman Bathyllus, a pantomime dancer of whom he was said to be excessively fond. In *On Providence* 3.10, Seneca reports, perhaps on the basis of Maecenas's own works, that Maecenas's wife, Terentia, rejected him daily, and that it was because of his resulting insomnia that he tried to drown himself in wine, music, and other pleasures.

**114.5** The prose fragments Seneca quotes in this letter are from works lost to us.

**114.13** Gaius Gracchus, L. Licinius Crassus, and Curio were orators of the second and early first centuries BCE. Appius Claudius Caecus and Tiberius Coruncanius lived two centuries earlier; their archaic Latin, like that of the even older Twelve Tables (Rome's oldest code of law, dating to the mid-fifth century BCE), would have sounded extremely out of place in the Neronian period.

**114.17** Lucius Arruntius (consul in 22 BCE) was a younger contemporary of the historian Sallust, better known for his military achievements in the civil wars than for his historical writings, which are mentioned only in this passage. The linguistic peculiarity lies in Sallust's and Arruntius's unidiomatic use of certain common words; for instance, in expressions involving the verb *facere*, "to do or make"; here, "effect."

**114.23**  Virgil, *Georgics* 4.212–13.

**115.5**  Virgil, *Aeneid* 1.327–28, 330.

**115.11**  The account of corruption in this paragraph closely resembles that given by Cicero in *Tusculan Disputations* 3.2–3 and by Calcidius, *On the Timaeus of Plato* 165–66 [= *SVF* 3.229]. For the doctrine, see the note on 31.2.

**115.12**  Ovid, *Metamorphoses* 2.1–2.

**115.13**  Ovid, *Metamorphoses* 2.107–8.

**115.14**  The last of these eight passages is from Euripides, as Seneca will shortly explain; the first seven have not been identified. The metrical Latin translations are likewise by an unknown hand, unless they are Seneca's own. The first fragment is extant also in Greek; see Kannicht and Snell 1981, frag. 181, and for possible Greek parallels for the others, frag. 461 in the same volume.

**115.15**  The Euripides passage is extant in Greek in its entirety, with attribution to the lost *Danae*, where the words would be appropriate to the cruel father Acrisius upon his discovery of Danae's seduction (Kannicht 2004, frag. 324). However, Seneca identifies the passage just below as being from the *Bellerophon*. Either Seneca misremembers, or Euripides used the same lines in two different works.

**116.1**  For the Peripatetic position, see the note on 85.3. Seneca now augments the arguments given in 85.3–9, drawing attention to the fact that for Stoics too, the capacity for affective response is natural in human beings: their objection is not to affective responses as such but to the improper evaluation of external objects that is implied in the ordinary person's emotions. See further the notes on 9.3, 75.12, and 85.9, with Graver 2007.

Desire (*cupido*, Gk. *epithumia*) differs from wanting (i.e., pursuit on the basis of "selection"; see the note on 92.11) in that it regards its object as a genuine good rather than as a preferred indifferent. As such, it was classified by Stoics as an emotion and excluded from the ideal human condition.

**116.5**  Panaetius of Rhodes assumed leadership of the Stoic school in Athens about 129 BCE. His statement here is in keeping with his interest in practical ethics.

**117.1**  Although mention of the good suggests ethics, the question being asked really belongs to metaphysics. Wisdom (*sapientia*), in Stoic ontology, is a body: like the virtues, it is the human mind in a certain disposition, and the mind, in its identity as *pneuma*, is itself corporeal; compare 113.1.

By contrast, "being wise" (*sapere*) is incorporeal; it is just something that might be said of a person. For reasons Seneca is about to explain, the term "good" is properly applied only to what is corporeal.

**117.2** Compare 106.4–6, and see the notes on 58.11 and 44.6.

**117.3** "Supervenient" translates Seneca's term *accidens*, used in a technical sense for the events of which corporeals are the substrate; see *OLD* s.v. *accido* 8b, and compare Cicero, *On the Nature of the Gods* 2.82.

**117.5** Seneca's words "choiceworthy" (*expetendum*) and "choosable" (*expetibile*) correspond loosely to the distinction made by Greek Stoics between the *haireton* ("choiceworthy") and the *haireteon* ("what must be chosen"). The shorter adjective was restricted to (corporeal) goods; see Stobaeus 2.7.6f, 78W = *SVF* 3.89, 2.7.11f, 97–98W [LS33J].

**117.6** "Preconception" (*praesumptio*) renders the Greek technical term *prolēpsis*, which the Stoics used to signify universally valid and naturally acquired conceptions, especially in the domain of ethics: see Diogenes Laertius 7.53–54 [LS 39D, 40A]; Plutarch, *On Stoic Self-Contradictions* 1041e [LS 60B]. Cicero similarly attributes to the Stoics the claim that beliefs in divinities and in the afterlife are shared by all peoples due to "implanted preconceptions," and that universality counts as evidence in support of those views (*Tusculan Disputations* 1.29–32, *On the Nature of the Gods* 2.5, 2.12).

**117.10** In Stoic metaphysics, every causal interaction consists of one body acting upon another body to produce an effect; that effect is what is expressed in language concerning the interaction. For instance, a knife acts upon flesh to produce the effect *being cut*; and similarly wisdom, which is a disposition of the wise person's corporeal mind, acts upon that person to produce the effect *being wise*. See Stobaeus 1.138.17–139.4 [LS 55A]; Sextus Empiricus, *Against the Mathematicians* 9.211 [LS 55B]. Seneca's ensuing polemic repeatedly ignores this metaphysical distinction.

**117.12** Stoic logic was influenced by earlier thinkers, notably by the dialecticians of the Megarian school. (It was they who had propounded the logic puzzles called *sophismata*; see the note on 45.5.) Compare Cicero, *Tusculan Disputations* 4.21, where the "logicians" are said to have distinguished between the longing "to have wealth," i.e., longing to have wealth predicated of oneself, and longing for material possessions as such.

**117.13** There was no single equivalent in Latin for the Greek *lekton* ("thing said" or "sayable"; LS chap. 33). Seneca here mentions three possible translations: *effatum* ("proposition"), *enuntiativum* ("predication"), and *dictum* ("what is said"). Compare Cicero, *Prior Academics* 2.95, and see Inwood 2007a, 297.

**117.19** See the note on 65.16.

**118.1** Cicero, *Letters to Atticus* 1.12.4. For Seneca's use of this collection, compare 21.4 and 97.2–10.

**118.2** Cicero, *Letters to Atticus* 1.12.1. An annual interest rate of 12 percent was exorbitant even for Roman moneylenders.

**118.4** For Vatinius see the note on 94.25.

**118.8** Since misconceptions about what is good are responsible for human misery, the project of developing a correct conception holds the key to happiness. In the investigation that follows, Seneca adheres to the usual Stoic assumption that the good is that which benefits (i.e., which renders a person happy; see the note on 44.6), but seeks to specify as well what it is about genuinely good things that enables them to benefit us. A crisply formulated definition (at the end of 118.12) is thus added to the extensive discussions of Stoic notions of value that have been offered in earlier letters.

**118.13** The opponent refers to a view shared by Stoics and Peripatetics, that the good is characteristically in accordance with nature. Seneca grants this much, but denies that the phrase "in accordance with nature" adequately identifies the distinctive property of the good. For a Stoic, a thing is not good unless it is *completely* in accordance with nature, with completeness thought of as a limit, like straightness in 66.8–9. See further the notes on 44.6 and 113.5.

**119.2** Cato the Elder; see the note on 11.10.

**119.3** Given the structure of the sentence, a Tibur cup must be a rustic drinking vessel, perhaps of earthenware or of the white stone that was an export of that town.

**119.5** The phrase "natural wealth" suggests Epicurean recommendations about limiting one's desires to minimal body needs; compare 4.10–11.

**119.6** The proscriptions under Sulla (82 BCE) awarded a portion of the proscribed citizen's estate to his killer, with the remainder accruing to the state treasury. Compare *On Providence* 3.7, *On Benefits* 5.16.3.

**119.7** The Epicurean associations are now confirmed: compare 4.10, where the same saying of Epicurus is quoted, and see also 25.4, 110.18, and the note on 25.4.

For Alexander see the note on 59.12, and compare 94.63.

**119.9** Crassus was famous for his wealth; see the note on 4.7, and compare *On the Happy Life* 21.3. Licinus was a freedman of Julius Caesar who amassed a large fortune as procurator of Gaul.

**119.13** Horace, *Satires* 1.2.114–16.

**120.1** In Stoic ethics, what is good and what is honorable are conceptually distinct (*divisa*) but not different in extension (*diversa*): everything that is good is also honorable, and everything that is honorable is also good. This is not the case for the other ancient schools, notably the Peripatetics (see the note on 85.31), who define goodness at least partly in terms of instrumental utility and thus maintain that there are other goods besides virtue.

**120.2** The opponent's explanation of the honorable would be unobjectionable to a Stoic; see the note on 95.5.

**120.4** While nature does provide us at birth with the instinctive tendencies that favor our development toward virtue (see the note on 94.29), there is no innate knowledge as such, nor are we born with any articulated concepts. Our entire set of concepts and beliefs must be built up from experience. The problem, then, is how we acquire even a conception of the human good, given that the good as Stoics define it (i.e., as the perfection of our rational nature) lies outside our experience.

The word *analogia* was of Greek origin. The preeminent Roman scholar to use the word was Varro, writing on linguistic theory in books 8–10 of *On the Latin Language*.

**120.6** See the note on 98.13.

**120.7** The heroic stand by Horatius Cocles was said to have defended Rome from an attack by the Etruscan king Lars Porsenna in the last decade of the sixth century BCE. A longer version of the story appears in Livy 2.10.

**120.11** See the note on 67.10.

**120.12** Namely, the insight that the happy life flows smoothly and is completely under its own control.

**120.14** See the note on 41.5.

**120.18** The theme is repeated from 24.19–20.

**120.19** For Vatinius and Cato, see the note on 94.25. Manius Curius Dentatus (early 3rd c. BCE) was legendary for frugal living, as were Fabricius and Tubero (see the note on 95.72). For the wealthy Licinus, see the note on 119.9; for Maecenas, on 19.9 and 114.4; for Apicius, on 95.42.

**120.20** Horace, *Satires* 1.3.11–17.

**121.1** This statement implies that Posidonius (see the note on 78.28) and the second-century-BCE Stoic Archedemus (Diogenes Laertius 7.84 [LS 56A]) are the primary sources for the discussion that follows.

**121.4** For the corrupting influence of well-meant prayers, compare 31.2, 94.53–55, 115.11.

**121.5** Stoics argued that the capacity for perception exhibited by animals (i.e., by animate creatures) includes a capacity for reflexive perception of one's own physical structure and abilities. The topic is highly relevant to their ethics, since one way of justifying the Stoic position on the human good was to appeal to our awareness of our own constitution as rational beings and our natural instinct to preserve it; see Cicero, *On Ends* 3.16–24, 62–68; Diogenes Laertius 7.85–86 [LS 57A]. Seneca's treatment of this strand of Stoic thought has much in common, especially his animal examples, with the *Elements of Ethics* by Hierocles (text and commentary in Bastianini and Long 1992; translation in Ramelli and Konstan 2009).

**121.6** For these performances, see the note on 47.17.

**121.10** For the terminology, see the note on 50.6.

**121.14** For this process of instinctual attachment (*oikeiōsis*), see the note on 9.17.

**121.18** Compare 82.15, 116.3.

**122.2** Virgil, *Georgics* 1.250–51.

**122.10** Nothing is known about Acilius Buta beyond what Seneca says here.

**122.11** Julius Montanus, a contemporary of Ovid, was otherwise well regarded for his poetry (Ovid, *Epistles from Pontus* 4.6.11–12; Seneca the Elder, *Controversiae* 7.1.27). The two passages quoted here are the only lines of his poetry that survive.

Pinarius Natta appears in Tacitus, *Annals* 4.34, as an associate of Sejanus (see the note on 55.3).

**122.12** Marcus Vinicius, consul in 30 CE, was an important political figure under Tiberius, Caligula, and Claudius; he was the son of the Publius Vinicius mentioned in 40.9. His equestrian associate Varus is not otherwise known.

**122.15** Albinovanus Pedo was a close associate of Ovid; he too was well known as a poet, but is mentioned here for his wit in conversation. Sextus Papinius is either the consul of 36 CE, or his son of the same name, who according to Tacitus, *Annals* 6.49.1, committed suicide because of sexual abuse by his mother.

In the course of reckoning up his household accounts, Papinius has one or more of his slaves whipped, presumably for mishandling the master's money. Pedo does not appear to regard the procedure as unusual in itself: like all Papinius's activities, it is peculiar only in that it takes place during the night.

**122.16** There is a play on words: *lychnobius* is both *lychno-bios*, "one who lives by the lamp," and *lichno-bios*, "one who lives greedily" (Summers 1910). There may also be a further witticism, in that the olive oil used in the lamps might instead have been eaten, as in Varro, *Menippean Satires* 573.

**123.1** Seneca's villa in the Alban Hills would have been located about fifteen miles southeast of Rome.

**123.4** A state dinner given by a newly elected magistrate, normally at great expense; compare 95.41.

**123.7** Compare 87.9.

**123.10** The speech that follows is that of a crass hedonist who offers as a pretext the Epicurean claims that virtue is an empty name (cf. Cicero, *On Ends* 2.48) and that sensual pleasure is the goal of existence. Compare 21.9. The commonplace that life is "irretrievable" recalls Virgil in *Georgics* 3.284 and *Aeneid* 10.467–68; compare Seneca's own treatment of the theme in 108.24.

**123.12** The voice of the Sirens; compare 31.2 and 88.7, and see the note on 31.2.

**123.13** In order to make a fully rational decision, one needs not only to understand the Stoic position on naturally preferred and dispreferred indifferents (see the note on 31.6) but also to correct for the natural preference itself.

**123.15** The second speaker, likewise a crass hedonist, gives a philosophical veneer to his position by referring to the Stoic doctrines that the wise person falls in love and possesses knowledge of proper conduct at drinking parties (Stobaeus 2.5b9, 65–66W [*SVF* 3.717]; Diogenes Laertius 7.129–30).

**124.1** Virgil, *Georgics* 1.176–77.

Both nonhuman animals and human infants lack the ability to use spoken language; the Latin word *infans* actually means "nonspeaker." However, it is not speech in itself that puts mature human beings into a different ethical category; rather, it is the rational capacities that are typically manifested in the use of language.

**124.2** Hedonist philosophers, among whom Seneca is especially concerned with the Epicureans, maintain that our instinctive attraction to pleasure and aversion to pain are indicative of what is good or bad for us. Seneca objects that on this basis it will be difficult to refute the crass hedonist who uses Epicureanism as a pretext for an entirely unregulated manner of living. Compare 123.10, and see the note on 21.9.

**124.5** Vision is our most accurate sense; when dissimilar objects are very small, we need vision to tell them apart. If any of our senses were able to tell us whether an object is good or bad, it would have to be vision. But in fact, we cannot *see* goodness or badness. It follows that the good is grasped only by the intellect.

**124.11** Compare 118 13–16 and 120.15–16.

**124.17** The point about memory and anticipation appears in similar terms in Cicero, *On Duties* 1.11.

**124.18** Animal behavior is disordered and unsystematic in the sense that non-human animals, by their focus only on the immediate present, lack the capacity to subject their behavior to a rational plan. Consequently, they have no access to the good as Stoics understand it. Compare *On Anger* 1.3.7.

**124.23** See the note on 59.18.

**124.24** The extant collection ends with a return to the theme of the wise person's powerful sense of joy; compare 4.1, and see the note on 23.3.


## Fragments

1   The "unwashed" are early Romans, whose lack of refinement in literary matters matches their rugged disregard of personal hygiene. "Those who wear perfume" are Seneca's contemporaries.

2   Marcus Cornelius Cethegus was a contemporary of Ennius and a victor in the Second Punic War. The lines are also quoted by Cicero in *Brutus* 58–59, with attribution to book 9 of the *Annals*. Seneca's objection to them may be that the words "the ones who lived and spent their lives in those days" add little to the thought, or that the metaphors of the last line are overly elaborate.

3   We can only guess that Sotericus is a craftsman whose articles of furniture are tasteless in design or clumsily made.

4   The compound words "sweet-speaking" (*suaviloquens*) and "brief-speaking" (*breviloquentia*) recall Ennius's fondness for such compounds.

The first of these was used by Ennius with reference to the oratory of Cethegus, as quoted by Cicero in *Brutus* 58:

> Also Cornelius, the orator
> Marcus Cethegus, with sweet-speaking mouth,
> colleague of Tuditanus, son of Marcus.

5    Aulus Gellius introduces this fragment as if taken from a different Senecan context. Compare 2.6, both for the turn of phrase and for the thought.

Angle brackets indicate words that are not in the manuscripts.

| | | | |
|---|---|---|---|
| **1.1** | *maxima . . . magna.* | **51.1** | *editum illum ac.* |
| **11.5** | *lenti.* | **52.5** | *alterum.* |
| **12.6** | *includit.* | **52.5** | *<in aperto est>.* |
| **12.7** | *<unus>.* | **53.9** | *adesse.* |
| **12.7** | *<licet dies sit>.* | **51.4** | ~~*et.*~~ |
| **13.14** | omit *ibi.* | **56.3** | *Crispum.* |
| **14.13** | *et probris infandis.* | **58.10** | *animam.* |
| **15.4** | *usu redde facile.* | **65.15** | *potiora.* |
| **15.8** | *et latus.* | **66.12** | *oriuntur.* |
| **15.8** | *media oris vi abeat nec.* | **67.5** | *<tormenta non optabilia sunt>.* |
| **15.9** | *munus Graecum.* | **71.19** | *nobis.* |
| **19.6** | *<scias>.* | **71.20** | *rigida re quid amplius intendi* |
| **20.11** | *gloriosus.* | | *potest?* |
| **21.4** | omit *<sibi>.* | **73.6** | *<ista>.* |
| **21.10** | *et inscriptum videris.* | **74.9** | *destituti.* |
| **22.13** | *arculas advoco.* | **74.18** | *ut non deseratur.* |
| **29.6** | *M. Lepidi philosophum.* | **78.15** | *illa.* |
| **32.3** | *inniti sibi.* | **78.17** | *exsurgit.* |
| **33.5** | omit *<continuando>*; move *et* | **82.2** | no lacuna. |
| | to follow *per lineamenta sua.* | **82.15** | no lacuna. |
| **34.3** | *quid aliud.* | **84.1** | omit *<non>.* |
| **36.9** | *aliquis.* | **86.14** | *quid quod vidi illud arbustum* |
| **37.3** | *vim.* | | *trimum et quadrimum haud* |
| **40.2** | *una.* | | *fastidiendi fructus deponere.* |
| **40.2** | *iuveniori oratori.* | **87.3** | *non magis hora.* |
| **40.7** | *pondere se rapit.* | **87.24** | *honesta enim actio recta* |
| **40.9** | *ut P. Vinicius qui titubat.* | | *actio est.* |
| **40.10** | *numquid dicas.* | **88.4** | *<videndum>.* |
| **42.10** | *lacrimis.* | **88.44** | *uni diversum.* |
| **48.8** | *laqueist timore pendenti* | **90.28** | *perpetuae.* |
| | *rumpens.* | **90.36** | *secutast.* |
| **48.9** | *quae* (no lacuna). | **92.2** | *securos.* |
| **49.10** | *da aequanimitatem.* | **92.6** | *<pusillum, si beatam>.* |
| **50.5** | omit *<si>.* | **92.29** | *illa alte haerens et exagitata.* |

92.34   *exurat.*

94.7   omit <*diu*>; insert <*semper*> after *quemquam.*

95.16   *viscerum.*

95.26   *echinis totam dissecti structique.*

98.14   See commentary.

102.3   *negat.*

102.28   *necessariis* (no lacuna).

102.30   *sed ille quoque.*

104.11   *ut virides frondes.*

104.27   *foris vero.*

104.29   *in pace.*

104.29   *in servis se libertati addixisse.*

105.3   *parva si notabilia sunt, si rara.*

107.1   <*deesset aliquid nunc*>.

107.5   *deincepsque* <*accidet*> *multa et varia sunt* <*quae*>.

108.7   *galli.*

108.21   *crudelitatis.*

108.31   *et alii quiqui.*

109.16   *quam in suo.*

109.18   *exigua video.*

113.20   *exibit.*

113.20   <*cenare bene*>.

113.25   <*lis est*>.

113.31   *doce.*

114.2   *dicenti.*

114.10   *et ignota ac.*

114.16   no lacuna.

122.4   *sub arta umbra.*

123.3   *ad voluptatem prohibentes.*

123.5   *aliquod enim.*

123.10   *eo.*

123.10   *sine tibi interire.*

123.12   *in turpem vitam misera nisi turpi spe inludunt.*

124.14   *qua.*

# References

## Editions and Translations

Beltrami, A., ed. 1937. *L. Annaei Senecae ad Lucilium epistulae morales*. Rome: Typis Regiae Officinae Polygraphicae.

Fantham, E., trans. 2010. *Seneca: Selected Letters*. Oxford: Oxford University Press.

Gummere, R. M., ed. and trans. 1917–25. *Seneca: Ad Lucilium Epistulae Morales*. 3 vols. Loeb Classical Library. Cambridge, MA: Harvard University Press.

Hense, O., ed. 1914. *Seneca: Opera quae supersunt*. Leipzig: Teubner.

Inwood, B. 2007a. *Seneca: Selected Philosophical Letters*. Oxford: Oxford University Press.

Préchac, F., ed., and H. Noblot, trans. 1945–64. *Sénèque: Lettres à Lucilius*. Paris: Les Belles Lettres.

Reynolds, L. D., ed. 1965a. *Seneca: Ad Lucilium Epistulae morales*. 2 vols. Oxford: Clarendon Press.

Summers, W. C., ed. 1910. *Select Letters of Seneca*. London: Macmillan.

Veyne, P., ed. 1993. *Sénèque: Entretiens, Lettres à Lucilius*. Revised translation, introduction, and notes. Paris: Laffont.

## Secondary Works

Abel, K. 1981. "Das Problem der Faktizität der senecanischen Korrespondenz." *Hermes* 109: 472–99.

Algra, K. 2003. "Stoic Theology." In *Cambridge Companion to the Stoics*, ed. B. Inwood. 153–78. Cambridge: Cambridge University Press.

Barnes, J. 1997. *Logic in the Imperial Stoa*. Leiden: Brill.

Bastianini, G., and A. A. Long, eds. 1992. "Ierocle: Elementi di Etica." In *Corpus dei papiri filosofici greci e latini*, vol. 1.1.2, 268–362. Florence: Olschki.

Brennan, T. 2005. *The Stoic Life: Emotions, Duties, and Fate*. Oxford: Oxford University Press.

Buecheler, F., and A. Riese, eds. 1894–1926. *Anthologia Latina*. 2 vols. Leipzig: Teubner.

Cancik, H. 1967. *Untersuchungen zu Senecas Epistulae Morales = Spudasmata*, vol. 18. Hildesheim: Olms.

Cancik, H., and N. Schneider, eds. 2002–10. *Brill's New Pauly: Encyclopaedia of the Ancient World*. Leiden: Brill.

Cooper, J. 2012. *Pursuits of Wisdom: Six Ways of Life in Ancient Philosophy from Socrates to Plotinus*. Princeton, NJ: Princeton University Press.

Damschen, G., and A. Heil, eds. 2014. *Brill's Companion to Seneca*. Leiden: Brill.

Dillon, J. 1996. *The Middle Platonists: 80 B.C. to A.D. 220*. 2nd ed. Ithaca, NY: Cornell University Press.

Edwards, C. 1997. "Self-Scrutiny and Self-Transformation in Seneca's Letters." *Greece & Rome* 44: 23–38.

Foucault, M. 2001. *L'herméneutique du sujet: Cours au Collège de France (1981–1982)*. Paris: Gallimard. Trans. G. Burchell (2005) as *The Hermeneutics of the Subject*. New York: Palgrave Macmillan.

Friedrich, O. <1880> 1964. *Publilii Syri Mimi Sententiae*. Hildesheim: Olms.

Gill, C. 2009. "Seneca and Selfhood: Integration and Disintegration." In *Seneca and the Self*, ed. S. Bartsch and D. Wraye, 65–83. Cambridge: Cambridge University Press.

Graver, M. 2007. *Stoicism and Emotion*. Chicago: University of Chicago Press.

———. 2009. "The Weeping Wise: Stoic and Epicurean Consolations in Seneca's 99th Epistle." In *Tears in the Graeco-Roman World*, ed. T. Fögen, 235–52. Berlin: De Gruyter.

———. 2012. "Seneca and the *Contemplatio Veri*." In *Theoria, Praxis, and the Contemplative Life after Plato and Aristotle*, ed. T. Bénatouïl and M. Bonazzi, 73–98. Leiden: Brill.

———. 2014. "Honeybee Reading and Self-Scripting: *Epistulae Morales* 84." In *Seneca Philosophus*, ed. J. Wildberger and M. Colish, 269–93. Berlin: De Gruyter.

———. 2015. "The Emotional Intelligence of Epicureans: Doctrinalism and Adaptation in Seneca's Epistles." In *Roman Reflections: Essays on Latin Philosophy*, ed. Katharina Volk and Gareth Williams. Oxford: Oxford University Press, 2015.

Griffin, M. 1968. "Seneca on Cato's Politics: *Epistle* 14. 12–13." *Classical Quarterly* 18: 373–75.

———. 1992. *Seneca: A Philosopher in Politics*. 2nd ed. Oxford: Clarendon Press.

———. 2013. *Seneca on Society: A Guide to "De Beneficiis."* Oxford: Oxford University Press.

Grimal, P. 1978. *Sénèque ou la conscience de l'Empire*. Paris: Les Belles Lettres.

Hachmann, E. 1995. *Die Führung des Lesers in Senecas "Epistulae Morales."* Münster: Aschendorff.

Inwood, B. 1995. "Seneca in His Philosophical Milieu." *Harvard Studies in Classical Philology* 97: 63–76. Reprinted in Inwood (2005), 7–22.

———, ed. 2003. *Cambridge Companion to the Stoics*. Cambridge: Cambridge University Press.

———. 2005. *Reading Seneca: Stoic Philosophy at Rome*. Oxford: Clarendon Press.

————. 2007a. *Seneca: Selected Philosophical Letters*. Oxford: Oxford University Press.

————. 2007b. "The Importance of Form in the Letters of Seneca the Younger." In *Ancient Letters: Classical and Late Antique Epistolography*, ed. R. Morello and A. Morrison, 133–48. Oxford: Oxford University Press.

————. 2007c. "Seneca, Plato and Platonism: The Case of Letter 65." In *Platonic Stoicism, Stoic Platonism: The Dialogue between Platonism and Stoicism in Antiquity*, ed. M. Bonazzi and C. Helmig, 149–68. Leuven: Leuven University Press.

Inwood, B., and L. Gerson. 1997. *Hellenistic Philosophy: Introductory Readings*. 2nd ed. Indianapolis: Hackett.

Kannicht, R. 2004. *Euripides*. Tragicorum Graecorum Fragmenta. Vol. 5. Göttingen: Vandenhoeck and Ruprecht

Kannicht, R., and B. Snell. 1981. *Fragmenta Adespota*. Tragicorum Graecorum Fragmenta. Vol. 2. Göttingen: Vandenhoeck and Ruprecht.

Ker, J. 2009. *The Deaths of Seneca*. Oxford: Oxford University Press.

Kidd, I. G. 1988. *Posidonius II: The Commentary*. 2 vols. Cambridge: Cambridge University Press.

Laarman, M. 2014. "Seneca the Philosopher." In Damschen and Heil (2014), 53–71.

Lapidge, M. 1992. "The Stoic Inheritance." In *A History of Twelfth-Century Western Philosophy*, ed. P. Dronke, 81–112. Cambridge: Cambridge University Press.

Leeman, A. D. 1951. "The Epistolary Form of Sen. *Ep.* 102." *Mnemosyne* 4: 175–81.

————. 1953. "Seneca's Plans for a Work 'Moralis Philosophia' and Their Influence on His Later Epistles." *Mnemosyne* 6: 307–13.

Long, A. A. 1992. "Stoic Readings of Homer." In *Homer's Ancient Readers*, ed. R. Lamberton and J. Keaney, 41–66. Princeton, NJ: Princeton University Press. Reprinted in Long (1996), 58–84.

————. 1996. *Stoic Studies*. Cambridge: Cambridge University Press. Reprint, Berkeley: University of California Press, 2001.

————. 2006. *From Epicurus to Epictetus: Studies in Hellenistic and Roman Philosophy*. Oxford: Clarendon Press.

Long, A. A., and D. N. Sedley, eds. 1987. *The Hellenistic Philosophers*. 2 vols. Cambridge: Cambridge University Press.

Mastandrea, P. 1988. *Lettori Cristiani di Seneca Filosofo*. Brescia: Paideia Editrice.

Maurach, G. 1970. *Der Bau von Senecas Epistulae Morales*. Heidelberg: C. Winter.

Mazzoli, G. 1989. "Le 'Epistulae Morales ad Lucilium' di Seneca: Valore letterario e filosofico." In *Aufstieg and Niedergang der Römischen Welt*, vol. 2.36.3, 1823–77. Berlin: De Gruyter.

Ramelli, I., and D. Konstan. 2009. *Hierocles the Stoic: "Elements of Ethics," Fragments, and Excerpts*. Atlanta: Society of Biblical Literature.

Rawson, E. 1985. *Intellectual Life in the Late Roman Republic*. Baltimore: Johns Hopkins University Press.

Reydams-Schils, G. 2010. "Seneca's Platonism: The Soul and Its Divine Origin." In *Ancient Models of Mind: Studies in Human and Divine Rationality*, ed. A. Nightingale and D. Sedley, 196–215. Cambridge: Cambridge University Press.

Reynolds, L. 1965b. *The Medieval Tradition of Seneca's Letters*. Oxford: Oxford University Press.

Ross, G. M. 1974. "Seneca's Philosophical Influence." In *Seneca*, ed. C. D. N. Costa, 116–42. London: Routledge and Kegan Paul.

Russell, D. A. 1974. Letters to Lucilius. In *Seneca*, ed. C. D. N. Costa, 70–95. London: Routledge and Kegan Paul.

Schafer, J. 2009. *Ars Didactica: Seneca's 94th and 95th Letters*. Hypomnemata 181. Göttingen: Vandenhoeck and Ruprecht.

———. 2011. "Seneca's *Epistulae Morales* as Dramatized Education." *Classical Philology* 106: 32–52.

Sedley, D. 1997. "The Ethics of Brutus and Cassius." *Journal of Roman Studies* 87: 41–53.

———. 2005. "Stoic Metaphysics at Rome." In *Metaphysics, Soul and Ethics: Themes from the Work of Richard Sorabji*, ed. R. Salles, 117–42. Oxford: Clarendon Press.

Setaioli, A. 1988. *Seneca e i Greci*. Bologna: Pàtron.

———. 2000. *Facundus Seneca: Aspetti della lingua e dell'ideologia senecana*. Bologna: Pàtron.

———. 2003. "Seneca e Cicerone." In *Aspetti della fortuna di Cicerone nella cultura latina: Atti del III Symposium Ciceronianum Arpinas*, ed. E. Narducci, 55–77. Florence: Felice Le Monnier.

———. 2014. "*Epistulae Morales*." In Damschen and Heil (2014), 191–200.

Sharples, R. W., ed. 2010. *Peripatetic Philosophy, 200 BC to AD 200: An Introduction and Collection of Sources in Translation*. Cambridge: Cambridge University Press.

Skutsch, O. 1985. *The "Annals" of Q. Ennius*. Oxford: Clarendon Press.

Traina, Alfonso. 1995. *Lo stile "drammatico" del filosofo Seneca*. 5th ed. Bologna: Pàtron.

Trillitzsch, W. 1971. *Seneca im literarischen Urteil der Antike: Darstellung und Sammlung der Zeugnisse*. Amsterdam: Hakkert.

Usener, H. 1887. *Epicurea*. Leipzig: Teubner.

Vahlen, J. 1903. *Ennianae Poesis Reliquiae Iteratis Curis*. Leipzig: Teubner.

von Albrecht, M. 2014. "Seneca's Language and Style." In Damschen and Heil (2014), 699–744.

von Arnim, H., ed. 1921–24. *Stoicorum Veterum Fragmenta*. 4 vols. Leipzig: Teubner.

Vottero, D. 1998. *Lucio Anneo Seneca: I Frammenti*. Bologna: Pàtron.

Warmington, E., ed. 1956–1982. *Remains of Old Latin*. 3 vols. Cambridge, MA: Harvard University Press.

Wilcox, A. 2012. *The Gift of Correspondence in Classical Rome: Friendship in Cicero's "Ad Familiares" and Seneca's "Moral Epistles."* Madison: University of Wisconsin Press.

Wildberger, J. 2006. *Seneca und die Stoa: Der Platz des Menschen in der Welt*. 2 vols. Berlin: De Gruyter.